Regionalism in the
New Asia-Pacific Order

Regionalism in the New Asia-Pacific Order

The Political Economy of the Asia-Pacific Region, Volume II

Joseph A. Camilleri

Professor of International Relations,
School of Social Sciences, La Trobe University, Melbourne

Edward Elgar
Cheltenham, UK • Northampton, MA, USA

Published by
Edward Elgar Publishing Limited
Glensanda House
Montpellier Parade
Cheltenham
Glos GL50 1UA
UK

Edward Elgar Publishing, Inc.
136 West Street
Suite 202
Northampton
Massachusetts 01060
USA

A catalogue record for this book
is available from the British Library

ISBN 1 85898 835 7 (cased)

Printed and bound in Great Britain by MPG Books Ltd, Bodmin, Cornwall

Contents

Figures

Tables

Abbreviations and acronyms

ABAC	APEC Business Advisory Council
ADB	Asian Development Bank
AEBF	Asia–Europe Business Forum
AECF	Asia–Europe Cooperation Framework
AEH	ASEM Education Hubs
AEU	Asia–Europe University
AFTA	ASEAN Free Trade Area
AIA	ASEAN Investment Area
AIC	ASEAN Industrial Complementation scheme
AICO	ASEAN Industrial Cooperation Organisation
AIJV	ASEAN Industrial Joint Venture
AMDA	Anglo-Malaya Defence Agreement
AMF	Asian Monetary Fund
AMM	ASEAN Ministerial Meeting
ANU	Australian National University
ANZAM	Committee formed to oversee joint military exercises between British, Australian, New Zealand and Malayan forces
ANZUS	Treaty with Australia and New Zealand
APCC	Asia-Pacific Cultural Centre
APEC	Asia-Pacific Economic Cooperation
APMCS	Asian and Pacific Maritime Cooperation Scheme
APO	Japan Productivity Organization
APPU	Asia-Pacific Parliamentarians' Union
APU	Asian Parliamentarians' Union
ARF	ASEAN Regional Forum
ASA	ASEAN Swap Arrangement
ASC	ASEAN Standing Committee
ASEAN	Association of Southeast Asian Nations
ASEAN+3	ASEAN plus China, Japan and South Korea
ASEAN PMC	ASEAN Post-Ministerial Conference
ASEAN-ISIS	ASEAN Institutes of Strategic and International Studies
ASEANPOL	Meeting of the Chiefs of National Police of ASEAN member countries
ASEM	Asia–Europe Meeting
ASPAC	Asian and Pacific Council
ATF	ASEM Trust Fund

AUSBC	ASEAN–US Business Council
BIMP-EAGA	Brunei–Indonesia–Malaysia–Philippines East ASEAN Growth Area
BPA	Bilateral Payments Arrangements
CAP	collective action plans
CBMs	confidence-building measures
CCOP/SOPAC	Committee for Coordination of Joint Prospecting for Mineral Resources in South Pacific Offshore Areas
CEPT	Common Effective Preferential Tariff
CER	Closer Economic Relations (between Australia and New Zealand)
CIDA	Canadian International Development Agency
CSBMs	confidence and security building measures
CSCAP	Council for Security Cooperation in the Asia Pacific
CSCE	Conference on Security and Co-operation in Europe
CSPCP	Conference of South Pacific Chiefs of Police
CTI	Committee on Trade and Investment
DFAT	Department of Foreign Affairs and Trade (Australia)
DPRK	Democratic People's Republic of Korea
DRV	Democratic Republic of Vietnam
EAEC	East Asia Economic Caucus
EAEG	East Asia Economic Group
ECAFE	Economic Commission for Asia and the Far East (UN)
ECOCEN	Economic Cooperation Centre
EEZ	exclusive economic zone
EPG	Eminent Persons Group
ERTMs	environment-related trade measures
ESCAP	Economic and Social Commission for Asia and the Pacific
EU	European Union
EURATOM	European Atomic Community
EVSL	early voluntary sector liberalization
FDI	foreign direct investment
FPDA	Five-Power Defence Arrangement
FUNCINPEC	Front Uni National pour un Cambodge Indépendant, Neutre, Pacifique et Coopératif
G7	Group of Seven
G77	Group of Seventy-Seven
GATT	General Agreement on Tariffs and Trade
GDP	gross domestic product
GEF	Global Environmental Facility
GEM	group of experts meeting
GNP	gross national product
GSP	Generalized Scheme of Preference

HPA	Hanoi Plan of Action
IADS	Integrated Air Defence System
IAEA	International Atomic Energy Agency
IAP	individual action plan
ICT	information and communication technology
IGCC	Regional Organization for Inter-governmental Co-operation and Coordination in Family and Population Planning
ILO	International Labour Organization
IMC	Informal Meetings on Cambodia
IMF	International Monetary Fund
IMS-GT	Indonesia–Malaysia–Singapore Growth Triangle also known as SIJORI
IMT-GT	Indonesia–Malaysia–Thailand Growth Triangle
INTERFET	International Force on East Timor
IPR	intellectual property rights
ISEAS	Institute of Southeast Asian Studies
ISG	Intersessional Support Group
ISIS	Institute of Strategic and International Studies
ISM	Intersessional Meeting
ITA	International Technology Agreement
JERC	Japan Economic Research Center
JIIA	Japan Institute of International Affairs
KEDO	Korea Energy Development Organization
LDP	Liberal Democratic Party (Japan)
LWR	light-water reactor
MAPHILINDO	Malaysia–Philippines–Indonesia
MITI	Ministry of International Trade and Industry (Japan)
MOFA	Ministry of Foreign Affairs (Japan)
NAFTA	North American Free Trade Area
NATO	North Atlantic Treaty Organization
NETs	natural economic territories
NIE	newly industrializing economy
NGO	non-governmental organization
NPCSD	North Pacific Cooperative Security Dialogue
NPT	Nuclear Non-Proliferation Treaty
NRI	Nomura Research Institute
ODA	overseas development assistance
OECD	Organization for Economic Cooperation and Development
OPTAD	Organization of Pacific Trade, Aid and Development
OSCE	Organization for Security and Cooperation in Europe
PAFTA	Pacific Free Trade Area
PAFTAD	Pacific Trade and Development Conference
PAS	Parti-Islam Se-Malaysia (Malay Islamic Party)

PBC   Pacific Basin Council
PBEC   Pacific Basin Economic Council
PBF   Pacific Business Forum
PECC   Pacific Economic Co-operation Council
PFP   Partners for Progress
PFTA   Pacific Free Trade Area
PNG   Papua New Guinea
PRC   People's Republic of China
PRK   People's Republic of Kampuchea
PTA   preferential trade arrangement
ROK   Republic of Korea
SEACEN   Southeast Asian Central Banks
SEAFDC   Southeast Asia Fisheries Development Center
SEAMCED   Ministerial Conference for the Economic Development of
              Southeast Asia
SEANWFZ   Southeast Asian Nuclear Weapons-Free Zone
SEAP   Southeast Asian Promotion Center for Trade, Investment and
              Tourism
SEARTCD   Southeast Asian Agency for Regional Transport and
              Communications Development
SEATO   Southeast Asia Treaty Organization
SEOM   Senior Economic Officials Meeting (ASEAN)
SGATAR   Study Group on Asian Tax Administration and Research
SIJORI   Singapore–Johore–Riau Growth Triangle
SLORC   State Law and Order Restoration Council
SOM   Senior Officials Meeting (ASEAN)
SOMTI   Senior Officials Meeting on Trade and Investment (ASEAN)
SPARTECA   South Pacific Regional Trade and Economic Co-operation
              Agreement
SPLMC   South Pacific Labour Ministers' Conference
TAC   Treaty of Amity and Cooperation
TCSP   Tourism Council for the South Pacific
TREMs   trade-related environmental measures
TWG   technical working group
UKUSA   United Kingdom–US–Australia Agreement
UNCTAD   United Nations Conference on Trade and Development
UNDP   United Nations Development Programme
UNEP   United Nations Environment Programme
UNESCO   United Nations Educational, Scientific and Cultural
              Organization
UNIDO   United Nations Industrial Development Organization
UNTAET   United Nations Transitional Authority in East Timor
USAID   United States Agency for International Development

VIE	Virtual Information Exchange
WEC	West–East Corridor of the Mekong Basin
WTO	World Trade Organization
ZOPFAN	Zone of Peace, Freedom and Neutrality

Preface

Conceived in the mid-1990s, this companion volume to *States, Markets and Civil Society in Asia Pacific* (first published by Edward Elgar in November 2000) has been long in the making. Different interests and priorities have inevitably competed for the scarce resource we call 'time'. On reflection, however, the time it has taken to write this second volume is also a function of what has been a rapidly changing and increasingly disconcerting global and regional landscape. The kaleidoscope of ambiguity and uncertainty that is now integral to political discourse greatly complicated the already hazardous task of interpretation. Such dramatic events as September 11, the Bali explosions and North Korea's apparent acknowledgement of its hitherto secret nuclear weapons programme were merely symptomatic of deepening international cleavages. They did nevertheless point to the need for painstaking analysis that is sensitive both to the patterns of emerging trends and to the unexpected.

As its title indicates, the first volume was an attempt to bring the three analytical categories of state, market and civil society into a unified framework, within which it might be possible to explore the political economy of the Asia-Pacific region. The rationale for this conceptual point of departure, relevant as much to the second as to the first volume, is not always clearly understood and is therefore worth restating here. Though analytically distinct, state, market and civil society are three closely related categories. They are not, as is sometimes thought, three discrete actors but three overlapping arenas in which diverse actors compete and co-operate. Terrorist groups, as the world is rapidly discovering, operate simultaneously in all three arenas. From civil society and its discontents they draw inspiration and support; through the market they channel resources and calculate the impact of their strategies; to the state they direct their demands and their attacks. The specific relationships and modes of action may be different, but the triadic connection holds as much for industrialists, financiers, Jews, Catholics, town planners, scientists and security analysts as it does for terrorists. It is this triadic connection between the political, economic and socio-cultural domains, which gives form and content to the contemporary organization of human affairs.

In identifying and explaining the interconnections of state, market and civil society shaping the geopolitics and geoeconomics of the Asia-Pacific region, the first volume put the spotlight on the national domain. Here the accent was on the policies of both state and non-state actors, on domestic and external influences, and on the changing complexion of economic, social and cultural life. Considerable attention was directed to diplomatic, strategic, economic and cultural interactions. The global and regional backdrop was ever present, but the focal point of analysis was that provided by national polities, national economies and national societies, be it those of the United States, China, Japan, South Korea, Malaysia, Indonesia, Australia, Canada or the Pacific islands. Market and civil society were considered at length in so far as they intruded into the national domain. This present volume is also concerned with the interconnections of state, market and civil society, but the spotlight is very much on the regional domain, on the regional and sub-regional institutions which states, markets and civil society have spawned as they contend with the multiple challenges of modernity.

Much has been written over the last ten years on regionalism generally and on Asia-Pacific regionalism in particular. Why add yet another volume to what is already a large if not always distinguished body of literature? The intention here is not, as is often the case, to dissect this or that organization – the Association of Southeast Asian Nations (ASEAN), the ASEAN Regional Forum (ARF), or the Asia Pacific Economic Cooperation (APEC) grouping – or even to assess its chances of survival. The aim rather is to describe and interpret the evolution of Asia-Pacific regionalism. We begin with a brief survey of the colonial and pre-colonial periods to establish the longstanding roots of regionalization in this part of the world, before proceeding to an examination of the multilateral processes and mechanisms that gave regional expression to the logic of the Cold War. This evolutionary perspective is revealing because it points to both continuities and discontinuities, to unfolding secular trends but also to new thresholds. ASEAN provides us with a convenient landmark because, though formed in the midst of Cold War tensions and the ideological polarization of communism and anti-communism, it foreshadows a different kind of regionalism, one that cultivates a different security discourse, gives rise to different forms of interaction, and places the initiative in the hands of different actors.

However, as the chapters that follow will show, the transition to a new kind of regionalism that was meant to typify the post-Cold War period was a slow, tortuous and contradictory process. Though ASEAN itself remains the most accurate barometer of that contradiction and complexity – hence the sustained attention it receives in this volume – other attempts at institutional innovation also pointed to conflicting interests and perceptions and to the pervasive gap between promise and performance or, as the jargon of security studies would have it, between declaratory and operational policy. Reduced to its essentials, this study poses three key questions: has Asia-Pacific regionalism since the late 1980s sought to institutionalize a new conception of security? Does regional multilateralism in its diverse manifestations offer Asia Pacific, actually or potentially, a helpful path for negotiating the often slippery geopolitical, economic and cultural terrain? Does the emerging regional architecture in Asia Pacific show signs of integrating state, market and civil society in ways that are likely to make for a solid, enduring and convivial 'house'? In Chapters 4–8 the focus shifts from ASEAN to the ARF and APEC, back again to ASEAN, and then to a range of other track-one as well as track-two and track-three organizations, but each chapter explores, at least implicitly, the same three questions.

It is only in Chapters 9 and 10, however, that all three questions are brought together and explicitly addressed. Here the notion of 'comprehensive security' effectively becomes the yardstick used to characterize and evaluate the recent trajectory of Asia-Pacific regionalism. It is in these two chapters that the study grapples with the long-term implications of the two contrasting architectural blueprints: 'Asia Pacific' and 'Pacific Asia'. The aim, it should be stressed, is not to pass judgement on the intellectual and political merit of either blueprint, but rather to examine the ideological and cultural premises upon which each blueprint is predicated, and to assess whether the two blueprints are mutually exclusive or whether regional and global multilateralism provides a basis for fruitful if uneasy coexistence. No single exploration, not even a two-volume study, can do justice to such an ambitious enterprise. The hope simply is that this study will have shed enough light to illuminate some of the ground already traversed and cast into sharper relief at least a few of the roadblocks likely to be encountered in the journey that lies ahead.

As noted in the preface to the first volume, this study would not have seen the light of day were it not for the support it received from so many quarters. I owe a profound intellectual debt to many scholars, officials, journalists and practitioners, many of whom are cited in the pages that follow. May I mention in this regard my rewarding association with the Council for Security Cooperation in the Asia Pacific, especially its Australian Committee and its two Co-Chairs, Desmond Ball and Stuart Harris. Let me also acknowledge that this project would not have been possible without the generous support of the Australian Research Council or the invaluable contribution of my research assistants and friends, Andrew Cock, Amnon Varon, Michalis Michael, Eşref Asu and Michael O'Keefe. A special word of thanks go to the last two, to Michael on whom I came to rely for the entire duration of the project, and to Eşref whose methodical and highly professional input was crucial to the last stage of the project.

I am especially grateful to La Trobe University, to the Borchardt Library for its unfailing assistance, and to the School of Social Sciences and the Politics staff for their continuing and multifaceted assistance. I am greatly indebted to the administrative staff for their enthusiastic co-operation, in particular to Liz Byrne, Nella Mete and Nicole Oke, and to Eva Fabian for so efficiently producing the camera-ready copy. The largest debt, of course, I owe to my wife, Rita. She not only endured my less than agreeable moods and uncommunicativeness during prolonged periods of research and writing, but also gave me at the most critical moments unfailing support and encouragement.

Joseph Camilleri

1. Conceptualizing region and regionalism

Interest in the study of regions has waxed and waned largely in response to shifts in the pattern of political, economic and strategic interaction both within and across state boundaries. The Second World War and subsequent efforts to reconstruct the ravaged economies of Western Europe served as a powerful stimulus for greater conceptual sophistication in the analysis of regions and regional integration. Using Europe as their main political laboratory, Haas, Mitrany and Deutsch were especially influential in the formative stages of theoretical inquiry.[1] The rapid evolution of regional organizations in Western Europe, beginning with the Coal and Steel Community and the European Atomic Community (EURATOM), seemed to indicate a new threshold in regional practice and a new challenge to the conceptual understanding of regional institutionalization in both its functional and political manifestations. However, with the loss of impetus which the idea of European unity experienced during the late 1960s and early 1970s, and the failure of that idea to be replicated in other parts of the world, regional integration theory entered a period of visible decline.[2] It appeared as if regional formations, particularly those with supranational aspirations, were being squeezed by two powerful forces: both older and newer versions of nationalism emanating from 'below', and global patterns of interdependence pressing from 'above'.

No sooner, however, had disillusionment set in, than a combination of factors – some well understood at the time but others only dimly perceived – would generate during the 1980s renewed though substantially modified enthusiasm for the theory and practice of regionalism. The 'new regionalism', as it subsequently came to be known, was less addicted to notions of supranational integration and more sensitive to the importance of looser regional linkages and exchanges. One observer characterized the new regionalism in the following terms:

> The revival of the European Community, the rise of effective comprehensive regional organizations outside of Western Europe, the emergence of 'trading blocs', the development of a mediatory role for regional organizations in the area of conflict resolution, the new linkages that they have formed with national and international institutions . . . and many other trends all suggest that the new regionalism is more than just a revival of the old, and that it is becoming a significant new factor in international relations.[3]

The widespread resurgence of regionalism was a complex phenomenon to which many disparate influences had contributed, but none was more pervasive than the internationalization of trade, production and finance.

What these pendulum swings in the vigour of regional discourse suggest is that the ebb and flow of ideas and periodic articulation and reorganization of political space which they express are themselves symptomatic of a complex evolutionary process. Regional systems, including their geographical, economic, politico-military and normative characteristics, are constantly evolving in response to new challenges posed by changing internal and external environmental conditions. An evolutionary perspective is therefore essential to an understanding of the scope and limitations of regionalism at any given time and place.

DEFINING REGION AND SUB-REGION

The case for historical contextualization does not obviate the need for definitional clarity. After all, the delineation of space, whether regionally or otherwise, is largely a subjective construct. Regions can be endowed with different meanings and be made to perform diverse functions – which meanings and which functions at a particular moment will depend as much on the perspective of the observer as on the phenomenon to be observed. To cite a few examples, Michael Haas follows Brecher in identifying regional systems in terms of three key elements: geographical delimitation of space, multiple actors, and a relatively self-contained network of political and military interactions.[4] Others employ the term 'proximity'[5] to convey the institutional dimension of interaction. Others still emphasize the role of 'economic interdependence', 'shared political attitudes and behavior' and even social and cultural homogeneity.[6] The definition advanced by Cantori and Spiegel stresses geographical proximity; international interaction; common bonds (ethnic, linguistic, cultural or social); and a sense of identity, which may assume high visibility in relations with states external to the region.[7]

The problem that emerges from these and other definitional exercises is not so much the gap that separates them as the vagueness common to many of the proposed conceptual categories. That vagueness – and the numerous differences in definitional emphasis and content arising from it – reflects in part the subjective element of the enterprise. In order to condense the commonly cited attributes of region into a more parsimonious set of necessary and sufficient conditions, Thompson privileges geographical proximity, regularity and intensity of interactions, and shared perceptions of the region as a distinctive theatre of operations.[8] Yet none of these three conditions, least of all the last one, can be formulated, let alone applied, with any degree of precision. Similarly, the general proposition that regions 'can be . . . conceived as "an intermediate form of community" between the national community of the state and the potential global community of humankind'[9] is plausible enough, but it fails to account for the size, boundaries or qualitative attributes of a region. If, for example, regular interaction is to be treated as a prerequisite of regional identity, several questions still remain to be addressed: how much and what kind of interaction? How does interaction at one level (for example, security or human rights) affect or is affected by interaction at another level (for example, economy or environment)? Who or what are the constituent units of regions – is it just states or both states and non-state actors?

To explore these questions in greater depth, it may be useful to revisit the elusive but closely related categories of boundaries and identity, for they are central to any conception of regional space. To put it differently, what are the influences which bear upon the construction of regional identity and regional boundaries? For analytical convenience we may distinguish between endogenous influences (those emanating from within the region or peculiar to the space encompassed by the region) and exogenous influences (those emanating outside the region or associated with space external to the region). Similarly, both sets of influences may be further subdivided into those that have a material or ideational basis, remembering, however, that useful though they are, such distinctions are ultimately artificial constructs, which, if taken too far, can obscure rather than illuminate.

Among the more important endogenous influences are those of geography and demography on the one hand and history and political culture on the other. Geography governs climate, size, topography, strategic location, and availability of raw materials, while demography indicates the size of the population and its age, sex and spatial distribution both within and between countries. Geographical and demographic factors combine at any given historical moment and in the context of prevailing technological possibilities to shape settlement patterns, population flows, communication and transportation systems, economic exchanges and strategic relationships. Yet these material constraints and opportunities impinging on human activity do not fully define it. We must turn to history to see what continuities or discontinuities in cultural, political and economic experience have emerged, and how these have shaped over time perceptions of amity and enmity and practices of co-operation, competition and conflict. An analysis of these practices and perceptions sheds useful light on the formation and subsequent development of regions, understood here not only as the physical space within which material exchanges routinely occur but as the socio-cultural space which conditions relatively constant expectations of interactional outcomes, positive or negative as the case may be.

Set against this wider historical canvas, one feature, itself a complex blend of ideational and institutional processes, namely political culture, looms large in the definition of regional boundaries and identity. Religious, ethnic, national, ideological and other ideational symbols and values give shape and meaning to societal affinities and solidarities on the one hand and conflicts of interest and perception on the other. These images of 'self' and 'other' help to frame the contours of individual societies and communities, but over time they can also acquire a regional dimension. In a sense the definition of a region and the values and purposes it represents become an integral part of the self-understanding of the societies which constitute the region, although that self-understanding may differ considerably in normative or cognitive structure from one society to another. In other words, normatively and cognitively speaking, interdependence does not mean – and is not conditional on – unqualified commonality or homogeneity. Shared knowledge and learning need not imply intersubjective harmony.[10] Two implications of this proposition are worth highlighting. First, differences and even perceptions of difference may well be integral to the construction of regional identity. Indeed, strategic, economic or cultural fault-lines may emerge as defining features of the regional landscape. Secondly, neighbouring states and communities may come to value any number of material exchanges, be it trade, technology flows or population movements, despite the substantial cultural or ideological distance that separates them. Material incentives may be at least as important as ideational affinities in binding a region together, although it should be noted that, analytically useful as the distinction between the material and the ideational may be, the two realms are in reality so closely interconnected as to be mutually constitutive.[11]

Ideas, symbols, values, or even affinities and solidarities, do not exist in a vacuum. They are of necessity internalized by agents, that is, individuals or collectivities of one kind or another. To put it differently, regional intercourse can be mediated by soldiers, diplomats, traders, financiers, guest workers, missionaries, intellectuals, tourists or refugees – to name a few of the more obvious categories – acting either as individuals or as members of their respective groups or associations, or as is more likely in their dual capacities. There is no denying, however, that collectivities are especially influential if for no other reason than that they bring far greater power and resources to bear on the form and content of regional interaction. More than that, collectivities are, by virtue of their institutional endowment, able to give expression to and legitimize ideas, symbols and values in ways which influence the perceptions and behaviour of their members, and, whether negatively or positively, the images and perceptions of other collectivities.

Understandably perhaps, much of the literature has tended to privilege states as the collectivities whose practice and discourse are likely to have the greatest impact on the formation of regions, the delineation of their boundaries, and the shape of their internal and external relationships. Inter-state relations – and the geopolitical and strategic norms on which they are premised – no doubt endow most regions with their political complexion. Such principles as sovereignty and the authority patterns which they imply both within and between states, leverage over the use and threat of force as manifested in military postures and capabilities, diplomatic conventions, and legal and organizational arrangements all testify to the relevance of state-centric perspectives on regional order. Yet individual states and the state system as a whole may be best characterized as intermediate agencies (or intermediaries) in the definition and development of regions. Important though they are in their own right, states are also a conduit for the diverse influences – geographical and demographic, as well as historical, political and socio-cultural – that simultaneously facilitate and impede the construction and evolution of regional space and time. These influences and the sites where they operate, primarily through markets and civil society, must therefore be made an integral part of the analysis.

Regions are not, however, self-contained entities. They are subject to any number of exogenous influences. These may well prove as decisive as endogenous influences in shaping the structure, composition and ethos of a given region, particularly if they evoke or provoke on the part of member states and their respective societies common or complementary responses based on shared experiences and interpretations. Such responses, it should be noted, need not be uniform across time or space – they can range from enthusiastic acceptance to grudging compliance or even active resistance. The external environment, in other words, is likely to present a region and its members with a mix of risks (threats) or opportunities (benefits), which bears upon virtually every area of social, political and economic life.

Exogenous influences may take different forms and originate from different sources. They may arise from the policies of states, transnational corporations, financial markets, international governmental institutions or non-governmental organizations. However, when it comes to external security, the member states of any region are likely to focus on the strategic orientation of external states, seeing in them the potential either for protection or for domination and hegemony. A great power may be geographically external to the region yet geopolitically integral to it, as was the case with the United States in both Northeast and Southeast Asia for the best part of 50 years after the Second World War. In responding, then, to external challenges states may opt for a variety of co-operative regional arrangements with a view either to resisting the hegemonic aspirations of an external power, or to benefiting from its protective umbrella. Such co-operation may entail alliances, balance of power strategies, institutionalization of confidence-building measures, or more ambitious security regimes. The same regional ambivalence to external pressure is evident in the economic arena. Whereas states may in certain circumstances be inclined to resist foreign penetration of their economies by erecting trade barriers or capital controls, they may in different circumstances opt for accommodation with foreign interests or prevailing economic orthodoxy, hoping instead that trade liberalization or financial deregulation will deliver competitive advantage in the international marketplace. How individual states and regions as a whole at a given moment respond to exogenous influences depends on the complex interplay of state, economy and civil society on the one hand, and the equally complex relationship between the local, national, regional and global tiers of governance on the other.

REGIONALISM AND REGIONALIZATION

High levels of interaction between neighbouring states are normally considered central to the formation and growth of regions. Interaction, however, has both quantitative and qualitative dimensions. Trade, financial flows, technology transfers and population movements are no doubt important indicators of regionalization, yet there is more to the phenomenon than the volume of these flows. At least as relevant are the division of labour within transnational firms, the strategic alliances among firms, and the development of regional business networks, growth triangles, industrial corridors, and the dense societal networks that connect families, firms and industries. In the economic arena the emergence of transnational technology complexes and production structures closely correlates with the development of regionally significant clusters. Qualitative interaction is if anything even more significant when it comes to geopolitical and cultural relationships, since these operate through formal and informal channels, through both states and non-state actors. In the Asia-Pacific region, for example, the pre-colonial, colonial and post-colonial periods have given rise to a succession of symbols, values, experiences and movements that have richly contributed to the emergence of regional and sub-regional consciousness.

Regional interaction – even interdependence – does not occur in a vacuum. As already noted, material and ideational processes and exchanges can give rise to a sense of regional identity, regional patterns of economic and social activity, and regional forms of organization. Whether or not and to what extent regionalization does in fact emerge is a function of a number of key variables, notably the configuration of power within and between regions, axes of conflict internal or external to the region, the degree of cohesion and homogeneity in intra-regional relationships, and the region's relative openness or closure to the outside world. These variables combine in different ways at different times to produce different outcomes, but each variable will to a greater or lesser extent help to shape the evolving regional landscape.

Power relations are instructive in that they indicate the way powerful states, groups and individuals influence outcomes, not least those that have a direct bearing on the formation of regions. Power here is used in its wider sense to denote the demographic and cultural as well as military and economic assets at the disposal of states and non-state actors. As we shall see in the next chapter, China, Japan and the United States have by virtue of their respective spheres of influence, created in different periods and sustained by vastly different forms of power, played a major part in the development of regional affinities and interdependencies. It is, however, conflict – actual or potential, real or imaginary – which endows power relations with content and meaning. It is the major axes of conflict, whether among regional powers or between regional and external powers, which bestow on the security dilemma its distinguishing regional characteristics. Buzan's notion of the *regional security complex* is presumably an attempt to connect regional security responses with prevailing patterns of regional conflict.[12] The ensuing regional security complexes may rest on the dominance of regional or global hegemons, great power concerts, various types of military alliance, and other multilateral security arrangements reflecting varying levels of institutionalization and normative convergence.[13] To suggest, however, that these complexes or security communities are situated somewhere between 'the "logic of anarchy" (of the state system) and the "logic of community" (of a potential world community of humankind)'[14] does not adequately characterize them. Still less does it explain why any security arrangement occupies a particular point on the continuum at a specific moment, or why there is likely to be movement from one moment to the next.

A fuller grasp of the dynamics of regionalization requires that considerations of power and conflict be complemented and qualified by the role of homogeneity and community. In other words, both difference and identity, division and cohesion must be regarded as integral to the growth of regional exchanges and institutions. Heterogeneity – and the prospect of division and conflict – far from being injurious to regionalization may well provide a set of states (as well as other actors) with a powerful incentive to manage and even prevent conflict. In the European context, it is arguably Franco-German hostility, resulting in three major wars in the space of a few decades, which more than any other factor paved the way for European integration. Notwithstanding marked ethnic, linguistic, religious and economic differences, perhaps because of them, Western European political and intellectual elites now turned to the idea of European unity in the hope of averting future wars and stemming the tide of European decline. The important point to note is that homogeneity and heterogeneity are ultimately subjective notions, not easily definable in terms of quantitative criteria. The differences separating France and Britain, Portugal and Denmark, or even Greece and Turkey may at a certain point in time appear unbridgeable, yet social and economic change can even in a relatively short time-span drastically diminish their significance and give rise to new possibilities scarcely imaginable even a few years earlier.

None of this is to suggest that difference and division constitute an adequate foundation for regionalization, but rather that what gives impetus to and sustains the process is a peculiar blend of difference and commonality, division and cohesion. To this extent at least, Deutsch is right to emphasize the importance of communication, that is of shared knowledge and perceptions. The experiences associated with past wars and the awareness of conflicting interests and perspectives can help to forge among elites but also among the wider public a sense of community, that is a readiness to seek common ground and new forms of collaboration. The ensuing growth of transaction flows may be interpreted as the outward or quantitative manifestation of this 'sense of community', by which Deutsch had in mind a set of mental and emotional dispositions, including 'mutual sympathy and loyalties . . . partial identification in terms of self images and interests . . . mutually successful predictions of behaviour mutual attraction and responsiveness in the process of decision-making'.[15] Deutsch's 'transactionalist' perspective with its implicit emphasis on ideational and normative influences has rightly been described as offering an alternative to the language of power.[16] However, as Deutsch himself intimates, though never fully elaborates, there are clear limitations to the theory and practice of community, in a regional as in any other political setting. While international and transnational interactions are no doubt instrumental in shaping and reshaping shared identities as well as in defining and redefining state interests, the outcome is invariably a composite one, in which the experience of difference coexists with shared identity and conflict with co-operation.

To surmount or at least bypass these conceptual difficulties, the transactionalist model favoured by Deutsch and his associates developed the notion of 'security community', that is, a regional association where by definition the imperative to co-operate has achieved primacy over conflictual tendencies. While competing interests, disagreements and power asymmetries may persist, the members of a security community are said to engage in an informal governance system based on shared meanings and a collective identity which predisposes them to the peaceful settlement of disputes. Such communities are characterized by a high degree of trust, common aspirations, low probability of armed conflict, and clear differentiation between life within and outside the community. More concrete indicators of the existence of a security community may be found in the normative discourse of member states, common definitions of external threats, various forms of joint military preparedness, relaxation of border controls, and a wide range of multilateral institutional arrangements.[17] This formulation is nevertheless problematic, not because it lacks parsimony, but because it begs two fundamental though closely related questions: is peaceful governance a *sine qua non* for the existence of a region? Is the co-operative ethos prevailing within a region attainable only at the expense of mistrust and antagonism in relations between regions? There is, of course, no simple or uniform answer to either question. On the other hand, such notions as *security community* and *regional security complex* are open to criticism in that, unwittingly or otherwise, they apply to a regional setting the crude principle of the amity–enmity complex.[18]

Both questions are nevertheless illuminating for they permit a closer examination of the last of the four variables we have identified as central to the processes and modalities of regionalization, namely the relative openness or closure of one region *vis-à-vis* other regions and the global system as a whole. Openness in this context refers to the extent and intensity of interaction between one region and its external environment or to be more exact to a region's capacity and propensity for such interaction. Here it is worth stressing that openness or closure are not necessarily antithetical, and certainly not mutually exclusive. Openness in the context of economic exchange may, for example, coexist with high levels of cultural insularity. Forms and degrees of openness are in any case unlikely to be static. Financial, commercial, technological and demographic movements across regional boundaries will normally be subject to periods of ebb and flow, which often overlap and intersect and must themselves be situated within an evolutionary framework.

It will come as no surprise that the complexities of openness and closure have assumed unusual prominence in the age of globalization. The expansion of the capitalist world economy, in particular the vastly increased mobility of capital, labour and information, has greatly multiplied and diversified the linkages between regional subsystems and the world system. To this extent, globalization has arguably given rise to greater homogeneity, both within and between regions. Paradoxically enough, by virtue of the competitive dynamic which animates it, global capitalism has also engendered a series of new economic and political divisions both within and between regions.[19] Difficult questions immediately arise as to the precise relationship between regionalization and globalization. Are these to be considered quite separate, perhaps, parallel or overlapping trends? Or, are they convergent or even mutually constitutive trends? Expressed a little differently, does one complement and even reinforce the other? Or, again are they largely antithetical trends, and is regionalization best understood as a response to the challenge of globalization, as an attempt on the part of nations and communities to salvage something of their autonomy and distinctiveness by pooling resources or developing common institutions?[20] Even if this third interpretation is assumed to offer the most persuasive account of regionalization, the ensuing world order would not necessarily be more pluralistic and regions would not be transformed into diverse and autonomous entities occupying political space freed of the constraints of economic, technological and cultural globalization. In other words, regional formations, initiatives and institutions, regardless of their underlying premises and objectives, might not be able to withstand the intrusiveness of globalizing influences. Even with the creation of trade blocs, mercantilist notions of integration, and the adoption of redistributive principles in social and economic policy, regions would still be obliged to take cognisance of the international division of labour and the competitive ethos which sustains it. Similarly, regions, regardless of their internal capabilities and co-operative arrangements, can neither ignore nor extricate themselves from the internationalization of the security dilemma.[21]

It is neither possible nor appropriate to examine within the confines of this chapter the complexities of the elusive and still rapidly evolving phenomenon that is globalization. A few observations may nevertheless be helpful in clarifying the implications for regionalization. Though globalization in itself is not a new phenomenon, the most recent phase – often associated with the last three decades of the twentieth century – has been characterized by the increasing mobility of capital, and with it the tendency for production to be organized on a global scale. Integral to this trend has been the shift to 'flexible production' made possible in large measure by the revolution in information technology and the consequent creation and maintenance of global production networks.[22] A second distinguishing feature of contemporary globalization has been the phenomenal expansion of international financial flows, with the global movement of capital far outstripping the total value of world trade. The sheer speed and magnitude of financial transactions have combined with their speculative character to shape both the pattern of production and its geographic location. The judgements and decisions of large corporations, banks and foreign exchange markets testify to the structural power of internationally mobile capital, which both states and inter-state organizations have no option but to recognize and accommodate. Though the circumstances of states vary considerably, both in terms of internal and external influence, the freedom of action available to national policy-makers is severely constrained by the mere fact that strategically placed financial interests have it within their power to bestow their favour on compliant governments and to withdraw it from recalcitrant ones. Though globalization affects different regions and different parts of the same region differently, no region can escape its impact or remain immune to the interconnectedness of global production networks and the intrusiveness of financial markets.

Regionalization may indeed be seen as an indispensable conduit for globalization in that the 'post-Fordist' emphasis on flexible production techniques and the flexible deployment of labour itself necessitates the emergence of regional trading blocs or 'free trade areas'. These regional arrangements, which are overtly at odds with global multilateral norms and institutions, are nevertheless favoured precisely because it is only through the integration of key commodity and service industries that major corporate interests can take full advantage of their newly found flexibility. They are as a consequence able to devise strategies better adapted to the social, economic and financial conditions obtaining in different countries and even different localities in the same country. States too may be attracted by the regional option in that it offers the prospect of institutional arrangements which can, in the face of globally induced tensions and dislocations, facilitate the task of collective management but without the intrusiveness of global standard-setting and regulatory and enforcement mechanisms. Refugee flows, transnational crime, air pollution or piracy may be symptoms of global pathologies, but the more effective /or at least more palatable remedies may be more accessible at the regional than global level.

All regional trading blocs do not, however, perform the same functions or conform to the same logic. Varying degrees of openness or closure are reflected in highly variable policies on appropriate levels of protection for domestic industries. In this sense, economic regions may be described as sites of contention between interests that can successfully negotiate the competitive environment of an unrestricted global marketplace and those intent on securing at least temporary protection from such competition by erecting regional barriers to trade and financial flows. Regionalism, like nationalism, can therefore embrace globalizing trends and influences, but it can also act as a countervailing force, in the cultural and political as much as in the economic sphere. More specifically, regional collaboration may serve to counter the homogenizing tendencies that accompany cultural globalization. Spread by educational institutions and the world media and sustained by the ideological preferences and practices of political, business and professional elites, resistance to these tendencies is often expressed by the affirmation of distinct identities and cultural and religious traditions, whether at the local, national or regional level. The assertion of 'Asian Values' or the 'Asian Way' in contradiction to 'Western' or 'liberal' values offers one, albeit striking, illustration of the kind of inter-regional fault-lines that elites, competing for influence and legitimacy on the national and international stage, have been instrumental in etching on to the global geoeconomic landscape.

But if regionalism can be depicted as a consequence of – or reaction to – globalization, it can also be interpreted as a stimulus to globalization. Regional pressures towards the homogenization of economic policies, whether based on the desire to attract foreign investment and technology, or on the perceived need to engage in more effective bargaining at global multilateral fora, become powerful instruments for incorporating national and regional bureaucracies into the emerging ethos and rationality of global practices and institutions. To this extent, it may be more accurate and analytically more useful to view regionalization and globalization as mutually reinforcing processes, as different parts of a larger dialectic that oscillates between and encompasses closure and openness, homogeneity and heterogeneity, conflict and co-operation. The renewed interest in regions and regionalism is in large measure attributable to this dialectic and its multiple and far-reaching implications for governance. The crucial question here is the adequacy of existing institutions for managing the new and complex web of geopolitical and geoeconomic developments, and the extent to which institutional innovation can remedy any observable normative or organizational deficit. How, in other words, does regionalism relate to regionalization? To what extent are the functional and institutional arrangements that have emerged over the last 30 years a response to rising levels of regional or global economic interaction and interdependence? And how does regional governance relate to the increasingly intricate and at times opaque framework of global governance?

REGIONAL MULTILATERALISM: A TYPOLOGY

We have already had occasion to refer to both *regionalism* and *regionalization*. It may be useful at this point to distinguish a little more clearly between the two concepts. Whereas regionalization refers to the diverse flows and processes, be they economic, technological, or socio-cultural, that bind together the constituent entities of any given region, regionalism describes the tendency of a region and its constituents to preserve or expand the benefits of regional interaction by developing institutions and mechanisms of various kinds that set, monitor and enforce the standards of interaction.[23] In this sense, regionalism is simply another name for regional multilateralism. It is worth stressing, however, that, while states will generally play a key role in establishing and consolidating regional institutions and mechanisms, there is no reason to conceive of the phenomenon as exclusively state-centric. Though politicians, diplomats, bureaucrats and generals are central figures in the regionalist project, so are merchants, industrialists, intellectuals, professionals and social activists. What differentiates these actors is the political space they occupy, the different forms it assumes in each case, and the different basis on which it is delineated. Second-track and third-track diplomacy are terms that have recently come into prominence precisely in order to express the multiplicity and diversity of spatial forms which first-track diplomacy cannot fully capture.[24] We shall presently return to the respective roles of state and non-state actors, but suffice it here to say that multilateralism, in its regional as much as in its global dimension, is a multifaceted phenomenon whose distinguishing characteristic is the interconnectedness of both normative and organizational strands.

To convey something of the richness and intricacy of regional forms, we propose to construct a typology based on five main categories: membership, structure, function, external orientation and architecture. Membership refers to the kinds of entities that are involved in multilateral relations. One of the more important contributions of functionalism and especially neo-functionalism has been the increasing emphasis placed upon civil society and the ensuing network of linkages which cut across state boundaries and to varying degrees limit the state's freedom of action. States, important as they are, share the stage with several other types of actors, notably those that spring from or function within civil society (for example, professional associations, labour unions, religious groups, 'epistemic communities',[25] social movements) and those that operate in the marketplace, that is, the firms and individuals that are engaged in the production, exchange and distribution of goods and services. To the extent that the networks of linkages to which these actors contribute assume a distinctly regional profile, it may be appropriate to refer to regional markets, regional economies, and even regional civil society. Sustaining each of these regional sites will be a certain institutional infrastructure which complements, confronts, or in some way connects with state-centric institutions. Distinct from, though closely related to, this categorization is that which differentiates between actors in terms of the political space they occupy. We may speak of national actors, that is actors whose political space or range of action is co-extensive with the boundaries of the state. In this sense, firms, civil society organizations and states themselves can all qualify as national actors. However, states can also give rise to international actors (inter-state governmental organizations) and supranational actors (highly integrated regional institutions), whose activities and *modus operandi* encompass two or more states. On the other hand, civil society organizations can also assume a multiplicity of profiles – national, subnational and transnational – that is to say their activities may range across the entire national space, some fraction of it, or across the space of two or more states.

Another important characteristic of regions is their internal structure, that is the types of linkages that connect their constituent entities. These can range from relatively unstructured, highly informal consultative arrangements, through to unwritten customs and conventions, more formal legal arrangements as expressed in memoranda, agreements and treaties, and specific organizational arrangements involving bureaucratic and political participation at varying levels of seniority, budgetary allocations, secretariats, administrative infrastructure, and in some instances even a legislative and judicial framework.[26] Environmental factors are likely to account for considerable variations in institutionalization across regions – but also across policy areas within the same region – in terms of complexity, formality, resource allocation and the pooling or delegation of sovereignty.

Regional arrangements may also be distinguished by reference to the functions they serve. Whereas some have a primarily geopolitical or security focus, others function largely in the economic arena. This distinction, however, runs the risk of oversimplification, for security and economy are not discrete but closely interconnected spheres of activity. Moreover, they do not exhaust the wide range of functions performed by regional organizations, nor do they convey the diverse organizational forms through which security and economic co-operation can be expressed. In the security context, collaborative arrangements may take the form of military alliances, regional concerts, collective security organizations, or more *ad hoc* confidence-building mechanisms. Similarly, in the economic arena, varying levels of regional integration may be envisaged from limited attempts at sectoral co-operation, to free trade associations, customs unions, common markets, and economic unions.[27] In any case, regionalism may be motivated by any number of objectives. A regional formation, whether as a consequence of its security and economic functions or quite independently of them, may serve a wider normative or agenda-setting purpose. Its main function might be to enhance common understanding and communication among its members either as an end in itself or as a means to achieving certain practical outcomes. Conversely, regional collaboration may eschew larger cultural or ideological goals and concentrate instead on any number of highly concrete technical tasks, involving the shared expertise of the bureaucratic and professional classes in such diverse fields as health, education, transport or environment. In practice, most regionalist projects are likely to involve a range of functions and engage a variety of actors, giving rise to multiple and diverse forms of interaction.

The variability of institutional forms is not, however, confined to issues of internal structure and organizational culture. It is also characteristic of regional responses to the external environment. Here too variability has a great many dimensions, but two merit particular attention. The first is best expressed by the notions of *openness* and *closure* and the second by *inclusiveness* and *exclusiveness*. Though the two sets of ideas are closely related – they both connote the degree to which threats to internal cohesion are attributed to external agencies – they allude to somewhat different types of threat perception, and certainly to different responses. Openness and closure refer to those material and ideational factors which predispose certain regions to pursue high levels of interaction with the outside world – reflecting varying levels of dependence and interdependence – and other regions to pursue policies of self-reliance or even self-sufficiency. Openness may manifest itself in trade and investment policies or in security arrangements, both of which may give rise to extensive or intensive inter-regional exchanges, but also to substantial linkages between regional and global institutions. In practice no regional formation is likely to be completely open, that is to allow the totally unfettered movement of people, ideas, information, commodities and capital across its boundaries or on the other hand to be hermetically sealed, that is, to avoid all commercial, financial, political or cultural transactions with external actors, be they states, other regions, or global multilateral organizations. Most regions will pursue a mix of openness and closure, with the quality of that mix varying from region to region, and from one policy area to another within the same region.

Inclusiveness refers instead to those material and ideational conditions which predispose regional organizations to extend membership to any state which qualifies by virtue of geographical proximity and readiness to comply with regional norms and policies. By contrast an exclusivist stance normally rests on the view that the existing membership should be consolidated, and that to accept new members, regardless of geographical location or willingness to abide by existing institutional norms and practices, would be to endanger the region's cohesion, stability and organizational effectiveness. The intensity of the depth-versus-breadth debates that have punctuated the recent history of the European Union and ASEAN are indicative of the far-reaching implications of the questions involved, and of the difficulty of bringing those debates to some consensual finality.

It remains to say a word about architecture,[28] which in one sense represents a summation of the other dimensions, but in effect tells us something of a region's underlying logic, or expressed a little differently, something of the design which is in the minds of its leading architects. At any given moment the architecture as it appears to the observer will not necessarily match the original design, and in any case both design and architecture are likely to evolve over time. Architecture is nevertheless a useful concept for it points to those structural and 'stylistic' features which give shape and content to the relationships between the region and its sub-regions. More generally, it highlights the different forms of nesting which link the regional, sub-regional and global tiers of governance. More than that, a region's architecture is likely to reveal something of the normative design – or in some instances competing designs – that animates the regional project. In line with Paul Taylor's illuminating typology, we may describe a region's organizational architecture primarily in terms of *adjustment* (various forms of inter-governmental co-operation designed to assist governments to carry out the multiple new tasks which inevitably arise from new political circumstances, in particular from technological change and other aspects of economic modernization), *integration* (involving the refashioning of the state system as a consequence of substantial changes in societal attitudes and values or attempts by policy elites to reconcile their differences), or *transformation* (associated with deeper normative change, which may result in new forms of global or regional federalism described by Dag Hammarskjöld as 'sophisticated constitutionalism').[29]

REGIONALISM: THE ROLE OF POWER

One of the noteworthy deficiencies of both functionalism and neo-functionalism has been the tendency to portray multilateralism as a technical project, as one in which the scope and authority of international institutions can expand by dint of the 'spill-over' effect, with innovative leadership and non-state actors helping to give the process greater impetus and legitimacy. Insightful though it may have been, this attempt to elucidate the inner dynamic of institutional growth was unnecessarily unidimensional in the sense that it understated the impediments to multilateralism and gave pride of place to technical or functional considerations at the expense of political or structural determinants. Power in particular, though it may assume different forms and originate from different sources, must be made an integral part of the equation, for it invariably influences and even shapes the creation, development and consolidation of multilateral processes and institutions, as well as their impairment and eventual disintegration. Power, whether expressed in material or ideational terms – the two, we have noted more than once, are closely entwined and often mutually reinforcing – is indispensable to any coalition of interests intent on establishing and sustaining a multilateral project. Power has many ingredients – economic, military, organizational or cultural – and is not amenable to precise measurement, yet its relative distribution both globally and regionally is bound to have a profound impact on regional multilateralism, advancing or retarding its prospects as the case may be.

We begin with an analysis of the global structure of power, for the systemic environment sets the context – the web of constraints and opportunities – within which subsystems or regions must function. This is especially the case in the era of globalization where no region is sufficiently self-contained to be immune to outside pressure. A systemic perspective must, however, encompass both the political and economic dimensions of power, and cannot therefore be reduced to the power of states. On the other hand, if we treat states not just as agents and repositories of power but as sites where a great many other actors exercise and compete for power, then the state system taken as a whole can be used as an approximate guide to the global distribution of power. In this sense it may be useful to begin by distinguishing between international structures on the basis of key geopolitical variables. We may, for example, conceive of a unipolar model in which only one centre of power is capable of pursing global objectives and strategies; a bipolar model sustained by one major axis of systemic conflict, and opposing blocs or alliance systems over which one centre of power exercises hegemonic leadership; and a multipolar model characterized by multiple, fluid alliances and coalitions.

As a generalization, regional formations can expect to enjoy relatively high levels of autonomy in multipolar systems and relatively low levels of autonomy in unipolar systems. Bipolarity would make for less uniform outcomes, with levels of autonomy likely to be lowest for regions that were closely integrated into one or other of the two opposing spheres of influence.[30] The structural differences between the three models would also manifest themselves in different crisis management strategies and different rates of success in conflict resolution (about which more later). Suffice it here to say that the contemporary world system is best described as a complex and dynamic mosaic of all three structures, which reflects the powerful and contradictory pressures associated with rapid strategic, economic, technological, cultural and institutional change. In other words, the post-Cold War system is likely to be characterized by substantial variation from region to region with respect to levels of autonomy, patterns of institutional innovation and consolidation, crisis management techniques, and approaches to conflict resolution.

In examining systemic influences on regional arrangements and institutions we have thus far concentrated on the global configuration of power. Equally important, however, is the specific role of individual dominant powers. Dominance here is used loosely to refer not only to hegemony but to a wide range of relationships through which external powers are able to exercise systematic leverage over regional affairs. We may, for example, speak of the Soviet Union, the United States, China and in later years Japan, as having wielded considerable though variable influence on Southeast Asia during the Cold War period. Military capabilities of one kind or another were critical to US, Soviet and Chinese influence, but many of the protagonists were also able to rely on other forms of power in which they enjoyed a degree of comparative advantage: Japan relied mainly on its economic muscle, China on its physical proximity and demographic weight, and the United States on its organizational power.

Dominant external powers are no doubt integral to any regional equation, yet dominance is not synonymous with institutional leadership, and this for two reasons. First, certain ingredients of power that make for dominance, especially military and economic assets, may not be accompanied by the necessary organizational know-how and infrastructure, diplomatic skills, or normative, ideological or intellectual legitimacy. In other words, a dominant power need not necessarily be hegemonic. As Robert Cox has so incisively argued,

> [Hegemony presupposes] dominance of a particular kind where the dominant state creates an order based ideologically on a broad measure of consent, functioning according to general principles that in fact ensure the continuing supremacy of the leading state or states and leading social classes but at the same time offer some measure or prospect of satisfaction to the less powerful.[31]

For Cox, the hegemonic order is underpinned by a structure of values and understandings as much as it is by a structure of power. These two structures, which complement and reinforce each other, derive not merely from the power of the dominant state but from the practices and ideologies of its most powerful social strata. It is these practices and ideologies which inspire emulation or elicit the acquiescence of the dominant social strata of other states.[32]

Giving expression to the same idea, Gamble and Payne describe hegemony as a 'rare and very powerful political relationship' where the incorporation of subordinate groups involves the granting of special privileges and benefits. As a consequence, hegemony implies 'not simply the acceptance of a common set of ideological principles but the construction of a new identity in which both leader and subordinate share'.[33] Arguably, during the Cold War years both the United States and the Soviet Union exercised hegemonic leadership within their respective camps, but any implied symmetry between the two centres of power would be seriously misleading. Moscow's dominance was too dependent on the instruments of political and military coercion and too constrained by the weakness of the Soviet economy, for it to enjoy the necessary degree of legitimacy. US power, by contrast, had at its disposal a much larger and more sophisticated economic and technological base, and an elaborate organizational infrastructure endowing it with a global reach which no competitor could match. To put it differently, the American state acting in conjunction with American capital was able to institutionalize the core–periphery division of labour on a global scale. The General Agreement on Tariffs and Trade (GATT), the International Monetary Fund (IMF), the World Bank and the United Nations (UN) system itself were but the most obvious manifestations of US *global hegemony*, that is, of the subtle mix of formal and informal inducements and constraints which incorporated allies, friends and neutrals alike into a complex web of dependence.

Yet, US institutional leadership in the post-1945 period, though extensive and deeply embedded, was neither universally accepted nor uniformly effective.

In Asia Pacific, for example, the economic and military order associated with *Pax Americana* reflected and sustained a structure of intersubjective meanings which was never fully internalized by the polities or cultures of the region. Much of the opposition to US dominance, it is true, derived from the ambitions of a rival hegemonic project centred on Soviet power and leadership. Nevertheless two of the most intense conflicts of the Cold War period, the Korean and Vietnam wars, were not mere manifestations of strategic bipolarity. They also expressed on the one hand the strength of Vietnamese and Korean nationalism and on the other the revival of China's political self-confidence and the determination of its communist leadership to resist Western dominance and at least partially erase the profound sense of past humiliations. Equally relevant in this context were the numerous and diverse revolutionary movements, including communist parties of varying ideological complexion, which sought to arrest and even reverse the penetration of US influence.

At one level the end of the Cold War could be said to represent the ultimate triumph of American power. At a deeper level that triumph, most conspicuously reflected in the durability of US alliances and US military supremacy, merely obscured the new complexity and polarization of regional geopolitics. The 'Asian versus Western values' debate, the trade frictions between the United States and the main East Asian economies, the uneven development between and within national economies, and the consequent pressures for the reorganization of existing regional institutions and establishment of new ones pointed to the fluidity of the post-Cold War period. The material power relations underpinning US hegemony may not have visibly changed, but new axes of conflict and new forms of contestation were beginning to corrode the ideological framework of US hegemony. In that sense the institutions of the Cold War period, even the most solidly based military alliances, seemed ill-equipped to cope with the challenges posed by rapidly evolving economic conditions and cultural perceptions. The terrorist attacks on the United States on 11 September 2001 and the ensuing 'war on terror' were a dramatic manifestation of this trend.

The emergence of new multilateral institutions or the consolidation of existing ones may therefore be seen as one logical consequence of the decline of global hegemony, which is not to say that this is a necessary or even probable consequence. Multilateralism may be more accurately described as the terrain of contestation within the core – in part between existing and aspiring hegemons – as well as between the core and the periphery. Both of these possibilities manifested themselves at different times and with different degrees of intensity during the Cold War years and in somewhat different guise during the post-Cold War period. The various attempts of the non-aligned movement and the G77 to use multilateral institutions, in part through the UN system, to curb hegemonic power are a case in point. So are West European and Japanese initiatives aimed at limiting the tendency of US policy-makers to act unilaterally whether on economic or security issues. Contestation, however, has regional as well as global dimensions. In the Asia-Pacific context, the growth of the Association of Southeast Asian Nations (ASEAN), the subsequent establishment of the Asia Pacific Economic Cooperation (APEC) group, the ASEAN Regional Forum (ARF) and ASEAN+3 (ASEAN + China, Japan and South Korea) may be partly understood as responses to diminished US hegemony – or at the very least to the perception of such diminution.

Not surprisingly, the post-Cold War period has given rise to numerous and often conflicting interpretations of the evolving geopolitical and geoeconomic landscape. Precisely because it is a transitional period, the analysis of emerging trends has had to contend with multiple – and often highly elusive – variables. For some the decline of US hegemony is evident in the rise of new regional centres of power, and in the case of Asia Pacific of regional hegemons, notably China and Japan. The implications for multilateralism may vary considerably, pointing at one extreme to *regional hegemony* (that is, the dominance of a regional hegemon) or at the other extreme to regional autonomy (arising from a new equilibrium between the emerging regional hegemon and the declining global hegemon). Others, less persuaded by the putative signs of greater multipolarity, point instead to the durability, even consolidation, of US hegemony and to the pervasive US role in the functioning of most global and regional institutions. Others still regard America's global military reach as constrained in practice by domestic influences, ranging from the psychology of internal introversion to the paralysing fear of sustaining casualties in any military conflict, and the preoccupation with maximizing economic opportunities in a highly competitive global market. As a consequence, the argument runs, the United States, notwithstanding its awesome military capabilities, is compelled to pursue the politics of coalition-building. The net effect of such a strategy is to encourage the establishment of *ad hoc* coalitions which depend for their success, and especially for their legitimacy, on varying degrees of co-operation with global and regional institutions. Though multilateralism of this kind does make for greater participation in international decision-making by those situated at the periphery of the world system, proponents of this model tend to focus attention on the emerging concert of powers, a mechanism which is essentially informal in structure and can function either regionally or globally, but often with uneven or intermittent success. These diverse models or scenarios are not necessarily mutually exclusive; they may indeed coexist or even complement one another. Given the plurality of competing interests and capabilities which are shaping this period of transition, we should expect to find a considerable degree of flux and heterogeneity in regional architecture, with varying levels of institutional innovation giving expression to complex but diverse forms of interaction between economy and security on the one hand, and between regional and sub-regional levels of coordination on the other.

REGIONALISM: THE ROLE OF CONFLICT

As with power so with conflict, the implications for institutional innovation are often contradictory. Both inter-societal and intra-societal conflict can have far-reaching consequences for regional identity and institution-building, but the linkages between the type of conflict, the mechanisms which it brings into play and the outcomes that it produces are neither uniform nor unidirectional. A few key distinctions may shed useful light on the analysis of this complex set of linkages.

Intra-societal conflict, be it economic, ethnic, racial, religious or ideological in origin or character, can in certain circumstances become a catalyst for institutional innovation. To cite an obvious example, ASEAN was conceived by its founders largely, though not exclusively, as performing an internal security function. It soon became a legitimating mechanism for overcoming, or at least minimizing, the vulnerability of governments to pressure exerted by communist and other revolutionary movements A regional umbrella came to be seen as an indispensable aid to national resilience. Over time, however, as we shall see in the case of ASEAN, a regional organization may acquire entirely new functions, or it may continue to perform similar functions but with significant changes of emphasis or strategic approach. Changes in the political complexion of states, for example the uneven but steady transition from authoritarian to more liberal forms of government, may itself contribute to regional co-operation, or at least endow regionalization with new institutional possibilities.[34] Equally, regional initiatives, inspired in part or in whole by internal considerations of political stability or economic prosperity, may subsequently assume, implicitly or explicitly, an external security function and give rise to new instruments of conflict prevention or conflict management.

That having been said, intra-societal conflict may also act as an impediment to institutional innovation. Any number of factors associated with internal instability may militate against regional co-operation. National governments, whose decision-making processes are largely ineffectual or whose hold on power is precarious, are unlikely to be able to commit the energy and resources needed to sustain regional institution-building. The difficulties experienced by ASEAN at the height of the East Asian financial crisis in 1997–98 is a case in point. Similarly, the incompatibility of interests and perceptions which lie at the root of intra-societal conflicts may well have a spill-over effect and exacerbate inter-state conflicts, or at least place severe limitations on regional co-operation. The political turbulence associated with leadership change in Indonesia and increasing social and religious ferment in Malaysia in the late 1990s may offer another partial explanation of ASEAN's temporary paralysis.

The dual possibilities implicit in intra-societal conflict are equally evident with inter-societal conflict. Here again conflict may serve as a catalyst for institutional innovation. As Western European integration has amply demonstrated, the painful lessons of the last war (the Second World War) and the cumulative damage resulting from intermittent hostilities (decades of Franco-German enmity) can provide a powerful incentive to devise new institutions capable of cementing a durable peace. That option may be all the more attractive to the extent that institutional integration carries the promise of substantial improvements to the economic and social well-being of member nations. Yet, inter-state conflict may have exactly the opposite effect. It may impede regional institutionalization, and encourage instead various forms of regional segmentation, be it ideological, economic or strategic, with entire regions or sub-regions sharply divided into opposing blocs or spheres of influence. This was precisely the impact of the Cold War in central Europe, the Middle East, and the rimlands of Asia, where the establishment of alliances and counter-alliances, the progressive build-up of offensive capabilities and the mutual mistrust and suspicion they encouraged had a profoundly deleterious effect on the normative and institutional foundations of regional identity formation.

The preceding analysis is useful not for its predictive capacity – it clearly does not enable us to determine with any degree of reliability the institutional outcomes of internal or international conflict – but for its insights into the complex and at times contradictory relationship between conflict and institution-building. Enough has already been said to indicate that the two are not mutually exclusive. The clash of interests and perceptions, of strategic calculations and cultural traditions may at a given moment make way for a greater degree of mutual accommodation, which may range from passive coexistence to active co-operation. Whether or not conflict leads in this direction – and the particular path that is followed – will be shaped by the complex interplay of security and economy, and political processes operating nationally, regionally and internationally. We shall return to these complexities later in this chapter and at greater length in subsequent chapters.

Given that regional multilateralism may be encouraged by the frequency or intensity of conflict or, more accurately, by the perceived need for conflict management, it is not surprising that multilateral arrangements should focus on the creation of conflict-resolving or at least conflict-stabilizing mechanisms.[35] These may vary considerably in form, scope or strategic orientation. In the field of conventional security, they are likely to encompass in the first instance a range of confidence- and security-building measures, designed to achieve primarily political and psychological outcomes, though they may also have important military ramifications. More ambitiously, multilateral initiatives may emerge in the areas of disarmament and arms control, crisis and conflict prevention, and even peacekeeping and peace enforcement

In the field of non-conventional security, the potential agenda is virtually limitless, ranging across such diverse fields as piracy, terrorism, transnational crime, population movements, the environment, and foreign debt. Here too, regional multilateralism can serve a great many functions, from setting and monitoring standards in environmental protection, to strengthening human rights institutions, to promoting state-centric or transnational forms of technical and economic co-operation, to negotiating and implementing trade agreements, to fostering cultural exchanges and dialogue. In seeking solutions to transnational problems multilateral approaches are well suited to exploiting the advantages of neighbourhood and proximity, expanding or complementary markets, economies of scale, and regional clustering arising from favourable labour, fiscal or resource conditions.

Yet multilateralism is no panacea. The complex and diverse transnational challenges that often exceed the problem-solving capacities of national governments are not all necessarily amenable to regional solutions. Indeed, multilateralism may in certain circumstances merely serve to exacerbate conflict. The formation of regional trading blocs may be a case in point. Regionalist projects, while helping to eliminate trade barriers within the region, may attempt to insulate the regional economy from foreign competition and in the process become exclusivist and protectionist in orientation. This 'strategic trade' approach may be motivated by legitimate social and economic objectives, but inherent in it is the possibility that it will be used to buttress the vested interests of regional firms and industries, the end result of which may be a collision, or at least uneasy stand-off, between regional blocs. While the European Union, the North American Free Trade Area (NAFTA), and the much less formalized regional production alliance centred around Japan are all rhetorically committed to free trade principles, in practice all three pursue to varying degrees and in different ways training, research, investment, public procurement and infrastructure policies designed to maximize their respective trading interests.[36] In these circumstances it is arguable that regionalism may accentuate rather than moderate the competitive dynamic driving the contemporary global economy.

The notion of exclusive (or closed) as distinct from inclusive (open) regionalism has been most clearly applied to international trade, with principles of free trade sharply – often somewhat simplistically – juxtaposed with those of managed or strategic trade. The polarizing tendencies of regional multilateralism are not, however, confined to trade or the economic arena more generally. They are equally evident in the geopolitical organization of regional space, where the competition between imperial powers can give rise to military alliances or other mechanisms for maintaining and expanding economic and military spheres of influence. The division of post-1945 Europe into two opposing strategic and ideological blocs is a classic instance of this phenomenon. In addition to the more obvious economic and strategic dimensions, inter-regional rivalries can also appear in cultural, religious or civilizational garb, with regional alliances or coalitions giving expression to common or unifying principles and beliefs. In this case symbols and loyalties, though crucial to the processes of regional cohesion, are likely to have a sharply polarizing effect on inter-regional relations. In reality, the economic, geopolitical and ideational origins of regional identity formation are seldom independent or mutually exclusive of one another. Generally, all three dimensions will be in evidence, though there may be moments when one dimension is dominant and others when it is barely visible, at least to the naked eye. The factors making for inter-regional conflict or accommodation cannot therefore be reduced to a single category, nor can they be adequately encompassed by a snapshot of reality that is fixed in time and space.

A FEW CONCLUDING OBSERVATIONS

What emerges from the foregoing survey is the multidimensional character of regional multilateralism – the multiple purposes which it can serve and the numerous forms it can take. Multilateral institutions may give expression to the interests and power of a global or regional hegemon. Alternatively, they may reflect a more co-operative and less monolithic order more in keeping with the structural needs of a global or regional concert of powers. There is more, however, to regional multilateralism than this range of possibilities. Institution-building need not be directed to system-maintenance, understood as the development and consolidation of a regional order consistent with the interests of the powerful, be they one or many. On the contrary, it may be propelled by, or facilitate, a process of system-transformation. It is even conceivable that in certain circumstances institutional change may have as its underlying logic resistance to internally or externally imposed homogeneity. Periodic, and thus far largely unsuccessful, attempts to forge Arab unity in the Middle East, and the assertion of Asian values by East Asian governments represent different versions of the same strategic approach, namely the attempt to use the regional formula to undermine or at least weaken the prevailing hegemonic order. Regional multilateralism, it is true, will seldom have a purely subversive function, but it often constitutes 'a site of struggle between conservative and transformative forces' and is itself in part a response to the stresses and strains bearing upon both national and global institutions.[37]

To put matters a little differently, regional multilateralism cannot but reflect the changing context in which power is exercised and wealth is accumulated and distributed. As Robert Cox has observed, the evolving global economic order may well hold the key to the growth of regional institutions. They are after all part of the historical dialectic which prompted Karl Polanyi to describe the political economy of nineteenth century Europe in terms of a 'double movement', that is, a movement with two distinct phases. He associated the first phase with the introduction of a self-regulating market which limited the role of the state to the performance of highly specialized functions, notably the preservation of domestic order and stability as well as external security.

However, as society became vulnerable to the unplanned and destabilizing consequences of market-driven behaviour, a second phase would unfold with renewed emphasis on regulating and civilizing the market.[38] As others have observed, a similar double movement appears to have been at work in the twentieth century, hence the periodic fluctuations between trade liberalization and financial deregulation policies on the one hand and trade protectionism and financial controls on the other.

In the first 70 years of the twentieth century, free-market doctrines were tempered by the imperatives of war, not least the Cold War, the Great Depression, and the consequent popularity of collectivist projects, notably Keynesianism, welfarism and state socialism. The subsequent few decades would see a drastic swing of the pendulum with the pressures sustaining the globalization of production, trade and finance assuming unprecedented potency. Perhaps we are now witnessing the early signs of yet another swing which we associate with the discontents of globalization and the rising consciousness of its socially and environmentally disruptive ramifications. These two conflicting tendencies have clearly influenced the scope and function of multilateralism. They largely account for the quantitative and qualitative ebb and flow that has characterized the development of many regional institutions. Central to this ebb and flow have been the profound divisions within policy communities, namely between advocates of enlarged membership (breadth) and openness on the one hand and more intensive forms of regional integration (depth) and even closure on the other. This is not to say that these two sharply contrasting and internally consistent formulations hold a monopoly on the regionalist agenda. On the contrary, the evolution of regionalist theory and practice has seen a good deal of *ad hoc* improvisation, with the key ideational and material building-blocks of regionalism giving rise to highly diverse and complex combinations of codes of conduct and structure. Nevertheless, there is no denying that regional institutionalization is primarily the product of two powerful but contradictory impulses: on one side the drive towards the unfettered flow of goods and services capital, labour and information, encapsulated by such terms as globalization and 'borderless world', and on the other the willingness of states to experiment with regional arrangements in the hope of taming the globalization tiger, even when this might entail a partial renunciation of their sovereign authority, or the delegation or pooling of that authority.

The chapters that follow are an attempt to situate this dialectical process in the Asia-Pacific context. The focus here will be on the dynamics of regional interdependence and the scope and functions of regional institutions, whether of the closed or open variety. The aim is to determine whether and how the polities and societies of Asia Pacific are coping with the mounting tensions created by rapid market globalization and partly as a consequence the diminishing efficacy of national governance. Increasing interdependence by its very nature generates pressures for new forms of global and regional governance, which often translate into new networks and organizations and new patterns of social interaction with non-state actors performing increasingly important and diverse roles, but with states still heavily involved in the negotiation of agreements and implementation of decisions.[39]

It is precisely because regionalist projects are characterized by ambiguity and even contradiction that the definition and formation of regions cannot be considered an immutable process. On the contrary the way regions organize themselves, set their boundaries and develop their identities is necessarily subject to periodic change. The analysis of regionalism must therefore adopt an evolutionary perspective which takes account of the changing structural conditions – embedded in the physical, economic and geopolitical environment – to which institutions must adapt as well as of the changing perceptions and self-understanding of relevant actors.[40] The evolutionary approach is particularly useful in identifying the phases that characterize the trajectory of a regionalist project and the thresholds which separate one phase from another. A threshold here simply refers to that unique conjuncture of endogenous and exogenous influences which significantly alters the dynamics of challenge and response. It points to a new pattern of adaptation, with consequent changes for a region's membership, policies and organizational structure. Though some influences will prove more decisive than others, it is the peculiar convergence of influences at a given time and place which confers on the threshold its potency and distinctiveness. While the end of the Cold War and the changing international hierarchy of power which accompanied it were critical to the subsequent evolution of regional arrangements in Asia Pacific as elsewhere, so too was the rapidly changing international division of labour, and with it the reorganization of the world's financial and trading systems. To these factors must be added the growth of a large middle class, the democratization of political processes and institutions, and the associated uncertainties generated by the problems of leadership succession. As this study will reveal, contemporary Asia-Pacific multilateralism is the product of a tangled and still evolving web of political, economic and cultural trends unfolding simultaneously at the national, international and transnational levels, and in the process creating new sites of contestation, negotiation and conflict management.

NOTES

1.   Ernest Haas, 'The Challenge of Regionalism', *International Organization*, 12 (4), Autumn 1958, 440–58; Karl W. Deutsch et al., *Political Community and the North Atlantic Area*, Princeton, NJ: Princeton University Press, 1957; David Mitrany, *A Working Peace System*, Chicago: Quadrangle Books, 1961. Other significant contributions in this relatively early phase included Amitai Etzioni, *Political Unification*, New York: Holt, Rinehart & Winston, 1965; Bruce M. Russett, *International Regions and the International System: A Study in Political Ecology*, Chicago: Rand McNally, 1967; Joseph S. Nye (ed), *International Regionalism*, Boston, MA: Little Brown, 1968.

2.   See Ernest Haas, *The Obsolescence of Regional Integration Theory*, Berkeley, CA: Institute of International Studies, University of California, Research Series No. 25, 1975; also Charles A. Duffy and Werner J. Field, 'Wither Regional Integration Theory?', in Werner J. Field and Gavin Boyd (eds), *Comparative Regional Systems*, New York: Pergamon Press, 1980.
3.   Norman D. Palmer, *The New Regionalism in Asia and the Pacific*, Lexington, MA: Lexington Books, 1991, pp. 16–17.
4.   See Michael Haas, 'International Subsystems: Stability and Polarity', *American Political Science Review*, 64 (1), 1970, 101; Michael Brecher, 'International Relations and Asian Studies', *World Politics*, XV, January 1963, pp. 221–35.
5.   Raimo Väyrynen, 'Regional Conflict Formations: An Intractable Problem of International Relations', *Journal of Peace Research*, 21 (4), 1984, 340.
6.   Bruce Russett, 'Delineating International Regimes', in J. David Singer (ed), *Quantitative International Politics: Insights and Evidence*, New York: The Free Press, 1968, pp. 318–19.
7.   Louis J. Cantori and Steven L. Spiegel (eds), *The International Politics of Regions: A Comparative Approach*, Englewood Cliffs, NJ: Prentice-Hall, 1970, pp. 6–7.
8.   William R. Thompson, 'The Regional Subsystem: A Conceptual Explication and a Prepositional Inventory', *International Studies Quarterly*, 17 (1), March 1973, 89–117.
9.   Arie M. Kacowicz, 'Regionalization, Globalization and Nationalism: Convergent, Divergent, or Overlapping?', *Alternatives*, 24 (4), October–December 1999, 530.
10. This observation may apply as much to national identity as to regional identity, although transposing the argument from one level to another needs to proceed with greater caution than is the case, for example, in Andrew Hurrell, 'Regionalism in Theoretical Perspective', in Louise Fawcett and Andrew Hurrell (eds), *Regionalism in World Politics: Regional Organization and International Order*, Oxford: Oxford University Press, 1995, pp. 58–66.
11. In this sense, while constructivist formulations represent a welcome antidote to the sterility of realist theory, there is often a tendency, implicit if not explicit, to privilege the ideational realm to the point of detaching it from its material base, and in the process limiting the capacity to illuminate the subtle relationship between an agent's socio-cultural and physical environment. Even as sophisticated a contributor to constructivist thinking as Alex Wendt does not altogether avoid this trap (see 'Anarchy is What States Make of It: The Social Construction of Power Politics', *International Organization*, 46, Spring 1992, 391–425; also 'Collective Identity Formation and the International State', *American Political Science Review*, 82 (2), June 1994, 385–6).
12. See Barry Buzan, *People, States and Fear: The National Security Problem in International Relations*, Brighton, Sussex: Wheatsheaf Books, 1983, pp. 104–10.
13. See Kacowicz, 'Regionalization, Globalization and Nationalism', p. 531.
14. Ibid., p. 543.
15. Deutsch et al., *Political Community*, p. 36.
16. Emanuel Adler and Michael N. Barnett, 'Governing Anarchy: A Research Agenda for the Study of Security Communities', *Ethics and International Affairs*, 10, 1996, 67.
17. Ibid., pp. 92–3.
18. In its crudest ethological form, the principle was applied by Robert Ardrey to the interpretation of nationalism. See *The Territorial Imperative*, London: Collins, 1967, pp. 291–344.
19. See Väyrynen, 'Regional Conflict Formations', p. 338.
20. For a fuller examination of these three scenarios, see Kacowicz, 'Regionalism, Globalization and Nationalism', pp. 532–4.
21. See Joseph A. Camilleri and Jim Falk, *The End of Sovereignty: The Politics of a Shrinking and Fragmenting World*, Aldershot, UK: Edward Elgar, 1992, pp. 147–8.
22. For a useful discussion of this trend and its implications, see Philip G. Cerny, 'Globalization and the Changing Logic of Collective Action', *International Organization*, 49 (4), 1995, 612–17.
23. Although these terms are not always used with the care and precision they deserve, a useful analysis at least of the underlying currents which they represent is offered by Mario Telò, 'Between Trade Regionalization and Deep Integration', in Mario Telò (ed), *European Union and New Regionalism: Regional Actors and Global Governance in a Post-Hegemonic Era*, Aldershot, UK: Ashgate, 2001, pp. 71–95.

24. See, for example, Stuart Harris, 'The Regional Role of Track Two Diplomacy', in Hadi Soesastro and Anthony Bergin (eds), *The Role of Security and Economic Cooperation Structures in the Asia Pacific*, Jakarta: Centre for Strategic and International Studies, 1996; Herman Joseph S. Kraft, 'Track Three Diplomacy and Human Rights in Southeast Asia: The Case of Asia Pacific Coalition for East Timor', Paper presented at the Global Development Network 2000 Conference, Tokyo, 13 December 2000.
25. See P.M. Haas, 'Obtaining International Environmental Protection through Epistemic Consensus', *Millennium Journal of International Studies*, 19, 1900, pp. 347–63.
26. Paul Taylor, *International Organization in the Modern World: The Regional and the Global Process*, London: Pinter, 1993, pp. 24–46.
27. See Richard Gibb, 'Regionalism in the World Economy', in Richard Gibb and Wieslaw Michalak, *Continental Trading Blocs: The Growth of Regionalism in the World Economy*, Chichester: John Wiley & Sons, 1994, pp. 22–8.
28. In the early 1990s, the notion of 'architecture' became widely, if somewhat loosely, used, especially in the Asia-Pacific context. See, for example, Jusuf Wanandi, 'Developing the Regional Security Architecture: The Road Ahead', Paper presented at the 10th Asia-Pacific Roundtable, Kuala Lumpar, 5–8 June 1996.
29. Paul Taylor, 'A Conceptual Typology of International Organization', in A.J.R. Groom and Paul Taylor (eds), *Frameworks for International Co-operation*, London: Pinter, 1990, pp. 12–26.
30. Several of these categories and their interconnections are examined in Benjamin Miller, 'International Systems and Regional Security: From Competition to Co-operation, Dominance or Disengagement?', *Journal of Strategic Studies*, 18 (2), June 1995, 52–100, but the argument we develop here is both less mechanistic and less prescriptive.
31. R.W. Cox, *Production, Power and World Order: Social Forces in the Making of History*, New York: Columbia University Press, 1987, p. 7.
32. Robert W. Cox, 'Multilateralism and World Order', *Review of International Studies*, 18, 1992, 179. For a useful examination of divergent interpretations, see Richard Rosecrance, 'Regionalism and the Post-Cold War Era', *International Journal*, XLVI, Summer 1991, 373–93; also Joseph A. Camilleri, 'Alliances in the Emerging Post-Cold War Security System', in Richard Leaver and James L. Richardson (eds), *Charting the Post-Cold War Order*, Boulder, CO: Westview Press, 1993, pp. 81–94.
33. Andrew Gamble and Anthony Payne, 'Conclusion: The New Regionalism', in Andrew Gamble and Anthony Payne (eds), *Regionalism and World Order*, London: Macmillan, 1996, p. 261.
34. Hurrell, 'Regionalism in Theoretical Perspective', p. 69.
35. For a sober assessment of the scope and limitations of regionalism as a conflict-resolution mechanism, see Charles van der Donckt, 'Looking Forward by Looking Back: A Pragmatic Look at Conflict and the Regional Option', *Pacifica Review: Peace Security and Global Change*, 8 (1), 1996, 43–61.
36. For some this competitive dynamic is in part sustained by three regionally specific but distinctive models of capitalism. See, for example, Michel Albert, *Capitalism against Capitalism* (trans. Paul Haviland), London: Whurr, 1993.
37. Cox, 'Multilateralism and World Order', p. 177.
38. See Karl Polanyi, *The Great Transformation: The Political and Economic Origins of Our Time*, Boston, MA: Beacon, 1957, pp. 223–48.
39. See Gamble and Payne, 'Conclusion: The New Regionalism', pp. 251, 263.
40. The case for examining more closely, both conceptually and empirically, the 'interplay between regional economic integration and identity', and more specifically 'the interplay between power and purpose and between identity and interest' is well made by Richard Higgott, 'The International Political Economy of Regionalism: The Asia-Pacific and Europe Compared', in William D. Coleman and Geoffrey R.D. Underhill (eds), *Regionalism and Global Economic Integration: Europe, Asia and the Americas*, London: Routledge, 1998, p. 46.

2. Asia Pacific as region

Region is a fluid, some may say elusive, but none the less useful concept for bringing a degree of clarity, if not order, to the multifaceted and ceaselessly changing patterns of interaction across state boundaries. There is, of course, no single 'regional' narrative. Regions can emerge and survive in vastly different circumstances. They are, as we have seen, the product of both endogenous and exogenous influences, ideational and material currents, statist and non-statist discourses and practices. Each region is therefore likely to have its own political complexion reflecting a particular configuration of power within and outside its boundaries and a distinctive mix of conflictual and co-operative relationships. Similarly, the degree of openness or closure in relations with the outside world is likely to differ markedly from region to region. Almost by definition a region's cohesion will be predicated on a certain convergence of attitudes, norms and expectations, but such convergence may coexist with considerable religious, linguistic, cultural divergence. Indeed, complementarity of needs, resources and capabilities may be at least as significant a catalyst for regionalization as cultural or political affinity.

This brief restatement of the argument outlined in the preceding chapter suggests that region may be most usefully considered a site of patterned interaction, which, though it will at any given moment have a spatial or geographical expression, need not be confined to a fixed space. There are, indeed, good grounds for defining region as a site of contestation for the periodic reorganization of political space. It comes therefore as no surprise that in Asia Pacific the delineation of region and sub-regions has been a subject of intense debate. For the greater part of the 1980s and 1990s two geographically distinct representations of the region, *Pacific Asia* and *Asia Pacific*, fiercely competed for academic and political legitimacy. The focus on Pacific Asia, often referred to as East Asia, was partly a response of the rapid industrialization of a number of Asian economies and the pivotal role played by Japan in giving impetus to and sustaining a process that had seemingly transformed East Asia into one of the three centres of gravity in the world economy.[1] Asia Pacific on the other hand, pointed to a much larger region which encompassed the Pacific Ocean and more importantly retained the United States as integral to the region's economic and strategic landscape.

Whether Pacific Asia constitutes a coherent regional entity or is merely the core of a larger Asia-Pacific entity is a question that is not amenable to a simple or definitive answer. The question itself requires considerable refinement and elaboration and prompts several subquestions: what is the exact spatial delineation envisaged for Pacific Asia or Asia Pacific? Do the proposed boundaries apply uniformly across the geopolitical, geoeconomic and cultural arenas, or does each arena have its own distinct boundaries? Are they susceptible to expansion or contraction with changing political circumstances? Clearly, how these questions are answered will depend in part on which fields of interaction are given primacy, or which period of history is under consideration. As the pages that follow will show, different ways of framing the question are likely to yield different answers. Suffice it for the moment to say that regionalization in Asia Pacific as elsewhere is an evolutionary process, which in some sense mirrors and reinforces the evolution of the world system. Regionalization may be described as a partial and often incremental response to the multiple challenge posed for states and other actors by changes to their internal and external environment. At issue here are not only the boundaries of regions, that is the various ways political space is defined and organized, but the very emergence, transformation and eventual dissolution of regions. To put it differently, the patterns and forms of regional interaction are neither static nor uniform. They are part of a dynamic process which finds expression in the periodic reconfiguration of power relations, and axes of conflict which in turn serve as catalysts for normative and institutional change.

An evolutionary approach is well suited to mapping the emergence and subsequent development of a region, and the thresholds that separate one phase from another. A threshold here simply refers to that unique conjuncture of influences – endogenous and exogenous, ideational and material, integrative and disintegrative – which significantly alters the dynamic of challenge and response as experienced by regional formations and their constituent members. Though some influences may prove more decisive than others, it is the peculiar convergence of influences at a given time and place which confers on the threshold its potency and distinctiveness. In other words, by applying an evolutionary and therefore historical perspective to the Asia-Pacific region it may be possible to perform three important analytical tasks: to identify the key influences which have thus far shaped the trajectory of regionalization; to specify the phases which have characterized this trajectory; and to elucidate the contradictory tendencies which are currently buffeting regional processes and institutions, the outcome of which will govern the future form and direction of Asia-Pacific regionalization.

HISTORICAL OVERVIEW

It has often been said that 'Asia' is largely an artificial construct, a product of the Western imagination, of the West's attempt to differentiate itself from the East. A sense of Asian identity, the argument runs, emerged only in the wake of Western colonization. Nationalism, freedom, independence were predominantly Western concepts which Asians subsequently deployed to oppose Western domination.[2] There is no disputing the fact that Asia has been the site of extraordinary cultural or civilizational diversity, giving birth or shelter to most of the world's major religious and ethical traditions, including Hinduism, Buddhism, Taoism, Confucianism, Shintoism, Islam and Christianity. Over thousands of years the history of East and Southeast Asia has been punctuated by a number of invasions and mass migrations which through a subtle mix of collision and coexistence have strikingly coloured the continent's cultural and geopolitical landscape. It is nevertheless safe to say that prior to the advent of European imperialism, East or Pacific Asia, as distinct from other parts of Asia, had despite the powerful Islamic challenge retained a recognizable and relatively self-contained pattern of interaction between its constituent units. The central but by no means sole element in that distinctive configuration of power and norms was the Sino-centric world order. The 'Middle Kingdom' had over several centuries extended its Confucian civilization together with its writing system, examination system and bureaucratic institutions to Japan, Korea and parts of Southeast Asia, which in return paid tribute to the Chinese emperor. This Chinese 'cultural area' represented a hierarchical order which, even when headed by non-Chinese dynasties, for example the Mongols from 1279 to 1368 and the Manchus from 1644 to 1912, managed to maintain the moral and political authority of the imperial order. Tributary states were prepared to accept their subordinate status because Chinese hegemony relied primarily on cultural and economic levers rather than military coercion.[3] To the extent that they had access to Chinese markets, a guarantee of non-intervention in their domestic affairs and a measure of Chinese military protection against external threats, these states had a vested interest in the consolidation of the Sinic sphere of influence.

While functioning as a relatively closed regional system, the Chinese world order would be periodically subjected to external pressure, most dramatically at the hands of the European colonial powers. Even before the Spanish occupation of the Philippines in 1570, rapidly growing trade between Spain and the Americas had released vast volumes of silver into the Asia-Pacific region and initiated a commercial boom based on the increased circulation of currency and greatly expanded markets. Spanish, Portugese and Dutch traders were responsible for the introduction of new agricultural crops, including cassava, maize and sweet potato, to which were added pepper, the finer spices and tobacco. The net effect was to transform the agricultural systems of Southeast Asia and southern China, and to shift the emphasis from subsistence to cash crop cultivation. New and expanded markets, facilitated by the infusion of European capital and transport infrastructure, paved the way for the resurgence of Chinese business and indigenous production networks, and the emergence of an influential merchant class.

In the course of the nineteenth century the impact of European colonialism would become pervasive, most obviously through the establishment of territorial control over much of the region and the introduction of European social and political institutions. By the close of the century, much of East Asia or the 'Far East' had been integrated, whether as formal colonies or spheres of influence into one or other of the European empires.[4] The Treaty of Nanking concluded at the end of the Opium War of 1840–42 saw Britain take the lead in forcibly opening China's markets, soon followed by France and the United States, and eventually by most of Europe's middle powers. In a parallel development the United States focused on Japan, with Matthew Perry's expedition eventually compelling the Japanese to conclude the Treaty of Kanagawa in March 1854, reinforced and extended in June 1858 by the Treaty of Amity and Commerce.[5] Japan was now required to open up its ports to foreign trade, impose customs on both exports and imports, and extend extraterritorial rights to US nationals.[6] Western imperial powers may thus be said to have created a new hegemonic regional order.

Unlike the first hegemonic cycle, which we associate with the period of prolonged Chinese dominance, Western hegemony was far more diffuse with several centres of power fiercely competing for markets and influence. Competition was, however, tempered by intermittent outbreaks of co-operation aimed at preventing the spoils of colonization from being entirely dissipated by intercine inter-imperialist conflicts.[7] As with colonial practice elsewhere, the imperial powers sought to absorb indigenous elites into their respective bureaucracies. Indeed, these elites often became 'indispensable agents of colonial governments' providing a bridge between their administration and 'old village structures such as the *Barangay* in the Philippines, the *desa* in Java, and the *Kampung* in the maritime Malay world'.[8] There was nevertheless a unique feature to European colonialism – or to be more precise, merchant capitalism – in East Asia, namely reliance on the entrepreneurial skills of Chinese clans and family networks. Intent on expanding their capital base, Chinese businesses operating from southern China and much of Southeast Asia ventured into trading, shipping, retailing, and even tin mining, timber processing and sugar milling, and in the process became vital cogs in European and US trade and investment strategies.[9]

What, then, are we to make of this second hegemonic cycle? At one level it is arguable that European and American colonialism disrupted the Sino-centric world order and with it the normative and institutional framework which had endowed East Asia with a measure of cultural and political cohesion. The colonial experience was doubly disruptive in that it inflicted irreparable damage on the legitimacy and efficacy of Chinese imperial authority, establishing in its place a series of discrete administrations and 'spheres of influence' which tied different parts of East Asia to the interests, institutional practices and educational systems of different colonial powers. The resulting vertical social, economic and bureaucratic linkage weakened any sense of regional identity and accelerated East Asia's absorption into the emerging international commodity and financial markets. At another level, the evidence suggests that the colonial experience produced similar effects, that is, commercialization of agriculture, rise of merchant class, urbanization, vulnerability to external markets, and similar responses, including sharp debates about the direction and pace of modernization, intensified search for identity, and rise of national movements. Though these largely unforeseen effects of colonialism did not themselves lead to regional policies or programmes, they did create a climate of opinion, especially among the educated elites, which was regional in its geographical scope and, potentially at least, in its psychological and political consequences.

Soon, however, the intrusion of an altogether new variable, that is Japan's industrialization and economic expansion, would drastically alter the regional equation. By the end of the nineteenth century Japan had embarked on a strategy of regional empire-building. Three forays into Northeast Asia would signal the rise of Japan's military and economic power. By 1876 Japan had extracted from Korea an agreement (the Kanghwa Treaty of 27 February 1876) which resulted in the opening of three Korean ports (Fusan, Jinsen and Gensan) to Japanese trade.[10] In September 1894 Japan, having formally declared war on China on 1 August, defeated the Chinese fleet in the battle of the Yellow Sea at the mouth of the Yalu River. Following a succession of defeats China sued for peace, and in the Treaty of Shimonoseki (17 April 1895) ceded the Liaotung Peninsula, the island of Formosa, and the Pescadores, paid Japan a substantial indemnity, and opened four cities (Shashi, Chungking, Suchow and Hangchow) to Japan for commercial and industrial purposes.[11] In February 1904, Japan declared war on Russia, ostensibly to protect Korean independence, and, having inflicted a costly defeat (Russian casualties in killed and wounded were estimated at 150,000), secured through the treaty of Portsmouth in September 1905 several key concessions. Russia recognized Japan's paramount interests in Korea, transferred to Japan its rights in the Liaotung Peninsula, and ceded to it the southern section of the Manchurian Railway and the southern half of Sakhalin Island.[12]

By the turn of the century Japan had established its credentials as a rising imperial power. More than that, its military victories helped to finance the development of Japan's heavy industry, opened new markets for its textiles and other manufactures, and gave it access to territories rich in minerals, railroads and internal waterways. Subsequent Japanese investments in industrial infrastructure in Korea and Formosa, coupled with the transfer of technology and new administrative arrangements, subsequently reshaped these economies in ways designed to meet the needs of Japan's economy. By the late 1920s, Korea and Taiwan supplied 80 per cent of Japan's rice imports, two-thirds of its sugar, and a sizeable proportion of its minerals and timber.[13] A similar pattern was in evidence in Manchuria where extensive investments in transport infrastructure helped to secure for Japan a substantial supply of iron ore.

Japanese imperialism, then, had a dual rationale: on the one hand, to gain the necessary access to markets and resources in Northern Asia to sustain its industrial development, and on the other to strengthen its hand *vis-à-vis* the other imperialist powers, partly by building up its military strength and partly by endowing its diplomacy with the rhetoric of anti-imperialism and pan-Asianism. Japan sought to demonstrate its 'Asianness' by stressing its indissoluble links with the Chinese culture, and its respect for the Confucian tradition. Conversely, Japanese assimilation policies sought to convey the notion that all colonized peoples who came under Japanese imperial rule would form an integral part of the imperial family and share equally in the emperor's benevolence.[14] To succeed, both prongs of the strategy required Japan to forge a regional network of relationships and sphere of influence, which inevitably provoked the anxiety and suspicion of Western imperialist states. Paradoxically, the very attempt to foil or neutralize Western responses would lead Japan to rely even more on East Asian market penetration and territorial annexation. A critical point in this story was reached with the Washington Conference of 1921, which imposed severe limitations on the size of the Japanese navy, just when Japan seemed within reach of hegemony over Asia. The ensuing five-power naval treaty fixed the ratio of naval capabilities at 5:5:3:1.75:1.75 for the United States, Great Britain, Japan, France and Italy, respectively.

Notwithstanding these limitations and the political frictions which they implied, Japan continued to expand its economic stake in the region. By 1931, Japanese investments in China had equalled those of Great Britain and exceeded those of all other countries combined.[15] Japan's trade with Indonesia and Malaysia was making similar inroads. Japanese interests, it seemed, could be advanced within the existing strategic equilibrium. This impression was reinforced by reforms within Japan, notably the adoption by the Diet in March 1925 of the Universal Manhood Suffrage Bill, and modest reforms in Korea and Taiwan, including increased opportunities for political self-expression and a more equitable judicial system. This period of geopolitical compromise would soon give way to intensified rivalry. Japanese governments, squeezed on several fronts, now felt obliged to define economic interests by turning increasingly to military power. Petri identifies three key contributing factors: the rise of Chinese nationalism and the growing threat to the Japanese presence posed by the Kuomintang; Japan's increasing vulnerability to the protectionist policies of its trade rivals, which risked eroding its access to international markets; and the sharp fall in commodity prices during the Great Depression, which in turn had a devastating impact on Japanese agriculture.[16] The 1931 invasion of Manchuria and the ensuing wave of public and private investments were clearly designed to achieve a much higher level of complementarity with the Japanese economy. Japan's continuing territorial expansion into China, resulting in the capture of Nanking and much of the Yangtze valley, was but the most striking episode in a concerted attempt to establish the so-called Greater East Asia Co-Prosperity Sphere centred on Japan, Manchuria and China, but also incorporating Korea, Formosa and much of Southeast Asia. Though, as a consequence, the region's trade with the West collapsed, the diminished safety of trade routes meant that the processes of economic integration with Japan would henceforth make relatively little progress. These considerations were no doubt influential in Japan's decision to wage war in the Pacific and proceed with the complete incorporation of its colonial economies. Tokyo's single-minded objective was to create regionally the industrial infrastructure it needed to produce the raw materials – not just coal and iron but tin, rubber, bauxite, tungsten, nickel and chromium – on which its heavy industries had become almost totally reliant.

The increasingly coercive quality of Japanese imperial politics through the 1930s was accompanied by a clearly visible shift in Japanese official discourse. More and more emphasis was placed on the obligations rather than the rights of colonized peoples, with Japan's overseas possessions often referred to as the 'outer territories', the mere extensions of a single Japanese nation. Japanese domination was openly advanced as the only means of liberating Asia from the yoke of Western colonialism. Not surprisingly, the East Asian response to Japan's self-proclaimed role as liberator was less than enthusiastic. But the deep resentments provoked by Japanese expansionism, not least the economic hardships and military atrocities associated with Japanese occupation, gave rise to a more determined nationalism, more experienced leaders and more enterprising indigenous business communities. Inspired in part by the Japanese model, a new business ethos gradually emerged linking public and private interests. The Asian response to Japanese imperialism had two seemingly contradictory dimensions: on the one hand, emulation of Japanese discourse and practice, and on the other rejection of Japanese hegemony. To this extent at least, Japan's short-lived imperialist experiment had served as an important catalyst not only for East Asia's immediate political and economic transformation but for reshaping the region's cultural traditions and political aspirations.

With Japan's defeat and the end of the Pacific War, political independence soon became the established norm throughout East Asia, although the strategies, institutional arrangements and timelines which characterized the transfer of power varied considerably from country to country. Unresolved internal conflicts, for example the unfinished civil war in China, and the reluctance of certain colonial powers to oversee a prompt and peaceful transition to independence, notably France in Indochina, were compounded by the polarizing effects of the Cold War. At first sight it appeared as if old and new political divisions, mirrored and reinforced by East Asia's cultural heterogeneity, would deal a fatal blow to any prospect of regional identity formation. Yet, despite the asymmetries and unresolved tensions which Western colonialism had left in their wake, East Asian societies had been deeply and irrevocably influenced by the powerful currents of economic and political modernization. They had become an integral part as much of the world economy as of the international security system. It would be inaccurate, however, to conclude that these historical influences had served merely to connect East Asia more closely with the outside world. In the process, new and highly specific patterns of connectivity, notably in regional trade, had been established linking different parts of East Asia with the rest of the Pacific basin.

REGIONALIZATION AFTER 1945

The tendency towards greater regional interaction would gain new momentum during the second half of the twentieth century, although the trend varied greatly in intensity from one country to another and one period to the next. The unevenness of the trend led some observers to question its long-term significance, but indicative of the emerging reality were the numerous analytical models and concepts advanced both to characterize and explain the phenomenon. The 'Asian economic miracle', the 'Pacific Century', the 'Pacific Community', or simply the 'Asia-Pacific idea',[17] were a few of the terms devised to describe what was a still unfolding, diffuse and highly contested sequence of events. Some emphasized the hegemonic role of the United States, in particular the integrationist implications of US containment policies and the associated web of military alliances, deployments, and procurement and training programmes on the one hand and aid, trade and capital flows on the other.[18] The geopolitical reach of the American state and the closely connected spread of American capital were seen as the twin engines of Pacific Asia's integration into the global political economy. Others pointed to the growth of exports, which, in the case of Japan and later the newly industrializing economies (NIEs), enabled resources to be allocated on the basis of comparative advantage, thereby enabling these economies to penetrate external markets and overcome the limitations of their relatively small domestic markets.[19] Others still attached greater importance either to the developmental state[20] or to culture,[21] which they invariably depicted as the principal agent of transformation, and not infrequently as the factor which most powerfully expressed and reinforced the commonalities underpinning East Asia's contemporary political evolution.

No doubt each of these competing interpretations tells us something of recent trends, yet none fully captures the complexity of this multidimensional and contradictory phenomenon. That a great many external influences, not least the American economic and geostrategic presence, have impinged on the processes of East Asian regionalization is clear enough. On the other hand, the full impact of that presence, and the way it has intruded into the policies, institutions and external linkages of different countries cannot be ascertained without reference to the traditions, political culture and demographic and economic circumstances of each of these countries as well as to the many other external influences bearing upon their policies and perspectives. In grappling with the intricacies of Asia-Pacific regionalization it is well therefore to be suspicious of reductionist or unidisciplinary interpretations. It is not just a question of avoiding the dangers of oversimplification or of relating the domestic and the international, but of combining theoretical and empirical insights in ways that are analytically illuminating yet mindful of complexity and contradiction.

To illustrate the conceptual puzzle posed by Asia-Pacific regionalization, it is useful to begin by briefly examining the hegemonic role of the United States. Embedded in the logic of strategic containment and economic liberalism, US policies in the immediate aftermath of the Second World War set out to reconstruct the political economy of the region. Within this grand design the economic reconstruction of Japan would play a pivotal role as bulwark against the expansion of Soviet power. To perform the strategic function assigned to it the Japanese economy had to be given 'assured access to both raw materials in East and Southeast Asia and to high-income markets in North America'.[22]

US planning was therefore intent on dismantling the relational networks constructed by European metropolitan powers in Southeast Asia as a necessary condition for transforming Japan into a surrogate for US hegemony. Ironically, Japanese interests were now being assisted to achieve in the marketplace what had been denied to them on the battlefield, namely an economic sphere of influence. Production processes in East and Southeast Asia were gradually reorganized into networks geared to the requirements of Japanese industrialization. This view was openly articulated by the influential Institute of Pacific Relations which at its 1947 conference recommended that active steps be taken to help Japan 'regain something of her old position as the mainspring of the Far Eastern economy as a whole'.[23]

For the best part of three decades, US military and economic power would underpin the reorganization of East Asia's political economy. Quite apart from the leverage afforded by its military alliances, arms transfers, and extensive network of military facilities and deployments, the United States played a crucial role in regional affairs by virtue of the size of its markets, the technological edge of its industries, and the marketing, managerial and organizational strength of its industrial and financial enterprises. To argue that US hegemony exercised a decisive influence in the regionalization of economic and political life in Asia Pacific is not, however, to suggest that it was the only contributing factor, or that regionalization would necessarily lose momentum once US hegemony began to erode.

Notions of diminishing US hegemony need in any case to be treated with caution. As we argue in the first volume, the recent evolution of the political economy of Asia Pacific is best encapsulated by reference to three competing yet overlapping tendencies: residual hegemony, increasing interdependence and intensifying competition.[24] It is precisely because of the combined impact of these last two tendencies that the decline of America's hegemonic position, certainly when compared to its heyday in the 1950s and 1960s, has coincided with a more highly developed pattern of regional interaction.

The rise of both Japan and China as major centres of power provided important avenues for the development of new regional networks which partially offset East Asia's longstanding dependence on US markets and security commitments. As Richard Stubbs and others have observed, the growth of Japanese capital exports since the 1970s was accompanied by the diffusion of Japan's industrial structures and practices.[25] Throughout much of Southeast Asia, Japanese parent companies had established multi-tiered networks of subcontracting firms which came to play an indispensable role in the expansion of the region's manufacturing sector. In many cases, Japanese business was able to reknit political and personal connections which had existed prior to the Second World War. New, often informal but finely targeted arrangements between Japanese corporations and Southeast Asian political elites, lubricated by substantially greater volumes of Japanese aid, foreign direct investment and technology transfers, helped to create an increasingly integrated regional economy centred on Japan.[26]

Another important factor contributing to regional economic integration was the rapid growth of China's economy during the 1980s and 1990s, and the gradual emergence of a 'Greater China'. The precise geographical delineation implied by the concept of a Greater China bloc or area remains at best elusive and at worst highly contested, but there is no denying that the concept points to the development of economic networks and complementarities of far-reaching regional significance. For some the construction of Greater China, often seen as encompassing China, Hong Kong, Macau and Taiwan, rests on two sets of policies pursued by Beijing with varying degrees of success since the early 1980s:

> The first relates to a national reunification policy which builds on the concept of 'one country, two systems'. The second is based on an Open Door policy which enables China to envision economic development by encouraging local incentives, especially in the Southern provinces (Guangdong and Fujian) close to Hong Kong and Taiwan.[27]

The geopolitical thrust of Beijing's reunification plans, particularly in relation to Taiwan, and the opportunities for more intensive economic interaction afforded by the modernization drive gave the prospect of a Greater China added momentum and potency. The return of Hong Kong and Macau to Chinese sovereignty and the development of special economic zones located in Guangdong and Fujian were important signposts along the way.[28] Such a reading of emerging trends, however, runs the risk of overstating Beijing's capacity to steer events in a particular direction. Important in this respect has been the role of other actors, including provincial and local governments in coastal China as well as business interests based in Hong Kong and Taiwan, with a major stake in developing manufacturing and financial networks capable of combining 'Taiwan's capital and its technical and managerial know-how, Hong Kong's intermediation services and China's cheap labour and material resources'.[29] In any case the informal but pervasive Chinese 'commonwealth' built on ethnic ties, family clans, and the affinities born of a common culture and business ethic also extends to much of Southeast Asia.[30] While exercising profound influence on the structures and relationships of Southeast Asia's economies, the overseas Chinese are at the same time engaged in multiple commercial and financial activities which bring them into close contact with China's large and medium-sized firms and with the various layers of its elaborate bureaucracy.[31] The net effect of these overlapping and intersecting networks, increasingly regularized but still largely informal, is to create a multi-spatial regional production process mirrored and reinforced at the discursive level by linguistic, cultural and intellectual commonalities and complementarities.

The picture that emerges from this initial exploration of regionalizing tendencies in Asia Pacific after 1945 is one of complexity and disconnectedness. It is as if three major centres of economic and geopolitical gravity, the United States, Japan and China, instigated or at least encouraged the formation of regional networks and identities, but with each centre pursuing its own distinctive interests and *modus operandi*. These networks and identities were not co-extensive in either time or space. Nor were they predicated on the same rationale or organizational form. Yet, they were not entirely unconnected. They are best understood as three distinct but interwoven patterns, each meshing into the rich and evolving tapestry of Asia-Pacific regionalization. Here it may be useful to develop a few of the more important connecting strands.

The first and most obvious point of connection was the working of exogenous market forces, sometimes loosely referred to as globalization. The regionalization of economic activity associated with the regional interests, networks and practices of the major centres of power was in part a reflection of the expanding interconnections between them, and more generally the internationalization of trade and finance.[32] In the case of the United States and Japan in particular, both state and capital were actively engaged in the penetration of global markets, not least each other's domestic markets, facilitated in part by the liberalization of the international trading regime, the accelerating improvements in world communications and transport, and the progressive liberalization of international capital flows.

The dependencies and interdependencies generated by a more integrating world economy will receive more detailed attention in subsequent chapters. Relevant for our analytical purposes here is the role of predominantly endogenous linkages, especially those manifested in the Sino–Japanese relationship. This is not to underestimate the marked differences between the Chinese and Japanese patterns of regional extension. The relationship between Japanese parent companies and their subsidiaries in Asia points to a far more hierarchical decision-making structure than in the Chinese case.[33] Moreover, Japanese corporate networks relied largely on Japanese sources of technology, whereas Chinese networks tended to be far more open and flexible in acquiring technical capabilities.[34] However, the similarities are at least as striking as the differences. Notable in this respect is the well-known Japanese emphasis on flexibility, partly reflected in 'just-in-time' strategies, and in the Chinese case in a willingness to share information and resources, and to respond to changing market conditions, if necessary by shifting to the development of new products or industries.[35] More important still was the common Chinese and Japanese tendency to operate through networks, although, as we have already noted, Chinese networks tend to be organizationally more diffuse than their Japanese counterparts. Here, commonality and difference combined to produce complementarity, with large Japanese corporations collaborating with small and medium-sized Chinese family firms 'to form country-specific as well as region-wide production networks'.[36] A third similarity between Chinese and Japanese firms was their pragmatic attitude to the public–private divide, a readiness to enter into formal and informal arrangements with governments, and where opportunities presented themselves to participate in joint ventures with state enterprises.

Important as Chinese and Japanese networks have been in sustaining rapidly rising levels of economic interaction in East Asia, US power and capital would, if anything, play an even more decisive role. As noted earlier, the importance of the US domestic market in sustaining East Asia's export orientation cannot be overstated. In 1993, the United States accounted for 29.4 per cent of Japan's exports, with comparable levels of trade dependence evident for China (29.0 per cent) and Taiwan (28.3 per cent).[37] Quite apart from the sheer volume and strategic significance of bilateral trade in cementing the complex triangular relationship between China, Japan and the United States, the flow of US capital and technology and the dominance of the US dollar in international trade and foreign exchange markets were also important mechanisms contributing to the interpenetration of national economies. In China's case, the US pull factor was also evident in the growing number of Chinese students entering the United States (up from 1,330 in 1979 to 13,491 in 1990) and the corresponding rise of US tourists visiting China (up from 101,500 in 1980 to 233,000 in 1990).[38]

The preceding survey of the post-1945 period has done no more than describe a few of the salient factors sustaining the momentum for Asia-Pacific economic and technological regionalization. The emphasis thus far has been on the initial impetus provided by US hegemony and the subsequent emergence of a Japanese regional production network and a Greater China bloc. It is worth stressing, however, that Japan and China as rising regional hegemons had not, either individually or collectively, supplanted the United States, whose far-reaching, multifaceted though slowly eroding, presence is best depicted as 'residual hegemony'.[39] What we have seen instead is a complex triangular relationship in which competition and even tension coexist with varying degrees of accommodation, in which both diverging and converging interests find expression in multiple linkages and channels of communication. There is nevertheless more to East Asian regionalization than the dynamics of conflict and co-operation between three distinct spheres of influence. The scale, pace and structure of East Asia's export-oriented industrialization, particularly its staggered impact first on South Korea, Taiwan, Hong Kong and Singapore, then on the ASEAN countries, China and more recently Vietnam, are an essential part of any plausible explanatory framework.

Both the inner dynamics and outward manifestation of East Asia's industrialization are examined at length in *States, Markets and Civil Society in Asia Pacific*.[40] Suffice it here to say that the increasing importance of intra-regional trade, measured in both absolute and relative terms, was a byproduct of the prolonged period of economic growth and the sustained export orientation of both established extractive and emerging manufacturing industries. As a consequence, East Asia's share of world trade would rise from 10.8 per cent in 1970 to 19.4 per cent in 1990,[41] and Pacific basin countries would account for a large and growing proportion of its exports and imports. As Table 2.1 shows, once the United States, Canada, Australia and New Zealand, including US–Canadian bilateral trade, are brought into the equation, we discern an appreciable rise in intra-Pacific trade as a proportion of the total external trade of Pacific basin countries. The share of intra-Pacific exports in total exports rose from 47.3 per cent in 1965 to 61.2 per cent in 1984, while the corresponding rise for imports was from 51.6 per cent to 58.3 per cent.[42] Even if North America is excluded from the calculation, a roughly comparable result obtains, with East Asia's intra-regional exports as a proportion of its total exports rising from 31 per cent in 1970 to 39 per cent in 1990.[43] Instructive though they are, these trends nevertheless need qualification. First, the trend was not uniform across all countries: the increase in intra-regional trade was especially marked for such countries as China, Indonesia and the Philippines; it was much less so for Japan, Korea or even Malaysia; and in Taiwan's case intra-regional trade accounted for a diminishing share of its total trade.[44] There were also striking variations in time frame between the trading patterns of different countries. Whereas Indonesia's, Malaysia's, New Zealand's and Canada's intra-Pacific exports as a proportion of their total exports rose steadily from the mid-1960s to the mid-1980s, Thailand, Hong Kong, South Korea and Papua New Guinea recorded a corresponding decline. Moreover, when compared to the pattern for exports, the share of intra-Pacific imports in the total imports of Pacific basin countries during this 20–year period rose more modestly and less evenly.[45] Finally, it is worth noting that if we consider East Asia rather than the Pacific basin as a whole, regional trade as a proportion of total trade was for many countries still lower in 1990 than it had been prior to the Second World War. The proportion for China was 59 per cent in 1990 compared to 70 per cent in 1938, and for Japan, Korea and Thailand it was 29 per cent and 70 per cent, 40 per cent and 100 per cent, and 51 per cent and 65 per cent, respectively.[46]

Allowing for variations in the pattern of trade regionalization, depending on how the region is defined (as Pacific Asia or Asia Pacific) and the period under consideration (for example, the 1970s or the 1980s), there is no question about the general direction of the trend. Several factors had contributed to the intensification of regional trade, but none was more important than the gradual relocation of the less capital- and technology-intensive manufactures first from Japan to the four tiger economies, and subsequently to the ASEAN countries and China. As these economies expanded, the conditions were created for additional investments in communications and transportation and other industrial infrastructure, which expanding Japanese aid flows helped to sustain. Japanese and to a lesser extent US foreign direct investment (FDI) played a critical role in the development of trade linkages, although by the late 1980s both South Korea and Taiwan had also become major investors in East Asia. Japanese FDI flows assumed, however, strategic importance by virtue of scale and the global production strategies on which they were predicated. A number of large Japanese corporations established production facilities spanning the entire region. To cite one striking but not untypical example, Toyota had over a period of 40 years substantially dispersed its production network with the result that by 1999 its overseas operations accounted for almost 30 per cent of its global production, with Asia and Oceania producing 273,000 vehicles down from 313,000 in 1995. By 2000 Toyota had six manufacturing centres in China, four in Thailand, two each in Malaysia and the Philippines, and one each in Indonesia, Taiwan, Vietnam and Australia, with a combined workforce of some 32,000, with substantial trade in parts and materials between these subsidiaries and between them and the parent company.[47] Precisely because of their increasing technological sophistication, the new industries which Japan established in Asia and Oceania were designed to serve as a global export platform, a source of exports to the Japanese domestic market but also an outlet for the large volume of technology-intensive inputs and capital goods which Japan could rapidly export.

Partly because of Japan's central role in developing the complex structure of intra-regional trade and investment, the 'flying-geese' model of East Asian economic development gained wide currency in Asia and beyond.[48] A four-tier model of industrialization was envisaged whereby technology, goods and capital would be successfully transferred from the first tier (Japan) to the second tier (the first generation of NIEs), and eventually to the third tier (the industrializing ASEAN economies), and the fouth tier (principally China).[49] Reflecting their different levels of development, these economies would occupy different but

Table 2.1   Asia-Pacific exports 1960–99 (value in $ million at current prices and percentages as a proportion of country's total exports)

	1960		1966[1]		1970		1975		1980		1985		1990		1995		1999	
	$m	%	$m	%	$m	%	$m	%	$m	%	$m	%	$m	%	$m	%	$m	%
Japan–US	1,107	27.3	3,010	30.8	6,015	31.1	11,246	20.2	31,910	24.5	66,684	37.6	91,121	31.7	122,034	27.5	130,195	31.0
Japan–China	3	0.1	315	3.2	569	2.9	2,258	4.0	5,109	3.9	12,590	7.1	6,145	2.1	21,934	4.9	43,070	10.2
Japan–Russia[2]	60	1.5	215	2.2	341	1.8	1,626	2.9	2,796	2.1	2,772	1.6	2,563	0.9	1,170	0.0	483	0.1
China–US	–	–	–	–	–	–	159	2.7	983	5.4	2,336	8.5	5,314	8.5	24,744	16.6	42,003	21.5
China–Russia	848	44.9	145	9.9	20	1.4	150	2.8	228	1.3	1,037	3.8	2,048	3.3	1,674	1.1	1,497	0.8
ASEAN4[3]–US	619	22.6	736	21.4	892	19.5	3,385	21.9	8,839	18.7	9,070	19.8	16,695	19.3	38,084	19.7	51,579	22.6
ASEAN 4–Japan	357	13.0	849	24.7	1,361	29.8	5,146	33.3	16,273	34.5	14,204	31.0	21,020.5	24.4	33,764	15.5	34,901	15.3
ASEAN 4–China	38	1.4	–	–	22[4]	0.5	94	0.6	386	0.8	597	1.3	1,828.9	2.2	5,501	2.8	7,875	3.4
ASEAN 4–NIEs[5]	510	18.6	198	5.7	840	18.4	2,316	15.0	8,276	17.5	9,133	19.9	18,928[10]	21.9	48,060	24.8	57,679	25.3
NIEs–China	49	2.4	12[6]	0.4	33.3[7]	0.5	137	0.6	1,559[8]	2.2	8190[9]	7.2	23,385[10]	8.7	84,597	16.0	95,127	17.1
NIEs–Japan	174	8.4	317	9.9	895	14.1	2,845	13.0	7,564	10.6	42,433	37.2	30,271	11.3	50,059	9.5	46,59	8.4
NIEs–US	235	11.3	605	18.8	2,032	32.0	5,699	26.2	18,601	25.9	46,766	41.0	72,223	27.0	110,007	20.8	124,058	22.3
Australia–US	136	6.6	412	13.0	612	12.8	1,210	10.1	2,570	11.6	2,344	10.3	4,283	10.7	3,358	6.4	5,398	9.6
Australia–China	23	1.1	165	5.2	129	2.7	326	2.7	796	3.6	865	3.8	959	2.4	2,293	4.3	2,630	4.7
Australia–Japan	313	15.2	586	18.5	1,254	26.3	3,471	29.0	5,871	26.6	6,065	26.7	10,232	25.7	12,184	23.1	10,779	19.2
Australia–ASEAN4	51	2.5	119	3.8	204	4.3	644	5.4	1,228	5.5	969	4.7	2,561	6.4	5,380	10.2	4,182	7.4
Australia–NIEs	59	2.9	155	4.9	256	5.4	744	6.2	1,860	8.4	2,754	12.1	6,359	16.0	11,817	22.4	11,249	20.0
Canada–US	3,110	56.6	5,786	60.3	10,437	62.3	21,170	62.1	41,068	60.8	68,283	75.0	95,388	74.7	152,896	79.5	208,013	87.2
Canada–China	9	0.2	171	1.8	135	0.8	371	1.0	742	1.1	929	1.0	1,320	1.0	2,293	1.2	5,254	2.2
Canada–Japan	182	3.3	366	2.8	777	4.6	2,081	6.1	3,751	5.5	4,222	4.6	7,135	5.6	8,531	4.4	1,673	0.7
Canada–ASEAN4	24	0.4	39	0.4	67	0.4	163	0.5	432	0.7	470	0.5	1,068	0.8	1,442	0.7	984	0.4
Canada–NIEs	31	0.6	37	0.4	68	0.4	198	0.6	932	1.4	1,206	1.3	2261	1.8	4,738	2.5	2,965	1.2

Notes

1. For this purpose the year 1966 instead of 1965 as during the years 1964–65 Malaysia and Singapore were united as one trading state.
2. Before 1991 referred to as 'USSR'.
3. ASEAN 4: Indonesia, Philippines, Thailand, Malaysia (Federation of Malaya).
4. From the ASEAN 4, only Malaysia exported to China in 1970.
5. NIEs (newly industrializing economies): Hong Kong, Singapore, Republic of Korea, Taiwan.
6. This figure comprises only Hong Kong's trade.
7. These figures comprise trade for Hong Kong (export: $10.6m, import: $467m) and Singapore (export: $22.7, import: $125.9m).
8. No figures available for Taiwan–China.
9. No figures available for Taiwan and Korea.
10. No figures available for Korea.

Sources:
International Monetary Fund (IMF), *Direction of Trade Annual*, 1964–68, 1958–62; IMF, *Direction of Trade Statistics Yearbook*, 1982, 1987, 1992, 1997, 2000; *The Far East and Australasia, 1982–83* (14th edn, London: Europa, 1982), 1989 (20th edn, 1988), 1993(24th edn, 1992), 1997 (28th edn, 1996), 2001 (32nd edn, 2000); *China Facts & Figures Annual*, John L. Scherer (ed), vol. 1, 1978 (Gulf Breeze, FL, Academic International Press, 1978).

complementary roles within the regional division of labour. As each moved up the ladder of development, it would be better placed to contribute to the growth of those situated at the lower tier of industrialization. The explanatory utility of the flying geese model is subject to a number of limitations. Noteworthy among these is its emphasis on the national dimensions of industrialization, which tends to understate the strategic role of capital. Yet, it is regional and global corporate strategies, whether through intra-firm integration or inter-firm collaboration, which establish the conditions of competitiveness and provide the impetus for the continuous reorganization of industry.

In this context, two propositions central to the flying geese model, namely 'horizontal integration' and 'economic complementarity',[50] merit attention for they suggest a pattern of economic regionalization which is in some respects seriously misleading. First, the East Asian division of labour had by the late 1980s acquired a distinctly vertical profile in that Japanese capital was the primary engine driving the diffusion of economic roles and the structure of product cycles. The environment within which NIE and ASEAN enterprises operated was shaped largely by Japanese industrial and financial firms and their production and investment strategies. As a consequence the ASEAN economies had become a production platform geared to serving the Japanese market, providing Japanese capital with enhanced export opportunities, and displacing environmental hazards from the core to the periphery of the region. Secondly, the four tiers of East Asian industrialization had given rise to competition as much as to complementarity. Faced with the rapid growth and increasing competitiveness of Korean and Taiwanese electronic industries, Japanese enterprises sought to retrieve lost ground by establishing productive facilities in Southeast Asia where they could combine their technological, financial and marketing muscle with cheap local labour. Similarly, once China had by the mid-1980s added its vast reservoir of cheap labour to the regional economy, a new competitive dynamic soon emerged between ASEAN and Chinese export industries, especially in textiles and clothing but also electrical appliances and wood manufactures. Without question the regionalization of trade, aid, capital flows and technology transfers had become an integral part of East Asian industrialization, but this is not to say that all participating economies were equally influential in shaping the increasingly dense network of transactions or derived equal benefit from it. Nor did it necessarily mean that the network was uniformly spread across East Asia, or indeed that it was confined to East Asia.

Thus far the discussion has centred largely on regionalization in the economic domain, but the phenomenon was not entirely driven by economics. While the 'strong state' thesis should not be overstated, the authority and resources of many East Asian states were instrumental, especially in the early stages of industrialization, in expanding the economic and social infrastructure, developing institutional mechanisms for macroeconomic management, and for cultivating policy networks linking the business community with the bureaucracy, and often the military.[51] It is in large part this commonality of experience, aptly expressed by the term 'authoritarian developmentalism', which underpinned the notion of an 'Asian Way' or the 'Oriental Alternative'.[52] Commonly depicted as the expression of East Asia's cultural heritage, and of its attachment to, or at least affinity with, Confucianism (understood as a code word for a social model based on human emotional bonds, respect for authority, and group harmony),[53] the Asian way was as much a political as a social construct. It was first and foremost an attempt by economic and political elites to enhance the legitimacy of the development model which they were intent on pursuing and not infrequently the wealth and power which they derived from it. The 'Asian values' discourse, to which we return in Chapter 9, did nevertheless have substantial resonance among Asian publics, and its distinctly non-Western or even anti-Western tone did provide, if not a common language, at least a rhetorical bridge between otherwise economically, ethnically and linguistically diverse East Asian polities.[54] Also relevant in this context is the notion of an East Asian strategic culture, which gained currency during the 1980s and 1990s, most explicitly in the writings of a number of Western scholars struck by the patient, informal, pragmatic, consensual and incremental approach of Asian diplomacy, which they contrasted with the Western preference for legal and institutional arrangements, and the sharp delineation of rights and obligations.[55] Here again, the claims for Asian distinctiveness may have been overstated but Asian, and in particular ASEAN, leaders went to considerable pains to cultivate a diplomatic ethos and style respectful of one another's state-building, in part through consistent invocation of the twin principles of state sovereignty and non-interference in the internal affairs of other states.

The regionalization of political discourse was not, however, a purely statist phenomenon. The emerging maps of knowledge and networks of political mobilization did not all emanate from actual or aspiring centres of hegemonic power, be it Washington, Tokyo or Beijing, or for that matter from other states in the region. A great many intellectual currents, social movements and political campaigns gave rise to often informal but strategic transnational coalitions. These centred on a wide spectrum of expectations and demands, varying from the repressed claims of the 'comfort women' forced into sexual service by the Japanese military in the Second World War, to mounting protests against French nuclear testing in the Pacific, indigenous struggles to reclaim land and cultural dignity (in Australia, New Zealand, Hawaii, Taiwan, Malaysia, the Philippines); and increasingly vocal and coordinated responses to environmental hazards associated with such practices as deforestation, sulphur and other emissions, overfishing, or shipment of highly toxic nuclear and chemical materials. The regionalization of social activism is examined more closely in later chapters. It is, however, worth noting here that the phenomenon was by no means confined to non-government organizations (NGOs) of Western inspiration, but encompassed a growing number of professional, labour, religious, women's and other networks and associations, many of which were deeply rooted in local cultures and traditions.

Our discussion of regionalization has until now assumed that the various manifestations of the phenomenon and the forces contributing to its momentum necessarily spanned the entire region, however one might choose to define its boundaries. Yet there is no reason to suppose that regionalization had to proceed uniformly across the region. Sub-regional patterns of interaction and the formation of sub-regional clusters can themselves be an important indicator of regionalization, though the linkages between the regional and sub-regional may not always be direct or transparent. Significant ideational and material factors contributed to a dense Southeast Asian network of social, economic, religious and political ties that predated the Second World War. Neither the artificial divisions imposed by colonial rule nor the polarization introduced by the Cold War could erase the experience of spatial and social proximity derived from diasporic networks and other forms of cultural and economic interaction. In that sense, the 'vernacular language'[56] of Southeast Asian identity may be said to have preceded the statist discourses that developed in the wake of decolonialization. Not surprisingly the policy elites that emerged in the post-independence period in the political, bureaucratic, business, media and intellectual arenas were soon connected by a multiplicity of channels which greatly facilitated the transmission and development of ideas, and eventually the establishment of regional institutions.[57] In that sense, the construction of Southeast Asian regionalism was both a society-centred and a state-centred project.

Writing in 1988, Barry Buzan identified four Asian security complexes: South Asia, Southeast Asia, Northeast Asia and the South Pacific, the last three of which are directly relevant to our analysis of the Asia-Pacific region. Focusing principally on the Southeast Asian complex, he noted the absence of any single country capable of dominating the local security environment, and of any single or rigid pattern of relations dominating the history of the complex.[58] Even the principal division which he identified, namely that 'between capitalist ASEAN and the Vietnamese communist empire', was primarily a manifestation of the Cold War overlay, which would soon be overtaken by events, notably the UN-supervised Cambodian peace process and Vietnam's eventual admission to full membership of ASEAN. Though a number of unresolved local territorial and other disputes might be a source of intermittent friction in Southeast Asian relations, for Buzan it was largely regional considerations, notably China's role and great power rivalry, namely between China and the Soviet Union, and to a lesser extent between the Soviet Union and the United States, which conferred on the complex its defining characteristics. The end of the Cold War and the intensification of Sino–American tensions, coupled with China's increasing assertiveness, have in one sense produced a substantially different environment to the one envisaged by Buzan. Neither of these developments, however, nor the economic and political difficulties experienced by a number of Southeast Asian states in the 1990s have changed the geographical contours of the Southeast Asia complex or dramatically altered the inclination of national policy elites to think of Southeast Asia as a natural arena for security and economic dialogue.

In the case of the South Pacific, more accurately designated as Oceania, the heavy dependence of micro-states on metropolitan assistance (usually from the ex-colonial power) has paradoxically stimulated various forms of regional interaction. The networking established by Christian missions, first on a denominational basis and subsequently through ecumenical collaboration via the Pacific Conference of Churches, was mirrored by various forms of colonial integration and eventually by inter-colonial regionalism beginning with the establishment of the South Pacific Commission in 1947. Another important institution contributing to regional dialogue and identity formation was the UN system as a whole and in particular its specialized agencies and regional organizations to which Pacific islands increasingly turned for financial and technical assistance. Equally significant was the role of international firms with a dispersed stake in the region, and the various regional consultative forums which they helped to establish, notably the Pacific Basin Economic Council (PBEC) and the Pacific Economic Co-operation Council (PECC).[59] Through a steady expanding network of conferences and multilateral institutions, devoted primarily to functional co-operation, a sense of political commitment, often referred to as the 'Pacific way' or 'Pan-Pacific nationalism' gradually emerged linking the more culturally distinct Melanesian, Polynesian and Micronesian identities.[60] Notwithstanding the meandering and at times faltering pace of South Pacific regionalism in the post-independence period, Pacific leaders were eager to widen the political space available to them for the expression of indigenous values and control in the face of unresolved ethnic and tribal conflicts on the one hand and continuing vulnerability to powerful external pressures on the other.

It remains to say a word about the third sub-region of relevance to our analysis, variously referred to as Northeast Asia or the North Pacific, depending on whether or not it is thought necessary to include the United States and Canada. The debate is in many ways an artificial one since Northeast Asia's geopolitical and economic landscape must take full account of the pervasive presence of American interests and power. With this crucial caveat in mind, it may nevertheless be useful to sketch, however briefly, the scope and limitations of regional interaction in Northeast Asia, the principal constituents of which are China, Japan, the two Koreas, Taiwan and the Russian Far East. Conscious of the multiple tensions that have beset this part of the world for the greater part of the twentieth century, most observers have tended to emphasize the obstacles to regionalization. Studies of the post-1945 period have invariably focused on Cold War rivalries most strikingly manifested in the division of the Korean peninsula and the China–Taiwan dispute, but also on the unresolved territorial and other tensions between China and Russia, and China and Japan, and the continuing antipathies between Japan and Korea. Important as these limiting factors have been, a number of more recent developments, notably the dissolution of the Cold War system, the introduction of market reforms in China, and above all the sustained expansion of several Northeast Asian economies have created more favorable conditions for higher levels of regional interdependence.

Trade and to a lesser extent capital, technology and labour flows are perhaps the most important indicators of this trend. Whereas in 1975 intra-regional trade accounted for 30.6 per cent of East Asia's total trade, by 1992 the proportion had risen to 45.0 per cent.[61] If to this figure is added East Asia's trade with North America, which in 1992 represented 22.9 per cent of its total trade, the enormous concentration of intra-Pacific trade becomes readily apparent. Intra-regional FDI flows, at least in absolute terms, were much less impressive than intra-Pacific flows, given that a large share of Japanese and Korean investments were directed to North America, especially the United States. Intra-regional FDI flows during the 1980s and 1990s nevertheless followed a steep upward curve, with Japanese investments to China rising from $100 million in 1985 to $1691 million in 1993, and South Korean investments to China rising even more dramatically from $0.1 million in 1985 to $639.4 million in 1993.[62] However, as we were at pains to show in *States, Markets and Civil Society in Asia Pacific*, the burgeoning web of economic transactions both within Northeast Asia and across the North Pacific unfolded within a fiercely competitive environment, which could not but influence the decisions and strategies of corporations, banks and other key regional players. At one level increased economic and functional interaction might be expected to exert powerful pressures for institution-building, but, as we shall see in later chapters, the precise form which such institutions might take, the objectives. they would serve, the balance that would be struck between protectionist and liberalizing tendencies and the way membership would be constituted, were economically and politically sensitive questions which would inevitably lead to protracted and contested negotiation.

Another complicating variable in the regional equation was the steady development of regional clusters, variously described as growth areas, growth triangles, growth polygons or natural economic territories.[63] These clusters included the Southern Growth Triangle also known as SIJORI (comprising Singapore, Johore in Malaysia, and the Riau Islands in Indonesia), the Northern Growth Triangle (consisting of the Northern States of Peninsular Malaysia, several provinces in Southern Thailand, and North Sumatra and Aceh in Indonesia), and East Asia Growth Area (EAGA) comprising Brunei, North Sulawesi and West Kalimantan in Indonesia, Sabah, Sarawak and Labuan in

Malaysia, and Mindanao and Palawan in the Philippines. These and other clusters, each with its own characteristics and at different stages of development, were based in part on geographical proximity and historical linkages. More importantly perhaps, this form of 'soft regionalism' reflected the powerful pressures associated with the globalization of markets, capital flows and technology linkages, which could not be easily accommodated within state boundaries or adequately mobilized by existing regional institutions.

Though later chapters will subject many of these trends to detailed scrutiny, one feature of contemporary Asia-Pacific regionalization should already be apparent. Regionalizing tendencies were not spatially, temporally or institutionally uniform. They had not given rise to a single, coherent, clearly demarcated economic, let alone political or cultural region. Identifiable patterns of sustained interaction had emerged, primarily but not exclusively in the economic arena, which in some respects encompassed the entire Asia-Pacific region, but in other respects were limited to Pacific Asia, or to a number of sub-regions or, as we have just seen, to clusters which cut across the boundaries of two or more neighbouring states. These distinct, often overlapping, at times competing patterns of regional interaction were not, on the other hand, entirely haphazard or discrete phenomena. As indicated earlier, the diplomatic, economic or normative influence exercised at different times and in different ways by China, Japan or the United States helped to confer on the Asia-Pacific region a greater degree of political coherence than might otherwise have been the case. Especially striking from the early 1980s onwards were the multiple points of connection which these three centres of power had established by virtue of their overlapping membership of the three sub-regions – the United States remained politically and strategically omnipresent; Japan had developed a major economic stake in all three sub-regions and become a significant player in several areas of regional conflict; China had important ties with Russia, North Korea and Vietnam, had been a key protagonist in the Cambodian conflict and was central to the Spratlys dispute, was developing a multidimensional relationship with ASEAN, and had extensive symbolic and practical connections with the economically influential Chinese communities of Southeast Asia. To this must be added the role of one or two strategically placed semi-peripheral or middle powers, notably Australia, Malaysia and South Korea, which by virtue of their geographic location, physical assets, and multifaceted economic and diplomatic relationships, had helped to build usable, though still fragile, bridges between two or more sub-regions – in Australia's case between Oceania and Southeast Asia, and in the case of Malaysia and South Korea between Southeast and Northeast Asia.

Without underestimating the increasing volume and concentration of regional and sub-regional trade, or the rising density of capital and information flows, the Asia-Pacific region, it must be said, remained vulnerable to potentially disintegrative tendencies. The notion of an emerging Pacific Community had to contend with the still unresolved political and psychological tensions associated with sharply diverging views on the identity and membership of that community. At issue in particular was the current and future role – economic and cultural as much as strategic – of the United States, and to a lesser extent that of Canada, Australia and New Zealand. Were these economies and polities to be treated as integral to the region's structure and ethos, or were they more accurately characterized as influential outsiders?

The limitations to regionalization were not, however, simply the product of competing regional designs or projects, or for that matter of the periodic shifts in the distribution of economic power and political initiative (about which more later). The evolution of regional interaction had for some time been, and was likely to remain, a contradictory and contested process. Countervailing tendencies originated both from below and from above. At the national and subnational levels the ethnic, religious and economic divisions which state-building had failed to overcome posed a threat to the dynamic of regionalization, by creating either domestic political instability, which might in turn divert attention and resources from regional interaction, or by endowing religious, cultural or political fault-lines with a regional dimension. At the international level, the globalization of production and distribution structures coupled with increased capital mobility, the transnationalization of financial institutions, and accelerated deterritorialization of technical innovation, had substantially limited the capacity of geographically delineated spaces, including regional space, to develop formal or new informal mechanisms capable of sustaining and guiding regional interdependence. The economic and political crisis experienced by Indonesia in the late 1990s was indicative of the enormous pressures bearing upon the Indonesian state both from below and from above. The mutually reinforcing impact of these pressures could not but spill over into the regional domain given Indonesia's pivotal role in ASEAN and Southeast Asia more generally. The repercussions of the East Asian financial crisis varied considerably in scale and intensity from country to country, as did the sources of political discontent. None the less these closely interacting constraints on the efficacy of state action had noticeably, though perhaps only temporarily, reduced the capacity of these societies to maintain the impetus of economic and political integration.

Regionalization in Asia Pacific could not escape the far-reaching, though often dimly perceived, effects of pendulum swings associated with cyclical factors or 'conjunctures'. Yet, viewed from the perspective of the *longue durée*, regionalization was here to stay. Conflicting interests and perceptions and shifting policy orientations on the part as much of firms as of states had given rise to competing delineations of regional space and architectural blueprints. At stake were not merely issues of institutional membership and structure, but the interplay of security, economy and culture, of statist and non-statist discourses, of regionalization and globalization, and increasingly of the national, regional and global tiers of governance. The chapters that follow will place these interrelationships in their historical context, and in the process attempt to trace how they have evolved over time, and illuminate the implications of that trajectory.

NOTES

1. For an examination of the historical, cultural, demographic, political and economic factors pointing to the formation of an East Asian region, see Alexander B. Murphy, 'Economic Regionalization and Pacific Asia', *Geographical Review,* 85 (2), April 1995, 127–40.

2. See, for example, Gerald Segal, '"Asianism" and Asian Security', *The National Interest,* Winter 1995–96, p. 59.

3. See Marc Mancall, 'The Ch'ing Tribute System: An Interpretive Essay', in John K. Fairbank (ed), *The Chinese World Order: Traditional China's Foreign Relations,* Cambridge, MA: Harvard University Press,1968, pp. 63–89.

4. See Frances V. Moulder, *Japan, China and the Modern World Economy: Toward a Reinterpretation of East Asian Development ca. 1600 to ca. 1918,* Cambridge: Cambridge University Press, 1977, pp. 91–146.

5. For a highly revealing account of US interests and perspectives, see Roger Pineau (ed), *The Japan Expedition 1852–1854: The Personal Journal of Commodore Matthew C. Perry,* Washington, DC: Smithsonian Institution Press, 1968, pp. 157–76.

6. See Chitoshi Yanaga, *Japan since Perry,* Handen, CT: Archion Books, 1966, pp. 20–25.

7. This periodization of hegemonic regimes may be contrasted with Chung-in Moon's three hegemonic cycles which omit any mention of the European colonial phenomenon. He focuses instead on the hegemonic roles of China, Japan (culminating in the Greater East Asia Co-prosperity sphere) and the United States which, we are told, in line with its Containment strategy played the role of 'benign hegemon' (see Chung-in Moon, 'Economic Interdependence and the Implications for Security in Northeast Asia', *Asian Perspective,* 19 (2), Fall–Winter 1995, 29.

8. J. Kathirithamby-Wells, 'The Old and the New', in Richard Maidment and Colin Mackerras (eds), *Culture and Society in the Asia-Pacific,* London: Routledge, 1998, p. 19.

9. Ibid., p. 22.

10. Chitoshi Yanaga, *Japan since Perry*, pp. 186–7.

11. Ibid., pp. 243–7.

12. Ibid., pp. 304–13.

13. This assessment is made by Peter A. Petri, 'The East Asian Trading Bloc: An Analytical History', in J. Frankel and M. Kahler (eds), *Regionalism and Rivalry: Japan and the US in Pacific Asia,* Chicago: University of Chicago Press, 1993, p. 3. See also Ramon H. Myers and Mark R. Peattie (eds), *The Japanese Colonial Empire, 1895–1945,* Princeton, NJ: Princeton University Press, 1984.

14. The ideological underpinnings of Japan's assimilationist strategy are clearly identified by Mark R. Peattie, 'The Japanese Colonial Empire', in Peter Duus (ed), *The Cambridge History of Japan,* Vol. 6, *The Twentieth Century,* Cambridge: Cambridge University Press, 1988, pp. 240–42.

15. A perceptive account of the structure, ethos and growing assertiveness of Japanese imperialism during this period is provided by W.G. Beasley, *Japanese Imperialism: 1894–1945,* Oxford: Clarendon Press, 1987.

16. Petri, 'The East Asian Trading Bloc', pp. 33–4.

17.	See Mark Borthwick, *Pacific Century: The Emergence of Modern Pacific Asia*, Boulder, CO: Westview Press, 1992, pp. 507–46; also World Bank, *The Asian Miracle: Economic Growth and Public Policy*, Oxford: Oxford University Press, 1993.

18.	See, for example, Walden Bello and Stephanie Rosenfeld, 'Dragons in Distress: The Crisis of the NICs', *World Policy Journal*, 7, 1990, 431–68.

19.	This neo-classical perspective on the dynamics of East Asia's regionalization is clearly evident in Bela Balassa, 'The Lessons of East Asian Development: An Overview', *Economic Development and Cultural Change*, 36 (3), Supplement, 1988, S273–90. For a sharper analysis of East Asian economic growth, the contribution of trade to that growth, and the strong trade complementarity between the resource-rich countries of the Pacific and the rapidly industrializing East Asian economies, see Peter Drysdale, *International Economic Pluralism: Economic Policy in East Asia and the Pacific*, Sydney: Allen & Unwin in association with the Australia–Japan Research Centre, Australian National University, 1988, pp. 60–83.

20.	See M. Castells, 'Four Asian Tigers with a Dragon Head: A Comparative Analysis of the State, Economy and Society in the Asian Pacific Rim', in R. Appelbaum and J. Henderson (eds), *States and Development in the Asian Pacific Rim*, Newbury Park, CA: Sage, 1992; R. Wade, *Governing the Market: Economic Theory and the Role of Government in East Asian Industrialization*, Princeton, NJ: Princeton University Press, 1990.

21.	See Hung-Chao Tai, 'The Oriental Alternative: A Hypothesis on East Asian Culture and Economy', in Hung-Chao Tai (ed), *Confucianism and Economic Development: An Oriental Alternative?* Washington, DC: Washington Institute Press, 1989; Roy Hofheinz and Kent E. Calder, *The East Asia Edge*, New York: Harper & Row, 1982, pp. 41–5, 109–13.

22.	Ravi Arvind Palat, 'Introduction: The Making and Unmaking of Pacific-Asia', in Ravi Arvind Palat (ed), *Pacific-Asia and the Future of the World-System*, London: Greenwood, 1993, pp. 9–10.

23.	Institute of Pacific Relations (in Frankel and Kahler, *Regionalism and Rivalry*, p. 36).

24.	See Joseph A. Camilleri, *States, Markets and Civil Society in Asia Pacific: The Political Economy of the Asia-Pacific Region,* Vol. I, Cheltenham, UK: Edward Elgar, 2000, pp. 148–9, 226–8.

25.	Richard Stubbs, 'Asia-Pacific Regionalization and the Global Economy: A Third Form of Capitalism?', *Asian Survey*, 35 (9), September 1995, 793.

26.	This analysis is based in part on the more detailed examination of trends in Camilleri, *States, Markets and Civil Society*, pp. 67–79. Also relevant are a number of studies which have focused on the 'keiretsu' structure of Japan's large corporations and its implications for Japan's regional policies. See, for example, Walter Hatch and Kozo Yamamura, *Asia in Japan's Embrace: Building a Regional Production Alliance*, Cambridge: Cambridge University Press, 1996; Edward J. Lincoln, *Japan's Rapidly Emerging Strategy toward Asia*, Paris: OECD, 1992; Mitsubiro Seki, *Beyond the Full-Set Industrial Structure: Japanese Industry in the New Age of East Asia*, Tokyo: LTCB International Library Foundation, 1994; Richard Doner, 'Japan in East Asia: Institutions and Regional Leadership', in Peter J. Katzenstein and Takashi Shiraishi (eds), *Network Power: Japan and Asia*, Ithaca, NY: Cornell University Press, 1997, pp. 197–233.

27.	Ngai-Ling Sum, '"Greater China" and the Global–Regional–Local Dynamics in the Post-Cold War Era', in Ian G. Cook, Marcus A. Doel and Rex Li (eds), *Fragmented Asia: Regional Integration and National Disintegration in Pacific Asia*, Aldershot, UK: Avebury, 1996, p. 59.

28.	For a brief survey of these expanding linkages, see Camilleri, *States, Markets and Civil Society*, pp.106–12; also J.A.C. Mackie, 'Overseas Chinese Entrepreneurship', *Asia-Pacific Economic Literature*, 6, May 1992, 41–64; John Kao, 'The Worldwide Web of Chinese Business', *Harvard Business Review*, 71, March–April 1993, 24; special issue devoted to the discussion of 'Greater China' in *The China Quarterly*, 136, December 1993; Hsin-

Huang, Michael Hsiao and Alvin Y. So, 'Ascent through National Integration: The Chinese Triangle of Mainland–Taiwan–Hong Kong', in Palat (ed), *Pacific-Asia and the Future of the World-System*, pp. 35–50.

29. Suisheng Zhao, 'Soft versus Structured Regionalism: Organizational Forms of Co-operation in Asia-Pacific', *Journal of East Asian Affairs*, 12 (1), Spring 1998, 114.

30. Peter J. Katzenstein, 'Introduction: Asian Regionalism in Comparative Perspective', in Katzenstein and Shiraishi (eds), *Network Power*, p. 38.

31. See Wang Gungwu, *China and the Chinese Overseas*, Singapore: Times Academic Press, 1991; G. Hamilton (ed), *Business Networks and Economic Development in East and Southeast Asia*, Hong Kong: Centre of Asian Studies, University of Hong Kong, 1991.

32. The bilateral and trilateral linkages between these three centres of power are examined in Camilleri, *States, Markets and Civil Society in Asia Pacific*, pp. 157–215.

34. See Joel Kotkin, *Tribes: How Race, Religon and Identity Determine Success in the New Global Economy*, New York: Random House, 1993, pp. 165–200; Hatch and Yamamura, *Asia in Japan's Embrace*, pp. 56–61, 70–71.

35. This difference is heavily emphasized in Katzenstein, 'Introduction: Asian Regionalism in Comparative Perspective', pp. 39–40.

36. See Farid Hariato, *Oriental Capitalism*, Toronto: Centre for International Studies, University of Toronto, 1993, pp. 19–20; Danny Kin-Kong Lam and Ian Less, 'Guerilla Capitalism and the Limits of the Statist Theory: Comparing the Chinese NICs', in Cal Clarke and Steve Chan (eds), *The Evolving Pacific Basin in the Global Economy: Domestic and International Linkages*, Boulder, CO: Lynne Rienner.

36. Stubbs, 'Asia-Pacific Regionalization and the Global Economy', p. 795.

37. Parthay Gangopadhyay, 'Patterns of Trade, Investment and Migration in the Asia-Pacific Region', in G. Thompson (ed), *Economic Dynamism in the Asia-Pacific: The Growth of Integration and Competitiveness*, London: Routledge in association with the Open University, 1998, p. 103.

38. Harry Harding, *A Fragile Relationship: The United States and China since 1972*, Washington, DC: Brookings Institution, 1992, p. 367.

39. The concept is developed at some length in Camilleri, *States, Markets and Civil Society in Asia Pacific*, pp. 151, 175–8, 211–15.

40. Ibid., pp. 83–105.

41. See Table 6.1 in Soogil Young, 'East Asia as a Regional Force for Globalization', in K. Anderson and R. Blackhurst (eds), *Regional Integration and the Global Trading System*, New York: Harvester/Wheatsheaf, 1993, p.182. East Asia here comprises Japan, the four NIEs, the ASEAN four (Thailand, Malaysia, Indonesia and the Philippines) and China.

42. See Table 17 in Willy Kraus and Wilfrid Lütkenhorst, *The Economic Development of the Pacific Basin: Growth Dynamics, Trade Relations and Emerging Cooperation*, New York: St. Martin's Press, 1986, p. 117.

43. See Table 6.3 in Young, 'East Asia as a Regional Force for Globalization', p. 131.

44. See Table 1.2 in Petri, 'The East Asian Trading Bloc', p. 30.

45. Kraus and Lütkenhorst, *The Economic Development of the Pacific Basin*, p. 117.

46. Petri, *The East Asian Trading Bloc*, p. 30.

47. See 'Toyota and the World 2002' Databook, pp. 1, 3, 12, 23, 54, 58, at http://www.toyota.co.jp/IRweb/corp_info/datacenter/2002/2002databook_3.pdf (sighted on 2 October 2002).

48. The model is examined in Camilleri, *States, Markets and Civil Society*, pp. 101–6. One of the first proponents of the model was Kanane Akamatsu, 'A Historical Pattern of Economic Growth in Developing Countries', *The Developing Economies*, 1, March–April 1962, 3–25. For a sophisticated analysis of the interaction of the relevant economies and their respective industries, see Terutomo Ozawa, 'Pacific Economic Integration and the "Flying

Geese" Paradigm', in Alan M. Rugman and Gavin Boyd (eds), *Deepening Integration in the Pacific Economies: Corporate Alliances, Contestable Markets and Free Trade*, Cheltenham, UK: Edward Elgar, 1999, pp. 55–91. A mildly critical but generally supportive review of the model in the wake of the 1997 financial crisis is offered by one of its leading Japanese exponents, Kiyoshi Kojima, 'The "Flying Geese' Model of Asian Economic Development: Origin, Theoretical Extensions, and Regional Policy Implications', *Journal of Asian Economics*, 11, 2000, 375–401.

49. See William McCore, *The Dawn of the Pacific Century: Implication of the Three Worlds of Development*, New Brunswick, NJ: Transaction Publishers, 1993.

50. See Robert A. Manning and Paula Stern, 'The Myth of the Pacific Community', *Foreign Affairs*, 73 (6), November–December 1994, 82–3.

51. The case for the 'developmental state' is critically reviewed and a more nuanced interpretation presented in Camilleri, *States, Markets and Civil Society*, pp. 360–74.

52. See Balihari Kausikan, 'Asia's Different Standard', *Foreign Policy*, 92 (3), Fall 1993, 24–41. A more explicit connection between cultural values and economic practice is proposed by Hung-Chao Tai, 'The Oriental Alternative', pp. 10–36.

53. Confucianism is not, however, as cohesive a religious–ideological system as is sometimes argued or implied. The ambiguities of the Confucian heritage are elucidated in G. Rozman, 'Comparisons of the Modern Confucian Values in China and Japan', in G. Rozman (ed), *The East Asian Region: Confucian Heritage and its Modern Adaptation*, Princeton, NJ: Princeton University Press, 1991, pp.157–203.

54. For a critical assessment of the 'Asian Values' discourse, see Alan Dupont, 'Is there an Asian Way', *Survival*, 38 (2), Summer 1996.

55. See Desmond Ball, 'Strategic Culture in the Asia-Pacific Region', *Security Studies*, 3 (1), Autumn 1994, 44–74.

56. Diana Wong, 'Regionalism in the Asia-Pacific – A Response to Kanishka Jayasuriya', *Pacific Review*, 8 (4), 1995, 686.

57. See Richard Higgott, 'Ideas, Identity and Policy Coordination in the Asia-Pacific', *Pacific Review*, 7 (4), 1994, 367–79. For insights into the national manifestations of those policy elites, see David Camroux, 'The Asia-Pacific Policy Community in Malaysia', *Pacific Review*, 7 (4), 1994, 421–33; K. Jayasuriya, 'Singapore: The Politics of Regional Definition', *Pacific Review*, 7 (4), 1994, 411–20.

58. Barry Buzan, 'The Southeast Asian Security Complex', *Contemporary Southeast Asia*, 10 (1), June 1988, 5.

59. See Ron Crocombe, 'South Pacific Regionalism', in Y. Ghan (ed), *Small States: Pacific Experiences*, London/Suva: Commonwealth Secretariat and University of the South Pacific, 1990, pp. 229–33.

60. For an early exposition of these trends, see Greg Fry, 'Regionalism and International Politics of the South Pacific', *Pacific Affairs*, 54 (3), Fall 1981, 456–68.

61. Masani Yochida, Ichiro Akimune, Masayuki Nohara and Kimitoshi Sato, 'Regional Economic Integration in East Asia; Special Features and Policy Implications', in Vincent Cable and David Henderson (eds), *Trade Blocs? The Future of Regional Integration*, London: Royal Institute of International Affairs, 1994, p. 68.

62. FDI flows contributed significantly to China's integration with the regional economy. See Allen Y. Tso, 'Foreign Direct Investment and China's Economic Development', *Issues and Studies*, 34 (2), February 1998, 1–34.

63. For a comprehensive overview, see Chia Siow Yue and Lee Tsao Yuan, 'Subregional Economic Zones: A New Motive Force in Asia-Pacific Development', in C. Fred Bergsten and Marcus Noland (eds), *Pacific Dynamism and the International Economic System*, Washington, DC: Institute for International Economics, pp. 225–69.

3. Regionalism in the era of bipolarity

Regionalization, we have been at pains to establish, is hardly a new phenomenon in Asia Pacific. The closely interwoven cultural, economic and geopolitical strands which lend the pattern of regional interaction its unique texture have a long though chequered history. So has the growth of regionalism. In this chapter we focus attention on the evolution of multilateral advocacy and practice. Organizations will necessarily be the subject of more extensive analysis but without neglecting a range of other multilateral initiatives, including treaties, agreements, memoranda of understanding, conferences, declarations and joint activities of various kinds. While states will be treated as central to the process, there is no implicit assumption that multilateralism is an exclusively state-centric process, or that non-state actors may not in certain periods or circumstances play an influential role. As we shall see, states, markets and civil society have all contributed to the shape and content of Asia-Pacific regionalism. It is the complex dynamic of these three layers of interaction which have endowed the multilateral agenda in this region with its distinctive ethos and profile.

For reasons that will soon become apparent, the Cold War years represent a watershed in the evolution of Asia-Pacific regionalism. This is not to say that the effects of strategic and ideological bipolarity were uniformly experienced across time or space. Substantial discontinuities characterized the evolution of the international system during these four decades both between different parts of the world and from one phase to the next. The fluctuation between Cold War and détente were themselves symptomatic of tendencies and counter-tendencies, of tensions within and between alliance systems, and of other complex factors making simultaneously for order and disorder. The tendency of the East–West confrontation to impose bipolarity on a global scale was never fully realized. Other actors, priorities and processes gave rise to a multiplicity of trends and counter-trends which could not be easily accommodated by the logic of the Cold War. The evolving form and content of regionalism, from the mid-1940s to the late 1980s, in Asia no less than in Europe, could not but reflect these competing tendencies. Our examination of Asia-Pacific regionalism as it unfolded during this extended period will therefore need to be informed in the first instance by the contrasting implications of Cold War dynamics, functional co-operation and economic transnationalism.

COLD WAR DYNAMICS

The impact of the Cold War on the development of regional institutions was perhaps less striking but no less instructive in Asia than in Europe. Several distinguishing characteristics of the bipolar era are worth noting at the outset. The integrative tendencies operating within each alliance system, at least at the height of the Cold War, transformed the bloc into a key unit of international decision-making, with ideology serving simultaneously as an instrument of domestic legitimation and a vehicle for the internationalization of conflict. Each bloc spawned a web of bilateral and multilateral agreements governing the establishment and operation of military bases, stationing of troops, combined military exercises, joint weapons procurement policies, and above all the adoption of the strategy of extended deterrence. To a greater or lesser extent these agreements constituted the legalized intrusion of the superpower inside the boundaries of its allies,[1] a phenomenon which was to receive its starkest expression in the Brezhnev doctrine of *limited sovereignty*.[2]

The ostensible commonality of perception and response could not obscure the fact that the two alliance systems were instruments in the global context for geopolitical and ideological influence, which was in turn critical for the reorganization of the post-1945 international economic order.[3] Alliance formation offered the superpowers the opportunity to maintain and expand their respective strategic and economic spheres of influence, although there were significant differences in the resources and alliance management strategies used by the two sides, and in the success with which they pursued their respective goals and maintained their institutional and ideological primacy. The asymmetrical qualities of the two blocs were nowhere more apparent than in Asia Pacific, where the United States enjoyed distinct strategic and economic advantages over its arch rival.

The underlying rationale and institutional framework of Cold War alliances in Asia are reviewed in *States, Markets and Civil Society*.[4] Suffice it here to say that its decisive military victory over Japan gave the United States in the immediate aftermath of the war a formidable capacity to apply its containment policy to shape the political complexion of the emerging regional order.[5] The relative impotence of junior allies to influence US occupation policy in Japan was indicative of things to come. The Far Eastern Commission established in December 1945 was intended to formulate the policies, principles and standards with which Japan would have to comply in fulfilment of the terms of surrender. In practice Commission members were unable, either individually or collectively, to exercise much influence over decision-making, which rested largely with the Allied Council.[6] Though it included China, Britain and the Soviet Union, the Council itself merely served to strengthen and legitimate US dominance. Located in Washington and chaired by US Supreme Commander Douglas MacArthur, who exercised sole executive authority over the occupying administration, the Allied Council had little option but to reflect US interests and priorities. Not surprisingly the Peace Treaty concluded in September 1951, while it placed restrictions on future Japanese rearmament, provided the United States with the necessary platform to conclude a bilateral security treaty with Japan and virtually free rein to maintain bases in Japan and use them in support of operations in other parts of East Asia.

The San Francisco security system, as it came to be known, would over the following three years give rise to a loose but comprehensive network of defence arrangements with countries situated along the Western Pacific rim. Bilateral treaties were concluded with the Philippines (August 1951), South Korea (August 1953) and Taiwan (December 1954).[7] The ANZUS treaty with Australia and New Zealand in September 1951 widened still further the perimeter of US power projection, although the 1947 UKUSA agreement had already established the framework for intelligence co-operation with Australia, Canada and Britain, notably in the areas of signals and communications. The ANZUS Treaty established a Council comprising the three foreign ministers or their deputies, whose primary task was to review the strategic outlook for the region. As of 1952 it was complemented by annual meetings of military representatives, which would oversee the organization of joint military exercises, and foster the larger framework of defence collaboration, including American use of Australian military facilities and the establishment of new facilities serving primarily US military requirements.[8]

ANZUS was one of the few initial attempts by the United States to experiment with a multilateral approach to collective security in the Asia-Pacific region. Earlier proposals envisaging the inclusion of other parties, including the Philippines and even Indonesia, soon foundered in the face of practical difficulties and the complexities of reconciling diverging national strategic perceptions and cultures. In any case, US policy-makers generally and military planners in particular saw little advantage in replicating the NATO model in Asia. More attractive was the network of bilateral arrangements, which promised to perform the same function but circumvent the need for multilateral consultation. From Washington's vantage point multilateral processes were more likely to restrict than enhance its diplomatic and strategic freedom of action. Notwithstanding the strategic calculus underlying US containment policy in Asia Pacific, the multilateralist project was not, however, entirely abandoned for implicit in it was the potential for coordination and legitimation which bilateralism could not easily match.

It is not surprising therefore that, against a backdrop of domestic political turmoil throughout Southeast Asia – much of it associated with the rapid and often unpredictable pace of decolonization – and the establishment of communist rule in China, the United States should have revisited the merits of collective defence. An early indication of this possibility came with the Agreement for Mutual Defence Assistance in Indochina. Concluded in

December 1950, the agreement between the United States, France, Cambodia, Laos and Vietnam provided for US military aid, including equipment, material and services, to the three Indochinese governments to which France had granted a measure of autonomy while retaining firm control of their foreign relations and armed forces. In practice, the flow of aid was specifically designed to support the French war effort against the Vietminh, which Washington portrayed as integral to the 'free world's stand against Communist expansionism'.[9]

This early attempt to explore multilateral avenues for incorporating Vietnam into the American strategic orbit was destined to fail for it was premised on France's capacity to reassert its political authority in Indochina or at least to crush the military threat posed by the Vietminh. By mid-1953 it became apparent that, despite substantial US military support, the French could not dislodge the Vietminh, who now effectively controlled most of Tonkin and Annam, and the northern districts of Cochin China. In September 1953, France, again with strong US encouragement, would initiate one final military onslaught to recover lost ground, but the fall of Dien Bien Phu on 7 May 1954 effectively put an end to French colonial rule in Indochina. To offset the weakened Western position in Southeast Asia, the United States proceeded to construct a more elaborate multilateral security system. A Five Power Staff Agency formed in January 1953 and representing the United States, Britain, France, Australia and New Zealand convened a conference in Manila in September 1954, with Thailand, the Philippines and Pakistan as the only three Asian participants – Burma, Ceylon, India and Indonesia had been invited but did not attend.

The ensuing Southeast Asia Collective Defence Treaty, which came into force in February 1955, established a Council of Ministers whose inaugural meeting agreed to form a more permanent body known as the Southeast Asia Treaty Organization (SEATO). The principal clause of the treaty outlined the circumstances in which its members would act against aggression:

> Each Party recognizes that aggression by means of armed attack in the treaty area against any of the Parties or against any State or Territory which the Parties by unanimous agreement may here after designate, would endanger its own peace and safety, and agrees that it will in that event act to meet the common danger in accordance with its constitutional processes.[10]

The fact that the American obligation was explicitly limited to cases of 'communist' aggression underscored the Cold War logic that inspired it, as did a subsequent statement by Australian Foreign Minister Richard Casey: 'resistance to Communism is the immediate objective of the treaty, and it is for this principal purpose that the Australian government is prepared to commit itself to this treaty'.[11] As doubts emerged about SEATO's capacity to act in Southeast Asia as the United States intended, in part because of France's and Pakistan's increasing reluctance to support US initiatives, the Kennedy administration concluded a bilateral agreement with Thailand in March 1962, which radically redefined the SEATO obligation. The treaty, it was now argued, required members to act individually against 'communist aggression', where agreement could not be reached on collective action.

Although the Manila Pact – and its offshoot SEATO – was the most conspicuous multilateral security initiative in the Asia-Pacific theatre of the Cold War, it was by no means the only attempt to institutionalize the containment doctrine and its obverse, the domino theory. In Malaya, Britain had imposed 'Emergency' rule in June 1948 with a view to removing the threat of 'communist subversion' posed by guerilla attacks near the border with Thailand. With the establishment of the Federation of Malaya in February 1948, the Far East Command operated under the British Commander-in-Chief of the Far East and comprised a UK infantry brigade and various air and naval units, and a battalion each from Australia and New Zealand. As part of this arrangement a Chief of Staff Defence Committee, which came to be known as the ANZAM Committee, was formed to oversee joint military exercises between British, Australian, New Zealand and Malayan forces.

With the Federation of Malaya achieving full independence in October 1957, the *ad hoc* ANZAM security framework was replaced by the Anglo-Malaya Defence Agreement (AMDA). Australia and New Zealand soon associated themselves with AMDA by exchanging separate sets of letters with Malaya during March and April 1959. With the creation of the Malaysian Federation in September 1963, the scope of the AMDA arrangements was extended to cover all states in the new federation. Once again Australia and New Zealand exchanged letters with Malaysia to formalize their association with the revised AMDA. While Malaya/Malaysia and Britain were primary members of AMDA, Australia and New Zealand played an important role as 'associated powers', not least through the ANZUS connection which helped to establish a bridge between the diminishing British presence East of Suez and the rapidly expanding US presence in Southeast Asia. With the release in 1967 of the White Paper, *Britain East of Suez*, London signalled its intention to phase out most military commitments in Asia by 1971. A ministerial meeting held in London issued a communiqué on 16 April 1971, which eventually became the founding document of the Five-Power Defence Arrangement (FPDA). It envisaged two key functions: continued defence co-operation among the parties, and, in the event of an actual or threatened armed attack against either Malaysia or Singapore, a process of consultation to determine what measures should be taken jointly and separately in response to such attack or threat.[12] At a five-power ministerial meeting convened in Kuala Lumpur in June 1971 agreement was reached to create side by side with the FPDA an Integrated Air Defence System (IADS). These arrangements were riddled with ambiguity, most obviously in relation to the threat perceptions on which they rested and the responses they foreshadowed in the event of aggression. They were also vulnerable to the unresolved tensions between the principal parties, Malaysia and Singapore. It is, however, clear enough that the British withdrawal East of Suez had prompted the British, Australian and New Zealand governments to devise new ways of stabilizing the Southeast Asian region, not least the Strait of Malacca, consistent with larger Western trade and security interests.[13]

In this all too brief survey of multilateral security arrangements mention must be made of the Asian and Pacific Council (ASPAC) established in June 1966 primarily though not exclusively at South Korea's instigation. Seoul had originally proposed the more ambitious anti-communist collective defence system known as the Asian and Pacific Treaty Organization (APATO), but the mixed response it received compelled it to lower its sights, and pursue instead a looser co-operative arrangement. Although ASPAC was conceived very much with Cold War objectives in mind, its mandate was couched in the language of regional collaboration and solidarity. The geographical scope of the security community it envisaged, however, remained unchanged – the unstated intention was to encompass all of the Asian and Pacific members of the US-centred alliance system except for the United States itself. At the inaugural 1966 meeting nine countries were considered members of the initiative: Australia, Japan, Republic of Korea (ROK), Malaysia, New Zealand, the Philippines, Taiwan, Thailand, Vietnam (South), with Laos accorded observer status. It soon became apparent that diverging interests and perceptions would limit ASPAC's organizational capacity and infrastructure, and confine its agenda to functional rather than overtly military co-operation. Indicative of these limitations was the absence of a permanent secretariat and the emphasis on fostering relatively autonomous functional projects: the Tokyo-based Asian and Pacific Maritime Cooperation Scheme (APMCS), the Economic Cooperation Centre (ECOCEN) in Bangkok, the Registry of Scientific and Technical Services (Canberra), the Cultural and Social Centre (Seoul), and the Food and Fertiliser Technology Centre (Taipei). Though some of these projects were, by virtue of their functional utility, able to survive, ASPAC's overriding agenda, which was to promote an anti-communist coalition aimed in part at thwarting China's admission to the UN, would soon be overtaken by events. The Nixon doctrine, Sino–American rapprochement and China's successful bid for UN membership in 1971 combined to deprive ASPAC of its legitimacy. With most members unwilling to host the 1973 annual meeting, ASPAC died a natural death.[14]

ASPAC's early demise was but the most striking symptom of a wider and deeper geopolitical current which, even at the height of the Cold War, called into question the dominance of ideological and strategic bipolarity. Central to this counter-tendency was the preoccupation of many Third World governments, the Asia-Pacific region very much included, with the multiple challenges posed by decolonialization, independence, development and issues of race. Non-alignment and pan-Asianism, the two movements which perhaps most vividly captured this mood, were sufficiently potent to give rise to what may be loosely described as 'Asian diplomacy'. As one historian has put it, 'The Geneva and

Colombo conferences, including the itinerant diplomacy associated with them, were the last important stages leading up to Bandung: An Asian system of powers was coming into being'.[15] Though this description may overstate the trend, the Conference on Indonesia and the Colombo, Geneva and Bandung conferences which followed did endow Asian diplomacy with a tone and an ethos which the Cold War marginalized and obscured but never entirely extinguished.

The conference on Indonesia, which met in New Delhi in January 1949, was attended by 15 countries, including Afghanistan, Australia, Burma, Ceylon, India, Pakistan and the Philippines. Its key resolution, which was conveyed to the Security Council, condemned the Dutch military action launched on 18 December 1948 as a breach of the peace and an act of aggression, and recommended to the Security Council the staged withdrawal of Dutch forces from all areas occupied as a consequence of that action, and the establishment of an interim Indonesian government pending the elections for a constituent assembly to be completed by 1 October 1949.[16] In what was perhaps the first significant Asian diplomatic initiative of the post-1945 period, the conference on Indonesia had a marked impact on world opinion as well as on the Security Council's deliberations. Indicative of the same sense of emerging Asian solidarity was the Colombo Conference which opened in April 1954. Four governments (India, Pakistan, Burma and Indonesia) had accepted Ceylon's invitation with the clear expectation that the Indochina question would loom large in their deliberations. Paving the way for subsequent negotiations, the Conference called for the complete independence of Indochina and requested the negotiating parties (France, the Democratic Republic of Vietnam [DRV] and the Associated States Cambodia, Laos and [South] Vietnam) to report to the Geneva Conference, which would in turn report to the UN. A week later the Indochina phase of the Geneva Conference got under way (8 May 1954) exactly a day after the fall of Dien Bien Phu. Though none of the Colombo powers was a participant at the Conference, their voice and especially India's would visibly affect its proceedings and conclusions. Equally instructive was China's participation side by side with the other four greater powers. In addition to the bilateral armistice agreement between France and the DRV, the conference produced the multilateral Final Declaration which received the endorsement of all participants except for the United States. With the Cold War still gaining momentum, a predominantly Asian initiative had effectively isolated the United States. The declaration explicitly stated that the military demarcation line between the two regrouping zones was in no way to be interpreted as constituting a political or territorial boundary, and provided for the complete reunification of Vietnam following the conduct of free general elections under the supervision of an International Control Commission to be chaired by non-aligned India. While the normative position adopted in Geneva was not accompanied by clearly defined implementation mechanisms and could not be expected to withstand the mounting geopolitical pressures arising from Cold War rivalries in general and US containment policies in particular, it had nevertheless challenged the emerging orthodoxy which viewed ideological bipolarity as the overriding organizing principle of Asian politics.

The pan-Asianist impulse had in any case yet to run its full course. Disturbed by the polarizing implication of SEATO's creation and convinced of the beneficial effects which China's inclusion in the United Nations would have on regional security, Nehru became increasingly drawn to the idea of a pan-Asian conference. To this end a meeting of the Colombo powers was held in Bogor in late December 1954. Despite sharply conflicting views as to which countries should be invited – the most contentious issue revolved around China's and Taiwan's participation – the meeting resolved that the Conference should proceed. The People's Republic of China (PRC) was to be invited as were the four Indochina states, but North and South Korea as well as Mongolia would be excluded.[17] When Sukarno opened the Asia-Africa Conference in Bandung on 18 April 1955, 29 countries were represented, the five Colombo powers and 24 of the 25 governments that had been invited.[18] The notable achievement of the Conference was precisely its membership, bringing together as it did a number of non-aligned countries but also many others that were formally or informally aligned with the United States or the Soviet Union.

Given the diversity of interests and ideological positions, the Conference yielded few concrete agreements. Yet the 'spirit of Bandung', as it came to be known, had far-reaching ramifications. The Conference gave China a much needed stage on which to demonstrate its diplomatic independence; it enabled Zhou Enlai to make a number of conciliatory overtures to the United States and China's neighbours; above all it helped to cement China's place in Asian diplomacy.[19] The Bandung Conference also established the credentials of the non-alignment movement as a new but influential forum on the world stage, one that would strengthen the determination of its members to defend the hard-fought gains of political independence and assist others to remove the yoke of colonialism. Yet Cold War rivalries could not be altogether cast aside. The intrusion of ideological and geopolitical cleavages often pitted states aligned or associated with the West against the non-aligned, of which India, Indonesia and Burma were the most vocal. The inclusiveness that had been achieved at Bandung would not long survive the close of the Conference, although the idea itself, the notion of an Asian system of powers, would, latently at least, continue to exercise the Asian imagination.

In the aftermath of Bandung, the tone and agenda of Asian diplomacy would be shaped largely by the two dominant Cold War formations. Yet, this is not to say that the two opposing alliance systems were entirely stable or free of tension. Of the multiple factors at work, a few are worth highlighting: the deep divisions within alliances (most dramatically manifested in the Sino–Soviet dispute); the need for coexistence, and even a measure of co-operation across the Cold

War divide (as exemplified by relations between China and a number of Southeast Asian countries during the 1950s, especially after the Cultural Revolution; the mounting costs of hegemony differentially but just as acutely experienced by both superpowers, with Vietnam and Afghanistan apt reminders of the immense expenditure of energy, resources and prestige which the hegemonic project often entailed and of the continuing viability of the non-alignment option even during the height of the Second Cold War). Even before 1989 the strains of alliance management had become apparent in the dissolution of some Cold War arrangements (for example, Sino–Soviet alliance, SEATO, ASPAC) and the paralysis of others (for example, US–New Zealand), or more often in the periodic revamping of the relationship (for example, US–Japan, China–Vietnam).

It cannot be stressed enough that Asia-Pacific multilateralism from the 1950s to the 1980s was largely but never fully shaped by the logic of the Cold War. The ideological and geopolitical polarization of international relations was itself a contradictory process which over time would place severe limitations on the capacity of the superpowers to incorporate the entire world into their respective camps. Two contradictions had especially telling effects. The first related to the complex challenge of alliance management. US hegemony, we have seen, was in no small measure built upon Japanese reindustrialization, for Japan was seen as playing a critical role in advancing US security and economic interests in the region. Similarly, though to a lesser extent, the Soviet Union would contribute to China's economic reconstruction. In this sense, both superpowers may be said to have directly assisted the emergence of future rivals. While neither Japan nor China had any prospect of competing with the United States and the Soviet Union in the global projection of power, they certainly could in time develop the capacity and the will to act as regional hegemons. As far back as the early 1960s Japan began, rather cautiously it is true, to sponsor and even initiate a number of low-level multilateral arrangements. Japanese proposals and participation were invariably driven by considerations of Japanese interests and strongly influenced by the pervasive state–industry nexus which underpinned the core of Japan's external economic and domestic policies. If ties between China and the Soviet Union deteriorated sharply in the late 1950s, it is in no small measure because Moscow became increasingly suspicious of Beijing's intentions and fearful that Chinese power, prestige and wealth might in due course expand at its own expense.

The second contradiction had to do with the very dynamic of capitalist accumulation, predicated as it was upon the opening up of markets, that is, the breaking down of barriers to the movement of capital, money and technology. In other words, whereas the logic of the Cold War was premised on the rigid division between two opposing social and economic systems, in practice one of the two protagonists was, by dint of economic interest, technological capability and ideological predisposition, committed to economic globalization.

The Soviet Union too may have had global aspirations in the sense of constructing a global socialist commonwealth, but, given the limitations of Soviet economic and political institutions and assets, the project lacked the agency and structural potency needed to make it all feasible, let alone bring it to actual fruition. The mutually reinforcing impact of these two countervailing tendencies – the centrifugal forces operating within the two alliance systems and the centripetal forces at work in the emerging global economy – would significantly impinge on the multilateral agenda, not least at the regional level.

FUNCTIONAL REGIONALISM

In Asia-Pacific the contradictions inherent in ideological and strategic bipolarity would soon pave the way for a great many regional initiatives which, though often required to function within the constraints of Cold War politics, were entrusted with tasks and structures which could not be easily or entirely subsumed under the logic of the Cold War. These multilateral arrangements developed in different settings, served different purposes, and conferred a leadership role on different actors. For reasons already alluded to, few if any multilateral institutions, especially of the inter-governmental variety, came into being at the instigation of communist states. Neither China nor the Soviet Union thought it productive or feasible to engage in multilateral activism, except at the level of party-to-party relations. One of the few exceptions was the Conference of the Foreign Ministers of Kampuchea, Laos and Vietnam. Established in January 1980 a year after Hanoi's military intervention in Cambodia, it resulted in the overthrow of the Pol Pot government and the installation of the pro-Vietnamese Heng Samrin administration. Designed to strengthen security, economic and technical collaboration between the three Indochinese states, this trilateral association was able to present a united stance on the Cambodia conflict and establish a number of commissions, but by the time it was dismantled in 1989 little headway had been made on specific projects or on political co-operation more generally.

Leaving aside the security arrangements spawned by the Cold War, the engine propelling institutional innovation in Asia Pacific was driven largely by the United Nations and its agencies or by governments aligned with or sympathetically disposed to the United States. In this region, no less than in Europe, the Western camp had at its disposal a more sophisticated economic and technological base, a more extensive and diversified institutional infrastructure, and a larger and geographically more dispersed membership. Western-inspired regional initiatives duly reflected these advantages and at times gave the impression of inclusiveness even though compliance with notions of the free market was often treated as a condition of membership.[20] Having played the decisive role in the development of a regional security architecture, the United States adopted a lower profile in the promotion of functional multilateralism, preferring to delegate that role to its allies. US initiatives were few in number, modest in scope, and often did not directly involve the government of the United States: in November 1965 the Southeast Asia Ministries of Education Organization was created with US diplomatic and financial support; in December 1971 the Pacific Asian Congress of municipalities came into being largely as a result of the efforts of Mayor Frank Fasi of Honolulu; at the initiative of the chief justices of American and Western Samoa a meeting of chief justices and attorneys from some 20 Pacific countries, including the United States, was held in January 1972, from which emerged an annual forum known as the South Pacific Conference on Law and Law Enforcement; at the instigation of the East–West Center (established by the US Congress in 1960 but with the participation of several Asia-Pacific countries) the Pacific Islands Conference was formed in March 1980 with a broad brief to examine the problems of development experienced by Pacific island nations.

Taking advantage of its remarkable post-war economic recovery and relatively unburdened in the security arena, where the United States had assumed primary responsibility, Japan sought from the early 1960s to expand its economic sphere of influence. Here again the initiative did not always come from the government itself although the close nexus between state and industry on the one hand and between government and the ruling Liberal Democratic Party on the other meant that all initiatives, whether bearing the official imprint or not, effectively had a measure of government support. The Japan Productivity Organization (APO) formed in April 1961 was, as its name implies, entrusted with the task of increasing the economic productivity of Asian countries, principally through technical assistance and training, and the funding of research and technology transfer.[21] In December 1965 an Asian Parliamentarians' Union (APU) was created, with the Japanese Liberal Democratic Party (LDP) assuming a leadership role. By virtue of its origins, the APU functioned, particularly in its early days, as an anti-communist organization, although with increasing Pacific island membership it felt it necessary to rename itself the Asia-Pacific Parliamentarians' Union (APPU) and to call for an end to French colonial rule and to nuclear weapons testing. The improvement in China–Japan relations, particularly after normalization in September 1972, coupled with the misgivings expressed by a number of Asian governments about the organization's ideological profile also contributed to a noticeable toning down of its anti-communist rhetoric.

Encouraged by these early developments the Japanese Foreign Ministry set out to give flesh to Prime Minister Eisaku Sato's 'Asian diplomacy' by convening in April 1966 the inaugural Ministerial Conference for the Economic Development of Southeast Asia (SEAMCED). Six countries (Japan, Laos, South Vietnam, Malaysia, the Philippines and Thailand) initially attended the Conference but were joined in subsequent years by Indonesia, Australia, New Zealand, the Khmer Republic and Burma. SEAMCED functioned as an umbrella for numerous subsidiary bodies, notably the Southeast Asia Fisheries Development Center (SEAFDC), the Southeast Asian Agency for Regional Transport and Communications Development (SEATAC), the Southeast Asian Promotion Center for Trade, Investment and Tourism (SEAP CENTER), the Regional Organization for Inter-governmental Co-operation and Coordination in Family and Population Planning, and the Study Group on Asian Tax Administration and Research (SGATAR). These became the principal mechanisms through which Southeast Asian countries would identify useful projects and Japan would funnel the necessary equipment, technical assistance and finance. Given its substantial maritime interests, not least its concern with the physical security of oil transit routes, particularly in the Strait of Malacca, Japan pressed, in conjunction with ASPAC, for the establishment of the APMCS. However, with the increasing difficulties besetting ASPAC and with Indonesia insisting on acceptance of the archipelagic principle, Japan soon lost interest in the scheme. More successful was the proposal for a hydrographic survey which Singapore, Indonesia, and Malaysia approved in November 1971, paving the way for the tripartite Council which, with the aid of Japanese funding and expertise, would oversee navigational safety in the Malacca and Singapore straits.

Notwithstanding the pre-eminence of US strategic power and Japanese economic muscle, several other countries, often pursuing quite different objectives and responding to quite different pressures, also played a part in the development of the multilateral agenda. By far the most active in this respect were other allies to the United States. In July 1961 the South Korean Postmaster-General with the support of his Philippines counterpart successfully pressed for the formation of an Asian bloc within the Universal Postal Union. By July 1966 the required number of ratifications enabled the new organization to get off the ground. A bolder Korean initiative and one more directly linked to Cold War considerations, led to the creation of the Asian and Pacific Council in June 1966. However, as we have already seen, ASPAC proved a rather short-lived experiment as did several of the projects it had spawned; its cultural arm (CULSOCEN), which had relied heavily on South Korean financial support, continued to operate from its offices in Seoul, but at a much reduced level of activity.

Taiwan's forays into the multilateral arena were also moulded by the logic of the Cold War, although in this case the transparent objective was to endow the Taipei regime with greater international legitimacy. The establishment of the Food and Fertilizer Technology Centre as an ASPAC project in June 1969 and of the Asian Vegetable Research and Development Centre in May 1971 provided Taiwan with useful channels for dispensing financial and technical assistance, thereby demonstrating its contribution to functional co-operation and its credentials as a good 'regional citizen'. The Asia-Pacific Cultural Centre (APCC) which was formed in late 1972 as an offshoot of the APU (subsequently APPU) performed a more or less similar function.

In Southeast Asia the initiative among US allies rested primarily with Thailand and the Philippines. Though party to several agreements, Thailand's principal multilateral achievement was to secure ASPAC support in June 1970 for a regional ECOCEN which was duly opened in April 1971. Having commissioned a number of studies, the Centre was nevertheless closed after a relatively short life, suffering the same fate as its progenitor, ASPAC. In pursuit of a more energetic regional diplomacy, the Philippines was instrumental in getting several functional arrangements off the ground. Notable among these were the Informal Meetings of Directors-General of Civil Aviation (1961), the Asian Judicial Conference (1963), the Study Group on Asian Tax Administration and Research (1971), the Taxation and Customs Cooperation Conference (1972), the Association for Science and Co-operation in Asia (1972), and ASEANPOL, the Meeting of the Chiefs of National Police of the ASEAN countries (1981). These initiatives varied widely in scope, membership, effectiveness and longevity. They were in that sense an accurate barometer not only of Philippine activism, but of the conflicting tendencies underlying the geopolitics of the Asia-Pacific region.

Malaysia too was keen to explore the possibilities of regional co-operation as a way of harnessing external financial and technical resources in support of development projects and policies. Dissatisfied with the proliferation of UN programmes on family and population planning, the Malaysian government convened a Southeast Asian ministerial conference in October 1970 which gave birth to the Inter-Governmental Co-operation and Coordination (IGCC) Organization. After a decade of moderate activity, IGCC closed its doors in 1982 following a decision by the US Agency for International Development (USAID) to terminate funding for such programmes. Another Malaysian initiative led to the formation of the Southeast Asian Agency for Regional Transport and Communications Development (SEARTCD), whose offices opened in Kuala Lumpur in January 1973. Like so many others during this period, these multilateral arrangements proved extremely fragile, susceptible as they were to multiple pressures, from the fluctuating interest of external donors, to the variable and sometimes diverging needs of Southeast Asian economies, and to the tensions associated with the end of the Vietnam War and the advent of communist regimes in Cambodia, Laos and most importantly reunified Vietnam.

To complete this all too brief survey of Asia-Pacific multilateralism in the Cold War context, reference must be made to the Australian contribution and to South Pacific activism more generally. Mindful of Australia's size, location, resources and close ties with Britain and the United States, Australian governments were keen to establish their credentials as supportive of Southeast Asian and South Pacific developmental aspirations, but in ways which would not prejudice Western interests, and especially the strategic connection with the United States. Nothing more clearly revealed these twin objectives than the Australian role in the formation and subsequent development of the Colombo Plan, originally known as the Colombo Plan for Co-operative Economic Development in South and Southeast Asia. In practice, the Colombo Plan was not a fully-fledged multilateral organization, functioning instead as a forum for developing countries to identify their needs and secure aid from donor countries, usually on a bilateral basis. Set up in July 1951 on a five-year trial basis, in response to two distinct but parallel proposals, one advanced by Ceylon and the other by Australia, the Colombo Plan was regularly renewed every five years until 1980, when it was extended for an indefinite period. In 1977 its scope had already been widened functionally and geographically to allow for greater investment of resources to meet social needs and the inclusion of the island nations of the South Pacific. The organization was accordingly renamed the Colombo Plan for Co-operative Economic and Social Development in Asia and the Pacific. Though it funded a large number of irrigation schemes, industrial projects, and provided training and technical services, and thousands of scholarships to Asian students many of whom came to Australia, the Colombo Plan was also viewed by the Australian government as a useful vehicle for extending Western influence. It served Cold War objectives as a platform for a sophisticated propaganda strategy, which included the funding of Asian newspapers with anti-communist leanings, but also as a conduit for training Asian intelligence officers in counter-subversion techniques and funding the supply of radio equipment, which in turn increased the audience for Radio Australia's Asian language programmes.[22]

The Cold War impulse, though often qualified or unobtrusive, was also evident in a number of other Australian initiatives. The South Pacific Commission was formed in February 1947 before East–West antagonisms had fully matured. However, in signing the Canberra Agreement establishing the Commission, Australia and to a greater or lesser extent the other five signatories (Britain, France, the Netherlands, New Zealand and the United States) had made a judgement that only by promoting the social and economic development of the region could they hope to create the conditions for political stability on which the defence of Western interests ultimately depended. Indicative of the same preoccupation with domestic stability was the decision in 1950 to expand the Australian annual conference of police commissioners to allow for international membership.[23] In October 1957, following an Australian proposal to extend the existing Commonwealth practice, an agreement was reached to establish a Council bringing together on an annual basis the Central Banks of Southeast Asia, New Zealand and Australia (SEANZA). In 1967, the Australian government successfully advocated the creation within ASPAC of a Registry of Scientific and Technical Services. Following normalization of relations with China under Gough Whitlam, Australia terminated its participation in ASPAC, and as a consequence phased out the Registry operation.

Finally, mention must be made of the Whitlam initiative which led to the formation of the South Pacific Labour Ministers' Conference (SPLMC) in 1973. Intended largely as the Pacific equivalent of the Conference of Asian Labour Ministers (CLAM), SPLMC lasted for a decade, by which time its purpose was effectively absorbed by CLAM, now renamed the Conference of Asian and Pacific Labour Ministers.

Australia's multilateral diplomacy during this period was the byproduct of two interconnected sets of objectives: one driven primarily by functional and the other by geographical considerations. On the one hand, Australia had, by virtue of its alliance with the United States and its identification with Western interests more generally, sought to position itself in Asia in the context of Cold War rivalries, although at least as much with the Chinese threat in mind. Yet, Australia's geographical location also required it to develop extensive links with East Asia as a whole, and especially with Southeast Asia and the South Pacific. Geographically speaking at least, Australia constituted, whether consciously or not, an important though fragile bridge between Southeast Asian and South Pacific institution-building. In the latter case two other countries, New Zealand and Fiji, played an active role, which is not to say that smaller island states, for example Vanuatu,[24] did not also contribute to the multilateral agenda. Apart from its wide-ranging participation, often as a foundation member, in regional and sub-regional organizations, and its support for the US-sponsored system of collective security in Asia Pacific, New Zealand diplomacy was characteristically pro-active, especially with respect to the Southwest Pacific.[25] The historical connection between the Maori and Polynesian societies and the settlement in New Zealand of a large number of migrants from several Pacific islands were important contributing factors, as were New Zealand's special ties with the Cook Islands, Niue and the Tokelau Islands.[26]

Of the newly independent South Pacific states, Fiji probably made the most sustained contribution to the regionalist agenda. It played an influential role in the early discussions which set the stage for the establishment in 1968 of the short-lived Pacific Islands Producers' Association (PIPA). Fijian initiatives with more durable results included the formation of the Conference of South Pacific Chiefs of Police (CSPCP) in 1970, the Committee for Coordination of Joint Prospecting for Mineral Resources in South Pacific Offshore Areas (CCOP/SOPAC) which received strong ECAFE (UN Economic Commission for Asia and the Far East) support and held its inaugural meeting in November 1972, and the Tourism Council for the South Pacific (TCSP) which, with substantial European funding, got off the ground in March 1983. Undoubtedly, however, Fiji's most significant intervention had come much earlier when its first Prime Minister, Ratu Mara, mindful of the imminent independence of several small Pacific island states, put forward the idea of a new regional organization that would go beyond the technical functions performed by the South Pacific

Commission, viewed widely as the creation of the colonial powers. This was to be a relatively informal organization but one which, by virtue of bringing together every year the heads of government of all independent Pacific island states, would set an agenda for regional co-operation in the social, economic and political arenas. Established in August 1971, the South Pacific Forum had seven founding members – the Cook Islands, Fiji, Nauru, Tonga and Western Samoa as well as Australia and New Zealand – but by 1986 its membership had risen to 15. Within the space of a few years, the South Pacific Forum had become the centrepiece of South Pacific co-operative regionalism and, despite its many limitations, one of the more innovative attempts at institution-building in Asia Pacific.

In characterizing the trajectory of regional and sub-regional institutions, the emphasis thus far has been on identifying the states, be they external or internal to the region, great powers, middle powers or small powers, which were able at different moments during this forty-year period, to shape the regional agenda or at least crystallize existing trends whether by injecting funds, advocating new ideas or facilitating consultative processes. One other actor, the United Nations, would play a key role in the development of Asia-Pacific regionalism. The UN Charter was after all predicated on the assumption that the UN system would perform its functions in close collaboration with regional arrangements, providing the necessary impetus for their formation and drawing sustenance from them. Predictably, the UN would funnel much of its involvement and resources through the Commission established in 1947 expressly to deal with Asia-Pacific affairs. ECAFE was primarily focused on issues of development, except that over time, as the decision in 1974 to rename it the Economic and Social Commission for Asia and the Pacific (ESCAP) clearly indicates, the development objective acquired a social as well as an economic dimension and was extended to encompass the whole of the Asia-Pacific region. Meeting annually at ministerial level to monitor programmes in the region, equipped with a permanent secretariat, and benefiting from substantial US and increasing Japanese funding, ECAFE was instrumental in launching a great many projects and sponsoring a number of new regional initiatives, of which the most significant was the formation of the Asian Development Bank (ADB) in December 1965. Mandated to foster regional economic growth and co-operation and to accelerate the economic development of the less-developed member countries, the ADB's main activities centred on mobilizing public and private capital in support of development projects, and assisting in the formulation and implementation of development policies, including better utilization of resources, expansion of foreign trade, especially intra-regional trade, provision of technical assistance, and coordination of efforts with other inter-governmental organizations as well as with the private corporate and financial sector, both nationally and internationally. Within a few years Japan would emerge as an increasingly important source of financial resources, and the principal architect in the development and subsequent reorganization of several funds, including the Agricultural Special Funds and the Multi-purpose Special Funds (1968), the Asian Development Fund (1974), the Asian Development Equity Fund (1988), and the Japan Special Fund (1989). By the end of 1987, the ADB had been instrumental in providing some 400 soft loans valued at $1.7 billion. None of this is to suggest that the ADB's performance was not the subject of criticism, especially among those who questioned the development model on which its lending policies were predicated. The Asian Development Bank was nevertheless for many years the principal regional vehicle for channelling scarce financial resources to the developing economies of Southeast Asia and the South Pacific.

Though none of ESCAP's other institutional offshoots had the same leverage or access to resources as the ADB, they were none the less indicative of the range of functions it was able to perform. With a view to expanding intra-regional trade, ECAFE convened a series of meetings to consider the possibility of mutual tariff reductions, which eventually led in July 1975 to the Agreement on Trade Negotiations, also known as the Bangkok Agreement. The idea of an Asian Telecommunity, having received formal endorsement in 1968, gained the support of the International Telecommunication Union and funding from the ADB and the World Bank. The Asia-Pacific Telecommunity, as the institutional expression of that idea, came formally into being in March 1979. Its primary task was to facilitate the planning, programming and development within the region of intra-regional and international telecommunication networks to meet immediate and future requirements.[27] In October 1974, ESCAP joined with UNCTAD (UN Conference on Trade and Development) to convene the Roundtable Meeting on Asian Reinsurance Corporation. Its main function was to operate as a professional reinsurer and a source of information and expertise for the national insurance and reinsurance markets of member states. Two further initiatives, both of which came to fruition in 1982, are worth noting: the Intergovernmental Constitutive Forum of Developing Tropical Timber Producing/Exporting Countries and the Regional Consultative Group on Silk. In the former case the organization was given the difficult, not to say contradictory, task of assisting the industry to maximize its earnings on the one hand and minimize the damaging ecological practices of the past on the other. In the latter case, the silk-producing countries of the ESCAP region had a simpler purpose in mind: to promote the production, processing and marketing of silk.

While ECAFE/ESCAP was the main conduit through which the UN contributed to regionalism, other UN agencies also played a part. Acting in conjunction with ESCAP, UNIDO (UN Industrial Development Organization) initiated a series of talks in July 1970 which in due course (July 1972) gave rise to the Pepper Community with India, Indonesia and Malaysia as the three founding members, followed by Brazil in 1981. In 1976 the UNDP (UN

Development Programme) funded the National Broadcasting Centre of Malaysia, and a year later UNESCO (UN Educational, Scientific and Cultural Organization) sponsored two inter-governmental meetings with a view to expanding the scope of the Malaysian facility. In August 1977, agreement was reached to establish the Asia-Pacific Institute for Broadcasting Development with the aim of improving the professional capability of national broadcasting systems by developing systematic training and research programmes and creating a network of collaborating institutions. In July 1978, the Food and Agricultural Organization convened a conference which agreed to establish the Centre on Integrated Rural Development for Asia and the Pacific. Here again, the overriding institutional task was to create a regional network of national institutions as a way of improving the production, income and living conditions of small-scale farmers and other needy rural groups.[28]

The UN system had helped to solidify the region's multilateral infrastructure, widening the range of functions performed by regional institutions and enhancing the level of participation.[29] By dint of its universal membership and mandate, institutions sponsored or assisted by the United Nations could be expected to have a more inclusive membership than those largely initiated by the United States and its allies. The UN's direct or indirect presence in the consultative processes that preceded and followed the creation of new regional arrangements constrained the intrusion of Cold War tensions into the regional agenda, and offered non-aligned states a more congenial environment within which to pursue the twin objectives of development and decolonization. It is worth stressing, however, that virtually every organization that was formed under UN auspices or with UN support was premised, explicitly or implicitly, on free market principles, and to that extent at least was unlikely to strike a responsive chord with any of Asia's communist governments. During the 1950s and 1960s China was highly critical of international institutions, whether regional or global, portraying them as a tool of the great powers, and of the United States in particular.[30] Market-oriented organizations were branded as anti-socialist and antithetical to the Maoist principle of self-reliance.[31] Following its admission to the UN, China began to moderate its criticism of inter-governmental institutions but by the end of the 1970s it had joined only three regional organizations, the Asia-Pacific Postal Union, the Informal Meeting of Director Generals of Civil Aviation, and the Asia-Pacific Telecommunity.

ECONOMIC TRANSNATIONALISM

In *States, Markets and Civil Society* an extensive account is given of the complex and growing links that emerged among East Asian economies and between them and the US economy in the 1960s and 1970s. The dynamic of this process was well understood even at the time by influential business and policy-making circles, especially in the United States. Addressing the National Press Club in

Canberra in August 1976, US Deputy Secretary of State, Charles Robinson
put it rather succinctly:

> The People of the Pacific basin have been brought together in an increasingly
> complex web of economic, social, cultural and security relationships. A significant
> factor in that progress has been the fantastic growth of the Japanese industrialized
> society, the strong pull of the United States and the growth of the Japanese
> industrialized society, the strong pull of the United States and Japanese economies
> on each other, and the impact of that relationship on others in the region.[32]

By the late 1970s the entry of Japanese capital into the United States, not least
in the automobile manufacturing sector, had substantially increased the
production and technology interdependencies of the two countries. These
interconnections in turn had a profound influence on the rate and pattern of
growth recorded by the newly industrializing economies of Northeast and
Southeast Asia.

Undoubtedly, the most visible, and in a sense the most important, links
between these Asia-Pacific economies had developed in the area of trade. For
our present purposes here it will suffice to highlight a few key indicators of
market integration. By the late 1970s the United States accounted for 20 per
cent of ASEAN's exports and 16 per cent of its imports. In the case of Japan,
the proportions were even higher with 25 per cent and 27 per cent, respectively.
In the space of just three years two-way trade between the United States and
five ASEAN countries (Indonesia, Malaysia, Philippines, Singapore and
Thailand) had increased from $10.0 billion in 1976 to $16.9 billion in 1979.
During the same period Japan's two-way trade had increased from $63.6 billion
to $110.1 billion, and China's two-way trade from $10.9 billion to $20.9
billion.[33] Trade links were completed and in large measure sustained by the
large and growing network of other transactions already outlined in the previous
chapter and in the companion volume. Economic and technical assistance,
financial flows, tourism, migration and student exchanges were all, as we have
seen, important elements of this transactional network. Two elements are worth
restating here. The first, which derives from trade, refers to the mutual
dependence of all these economies on major sea lines of communication; the
second relates to foreign direct investment (FDI) flows, primarily originating
from Japan and the United States. US FDI to Asia would double from
approximately $16 billion in 1980 to $32 billion in 1988, with Japanese FDI
flows during that eight-year period increasing even more sharply from just
$10 billion to well over $40 billion.[34]

It should be readily apparent from the scale, scope and function of these
flows that they involved both state and non-state actors. By the 1990s not only
governments but industrial corporations, banks and a range of other commercial
and financial enterprises had become major stakeholders in the diverse but
interconnected processes contributing to market and financial integration in

the Asia-Pacific region. Both state and non-state actors were to this extent at least increasingly disposed to exploring from their respective vantage points the benefits of various multilateral options. Political, business and academic elites were increasingly attracted by what they saw as the new incentives and opportunities offered by competitive interdependence.[35] Not surprisingly perhaps, within the academic community it was primarily economists drawn from Japan, the United States, Australia and to a lesser extent South Korea and Southeast Asia who would pioneer the concept of a Pacific economic community. To varying degrees most of the contributors to this policy-oriented literature were preoccupied with one central question: could a loose and experimental consultative regional forum be created, which, in the interests of expanding regional commerce and foreign direct investment, would facilitate the coordination of trade, investment, monetary and even fiscal policies, while at the same time taking full account of the region's cultural, political and economic diversity?

While the emerging 'Pacific Community' literature derived most of its appeal and coherence from this single and deceptively simple formulation, sceptics continued to question not only whether multilateral approaches were at all feasible, but whether Asia Pacific constituted a region in any accepted sense of the word.[36] Something of the complexity of the issues involved was conveyed by the multiple terms used to designate the idea: Pan-Pacific association, Pacific basin co-operation, Pacific community, Pacific economic community.[37] The proliferation of labels pointed to a number of critical yet unresolved questions. The first set of questions revolved around the purpose or purposes which multilateral institutions would serve in the Asia-Pacific context. Would they, for example, be restricted to co-operation in the economic arena alone? If so, with what objectives in mind? And, in what areas of economic activity? Could economic integration, however modest, be divorced from political and security considerations? A second set of questions related to the issue of leadership: at whose initiative would the multilateral project get under way? Should it be left to the initiative of one or other great power, in the expectation that only great power leverage could bring the project to successful fruition? Might not such an approach create resentment amongst small and medium powers? If, on the other hand, the process of regional integration were to proceed in a consensual way, it would presumably need to rest on a substantial commonality of interests, which could not be easily demonstrated given vast differences in wealth, income distribution, industrial capacity, technological dependence and levels of trade protection. A third but closely related dilemma centred on the vexed question of membership: should regional institutions seek to maximize commonality of views and interests by opting for a highly selective or 'exclusive' approach to membership, or should the emphasis be on incorporating virtually the whole Pacific basin even if this meant narrowing common ground and reducing the prospects for effective collaboration? Several criteria could obviously be used to define membership: geographical proximity or coherence, political or ideological cohesion, and compatibility or complementarity of economic systems and stages of development. To concretize the difficulties, would the 'Pacific Community' include all five advanced countries (the United States, Japan, Canada, Australia and New Zealand) any or all of the communist states, the three Chinas (PRC, Taiwan and Hong Kong), the Pacific micro-states, any or all of the Latin American Pacific states, any or all of the South Asian states?[38] The last cluster of questions, derived from the previous three, concerned the structure and *modus operandi* of any proposed regional organization. Would it be of a purely consultative kind or would it seek to coordinate policy, or more ambitiously still, would it make biding decisions with respect to policy formulation and even policy implementation?

Predictably, answers to these questions could not but reflect the diversity of interests and perceptions. Even among the advocates of regionalism views differed considerably with respect to both objectives and strategies. Views would in any case change with the passage of time, and change itself was unlikely to be uniform or universal. Numerous studies have traced the evolution of proposals and initiatives from the early 1960s to the early 1980s. The aim here is not to present yet another historical account, but to identify a number of thresholds and discontinuities in this evolutionary process.

During the 1960s it was perhaps Japan more than any other country which gave impetus to various notions of regional cooperation. At first, advocacy of such ideas came almost exclusively from unofficial sources, that is, from academics or politicians speaking in their individual capacities. Almost invariably, the accent was on the economic rather than the political, strategic or cultural dimensions of regionalism. Morinosake Kajima, a businessman and LDP politician, is often credited with articulating one of the earliest proposals for a Pan-Pacific organization. Primarily Asian in its orientation, the proposal reflected Japan's expanding regional economic interests. It envisaged an Asian Development Fund which, partly modelled on the Marshall Plan, would disburse grants rather than credits and so help to allay residual Asian suspicions of Japanese intentions.[39] A more influential contribution came soon after with the establishment of the Japan Economic Research Center (JERC) which became a major institutional vehicle for the dissemination of ideas on regional economic co-operation. Particularly significant was a series of studies undertaken by Professor Kiyoshi Kojima of Hitosubashi University, who proposed in 1965 the establishment of a Pacific Free Trade Association (PAFTA) which would be confined to five developed economies, the United States, Canada, Australia, New Zealand and Japan.[40] It soon emerged, however, from Kojima's own research that in the prevailing circumstances the elimination of tariffs might simply magnify the trade surpluses of some countries and trade deficits of others.[41]

In 1967, the notion of Pacific basin co-operation gained further momentum with Foreign Minister Takeo Miki's formal support for the development of a

Japanese Asia-Pacific policy, the centrepiece of which would be a region-wide approach to the problem of poverty based on the combined efforts of developed and developing economies.[42]An expanded and more concrete version of this idea came to be known as the OPTAD concept. Calling for the establishment of an Organization of Pacific Trade, Aid and Development, it was first presented in 1968 at the Conference on Pacific Trade and Development, organized by JERC and addressed by Foreign Minister Miki. A series of annual meetings then followed, which attracted a large and increasing number of policy-oriented economists and became known as the Pacific Trade and Development Conferences.[43] Though no major proposals would emerge over the next few years, Japanese interest in the subject was also kept alive by a number of studies commissioned by the Japan Institute of International Affairs and the Institute of Developing Economies, which were closely linked to the Ministry of Foreign Affairs and the Ministry of International Trade and Industry (MITI), respectively.

The other noteworthy development was the formation in April 1967 of the business organization, the Pacific Basin Economic Council (PBEC) comprising five national committees (Australia, Canada, Japan, New Zealand and the United States). Premised on the view that these economies had become increasingly interdependent, the PBEC was primarily concerned to promote trade and investment opportunities in the region, without allowing continuing debate on the precise geographical boundaries of the region to stall the process. Though its strategic focus was on identifying regional co-operation mechanisms that would allow both the private and public sectors to play their part in the achievement of that objective, its attitude to the idea of a 'Pacific economic community' remained at best ambivalent.[44]

By the end of the decade Australia and Japan, drawn together by a flourishing bilateral trade relationship, both developed economies but highly exposed to any increased European or US protectionism, had taken the initiative to explore possibilities for greater regional collaboration. In October 1972, at a joint ministerial conference the two countries agreed to fund the establishment of the Australia, Japan and Western Pacific Economic Relations Research Project to be conducted by the JERC and the ANU's Research School of Pacific Studies, and headed by Saburo Okita and Sir John Crawford. Though their joint report, presented to the Australian and Japanese governments in 1976, made several recommendations for speeding up the development of regional economic links, including the establishment of an OPTAD, it did not elicit any immediate or tangible response.[45] In March 1977, in an endeavour to break through the apparent impasse, Jiro Tokuyama of the Nomura Research Institute flagged the idea of an inclusive Pacific Economic Basin which would bring together the five developed economies but also the ASEAN countries, South Korea, Taiwan, and perhaps China and Mexico. The abundance of raw materials and the large population to be found in this rather large but rapidly integrating region, coupled with the advanced technologies and affluent and sophisticated markets of the United States and Japan, were viewed as necessary and sufficient conditions for the sustained growth of the Pacific basin economy.[46]

The competition of ideas in an arena where state actors had thus far confined themselves largely to general affirmations of the value of greater regional collaboration elicited the most striking official intervention yet with Prime Minister Ohira's decision in December 1978 to establish a private consultative group to investigate ways of enhancing regional economic co-operation. Though Ohira discounted the prospects of European-style regional integration, he saw merit in a looser 'Pacific Ocean Community' within which Japan could offer stable markets for agricultural and other primary products and the Japanese yen as a vehicle for greater access to financial resources. The stage was thus set for a more concerted approach to the development of co-operative regionalism. Particularly influential was a discussion paper on the OPTAD concept commissioned by the US Senate Committee on Foreign Affairs and prepared by Drysdale (Australian National University) and Patrick (Yale University). Depicting the Pacific region as a new centre of world economic activity but noting the discrepancy between high and rising levels of economic interdependence on the one hand and the relatively low levels of institutional co-operation on the other, the authors proposed the creation of a new organization which would serve primarily as a forum for the discussion and the harmonization of policies, particularly in the areas of trade, development financing, FDI, and security of raw material and energy supplies.[47] The next major step came in a landmark seminar held in September 1980 at the ANU and sponsored by the Australian government, which examined not only the possible objectives, priorities and membership of a 'Pacific Community' but also the steps that should form part of any transitional strategy. To this end the seminar recommended the creation of a standing committee which would in turn establish task forces to undertake major studies on different aspects of Asia-Pacific multilateralism. Despite misgivings in several quarters, not least within ASEAN, the ANU seminar had, by giving issues of implementation the sharp edge they had previously lacked, set the stage for a politically driven dialogue in which governments would now play a more conspicuous role.

The call in 1980 by the Australian and Japanese prime ministers for a new regional initiative became the catalyst for the decisive next step in this process, the creation of the Pacific Economic Co-operation Council (PECC). At its next three meetings (Bangkok 1982, Bali 1983, Seoul 1985) PECC, with the active involvement of its three key constituents (business, government and academia) – they were also its key constituencies – set in train a series of task force activities, regional study groups and consultations. In 1986, PECC expanded its membership to include representatives from Beijing and Taipei, raising the number of national committees to 15. Within the space of ten years, PECC would boast 20 member committees (Australia, Brunei, Canada, Chile,

China, Hong Kong, Indonesia, Japan, Korea, Malaysia, Mexico, New Zealand, Peru, the Philippines, the Soviet Union, Singapore, Chinese Taipei, Thailand, the United States and the Pacific island states), and two institutional members (PBEC and the Pacific Trade and Development Conference: PAFTAD) which had no vote on its standing committee but participated fully in its main activities (see Figure 3.1).

Though it did not lead to the rapid formation of a new regional organization, the PECC initiative was nevertheless significant in several important respects. First, by making membership widely accessible, it helped to defuse many of the divisions which had until now posed a major conceptual and practical obstacle to innovation. By bringing in a number of Pacific Latin American countries and the Pacific island nations, it deflected the argument that the 'Pacific Community' was first and foremost an instrument designed to cement US interests and dominance. More importantly perhaps, by including the three Chinas it sidestepped the vexed question of the Taiwan dispute. In other words, the membership issue was resolved by adopting the principle, in practice if not formally, that the Asia-Pacific region consisted of the Pacific basin, that is, all the island nations stretching across the Pacific Ocean and all the countries bordering that ocean. The absence of certain countries (for example, Vietnam, Ecuador) was the result not of some new exclusionary principle but either of a lack of interest on the part of the country concerned or of some temporary political difficulty.

Secondly, the PECC experiment rested on the notion that the constituent units of the co-operative framework were economies rather than states. This conceptual point of departure had two implications: (i) it eased the problem posed by the unfinished and contested business of Chinese national reunification (by admitting three separate Chinese economies rather than three independent Chinese polities) and, hypothetically at least, made it possible to do the same with Korea at some unidentified future date; (ii) and perhaps more importantly, it placed the emphasis on economic regionalism, and thereby conferred on business interests, perspectives and participation a status they could not otherwise have enjoyed. The central role of the corporate sector in defining both policy agenda and organizational complexion became one of the distinguishing characteristics of the emerging multilateral project in Asia Pacific.

Thirdly, by adopting, and in a sense pioneering, a track-two approach, PECC highlighted the contribution which non-state actors could make to the regionalist project in both the preparatory and more advanced stages of development. Mention has already been made of the crucial role played by the private sector in industry and finance. The third player in this instance, the academic community – policy-oriented economists in the main – pointed to the highly effective role of epistemic communities in elaborating the conceptual framework within which the policy and institutional agenda could be publicized and

Figure 3.1   Organizational structure of PECC

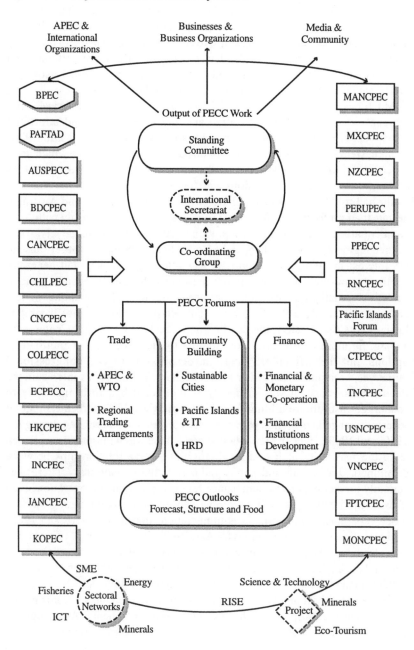

Source: PECC Secretariat

eventually legitimized. It is worth stressing, however, that PECC, important as it was in facilitating the cross-fertilization of ideas and in narrowing the cultural gap separating the academic, business and policy-making communities in different countries, remained an exclusive club in that it appealed to a relatively small, carefully selected (or self-selected) group of academics, officials and business leaders, many of whom had over time cultivated close personal or ideational connections within and across national boundaries.

Much has so far been made of the particular impetus which Asia-Pacific regionalism derived from Australian and Japanese official and unofficial initiatives. A degree of convergence became evident from the mid-1970s onward, stemming in part from a common pan-Pacific perspective which itself reflected the extensiveness but also the intensity of Japan's and Australia's economic and strategic connections with the United States. The other common factor had to do with the ambivalence with which both Japan and Australia, despite their profoundly different histories, viewed their relationship with Asia. Neither party could contemplate a predominantly, let alone exclusively, Asia-centred regionalism. What, then, of the United States? While not entirely absent, US interest in multilateral proposals was relatively low-key and generally confined to business leaders with a strong stake in the Pacific economy and to a relatively small group of officials and academics with a longstanding interest and expertise in Asia-Pacific affairs. The Hudson Institute, the Brookings Institute, the Asia Society, the Pacific Forum, and the East–West Center were among the more conspicuous contributors to the discussion of multilateral options, but the official US position, despite one or two congressional initiatives,[48] remained guarded or at best hesitant. Washington's interest in the Pacific basin concept was primarily economic. It had little incentive to encourage institution-building of a kind which would disturb the bilateral security arrangements it had painstakingly constructed and refined during the 1950s and 1960s. Even in the economic arena there was widespread scepticism as to the feasibility of institutionalizing the diverse relationships between developed, developing and newly industrializing economies.[49] There was certainly no inclination to countenance regional economic co-operation, even if its institutional expression were relatively modest, except among market-based economies.[50] In short, US administrations during the 1970s and 1980s tended to view multilateral options for Asia Pacific in the context of two primary considerations: their likely impact on the highly advantageous strategic status quo, and the likelihood that they could help to prise open East Asian economies, notably Japan's, as a way of reducing the chronic US trade deficit.

The 'Pacific Community' concept would encounter scepticism from another influential quarter, ASEAN. As the most successful experiment in Asian regional co-operation to date, ASEAN was concerned that a pan-Pacific organization might slow down the momentum of its own development. Expressing a Malaysian point of view, which was not, however, unrepresentative of ASEAN thinking, Ghazali Shafie noted that a Pacific Community held considerable geopolitical, strategic and economic attractions for the United States, Japan and Australia.[51] The implication was that the pan-Pacific concept was more likely to advantage the interests of great rather than smaller or middle powers, advanced rather than developing economies. ASEAN countries had yet to be convinced that a new regional grouping would not be directed against another power – or be so interpreted by that power, possibly China or Vietnam – in ways that were not necessarily consistent with ASEAN interests. They were no doubt also concerned that such a grouping might create divisions with ASEAN itself or between ASEAN and other countries, perhaps parts of the developing world. There was, moreover, a nagging anxiety, admittedly more prevalent in some quarters than others, that a Pacific Community might place the ASEAN economies in a position of permanent dependence on the world's major centres of industrial, financial and commercial power.[52] Indeed, it was by no means clear how ASEAN industries would cope with substantially reduced levels of protection and increasing competition between ASEAN and NIE exports in advanced industrial markets. Perhaps the greatest anxiety was that a larger Pacific organization might jeopardize ASEAN's internal moves towards more effective economic, functional and political integration. To put it simply but not inaccurately, ASEAN had not yet been persuaded that a Pacific Community would yield sufficient benefits to outweigh any damage that may be done to its existing bilateral and multilateral relationships.[53] Given these misgivings, ASEAN itself refrained from taking any official steps in support of Pacific economic co-operation, leaving it to member states, particularly Thailand and Indonesia, to explore possibilities. As of July 1984, ASEAN as a whole was nevertheless able through the ASEAN Post-Ministerial Conference to exchange views directly with the five developed Pacific economies.

The 'Pacific Community' or 'Pacific basin' co-operation concept had by the mid-1980s made some headway in establishing itself in an academic and policy discourse. Yet, while the concept elicited relatively strong interest from Japan, Australia and South Korea, responses from other quarters varied considerably in enthusiasm and intensity. In the case of some key actors, notably the United States, the idea had yet to gather sufficient momentum for it to register as a priority item on the policy agenda. For others, in particular Pacific island leaders, who were hardly significant players in the main game, the attitude was one of studied caution coupled with sharp criticism of the lack of adequate consultation.[54] The perspectives and policies of states were not, however, the only barometer of the prevailing political climate. The formation of PECC was perhaps a more accurate indicator not only of the preferences and priorities of important non-state actors, notably business interests, but of the influence which they would eventually bring to bear on the policy-making process.

The PECC phenomenon and the interests and perceptions which gave it birth and sustenance are examined at greater length in Chapter 5. Suffice it here to say that by the mid-1980s several difficulties, many of them with a clear economic dimension but all of them intensely political, still confronted the 'Pacific Community' project. Each of these difficulties revolved around fault-lines which, if not carefully handled, could scuttle the project even before its inception. The first and most obvious was the core–periphery division which separated the most advanced economies, the United States and Japan, from the least-developed economies, Indonesia and the Philippines, not to mention Burma and the Indochinese states. The second fault-line derived from the cultural as much as geographic distance separating the eastern and western rims of the Pacific basin, and was most strikingly expressed by the two competing visions of 'Asia Pacific' and 'Pacific Asia'. The third fault-line between existing and aspiring or potential hegemons pointed to the simmering tensions, predominantly but not exclusively related to trade, between the two dominant centres of the regional economy, the United States and Japan. Finally, a geostrategic and ideological fault-line had for the best part of four decades pitted the United States against the Soviet Union and China, with the Korea and Taiwan conflicts living proof of the continuing potency of that confrontation.

NOTES

1. See J.A. Camilleri, 'The Cold War', in Max Teichmann (ed), *Power and Policies: Alignment and Realignments in the Indo-Pacific Region*, Melbourne: Cassell Australia, 1970, pp. 16–24.
2. For the ideological defence of the Brezhnev doctrine see the article by S. Kovalev, 'Sovereignty and the Internationalist Obligations of Socialist Countries', *Pravda*, 26 September 1968, in *Current Digest of Soviet Press*, XX (39), 16 October 1968, pp. 10–12.
3. For a fuller analysis of the functions of the Cold War, see Fred Halliday, *The Making of the Second Cold War*, London: Verso, 1983, pp. 42–5; also Joseph A. Camilleri and Jim Falk, *The End of Sovereignty? The Politics of a Shrinking and Fragmenting World*, Aldershot: Edward Elgar, 1992, pp. 158–60; see Michael Cox, 'From the Truman Doctrine to the Second Seapower Détente: The Rise and Fall of the Cold War', *Journal of Peace Research*, 27 (1), 1990, 30–31.
4. Joseph A. Camilleri, *States, Markets and Civil Society in Asia Pacific: The Political Economy of the Asia–Pacific Region*, Vol. I, Cheltenham, UK: Edward Elgar, 2000, pp. 13–20.
5. For an illuminating official account of US occupation policy, see 'Far Eastern Commission Basic Post-Surrender Policy for Japan', adopted 19 June 1947, in *Japanese Peace Settlement: Documents*, Canberra: Department of External Affairs, August 1947, pp. 135–44.
6. See W. Macmahon Ball, *Japan: Enemy or Ally?*, New York: John Day, 1949, pp. 14–42.
7. See Stephen E. Ambrose, *Rise to Globalism: American Foreign Policy since 1938*, 6th rev. edn, Harmondsworth, Middlesex: Penguin Books, 1991, pp. 97–109; J.P.D. Dunnabin, *The Cold War: the Great Powers and their Allies*, London: Longman, 1994, pp. 96–100; Robert E. Harkavy, *Great Power Competition for Overseas Bases: The Geopolitics of Access Diplomacy*, New York: Pergamon Press, 1998.
8. See Joseph A. Camilleri, *The Australia–New Zealand–US Alliance: Regional Security in the Nuclear Age*, Seattle, WA: University of Washington Press, 1987, pp. 1–16.
9. See George McTurnan Kahin and John W. Lewis, *The United States in Vietnam*, Ithaca, NY: Delta, 1967, pp. 28–35.
10. Article IV paragraph 1 of the Treaty.
11. Statement to the House of Representatives made on 27 October 1954, *Commonwealth Parliamentary Debates* (hereafter referred to as *CPD*), House of Representatives (H of R), vol. 5, p. 2387.

12. See Chin Kin Wah, *The Defence of Malayisa and Singapore: The Transformation of a Security System 1957–1971*, Cambridge: Cambridge University Press, 1983, pp. 144–78, 192– 94.
13. See T. B. Millar (ed), *Britain's Withdrawal from Asia: Its Implications for Australia*, Proceedings of a Seminar conducted by the Strategic and Defence Studies Centre, Australian National University, Canberra, 29–30 September 1967; *Cmnd 4521, Supplementary Statement on Defence Policy 1970*, London: HMSO, October 1970, pp. 4–5.
14. See Joint Communiqué issued at the end of the First Ministerial Meeting, Seoul, 14–16 July 1966, in Department of External Affairs, *An Introduction to the Asian and Pacific Council (ASPAC)*, Canberra, 1968, pp. 22–5.
15. A.W. Stargardt, 'The Road to Bandung: The Emergence of the Asian System of Powers', *Monographs in Asian Diplomatic History*, Cambridge Project on Asian Diplomatic History, 1992, p. 35.
16. The Resolution (Document S/1222) was adopted on 22 January 1949.
17. For a highly revealing account of the Bogor meeting, see Stargardt, 'The Road to Bandung', pp. 38–9.
18. The following accepted the invitation to attend: Afghanistan, Cambodia, China, Egypt, Ethiopia, the Gold Coast, Iran, Japan, Jordan, Laos, Lebanon, Liberia, Libya, Nepal, the Philippines, Saudi Arabia, the Sudan, Syria, Thailand, Turkey, the Democratic Republic of Vietnam, the State of Vietnam, and Yemen. Only one African state, the Central African Federation, declined on the grounds that it had yet to achieve full independence.
19. See Roslan Abulgani, *The Bandung Connection: The Asia–Africa Conference in Bandung in 1955*, translated by Molly Bondan, Jakarta and Singapore: Gunung Agung, 1981, pp. 151–5.
20. Much of the information and empirical material on functional co-operation during the 1950s and 1960s is drawn from the following excellent surveys: L.P. Singh, *The Politics of Economic Cooperation in Asia: A Study of Asian International Organizations*, Columbia, MO: University of Missouri Press, 1966; Michael Haas, *Basic Documents of Regional Organizations*, Dobbs Ferry, NY: Oceania Publications, 1974; J.N. Shubert, 'Toward a "Working Peace System" in Asia: Organizational Growth and State Participation in Asian Regionalism', *International Organization*, 32, Spring 1978, 425–62; A. Jorgensen-Dahl, *Regional Organisation and Order in Southeast Asia*, London: Macmillan, 1982; R.A. Scalapino, A. Sato and S. Han (eds), *Pacific Asian Economic Policies and Regional Interdependence*, Berkeley, CA: University of California Press, 1988; Michael Haas, *The Asian Way to Peace: A Study of Regional Cooperation*, New York: Praeger, 1989.
21. In 1986, Japan's financial contribution ($1.85 million) accounted for close to 60 per cent of all member assessments.
22. For a detailed exposition of the role which the Colombo Plan would perform in the creation of an Australian propaganda strategy, see Daniel Oakman, 'The Politics of Foreign Aid: Counter Subversion and the Colombo Plan 1950–1970', *Pacifica Review: Peace, Security and Global Change*, 13 (3), October 2001, 255–72.
23. The organization came to be known as the Conference of Commissioners of Police of Australia and the South-West Pacific Region.
24. On Vanuatu's initiative, a meeting of attorneys general held in Vila in late 1981 agreed to form the Pacific Islands Officers' Meeting as a consultative mechanism for improving the administration of justice in the region. By 1987, 14 countries had joined the organization.
25. New Zealand Labour governments under Norman Kirk and Wallace (Bill) Rowling pioneered proposals for the establishment of a South Pacific Nuclear Free Zone, NZ Southwest Pacific diplomacy. See Ray Goldstein with Rod Alley (ed), *Labour in Power: Promise and Performance: Evaluation of the Work of the New Zealand Government from 1972 to 1975*, Wellington: Price Milburn for New Zealand University Press, 1975.
26. See Roderic Alley (ed), *New Zealand and the Pacific,* Boulder, CO: Westview Press, 1984.
27. For more details of the Asia-Pacific Telecommunity (APT) Secretariat, see APT website at http://www.aptsec.org/ .
28. See various publications sponsored by the Centre for Integrated Rural Development for Asia and the Pacific, including Emmanuel D'Silva and Kaye Bysouth, *Poverty Alleviation through Agricultural Projects*, Washington, DC: World Bank, 1992.

29. For an indication of the substantial issue coverage achieved by Asian organizations, see James N. Schubert, 'Toward a "Working Peace System" in Asia: Organizational Growth and State Participation in Asian Regionalism', *International Organization*, 32 (1), Winter 1978, 425–40.
30. See Samuel Kim, 'Mainland China and a New World Order', *Issues and Studies*, 27 (11), November 1991, 5.
31. Herbert S. Yee, 'China and the Pacific Community Concept', *World Today*, February 1983, 70–71.
32. Charles Robinson, National Press Club, Canberra, August 1976.
33. All these figures are drawn from the *Direction of Trade Statistics Yearbook* (relevant years) published by the International Monetary Fund.
34. See Mark Borthwick, *The Pacific Century: The Emergence of Modern Pacific Asia*, Boulder, CO: Westview Press, 1992, p. 514.
35. This term is used in Camilleri, *States, Markets and Civil Society* to convey the complex blend of competition and co-operation characteristic of the relationship between the major centres of power, both globally and in Asia Pacific (see pp. 148–52).
36. Notable among the sceptics was Gerald Segal who insisted on the need to distinguish between the dynamism of a number of Pacific economies, that is 'economic successes', and what he termed 'Pacific Consciousness'. See Gerald Segal, *Rethinking the Pacific*, Oxford: Clarendon Press, 1990, pp. 369–91.
37. For a useful survey of competing concepts and labels, see Willy Kraus and Wilfred Lütkenhorst, *The Economic Development of the Pacific Basin: Growth Dynamics, Trade Relations and Emerging Cooperation*, New York: St. Martin's Press, 1986, pp. 92–7, see also David M. Connolly, 'Progress and Prospects for a Pacific Basin Community', in *Forum on the Pacific Basin: Growth, Security and Community*, A Conference Sponsored by the Asia and World Forum (Taipei), the Centre for the Study of Security Issues (Tokyo), the Foreign Policy Research Institute (Philadelphia), and the Institute of International Studies (Seoul), Taipei, 28–30 May 1980, pp. 235–7.
38. This was very much the view advocated in Australia by Sir John Crawford. See his paper 'The Pacific Basin Cooperative Concept', Australia–Japan Economic Relations Research Project, Research Paper No. 70, August 1980, p. 9.
39. See King-yuh Chang, 'Building the Pacific Community: An Incrementalist Approach', *Korea and World Affairs*, 7, Summer 1983, 222–3.
40. Much of the historical material for this analysis draws on Hadi Soesastro, 'Pacific Economic Co-operation: The History of an Idea', in Ross Garnaut and Peter Drysdale, with John Kunkel (eds), *Asia-Pacific Regionalism: Readings in International Economic Relations*, Pymble, NSW: HarperEducational in association with the Australia–Japan Research Centre, 1994, p. 79.
41. See K. Kojima, *Economic Co-operation in a Pacific Community*, Tokyo: Japan Institute of International Affairs; see also Mitsuro Donowaki, 'The Pacific Basin Community', in Hadi Soesastro and Han Sung-joo (eds), *Pacific Economic Co-operation: The Next Phase*, Jakarta, Centre for Strategic and International Studies, 1983, p. 235.
42. Soesastro, 'Pacific Economic Cooperation', p. 80.
43. Donowaki, 'The Pacific Basin Community', p. 235. For a more detailed account of the origins and role of the PAFTAD Conference series, see Peter Drysdale, 'The Pacific Trade and Development Conference: A Brief History', Australia–Japan Research Centre, Australian National University, Research Paper No. 112, June 1984; also Takashi Terada, 'The Japanese Origins of PAFTAD: The Beginning of an Asian Pacific Economic Community', *Pacific Economic Papers*, No. 292, Canberra: Australia–Japan Research Centre, Australian National University, June 1999.
44. See Lawrence T. Woods, 'A House Divided: The Pacific Basin Economic Council and Regional Diplomacy', *Australian Journal of International Affairs*, 45 (2), November 1991, 264–79.
45. The report was later published as a book: Sir John Crawford and Saburo Okita (eds), *Raw Materials and Pacific Economic Integration*, Canberra: Australian National University Press, 1978.
46. Connolly, 'Process and Prospects for a Pacific Basin Community', pp. 230–31.

47. P. Drysdale and H. Patrick, *An Asian-Pacific Regional Economic Organization: An Exploratory Concept Paper*, Washington, DC, 1979, also P. Drysdale, 'The Proposal for an Organization for Pacific Trade and Development Revisited', *Asian Survey*, XXIII (12), December 1983, 1293–303.
48. See in particular, 'The Pacific Community Idea', Hearing Before the Subcommittee on Asian and Pacific Affairs of the Committee on Foreign Affairs, House of Representatives, 96th US Congress, first Session, Washington, DC, 1979.
49. For an analysis of these constraints, see Gavin Boyd, 'Pacific Community Building', in Gavin Boyd (ed), *Regionalism and Global Security*, New York: Pergamon, 1984, pp. 84–9. The caution characteristic of official US attitudes is well illustrated in Paul Wolfowitz, 'US Interests and the Emerging Pacific Community', in Robert L. Downer and Bruce J. Dickson (eds), *The Emerging Pacific Community: A Regional Perspective*, Boulder, CO: Westview Press, 1984, pp. 23–31.
50. There was, on the other hand, a growing realization, especially among the academic and business communities, that much could be gained from loose consultative arrangements, particularly with a focus on trade and other economic issues. See, for example, the report prepared by the Pacific Basin Congressional Study Group of the Center for Strategic and International Studies, in Downer and Dickson (eds), *The Emerging Pacific Community*, pp. 13–19. See also Richard Sneider, 'The Evolving Pacific Community – Reality or Rhetoric?', in R. Hewett (ed), *Political Change and the Economic Future of East Asia*, Honolulu: University of Hawaii Press, 1981, pp. 40–43.
51. See 'Toward a Pacific Basin Community: A Malaysian View', in *Pacific Region Interdependencies: A Compendium of Papers Submitted to the Joint Economic Committee, Congress of the United States, 15 June 1981*, Washington, DC: US Government Printing Office, 1981, p. 74.
52. A version of these misgivings is outlined by Obaid ul Haq, 'The Pacific Basin Community: Problems and Prospects', in Downer and Dickson (eds), *The Emerging Pacific Community*, pp. 4–41.
53. For another rendition of this argument, see Michael Yahuda, 'The "Pacific Community": Not Yet', *Pacific Review*, 1 (2), 1998, 124. Other accounts of the ASEAN perspective are offered by A.H. Zakaria, 'The Pacific Basin and ASEAN: Problems and Prospects', *Contemporary Southeast Asia*, 2 (4), March 1981, 332–41; R.M. Nicholas, 'ASEAN and the Pacific Community Debate: Much Ado about Something', *Asian Survey*, 21 (12), 1981, 1197–210.
54. See the assessment offered by Anthony Haas in *Linking the Pacific: A Report of an International Seminar on New Zealand and the Pacific Basin Concept*, Wellington, NZ: New Zealand Institute of International Affairs, April 1980, p. 15.

4. ASEAN: transition to the new regionalism

Conceived primarily as a response to the challenges posed by internal and regional security, the ASEAN experiment was nevertheless deeply influenced by the Cold War climate of ideological and strategic rivalry and by the uncertainties surrounding the triangular relationship between the United States, the Soviet Union and China. In addition, ASEAN has had to contend with the multiple pressures associated with increasing regional and global economic integration, a trend which led most of its members to adopt a sustained export-led growth strategy. It would be a mistake, however, to interpret ASEAN's contribution to the fabric of regional co-operation in purely reactive terms.[1] ASEAN soon emerged as a dynamic institution responding to, but also anticipating, many of the changes that would periodically reshape the geopolitical and geoeconomic landscape. Arguably the most successful and certainly the most durable initiative in Asian multilateral diplomacy since 1945, ASEAN would exert a decisive influence over virtually all subsequent attempts at institutional innovation in the region. Indeed, it would not be an overstatement to suggest that since its establishment in 1967, ASEAN has functioned as the principal barometer and catalyst of Asian regionalism.

ASEAN was not without its precursors.[2] The Association of Southeast Asia (ASA) comprising the Philippines, Malaya and Thailand was formed in 1961. Symbolically at least it was a significant step towards greater regional co-operation. Its administrative machinery and consultative arrangements would be carried over into ASEAN, but ASA itself soon floundered largely as a result of rising diplomatic tensions between the Philippines and Malaysia in 1963 over the Sabah issue. MAPHILINDO, formed by Malaysia, the Philippines and Indonesia, also in 1961, had an even shorter life, the precipitating factor in this case being the Indonesian policy of *konfrontasi* and Malaysia's consequent decision to withdraw from the organization.[3] Though abortive, both multilateral initiatives had one positive spin-off: they strengthened Southeast Asia's sense of regional identity, and provided Thailand and especially the Philippines with a greater appreciation of the potential for regional co-operation. The failure of Singapore's attempted integration into the Malaysian federation and its formal separation in September 1965 revealed once again that ethnic, ideological and geopolitical fault-lines still loomed large on the Southeast Asian landscape. Paradoxically, however, key regional players had a strong incentive to find ways of containing or managing these divisions, if for no other reason than that they threatened their own internal stability, and in extreme cases regime survival.

Of the numerous influences that helped shape the experiment, three are especially worthy of attention: domestic social and political conflict, bilateral tensions, and great power rivalry. From the onset of decolonization, emerging political elites, whether in Burma, Malaysia, the Philippines or Indonesia, were invariably challenged by insurgent movements and communist parties, which in turn provoked a range of coercive government strategies designed to eliminate or contain the challenge. Moreover, the retreat of empire had left behind, as in other parts of the colonial world, a pattern of territorial demarcation and political dominance which ethnic minorities were unwilling to accept. The significant Chinese and Indian minorities, which settled in much of Southeast Asia from the nineteenth century onwards, may have suited the purposes of the colonial power but in the post-colonial period soon became a source of recurring friction. Complicating these internal divisions were the longstanding suspicions and mistrust between neighbouring states, notably between Vietnam and Cambodia, Thailand and Vietnam, Malaysia and Thailand, and Malaysia and the Philippines.[4] Of the external powers, the United States and the Soviet Union exerted the most striking, if not the most enduring, influence by virtue of their global power projection and the polarizing implications of their alliances and counter-alliances. China and Japan were also an integral part of the power equation, the former by virtue of geography and demography, not to mention the role of the large resident communities of ethnic Chinese, and the latter by virtue of the unresolved legacy of the Second World War, and the far-reaching impact of its post-war economic resurgence.

This, then, was the complex domestic and international environment within which ASEAN's five founding members had to negotiate the framework of regional co-operation. Founded in August 1967, ASEAN was seen by many as a product of the Cold War, an anti-communist alliance, in which two of its members, Thailand and the Philippines, were close allies of the United States, members of SEATO, and actively involved in support of the US war effort in Vietnam. Two other members, Malaysia and Singapore, were members of AMDA (Anglo-Malaysian Defence Agreement, subsequently the FPDA) linking them to Britain, Australia and New Zealand, all allies of the United States. Thailand, the Philippines and Malaysia were also members of the anti-communist association, ASPAC, and Indonesia had just experienced a profound and bloody upheaval with the advent of General Suharto's fiercely anti-communist government.[5] This widely shared perception of the ideological complexion of the new organization – vociferously expressed by the communist powers and frequently though less forcefully articulated by academic and policy circles in the West – was not, however, entirely accurate.[6] The anti-communist outlook of the five ASEAN governments did not translate into a diplomatic posture whose style and content accorded fully with the logic of the Cold War.

Though Jakarta suspended diplomatic ties with the PRC in late 1967, ASEAN members generally adopted a nuanced position in their relations with the communist world, and several of them would soon move steadily towards diplomatic normalization with the PRC. More importantly perhaps, ASEAN's self-definition, viewed in terms of both formal and informal arrangements, pointed to functions which, though consistent with the requirements of regime survival, namely the survival of anti-communist governments, could not nevertheless be reduced to mere anti-communism. The Bangkok Declaration of 8 August 1967 envisaged that ASEAN would accelerate economic growth, social progress and cultural development; promote regional peace and stability; create the framework for regional co-operation; and discourage external interference.[7] While it could not wish away the reality of foreign military bases, the Declaration described them as 'temporary', and asserted that they could remain on Southeast Asian soil only so long as their presence had the 'concurrence of the countries concerned' and did not threaten directly or indirectly the national independence of states in the area'. At a more informal level, ASEAN was expected to facilitate 'subregional reconciliation, preserve the territorial status quo among members, assist in regime maintenance, and reduce the military role and influence of extra-regional powers'.[8]

APPROACH TO SECURITY

When the Bangkok Declaration was signed in August 1967, it could be argued that the five member states had relatively little in common, which perhaps explains why one of the organization's priorities was to encourage a sense of regional identity. A conscious desire to foster a feeling of togetherness and shared interests permeated ASEAN'S self-understanding,[9] and gave rise to mechanisms for regular and extensive interaction. On the other hand, the same lingering differences and suspicions help to explain why the Association, despite its underlying political purpose, chose to stress the less controversial areas of economic, technical, social and cultural collaboration. Great care was taken from the outset to avoid any action which might offend the sensitivities of any of its members. As a consequence, ASEAN initially developed as a loose organization with no central secretariat and a marked preference for informal meetings and ambiguous declarations. The Association's unique form of consultation and relationship-building, often depicted by reference to the twin notions of *musyawarah* (a consultative approach to the exercise of leadership) and *musfakat* (consensual approach to decision-making),[10] was first and foremost an attempt at conflict management and conflict prevention based on self-restraint.[11] To put it differently, ASEAN's consensual decision-making process set out 'to preserve peaceful relations between its members ... by way of avoidance, preservation and containment of sensitive issues that [could] lead to disruptive behaviour'.[12] It soon became the distinguishing characteristic of ASEAN's approach to security.

A second striking feature of the ASEAN experiment was the attempt to make socio-economic development an integral part of the security objective. As already noted, the Bangkok Declaration affirmed that acceleration of the economic growth, social progress and cultural development of the region was the necessary foundation for a prosperous and peaceful Southeast Asia. The priority ascribed to economic development reflected in part a shared sense of vulnerability to internal threats and a corresponding commitment to the preservation of political order. The doctrine of *national resilience*, which became an article of political faith in Indonesia from the late 1960s, was a reflection of the dual concern with internal and external security. It sought to harness ideological, political, economic, social, cultural and military resources into an overarching nation-building strategy. In due course, the concept would gain currency throughout ASEAN. Indeed, regional co-operation came to be seen as an instrument for promoting qualities of self-sufficiency and resourcefulness in each member state,[13] and regional stability as a necessary condition for mobilizing the domestic and international resources needed to sustain economic growth. By the mid-1970s *national resilience* and *regional resilience*, or differently expressed the comprehensive development of each society and comprehensive co-operation among them, became, at least at the declaratory level, the two closely interconnected pillars of ASEAN's comprehensive security policy.[14]

Phase I (1967–75)

Notwithstanding the initial emphasis on economic and functional co-operation, ASEAN's primary task during this first phase was to develop, slowly but surely, a security framework aptly described by Michael Leifer as an institutionalized vehicle 'for intra-mural conflict avoidance and management' on the one hand, and extra-mural 'management of order' on the other.[15] The rationale and scope of these twin functions were set out in a series of interlocking declarations. In the initial phase, which we associate with ASEAN's formative years (1967–75), the security preoccupations of member states were reflected primarily in two declarations: the Bangkok Declaration of August 1967, to which reference has already been made, and the Kuala Lumpur Declaration of November 1971, which among other things called for the establishment of a Zone of Peace, Freedom and Neutrality (ZOPFAN) in the region.

ZOPFAN, ASEAN's first common initiative, has its origins in the Malaysian proposal for the neutralization of Southeast Asia.[16] It attributed regional instability to great power rivalry in the region and committed its member states to establishing Southeast Asia as a zone from which would be excluded 'any form or manner of interference by outside powers'. The Declaration was not without its shortcomings.[17] Malaysian advocacy of the concept was not greeted with universal enthusiasm even within ASEAN. Thailand and the Philippines were concerned not to jeopardize their alliance relationship with the United States; Indonesia preferred to emphasize the principle of 'national resilience'; and Singapore held to the view that in the prevailing international climate, regional stability would be best served by the continued involvement of all major powers.[18] The Declaration did not specify a time frame or strategy for the achievement of its broad objective. Nor was it clear what sanctions were available to ASEAN for purposes of deterring or countering the external use of force in violation of ZOPFAN principles.

ZOPFAN did nevertheless set the tone for the organization's diplomatic ethos. The mid-1970s witnessed a significant improvement of relations between ASEAN members and the two major communist powers. Malaysia, the Philippines and Thailand extended diplomatic recognition to Beijing in May 1974, June and July 1975, respectively. Goodwill visits to Beijing by Singapore's Foreign Minister in March 1975 and the Prime Minister in May 1976 did not lead to full diplomatic normalization but did produce a noticeable expansion of cultural and economic ties. By 1976 all ASEAN countries had established diplomatic relations with the Soviet Union. The ZOPFAN idea, coupled with the slow but discernible contraction of the Western military presence on ASEAN soil, prompted the major communist powers to adopt a more favourable attitude to the organization.[19] Indicative of ASEAN's outlook at the conclusion of the Vietnam War was Jakarta's refusal to view the withdrawal of the US military presence from Southeast Asia as a threatening development. Foreign Minister Adam Malik counselled against any 'readjustment ... inspired by negative notions of fear or uncertainty or of perceived "vacuums" in power relationships', stressing instead 'the enlarged opportunities to implement a new framework of interstate relations' on the basis of the Bandung principles.[20]

Phase II (1976–78)

The second phase of ASEAN's development was ushered in by the first Heads of Government meeting held in Bali on 24 February 1976. Its two notable achievements were the Declaration of ASEAN Concord and the Treaty of Amity and Cooperation (TAC) in Southeast Asia. According to one assessment the Bali Summit expressed the organization's newly formed sense of political cohesion, which in turn made it possible to set economic growth and development objectives as central to ASEAN's agenda. The Declaration of ASEAN Concord, in particular, gave ASEAN economic ministers a brief to widen the scope of co-operative action, especially in the production of basic commodities (notably food and energy), the establishment of ASEAN large-scale industrial projects, preferential trading arrangements, price stabilization and export promotion. More significant perhaps, notwithstanding the cautiousness of the language used, was the recognition on the part of those gathered in Bali that political co-operation on issues of regional and global security was integral to the future of co-operative regionalism in Southeast Asia.[21]

At one level the TAC may be interpreted as a response to changing regional circumstances, in particular the reunification of Vietnam and the complete military withdrawal of the United States from Indochina. In other words, an attempt was made to adjust – but by no means abandon – the ZOPFAN neutralization principle by placing even greater stress on notions of sovereignty, independence, territorial integrity, and the renunciation of force in the settlement of disputes as guiding principles of regional relationships.[22] The contracting parties committed themselves to active collaboration in the economic and security ('peace and stability') arenas, and to this end undertook to coordinate their actions and policies by maintaining 'regular contacts and consultations with one another'. They also pledged to promote 'regional resilience', to strive to prevent disputes between them from arising, and, where such disputes did arise, to settle them 'among themselves through friendly negotiations'. The Treaty even provided for a High Council which would serve as a dispute settlement mechanism by offering its good offices or engaging in mediation, inquiry or conciliation. Indicative of ASEAN's inclusive approach was the added provision that accession to the Treaty would be open to all other states in Southeast Asia.

Complementing the Treaty's extra-mural contribution to regional security was one other provision in the Declaration of ASEAN Concord. It laid down for the first time a formal framework for ASEAN political co-operation, including periodic meetings of heads of government, improvement of the machinery for political co-operation, encouragement of peaceful settlement of intra-regional disputes, and greater harmonization of ASEAN views and positions. ASEAN came to be seen by its members, Indonesia included, as a vehicle through which they could more effectively advance their separate and collective interests. In the ensuing years the conflict over Cambodia and its implications for Vietnam's future role in Southeast Asia would seriously test ASEAN's collegial identity and diplomacy. ASEAN's handling of these issues became, as we shall see, a matter of considerable contention, not least within its own ranks. Yet both the organization and its member states recognized that domestic and regional security required ASEAN to persevere with both its intra- and extra-mural functions. Though declaratory policy was not always matched by operational policy, a framework had developed, at least embryonically, pointing to an emerging 'security community'.[23]

The intra-mural dimension of security was a particularly sensitive issue given the number of unresolved bilateral disputes and the preoccupation of every member state with matters of internal security, which invariably had, or were thought to have, external implications. Not surprisingly, the preference of ASEAN governments was for bilateral arrangements which in some instances preceded the formation of ASEAN. Malaysia and Thailand had signed a border defence agreement in 1965, but the two governments could not agree on 'hot pursuit' of communist insurgents across the border until 1970. Malaysia's security links with Indonesia, including joint naval exercises, the signing of a border agreement, and the development of a bilateral security dialogue, largely followed the establishment of ASEAN. By 1977 a series of bilateral agreements between Thailand and Malaysia, Thailand and the Philippines, and the Philippines and Singapore – to which should be added longstanding Indonesian and Filipino military collaboration and Singapore–Malaysia links, partly inspired by the FPDA arrangements – had created a network of interlocking intelligence and security exchanges. Another important dimension of this network was maritime security co-operation.[24] The 1974 Singapore–Indonesia agreement for a joint patrol of the Singapore and Malacca straits and the 1975 Phillippines–Indonesia joint sea patrol agreement were complemented by a cluster of agreements involving Malaysia, Indonesia and Thailand. Primarily designed to confront transnational threats to security, notably smuggling, gunrunning and piracy, these agreements also contributed to more effective collaboration between national security forces, though such collaboration fell short of standardized military procurement, military production, logistics arrangements or military doctrine.[25]

Phase III (1979–89)

ASEAN's extra-mural diplomacy during the 1980s operated at several interacting, at times contradictory, but often mutually reinforcing levels. Three levels are worth highlighting: the country-specific level, where the emphasis is on relations with individual countries; the conflict-specific level which refers to ASEAN's handling of conflicts of particular concern to its members; and the issue-specific level which illuminates ASEAN's approach to regional and global problems and to multilateral institutions. The aim here is not to offer an exhaustive historical account of ASEAN's external relations during this period, but to analyse three carefully selected facets of ASEAN diplomacy: relations with Vietnam (country-specific), Cambodia policy (conflict-specific), and attitudes to regional and global multilateralism (issue-specific). Each of these three facets is instructive in its own right, but also in terms of ASEAN's relations with the great powers, and the interaction between the intra- and extra-mural dimensions of diplomacy.

By the late 1970s Vietnam came to dominate ASEAN thinking on regional security. Although Hanoi was generally regarded as an obstacle to ASEAN–Indochinese reconciliation, there was nevertheless a widely though not universally held view that such reconciliation was both possible and desirable. Even after Vietnam's military intervention in Cambodia, Thailand's response was to avoid unnecessarily gloomy assessments of future relations, choosing instead to stress Vietnam's preoccupation with problems of economic reconstruction. In any case, ASEAN soon realized that Vietnamese actions in Cambodia and China's subsequent incursion into Vietnam were primarily a reflection of Sino–Vietnamese and Sino–Soviet tensions. In devising its Vietnam policy, ASEAN was anxious to attenuate Sino–Vietnamese hostility, but in ways which took into account the requirements of Thai security and US diplomatic sensitivities. As a consequence, ASEAN strongly and consistently condemned Vietnam's military presence in Cambodia, and called on Hanoi to withdraw troops, thereby making way for a neutral coalition government that would side with neither Vietnam nor China.

While all ASEAN governments were to a greater or lesser extent mistrustful of Vietnam's intentions and wary of Hanoi's ascendancy over the rest of Indochina, there were considerable differences of emphasis. At one end of the spectrum was Thailand, the ASEAN member which had developed the closest ties with China, and considered Vietnam's role in Indochina as posing a threat to its security, at least in so far as it enhanced Hanoi's capacity to support 'insurgency and secession – especially in northeastern Thailand'.[26] At the other end of the spectrum was Indonesia, which viewed China with even greater hostility and suspicion and tended to view Vietnam as a possible counterweight to Chinese regional dominance. By contrast the Thai government was prepared to permit the despatch of Chinese military equipment to the Khmer Rouge through Thai territory and turn a blind eye to the deployment of Chinese forces along Vietnam's northern border because the net effect of these actions was to constrain Vietnam's capacity to apply military pressure on Thailand. Yet Thai diplomacy had to be circumspect for fear of antagonizing other ASEAN members which saw little to be gained from overtly siding with either China or Vietnam.[27] Indeed, as a collective entity ASEAN took pains to remain, at least overtly, equidistant in the Sino–Vietnamese conflict, thereby preserving the image of neutrality which it had cultivated since its inception. The policy of equidistance was doubly useful for it relieved ASEAN of the need to declare its hand in the Sino–Soviet conflict, and at the same time enabled it to obscure the lack of internal consensus concerning the relative threat to regional security posed by China and Vietnam.

At their meeting in Kuantan (Malaysia), President Suharto and Prime Minister Hussein appeared, at least implicitly, to take ASEAN closer to Hanoi by questioning China's anti-Vietnamese strategy. The two leaders offered Vietnam another olive branch by suggesting that, once it had withdrawn its forces from the Thai border, ASEAN would be in a position to recognize the Heng Samrin regime in Cambodia, and Thailand might cease supporting the Khmer Rouge.[28] These overtures, sometimes referred to as the Kuantan principle, were justified and perhaps inspired by ZOPFAN notions of neutrality and regional independence, but they would soon, at least temporarily, be abandoned. Bangkok, intent on containing Vietnam through co-operation with China, was not prepared to accept the Indonesian–Malaysian proposal. In any event, Vietnam's own response was less enthusiastic, preferring to adopt a seemingly intransigent position and hoping that internal divisions within ASEAN would in due course work to its advantage. Whatever the underlying intentions of Vietnamese diplomacy, reports in late June 1980 that Vietnamese troops had entered Thai territory to disrupt the Thai army's plans to repatriate Cambodian refugees severely tarnished Vietnam's image and prompted all ASEAN members to brand Vietnamese actions as 'aggressive' and to solidify their support for Thailand. ASEAN policy was now actively seeking to weaken the Vietnamese-installed government of the People's Republic of Kampuchea (PRK) and hasten the withdrawal of Vietnamese forces from Cambodia. The ASEAN-initiated, UN-sponsored international conference on Kampuchea in July 1981 became the launching pad for a 'coercive diplomacy', which ASEAN states pursued through a wide range of bilateral and multilateral channels, notably the dialogue partnerships with the United States, the European Community, Japan, Canada, Australia and New Zealand, and membership of the UN, the Organization of Islamic Conference and the Commonwealth.[29] All the indications, at least in the early years of the Reagan presidency, were that ASEAN was prepared to act in unison with the United States and China, though perhaps for different reasons, in support of a strategy designed to bring maximum pressure to bear on Vietnam. The idea of offering Hanoi diplomatic or economic incentives which might persuade it to adopt a more flexible or accommodating stance on the conflict was no longer a decisive consideration in ASEAN thinking.

Although it held special security significance because of its geographical proximity and the historical context in which reunification had been achieved, Vietnam was not the only country which attracted ASEAN's sustained attention. The great powers, in particular China and the United States, and to a lesser extent the Soviet Union, could not but weigh heavily on ASEAN's extra-mural diplomacy. China's physical presence was even more striking than Vietnam's, and, in any case, relations with one country could not be disentangled from relations with the other. The Soviet Union, on the other hand, posed a less tangible or imminent threat. Though Moscow's power and influence were on the rise in different parts of Asia, and though its military presence in the Southeast Asian region appeared likely to expand by virtue of its alliance with Vietnam, the widely shared perception within ASEAN was that the Soviet build-up had to be considered in the larger context of Cold War rivalries. The projection of Soviet power in Southeast Asia was, it seemed, driven largely by Moscow's wish to establish its great power credentials in a region where the United States enjoyed undisputed military superiority, and to counter the influence of what was now perceived to be a distinctly unfriendly China. For many within ASEAN an uneasy balance between these three major centres of power offered the least unpalatable scenario, for it lessened the prospect that any of the three could impose hegemonic control over the region, thereby preserving for ASEAN and its member states a certain freedom of action which might not otherwise be available to them.[30]

Ambiguity, no doubt a distinguishing feature of Southeast Asian attitudes to China, was not entirely absent from the relationship with the United States. As already noted, most ASEAN states had cultivated either extensive military and economic ties directly with the United States (Thailand, the Philippines), or less directly by maintaining close ties with one or other of its allies (Malaysia, Singapore).[31] During the 1980s, US–ASEAN security co-operation was strengthened with regular high-level diplomatic and military consultations, combined military exercises, intelligence exchanges, policy coordination on the Cambodia conflict, and greater ASEAN interest in a continued US military presence in Southeast Asia.[32] In August 1989, Singapore took a step closer to alignment by offering to host US military facilities. It should be noted, however, that in explaining Singapore's motivation, Prime Minister Lee Kuan Yew placed the emphasis not on any Soviet threat but on the rise of new regional powers, Vietnam and India, and the likelihood of expanded Chinese and Japanese military capabilities.[33] Acceptance of the US military presence in the region, even at the height of the Second Cold War, did not derive from a perception that the Soviet Union posed a direct military threat to ASEAN. Nor did it signify a willingness on ASEAN'S part to join in the Reagan administration's anti-Soviet crusade.

The United States, for its part, had shown little enthusiasm for ZOPFAN, arguing that the neutralization of the region would diminish the capacity of the United States to discharge its obligations in the region, and more generally damage Western interests. Similarly, ASEAN's declared commitment to create a Southeast Asian Nuclear Weapons-Free Zone (SEANWFZ) provoked a distinctly negative US response. Right through the 1980s, US policy-makers insisted that such a zone would favour the Soviet Union at the expense of the United States, and diminish US deterrence capability. Washington saw the ASEAN proposal as setting a dangerous precedent likely to encourage the creation of other regional nuclear-free zones, thereby further circumscribing its strategic freedom of action, with respect to nuclear testing, port calls or the stationing of nuclear weapons.[34] Important as the US relationship was to each of its members, ASEAN, while relegating ZOPFAN to a relatively inconspicuous role in its extra-mural diplomacy, did not at any stage formally abandon its support for the concept. Similarly, though the enthusiasm or diligence with which ASEAN pursued the SEANWFZ proposal would wax and wane, the in-principle commitment to the objective remained firmly part of ASEAN's agenda right through the 1980s and beyond.

The continuities and ambiguities evident in ASEAN's approach to security at the country-specific level were equally apparent at the conflict-specific level.

Not surprisingly, the factors which helped shape ASEAN'S Vietnam policy also coloured its stance on the Cambodia conflict.[35] Acting with the support of Western powers and to a lesser extent China, ASEAN was able to formulate and execute a multifaceted strategy which had as its primary objective the containment of Vietnamese influence in Indochina and Southeast Asia more generally. Its advocacy of a comprehensive political settlement largely set the tone for the UN's own handling of the conflict. At ASEAN's initiative the General Assembly resolved in 1980 to call for the convening of an international conference on Kampuchea. Though boycotted by the Soviet bloc countries, the conference held in July 1981 issued a declaration which was subsequently endorsed by the UN and formed the basis for international consideration of the conflict.[36]

Apart from discouraging diplomatic recognition of the Vietnamese-backed Heng Samrin (PRK) government and continuing to press for Cambodia's UN seat to be filled by the Government of Democratic Kampuchea (DK) – a task in which it was largely successful, ASEAN also played a significant role in the formation of the Coalition Government of Democratic Kampuchea (CGDK) comprising the three Khmer resistance forces. This last element of the strategy would prove more problematic. The coalition's own legitimacy was severely tarnished by the inclusion of the Khmer Rouge who were known to have perpetrated the most unspeakable atrocities against the Khmer people. Moreover, to the extent that the coalition depended for its military muscle on Beijing's support for the Khmer Rouge, ASEAN had effectively made itself hostage to Chinese interests. In grappling with the first problem, ASEAN hoped that, with the aid of Sihanouk's leadership, the coalition would strengthen its credentials as the authentic mouthpiece of Cambodian nationalism. As for China's dominant influence over the coalition, ASEAN's strategy was to buttress the non-communist forces by facilitating arms supplies through Western channels.

By the mid-1980s, it became apparent that, however successful ASEAN's policies might be in containing Vietnam, they were not having the desired effect so far as resolution of the conflict was concerned. An increased awareness on ASEAN's part of the limitations of its strategy, coupled with Vietnam's desire to give greater priority to internal reconstruction, and the dual thaw in Soviet–American and Sino–Soviet relations prompted ASEAN to reconsider its position, and explore more assiduously the role which the UN might play in advancing the prospects of a comprehensive settlement.[37] Within ASEAN the two critical factors were Indonesia's willingness to assume a higher profile in peacemaking (hosting of the Jakarta Informal Meetings beginning in July 1988), and the change of government in Thailand (new Prime Minister Chatichai Choonhavan adopted the more moderate and incremental policy of 'turning the Indochina battlefield into a market place').[38] A number of internal and external factors combined to produce a new consensus in ASEAN's approach to the Cambodia problem.[39] Whereas ASEAN had hitherto used the UN primarily as a tool for isolating and punishing Vietnam and its client state in Cambodia, it was now intent on co-operating with the UN Security Council and with other regional players, notably Australia, with a view to the long-term resolution of the conflict. ASEAN diplomacy was not an insignificant factor in the relative success of the 1989 Paris Peace Conference co-chaired by France and Indonesia, and in the subsequent momentum given to the Australian peace initiative. The establishment of an effective international control mechanism to supervise and verify the Vietnamese withdrawal and an international peacekeeping force under UN auspices to maintain peace and order in Cambodia pending the holding of free elections became the twin pillars of ASEAN policy.[40]

Complementing and reinforcing the country- and conflict-specific elements of ASEAN's extra-mural diplomacy were the more explicit attempts to foster regional dialogue. The most important of these was the ASEAN Post-Ministerial Conference (PMC) which over time assumed the character of a multilateral security dialogue mechanism. During the 1970s, ASEAN had identified a number of countries as 'dialogue partners'. The annual post-ministerial meetings between ASEAN and Australia, Canada, the European Union, Japan, New Zealand, South Korea and the United States provided the organization with an invaluable opportunity to engage in a wide-ranging dialogue covering bilateral, regional and global issues. From 1984, ASEAN decided to follow up its annual ministerial meetings with a larger gathering in which all its dialogue partners were invited to participate. The progressive widening of the PMC's membership and agenda was supported by the development of an embryonic institutional infrastructure, including Senior Officials Meetings (SOMs) and meetings of the ASEAN states and dialogue partners.

For ASEAN, one of the PMC's main attractions was that it offered ASEAN's exports the prospect of more favourable terms of entry into external markets. It also provided a platform for the negotiation of a range of technical assistance programmes. The emphasis on economic objectives was seemingly reinforced by ASEAN's insistence that the PMC had no hidden agenda, and more specifically that it was 'neither intended to deal with the institutional aspects of the Pacific relations, nor be directed towards the establishment of a new regional institution'.[41] The PMC did nevertheless serve as an informal channel for exchanging views on diplomatic–security issues within ASEAN and between ASEAN and its dialogue partners. The PMC annual meetings had effectively become the largest regional platform for security dialogue.

The PMC was but a natural development in ASEAN's modest but persistent attempts to develop a global dimension to its extra-mural diplomacy. It consistently included in its ministerial deliberations international problems dealing with both economy and security. Frequent reviews of the international economic situation emphasized the North–South perspective on multilateral trade negotiations, the adverse effects of falling commodity prices on the export earnings of developing countries, and the need for more equitable international commodity agreements. ASEAN foreign and economic ministers repeatedly expressed concern over the disruptive effects of fluctuating exchange rates on the growth of world trade and the failure of international negotiations to produce a comprehensive solution to the debt burden of developing countries. Attention was also directed to geopolitical and strategic issues, including disarmament and arms control, the Arab–Israeli conflict, the Iran–Iraq war, Afghanistan, the situation in southern Africa, and UN reform. Given its limited capabilities, ASEAN's role was mostly one of moral exhortation, although on a few issues the formulation of a common position gave ASEAN countries a louder voice in international councils (for example, the UN General Assembly, UN agencies and programmes, the Non-Aligned Movement and the Organization of Islamic Conference) than might otherwise have been possible. In addition, where ASEAN's interests more closely matched its capacity to influence outcomes (for example, ASEAN co-operation, international trade negotiations, Indochinese refugees, the narcotics trade, and SEANWFZ), the questions involved were given systematic attention, and at times substantial resources were devoted to practical implementation.

Conclusions

What, then, may we reasonably conclude about ASEAN's approach to security during the 1970s and 1980s? Though a number of Western analysts rightly drew attention to the limitations of ASEAN policies and processes, two achievements, succinctly expressed by Noordin Sopiee, are worth highlighting.[42] First, ASEAN gave its members a greater sense of confidence in dealing with the external environment than at any time since decolonization. Perhaps the most telling factor in this was ASEAN's relative success in containing intra-regional tensions and rivalries, which in turn allowed member states to concentrate on domestic rather than external priorities. Secondly, and somewhat paradoxically, the new psychological climate made for a more self-assured and self-assertive diplomacy, which in turn nurtured within the ASEAN community the conviction that it could influence, and not merely be influenced by, regional and international politics. Reaching agreement the 'ASEAN Way', was, it is true, a slow and laborious process, involving extensive consultation and discussion, which did not always translate into sharply focused decisions or a concerted programme of action. The process itself, however, paid dividends in that it made the policy communities of each country more sensitive to one another's priorities and constraints and more aware of the potential but also limitations of consensual decision-making.

ASEAN enjoyed one other distinct advantage in that this was a sub-regional grouping comprising a core group of contiguous countries. Once ASEAN had demonstrated its durability, especially in the aftermath of the communist victory in Indochina, it became a pole of attraction for a number of organizations, both regional and international, governmental and non-governmental. By affiliating or coordinating their activities with ASEAN they could enhance the impact of their activities, and achieve more with fewer resources. Similarly, donor governments and agencies found it more attractive to channel their aid though the Association than through individual countries.[43] By the late 1970s, the growth of ASEAN prestige and influence had become something of a virtuous circle, with the Association attaining the status of a 'regional hub'. Not only did ASEAN extend dialogue or observer status to a number of external powers, but its links with diverse regional and international organizations made it uniquely placed to act as an intermediary between other regional initiatives, and between developed and less-developed economies in the region.[44] Jealous of the organizational pre-eminence it had achieved in Asian multilateralism, and fearful that other processes might weaken its unity and influence, ASEAN became negatively disposed to the emergence of other regional or sub-regional forums. In that sense ASEAN's success may be said to have weakened attempts to create a region-wide institutional framework and to that extent to have dampened, at least temporarily, the enthusiasm for a 'Pacific Community'.

ECONOMIC CO-OPERATION AND DIALOGUE PARTNERSHIPS

Although security in its various dimensions was one of ASEAN's primary concerns, it is worth remembering that, formally at least, co-operative relations to facilitate the economic development of member states constituted the Associations's overriding rationale. Functional and economic co-operation had in any case both intra- and extra-mural dimensions, and, as we shall see, significant implications for regional security. A word first about ASEAN's institutional capacity on which the effectiveness of such co-operation would in part depend. The skeletal organizational structure which ASEAN acquired in its formative stages included the annual ASEAN Ministerial Meeting (AMM) of foreign ministers, the Standing Committee chaired by the foreign minister of the country hosting the next AMM, preparatory meetings attended by the heads of the ASEAN national secretariats of each country, and the SOM, made up of the under-secretaries of foreign affairs. It was not until 1973 that the AMM agreed to the establishment of a Secretariat, and not until 1976 that Jakarta was selected as its location. Headed by a Secretary-General, the Secretariat was equipped with three bureaux to deal with economic affairs, science and technology, and social–cultural affairs respectively, and an administrative office, a public information office, and after 1981 a narcotics desk (see Figure 4.1).

Figure 4.1   Organizational structure of ASEAN

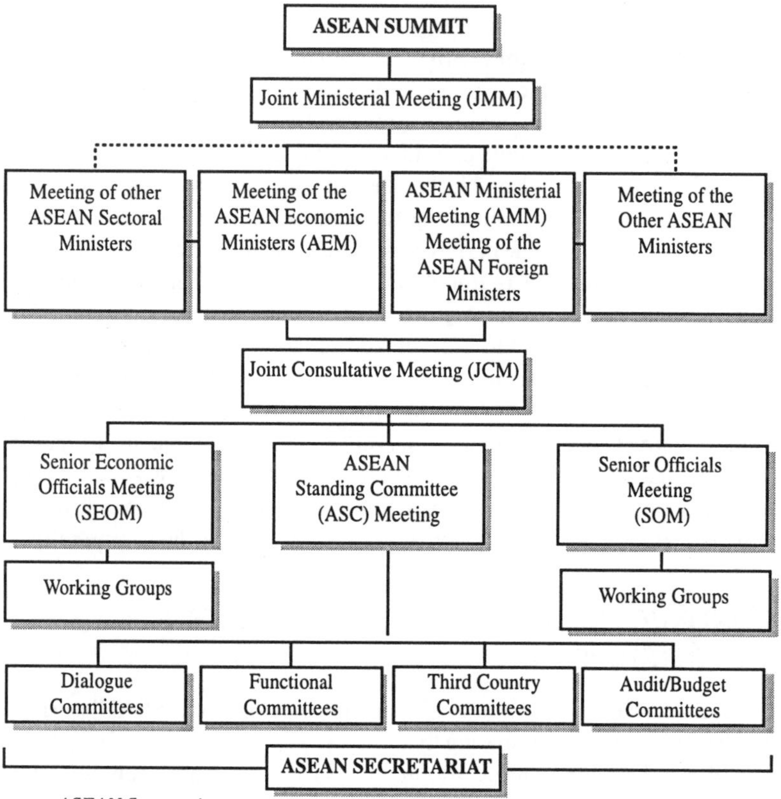

Source: ASEAN Secretariat

The elusiveness of the economic objective prompted the 1976 Heads of Government meeting in Bali to describe economic growth and development as 'the main foundation for the proposed Southeast Asia zone of peace, freedom and neutrality'.[45] Directed by the summit meeting to consider ways of implementing economic co-operation, the ASEAN economic ministers met in March 1976 to discuss the possibility of coordinated responses to natural disasters and other major calamities, greater collaboration in food and energy production, establishment of ASEAN large-scale industrial projects, preferential trade arrangements (PTAs), and the formulation of common positions at international trade and other negotiations.[46] The second meeting of the Heads of Government, which was held in Kuala Lumpur in 1977, agreed to the creation of a standby credit facility of $100 million – later increased to $200 million – to bridge the temporary international liquidity problems of member states. There was no shortage of initiatives: the ASEAN Industrial Project in 1976, the ASEAN PTA in 1977, the ASEAN Industrial Complementation Scheme (1981), and the ASEAN Industrial Joint Ventures in 1983. Collaborative activities were also initiated by the relevant ASEAN economic committees in finance and banking, food, agriculture and forestry, industry, minerals and energy, and transport and communications. With various degrees of private sector support and participation, several schemes were established, including the ASEAN Finance Corporation (1981), the ASEAN Reinsurance Pool (1982), and the ASEAN Bankers Acceptance Scheme.

Yet, the implementation of projects and proposals was painfully slow. The framework for industrial co-operation was not clearly defined, either in form or objective, partly because ASEAN had sought to accommodate two quite distinct strategies: market integration through trade liberalization on the one hand, and joint production endeavours through the integration of specific markets.[47] PTAs were intended to apply only to selected products: basic commodities, particularly rice and crude oil, products of ASEAN industrial projects, products for the expansion of intra-ASEAN trade; and other products as agreed upon from time to time. By 1986 the PTA still had negligible impact on intra-ASEAN trade,[48] and a definite timetable for the process of trade liberalization had yet to be set. The diverse character of member economies, the trade difficulties encountered by a number of them, the slow pace of bureaucratic negotiation, and above all the pressure exerted by powerful interest groups within each country made co-operative regionalism a more complicated task than the official rhetoric would indicate. It is against this backdrop that the 1987 Manila Summit set out to fast-track co-operative arrangements, while stopping well short of adopting sweeping new regional mechanisms or action programmes. The Summit did, however, recommend that intra-regional trade should by the end of the century cover a substantial share of the number and value of traded items under the PTA. It agreed on the progressive reduction of items which member countries could exclude from the application of the PTA, and on the deepening of the margin of preference for items currently covered by the PTA. The meeting also approved an immediate 'standstill of non-tariff barriers (NTBs)' and future negotiation of a gradual roll-back. Annual reviews of the progress of the improved PTA were to be conducted over the following five years, with further improvements to be considered at the end of the five-year period.[49]

It remains to say a word about the extra-mural dimension of ASEAN's attempts at economic integration. Of particular importance here were the crucial relationships with the advanced capitalist economies, in particular Japan, the United States, Europe, and to a lesser extent Canada and Australia. These were seen as the most likely sources of development aid, financial assistance and FDI, as well as the most important markets for Southeast Asian exports. In a sense, ASEAN was for many of its members a useful instrument which could focus the attention of the major centres of economic power in the West, including governments, the corporate sector and international financial institutions, on the region's economic potential and on its institutional capacity to harness that potential. The various attempts at coordinating and harmonizing industrial and trade policy were in part driven by these external considerations, which had, however, to contend with complex and often diverging domestic pressures, hence the often hesitant and intermittent quality of ASEAN's approach to regionalism. Later chapters will examine these efforts in greater depth. Here we confine ourselves to a few observations on the relationship with Japan and the United States, and more specifically on the factors which helped to shape ASEAN's economic dialogue with these two partners.

The oil crises and the prolonged economic recession which afflicted most Western economies during the 1970s strengthened in Japan the perception of ASEAN's economic importance. It is worth recalling that in 1975 ASEAN accounted for nearly one-fifth of Japan's oil imports, and one-third of its natural gas imports, almost the whole of its tin and rubber imports, over half its nickel, and more than one-third of its timber, copper and bauxite.[50] For Japan, economic aid to the ASEAN countries was a wise investment if it could obtain in exchange secure long-term access to their raw materials.[51] Japan's rapidly growing energy requirements largely explain the 250 per cent increase in its imports from ASEAN between 1975 and 1980, which resulted in ASEAN's share of Japan's total imports rising from 10.4 per cent to 15.1 per cent. During the same period Japan's exports increased by more than 170 per cent, and accounted for about one-tenth of Japan's total exports. Japanese FDI to ASEAN also rose both in absolute and relative terms – from $490 million in 1970 to $7,021 million in 1980, or, expressed as a proportion of total Japanese FDI, from 13.7 per cent to 19.2 per cent.[52] Japan and ASEAN had an added common interest, namely the safety of the sea lanes in Southeast Asia. The bulk of Japan's raw material imports, in particular oil from the Middle East and iron from Western Australia, passed through the straits of Malacca, Sunda and Lombok.

It is not difficult, then, to understand why the Japanese government should have singled out Southeast Asia as a focal point of its regional diplomacy. Prime Minister Fukuda's meeting with the ASEAN Heads of Government in August 1997 and the subsequent enunciation of the so-called 'Fukuda Doctrine' on 18 August 1977 were intended to signal the renewed vigour with which Japan would pursue its economic and diplomatic interests in the region.[53] The Doctrine, which was couched primarily in political terms, had three main pillars: Japan's rejection of military power and commitment to the peace and prosperity of Southeast Asia; Japan's intention to consolidate its relations with Southeast Asia in the social and cultural as well as the political and economic fields; Japan's wish to be an equal partner of ASEAN and its member countries, and in the process strengthen their solidarity and resilience.[54] Though formulated in broad political terms, the Doctrine nevertheless had important ramifications, some of which were canvassed at Fukuda's meeting with ASEAN leaders. These included Japanese support for ASEAN industrial projects, the doubling of Japan's official development assistance (ODA) over the following five years, and improvements to Japan's generalized system of preferences for ASEAN products. While it had proposed in 1972 that the Strait of Malacca should be internationalized, by 1978 Japan was ready to recognize the strait as constituting part of the territorial seas of the three regional states, Indonesia, Malaysia and Singapore.

ASEAN took advantage of Japan's overtures to press for greater access to Japanese markets, stabilization of the import of oil and natural gas, and a more generous programme in foreign aid and technology transfer. Preoccupied with its own economic difficulties, Japan's response was less than forthcoming. During Nakasone's tour of Southeast Asia in the early part of his prime ministership the best that Japan could offer was a 50 per cent increase of the ceiling of preferential tariffs for developing countries beginning in 1984; reactivation of a previous programme, whereby Japan would assist ASEAN enterprises in plant renovation; and an annual invitation to 150 young people from ASEAN countries to visit Japan. The only other measures involved limited scientific and technological collaboration, and a few bilateral co-operative projects.

The relationship was further complicated by Japan's steadily expanding military capabilities.[55] Hoping to contain adverse regional reaction, Nakasone proposed during his visit to Indonesia in May 1982 a $281 million loan for 1983, attempts to stabilize Indonesia's share of oil exports, and an increase in imports of Indonesian non-oil products.[56] In June 1985, Japan announced that tariffs on more than 1,800 processed agricultural and industrial products would be reduced 'in principle' by 20 per cent, and that tariffs on 42 primary and processed agricultural products and on 32 industrial products would be reduced or eliminated by 1987. Of particular interest to ASEAN countries were the proposed tariff reductions on boneless chicken, bananas and palm oil. While appreciative of these tariff cuts, ASEAN economic ministers used the opportunity of the joint meeting with their Japanese counterpart in June 1985 to urge Japan to take bolder steps to increase its imports of manufactured and semi-processed products from ASEAN, to reduce tariff and non-tariff barriers, and to increase the transfer of technology. Concerned by the continuing appreciation of the yen, ASEAN also requested that Japan introduce measures designed to alleviate the problem, especially the burden of debt servicing.[57]

The overall trend in Japan–ASEAN economic relations from 1981 to 1986 pointed to a relative decline. Two-way trade stood at $39,162 million in 1981 but fell to $28,640 million in 1986. Japanese FDI to ASEAN had reached $2,834 million in 1981 but shrank to $855 million in 1986, while Japan's official aid had rose only marginally from $799 million in 1981 to $914 million in 1986. Though ASEAN's manufactured exports to Japan between 1983 and 1987 had almost doubled as a proportion of total exports, the increase was more than offset by the decline in raw materials exports. As for Japanese foreign investment, an increasing proportion was now directed to Europe and the United States, the major export markets for Japan's industrial products. ASEAN's share had fallen from 31.8 per cent in 1981 to 4.6 per cent in 1987.[58]

None of this is to suggest that Japan had ceased playing a pivotal role in the development and structure of Southeast Asia's economies. In the late 1980s, several of the indicators of the ASEAN–Japan relationship resumed an upward curve. In 1988, Japan's imports of ASEAN manufactured goods rose to $6.6 billion, an increase of 44.8 per cent over the preceding year; total ODA loans to ASEAN and Myanmar amounted to 4.8 billion yen (or 43 per cent of total ODA loans); Japan's ODA to each of the ASEAN five countries exceeded the total received from all other OECD donors; Japan's FDI to ASEAN increased by 78 per cent over the previous year to some $47 billion (compared with $10 billion in 1980). Asia as a whole, and ASEAN in particular, had become the fastest-growing destination for Japanese FDI.[59] Several factors had contributed to this outcome: large wage differentials between the Japanese and ASEAN economies; the attractive tax incentives, promotional privileges and expanded public infrastructure offered by ASEAN countries; and Japanese assessments of Southeast Asia's relative political stability.[60] During his visits to Indonesia and the Philippines in April–May 1989, Prime Minister Takeshita promised that official aid to ASEAN would reach $50 billion over the following five years. Japan's salience to the development of Southeast Asia's regional economy was not in question.

Notwithstanding the increasing interdependencies between the Japanese and ASEAN economies, the relationship was far from symmetrical. Though ASEAN's manufacturing industries had benefited greatly from Japanese capital and technology transfers, they still found it difficult to penetrate the Japanese market. Moreover, the major influences shaping the extent and intensity of Japan's trade, financial and aid links with ASEAN had more to do with the changing complexion of Japan's own economy, the revised industrial and financial strategies of its corporate sector, and the evolution of global markets than with economic or political considerations peculiar to the bilateral relationship.

In the case of the United States, the other pole of attraction for ASEAN, trade constituted by far the primary focus of the relationship. In 1980, the United States already accounted for 16.7 per cent of ASEAN's total trade. Unlike the trend we have just observed in relation to Japan, ASEAN's exports to the United States continued to rise from $13.28 billion in 1980 to $16.87 billion in 1984, and after dipping in 1985–86 rose again to a new peak of $18.05 billion in 1987, by which time the United States accounted for over 22 per cent of ASEAN's total exports. Even more telling was the marked increase in ASEAN's trade surplus with the United States, which doubled from $4 billion in 1980 to $8 billion in 1987.[61] The growing importance of the US market for ASEAN exports would, however, be accompanied by periodic tensions reflecting the dynamism but also the weakness of the ASEAN economies. The dialogue process became one of the principal vehicles for articulating and negotiating the competing interests and priorities of the two sides.

The first meeting of the ASEAN–United States Dialogue in September 1977 canvassed three key themes – trade, investment and development assistance – all of which would regularly feature in subsequent discussions. ASEAN, as a major supplier of key commodities, was from the outset concerned to secure international arrangements designed to stabilize commodity export earnings. To this end it pressed hard for US support of commodity stabilization agreements and negotiation of a Common Fund. It also urged the establishment of a STABEX-type commodity earnings stabilization programme. While expressing sympathy for ASEAN's broad objective, the US delegation made it clear that ASEAN's specific proposal would not be supported. In the area of bilateral trade, ASEAN sought improved access to the US market, and in particular improvements to the US Generalized Scheme of Preferences (GSP). On the question of private foreign investment, the United States indicated a willingness to facilitate investments which contributed to ASEAN development objectives, but only 'within the framework of its general policies'. ASEAN representatives were reminded that investment decisions were ultimately made by private investors 'primarily in response to the existing investment opportunities and climate'.[62] US FDI in ASEAN would rise steadily through the 1980s, but at a slower rate than Japanese FDI. Finally, in recognition of the continuing need of ASEAN countries for concessional developmental assistance, the two sides agreed to set up a joint working group to define specific projects and make the necessary funding preparations. In many ways this was the least problematic of the three agenda items. By 1982, USAID had committed the modest but useful amount of $16.5 million to ASEAN regional projects. Over the next several years the working group would approve projects in the fields of energy, public health, agriculture, human resource development, narcotics control, research, and small and medium-sized enterprise support.

The trade relationship proved both more complex and more sensitive. By 1980, ASEAN had gained a number of GSP-related concessions, but was pressing for more substantial improvements, especially with regard to product coverage, competitive need limitations and rules of origin. To ASEAN's increasingly detailed proposals, the United States could respond only with limited gestures. In subsequent years, ASEAN's focus would turn increasingly to what it saw as the disturbing signs of rising US protectionism. A number of provisions in the US Trade and Tariff Act of 1984 were thought likely to prejudice ASEAN interests, in particular those relating to anti-dumping and countervailing duty laws, possible US retaliation against foreign trade barriers, and the new conditions attached to GSP eligibility. Equally troublesome were other protectionist bills before Congress, which might impose import quotas for textiles, shoes and copper, or use health, environmental or labour regulations to curtail ASEAN's preferential access to the US market. Partly with these fears in mind, ASEAN expressed interest in a joint initiative to liberalize two-way trade, but for the United States the proposed free trade arrangement with

Canada and the new round of multilateral trade negotiations were much higher priorities.

It is worth noting that both ASEAN and the United States had from the earliest stages of the dialogue process committed themselves to the active participation of the business sector. They warmly welcomed the formation of the ASEAN–US Business Council (AUSBC) in 1979, and soon after proceeded to invite private sector representatives to a number of Dialogue sessions. Beginning in 1983, the ASEAN and US delegations would meet with representatives of the AUSBC. While the US business community was, not surprisingly, interested in securing more favourable conditions for foreign investors in ASEAN countries, the US section of the AUSBC became a strong advocate for a number of official ASEAN positions, including simplification and liberalization of the US GSP system, additional US investment promotion missions to ASEAN, increased US participation in ASEAN industrial complementation schemes and joint ventures, and reduced US impediments to the export of ASEAN goods and services.[63] However, on the more sensitive trade issues the official US position reflected a wider range of economic and financial interests than those most prominently represented in the US section of the Business Council.

The US–ASEAN relationship was generally amicable but none the less asymmetrical. ASEAN's role was essentially that of a supplicant. ASEAN's export-oriented industrialization was dependent on access to US markets and on US investments and development assistance. US administrations, on the other hand, were in the enviable position of appearing generous, even when acceding only to requests that were readily affordable. ASEAN's costlier requests could be rejected on the grounds that they lacked congressional support, that the issues involved were a matter not for government but for the private sector, or that they could be more appropriately dealt with in the context of international negotiations. This is not to say that the dialogue process had no value for the United States. On the contrary, it was expected to facilitate three key US economic objectives: gain support for US positions in international trade negotiations, secure improved US access to ASEAN markets, and commit ASEAN to greater intellectual property protection – an objective which the United States could unilaterally pursue through domestic legislation in the area of copyrights, patents and trademarks. Moreover, ASEAN could perform a number of useful functions *vis-à-vis* US geopolitical interests in Asia. That having been said, the United States was far more important to ASEAN than ASEAN was to the United States. Their bargaining strengths were markedly unequal. The inducements and constraints which the United States could bring to bear on the relationship greatly exceeded those available to ASEAN.

This brief survey of extra-mural economic and functional co-operation would be incomplete without at least passing reference to the development of inter-regional links between ASEAN and the South Pacific Forum, if for no other reason than that they offer an instructive contrast between North–South and South–South relationships. Initial contacts in 1980–81 between the ASEAN Secretariat and the Forum Secretariat, the South Pacific Bureau for Economic Co-operation (SPEC), yielded little by way of concrete initiatives, but it did set in train a process of dialogue during the course of the 1980s. These discussions centred primarily on feasibility studies in the areas of investment co-operation, joint ventures, and human resources development projects. A Forum on ASEAN/South Pacific Investment Promotion in October 1986, attended by government and private sector representatives, was widely regarded at the time as pointing to significant opportunities for closer economic ties.[64] Several factors, however, made the going slow and difficult. The tensions in the Indonesia–Papua New Guinea (PNG) relationship associated with sensitive border crossings, refugee flows, Indonesian violations of PNG airspace, in particular refugee flows, and the relocation of families from Java to Irian Jaya, were an important contributing factor. Moreover, neither ASEAN nor the Forum was intellectually, economically or organizationally equipped to give inter-regionalism the necessary impetus. The scarce financial and technical resources at the disposal of the Pacific islands, the very low level of trade between Southeast Asia and the South Pacific, and the privileged position of metropolitan centres of economic and political power (Japan and the United States *vis-à-vis* ASEAN and Australia and New Zealand *vis-à-vis* the Forum) severely circumscribed the prospects of South–South co-operation. Yet, for all these difficulties, the principle of inter-regional cooperation had been firmly established.

In its first 20 years, ASEAN had managed, despite internal difficulties and the growing pressures exerted by a rapidly changing external environment, to take a few tentative but influential steps towards the 'new regionalism'. It embarked upon an ambitious programme of intra-mural and extra-mural collaboration, which, though it originated at the height of the Vietnam War and was in part inspired by a desire to defeat communist and other revolutionary movements, departed in several important respects from Cold War orthodoxy. First, despite the close security links between several of its members and the United States, ASEAN as a whole studiously avoided direct military alignment with either Cold War protagonist. Secondly, though all ASEAN members were in varying degrees suspicious of both Vietnamese and Chinese intentions, ASEAN's collective response steered clear of outright confrontation with either Hanoi or Beijing. By the late 1980s, ASEAN had found a way of striking a *modus vivendi* with both of them. Thirdly, and most importantly, ASEAN, precisely because it comprised newly independent Third World countries, sought from the outset to combine domestic and external security, economic as well as military security. Though guided by strongly anti-communist governments, ASEAN, despite or because of its inclination to compromise and improvisation, developed a collaborative methodology that seemed intuitively, if not always consciously or consistently, attuned to the increasingly complex and multifaceted agenda of regional and global security. At least at the declaratory level, ASEAN had established the foundations for a comprehensive security policy.

For all these promising developments, ASEAN policies raised more questions than they answered. Even on the issue of regional resilience, now one of the cardinal principles of ASEAN discourse, a considerable gap separated theory and practice. Three questions are worth highlighting. First, was ASEAN as a regional grouping sufficiently independent of Western, in particular US interests, to be able to fashion its own distinctive policies? To be more specific, did ASEAN have the intellectual and organizational capabilities – and the internal cohesion – to develop a relationship with the two major Asian powers, China and Japan, that was not a pale imitation of US strategic and economic priorities? The second question was closely related to the first: what would be ASEAN's regional identity? Was its future to be shaped primarily by an emerging 'Asian' or 'Pacific' consciousness? Thirdly, was ASEAN purely a creation of states, or to be more precise of governments preoccupied with regime survival? Or, was it a regional formation which, at least potentially, could involve larger societal forces? Could it give expression to the energies and aspirations of civil society? These questions, as we shall see, would be given increasing attention, if not definitive answers, in the immediate post-Cold War period.

NOTES

1. ASEAN has been the subject of numerous studies, a few of which have managed to combine historical insight with contemporary political analysis. See, for example, Alison Bronowski (ed), *Understanding ASEAN*, New York: St. Martin's Press in association with the Australian Institute of International Affairs, 1982.
2. See Philip Charier, 'ASEAN's Inheritance: The Region of Southeast Asia', 1941–61; *Pacific Review*, 14 (3), 2001, 313–38.
3. See J.A.C. Mackie, *Konfrontasi: The Indonesia–Malaysia Dispute 1963–1966*, Kuala Lumpur: Oxford University Press, 1974, pp. 200–238, 276–324.
4. For a lucid survey of these internal and external cleavages, see Michael Leifer, *Conflict and Regional Order in Southeast Asia*, Adelphi Papers 162, London: International Institute for Strategic Studies, 1980, pp. 4–13.
5. See Michael R.J. Vatikiotis, *Indonesian Politics under Suharto*, 3rd edn, London: Routledge, 1993, pp. 1–59; David Jenkins, *Suharto and his Generals: Indonesian Military Politics*, Ithaca, NY: Cornell University Press, Modern Indonesian Project, 1984, pp. 75–83.
6. Attention to the inadequacies of this simplistic interpretation is drawn by Lau Teik Soon, 'ASEAN and the Bali Summit', *Pacific Community*, 7 (4), July 1976, 536–8.
7. The text of the ASEAN (Bangkok) Declaration may be found in *ASEAN Documents Series 1967–1988*, 3rd edn, Jakarta: ASEAN Secretariat, 1988, pp. 27–8.
8. Michael Leifer, 'ASEAN: A Changing Regional Role', *Asian Survey*, 28 (7), July 1987, 764.
9. Bilson Kurus, 'Understanding ASEAN', *Asian Survey*, 33 (8), August 1993, 819–31.
10. See Arnfinn Jorgensen-Dahl, 'ASEAN 1967–1976: Development or Stagnation', *Pacific Community*, 7 (4), July 1976, 529–30.
11. Ibid., pp. 63–5.
12. See Kamarulzaman Askandar, 'ASEAN and Conflict Management: The Formative Years of 1967–1976, *Pacific Review*, 6 (2), 1994, 65.

13. See *Regionalism in South-East Asia*, Jakarta: Centre for Strategic and International Studies, 1975, p. 8.

14. Michael Leifer, *ASEAN and the Security of Southeast Asia*, London: Routledge, 1989, p. 4. See also Mohamed Jawhar, 'Managing Security in Southeast Asia: Existing Mechanisms and Processes to Address Regional Conflicts', *Australian Journal of International Affairs*, 47 (2), October 1993, 214.

15. See Michael Leifer, 'ASEAN as a Model of a Security Community?', in Hadi Soesastro (ed), *ASEAN in a Changed Regional and International Political Economy*, Jakarta: Centre for Strategic and International Studies, 1995, pp. 132–3.

16. The historical background to the ZOPFAN concept is surveyed in Heiner Hänggi, *ASEAN and the ZOPFAN Concept*, Singapore: Institute of Southeast Asian Studies Strategic Paper 4, 1991, pp. 5–20. See also Bilveer Singh, *ZOPFAN and the New Security Order in the Asia-Pacific Region*, Kuala Lumpur: Pelanduk Publications, 1992, pp. 11–68.

17. Ibid., pp. 37–50.

18. Muthiah Alagappa, 'Regional Arrangements and International Security in Southeast Asia: Going beyond ZOPFAN', *Contemporary Southeast Asia*, 12 (4), March 1991, 274.

19. Askander, 'ASEAN and Conflict Management', pp. 67–8.

20. Lau Teik Soon, 'ASEAN and the Bali Summit', pp. 539–40.

21. Adam Malik, 'Opening Statements to the Eighth ASEAN Ministerial Meeting, Kuala Lumpur, 13 May 1975', *Statements by ASEAN Foreign Ministers at ASEAN Ministerial Meetings 1967–1987*, Jakarta: ASEAN Secretariat, 1987, p. 195.

22. Sheldon W. Simon, *The ASEAN States and Regional Security*, Stanford, CA: Hoover Institution Press, 1982, p. 87.

23. Michael Leifer, 'The Extension of ASEAN's Model of Regional Security', in R. Cobbold (ed), *The World Reshaped, Vol. 2: Fifty Years after the War in Asia*, London: Macmillan, 1996, p. 138.

24. See Amitav Acharya, 'Regional Military–Security Cooperation in the Third World: A Conceptual Analysis of the Relevance and Limitations of ASEAN (Association of Southeast Asian Nations)', *Journal of Peace Research*, 29 (1), 1992, pp. 13–14.

25. J. Soedjati, 'ASEAN Regionalism and the Role of USA', *Indonesian Quarterly*, 12 (1), January 1984, 64.

26. See Simon, *The ASEAN States and Regional Security*, pp. 91–2.

27. Muthiah Alagappa analyses the Thai perspective in 'Regionalism and the Quest for Security: ASEAN and the Cambodian Conflict', *Australian Journal of International Affairs*, 46 (2), Winter 1993, 196; also Muthiah Alagappa, *The National Security of Developing States: Lessons from Thailand*, Dover, MA: Auburn House, 1987, pp. 78–147.

28. Simon, 'The ASEAN States and Regional Security', pp. 98–99.

29. For a fuller exposition of ASEAN's 'coercive diplomacy', see Alagappa, 'Regionalism and the Quest for Security', p. 198.

30. See Sheldon Simon, *The Future of Asian-Pacific Collaboration*, Lexington, MA: D.C. Heath, 1988, p. 71.

31. For a comprehensive but succinct survey of ASEAN–US military links, see John Saravanamuttu, 'Militarization in ASEAN and the Option for Denuclearization in South-East Asia', *Interdisciplinary Peace Research*, 2 (1), 1990, 45–8.

32. Muthiah Alagappa, 'US–ASEAN Security Relations: Challenges and Prospects', *Contemporary Southeast Asia*, 11 (1), June 1989, 3.

33. Leszek Buszynsky, 'Declining Superpowers: The Impact on ASEAN', *Pacific Review*, 3 (3), 1990, p. 259.

34. Alagappa, 'US–ASEAN Security Relations', pp. 8–9.

35. For an analysis of these ambiguities, reflecting in large measure ASEAN's complex relationship with the United States on the one hand and China on the other, see Leszek Buszynsky, 'ASEAN: A Changing Regional Role', *Asian Survey*, XXVII (7), July 1987, 767–75.

36. Alagappa, 'Regionalism and the Quest for Security', p. 199.

37. Early signs of this strategy appeared in the Joint Communiqués of the 19th ASEAN Ministerial Meeting, Manila, 23–28 June 1986, and 20th ASEAN Ministerial Meeting, Singapore, 15–16 June 1987, in *ASEAN Documents Series 1967–1988*, pp. 135, 144.

38. Ibid., p. 201.
39. See Tim Huxley, 'ASEAN Security Co-operation – Past, Present and Future', in Alison Bronowski (ed), *ASEAN into the 1990s*, London: Macmillan, 1990, pp. 96–100.
40. See Leifer, *ASEAN and the Security of Southeast Asia*, pp. 122–41; also Dewi Fortuna Anwar, 'Twenty Five Years of ASEAN Political Cooperation', in Soesastro (ed), *ASEAN in a Changed Regional and International Political Economy*, pp. 123–6.
41. Mochtar Kusumaantmadja, Minister for Foreign Affairs of Indonesia, address to the PMC, Jakarta, 12 July 1984.
42. See Noordin Sopiee, 'ASEAN and Regional Security', in Mohamed Ayoob, *Regional Security in the Third World: Case Studies from Southeast Asia and the Middle East*, London: Croom Helm, 1986, pp. 223–5.
43. Russell H. Fifield, *National and Regional Interest in ASEAN*, Singapore: Institute of Southeast Asian Studies, Occasional Paper No. 57, 1979, pp. 50–51.
44. See Chong Li Choy, *Open Self-Reliant Regionalism: Power for ASEAN's Development*, Singapore: Institute of Southeast Asian Studies, 1981, pp. 79–80.
45. *The ASEAN Report*, Vol. II, Hong Kong: Dow Jones Publishing (Asia), 1979, p. 2.
46. Ibid., pp. 2–3.
47. See R.B. Suhartono, 'ASEAN Approach to Industrial Co-operation', *Indonesian Quarterly*, XIV (4), October 1986, 519–20.
48. See Srikanta Chatterjee, 'ASEAN Economic Co-operation in the 1980s and 1990s', in Bronowski (ed), *ASEAN into the 1990s*, p. 66.
49. For a review of the economic decisions taken at the Manila Summit, see Steven C.M. Wong, 'The Third ASEAN Summit: Retrospect and Prospects', prepared for Paul Leong Khee Seong, Chairman of the ASEAN Chamber of Commerce and Industry's Group of Fourteen Working Committee on ASEAN Economic Co-operation and Integration, Kuala Lumpur, ISIS, July 1988.
50. See *Japan and ASEAN*, Tokyo: Japan Ministry of Foreign Affairs, 1978, p. 8.
51. See speech by Prime Minister Kakuei Tanaka during his visit to the Philippines in January 1974 (*Japan Times*, 9 January 1974, p. 4).
52. *Japan 1988: An International Comparison*, Tokyo: Keizai Kōhō Center, 1988, p. 50.
53. See Joint Statement of the Meeting of the ASEAN Heads of Government and the Prime Minister of Japan, Kuala Lumpur, 7 August 1977, in *ASEAN Documents Series 1967–1988*, pp. 511–14.
54. *Japan Times*, 19 August 1977, p. 14.
55. The implications of Japanese rearmament for ASEAN are examined by B.A. Hamzah, 'ASEAN and the Remilitarization of Japan: Challenges or Opportunities?', *Indonesian Quarterly*, XIX (2), 1991, 141–68.
56. See Hideo Matsuzaka, 'Future of Japan–ASEAN Relations', *Asia Pacific Community*, 20 Summer 1983, p. 15.
57. See Joint Press Release of the Second ASEAN–Japan Economic Ministers Meeting, Tokyo, 28 June 1985, in http:www:asean.or.id/dialog/prmiti2.htm (sighted on 20 September 1996).
58. Detailed statistical information is provided in Sueo Sudo, *The Fukuda Doctrine and ASEAN: New Dimensions in Japanese Foreign Policy*, Singapore: Institute of Southeast Asian Studies, 1992, pp. 216–17.
59. Hamzah, 'ASEAN and the Remilitarization of Japan', p. 159.
60. See Keith A.J. Hay, 'ASEAN and the Shifting Tides of Economic Power at the End of the 1980s', *International Journal*, XLIV, Summer 1989, 655.
61. International Monetary Fund, *Direction of Trade Statistics Yearbook*, 1987 and 1988.
62. Joint Communiqué of the First ASEAN–US Dialogue, Manila, 8–10 September 1977, at http://www.asean.or.id/dialog/PRUS1.htm (sighted on 19 March 1996).
63. See William E. Tucker, 'ASEAN's Economic and Strategic Significance', *Asia Pacific Community*, 16, Spring 1982, 43–44.
64. See Pamela Takiora and Ingram Pryor, 'The Pacific Islands and ASEAN: Prospects for Inter-Regional Co-operation', *Indonesian Quarterly*, XVI (1), 48–71; Pushpa Thampbipillai, 'ASEAN and the Pacific Islands: Bilateral and Multilateral Relations', *Indonesian Quarterly*, XVI (1), January 1988, 73–83.

5. Multilateral responses to competitive interdependence

In *States, Markets and Civil Society* we drew attention to the multiple trends that characterized the 1970s and 1980s and eventually transformed the geopolitical and economic landscape of the Asia-Pacific region.[1] Among these, several merit particular attention: the end of the Soviet–American ideological and strategic confrontation, the relative failure of Soviet and US interventionism, most spectacularly in Afghanistan and Vietnam respectively, the fragmentation of the Soviet empire, the slower and less visible decline of US influence, the growing assertiveness of new powers, notably China and Japan, the primacy of economic growth as an objective of national policy, and the economic performance of the newly industrializing economies. All of these developments and their far-reaching implications have been the subject of extensive analysis. Yet, several questions remain unanswered.

The overarching question is clear enough: how are we to make sense of these seemingly unconnected and at time contradictory trends? To pose this question is to invite a number of other equally intriguing ones. What do these trends tell us about the evolving interaction of economy and security during this 20-year period, and, by inference at least, about the institutionalization of economic and security relations during the 1990s? How have these linkages influenced the evolution of the Asia-Pacific region, its self-definition, and the relationship between region and sub-region on the one hand and between region and the world system on the other? The very formulation of these questions suggests the need for a historical–structural approach.[2] Here the notion of historical structure is used to refer to patterns of activity that entrench over relatively long periods of time a distinctive conjunction of material interests, intersubjective meanings and institutional practices. Clearly the scale and intensity of change are likely to be much greater between than within historical structures. In this sense a threshold may be said to separate one historical structure from another. By threshold we simply mean that unique combination of influences, which significantly alters the previously dominant pattern of interaction or historical structure. Applying this analytical framework to our inquiry the question becomes: does the confluence of events from the early 1970s to the early 1990s constitute a 'threshold' in the evolution of the modern world system generally and of the Asia-Pacific subsystem in particular?

Expressed more pointedly, do the 1990s point to a new way of visualizing and occupying political space, a new normative framework, and presumably a new or substantially reconfigured set of institutions, rules and procedures?

The purpose of this and subsequent chapters is to address these questions. While drawing on a number of historical studies which trace the development of existing multilateral organizations or the establishment of new ones, the aim here is not to offer a historical account as conventionally understood. What follows is not a blow-by-blow description of various moves on the multilateral chessboard, but a thematic presentation which places the recent evolution of Asia-Pacific regionalism in the context of 'competitive interdependence'. In that sense the primary aim is not to elucidate the origins of this or that regional organization, or indeed to evaluate its performance. Much of the literature, it should be noted, even when it is not primarily descriptive, which it is for the most part, tends to concentrate on the perceived strengths and weaknesses of various forms of institutional innovation. Even the more theoretically informed contributions seem preoccupied with judgements on the likelihood or actuality of success or failure.[3] When it comes, for example, to APEC or the ASEAN Regional Forum (ARF), the object of study tends to be the long-term prospects for organizational survival, the extent of support available to each organization, its level of activity, its capacity to influence outcomes. These are no doubt relevant considerations but they do not go to the heart of our inquiry, which has to do with the evolution of Asia-Pacific regionalism. The aim here is to ascertain whether the organization of political space within the region has changed over time, and, if so, what the implications might be for economy and security.

STRUCTURAL CHANGE

The three main regional subsystems comprising Asia Pacific (Northeast Asia, Southeast Asia and Oceania) experienced significant change as a consequence of the removal of Cold War overlay. By the end of the 1980s, strategic and ideological bipolarity was no longer the ordering principle for the organization of geopolitical space in Oceania; it was barely visible in Southeast Asia and of diminishing importance on the Korean peninsula and in Soviet–Japanese relations. Downward adjustments in US security commitments and the partial retrenchment of US forces deployed in the Asian rimlands formed part of the general readjustment in the regional constellation of power. The steadily improving US–Soviet relationship from 1985 onwards would coincide with the disintegration, loosening or at least transformation of a great many alliance arrangements, in particular USSR–Vietnam, USSR–North Korea, US–Philippines, US–New Zealand and US–South Korea. Partially offsetting the reduction of US troop levels and the closure of military bases in the Philippines was the bilateral agreement for the expanded use of Singaporean military facilities by US forces. Equally significant were the new burden-sharing arrangements between Japan and the United States governing the continuing deployment of US forces in Japan. The vast nuclear as well as conventional forward projection capability at the disposal of the United States coupled with widespread regional acceptance of the stabilizing value of its military presence reinforced the view that the region and the world system more generally had entered a 'unipolar moment'.

The removal of Cold War overlay did not mean an end to the many conflicts that had punctuated the Cold War period, notably the longstanding conflict between Japan and the Soviet Union, the unresolved Taiwan dispute, and the division of Korea. In any case a number of conflicts could not be attributed solely or even primarily to the imperatives of geopolitical bipolarity. Ball's often quoted list of 'sovereignty, legitimacy and territorial conflicts in East Asia' pointed to some 25 conflicts, including competing Russian and Japanese claims to the Kurile Islands, the Sino–Japanese dispute over the Senkaku (Diaoyutai) Islands, competing claims to the Paracel and Spratly Islands in the South China Sea, border disputes between China and Vietnam and Vietnam and Cambodia, and secessionist conflicts in Indonesia and Papua New Guinea.[4] There is no denying, however, that as Cold War rivalries subsided a psychological climate emerged far more conducive to the attenuation of local and regional tensions. Indicative of the new mood was the Soviet–American declaration issued in August 1990 in Irkutsk in which both Washington and Moscow acknowledged that they no longer considered each other adversaries in Asia Pacific.[5] The withdrawal of military forces, especially from Afghanistan and the Philippines, the gradual resolution of regional conflicts, for example in Cambodia, the partial demilitarization of borders, and the growing impetus for nuclear disarmament (establishment of nuclear weapons-free zones) were different manifestations of the same phenomenon. The normalization of Sino–Soviet/Russian relations, the gradual easing of tensions between Tokyo and Moscow, and the development of a continuing inter-Korean dialogue were other important features of the emerging landscape.[6]

Economic trends were equally complex and contradictory. At one level there were clear indications of a decline in US hegemonic power. After the mid-1980s the United States turned into a net debtor country, and by the early 1990s became the world's largest debtor. Persistent trade deficits with Japan and the East Asian newly industrializing economies and fierce trade wars with the European Community, especially in the agricultural sector but also in a number of manufacturing industries, suggested that the United States no longer exercised its former dominance in world trade. Increasing competition from its principal trading rivals had forced the United States to impose non-tariff barriers against a rising proportion of its imports. It is not that the United States had lost its status as the world's largest economy, but that the gap separating it from other economies was narrowing. Between 1965 and 1990, Japan's industrial production increased fivefold whereas it merely doubled in the United States. During the same period Japanese gross national expenditure rose from $90.8 billion to $2,961.0 billion. The corresponding figures for the United States were $705.8 billion (1965) and $1,512.5 billion (1990).[7] In 1992, Japan accounted for close to 39 per cent of total capital flows to Asian developing economies, whereas the corresponding figure for the United States was just under 20 per cent.[8]

Complementing Japan's rise as a centre of economic power was the emergence of a more productive and assertive semi-periphery in East Asia. One of the defining characteristics of East Asian industrialization was three-dimensional growth: increase in the export of manufactures, increasing ratio of manufacturing exports to total merchandise exports, and growth of the manufacturing sector as a proportion of GDP.[9] Taken together these two trends pointed to a significant shift in the structure of the world system, namely the diffusion of wealth and power within the core and the partial redistribution of economic benefits from core to semi-periphery. It should be stressed, however, that hegemonic decline was at best partial or relative. The US market continued to absorb the largest share of East Asian exports, and in that sense served as the primary locomotive of East Asian industrialization. In any case, beginning in the latter half of the 1980s the United States embarked on a series of financial, trade and technological countermeasures aimed at applying maximum pressure on trading partners and reasserting US economic leverage, both regionally and globally.

Notions of declining or emerging hegemony must be handled with care to avoid two distinct but closely connected pitfalls. First, hegemonic control cannot be equated with the agency or power of the state. Integral to any notion of economic hegemony in the era of advanced capitalism is the role of capital itself, since it is the decisions of private industrial, commercial and financial interests, at least as much as the decisions of states, which collectively structure the framework of international competition and the distribution of global economic power. Not surprisingly, it is largely business interests, reflected in and supported by academic advocacy and bureaucratic practice, which, beginning in the late 1970s, helped to establish the neo-liberal agenda as the foundation stone of economic policy. Though the pace and modalities of economic liberalization would vary from country to country, Australia, New Zealand, Canada, Indonesia, Thailand and other Southeast Asian economies were increasingly subjected to the strictures of trade liberalization and financial deregulation. The progressive lowering of tariff and non-tariff barriers to imports, the loosening of foreign exchange and investment controls, and more generally the reduced role of the state in the management of the national economy pointed to the increasing dynamism and mobility of transnational capital, especially American and Japanese capital, but also to the intensely competitive environment within which corporate strategies had to be formulated and executed.

The second factor qualifying the nature and functioning of hegemony was the increasing interpenetration, not to say integration, of national economies. Regionalization, as we have already noted in Chapter 3, was one obvious manifestation of this trend. Intra-Pacific trade as a proportion of total trade had risen from 56.9 per cent in 1980 to 68.5 per cent in 1989.[10] In monetary terms it had grown from $60.9 billion in 1970 to $939.3 billion in 1990.[11] Contributing to this trend was the relocation of manufacturing capacity from Northeast Asia to Southeast Asia (and later China), the increasing flow of East Asian exports to the United States, and the rapid expansion of FDI flows to Southeast Asia first from Japan and then South Korea and Taiwan. It is also worth noting that by 1990 the cumulative flow of Japanese investments to the United States stood at $130.5 billion.[12] In other words, the relatively simple notion of a US-centred North American trading bloc locked in fierce competition with a West European bloc and a Japan-centred East Asian bloc was but one element of a multifaceted reality. It was not just that an intricate web of interconnections had ensured the interdependence of the three blocs, but that the United States – US capital as well as the American state – was a core player in both the North American and Pacific regions.

The ambiguous role of the United States in Asia Pacific is central to the thesis we wish to advance and will be the subject of subsequent examination. For the moment suffice it to say that economic globalization and the collapse of strategic bipolarity ushered in a global geopolitical system that was unipolar in structure but was developing multipolar characteristics and a global geoeconomic system that was essentially multipolar but retained important elements of US hegemony. To put it simply, three contradictory yet complementary tendencies were shaping the evolution of the global political economy:

- *Residual US hegemony.* Despite the relative decline of its power, at least when measured in economic terms, the United States was nevertheless able, in part by relying on its formidable military and institutional capabilities, to maintain its ascendancy, although hegemonic control was more subtle, more vulnerable to resistance, and less statist or predictable than in the past.

- *Increasing interdependence.* The interpenetration of national economies and globalization of markets had made it necessary for states to pursue shared or complementary interests and to subject bilateral and multilateral arrangements to periodic review and renegotiation.

- *Intensifying competition.* Neither economic interdependence nor residual hegemony could ensure the harmonization of interests. On the contrary, competitiveness was the defining principle giving shape and content as much to corporate strategies as to state policies.[13]

To summarize, the late 1980s had ushered in a transitional period during which each of these three tendencies would uneasily coexist with but be unable to dominate the other two. Though a number of military alliances survived, primarily NATO in Europe and the security ties linking the United States with Japan, South Korea and Australia in Asia Pacific, these arrangements had neither the coherence nor cohesion of the Cold War years, and could no longer perform the same coordinating or stabilizing functions. As Chinese analysts would often observe in the early 1990s, the US–Soviet confrontation was no longer the fulcrum on which rested Asia-Pacific security.[14] Residual hegemony, increasing interdependence and intensifying competition would become the distinguishing hallmarks of the regional as much as global political economy, of the renewed impetus to multilateralism, regionally as much as globally.

It should be stressed, however, that the combination of unipolar and multipolar features characteristic of the world system was not uniformly replicated across the globe. Each region had its own distinctive history, geography and economy. In Asia Pacific rapid economic growth, unfolding in the context of a rapidly evolving international division of labour, was itself creating a new competitive dynamic both within and between national polities. Paradoxically, as we shall see, the vicissitudes of international trade were themselves a key factor propelling the new Asia-Pacific regionalism. The growing enthusiasm for, or at least diminishing resistance to, regional institutions was driven in part by the desire of some, not least the hegemon, to tear down the protectionist walls from behind which a number of East Asian economies had launched their export drives. For others, regional co-operation was a useful tool for solidifying the international push towards liberalization and weakening domestic opposition to it.

This overview of the structural conditions, which were to set the stage for the multilateral agenda of the late 1980s and early 1990s, would be incomplete without reference to another important trend, namely the economy/security nexus. It is precisely the interface between economic and geopolitical considerations that would provide much of the impetus for the discourse – and to a lesser extent the practice – of Asia-Pacific regionalism. Here we can do no more than identify a few key features of the nexus, though we shall have occasion to return to this theme in subsequent chapters.

As already indicated, economic growth in Asia Pacific necessarily involved a structural dynamic which thrived on competition for markets and resources at every level of organization both within and across national boundaries. China offers a striking example of the implications of this dynamic. As a consequence of China's modernization strategy significant parts of the Chinese economy were opened to the outside world, with foreign firms producing for the domestic market and Chinese firms making use of foreign capital, technology and managerial know-how to produce for the export market.[15] A number of local and provincial governments were now intent on developing extensive and sophisticated international transactions, exercising greater authority over economic policy, and retaining a greater share of the foreign exchange revenues derived from their internationally oriented economic activities.

There were three important dimensions to this trend which, individually and collectively, could not but influence the new regionalism. First, China's 'open door' policy was bound to strengthen the hand of the domestic constituency that supported the principles of trade and investment liberalization and participation in regional institutions committed to those principles. Secondly, the dynamic of rapid industrialization tended to produce losers as well as winners, with the former expressing their dissatisfaction through renewed advocacy of protectionist policies of one kind or another. In this sense, multilateral policies were likely to become entangled in the power play associated with economic and political fragmentation. Thirdly, the incorporation of the Chinese economy into the trading, productive and financial systems of the world economy was overseen by an authoritarian political system. Would such a system survive or would it eventually give way to more democratic arrangements? Whatever the outcome this would be a period of unpredictable flux which was bound to impact on China's external policies generally and more specifically on its commitment to regionalism. These three dimensions were to a greater or lesser extent applicable to developments in South Korea, Taiwan, Indonesia and other Southeast Asian countries.

The competitive dynamic underlying economic growth was also reflected in the emergence of a number of transnational security challenges. A detailed examination of these is outside the scope of this chapter, but a few observations will help to clarify the implications for multilateral discourse and practice.[16] Not surprisingly, economic competition accentuated the scramble for resources and strategic advantage, a trend to which the establishment of exclusive economic zones (EEZs) had given added impetus. The conflict surrounding the Spratly Islands was one manifestation of this trend. Though the dispute was a multifaceted one, important economic interests were at stake, notably access to potential offshore oil and natural gas deposits. Similar considerations underpinned competing claims to the Paracel Islands. It would not be an overstatement to suggest that tensions in the South China Sea were to a considerable degree driven by uncertainty over future energy supplies.[17] High rates of GNP growth inevitably meant rapidly rising energy demand. China's total energy consumption more than doubled in the space of 15 years, rising from 603 million tons of coal equivalent (mtce) in 1980 to 1290 mtce in 1995.[18] Indeed, by the early 1990s the region's actual and projected energy requirements greatly exceeded its reserves.[19] Regional production in 1995 could supply only 43 per cent of energy needs, and the proportion was expected to fall to 29 per cent by 2015.[20] Higher levels of energy sufficiency or arrangements able to deliver reliable access to energy supplies at relatively stable prices were now seen as central as much to security as to economic policy.[21]

Attempts by China and other regional powers, including several ASEAN states, to develop their naval capabilities, especially from the late 1980s onwards, were closely related to competing claims for disputed islands and to the wider strategic objective of ensuring access to energy supplies as well as to the transport networks needed to deliver them.[22] Protecting exclusive economic zones and maritime resources was another closely related objective, with the added complication that all Southeast Asian states had lodged overlapping claims with respect to their 200-mile EEZs. Given that 12 of the 15 maritime boundaries in the South China Sea were in dispute, naval expansion was seen by most claimants as necessary to lend added weight to their respective claims. Substantial GNP growth had thus provided many of these governments with the incentive but also the means to strengthen their external defence. Such an enhanced military posture was also portrayed as a prudent response to the mounting challenge posed by piracy,[23] refugee flows and the drug trade.[24]

Though there is no simple or automatic connection between the competitive dynamic of economic growth and that of military procurement and deployment, the 1985–95 period indicates a distinct trend towards increased military spending. In their analysis of defence expenditures in Indonesia, Malaysia, South Korea, Singapore, Thailand and the Philippines, Looney and Frederiksen have shown that, despite national variations, the rise in GNP was in almost every case accompanied by higher military budgets.[25] Between 1982 and 1991 Japan, South Korea, Taiwan, Singapore and Thailand registered increases in defence spending of between 34 per cent and 100 per cent in real terms.[26] Between 1985 and 1996, defence budgets increased in real terms by $2.3 billion in Singapore, $1.67 billion in Thailand, $1.4 billion in Indonesia and $1.1 billion in Malaysia. Arms transfers to East Asia as a proportion of the world total rose from 11.9 per cent in 1987 to 23 per cent in 1996.[27]

Beginning in the mid-1980s a number of Southeast Asian countries embarked upon naval modernization programmes, including acquisition of fast-attack craft and frigates, and Harpoon or Exocet anti-ship missiles.[28] A comparable trend was evident in the modernization of air forces, with most ASEAN countries placing orders for an array of advanced fighter/strike aircraft.[29] No doubt a great many factors had contributed to the arms build-up, including latent or overt tensions between neighbours (often in the context of territorial disputes), apprehension about China's future regional role, and the anticipated contraction of the US military presence. The fact remains, however, that East Asian governments perceived the strategic environment and defined their military priorities in part as a function of their economic policies and circumstances.

One other element in the linkage between economic policy and military capability merits particular attention. With the growth in economic and technological capabilities and the end of the Cold War, horizontal nuclear and missile proliferation acquired added impetus. The diffusion of nuclear technologies, even where there was no covert design for military diversion, created capabilities which might in time provoke temptations on the part of domestic elites and apprehensions on the part of neighbouring states. Though attention centred largely on North Korea's military ambitions, several other countries, notably South Korea, Taiwan and Japan, had the capability to go nuclear, and could in certain circumstances develop the incentive to go down that path. In any case the dynamic of horizontal proliferation depends not so much on the acquisition by one or more states of a sizeable nuclear or missile capability as on the perception that a potential adversary could at relatively short notice embark on such a path. The anticipated growth of research and commercial nuclear capabilities in the region tended to encourage this dynamic of nuclear ambiguity. The anxieties generated by the shipment of large quantities of plutonium from Europe to Japan and the latter's acquisition of a sophisticated delivery system (for example, H-2 rocket) stemmed precisely from such perceptions.[30]

It remains to say a word about the environmental impact of economic policy, for it too has widespread security implications. There is now a considerable body of literature, including official documentation, detailing the extent of environmental degradation in East Asia, and the mechanisms that constitute the economy–environment nexus.[31] Commercial logging and land clearance for agriculture have produced high levels of deforestation throughout the region. Annual rates of deforestation in Southeast Asia are said to have risen from 1.4 per cent in the 1980s to 1.8 per cent in the 1990s. Deforestation has in turn contributed to soil erosion, siltation and land degradation. Poor irrigation practices have led to soil salinity and water logging. The rapid growth in energy consumption has resulted in high levels of air pollution, hence the increased incidence of chronic health problems, notably respiratory disease. In addition to the long-term climatic impact of rising carbon emissions, economic activity in much of Southeast Asia has resulted in substantial water pollution and the progressive depletion of fresh water supplies.

Though the medium to long-term effects of environmental degradation do not easily lend themselves to definitive assessment, the available evidence pointed to a number of troublesome conclusions:

1. The pattern of agricultural and industrial development prevailing in many parts of East Asia was not ecologically sustainable.
2. Attempts by newly industrializing countries to maximize the international competitiveness of their products tended to militate against the adoption of a more effective environmental regime.
3. Increasingly environmental effects were transnational in scope as a result of high and rising levels of air and water pollution and the off-shore relocation of hazardous wastes and polluting industries.[32]
4. More effective environmental regulation might not be possible without acceptance of common standards and the establishment of regional and

international procedures and institutions capable of monitoring and enforcing such standards.

5. Failure to develop such a regime could give rise to heightened political tensions or even strategic rivalries.

The profile we have just sketched of the security challenges facing Asia Pacific in the early 1990s is neither detailed nor comprehensive. The wider security agenda now included a range of other issues, including ethnic conflicts of various kinds, complex and often highly contentious unregulated population movements, actual or potential food shortages, money laundering, people smuggling and other transnational criminal activities, terrorism and the AIDS pandemic. In any case, the widening security agenda was not purely the product of East Asian rapid industrialization. Many of the problems alluded to impinged directly or indirectly on the less-developed countries, including Vietnam, Cambodia, Laos and the Pacific island states as well as on the developed world, not least Japan, Australia, New Zealand and Canada. Enough has been said, however, to indicate why the economy–security nexus would have far-reaching ramifications for regional multilateralism. The new, often elusive, and invariably complex linkages between economy and security contributed much to the mood of uncertainty that soon enveloped the post-Cold War period. Could these linkages be managed in ways that preserved the fruits of economic development, yet without provoking conflicts likely to endanger internal or external security? Could adaptive responses to the new security challenges facing the region be developed within the framework of existing national, regional and global institutions? The magnitude and urgency of these questions could not escape the notice of epistemic and policy-making communities. Increasingly, though unevenly, efforts were made to come to terms with the conceptual and practical difficulties posed by the notion of 'extended security'.[33] To the extent that altered economic, political and strategic conditions on the one hand and a wider conception of security on the other were encouraging greater interest in institutional innovation, even those states most resistant to change were under mounting pressure at least to react to the proposals and initiatives of others.

By the late 1980s the idea that new forms of regional as much as global cooperation were needed to contain the structural instabilities generated by the end of the Cold War and economic globalization was rapidly gaining ground.[34] Relaxation of tensions on the one hand and new uncertainties on the other were combining to create a multilateral window of opportunity. This is not to say that the contours of a new co-operative order were easily discernible, or that new forms of collective management could be easily devised to accommodate an expanded and more diverse core as well as an ascending semi-periphery. The complex and contradictory tendencies we have identified were likely to push simultaneously towards co-operation and competition. Even those that were amenable to the idea of a new regionalism did not necessarily share a common agenda, nor could their diverse strategies and proposals be easily synchronized. Nevertheless the introduction of such concepts as *common security*, *co-operative security*, *economic security*, and even *comprehensive security* and increasing usage of such notions as *economic interdependence*, *dialogue*, *multilateralization* and *open regionalism* were indicative of the new intellectual climate.[35] The emerging discourse, though tentative and at times incoherent, pointed to new possibilities and provided new yardsticks by which to assess the future evolution of regional diplomacy.

AGENCY AND INSTITUTIONAL INNOVATION

It is one thing to say that the altered structural conditions outlined in the preceding section were conducive to institutional innovation, but quite another to specify the form and direction which such innovation might take and its implications for the emerging regional and global order. This more specific characterization of trends as they unfolded in the 1990s has to be located at the interface between structure and agency. Knowledge of structure may be compared to knowledge of rail tracks – necessary but insufficient knowledge if the aim is to ascertain which trains are travelling, or might travel, along which tracks and the length and duration of their journeys. For this purpose additional knowledge is needed about agency, which, to complete the metaphor, one might associate with the availability and quality of train drivers, and the instructions under which they are driving. The analogy cannot, of course, be taken too far since structure and agency are intimately interconnected and in the end mutually constitutive. Our purpose in this section is to identify agents of institutional change and in the process to situate them, their interests and actions in the context of structural constraints and opportunities.

The initiation of change, especially if it assumes organizational form, may be considered a key feature of leadership. At first sight it may seem as if only one of the three types of leadership posited by Oran Young is relevant to our notion of agency, namely 'intellectual leadership'.[36] On closer inspection all three types, 'entrepreneurial' (negotiating skills) and 'structural' (bargaining leverage in negotiations) as well as 'intellectual' leadership (the generation of ideas governing international regimes), are integral to the notion of agency. Similarly, all three are inextricably linked with structural conditions since these to a greater or lesser extent influence the skills and the ideas as well as the bargaining leverage that can be brought to bear in negotiations. Young's typology of leadership is analytically useful in so far as it conveys something of the different capabilities needed for effective leadership. On the other hand, the typology is unnecessarily restrictive in that it assumes that those capabilities are vested only in individuals and deployed only in the context of negotiation.

In reality, as Rapkin rightly argues, collectivities have interests, capabilities and a dynamic of their own, which are not fully captured by the attitudinal and behavioural characteristics of the individuals acting in their name.[37] However, whereas Rapkin conceives of these collectivities purely in terms of states, there is no reason why the attributes of leadership should not also be invested in a range of non-state actors. Moreover, leadership may involve any number of instruments (aid, trade, investment, sanctions, use of force) and settings (advocacy, adjudication, protest), which the overriding focus on negotiation may understate or even obscure. Leadership may also be exercised simply by virtue of the legitimacy enjoyed by the leader (be it individual or collectivity), by the high esteem in which the leader's values, norms, traditions and policies are held by others.[38]

Using this brief conceptualization as a backdrop, we can now depict a little more clearly the role of agency in the development of new regional organizations. In this and the next chapter the focus is on APEC and the ARF since these were the two major initiatives in Asia-Pacific regionalism during the 1990s. Other regional projects, both old and new, will be considered in Chapters 7 and 8. As already indicated, the idea of a 'Pacific Basin Community' was not the invention of the 1990s. It had been in gestation since the 1960s, although its leading exponents were business and epistemic communities rather than states. In Chapter 3 we saw that a number of non-governmental organizations, in particular the Pacific Basin Council (PBC), the Pacific Trade and Development Conference (PAFTAD) and the Pacific Economic Co-operation Council (PECC) had played an important part in formulating and promoting the idea. A number of academic institutions' think-tanks and research centres, notably the Australian National University, the Japan Economic Research Center, the East–West Center in Hawaii, the Asiatic Research Centre at Korea University, the Korea Development Institute, the Centre for Strategic and International Studies in Jakarta and the Institute of Strategic and International Studies in Kuala Lumpur, all in varying degrees and at different times performed a crucial facilitating, ideas-generating and legitimating role.[39]

Given overlapping membership and reciprocal representation on their governing bodies, these organizations mirrored and reinforced personal networks among the elites, which tended to 'facilitate cross-cultural co-operation, and help develop a convergence of ideas and understandings'.[40] The general consensus is that PECC, by virtue of its analysis and research capacity and comprehensive membership, bringing together as it did academia, government and business and representing virtually all of the region's economies, had become 'the most significant institutionalized expression of the concept of Pacific economic cooperation'.[41] PECC is widely credited with having provided the discursive and analytical framework which paved the way for the establishment of APEC and smoothed the path for its subsequent development. According to Elek, a leading Australian participant in the process:

What you will not easily find on the record is the many conversations which took place in the informal PECC/PAFTAD networks about what the Hawke initiative meant and how to make it work. Almost everywhere we went with Mr Woolcott, the PECC networks proved important.[42]

There is, in other words, a good deal to support Higgott's view that the organizational networks, which had PECC at their apex, constituted an influential epistemic community. They were able to mobilize governments to support the principle of Pacific economic co-operation in part by offering a compass which could help them navigate through the turbulence and uncertainty of the period.

These were in fact policy networks in the sense that they shared a common set of normative beliefs and professional judgements, 'an internalized and self-validating set of causal and methodological principles', a common policy project and an acknowledged research and analytical capability.[43] The argument here is that ideas found themselves in the policy process and became institutionalized not by accident but as a result of careful nurturing through formal and informal channels of communication and a sustained and legitimated process of interaction.[44] There was more, however, to the 'policy project' than 'regional economic cooperation'. What drove the multilateral project forward was not simply the general notion of interdependence or a conviction about the merits of greater consultation and coordination, but a common vocabulary and value system aptly described by Higgott as a blend of 'positivism, methodological individualism, and free trade economics'.[45] To be more specific, the policy network, which gave birth to APEC, was wedded to neo-liberal principles of economic growth and to trade and investment liberalization. Expressed a little differently, regional co-operation was seen as dependent on the establishment of institutions which recognized and enshrined the free play of market forces. In this important respect the private sector may be said to have been the engine of Asia-Pacific economic integration, even though academics or technical experts had the task of articulating the policies to be pursued, and governments that of translating those policies into concrete diplomatic, organizational and legal arrangements.

What emerges from the above discussion is that the state, though it remains the pre-eminent actor in Asia Pacific as elsewhere when it comes to legalizing and bureaucratizing institutional innovation, is not necessarily the primary architect of the institutional edifice. The argument needs to be further qualified or at least refined since the analysis thus far has focused on the economic dimension of regionalism. We might expect the state to play a more assertive role when it comes to security issues, although even here, as we shall see, the state's freedom of action may not be as great as is sometimes assumed. In the account that follows the spotlight is very much on the state, but the state understood not simply as an actor in its own right but as the arena within which a great many other actors – some operating within civil society and others in the marketplace, some occupying national, others international or transnational space – compete and co-operate.[46]

We begin this part of the analysis by examining the role of the major powers, the United States, China and Japan, before turning to the middle powers, in particular Australia and ASEAN. As has been well documented elsewhere, the United States was generally sceptical of the case for institutional innovation. As the dominant power in the region it could see little merit in any new organization which might erode its strategic and especially naval supremacy, and weaken or delegitimize its existing security arrangements. The view in Washington, under Reagan and in the early years of the Bush administration, was that a US-centred unipolar security system offered the best prospects for defending strategic interests, including protection of sea lanes, and securing access to markets and resources.[47] Yet, by the early 1990s a gradual but discernible shift was under way. Secretary of State James Baker enunciated three pillars around which a new Asia-Pacific architecture might be based: a framework for economic integration, a commitment to democratization and a renewed defence structure for the region.[48] More forthright support for the establishment of 'new mechanisms to manage or prevent emerging regional problems' had to await the advent of the Clinton administration.[49]

By contrast, the notion of some form of regional economic co-operation was favourably received at a much earlier stage. Washington, it is true, was not in the vanguard of those moving towards APEC's formation. By the same token the Reagan administration was giving thought to the institutionalization of economic relationships between East Asia and the United States as early as the summer of 1988. Australian Prime Minister Bob Hawke's speech in Seoul on 31 January 1989 and its apparent exclusion of the United States from the proposed new body proved something of a catalyst. By mid-1989 it was clear that Washington would be one of the participants in APEC's inaugural ministerial meeting in Canberra in November of that year.

What, then, might we conclude of the US role in the evolution of the new Asia-Pacific regionalism? Though not a prime mover, the United States could not indefinitely ignore the proposals and initiatives emanating from several other governments, not least those of its allies, in particular Canada, Australia and Japan. Simply put, a concerted multilateralist push materialized more quickly on the economic than the security front, and the United States had to respond accordingly. In any case, economic institutionalization had been under active consideration for more than two decades, whereas in the security arena sustained advocacy, at least among US allies, did not predate the end of the Cold War. There were, however, several more complex factors contributing to Washington's reassessment of its options. On balance the United States was more favourably disposed to economic than to security coordination for the simple reason that its relative position had weakened somewhat in the global economic arena, but no comparable weakening was discernible in the military arena. Moreover, a new regional economic institution might deliver to the United States what it had not thus far been able to achieve through bilateral pressure, namely enhanced access to East Asian markets. A 'Pacific partnership' was especially attractive if it could cement Japan's regional role while at the same time maintaining US primacy in the bilateral relationship with Japan. Nevertheless, given the dynamic unleashed by the decline of strategic and ideological bipolarity, the United States would sooner or later come to the realization that existing bilateral security arrangements were not enough to cope with the demands of increasing interdependence and the ongoing realignments of power.[50] A multilateral security forum might be necessary to incorporate China and Russia into a more durable and predictable regional order, and provide acceptable opportunities for more substantial Japanese involvement in regional affairs.

Like the United States but for quite different reasons, China too had shown little enthusiasm for regional multilateralism. It feared that participation in regional institutions might play into American hands. If the United States and its allies dominated such institutions, they could become a lever for the regional containment of Chinese power and influence.[51] An equally strong and related concern was the possibility that China's freedom of action with respect to Taiwan might be severely curtailed.[52] To put it simply, China was opposed to multilateralism constructed on unipolar foundations. In due course a number of factors would make it more amenable to multilateral dialogue. In the most immediate sense regional co-operation offered China the prospect of reducing its political isolation in the aftermath of Tiananmen. Important, however, as political considerations may have been, the decisive factor was economic. As indicated in Chapter 3 and in *States, Markets and Civil Society*, China's economic ties with the Asia-Pacific economies had grown substantially by the end of the 1980s. Economic modernization and more specifically the 'open-door policy', which had driven China's integration into the regional economy for more than a decade, led it in 1992 to accept the formula that provided for China's entry into APEC alongside Hong Kong and Taiwan.[53]

Beijing's changing attitude to multilateralism was also informed by the desire to play a more active role in regional affairs. Regional consultation and even coordination might offer China greater opportunities to establish its credentials as a new centre of power in the region, and do so in ways that would not fuel fears of an emerging Chinese threat. Yet, there was more to Beijing's change of heart than economic and security aspirations. A succession of statements and analyses by political leaders and experts alike suggest that by the early 1990s a significant shift had occurred in China's reading of the geopolitical and geoeconomic environment. Both the global and regional power configurations, it was argued, were moving steadily from unipolarity towards multipolarity. The United States was still the leading power in the region, but its influence was diminishing. It could no longer promote its economic, security and ideological priorities without at the same time taking into account the interests of other powers.[54] At the same time, Japan was actively adjusting its regional policies as part of a larger strategy of speeding up its transition from economic to political power. China, Japan, and in due course Russia and a greater ASEAN would together with the United States be the pillars of a new multipolar constellation. Not surprisingly, as of 1993 the Chinese Foreign Ministry let it be known that it was studying proposals for regional security co-operation and was willing to explore a common regional security mechanism.[55] Dialogues and consultations were now seen as meriting China's active involvement. A string of high-level endorsements of the idea followed in February–April 1994, paving the way for China's participation in the inaugural meeting of the ARF in July 1994.[56]

Of the three major regional powers, Japan made by far the most vigorous diplomatic efforts in support of APEC's and ARF's establishment. Yet, in each case a number of factors prevented it from assuming public or· decisive leadership. As noted in previous chapters and in *States, Markets and Civil Society*, Japan had been actively involved since the mid-1960s in advocacy of Pacific economic co-operation, but it was not until the 1980s that a number of strands in its foreign policy – internationalization, Asianization and nationalism – came together to produce a more clearly defined approach to regionalism. Initially, the focus had been on making PECC a viable and legitimate instrument of regional consultation. By 1988 the Ministry of International Trade and Industry (MITI) was ready, with the support of large business interests, to make a concerted push for a regional organization that would promote trade integration on the basis of consensual decision-making and 'openness to other nations'.[57] Although MITI could not press ahead with the desired vigour until mid-1989, primarily because of opposition from the small business lobby and the Ministry of Foreign Affairs (MOFA), it persisted with the refinement of its proposal in close consultation with Australian officials.[58]

When it came to security co-operation the Japanese government was initially less forthcoming, in part because of the cautiousness of MOFA, which was itself a reflection of Japan's reluctance to do anything that might rekindle regional anxieties about its future direction. Nevertheless, by 1991 the government was openly proclaiming the virtues of regional policy coordination on matters of security, including 'the reduction of tensions and creation of stability in such areas ... as the Korean Peninsula, Cambodia and the South China Sea'.[59] But on this occasion Japan was careful to distance itself from the Australian and Canadian proposals on the grounds that an institution akin to the Conference on Security and Co-operation in Europe (CSCE) was not well suited to Asian needs and circumstances.[60] In an address to the Diet in January 1991, Japanese Foreign Minister Nakayama Taro argued that expanded regional dialogue could best proceed through existing institutions, notably ASEAN, ASEAN PMC and APEC. In July 1991 Nakayama went further, and, in what came to be known as the Nakayama proposal, called for the creation of a security forum within the ASEAN PMC, and suggested that a Senior Officials Meeting be convened to consider options and report to a future meeting of the ASEAN PMC.[61] Once ASEAN endorsed the general idea, Prime Minister Kiichi Miyazawa reiterated in more forceful fashion the need for a new Asia-Pacific security organization in June 1992, and again in March 1993 through the enunciation of the 'Miyazawa Doctrine', which envisaged Russia's and China's participation in the proposed regional dialogue and security system.[62]

What considerations, then, had finally prompted Japan to embark on a sustained security initiative? While still preferring a bilateral framework for dealing with such issues as the Northern Territories dispute with Russia or the alliance with the United States, Japan could now see advantages in both *ad hoc* and more permanent multilateral mechanisms. Particularly appealing was the prospect of an institutional framework that could legitimize a more assertive Japanese role in regional diplomacy, while at the same time allaying Chinese, Southeast Asian and Australian anxieties. Conscious of the volatility – but also new opportunities – inherent in the post-Cold War environment, Japan was seeking to become a more independent actor by embedding its role in both established and emerging global and regional institutions. Japan was perhaps doing no more than catching up with other regional players, including such US allies as South Korea and Australia, which had already embarked upon a more independent diplomacy, or at least one less constrained by the rigidities of the Cold War era. Even if regional multilateralism did not appreciably enhance Japan's freedom of action, it could be reasonably expected to place additional constraints on Chinese and US unilateral action, which might otherwise prove highly damaging to Japanese economic or strategic interests.

By the late 1980s each of the three principal regional powers was willing, for different reasons and to different degrees, to entertain the development of new regional or sub-regional institutions. It was left, however, to small and middle powers, notably Australia and ASEAN, and to a lesser extent Canada, to exercise 'intellectual' and 'entrepreneurial' leadership by taking advantage of the more relaxed political and ideological climate. Though activated by different objectives, they sought to promote, through a range of proposals and initiatives, new or expanded co-operative arrangements, which might serve as a forum for negotiation, if not reconciliation, of conflicting regional interests. A separate but closely related concern, seldom articulated in public but none the less disquieting, was the need on the one hand to restrain the exercise of hegemonic power and on the other to minimize the likelihood of conflict between actual and potential hegemons. It is worth stressing in this context that many of the small and middle powers of the Asia-Pacific region felt increasingly vulnerable to developments in Europe and North America, especially in the economic arena. Steady progress in European integration, the expanding connections between Western and Eastern Europe coupled with the collapse of Soviet power, and the imminent establishment of a North American Free Trade Area pointed to the emergence of powerful trading blocs from which the countries of Asia Pacific might be excluded.[63]

It was the task of the Australian and ASEAN governments to offer a diagnosis of the predicament and, more importantly, institutional remedies, that would resonate with all relevant regional players. In Australia's case, though no concrete proposal would emerge until Hawke's Seoul speech in January 1989, interest in enhanced economic co-operation was of long standing in both official and unofficial circles. The path pursued by Australian diplomacy has been recounted in several studies and need not detain us here.[64] Suffice it to say that the Australian initiative was the product of complex but converging influences. Foremost among these was the Labor government's expectation that by subjecting Australia's financial and manufacturing sectors to international competition they would be better placed to take advantage of the dynamism of the East Asian economies. Another factor was Australia's frustration with the slow progress in the Uruguay Round negotiations, particularly with respect to agriculture. Fearing the possibility of an intensified trade war between the United States and Europe, the Hawke government hoped that an outward-looking Asia-Pacific grouping might help to reverse the trend. Having announced his intention to seek the attitudes of regional leaders to the creation of a 'more formal inter-governmental vehicle for regional co-operation', Hawke proceeded to mount a concerted diplomatic campaign, headed by the then Secretary of the Department of Foreign Affairs, Richard Woolcott. Priority was given to close coordination with Japan (working through both MITI and MOFA) and with ASEAN, in particular Indonesia. The primary aim was to secure agreement for an initial meeting in Canberra at ministerial level, with a clear focus on economic (and more specifically trade) as distinct from political issues. Though Australia favoured China's – as well as Hong Kong's and Taiwan's – participation, it was prepared to defer this sensitive issue to a later date.

For their part, the ASEAN countries had until recently questioned the value of a new regional grouping, with Malaysia perhaps the most sceptical among them. In July 1989 ASEAN collectively agreed to participate in the Australian-sponsored meeting, but at the same time expressed a number of caveats. It was concerned that any new regional organization should not overshadow but complement its own role and activities, that it should not lead to an exclusive trading arrangement, and that institutional innovation should be gradual and sensitive to the needs of developing economies.[65] Clearly, one of ASEAN's anxieties was that no actual or potential hegemon should come to dominate regional arrangements or derail the co-operative ethos it had painstakingly developed over the preceding two decades. The Australian government made it therefore one of its diplomatic priorities to gain ASEAN support, hence the importance attached to consultations with Jakarta, and to securing Suharto's personal endorsement of the proposal. Once ASEAN gave the green light, the major remaining hurdle had been overcome. Within ten months of Hawke's speech, the proposal was translated into a meeting of industry and foreign affairs ministers from 12 countries in Asia Pacific: the United States, Canada, Japan, South Korea, the six ASEAN states, Australia and New Zealand – an event widely regarded as one of the high points of Australia's multilateral diplomacy.

When it came to security co-operation, the Australian and ASEAN roles were partially reversed. In July 1990 Gareth Evans proposed the establishment of an institutional framework which might parallel the Conference on Security and Co-operation in Europe. It would address 'the apparently intractable security issues' in Asia and, like the CSCE, would comprise all the countries of the region and cut across ideological and strategic divisions imposed by the Cold War.[66] Though he took care to limit the scope of the proposal and obviate any inconsistency with existing alliance obligations, the response of the United States and, to a lesser extent, Japan was negative.[67] Even ASEAN governments took the view that it was preferable, at least initially, to develop the dialogue process at bilateral and sub-regional levels. The Australian proposal had widened the limits of academic and official debate and placed the notion of region-wide co-operative security higher on the regional agenda, but the initiative now lay elsewhere. As already indicated, Japan was instrumental in keeping the idea alive, in part through the Nakayama proposal, but by mid-1991 ASEAN had assumed primary responsibility for giving practical effect to the concept. Australia was prepared to let ASEAN make the running, with the emphasis now more on clarifying the conceptual underpinnings of dialogue than on offering institutional blueprints.

Over a period of two years, multiple and diverse currents would intersect and sufficiently overlap to produce a diplomatic agreement, though not necessarily a comprehensive meeting of minds. While the complex interconnection of factors, which contributed to the birth of the ASEAN Regional Forum (ARF), still awaits careful conceptualization, the sequence of key events is itself reasonably well documented. Central to the evolution of ASEAN's thinking was the role of the ASEAN Institutes of Strategic and International Studies (ASEAN-ISIS). The notion of a regional security forum was first broached by the ASEAN-ISIS directors at their fifth annual meeting in May 1990. A consensus, however, was not reached until their sixth annual meeting in Jakarta in early June 1991, which Satoh Yukioh, then Director of the Japanese Foreign Ministry's Information and Analysis Division, attended as guest speaker and observer. Important as this exchange between ASEAN and Japanese views would prove for the future course of events, there is reason to think that ASEAN-ISIS had already crystallized their thinking at an informal discussion immediately preceding the meeting. The ASEAN-ISIS Memorandum

No. 1, which emerged from that discussion, would form the basis of the declaration issued by the Jakarta meeting. It proposed the establishment of a regional security dialogue, which might take the form of an ASEAN PMC-initiated conference, and in which Russia, China and Vietnam would be invited to participate.[68] An ASEAN-sponsored conference held a few days later in Manila gave further impetus to the notion of an ASEAN-driven Asia-Pacific security dialogue.

ASEAN, however, was not yet ready to agree on a precise formula. The July AMM simply endorsed the broad principle. At the ASEAN PMC which immediately followed, the ASEAN countries showed little enthusiasm for the Nakayama proposal. The haste with which it had been presented was at odds with the ASEAN style, and threatened to preempt ASEAN's leading role. At their Singapore Summit in January 1992 ASEAN leaders had still not found an acceptable formula, but prodded by the Japanese initiative and a number of other developments, made it known that they were keen to see ASEAN PMC perform a more visible security role.[69] In July 1992, the ASEAN PMC issued the ASEAN Declaration on the South China Sea, which called for the peaceful settlement of disputes. In February 1993, ASEAN and Japan formally discussed the establishment of a new security forum, and in May of the same year ASEAN convened a consultative conference at deputy-ministerial level to flesh out the proposal. At their meeting in July 1993 the ASEAN foreign ministers endorsed the recommendation of a Senior Officials Meeting that China, Laos, Papua New Guinea, Russia and Vietnam be invited to join ASEAN and its dialogue partners within the framework of the 'ASEAN Regional Forum' to be convened in Bangkok in July 1994.[70]

The decision to create the ARF was the product of both converging and diverging interests. By mid-1993 the need for a security dialogue mechanism was widely accepted by small and great powers, theorists and practitioners alike. It was also commonly thought that such a mechanism should be region-wide and tailored to the region's complex history and the diversity of its strategic and political cultures. But there was substantial disagreement, whether explicit or implicit, as to the kind of security that such a mechanism should promote, the functions it should perform, the principal threats it should address, the degree of institutionalization that should accompany it, and the pace at which it should develop. At one end of the spectrum were the minimalists, notably China and the United States, whose concern was that institutional innovation might, unless carefully managed, restrict their freedom of action as actual or potential hegemons. At the other end were the maximalists, in particular Canada and Australia, who were attracted by more highly developed models of institutionalization and favoured inclusiveness of membership and agenda. In general terms ASEAN may be said to have occupied the middle ground, preferring an incremental approach that emphasized confidence-building, and saw co-operation in dealing with non-military threats as a useful stepping stone to handling more contentious inter-state disputes. The 'soft security' agenda seemed, at least at first sight, less likely to offend regional sensitivities.

It would be an oversimplification, however, to suggest that agreement was eventually reached because a formula was found that represented a compromise between the minimalist and maximalist positions and that ASEAN was best placed to devise such a formula. Such a reading does not do justice to the ambiguities, not to say contradictions, in the evolutionary process that led to the ARF's formation, gave it its distinctive profile, and placed ASEAN in the driver's seat. First, it is worth repeating that by the early 1990s the idea of institutionalizing co-operative security had gained wide currency across Asia Pacific. Track-two and even track-three forums had played a critical role in developing, articulating and legitimizing the idea. The ASEAN Institutes of Strategic and International studies (ASEAN ISIS) were but the most visible, perhaps most authoritative, manifestations of a phenomenon that encompassed virtually the entire region. Whatever its misgivings, no government was now prepared to be portrayed as obstructionist. Once it was accepted that a forum of one kind or another would come to pass, all great powers saw participation as preferable to seclusion. For the United States the primary concern was to prevent any new arrangement which would curtail its strategic dominance; for China to ensure that it was not subjected to regional containment; for Japan to find new and acceptable ways of pursuing a more activist regional diplomacy.

Great power interests and perceptions had thus converged to create a permissive environment but not necessarily shared goals. It was left to ASEAN, with some prodding from Japan and to a lesser extent Australia and Canada, to take advantage of the new environment and devise an acceptable formula. ASEAN was well placed to perform this task because none of the three great powers saw ASEAN as posing a threat to their interests, and each had reason to think that it could wield sufficient influence with ASEAN to be able to veto any unwelcome proposal. But there was more to it than acceptability in the abstract. ASEAN had both the will and the capacity to seize the initiative: the will because it wished to preempt initiatives by others that might diminish its status as the leading player in Asia-Pacific multilateralism; the capacity because the dialogue framework and PMC in particular already constituted a medium which all participants could use to articulate and promote their security concerns.

A CONCLUDING NOTE

Widely diverging interests and perceptions had combined in the vastly altered circumstances of the late 1980s and early 1990s to produce two new regional organizations. Though in both instances agency of different kinds played a critical role, it was the particular conjuncture of trends that endowed agency with its potency and plausibility. With APEC as with the ARF, leadership did not come from either the United States or China, although Japan did conduct, in concert with Australia and ASEAN respectively, an activist diplomacy. Both Australia in relation to APEC and Japan in relation to the ARF discovered for different reasons that ASEAN was critical to the viability of their respective proposals. This is not to say that ASEAN could exercise a power of veto, but that any region-wide multilateral initiative would in considerable measure depend for its legitimacy on ASEAN support and participation. The low level of institutionalization in Northeast Asia made that dependence even greater, thereby making ASEAN virtually indispensable to post-Cold War regionalism in Asia Pacific. It became the pivot around which the competing priorities of the great powers could be balanced, at times negotiated, though seldom reconciled.

ASEAN's centrality in the new regionalism was as much an indication of its weakness as of its strength. While reference is often made to ASEAN as if it were a single actor, the fact remains that the organization rested on an uneasy compromise between conflicting tendencies. Some member states (for example, Indonesia) were preoccupied with the potential threat posed by China's rise to power; others (for example, Thailand) were attracted by the prospect of closer economic and political ties with Beijing. Some saw a strong US military presence as an essential prerequisite for regional stability (for example, Singapore); others (for example, Malaysia) were concerned to maintain a regional equilibrium but without departing too drastically from the ZOPFAN principle. Some (for example, Singapore) were strong advocates of trade liberalization and financial deregulation; for others (for example, Malaysia) such a policy direction, unless carefully managed, risked undermining the foundations of economic development. In other words, ASEAN was a microcosm of the diverse policy preferences competing for ascendancy in the Asia-Pacific region as a whole. If other regional players treated the prospect of ASEAN exercising a leadership role within the emerging regional architecture with relative equanimity, it was because they knew that ASEAN lacked a unified position on the most contentious issues, let alone the capacity to impose it on others.

Agency and structure had combined in the late 1980s and early 1990s to make possible a degree of institutional innovation. At face value, the confluence of interests and perceptions was indicative of a significant threshold in the evolution of Asia-Pacific regionalism. It was not at all clear, however, what this threshold signified for the future. One set of unanswered questions related to the direction that these new organizations would take: the interests they would represent; the policies they would pursue; the decision-making processes they would develop. A second set of questions had to do with the systemic influences, geopolitical, economic and cultural, bearing upon Asia-Pacific regionalism. How would APEC and the ARF handle the globalizing impact of economic and technological change on the one hand, and global issues, networks and institutions on the other? More specifically, how well equipped were they to handle the economic/security nexus, and how would they approach the transnational challenges to security? A third set of questions, closely related to the previous two, raised the difficult problem of regional identity. At face value, both APEC and the ARF were, by virtue of membership and agenda, Pacific institutions. Yet, a number of actors were still committed to, or at least prepared to entertain, a different kind of regionalism, one whose membership and ethos were explicitly Asian, or even East Asian. Had Asia Pacific won the day against Pacific Asia, or were APEC and the ARF but the first move in a game that had barely begun? Were these two geographically distinct expressions of regionalism mutually exclusive? Or, might Asia Pacific and Pacific Asia be conceived as constructing two regional tracks, running parallel to each other, at times performing complementary functions, but pursuing contradictory objectives and priorities? Were APEC and the ARF likely to entrench the unipolar features of the post-Cold War system, or were they an expression of a new plurality in international relations and the bearers of a 'new regionalism'? It is to these questions that the next two chapters will turn their attention.

NOTES

1.   Joseph A. Camilleri, *States, Markets and Civil Society in Asia Pacific: The Political Economy of the Asia-Pacific Region*, Vol. I, Cheltenham, UK: Edward Elgar, 2000, pp. 51–5.
2.   See R.W. Cox, 'Social Forces, States and World Orders: Beyond International Relations Theory', *Millennium: Journal of International Studies*, 10 (2), Summer 1981, 126–55.
3.   John Ravenhill's recent study of APEC is perhaps the most insightful to date, yet it too tends to fall into this category (John Ravenhill, *APEC and the Consequences of Pacific Rim Regionalism*, Cambridge, Cambridge University Press, 2001).
4.   Desmond Ball, 'Arms and Influence', *International Security*, 18, Winter 1993/1994, 88.
5.   See William Tow, 'Regional Order in Asia Pacific', in Ramesh Thakur and Carlyle A. Thayer (eds), *Reshaping Regional Relations: Asia-Pacific and the Former Soviet Union*, Boulder, CO: Westview Press, 1993, pp. 278–81.
6.   See Richard L. Grant, 'Security Cooperation in the Asia-Pacific Region: An Introduction', in Desmond Ball et al., *Security Cooperation in the Asia-Pacific Region*, Honolulu: Pacific Forum/Center for Strategic and International Studies (CSIS), 1993, pp. 2–4; also Mike M. Mochizuki, 'Japan as an Asia-Pacific Power', in Robert S. Ross (ed), *East Asia in Transition: Toward a New Regional Order*, Armonk, NY: M.E. Sharpe, 1995, pp. 142–4.
7.   See Philip J. Meeks, 'Japan and Global Economic Hegemony', in Tsuneo Akaha and Frank Langdon (eds), *Japan in the Posthegemonic World*, Boulder, CO: Lynne Rienner, 1993, pp. 48–58.
8.   *Geographical Distribution of Financial Flows to Developing Countries: Disbursements, Commitments, Economic Indicators 1989/1992*, Paris: Organization for Economic Cooperation and Development, 1994.
9.   The dynamic of export-oriented industrialization as it unfolded in East Asia is examined in Camilleri, *States, Markets and Civil Society in Asia Pacific*, pp. 83–106.
10.   Cited in Ravenhill, *APEC*, p. 73.
11.   These figures appear in Hadi Soesastro, 'Implications of the Post-Cold War Politico-Security Environment for the Pacific Economy', in C. Fred Bergsten and Marcus Noland (eds), *Pacific Dynamism and the International Economic System*, Washington, DC: Institute for International Economics, 1993, p. 382.
12.   Ibid., p. 383.
13.   These tendencies and their impact on the Asia-Pacific region are examined in Camilleri, *States, Markets and Civil Society in Asia Pacific*, pp. 148–239.

14. See, for example, Guo Zhenyuan, 'Changes in the Security Situation of the Asia-Pacific Region and Establishment of a Regional Security Mechanism', *Foreign Affairs Journal* (Beijing), 29, September 1993, 38–47.
15. See Harry Harding, *China at the Crossroads: Conservatism, Reform or Decay*, Adelphi Paper 275, March 1993, pp. 40–41.
16. The discussion which follows is based largely on the analysis offered in Joseph A. Camilleri, 'Asia-Pacific in the Post-Hegemonic World', in Andrew Mack and John Ravenhill (eds), *Pacific Cooperation: Building Economic and Security Regimes in the Asia-Pacific Region, Boulder*, CO: Westview Press, 1995, pp. 181–90.
17. China's interests in the South China Sea are analysed in Leszek Buszynky, 'ASEAN Security Dilemmas', *Survival*, 34 (4) Winter 1992–93, 91–2; also Esmond D. Smith, 'China's Aspirations in the Spratly Islands', *Contemporary Southeast Asia*, 16 (3), 1994, 275–94.
18. See *State of the Environment China 1997*, http://svr1-pek.unep.net/soechina/drivf/driv31.htm_(sighted 19 February 1999).
19. See Fereidun Fesharaki, 'Energy and the Asian Security Nexus', *Journal of International Affairs*, 53 (1), Fall 1999, 88–9.
20. These figures are cited in Alan Dupont, *East Asia Imperilled: Transnational Challenges to Security*, Cambridge: Cambridge University Press, 2001, p. 72.
21. See Mark Valencia, 'Energy and Insecurity in Asia', *Survival*, 39 (3), 1997, 85–106; also Daniel Yergin, Dennis Eklof and Jefferson Edwards, 'Fueling Asia's Recovery', *Foreign Affairs*, 77 (2), March–April 1998, 34–50; Robert A. Manning, 'The Asian Energy Predicament', *Survival*, 42 (3), 2000, 73–88.
22. Changing patterns of supply and transport are examined in Fesharaki, 'Energy and the Asian Security Nexus', pp. 90–92.
23. Piracy grew steadily in Southeast Asia from the late 1980s especially in the major straits considered critical to regional and world trade. See: 'Maritime Piracy: A Global Overview', *Jane's Intelligence Review*, 12 (8), August 2000, 47–50; 'Piracy in Southeast Asia', Center for Strategic Studies, *Strategic Briefing Papers*, Vol. 3, Part 2, June 2000.
24. For an illuminating account of the implications of refugee flows and the narcotics trade, see Dupont, *East Asia Imperilled*, pp. 135–72, 194–211.
25. Robert E. Looney and P.C. Frederiksen, 'The Economic Determinants of Military Expenditure in Selected East Asian Countries', *Contemporary Southeast Asia*, 11 (4), March 1990, 274.
26. *SIPRI Yearbook 1991: World Armaments and Disarmament*, Oxford: Oxford University Press, 1991, p. 171; *SIPRI Yearbook 1992*, p. 260.
27. These figures are cited in Alan Collins, 'Mitigating the Security Dilemma the ASEAN Way', *Pacifica Review: Peace, Security and Global Change*, 11 (2), June 1999, 99–100.
28. 'Southeast Asian Navies Modernise', *Pacific Research*, 4 (2), May 1991, p. 10.
29. The trend is examined in Andrew Mack, 'Reassurance versus Deterrence Strategies for the Asia-Pacific Region', Working Paper 103, Peace Research Centre, Australian National University, Canberra, 1991, pp. 2–3. For details of later acquisitions, see Amitav Acharya, 'An Arms Race in Southeast Asia?', in Derek da Cunha (ed), *The Evolving Pacific Power Structure*, Singapore: Institute of Southeast Asian Studies, 1996, pp. 83–4; also Julian Schofield, 'War and Punishment: The Implications of Arms Purchases in Maritime Southeast Asia', *Journal of Strategic Studies*, 21 (2), June 1998, 83–4.
30. See A. Manning, 'Building Community or Building Conflict: A Typology of Asian Security Challenges', in Robert Ralph A. Cossa (ed), *Asia Pacific Confidence and Security Building Measures*, Washington, DC: Center for Strategic and International Studies, 1995, pp. 30–32; see also Selig S. Harrison, *Japan's Nuclear Future: The Plutonium Debate and East Asian Security*, Washington, DC: Carnegie Endowment for International Peace, 1996.
31. See Lorraine Elliott, 'Environmental Challenges', in Daljit Singh and Anthony Smith (eds), *Southeast Asian Affairs 2001*, Singapore: Institute of Southeast Asian Studies, 2001, pp. 68–81; Asian Development Bank, *Asian Environmental Outlook 2001*, Manila: Asian Development Bank, 2000; Dupont, *East Asia Imperilled*, pp. 47–68.
32. For a discussion of the regional implications of transboundary pollution in Asia Pacific, see Ian Townsend-Gault et al., 'Transboundary Ocean and Atmospheric Pollution in Southeast Asia: Prospects for Regional Co-operation', in Amitav Acharya and Richard

Stubbs (eds), *New Challenges for ASEAN: Emerging Policy Issues*, Vancouver: University of British Columbia Press, 1995; also Sang-Gon Lee, 'Transboundary Pollution in the Yellow Sea', in H. Edward English and David Runnals (eds), *Environment and Development in the Pacific: Problems and Policy Options*, New York: Addison Wesley Longman in association with the Pacific Trade and Development Conference, 1998.

33. 'Extended security' is a term used by Alan Dupont to denote the interconnections between state-centric and transnational challenges to security. See Dupont, *East Asia Imperilled*, pp. 7–11.

34. The fear of 'instability' is clearly acknowledged as a motivating force in the development of institutionalized arrangements in Ellis S. Krauss, 'Japan, the US, and the Emergence of Multilateralism in Asia', *Pacific Review*, 13 (3), 2000, 486.

35. These notions were appearing with increasing regularity even in the writings of Chinese scholars and experts, who had traditionally asserted the primacy of the sovereignty principle and the virtues of bilateralism. See Ji Guoxing, 'The Multilateralisation of Pacific Asia: A Chinese Perspective', *Asian Defence Journal*, 7, 1994, 20–24; also Banning Garrett and Bonnie Glaser, 'Multilateral Security in the Asia-Pacific Region and its Impact on Chinese Interests: A View from Beijing', *Contemporary Southeast Asia*, 16 (1), June 1994, 14–34.

36. Oran R. Young, 'Political Leadership and Regime Formation: On the Development of Institutions in International Society', *International Organization*, 45 (3), Summer 1991, 281–308.

37. See David P. Rapkin, 'Leadership and Cooperative Institutions in the Asia-Pacific', in Mack and Ravenhill (eds), *Pacific Cooperation*, p. 107.

38. This notion of legitimized leadership is closely related to Terada's notion of 'directional leadership'. See Takashi Terada, 'Directional Leadership in Institution-Building: Japan's Approaches to ASEAN in the Establishment of PECC and APEC', *Pacific Review*, 14 (2), 2001, 196–7.

39. Some of the more prominent individuals in this process are mentioned in Stuart Harris, 'Policy Networks and Economic Cooperation: Policy Coordination in the Asia-Pacific Region', *Pacific Review*, 7 (4), 1994, 390.

40. See Harris, 'Policy Networks and Economic Cooperation', p. 384.

41. David Arase, 'Pacific Economic Cooperation: Problems and Prospects', *Pacific Review*, 1 (2), 1988, 128.

42. Interview conducted by Takashi Terada and cited by him in *The Genesis of APEC: Australian–Japan Political Initiatives*, Pacific Economic Papers, No. 298, Canberra: Australia–Japan Research Centre, December 1999, p. 42.

43. Richard Higgott, 'APEC – A Sceptical View', in Mack and Ravenhill (eds), *Pacific Cooperation*, p. 89.

44. In Higgott's terminology these intellectual and organizational linkages constituted a 'policy network'. See Richard Higgott, 'Ideas, Identity and Policy Coordination in the Asia Pacific', *Pacific Review*, 7 (4), 1994, 373.

45. Richard Higgott, 'Economic Cooperation: Theoretical Opportunities and Practical Constraints', *Pacific Review*, 6 (2), 1993, 113.

46. The complex relationship between the state on the one hand and civil society and economy on the other is examined at length in Camilleri, *States, Markets and Civil Society in Asia Pacific*, pp. 354–82.

47. As late as October 1990, Richard Solomon, US Assistant Secretary of State for East Asian and Pacific Affairs, rejected region-wide solutions to regional problems, and in particular 'a Helsinki-type institution as an appropriate forum for enhancing security or promoting conflict resolution', *Pacific Research*, February 1991, 20. In July 1991 he re-emphasized the value of existing alliance arrangements (*New York Times*, 25 July 1991, p. A14).

48. James A. Baker III, 'America in Asia: Emerging Architecture for a Pacific Community', *Foreign Affairs*, 70 (1) Winter 1991–92, 1–18.

49. See statement by Winston Lord, US Assistant Secretary of State for East Asia and the Pacific, 'Lord Lays Out 10 Goals for US Policy in Asia', *US Information Service Official Text*, 5 April 1993, p. 10.

50. It is not so much, as Manning and Stern have argued, that US economic and security muscle, 'the two traditional pillars of American predominance in Asia' were 'diminishing assets',

but that these assets now had to perform different functions in what was a radically altered economic and strategic environment. See Robert A. Manning and Paula Stern, 'The Myth of the Pacific Community', *Foreign Affairs*, 73 (6), November–December 1994, 85.

51. See Garrett and Glaser, 'Multilateral Security in the Asia-Pacific Region and its Impact on Chinese Interests', pp. 25–6.
52. Ibid., p. 27.
53. See Weixing Hu, 'China and Asian Regionalism: Challenge and Policy Choice', *Journal of Contemporary China*, 5 (11), 1996, 46.
54. Ji Guoxing, 'The Multilateralisation of Pacific Asia: A Chinese Perspective', *Asian Defence Journal*, 7, 1994, 21.
55. *Foreign Broadcast Information Service (FBIS), Daily Report: China*, 23 April 1993, p. 1.
56. See Li Peng's Report to the Eighth National People's Congress, 10 March 1994, *FBIS Daily Report: China*, 28 March 1994, p. 47.
57. For a detailed account of the proposals contained in the June 1988 MITI report and the efforts of Japanese diplomacy to resolve internal differences while at the same time anticipating regional concerns, see Krauss, 'Japan, the US, and the Emergence of Multilateralism in Asia', pp. 474–9; also Yoichi Funabashi, *Asia Pacific Fusion: Japan's Role in APEC*, Washington, DC: Institute for International Economics, 1995, pp. 58–61.
58. See Donald Crone, 'The Politics of Emerging Pacific Cooperation', *Pacific Affairs*, 65 (1), Spring 1992, 75.
59. *Diplomatic Bluebook 1991*, Tokyo: Ministry of Foreign Affairs, 1991, pp. 27–8.
60. Ibid., p. 70.
61. Ibid., pp. 463–71.
62. See Young Sun Song, 'Prospects for a new Asia-Pacific Multilateral Security Arrangement', *Korean Journal of Defense Analysis*, 5 (1), Summer 1993, 196–7; also Paul Mitford, 'Japan's Leadership Role in East Asian Security Multilateralism: The Nakayama Proposal and the Logic of Reassurance', *Pacific Review*, 13 (3), 2000, 382–88; Akiko Fukushima, 'Japan's Emerging View of Security Multilateralism in Asia', in IGCC Study commissioned for the Northeast Asia Cooperation Dialogue VIII, Moscow, 11–12 November 1998, pp. 29–30.
63. See Crone, 'The Politics of Emerging Pacific Cooperation', p. 73.
64. One of the most detailed accounts is offered by Terada, *The Genesis of APEC*. See also 'Australian Prime Minister's Regional Economic Cooperation Initiative', *Backgrounder*, 18–31 May 1989; Gareth Evans, 'Australia's Regional Economic Cooperation: An Idea whose Time Has Come', speech presented at the opening of the 12th Australia–ASEAN Forum, Perth, 15 May 1989; *The Hawke Memoirs*, Melbourne: William Heinemann, 1994, pp. 430–33.
65. *Far Eastern Economic Review*, 17 August 1989.
66. Address to the Institute for Contemporary Asian Studies, Monash University, 19 July 1990, in *Monthly Record*, July 1990, pp. 424–5.
67. See Pauline Kerr, Andrew Mack and Pauline Evans, 'The Evolving Security Discourse in the Asia-Pacific', in Mack and Ravenhill (eds), *Pacific Cooperation*, pp. 236–9.
68. This record of events is documented in Mitford, 'Japan's Leadership Role', pp. 379–80.
69. PMC's extensive membership (ASEAN, United States, Japan, Canada, Australia, New Zealand, South Korea, European Community), which was soon to be expanded, was a distinct advantage.
70. See Amitav Acharya, *Constructing a Security Community in Southeast Asia: ASEAN and the Problem of Regional Order*, London: Routledge, 2001, pp. 168–72.

6. Limits of the new regionalism

The analysis developed in the preceding chapter suggests that the emerging multilateralism in Asia Pacific derived a good deal of its impetus from the converging interests, perceptions and preferences of key actors. Convergence must not, however, be confused with identity. A great many tensions were still evident, some of them the legacy of the Cold War, others with even longer historical roots, and others still the inevitable product of the deep contradictions inherent in the twin processes of globalization and regionalization. One of the central arguments of this study is that divergence is no less critical than convergence to an understanding of the new multilateralism. It is the interaction of these two opposing yet complementary tendencies, which helps to illuminate the construction of particular organizations – in this chapter the spotlight falls on APEC and the ARF – and more importantly the deeper geopolitical and geoeconomic foundations on which all such construction ultimately depends.

APEC and to a lesser extent the ARF, despite their very brief histories, have already attracted considerable attention within both the academic and policy-making communities. Regrettably, much of the writing has sought either to extol the virtues of one or other organization or to cast a sceptical eye on its prospects of success. In the case of APEC, the more critical studies have drawn attention to the inconsistencies of the organizational model,[1] others to the conflicting negotiating cultures which it encompasses,[2] and others still to the flawed conceptualization which underpins its approach to trade liberalization.[3] More policy-oriented studies have viewed with alarm APEC's slow progress, and variously drawn attention to its lack of direction, inefficient organization or inadequate resource base.[4] While each of these studies is of interest to the student of regionalism in Asia Pacific, the subject of our inquiry is not so much the organization in itself, but what attempts at institutional innovation can tell us about the dynamics of regionalization, and more specifically about the evolution of the economic and security landscape. To this end, use will be made of the five categories outlined in the first chapter: membership, organization, functions, regime and architecture. In tailoring these categories to suit the needs of this chapter, 'membership' and 'organization' will help us to analyse the competing attempts to define region and regionalism in the Asia-Pacific context. The analysis of 'functions' will shed light on the implications of the economy–security nexus and the emerging transnational challenges. Under 'regime' we explore the three tendencies we identified in the preceding chapter, namely residual hegemony, interdependence and competition, to see how leadership has been exercised in the region, with particular emphasis on the fluctuating relationship between state and non-state actors and between the private and public domains. Finally, 'architecture' will permit us to examine the underlying regional design to which these two institutions conform, and the linkages envisaged or implied between the sub-regional, regional and global tiers of multilateral construction.

APEC: COMPETING INTERESTS AND CONCEPTIONS OF REGIONALISM

Reference has already been made to the hyperbole with which those most directly associated with APEC have sought to portray the rationale and accomplishments of the organization. An extreme but not altogether unrepresentative version of the genre was a report prepared for APEC trade ministers by the Australian Department of Foreign Affairs in 2000. Reviewing APEC's first ten years, the report described the path chosen by APEC economies as one of 'openness, integration, institutional reform and better governance and cooperation', and the Asian financial crisis as a 'major hiccup'.[5] APEC itself was said to have 'provided the framework, and the Bogor goals a reference point, for the economic opening that has been indispensable for growth'.[6] Another observer saw in 'the imprecision of APEC's objectives' the means whereby 'the organization can offer its members the opportunity to play an evolving, undefined but potentially significant role in shaping the regional and global economic order'.[7] Numerous other studies, many of them by enthusiastic APEC advocates,[8] are useful because they tell us something of the intellectual origins of policies advocated by a number of countries, for example Australia, but they do not leave the reader much the wiser about the actual dynamics of the APEC experiment. Expressed a little differently, they fail to provide the evolutionary perspective needed for the analysis of any regional institution, let alone one which emerged in a period of substantial economic and political flux.

APEC's relatively short history may be described in terms of a number of distinct phases, each of which is marked by the particular interaction of competing interests and priorities. Many have indeed argued that in its initial phase APEC was preoccupied with defining key principles and objectives. The APEC Ministerial Meeting in Canberra in November 1989 affirmed that Asia-Pacific economic co-operation should recognize the diversity of the region, involve a commitment to open dialogue and consensus, strive to strengthen the open multilateral trading system, and collaborate with other governmental and non-governmental organizations in the region.[9] This first phase has been aptly described as 'OECD-style economic cooperation', with the emphasis on consultative activity rather than negotiation of formal agreements.[10] A second phase was perhaps ushered in by the Seoul Ministerial Meeting in November

1991, which entrusted APEC with the task of reducing barriers to trade and services as well as investment among participating economies, though in a manner consistent with GATT principles and without detriment to other economies. The commitment to this objective would be further strengthened at the Seattle Leaders' Meeting in November 1993, which established the Committee on Trade and Investment (CTI) and explicitly embarked upon a programme of regional trade liberalization.[11] Notionally, at least, the 1994 Bogor Summit could be seen as the beginning of a third phase, specifically aimed at trade liberalization through negotiated agreements for the removal of both tariff and non-tariff barriers. Helpful though it is, such a periodization does not fully capture the contradictions integral to APEC's evolution. A more thematic periodization is offered below in the discussion of 'functions'.

Membership

The story of APEC's membership is a relatively simple one. Twelve countries participated at the inaugural meeting in Canberra: Australia, New Zealand, the United States, Canada, Japan, South Korea and the six ASEAN states, Brunei, Indonesia, Malaysia, the Philippines, Singapore and Thailand. Three new members were added in November 1991: the People's Republic of China, Hong Kong, and Chinese Taipei. The Seoul meeting also agreed that membership would be open to any economy within the region which had extensive economic linkages within the region, and accepted the objectives and principles of the Seoul Declaration. Decisions on future membership would be made on the basis of consensus among existing participants. Mexico and Papua New Guinea joined in 1993, and Chile in 1994. The November 1997 Ministerial Meeting agreed that Peru, Russia and Vietnam would take their places the following year, but went on to institute a ten-year moratorium on APEC's enlargement. Yet, even by then, the organization's membership was a curious assortment, bringing under the one roof some of the world's most advanced as well as most backward economies.

Two distinct but closely related questions immediately arise: what was the common purpose or common project that would provide the necessary glue to hold the organization together? What logic, if any, would govern APEC's geographical extension? A persuasive and viable answer to the first question would presumably require that the common endeavour, however defined, yield, or be expected to yield, sufficient gains to all its members and that the costs of membership be distributed in such a way that for each member the gains exceed the costs. True enough, the gains – and for that matter the costs – need not be quantitatively or qualitatively identical for all members. While APEC was first and foremost an organization committed to economic objectives, it is not inconceivable that for some members the gains might be more political than economic. For Vietnam, for example, and perhaps for Russia, the expected gains, at least in the short to medium term, were as likely to be political as economic. For Vietnam participation in APEC was part of a wider strategy aimed at ending its former isolation, whereas for Russia it was recognition of the legitimacy of its aspiration to be a Pacific power. It is, in other words, possible to construct for each APEC member a distinctive profile which might help to explain the underlying logic of its participation. Such an explanation, however, would at best tell us why prospective members wanted to join, not why the core members were prepared to admit them to the organization.

At its inception APEC's composition – six ASEAN and six non-ASEAN states – gave an impression of cohesion reinforced by the fact that all non-ASEAN members were also dialogue partners of the Association. Both symmetry and cohesion, perhaps more apparent than real, were, however, called into question with the admission of the three Chinese economies in 1991. Although members of PECC since 1986, none of the three was a dialogue partner at the time. Moreover, from ASEAN's perspective China was a direct competitor for both foreign investment and export of manufactured products. The case for China's inclusion was nevertheless a strong one, given the size of its economy, its rapidly expanding regional trade, and its subsequent membership of ASEAN PMC. It was difficult to conceive of any regional grouping, whether primarily economic or political in inspiration and irrespective of the criteria of geographical definition, from which China would be permanently excluded. Moreover, China could be expected to add its considerable weight to the concerns and priorities of developing economies, which might otherwise be ignored given the glaring disparity in institutional leverage between the ASEAN and non-ASEAN economies. These same arguments were likely to be much less persuasive when it came to the admission of Mexico, Papua New Guinea, Chile, Peru or Russia.

ASEAN's marginalization within APEC was bound to create misgivings at least among those ASEAN members which were committed to advancing the Association's strategic role in regional institution-building and perceived an expanded APEC as posing a threat to that ambition. Though this view is most closely associated with Mahathir's Malaysia, it was not, as we shall see later in this chapter and more clearly in the next, confined to the government of one relatively small country. It was not, in any case, merely a question of consolidating ASEAN interests and identity. A closely connected thread in this complex web of overlapping and intersecting perceptions was the sentiment, more widely shared than is often acknowledged, that it was Asia, or to be more exact East Asia or Pacific Asia, that should constitute the focus of regional integration. That sentiment was expressed and justified in different terms by different players in different settings, with the accent at times on economic considerations, and at others on political or cultural ones.[12] But the undercurrent which it created within APEC, though often hidden from view, was, as our analysis will show, never far below the surface. On the other hand, the dominant conception of APEC as an Asia-Pacific construction had the United States as its most powerful advocate, with Australia and Canada among its more eloquent exponents, which is not to say that such a conception did not also have the support of key elements of the Japanese and South Korean policy-making elites.

Organization

A brief examination of the organizational infrastructure which APEC developed in its formative years will convey a clearer sense of these competing strands of regionalism (see Figure 6.1). Support for APEC's establishment was based in part on the understanding that it would be endowed with only the most skeletal infrastructure. The Australian vision was of a loose framework where the main objective would be not to produce a single internal market and customs union as in the European model but to facilitate more effective consultation and policy coordination among member economies. There is reason to think that the Australian government may have chosen to trim its sails to suit the prevailing political wind. At the Seattle Summit in 1993, Chinese President Jiang Zemin described Beijing's policy in the following terms: 'APEC should be an open, flexible and pragmatic forum for economic cooperation and a consultation mechanism rather than a closed, institutionalized economic bloc'.[13] It is this widely shared preference for low-key institutionalization, especially among Asian members, which prompted the decision to make the ministerial meetings the centrepiece of the organization. These meetings, held once a year to approve a budget and set policy direction, were supported by the Senior Officials' Meetings, which convened four times a year and served as 'a board of directors for the Secretariat and the Working Groups'.[14] It was not until 1993 that *ad hoc* arrangements paved the way for the first standing policy committee, the CTI, followed in 1994 by the Economic Committee. In due course the two committees would be supported by ten working groups and a number of subcommittees and experts groups. In addition, the 1992 ministerial meeting resolved to establish a small secretariat in Singapore as a support mechanism to facilitate and coordinate APEC activities. Eight years later the secretariat still exercised negligible autonomy, commanded a strictly limited research capability, and comprised only 23 seconded professional staff from member economies, and a similar number of locally recruited support staff.[15] It took patient and at times difficult negotiation to achieve even this modest organizational structure.

Nowhere were the tensions between different institutional approaches more evident than in the 1992 decision to establish the Eminent Persons Group (EPG). Given the task of articulating a vision of trade in the Asia-Pacific region to the year 2000, the EPG presented its initial report to APEC ministers in October 1993. Despite the favourable chairmanship of the United States, the report received a 'restrained response' and the EPG had its mandate renewed only for

Figure 6.1 Organization of APEC

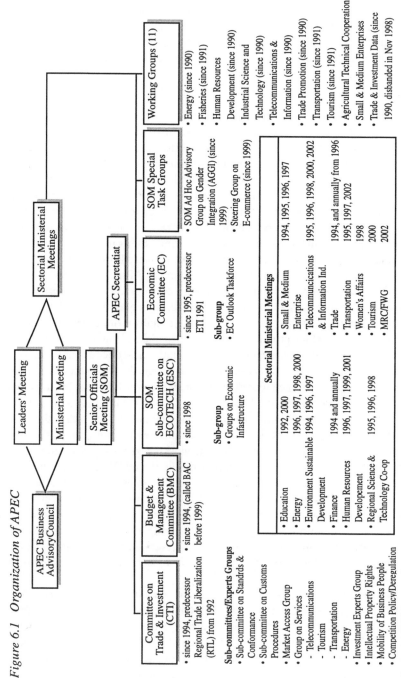

Source: APEC Secretariat

another year.[16] As Ravenhill makes clear, the EPG's main accomplishment was to place trade liberalization at the top of APEC's agenda, but in so doing it merely brought to the surface latent fears and reservations. For the developing economies the free trade objective, if pursued too fast and too aggressively, risked exposing several of their service and manufacturing industries to competitive pressures which they could not withstand. The EPG recommendations were widely seen as reflecting the interests of the advanced industrial economies.

The EPG's deliberations and recommendations received greater attention than they might otherwise have done because of another initiative, namely the advocacy of summit meetings, with the Australian government again playing a leading role. In April 1992, Prime Minister Paul Keating proposed regular heads-of-government meetings as a way of promoting greater Asia-Pacific regional co-operation. In letters to President George Bush, President Suharto and Japanese Prime Minister Kiichi Miyazawa, he suggested that such meetings, which might be held every two to three years, should be based on APEC membership.[17] The response of all three governments was considered critical to the success of the initiative: the United States and Japan because of the sheer weight of their economies, but also because a meeting of American and Japanese minds would serve as a practical demonstration of the usefulness of the APEC forum; Indonesia because of its leadership role in Southeast Asia and its capacity to neutralize negative reactions from other quarters. Though Suharto's initial reaction was guarded, Keating felt sufficiently encouraged to press ahead with his proposal. He advanced the argument that APEC provided Asian countries with a structure which could effectively contain US pressure on the sensitive issue of trade and human rights. US administrations, it was argued, were less likely to engage in offensive unilateral actions if they were obliged to meet their Asian counterparts regularly and at the highest level. The Keating strategy was seemingly validated by Suharto's agreement to attend the inaugural Leaders' Meeting in Seattle in November 1993.

The Bush administration's reaction to the proposal was also generally favourable, with Defense Secretary Dick Cheney describing it as 'basically sound policy'.[18] On the other hand, senior US officials made it known that the idea was somewhat premature given that the organization had hardly developed any secretarial or budgetary infrastructure. However, by April 1993, the Australian Foreign Minister, Gareth Evans, was confident that Australian diplomacy would soon bear fruit.[19] With unforeseen speed the United States, now chairing the APEC group, took up the Keating proposal and began sounding out APEC members about the possibility of a summit meeting to be hosted by President Bill Clinton. In July, the US President announced that he was proceeding with a heads-of-government meeting at Seattle, referring to APEC as 'the most promising forum' for debating trade issues. While reaffirming that the United States was ready to be a 'full partner in Asian growth', he took pains to emphasize the summit's purely economic agenda. As for Japan, the first clear indication of support came with the recommendation of a Foreign Ministry report that 'APEC should be expanded and strengthened to facilitate a loose economic unification in the region'.[20] The dominant view within the Japanese bureaucracy was that Tokyo could not afford to be seen as opposing any effort at trade liberalization, particularly one that was central to its relationship with the United States. The added endorsement of the proposal by such countries as South Korea and Singapore became the icing on the cake of Australian and US diplomacy.

Taken together, the EPG and summit initiatives prompted the Malaysian Minister for Trade and Industry to comment: 'APEC is slowly turning out to be what it wasn't meant to be, meaning that APEC was constituted as a loose consultative forum'.[21] This early crack in the multilateral edifice led a number of observers to conclude that a substantial gap separated the Asian and American approaches to institutional co-operation. The 'Asian evolutionary approach' with its emphasis on consensus and personal diplomacy was contrasted with the American 'legalistic and institutional' approach where the primary function of negotiation is to produce contracts, treaties and agreements. In one of the more sophisticated expositions of this argument, a distinction is drawn between the 'liberal' and 'cameralist' approaches to economic governance. In the liberal case, the construction of regional markets is conceived primarily in terms of 'liberalizing and "freeing" up economic processes', whereas in the cameralist framework the accent is on the contribution to national development and security.[22] APEC is said to embrace both political rationalities, the former identified with the United States, Australia, Canada and New Zealand, and the latter with the various countries of East Asia. APEC thus becomes the site of 'an unfolding struggle to define a new transnational political rationality', which, it is argued, will largely govern its future institutional evolution.[23]

Insightful though it may be, this characterization of the latent tensions within APEC is nevertheless deficient. Different negotiating styles and approaches to institutional development are no doubt part of the APEC equation, but they are perhaps no more than the outward manifestation of a deeper conflict of interests dictated by the vastly different economic circumstances and diplomatic experience of the relevant actors. If Japan, for example, was less than enthusiastic about negotiating binding trade and investment agreements, it was largely because it perceived this to be a strategy which generally worked to the advantage of the United States. Informal diplomacy, on the other hand, was more likely to weaken the hand of US and European negotiators,[24] and work in favour of the dominant regional economy and the tightly knit regional production networks centred around Japanese firms. Japanese governments had little incentive to pursue multilateral rule-making of a kind likely to prejudice the interests of politically well-connected sectors of the economy, notably agriculture or the construction and transportation industries.[25] In the case of ASEAN, two considerations, already alluded to, were uppermost in the minds of its members: first, that APEC should not be allowed to grow in size, influence and scope to the point of eclipsing ASEAN'S own leverage or influence in the region; and secondly, that APEC's institutionalization should not be allowed to proceed in ways likely to perpetuate the existing asymmetries of power and wealth within its ranks.

Given such disparate perspectives and priorities it is hardly surprising that APEC's first decade should have been characterized by a willingness, however grudging, on the part of members to accommodate conflicting interests and perceptions. Recognition of these economic and political realities is what in the end compelled APEC to adopt a relatively permissive approach to trade liberalization. The adoption of the 'flexibility principle' whereby APEC agreements were understood to be voluntary and non-binding simply made virtue of necessity. Differences in political culture and negotiating styles mirrored and reinforced the vast differences in the size, structure and technological sophistication of member economies. Such differences were inevitably reflected in the way national political and economic elites articulated their interests and engaged in coalition-building in support of those interests.

Here it is important to introduce another element of complexity, in that APEC, both formally and in practice, was an organization as much of economies as of states. It was not simply that APEC's mandate was essentially an economic one, but that the interests of capital were seen as central to that mandate. The interests of business became, at least in official discourse, virtually indistinguishable from the interests of national economies, and by implication from those of states. This is not to say that business circles in each of the member economies and the corporate sector as a whole were overly impressed with APEC's capacity to advance their respective interests. Yet, there is no disputing the fact that from its inception APEC saw the business community as its principal interlocutor. Most of those located inside or close to the APEC negotiating process made no secret of the fact that business was APEC's principal constituency, and that more effective ways had to be found for business to drive APEC's agenda.[26] In a speech delivered in October 1994, Joan Spero, US Under Secretary for Economic, Business and Agricultural Affairs, left her audience in no doubt as to the administration's thinking:

> APEC is not for governments, it is for you – you are the customer. Through APEC we aim to get governments out of the way, opening the way for business to do business. It is our goal to make APEC the most user friendly forum in the world. That is why business participates in APEC's working groups. That is why APEC established a business advisory group – the Pacific Business Forum – to advise APEC leaders this year on business priorities and vision for APEC's future. And that is why increasing the role of the private sector in APEC is a key objective for this year's meetings in Indonesia.[27]

The Pacific Business Forum (PBF) had been formed in 1993 with the express purpose of involving corporate interests more directly in shaping APEC's trade and investment liberalization policies and further developing business networks. The PBF's philosophy was best described as 'doing business better, faster and more effectively'.[28] Arrangements were also made for active private-sector representation in a range of APEC working groups, including telecommunications, transport and energy. In 1995 the Leaders' Meeting in Osaka agreed to establish the APEC Business Advisory Council (ABAC) which would replace the PBF and serve as APEC's peak advisory body. Its specific mandate was to communicate its views directly to leaders, especially on the implementation of the Osaka Action Agenda.[29] In the ensuing years ABAC would apply considerable pressure on political leaders to speed up trade and investment liberalization. Each year a string of recommendations would be made, including measures to accelerate banking and capital market reforms in member economies with a view to aligning them more closely with international financial standards, develop domestic bond markets and credible credit rating agencies, strengthen the enforcement of intellectual property rights (IPR), remove barriers to FDI, and encourage private-sector investment in information and communication technology (ICT).[30]

Simply put, business was from the outset given privileged access to APEC decision-making, in sharp contrast to the marginal role envisaged for other non-governmental organizations (NGOs), particularly those whose trade union, human rights, or environmental agendas placed them at odds with APEC's approach to free trade. Excluded from most official meetings, a number of NGOs proceeded to stage alternative summits and even protests, anticipating the much larger demonstrations that would confront the Seattle Ministerial Meeting of the World Trade Organization (WTO) in December 1999 and subsequent official or semi-official gatherings dealing with international trade and finance. In 1993, public rallies held in conjunction with the first APEC Leaders' Summit called for trade policy to place a higher priority on standards of environmental protection and worker health safety. An NGO meeting held in Kyoto to parallel the Osaka Leaders' Meeting stated that free trade would 'negate the development and democratic aspirations of people', and that 'economic growth and trade must serve human development and be based on the rights of individuals and people'.[31] Public agitation became even more visible in Manila in 1996 with a number of parallel civil society conferences and mass demonstrations staged across the Philippines. The 1997 Leaders' Meeting in Vancouver saw the first modest opening up of channels of communication. APEC's Human Resources Development Working Group was asked to 'increase labour force participation, including women and youth', and a new Ecotech subcommittee was established to coordinate the implementation of initiatives aimed at environmentally sustainable development. But by the end of the 1990s ABAC was still the only non-government group allowed extensive and regular participation in APEC's decision-making apparatus.

Functions

The privileged position which business enjoyed within the APEC family was not, however, primarily a function of its unique access to the corridors of power. What conferred on the business community a distinct advantage over other non-state actors was APEC's commitment to the 'Washington consensus'. By espousing the principles of free trade, financial and industrial deregulation, fiscal restraint, privatization, and 'transparency' in economic and political governance, APEC had in effect made its own the neo-liberal agenda which business generally, and large corporations in particular, had been expounding for some time. This is not to say that APEC was necessarily efficacious in translating theory into practice. For one thing, APEC members were not of ohe mind on how principles would be interpreted, objectives defined, and strategies implemented. This divergence was most clearly evident in the priorities and preferences of governments, but business itself was hardly a cohesive entity, with substantial differences emerging both within and between countries, especially on matters of trade. As a fledgling organization struggling to reconcile a number of unresolved differences within its ranks, APEC was bound to experience a period of continuing adjustment to changing circumstances. That trajectory is best captured by the following periodization: phase I (1989–92), phase II (1993–96), and phase III (1997–2001).

The early phase was one of quiet development, during which APEC pursued trade liberalization not directly through its own initiatives but by performing a lobbying role within a number of other international fora, in particular the Uruguay Round of GATT negotiations. APEC saw its primary function as one of trade facilitation. Modelling itself on the OECD, it undertook the collection of data on the economic performance and policies of member countries, with modest financial and technical assistance extended to developing economies to enable them to fulfil these tasks.[32] Early projects involved trade and investment data reviews, and low-level measures to facilitate trade, investment and technology transfers. As one observer put it, 'Non-ASEAN members were sensitive to the need to make the Association feel comfortable in the multilateral framework that it had reluctantly entered'.[33] Attempts, however, would soon be made to quicken the pace and scope of APEC activism, to the obvious discomfort of at least some of the less-developed member economies.

In August 1992, the Australian government, which had been a prime mover in APEC's early development, outlined publicly for the first time four major steps which APEC could take to advance the trade liberalization objective: reduce uncertainties in the regional market, address physical impediments to trade, harmonize national regulations and standards, and improve market access.[34] Free trade now became, especially among the English-speaking industrialized economies, the mantra which policy-makers, their advisers, and business representatives would endlessly repeat as if it held the secret to prosperity for all member economies. Contrary views or even reservations about the appropriate speed and modalities of trade liberalization were treated as if they exceeded the limits of legitimate discourse, even though the impressive performance of several East Asian economies during the 1970s and 1980s had rested, at least in part, on a strategic approach to trade. Political and social considerations which might moderate or even conflict with the commitment to free trade were either ignored or dismissed as short-term impediments. The fact that all governments have to contend with competing interests and claims, some of which may be severely disadvantaged by the undiluted application of free trade principles – and that these pressures inevitably influence political bargaining and even the electoral process – were regarded as tangential to APEC's agenda.[35]

This, then, was the prevailing political climate which saw the establishment of the Eminent Persons Group at APEC's Fourth Ministerial Meeting in 1992. The majority of EPG members were economists, closely associated with the development of PECC and well connected to the business community. Under Fred Bergsten's chairmanship, the EPG saw its task as devising a strategy for APEC which would give added impetus to the GATT negotiations, but would at the same time set the organization itself on the path of trade liberalization. Economic and technical co-operation, though a high priority for China and ASEAN, would receive scant attention.

The EPG's first report, which was to set much of the agenda for subsequent discussion, proposed that APEC should over time transform itself from a loose grouping into a regional free trade community, and that this goal be endorsed at the Seattle Summit. More specifically and immediately, it recommended an extensive series of trade and investment facilitation programmes, including the adoption of an Asia-Pacific investment code, the mutual recognition of product standards, and an effective dispute settlement mechanism. Given differences of view about the pace and direction of change, the Leaders' Meeting accepted the first two recommendations, but rejected the third. It also stopped short of renaming APEC the 'Asia Pacific Economic Community' as proposed by the EPG, but the joint statement issued at the conclusion of the meeting spoke of 'the emergence of a new voice for the Asia-Pacific in world affairs', and referred to the growing interdependence and sense of 'community' among member economies.[36] These visionary pronouncements were accompanied by a number of practical decisions: APEC members pledged to strive for a successful conclusion to the Uruguay Round by the 15 December 1993 deadline; another summit meeting would be held in Indonesia in 1994; a meeting of APEC finance ministers would be convened to discuss broad economic issues; a non-binding set of principles would be developed as a first step towards a regional investment agreement; and technology transfer programmes would be initiated to help Asian economies solve energy and environmental problems.[37]

Notwithstanding these achievements, the Seattle consensus masked underlying tensions, of which Mahathir's absence was but the most striking manifestation. The Malaysian Prime Minister warned that APEC was being transformed into a regional grouping whose primary objective was to serve the interests of the dominant member economies and strengthen the US bargaining position *vis-à-vis* Europe. To counter this tendency he proposed the establishment of an East Asian Economic Group (EAEG), an idea whose far-reaching implications will be examined in the next chapter. Clearly, Malaysia's aim was to wrest the initiative in regional multilateralism from the United States and its allies and to assert the notion of an Asian, or at least East Asian, identity.

Compounding this cleavage was the inability of the Seattle meeting to resolve two key issues: how fast trade liberalization should proceed within APEC, and whether or not such liberalization should be preferential or non-discriminatory. Differences of view had also surfaced in the EPG's own deliberations. Its recommendations had somehow to straddle two distinct positions. Both accepted that liberalization measures would need to be consistent with GATT. The United States (and its representative on the EPG, Fred Bergsten) favoured an APEC free trade area in which members eliminated barriers to regional trade, but not necessarily to trade with the rest of the world. Such an approach, it was argued, would apply added pressure on the Europeans to reciprocate APEC's trade concessions and enhance the likelihood of a successful conclusion to the GATT negotiations. Others, however, insisted that any liberalization should automatically flow to all GATT members. After protracted and at times intense debate, the EPG recommended in its second report a compromise position whereby individual members would decide for themselves whether to extend the benefits of trade liberalization to non-member economies. To maintain the momentum for liberalization, the EPG chose instead to recommend complete liberalization of trade within Asia Pacific by 2020.

The 1994 summit held in Bogor adopted the main thrust of the EPG recommendation with a deadline of 2010 for industrialized economies and 2020 for developing economies. The Pacific Business Forum, for its part, had stressed the need for APEC to press ahead with the elimination of trade barriers, reminding governments that business would invest only 'where bureaucracy is minimal and procedures straightforward and transparent'.[38] Mindful of the need for practical and achievable results in the acceleration of APEC's trade and investment facilitation strategy, the Leaders' Meeting asked ministers and officials to recommend initiatives on customs, standards, investment principles, and administrative obstacles to market access. The Leaders also agreed to strengthen co-operation within APEC, especially in education and training infrastructure, science and technology, and the environment.

In many respects, the Seattle and Bogor meetings were the high point of APEC's commitment to trade liberalization. Yet, several questions remained unanswered. Did the APEC agreement to remove trade barriers by 2020 apply to all trade, including such services as air travel, banking and insurance, or only to trade in goods? Would a number of countries be tempted to seek exemptions for particular industries? The South Koreans and the Japanese might, for example, seek to exclude agriculture. Even in Australia's case, no sooner had the Bogor Summit ended than difficult questions were being asked about the implications of the agreement for the politically sensitive textile, clothing, footwear, and motor vehicle industries. It was not yet known which members would extend the benefits of trade liberalization to non-members, and which would not. Nor was it entirely clear what criteria would be used to define the two categories: *industrialized* and *developing* economies, or how much disparity in the liberalizing capabilities of different economies APEC cohesion and sense of direction could withstand.

The summit meeting that followed in Osaka in 1995 managed to maintain the impression of forward movement. Sounding an optimistic note prior to the meeting, the Japanese Foreign Ministry suggested that APEC was 'now moving from a stage of "visions" and "concepts" to that of "actual implementation of measures"'.[39] The meeting did reaffirm the target dates of 2010 and 2020 for the removal of barriers to APEC trade, and each Leader presented an outline of measures that his economy had taken and would be taking to advance that commitment. To sustain the necessary momentum, the meeting adopted the Osaka Action Agenda which consisted of two prongs, the first dealing with the liberalization and facilitation of trade and investment, and the second with economic and technical co-operation. The Osaka Agenda was to be set in motion through a combination of individual action plans (IAPs) and a collective action plan (CAP). Each economy was requested to draw up a plan that would cover 15 specific areas, including tariffs, non-tariff measures, services, investment, standards and conformance, intellectual property rights, and competition policy. In addition agreement was reached on the principles that would guide the entire process of trade liberalization and trade facilitation. These included *comprehensiveness* (all impediments to free trade would need to be addressed), *comparability* (all 15 economies would be expected to make a comparable effort in advancing the trade and investment liberalization objective), and *flexibility* (each economy could tailor the specific timetable, approach, and priorities of its liberalization strategy to suit the particular stage of its economic development).[40] The difficulty with a number of these principles was twofold: either the principle did not lend itself to precise definition, or two or more principles could be read as inconsistent with each other. The principle of flexibility, in particular, conferred on each economy the responsibility of determining the contribution it would make in the light of its own circumstances, thereby negating, or at least diluting, the force of the other principles.

The 1996 Leaders' Meeting, which was held in Subic Bay, adopted the Manila Action Plan for APEC, which attempted to integrate the IAPs, CAPs, and a number of Progress Reports on Joint Activities. Judged in purely quantitative terms, the volume of APEC outputs was a solid one. The Leaders' Declaration was in any case careful to depict the Manila Plan as only the first step in 'an evolutionary process of progressive and comprehensive trade and investment liberalization'. However, on closer inspection it emerged that the IAPs submitted at Subic Bay did not by and large go beyond the commitments which APEC members 'had already agreed to unilaterally, within the WTO, or within another regional trade agreement'.[41] Reliance on voluntary, non-binding commitments and the absence of fixed and detailed timetables were not simply or even primarily concessions to the ASEAN diplomatic style but APEC's way of acknowledging the plurality of interests which it represented.

One other decision helped to convey the impression that the Subic Bay meeting had given renewed impetus to the APEC agenda. In the view of several APEC members, notably the United States, the APEC summit had, by endorsing the idea of an International Technology Agreement (ITA), helped to secure its adoption at the December 1996 WTO Ministerial Meeting in Singapore. The way had thus been opened for the elimination of tariffs on a range of information technology and telecommunications products by the year 2000. Yet the APEC endorsement was a qualified one, acknowledging once again the need for flexibility in implementation. This caveat was a concession to China and Malaysia which had argued that sectoral initiatives could be more appropriately developed in other industries, for example in textiles, where the United States still maintained relatively high levels of protection.

What emerges from this brief survey is that, even during this second phase when trade liberalization as both idea and policy objective appeared firmly entrenched, APEC's momentum was sustained largely by developing a discourse sufficiently ambiguous to accommodate widely disparate interests. The extent of that disparity and its impact on APEC's institutional and policy development would become more clearly visible during the third phase. A stream of APEC pronouncements and publications continued to preach the virtues of trade liberalization and to highlight the very substantial strides that had already been made. A report published in 1997 argued that as a result of the Manila Action Plan 'the real GDP of APEC economies would be raised by about 0.4 per cent, or a permanent increase of $69 billion per year in 1995 prices'.[42] Of this amount, $45 billion was attributed to trade facilitation and $23 billion to trade liberalization. A subsequent report calculated the gains (at 1997 prices) to be of the order of $75 billion.[43] The methodology, however, by which these conclusions were reached was not entirely convincing. To begin with these were figures for anticipated rather than realized GDP growth. More importantly, the connection between APEC initiatives, trade performance and GDP was not adequately demonstrated, and much less direct than was assumed. Even when

APEC economies registered substantial increases in export volume and income, or more generally in GDP growth, the many interacting factors contributing to such an outcome could not be easily disentangled, let alone a clear and precise weighting ascribed to any one of them.

By 1997 it was readily apparent that flexibility and consensus were the two key principles that could hold the organization together. To impose a more rigid discipline might be to invite even deeper cracks in the APEC edifice. At the same time the annual leaders' meetings had created expectations of continuing progress, which if not met might result in the gradual unravelling of the organization. Conscious of this dilemma and of the need to begin identifying sectors for more rapid liberalization, Canada as APEC host in 1997 saw the concept of 'early voluntary sector liberalization' (EVSL) as the most promising way forward. In the interests of achieving consensus, trade ministers attempted to strike a balance between the three main pillars of APEC's agenda, liberalization, facilitation and ecotech. The last two were seen as likely to be of greater appeal to developing economies which might otherwise conclude that greater sacrifices were expected of them than of the developed economies. Similar considerations prompted the ministers to strive for a balance in the sectors proposed for early liberalization. This fine balancing act eventually produced two lists: a list of nine sectors scheduled for immediate implementation, and a list of six sectors requiring further development. The following sectors were earmarked for immediate market-opening measures: environmental goods and services, energy, fish and fish products, forestry products, gems and jewellery, medical equipment and instruments, chemicals, and telecommunications. The Leaders' Meeting in Vancouver endorsed the package, which they found 'to be mutually beneficial and to represent a balance of interests'.[44] The Vancouver meetings nevertheless left four questions unanswered: (a) which products would be covered under each sector; (b) the extent of tariff reduction envisaged for each sector; (c) the speed at which such reductions would be occur; and (d) the differentiation that would be made between developed and developing economies.[45]

The lack of clarity on these aspects of the scheme made for conflicting interpretations. To prevent inertia setting in, officials from the United States, Canada, Australia, New Zealand, Hong Kong and Singapore pressed the view that all 15 sectors should be treated as a single package. Japan, on the other hand, insisted that voluntarism was integral to the concept, and accordingly refused to liberalize two highly sensitive sectors in the Japanese economy, fish and fish products and forestry products. Faced with Japanese resistance and reservations on the part of several other economies, the APEC Senior Officials Meetings in June and September 1998 duly concluded that 'flexibility' was the only way of resolving the problem.[46] Such a resolution, however, merely obscured the contradiction between two key principles espoused by APEC: the comprehensive and collective approach to trade liberalization favoured principally by the United States and flexibility tied to consensual decision-making advocated by most Asian members. In practice, flexibility meant that APEC would not reach agreement on EVSL, and that further progress on the issue would be left to WTO negotiations. As for the IAPs, they too seemed to be making relatively little headway, with ABAC and others questioning the transparency of these plans, and asking for greater clarity as to how they would advance the goals set in Bogor. By 1998 trade liberalization as APEC's overriding rationale appeared to lose much of the impetus it had acquired during the early and mid-1990s.

On trade and investment facilitation, broadly understood as action designed to reduce 'the cost or difficulty of doing business in another country', APEC developed a highly energetic programme involving some ten working groups as well as several groups of experts and special committees. Work was initiated in a great many areas, including customs modernization and customs co-operation, alignment with international standards, increased transparency for acquiring and using intellectual property rights, transparency in government procurement, review of technical regulations, improved mobility for business people, promotion of information technology, action plans for integrated transportation systems, and streamlining of tendering and regulatory processes for private firms in electricity generation.[47] Several steps were taken in each of these areas. The APEC Sub-Committee on Standards and Conformance had developed a programme for achieving uniform standards and measures in priority areas, notably in the electrical area. A mutual recognition arrangement on food and food products became operational in 1997. An agreement for the exchange of information on food recalls and food recall guidelines was reached in 1999.

In addition, APEC's Collective Action Plan on Investment organized several investment symposia, policy discussions to review the investment regimes of member economies, and policy dialogues to clarify the investment aspects of free trade areas to which APEC members belonged. In conjunction with the business sector, it prepared a menu of options for investment facilitation which member economies could include in their respective IAPs.[48] APEC also developed a list of Non-Binding Investment Principles designed to 'eliminate investment obstacles' and establish a free and open environment in the region. But, as the title indicates, adoption of the principles was purely voluntary, with few or no procedures to guide the process of implementation, although a survey of the IAPs of eight member economies indicated almost total compliance by Singapore, and substantial compliance by Australia and Canada, and to a lesser extent China, the Philippines and South Korea. As for competition policy and regulatory reform, here again APEC principles were non-binding to accommodate the different circumstances and priorities of member economies. Indeed, measures taken by APEC members in this connection were so diverse as to preclude any meaningful generalization.[49] To assist business mobility, the APEC Business Travel Card was introduced in 1997 and subsequently incorporated into IAPs, the aim being to improve service standards for processing applications by business executives, managers and specialists either for temporary residence permits, or, where certain requirements are met, for permanent residence.[50]

These and other initiatives, though they reflected a relatively high level of activism, were all predicated on the twin principles of flexibility and voluntary implementation. They were designed to avoid the impression of paralysis, while preserving the commitment to consensual decision-making. While they maintained relatively intact APEC's ideological commitment to the free market principles of trade liberalization, investment deregulation, and more generally business facilitation, they did so by providing each member economy with sufficient latitude to determine how quickly and extensively it would apply the principles, guidelines, recommendations and blueprints emerging with increasing regularity from APEC's multifaceted organizational framework. By the late 1990s, APEC had virtually abandoned any hope of adopting a clearly defined collective plan with specific commitments and targets for trade liberalization. The CTI continued to devote time and energy to CAPs, exploring new ways of producing 'tangible deliverables' and collective action on non-tariff measures of interest to the business sector.[51] Viewed in practical terms, however, the accent increasingly was on data gathering, monitoring, review, and advocacy functions more in keeping with the OECD model originally envisaged for APEC. The Shanghai Summit of November 2001 somewhat ritualistically reaffirmed the Bogor timelines, and set 2005 as the year for reviewing progress towards these goals. But in announcing a 'pathfinder' approach – whereby better-placed economies would proceed faster down the path of liberalization and set an example for others – APEC had in effect accepted that in the foreseeable future unilateral and bilateral arrangements might have primacy over multilateral ones.

A survey of the functions performed by APEC during this third phase merits two other observations. By the mid-1990s the developing economies became increasingly concerned that, given the generally higher levels of protection enjoyed by their industries, trade liberalization was likely to demand greater sacrifices of the developed countries. To offset this disadvantage they called on APEC to tolerate different speeds of liberalization, and just as importantly to mount a programme of development-oriented activities. China took up the cause, partly because it reflected its own needs, but also because it was a relatively painless way of gaining kudos among its Southeast Asian neighbours. In May 1996, Vice-Premier Zhu Rongji argued that the Asia-Pacific co-operation should encompass 'poverty elimination, environmental protection, technology transfer, infrastructure construction, and development in human resources'.[52] Chinese statements repeatedly emphasized the need for APEC's agenda to give the same priority to economic and technical co-operation as to trade and investment liberalization.[53] They called for more substantial technology transfers, and to this end established in January 1999 the APEC China Enterprises' Assembly. Comprising senior managers from 126 leading Chinese enterprises, the Assembly was to provide an avenue for the more effective use of information networks and financial support from APEC.[54]

The case for devoting greater energy and resources to development co-operation had by now become a recurring theme in ASEAN statements.[55] From the mid-1990s onwards, it is true, through a series of dialogues, seminars and other initiatives APEC set out to facilitate the availability of trained personnel in such areas as engineering and management, and enhance the capacity for infrastructure development (for example, Regional Integration for Sustainable Economies, Infrastructure for Sustainable Cities, APEC Infrastructure Facilitation Network). With Malaysia as Chair of APEC in 1998, greater attention was directed to human resource development, as evidenced by the Leaders' Declaration and its attachment, the Kuala Lumpur Action Programme on Skills Development, and APEC's support for the Asian Growth and Recovery Initiative designed to assist economies worst hit by the financial crisis. The following year the Human Resource Development Ministerial Meeting advocated that development and employment should be brought to the centre of APEC's economic policies.[56] Yet, most of these initiatives seldom went beyond studies, seminars, data gathering, and reaffirmation of the need for business to be more actively involved in development co-operation.

It is nevertheless the case that as time went on APEC discourse acquired more of a multidimensional character, especially in the wake of the 1997 financial crisis. The single-minded preoccupation with trade and investment could not indefinitely neglect a wide range of other policy concerns with which trade and investment were in any case integrally connected. Regional economic co-operation could not for long divorce itself from considerations of energy and environmental security. As early as November 1989, APEC ministers agreed to examine issues of energy resource supply and demand, early warning of natural disasters, and improved climate change studies. They also resolved to consider the interaction between environmental considerations and economic decision-making, with a view to strengthening marine resource conservation.[57] A meeting of ministers responsible for the environment in March 1994 developed an Environmental Vision Statement and Framework of Principles for Integrating Economy and Environment in APEC. The Osaka Action Agenda envisaged the future endorsement of policy principles which would address the risks and possible consequences of any future disruption to energy supply and demand, as well as the environmental effects of expanding energy consumption. In July 1996, an APEC ministerial meeting on sustainable development specifically pointed to the inter-relationship among poverty, unsustainable patterns of production and consumption, population, natural resource depletion and environmental degradation, and the potential for regional approaches in managing global environmental problems.[58] The meeting further recommended that the APEC Leaders at their Subic Bay meeting attach a high priority to clean oceans and seas in the APEC region.

An APEC workshop on trade and environment held in Beijing in July 1998 reviewed a number of trade-related environmental measures (TREMs) and environment-related trade measures (ERTMs), and re-emphasised the need for more effective coordination between these two areas of policy. However, for Chinese and other delegates, coordination did not mean the creation of uniform standards, but a highly differentiated approach reflecting the widely differing stages of development within APEC. Agreement could be reached only on broad principles: the need to accord sustainable development a much higher priority in their economic policies; to adopt and implement internationally recognized environmental and quality management standards; and promote regional co-operation in environmental protection, including institution-building, technology transfer and information exchange. When it came to energy policy the discussion was more focused, largely because it was driven by the business sector, or at least by business priorities, namely improving investor confidence and accelerating capital mobilization in APEC's energy sectors. Specific recommendations emerged for implementation of the APEC Natural Gas Initiative and for the restructuring and regulation of power production, the introduction of a competitive market in electricity generation and transmission, and facilitation of foreign ownership and control of electricity utilities.[59]

All of this suggests a comprehensive and widening agenda. Indeed, it is arguable that by the end of the decade, APEC had assumed a political function. At the most general level, the process of economic or even trade-related discussions could be viewed as a confidence-building measure likely to enhance regional security. More specifically, APEC provided a vehicle for diplomatic dialogue between the great powers, as much bilateral as multilateral. These opportunities were especially valuable at times of strain in the US–China relationship. A case in point was the meeting between Bill Clinton and Jiang Zemin at the 1999 Auckland APEC Summit – their first face-to-face contact since NATO's bombing of the Chinese embassy in Belgrade. A more direct multilateral engagement with security issues emerged again at the Auckland meeting where despite initial efforts to keep East Timor off the agenda, the New Zealand Foreign Minister Don McKinnon chaired a special ministerial session in response to the widespread violence which the Indonesia-backed militia had inflicted on East Timor. Notwithstanding Chinese and ASEAN reservations, and the unwillingness of the United States to lead a Kosovo-style operation, the scale of the emergency was such that the APEC meeting managed to prevail on the Indonesian government to accept the establishment of an Australian-led international peacekeeping force.[60]

Two years later the Shanghai Summit addressed another security issue, on this occasion in response to the 'September 11' terrorist attack on the United

States. It is worth noting, however, that the instructions in the APEC Leaders' Statement on Counter-Terrorism were directed not to foreign ministers, but to finance and transport ministries, and sought to freeze the funds of terrorist organizations and improve air and maritime security, in line with APEC's technical orientation. Equally instructive was that the support given to the United States was less than unequivocal. The Taliban was not mentioned by name; US-led strikes on Afghanistan were not endorsed, and emphasis was placed on the role of the United Nations. In October 2002, following the terrorist bombing in Bali, which killed close to 200 people – more than half of them Australians – the APEC Summit once again turned its attention to the terrorist threat. Meeting at Los Cabos in Mexico, the APEC Leaders issued the programmatic *Statement on Fighting Terrorism and Promoting Growth* which, in addition to reaffirming the commitments made in Shanghai, adopted the 'Enhancing Secure Trade in the APEC Region' (STAR) initiative.[61] The package included a number of measures to protect cargo, ships engaged in international voyages, international aviation and people in transit. In addition, agreement was reached on practical measures to prevent terrorist organizations from transferring and accessing funds. In particular, APEC Leaders undertook to ratify by October 2003 the International Convention for the Suppression of the Financing of International Terrorism, and to implement Security Council Resolutions 1373 and 1390. Other measures involved better monitoring of alternative remittance systems and non-profit organizations and enhancing law enforcement and regulatory capabilities. It remained to be seen, however, whether these measures would have the intended effect. Quite apart from the complex tasks of implementation and coordination, which APEC was poorly equipped to perform, were much larger issues which APEC had thus far evaded. No diagnosis of the terrorist threat was offered, and no attempt made to evaluate the underlying grievances which had contributed to it. Though by virtue of its mandate APEC meetings had made the obvious connection between terrorism and trade security, they were still a long way from connecting terrorism with the more encompassing notions of comprehensive or human security, or from linking APEC's initiatives with the security agenda of other regional organizations, notably the ARF.

APEC had entered its second decade with a broader, if still poorly defined, agenda. But on energy, environment and social, let alone political issues, APEC decisions were at best a promise of future action rather than actual achievement. Moreover, these decisions were invariably subordinated to the twin goals of trade and investment liberalization and facilitation, and premised on close partnership between government and business, with only minimal reference to other sectors of society with a stake in APEC outcomes. Linkages with other international organizations, with the possible exception of the WTO and other trade-related agencies, were poorly developed. APEC did acknowledge the UN's contribution to peacekeeping and peacebuilding in East Timor and to the international campaign against terrorism, but even here little thought had as yet been given to the possibilities of functional, let alone political coordination.

Power and Legitimacy

The discussion of membership, organization and functions has already highlighted the depth and durability of the tensions that arose both within and outside the forum. Influential voices, especially within the business communities of the industrialized economies, were highly critical of the limited scope and slow pace of trade liberalization. Others perceived APEC's neo-liberal agenda as damaging the weaker economies and ignoring the social and environmental consequences. Important as this tension was in APEC's evolution it did not fully describe the highly competitive environment within which APEC had to operate. Indeed, it is arguable that APEC mirrored and reinforced three principal fault-lines: one between the major economies, notably between the United States and Japan; another between the developed and developing economies; and a third between the included and the excluded, namely between governments and business on the one hand and significant elements of civil society on the other. This section focuses attention on the first two.

While it is true that the participation of the United States and Japan was crucial to the establishment and subsequent functioning of APEC, it is equally clear that the two were unable to exercise joint leadership in the development of the organization. Asia-Pacific economic co-operation held the prospect of expanded opportunities for US business and greater market access in countries, not least Japan, which had consistently accumulated large trade surpluses with the United States. Similarly, APEC offered Japan a forum within which it could assume a higher profile in regional affairs without provoking undue anxieties on the part of its Asian neighbours. It did not follow, however, as Rapkin and others have argued, that Japan would be prepared to use APEC as a forum for negotiating binding trade and investment agreements. On the contrary, neither Japan nor the United States was prepared to consult or compromise sufficiently for their divergent interests to be translated into common or at least compatible preferences.[62]

During the first term of Bill Clinton's presidency, APEC acquired much greater prominence in Washington's Asia-Pacific diplomacy. The motives were both varied and complex. As we have already observed, APEC was seen as a useful lever with which to extract additional concessions from the Europeans in international trade negotiations. More importantly, however, was the prospect of US firms making significant inroads into Asia's booming markets, especially in the motor car, semi-conductor, telecommunications, infrastructure and other industries in which the United States had established a sharp competitive edge.[63] An even more decisive, though closely related, consideration was the desire to derail attempts to construct an East Asian grouping, in which Japan would be the dominant force, and which might adversely affect US trade and other interests. As a trans-Pacific organization, APEC offered the most promising avenue for the pursuit of such a strategy, so long as it could be induced to adopt an aggressive trade liberalization agenda. The other caveat was that the reduction of trade barriers within APEC should proceed in ways that strengthened rather than weakened America's bargaining position *vis-à-vis* the European Union.[64] Given these desiderata, it is not surprising that US support for APEC should have been most visible during 1993–95. This was, after all, the period when it seemed that the EPG might be able to shape APEC's agenda in ways that were closely aligned with, if not directly inspired by, US priorities.

The US bargaining position was, however, more constrained than might appear at first sight. To begin with, useful as tariff reductions might be, US exporting firms seeking greater access to East Asian markets were more interested in reducing official and unofficial non-tariff barriers. Yet, US negotiators had relatively little to offer – except for WTO membership in China's case – which might entice their East Asian counterparts to remove these 'structural impediments'. The administration's hand was further weakened by mounting congressional resistance to principles of trade liberalization. Moreover, Washington did not seem well disposed to offering much by way of developing assistance, or indeed to funding other APEC initiatives which might be attractive to the ASEAN economies. The declining fortunes of the EPG in a sense reflected the relative weakness of America's hand. Increasing East Asian discomfort with EPG recommendations, which had already surfaced at the Seattle Leaders' Meeting, became increasingly evident after the presentation of its second report in 1994. At their meeting in September, the ASEAN economic ministers reacted negatively to any notion of binding investment principles or to the adoption of dispute settlement mechanisms, and agreed that the EPG should be dissolved. Following the tabling of its third report, which called for accelerated implementation of Uruguay Round commitments, the EPG had its mandate formally terminated at the Osaka meetings.

For its part, Japan was concerned that the 'dense web of mutually reinforcing ties – between government and business, between independent firms, and between management and labour',[65] which now tied the Japanese and other East Asian economies should not be jeopardized by APEC's free trade principles. There was little reason to expect that the United States would succeed in extracting from Japan at the APEC negotiating table concessions on agriculture and other vulnerable industries, which it had not managed to do in years of arduous negotiations either bilaterally or in the Uruguay Round. The relative weakness of Japanese governments during this period, coupled with a poorly performing Japanese economy and continuing rivalries between different arms of the bureaucracy, made such an outcome even less likely. Though Japan was keen to retain US economic and strategic engagement in Asia Pacific and to dissuade the United States from taking unilateral action in trade relations, hence its enthusiastic involvement in APEC, it was above all concerned to cement its pivotal role in the functioning of the regional economy. For Japan, slowing down the APEC push for trade liberalization had the added advantage of aligning it more closely with Chinese and ASEAN interests and perceptions.[66] Mirroring and reinforcing these multiple objectives was Tokyo's readiness to use APEC as a vehicle for development co-operation. This was very much the thinking that prompted Japan to introduce in February 1995 its proposal for a Partners for Progress (PFP) initiative, which envisaged the establishment of a pool of development funds to be dispensed under APEC auspices to developing member economies. By the time it made its way on to the Osaka Action Agenda, the Japanese proposal had been significantly diluted, but Tokyo had established its credentials as the major developed economy willing to make development aid the third pillar of APEC's policy framework.

ASEAN, too, was less than enthusiastic about the direction in which the United States was hoping to steer the organization. Not that ASEAN was able to speak with one voice on the two most contentious issues: APEC's role in trade liberalization, and the pace of its institutionalization. The approach agreed upon by ASEAN ministers in February 1990, better known as the 'Kuching consensus', had stressed the need for ASEAN to preserve its cohesion and identity, and for APEC to function as an outward-oriented organization committed to strengthening the openness of the international trading system. APEC was seen primarily as a consultative mechanism that would develop gradually and pragmatically, respect the different priorities and circumstances of its members, and assist them to identify common interests, which could then be more effectively articulated at international trading and other negotiations. The Kuching formula encapsulated many of the strands that would characterize Malaysia' highly sceptical attitude to APEC. Its advocacy of a separate East Asian grouping and Prime Minister Mahathir's decision to absent himself from the first Leaders' Meeting in Seattle reflected Malaysia's more assertive diplomatic style. By contrast, domestic and external influences prompted Suharto's Indonesia to accept the American and Australian arguments for faster trade liberalization. The success of the Bogor Summit is in many ways attributable to Suharto's decision to ignore both Malaysian misgivings and ASEAN's traditional insistence on consensual decision-making. That success could not, however, obscure wider ASEAN dissatisfaction with the agenda which the United States in particular was seeking to impose on APEC. Representing 16 per cent of APEC's population and a mere 2.9 per cent of its GNP, ASEAN could, even if fully united, expect to exercise at best limited influence over APEC's future direction. This growing realization was instrumental in weakening ASEAN support for APEC, and strengthening the hand of those who favoured a less directive role for APEC and a more nuanced approach to trade liberalization

In some respects China's circumstances differed markedly from those of most ASEAN countries. Chinese leaders remained firmly committed to preserving the Communist Party's dominant role in national economic policy and the apparatus of government more generally. This is not to say that they were opposed to trade liberalization. On the contrary, the opening up of the Chinese economy – with all the attendant pressures for economic restructuring, market competition, and compliance with international rules and regulations – was seen as the price that had to be paid if China was to gain access to the foreign markets, capital and technology deemed vital to the success of the modernization strategy. Access to US and Japanese markets had by the early 1990s assumed a high priority for China. By the late 1990s, APEC accounted for three-quarters of its trade and four-fifths of its incoming foreign investment.[67] In addition, Beijing entertained the hope that APEC might serve as a forum which could at least attenuate US unilateralism in trade relations, enhance its prospects of gaining admission to the WTO, and help legitimize its expanding influence in the region.

This having been said, China's vision for APEC was of a consultative arrangement which was gradualist and consensus-driven, and placed economic and technical co-operation on an equal footing with reduction of trade barriers. In this connection, Beijing's use of language bore a striking resemblance to that in which the Kuching consensus had been couched. In his speech to the 1998 Leaders' Meeting in Kuala Lumpur, Jiang Zemin offered the following caution 'countries should expand their opening-up programs in the light of their national conditions and in a step-by-step manner while paying attention to increasing their capabilities of preventing and withstanding risks'. He went on to observe: 'The trend of economic globalization is emerging in a context where there is no fundamental change in the inequitable and irrational old international economic order, which will inevitably widen the gap between poor and rich countries'.[68] Other Chinese commentators were less tactful in assessing the US vision for APEC. In the words of one analyst, the United States wanted 'to use APEC as a launching pad to catapult US corporations into the region's markets, targeting areas where the US deems itself to be competitive, such as aircraft, telecommunications, and banking'.[69] In other words, the Chinese leadership saw value in the APEC experiment, but only so long as it could be used to advance two closely related objectives: reducing the gap between advanced and industrializing economies, and strengthening the trend towards regional and global multipolarity. Where APEC policies and institutional arrangements ran counter to these objectives, more particularly where US actions seemed propelled by aggressive self-interested unilateralism, China could be expected to put its considerable weight behind moves to slow down APEC's momentum.

Two highly revealing episodes, the demise of the 'early voluntary sector liberalization' proposal and the mixed responses to the East Asian financial crisis, may help to clarify the competitive dynamic underlying APEC's evolution after1995. So far as EVSL is concerned, suffice it here to say that the episode highlighted the underlying conflict of interests between the US and Northeast Asian economies, and the inability of the United States to impose its will on APEC. Though Washington applied enormous pressure on Japan, which at first seemed almost completely isolated, the tide eventually turned. Tokyo launched an intense diplomatic campaign, which was fortuitously assisted by the onset of the financial crisis. The perception soon took hold that, whereas Japan was prepared to offer substantial funds to assist East Asia's economic recovery, the United States was content to act as a bystander, leaving it to the IMF to administer its rather unpalatable medicine. The decision to transfer the nine sectors to the WTO signalled that within APEC at least Japan was, despite its economic difficulties, a force to be reckoned with.

Just as Japanese intransigence had helped to scuttle the EVSL initiative, so US opposition effectively blocked the Miyazawa proposal, whereby a regional monetary fund would have been established, with Japan as its principal contributor, to assist East Asian economies most severely hit by the crisis. APEC enthusiasts would point to a number of initiatives taken by the organization in response to the crisis, notably the various programmes aimed at strengthening regional capital markets and developing or reorganizing pension systems, increased co-operation in financing infrastructure projects, development of credit-rating agencies, and introduction of more rigorous information-disclosure standards for firms planning to tap financial markets.[70] Reference is also made to the Executive Meeting of the East Asian and Pacific Central Banks, which agreed in August 1997 to the creation of a $10 billion facility to complement IMF measures, and to the establishment of the Manila Framework Group in November 1997, which set out to strengthen Asia's domestic financial systems and regulatory capacities, in part through the development of the Asian Surveillance Fund.[71] Leaving aside the questionable efficacy of these remedies, two aspects of the APEC response are worth noting. First, these initiatives were primarily designed to upgrade the financial infrastructure of these East Asian economies, that is to make it more 'open and accountable'. Much less emphasis was placed on actual financial assistance to governments struggling with large capital outflows, sharp currency and stock market depreciation, a succession of bank failures and business bankruptcies, and falling exports and government revenue. Secondly, they did nothing to address the international – as opposed to the domestic – factors which had contributed to the large and rapid movements of short-term foreign funds.

Japan's proposal, which envisaged the creation of a permanent Asian Monetary Fund (AMF) with a capitalization of $100 billion, had precisely these other objectives in mind. Equipped to provide prompt assistance to Asian countries facing serious economic and political instability, such a fund may have also helped to deter future speculative attacks on currencies. The United

States, and in particular the Treasury Department, opposed the Japanese initiative on the grounds that it was unnecessary – the IMF had sufficient resources to handle the crisis – and undesirable, since more easily accessible funds would erode the financial discipline that the IMF was seeking to impose as a condition of its assistance. Expressed a little more crudely but no less accurately, the United States wished to block the Miyazawa initiative because it threatened to weaken the IMF, the institution which tended to reflect US interests and priorities, and establish the AMF, a new institution which Japan would largely dominate. The combined impact of US and IMF hostility to the proposal, China's refusal to support any move which might enhance Tokyo's regional influence, and Japan's weakened position in the light of its own banking and financial difficulties soon brought the initiative to an abrupt halt. This is not to say that the APEC membership was generally satisfied with the outcome, or that the underlying contest for power and influence had escaped the notice of most members. Mahathir's Malaysia may have stood alone in its unflinching denunciation of international financial institutions, but the underlying sentiment struck a responsive chord in much of East Asia. Significantly, President Jiang Zemin used the occasion of the 1998 APEC Leaders' Meeting to call for a new international financial architecture which would more effectively supervise and regulate international capital flows, and enhance institutional capacity to reduce risks and provide relief.

What then might we conclude from these two episodes and more generally from APEC's trajectory over its first ten years? The first unavoidable conclusion had to do with the fragility of the APEC edifice. It is not that APEC was in any danger of disappearing from the regional landscape, but that its direction was at best uncertain, and at worst contradictory. 'Open regionalism' was itself a compromise formula that lent itself to ambiguous interpretation and erratic implementation. Regardless of the principles adopted in the early stages of its development, APEC encompassed different conceptions of regional co-operation, which themselves reflected diverging economic and geopolitical interests. For some, notably the United States, APEC's utility depended in part on its ability to act as an economic bloc. Such an arrangement held two distinct advantages: first, it would accelerate the process of trade liberalization within the bloc, thereby improving US access to East Asian markets; and secondly, it would strengthen America's hand (already strengthened by its dominant role within NAFTA) *vis-à-vis* the European Union. For others, a regional economic grouping was desirable, but one which did not include the United States, that is one which had a distinctive East Asian identity. 'Open regionalism' was perhaps no more than a short-term compromise to which a number of players were prepared to pay lip service, while still striving to achieve their preferred outcomes over the medium to long term. In that sense, the conventionally accepted dichotomy between the so-called 'American legalistic approach' and the 'Asian evolutionary approach' was a gross oversimplification which obscured as much as it clarified the evolving configuration of power and interests in the region.[72]

By the end of the 1990s, a second conclusion, closely related to the first, readily suggested itself. In the economic arena, which was APEC's primary field of action, no single centre of power could impose its will on the organization as a whole. The principal players – the United States and Japan, and to a lesser extent China and ASEAN – would each score partial and intermittent victories, but these were not extensive or durable enough to permit any one of them to set APEC's direction. As we have seen, success often meant blocking the objectives of others rather than achieving one's own. The fate of the EPG's recommendations, of the EPG itself, of the EVSL and Miyazawa initiatives, pointed to the absence of leadership, but not so much in the sense suggested by Ravenhill, namely the absence of 'heroes' or charismatic leaders.[73] Rather it pointed to the absence of the structural framework within which a single actor could exercise hegemony over the whole. APEC is therefore best understood as the product of 'competitive interdependence', a complex set of interacting but competing tendencies, in which 'residual hegemony' coexisted with 'increasing interdependence' on the one hand and 'intensifying competition' on the other. APEC summitry is in turn best understood as the most sophisticated institutionalized expression yet of 'competitive interdependence'. The evolving chemistry of APEC leaders' meetings, reflected in the twists and turns of the policy process which they oversee, was itself an indication of the fine yet fluid balance that existed among these three tendencies.

Architecture

Issues of architecture will be dealt with more fully in Chapter 10, but a few observations are worth making here for they arise directly out of the preceding analysis. APEC has been described as 'Pacific Rim regionalism', that is, an attempt to construct a regional organization incorporating littoral states situated along the eastern and western rims of the Pacific. Plausible though it is, this geographical representation is nevertheless misleading in that it overlooks the importance of the sea, the far-reaching implications of EEZs and the substantial commercial and military dominance which the great powers, notably the United States, exercise over this vast expanse of ocean. True enough, the vast majority of Pacific island states have not been admitted to APEC, yet their economic and military links to great and middle powers, in particular the United States and Australia, are so extensive as to warrant their inclusion, in practice if not in theory. APEC may therefore be more accurately represented as an attempt at 'Pacific Basin regionalism'.

By virtue of its comprehensive and diverse membership, APEC is arguably the most ambitious attempt to date at institutional innovation in the Asia-Pacific region. Yet, APEC's spatial delineation, which remained a source of considerable disputation throughout the first decade of its existence, does not of itself tell us much about its qualitative dimensions, or indeed its relationship to other forms of regional multilateralism. What APEC achieved in geographical breadth, it lacked in organizational and functional depth. The experiment in summitry may be interpreted in part as a response to these widely perceived deficiencies. The frequency and informality of the Leaders' Meetings were designed to strengthen the fabric of trans-Pacific relations, and in the process endowed the organization with a degree of legitimacy it would not have otherwise possessed. APEC had developed, seemingly by accident, an overarching institutional umbrella for the Asia-Pacific region. Though primarily focused on issues of trade, APEC summits were flexible enough to serve as a deliberative, even negotiating forum for a range of other issues, including the Asian financial crisis, East Timor, and the 'war on terrorism'.

The largely *ad hoc* character of APEC's development, however, left a number of critical questions about the region's institutional architecture largely unresolved. A good deal of ambiguity, for example, surrounded the likely division of functions between APEC and the other region-wide organization, the ASEAN Regional Forum. The frequently cited explanation that APEC was primarily responsible for promoting regional co-operation in the areas of trade and economic policy more generally, and that the ARF would concern itself principally with regional security raised more questions than it answered. As we have already observed, the dividing line between economy and security was an elusive one. Indeed, the line was especially blurred when it came to the wider security agenda, and to such issues as transnational crime, the drug trade, economically driven population movements, and the exploitation of fishing and forestry resources. Nor was it entirely clear how the economic and security dimensions of the East Asian financial crisis or future trade and investment relations between China and Taiwan could be neatly divided into separate compartments (see Figure 6.2).

The institutional division of labour gradually emerging in Asia Pacific had to contend with two other critical questions. The first concerned the relationship between APEC and what we have chosen to label 'sub-regional' organizations, either existing or in the making. The three most relevant sub-regions were North East Asia, Southeast Asia and the South Pacific. APEC had yet to define its relationship, formally or otherwise, with any one of them. Even in trade-related matters, it was not at all clear how APEC decisions would dovetail with, or be supported by, agreements or arrangements arrived at within ASEAN, the Pacific Islands Forum and its various subsidiary bodies, or the Closer Economic Relations Agreement between Australia and New Zealand. The problem was perhaps less pressing in the cases of Northeast Asia and the South Pacific, the former because of its low level of institutionalization, and the latter because of the limited overlap between APEC and Pacific Forum membership, and the economic marginality of the Pacific micro-states. Nevertheless both

Figure 6.2   Membership of key Asia-Pacific regional organizations

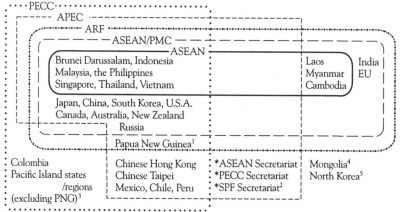

Notes
PECC: Pacific Economic Cooperation Council.
ASEAN: Association of Southeast Asian Nations.
ASEAN PMC: ASEAN Post-Ministerial Conference.
ARF: ASEAN Regional Forum.
APEC: Asia Pacific Economic Cooperation.

1.   Papua New Guinea attends ASEAN Ministerial Meeting as an observer.
2.   Those marked with an asterisk are participating as observers.
3.   Pacific island states / regions: Papua New Guinea, Fiji, Samoa, Solomons, Vanuatu, Tonga,
       Nauru, Kiribati, Tuvalu, Cook Islands, Niue, Micronesia, Marshall Islands, Palau.
4.   Mongolia's participation was approved in the 5th Ministerial Meeting in 1998.
5.   North Korea first participated in ARF in July 2000.

Source: Asia–Japan Center, October 2002

sub-regions were, for different reasons, expected to acquire added significance
in the years ahead. ASEAN sensitivities presented a greater challenge. By virtue
of its origins and the influence exerted by its most powerful member economies,
APEC reflected first and foremost the perspectives and priorities of advanced
industrial economies. By contrast, ASEAN and its offshoot, the ARF, bore
very much the imprint of the newly industrializing and less-developed societies
of the region. These tensions had yet to be fully addressed.[74] ASEAN had not
sought to become a tightly knit intra-regional economic grouping, but the role
that APEC would play in shaping the future direction of Southeast Asia's extra-
regional economic relationships was far from clear.

The second question had to do with APEC's extra-regional relationships, in
particular those with NAFTA and the European Union. The NAFTA factor
was especially troublesome, since its dominant member, the United States, as
well as Canada and Mexico, were members of both organizations. Was the
relationship to be conceived as essentially co-operative or competitive? APEC's

identity was no doubt central to all these questions. Whether APEC evolved into a fully-fledged common market, a 'Pacific OECD', or simply a network canvassing ideas and initiatives to be negotiated primarily in other fora would obviously impact on the wider Asia-Pacific architecture. But APEC's identity could not be treated as a given. Almost from its inception, APEC had functioned as a site as much for contestation as for co-operation, with both state and non-state actors attempting, with variable degrees of enthusiasm and success, to use this institutional experiment to advance their respective goals and strategies, or at least thwart those deemed injurious to their interests. More than ten years after its birth, APEC was still very much in a state of flux.

ARF: SECURITY CO-OPERATION IN THE BALANCE

The ASEAN Regional Forum is a more recent creation than APEC, which may help explain its relatively lower status, visibility and institutional infrastructure. While attracting a good deal of public and journalistic comment, the ARF did not command by the end of the 1990s anything like the attention which scholars and policy-makers were devoting to APEC. Its modest organizational foundations, limited objectives, and gradualist approach were important factors tending to lower expectations of the ARF's capacity to advance regional security, especially in its wider Asia-Pacific context. Yet, the formation of the ARF, its membership, ethos and mode of operation were equally revealing of the new regionalism and its underlying contradictions.

Membership

The first ARF meeting, which was held in Brunei in July 1994, had 18 participants: the six ASEAN members, Indonesia, Malaysia, Singapore, Thailand, the Philippines and Brunei, their dialogue partners, Japan, South Korea, the United States, Canada, Australia, New Zealand, and the European Union, as well as Russia, China, Vietnam, Laos and Papua New Guinea. As with APEC so with the ARF an institution was established, whose membership was trans-Pacific, encompassing small, middle and great powers and cutting across the ideological divisions of the Cold War period. Unlike APEC, the ARF comprised states rather than economies; its agenda revolved primarily around issues of security; and ASEAN saw itself and was seen by others as occupying the driver's seat. These three factors help to explain the EU's inclusion and Taiwan's exclusion. They also to a greater or lesser extent account for the subsequent decisions to admit Cambodia in 1995, India and Burma in 1996, Mongolia in 1999 and North Korea in 2000, by which time an understanding was reached that expansion had to give way to consolidation and the development of a more efficient process of co-operation. Cambodia's and Burma's admission foreshadowed their imminent membership of ASEAN which was now fully committed to encompassing the whole of Southeast Asia. India, on the other hand, offered the ASEAN countries a useful counterweight to China's influence in the region, and more generally strengthened the polycentric character of the organization, thereby lessening the prospect that any one great power would acquire the leading role which ASEAN had currently assumed. Partly in order to justify India's (as opposed to Pakistan's) admission, that same meeting adopted the criteria of commitment and geographic relevance as the basis on which the admission of new members would be considered. Commitment referred to a country's willingness to help achieve the ARF's key goals and to fully abide by the decisions and statements it had already made. The ARF's geographical footprint was said to cover Northeast Asia, Southeast Asia and Oceania.

Organization

Just as it had done with respect to membership, ASEAN was keen to maintain a relatively firm grip on the ARF's institutional development. ASEAN's thinking was of a forum in which all participants would feel comfortable, with the emphasis on the leisurely exchange of views rather than rapid decision-making, and confidence-building rather than conflict prevention or conflict resolution. To this end, the ASEAN interest in track-two diplomacy was from the outset injected into the ARF's agenda, for this was seen as a valuable mechanism for generating discussion on a range of issues which might otherwise remain undiscussed given government sensitivities. ASEAN also made it known that it was keen to retain chairmanship of the Forum, by having the chair rotating annually among its members, which in effect meant that annual ARF meetings would always be held in an ASEAN country. Indeed, the first ARF meeting requested its Chair, Brunei, to formalize the mechanics of the Forum, including the commissioning of papers from specific countries, convening of international workshops on specific problems, and arrangements for the following year's meeting and lead-up activities. By contrast, the Keating government, which had consistently pressed for a more extensive institutional infrastructure, advocated a number of specific trust-building measures, including exchanges on strategic perceptions, a regional securities studies centre, a regional arms register, and regional maritime safety and surveillance co-operation agreements.[75]

In its first few years the ARF seemed prepared to strike a middle path between ASEAN's low-key approach and the more ambitious programme favoured by countries like Australia. Tentative steps towards the creation of an institutional infrastructure were taken with the establishment of Senior Officials Meetings (SOMs), Intersessional Support Groups (ISGs) and Intersessional Meetings (ISMs). To enhance the ARF's regional credentials, the ISGs, best described as working groups set up to deal with specific issues, were to be co-chaired by one ASEAN and one non-ASEAN member, and could be convened in any member state. Increasing efforts to involve senior military officers in ARF discussions reflected a widely though not universally shared desire to enhance strategic consultation. Though not strictly speaking an ARF initiative, the first Forum for Defence Authorities, which was hosted by Japan in October 1996, brought together senior defence officials from the ARF's 21 members. While there were ample opportunities for the region's military establishments to exchange views on logistics, training, management and other problems of common interest (for example, Pacific Armies Senior Officers Logistics Seminar, Pacific Armies Management Seminars, Western Pacific Naval Symposium),[76] their institutionalized participation in the regional security dialogue represented a new development. At its fifth meeting in 1998 the ARF welcomed the practice of senior defence and military officials meeting informally during the course of ARF meetings, and encouraged their active participation at appropriate levels in all relevant meetings (see Table 6.1).

Other aspects of the ARF's organization and mode of operation will become apparent in the analysis that follows, which deals first with functions and then with issues of power and legitimacy. Suffice it here to say that by the late 1990s the organizational contours of the regional security dialogue initiated by the ARF were still not clearly defined. The cautious improvisation which had thus far governed its trajectory left several questions unanswered. Was ASEAN's leadership role a temporary device designed to nurture the organization during its infancy? Or was it meant as a long-term arrangement in recognition of the fact that leadership exercised by any one of the three great powers, namely the United States, China or Japan, would not be deemed acceptable by the entire membership? What precisely would be the relationship between the first and second tracks? How would that relationship be coordinated, and through what mechanisms? Finally, was there an expectation that, as the ARF became firmly established and its agenda widened, member states would endow the Forum with increased authority and resources? The ensuing discussion will shed light on some of these questions, but a more definitive analysis of trends and future possibilities will be left to the concluding chapter.

Functions

The early formulation of the ARF's functions bore the clear imprint of ASEAN's influence. An endorsement of TAC principles was contained in the Chairman's Statement issued at the first ARF meeting in July 1994. The Statement called for a study of 'the comprehensive concept of security, including its economic and social aspects, as it applies to the Asia-Pacific region', and went on to propose several other ideas as possible subjects of study, including confidence and security building, nuclear proliferation, peacekeeping co-operation and preventive diplomacy.[77] At its second meeting, ASEAN circulated 'The ASEAN

Regionalism in the new Asia-Pacific order

Table 6.1   ASEAN Regional Forum (ARF) first track meetings (1994–2002)

Dates	Meeting – Chair(s) – Place

NINTH ARF

| 31 July 2002 | ARF9 (Foreign Ministers Meeting) – Brunei – Bandar Seri Begawan, Brunei |

2001–2002 Intersessional Meetings

| 19–21 December 2001 | Intersessional Support Group (ISG) on Confidence Building Measures (CBMs) – India and Vietnam – New Delhi |
| 22–24 April 2002 | ISG on CBMs – India and Vietnam – Hanoi |

EIGHTH ARF

| 25 July 2001 | ARF8 (Foreign Ministers Meeting) – Vietnam – Hanoi |
| 17–18 May 2001 | ARF SOM (Senior Officials Meeting) – Vietnam – Hanoi |

2000–2001 Intersessional Meetings

18–19 April 2001	ISG on CBMs: Second Meeting – Republic of Korea and Malaysia – Kuala Lumpur
16–17 April 2001	Experts Group Meeting on Transnational Crime – Republic of Korea and Malaysia – Kuala Lumpur
1–3 November 2000	ISG on CBMs – Republic of Korea & Malaysia – Seoul
30–31 October 2000	Experts Group Meeting on Transnational Crime – Republic of Korea & Malaysia – Seoul

SEVENTH ARF

| 27 July 2000 | ARF7 (Foreign Ministers Meeting) – Thailand – Bangkok |
| 17–18 May 2000 | 7th ARF SOM – Thailand – Bangkok |

1999–2000 Intersessional Meetings

| 13–14 November 1999 | ISG on CBMs – Japan & Singapore – Tokyo |
| 5–7 April 2000 | ISG on CBMs: Second Meeting – Japan & Singapore – Singapore |

SIXTH ARF

| 26 July 1999 | ARF6 (Foreign Ministers Meeting) – Singapore – Singapore |
| 20–22 May 1999 | 6th ARF SOM – Singapore – Singapore |

1998–1999 Intersessional Meetings

4–6 November 1998	ISG on CBMs – Thailand & USA – Honolulu
3–5 March 1999	ISG on CBMs: Second Meeting – Thailand & USA – Bangkok
11–14 April 1999	Intersessional Meeting (ISM) on Disaster Relief – Russia & Vietnam – Moscow

FIFTH ARF

26–27 July 1998	ARF5 (Foreign Ministers Meeting) – Philippines – Manila
20–22 May 1998	5th ARF SOM – Philippines – Manila

Intersessional Meetings 1997–1998

4–6 November 1997	ISG on CBMs – Australia and Brunei – Brunei
18–20 February 1998	ISM on Disaster Relief – Thailand and New Zealand – Bangkok
4–6 March 1998	ISG on CBMs: Second Meeting – Australia and Brunei – Sydney

FOURTH ARF

27 July 1997	ARF4 (Foreign Ministers Meeting) – Malaysia – Kuala Lumpur
18–20 May 1997	4th ARF SOM – Malaysia – Pulau Langkawi

Intersessional Meetings 1996–1997

19–20 February 1997	ISM on Disaster Relief – Thailand and New Zealand – Wellington
6–8 March 1997	ISG on CBMs – China and Philippines – Beijing
26–28 March 1997	ISM on Search and Rescue Coordination and Cooperation – Singapore & USA – Singapore

THIRD ARF

22 July 1996	ARF3 (Foreign Ministers Meeting) – Indonesia – Jakarta
10–11 May 1996	3rd ARF SOM – Indonesia – Yogyakarta

Intersessional Meetings 1995–1996

18–19 Jan 1996	ISG on CBMs: First Meeting – Japan and Indonesia – Tokyo
4–7 March 1996	ISM on SAR – Singapore and USA – Honolulu
1–3 April 1996	ISM on Peacekeeping Operations – Malaysia and Canada – Kuala Lumpur
15–16 April 1996	ISG on CBMs: Second Meeting – Japan and Indonesia – Jakarta

SECOND ARF

1 August 1995	ARF2 (Foreign Ministers Meeting) – Brunei – Bandar Seri Begawan
22–24 May 19956	2nd ARF SOM – Brunei – Bandar Seri Begawan

FIRST ARF

25 July 1994	ARF1 (Foreign Ministers Meeting) – Thailand – Bangkok
23–25 May 1994	1st ARF SOM – Thailand – Bangkok

Source: Australian Department of Foreign Affairs and Trade

Regional Forum: A Concept Paper' which specifically encouraged ARF participants to associate themselves with the TAC. The Forum also established an Intersessional Support Group to be co-chaired by Indonesia and Japan to study confidence-building measures, and ISMs to study peacekeeping and search and rescue. These and other initiatives were seen as constituting the confidence-building stage or Stage One of the ARF process, which would lay the foundations for the next two stages, preventive diplomacy and conflict resolution, respectively.[78] Each of these three stages entertained two categories of measures, the first of which could be carried out in the short term, while the second would require careful consideration over a longer period of time. This evolutionary approach, clearly spelt out in the Concept Paper, bore ASEAN's distinctive imprint. It left the more difficult challenges to security, notably the resolution of territorial disputes, to a later stage, and placed the principle of sovereignty – and its corollary, non-interference in the internal affairs of other countries – at the heart of the Forum's mode of operation.

By the time of its third meeting in July 1996, the ARF was emerging as a multidimensional security dialogue mechanism. Though the emphasis was still on the elaboration of CBMs (for example, publication of defence policy statements, enhancing high-level defence contacts among ARF participants, support for the UN Register on Conventional Arms, voluntary exchange of information regarding military exercises and other global arms control and disarmament agreements), active steps were taken to improve regional search and rescue capabilities and to share peacekeeping experience and expertise more effectively among ARF participants. The proposed ISM on disaster relief and the encouragement given to ARF members to extend financial and political support to the Korean Peninsula Energy Development Organization (KEDO) were also indicative of a steadily expanding agenda. A Chinese proposal that 'the Forum start dialogue on defence conversion and begin at an appropriate time discussions on matters relating to comprehensive security cooperation' could be read as an exercise in self-legitimation, but also as evidence of an emerging regional or at least potential regional consensus about the multiplicity and interconnectedness of the issues comprising the new security agenda.

Following a request by the 1997 ARF Ministerial Meeting, a review was made of the implementation of agreed CBMs. Expressing satisfaction with the high degree of implementation, the 1998 ARF meeting decided that the review should be updated on an annual basis and that the ISG should consider two lists of new CBMs, one for implementation in the near future (Basket 1) and the other over the medium term (Basket 2). In the ensuing 12 months the ISG concluded that a number of Basket 1 CBMs were already at various stages of implementation, and accordingly placed the emphasis on those that had yet to receive much attention. ARF members were encouraged to exchange visits of their naval vessels, visit each other's military establishments and compile and circulate national lists of publications on CBMs as well as information on present levels of implementation. Basket 2 proposals to be considered included ARF liaison with other fora, a counter-narcotics project, and measures to prevent and combat the illicit trafficking in conventional small arms.[79]

Confidence-building measures had undoubtedly gathered momentum in the first phase of the ARF's development. Yet CBMs could not of themselves deliver regional security. Measures designed to make the defence activities and capabilities of ARF members more transparent could in any case be considered a two-edged sword. Enhanced transparency, to the extent that it reduced the possibility of strategic surprise, might generate higher levels of trust among the membership. On the other hand, it could also reveal the strategic weakness of various members, and to that extent might serve to increase anxieties, which could in turn lead to higher military expenditures, and eventually to a reciprocal arms build-up.[80] In any case, confidence-building had not as yet created a climate conducive to the resolution of disputes whether in South, Southeast, or Northeast Asia. There was certainly little evidence that the ARF process had much to contribute to the attenuation of tensions on the Korean peninsula, or in the China–Taiwan and India–Pakistan conflicts.

That having been said, there was a general expectation that successful CBMs might at least create within the ARF a greater willingness to explore the potential of 'preventive diplomacy'. At face value, there was a good deal of overlap between CBMs and preventive diplomacy. It was largely with a view to maximizing this overlap and accelerating the transition from one function to the other that the ISG on CBMs made four key recommendations to ARF senior officials and ministers: an enhanced role for the ARF Chair; a greater liaising role for the ARF with other parties, including other regional organizations; enhanced interaction between first-track and second-track fora, with the ARF Chairman playing a facilitating role; and better coordination between ARF meetings. In a series of preparatory meetings, an enhanced role for the ARF Chair was gradually fleshed out. In tandem with this new initiative, the Seventh ARF Meeting in July 2000 moved a little closer towards the establishment of an ARF Register of Experts/Eminent Persons, with ARF members invited to submit nominations.

Following these tentative first steps the ARF adopted at its Eighth Meeting in July 2001 three papers designed to provide a road-map for the gradual development of a preventive diplomacy capability. The paper on 'Concepts and Principles of Preventive Diplomacy' offered a snapshot of the ARF's understanding of the scope and limitations of preventive diplomacy. The paper on 'The Enhanced Role of the ARF Chair' sought to build upon and spell out more formally the coordination roles and functions which had already accrued through the practice of the last few years. The third paper set out the terms of reference for an ARF Expert/Eminent Persons Register. Participation in the register was voluntary and the views and recommendations of experts were non-binding. In the course of a two-year drafting process the contents of all three papers had been progressively diluted, revealing once again the constraints imposed by consensual decision-making in an institutional setting where the preferred pace and content of preventive diplomacy was still a matter of debate. Nevertheless the adoption of the three papers indicated a growing readiness on the part of the ARF membership to pursue a more action-oriented strategy.[81]

The first paper sought to go beyond the confidence-building efforts of the first few years by canvassing the development of new preventive diplomacy mechanisms. The approach would exclude the use of force; rely on such methods as negotiation, inquiry, mediation and conciliation; operate on the basis of consultation and consensus; apply only to conflicts between states; and be conducted in accordance with the principles of sovereign equality, territorial integrity and non-interference in the internal affairs of states. The second paper envisaged an enhanced role for the ARF Chair, which would include encouraging information exchange and dialogue between ARF members, submitting issues for consideration at ARF annual meetings, convening *ad hoc* meetings of all ARF members, and liaising with external parties, including international organizations and second-track bodies.

While cautiously exploring the possible application of preventive diplomacy techniques to regional conflicts, the ARF remained committed to developing a wider security agenda. The 'new' security issues were especially amenable to the ARF's agenda precisely because they were generally regarded as less sensitive than the traditional concerns of military security, but also because they required various forms of regional co-operation. Meeting in Bangkok in July 2000, ARF ministers stressed the importance of the economic, social and human components of human security, and specifically referred to the need for collective action to meet the challenges posed by globalization. In addition to work done over the preceding few years by way of setting the general direction of future co-operation, largely through ISMs, on such issues as search and rescue and disaster relief, increasing attention was directed to terrorism and transnational crime. Several meetings and working groups took up issues of piracy, illegal immigration, including trafficking in human beings, especially women and children, and illicit trafficking in drugs and small arms. Meetings of the ARF Experts' Group on Transnational Crime stressed the need for enhanced coordination and co-operation among ARF members. More specifically, support was expressed for practical measures aimed at more sustained contact between ARF enforcement agencies, better training of relevant personnel, a more effective framework of regional monitoring, and stronger support for international treaties and agencies.[82]

While transnational security issues had become a regular feature of the ARF agenda, there was still little evidence that the regional forum had either the inclination or the capacity to translate the new security discourse into policy initiatives. Several obstacles stood in the way. The first, though not necessarily the most important, had to do with the lingering attachment of political leaders and government officials to the more familiar politico-military discourse centred around issues of nuclear and missile proliferation, the production and stockpiling of anti-personnel landmines, the situation in East Timor and unresolved regional disputes, whether in the South China Sea or the Korean peninsula. More importantly perhaps, ARF governments, while intellectually persuaded of the validity of notions of comprehensive and even human security, were reluctant to engage in concerted action, either because they doubted that, given conflicting interests, agreement on practical measures would be forthcoming, or because they remained sceptical that such agreement, even if it materialized, would result in effective coordinated action on the ground. Lastly, and perhaps most importantly, governments were reticent to consider practical implementation, either because they were not themselves prepared to commit the necessary resources to the process or allow their freedom of manoeuvre to be restricted by collective decision-making. These familiar impediments to the regionalist project were nowhere more strikingly evident than in the ARF's early attempts to come to terms with the transnational challenges to security.

Power and Legitimacy

As we saw with APEC so with the ARF, functions and organization were inseparable from questions of power and legitimacy. In agreeing to the establishment of the ARF, ASEAN calculated that at least for the foreseeable future, regional security required a dialogue mechanism in which all great powers with interests in the region would be able to play a part. It would be misleading, however, to infer from this, as Acharya and others have done,[83] that ASEAN's policy of 'inclusiveness' signified the virtual abandonment of the ZOPFAN principle. The pragmatic, indeed inescapable, acknowledgement that the great powers and their rivalries continued to exercise a profound influence over the likely course of regional conflicts could not be equated with a policy of alignment with one or other of the great powers. Even those ASEAN countries which were most favourably disposed to a continuing, even expanded, US military presence in Asia Pacific, notably Singapore and the Philippines, saw this as an expedient device for countering China's rising geopolitical weight in the region. In any case, if the aim was to construct a region-wide security framework capable in due course of addressing such intractable problems as the China–Taiwan or Korean conflicts, the exclusion of the great powers would prove utterly self-defeating. In this sense, inclusiveness was first and foremost an attempt on ASEAN's part to establish a dialogue framework in which the great powers could fully participate, but which could not be subordinated to their individual or collective interests. ASEAN's determination to maintain a leadership role within the ARF was in part an expression of this design, namely the containment of great power rivalry, which is not to say that the strategy was rigorously formulated, or its execution doomed to success.

Though both Japan and Russia were in different ways and to different degrees relevant to the great power equation, the analysis here will be confined largely to China and the United States. In Beijing's case the decision to join the ARF in the first instance and its subsequent willingness to engage in a number of confidence-building measures were indicative of a significant shift in China's thinking on multilateral security co-operation. At the Second ARF Meeting in Brunei, Beijing signalled its willingness to allow the Spratlys to become a subject of multilateral discussion with ASEAN. Some chose to interpret this more accommodating stance as evidence that China wished to avoid isolation within the ARF.[84] There is reason to suggest, however, that Chinese calculations were both more complex and more ambitious. Beijing's willingness to implement CBMs, for example, its accession to the UN conventional arms register in 1993, the publication of a White Paper on arms control and disarmament in November 1995, and the signing of an agreement on prior notification of certain military manoeuvres and exchange of military observers in May 1996, was indicative of a strategic assessment of the evolving configuration of power both globally and regionally. While China was suspicious of, indeed hostile to, American notions of engagement, which it regarded as a more subtle but no less intrusive form of containment, it was amenable to ASEAN-style engagement, precisely because it accepted the legitimacy of Chinese influence. In the eyes of China's leaders, ASEAN and the ARF helped to reinforce the trend towards multipolarity, thereby constraining Washington's propensity to unilateralism. ASEAN's centrality within the ARF helped to consolidate two notions: first, that ASEAN was a significant player in its own right; and secondly, that all major powers – not just the United States – had a role to play in regional security. Both notions were seen as conducive to a multipolar security framework, and as providing China with greater leverage and greater opportunities to challenge, at least discursively, US policies and US-centred security arrangements.

For the United States, the establishment of the ARF was generally welcomed, but it was not an initiative in which it had invested much energy or one which it placed high on its diplomatic agenda. In the early 1990s, domestic and international influences, not least the end of the Cold War and opposition to the retention of US bases in the Philippines, had combined to make way for a reduced US military presence in the West Pacific. In line with the *East Asia Security Initiative* announced in July 1992, US force levels in East Asia were reduced from 132,000 to approximately 120,000 by the end of that year, and further reductions were projected which would result in a Pacific base force of 100,000 by the year 2000. Though these force levels were deemed sufficient to demonstrate US resolve and retain military predominance in the region, a more considered notion of Washington's future role emerged only gradually during the Clinton presidency. Under the slogan 'cooperative engagement' many of the earlier themes of US security policy were retained: strong bilateral alliances, respect for international norms, forward presence, and crisis response.

The creation of a 'New Pacific Community' became the focal point of the Clinton administration's approach, which sought to link economy, security and democracy.[85] Plans for a US military presence of 100,000 were cemented in 1998 in the Defense Department's *East Asia Strategic Report*. Even greater emphasis was now placed on retaining a lead in technological capabilities, strengthening existing alliance arrangements, notably with Japan, South Korea and Australia, and expanding security co-operation and military access in Southeast Asia. Enhancement of region-wide dialogue and confidence-building through the ARF was seen as a complementary but subsidiary objective. In this latter context, the United States expressed strong interest in 'the development of new mechanisms for transparency, confidence-building, including trilateral and multilateral meetings, defence forums, and combined education in the Asia-Pacific Center for Security Studies in Hawaii'.[86] While regularly participating in all ARF meetings, the US administration seemed content to let ASEAN states drive the agenda, concentrating its efforts in a few selected areas, for example in the ISGs dealing with search and rescue and confidence-building more generally.

US military engagement in the region was supported in Southeast Asia not only by US friends and allies but by ASEAN as a whole. The US presence was valued in that it encouraged Japan to adopt a less assertive defence posture than would otherwise be the case, and provided a useful counterweight to China's rising influence in the region. The ASEAN attitude could not, however, be interpreted as unqualified support for specific US deterrence policies, existing or projected military deployments, or military alliance arrangements. Rather ASEAN's strategy was to ensure that an equilibrium could be established such that no major centre of power could exercise hegemonic control over the region. Conversely, the ASEAN states saw little to be gained from a concert of powers, that is, a new security framework in which the great powers would determine outcomes with little or no reference to the interests or priorities of small and middle powers. As Acharya has observed, an Asian concert system modelled on Europe held little attraction for ASEAN since it would 'effectively marginalise ASEAN in the management of regional order'.[87]

Whereas ASEAN preferred the balancing of power to a concert of powers, it was nevertheless averse to the exclusive application of balance of power principles. From ASEAN's vantage point, attempts to achieve and maintain a great power equilibrium had to be qualified by and integrated with the establishment of multilateral dialogue mechanisms. One of the primary functions of security dialogue was, at least in principle, to subject the policies of all great powers to periodic scrutiny, particularly in the event that those policies adversely impacted on one or more ASEAN members. Placed in this context, multilateralism was seen as a useful constraint on the freedom of action available to great powers. This was the underlying rationale in ASEAN's efforts to place the Spratlys dispute on the ARF agenda. The mere discussion of this potentially divisive issue was thought to have a useful restraining effect on Beijing's South China Sea ambitions, if for no other reason than that it brought the international spotlight to bear on China's actions and policies, and obliged all ARF members, including the United States, to exercise greater vigilance.

True enough, there were diverse views within ASEAN regarding both the functions that the ARF could usefully and realistically serve and the most appropriate strategy for handling relations with China. It would, however, be a gross exaggeration to suggest that such diversity was equivalent to paralysis, or that as a result the ARF was at best an irrelevant sideshow.[88] Though China did frequently assert its sovereign authority over all of the disputed Spratly Islands, and sought to translate this claim into periodic displays of force – as in the Mischief Reef incident of 1995 and the subsequent expansion of its structures on the disputed reef in October 1998 – in practice it pursued a policy of relative moderation. Motivated in part by a desire to forge a close working relationship with ASEAN, China agreed at the 1995 ARF meeting to enter into a security dialogue with ASEAN, in which the South China Sea dispute would be one of the items of discussion. Subsequent ARF meetings, with China's implicit consent, repeatedly stressed the importance of self-restraint, welcomed the commitment of all countries concerned to resolve disputes by peaceful means and in accordance with the principles of international law, including the UN Convention on the Law of the Sea. The ASEAN–China Senior Officials Consultations, the exchange of views in the ARF, as well as the Informal Workshops on Managing Conflicts in the South China Sea were seen as contributing to this end. By the end of 2001 significant progress was reported on developing a Regional Code of Conduct between ASEAN and China, but a number of differences as much within ASEAN as between ASEAN and China had yet to be resolved.[89]

Architecture

The ARF had in its first eight years achieved a good deal less than its most enthusiastic supporters would have wished, which is not to say that it had achieved little or nothing of significance. The principle of 'co-operative security' on which the ARF experiment was premised had yet to be fully articulated, except at a high level of generality. ASEAN's leadership role within the ARF was constrained both by internal differences and by its limited capabilities. On the other hand, by virtue of occupying the driver's seat ASEAN had helped to gain recognition, in practice if not in theory, for the principle of multipolarity, thereby effectively precluding any one great power from seeking, let alone gaining, control of the regional security agenda. The principle of multipolarity, to the extent that it accurately expressed the emerging configuration of power and influence, gave the ARF solidity and durability of a kind that it might not otherwise have possessed. A decade after the initial decision to establish it in July 1993, there was little indication that any of its members was sufficiently disenchanted to rethink its membership of the ARF or support for its activities. The marriage of the ARF's two foundational principles, which might be best described as 'co-operative multipolarity', was of necessity one of uneasy coexistence in which competing poles might obscure or even moderate but hardly eliminate the intensity of their competition. The ambiguities surrounding the ARF's evolving agenda and rationale were as much a function of its own organizational and political profile as of its relationship to the wider regional architecture. Nevertheless, as Chapter 10 will explore in greater depth, the ARF's capacity to perform any of the functions it had set itself depended in part on how it would connect with other established or emerging regional arrangements.

Two related questions were involved here: was the underlying logic of the ARF's conception of security and its methodology consistent with that driving other regional dialogue mechanisms? And, even if they were, to what extent did the ARF connect with them in ways that were mutually reinforcing? Four sub-regional arrangements were especially relevant: first, and most obviously ASEAN itself; secondly, the ASEAN+3 dialogue linking Northeast and Southeast Asia; thirdly, the loose, largely *ad hoc* mechanisms that had recently emerged in Northeast Asia; and lastly the Pacific Islands Forum, the principal multilateral organization that linked the often overlooked yet strategically significant clusters of island states stretching across the Pacific.

ASEAN's central role has already been considered and will be further examined in the next chapter. Suffice it here to note that ASEAN's longstanding code of inter-state behaviour might not be easily transplanted to the much larger ARF grouping, which encompassed a more diverse array of political and strategic cultures, three poorly connected sub-regions, and actual or potential great power rivalries of uncertain scope and duration. Notwithstanding ASEAN's moral and diplomatic clout, serious questions arose as to ASEAN's leadership capabilities, especially during times of heightened tensions between the United States and China. In any case, as we shall soon see, the financial and political crises that beset much of Southeast Asia in the late 1990s called into question ASEAN's brand of normative and organizational leadership, not least within its own ranks. Would the ARF stand to gain from a more detached relationship with ASEAN, or were both organizations mutually dependent, whether by historical accident or geopolitical necessity, for their legitimacy and functional efficacy?

A second, somewhat contradictory trend had to do with the 'Asianization' of East Asian security.[90] The 1990s had witnessed a series of renewed, though not entirely successful attempts to cultivate an 'East Asian consciousness' whether in relation to human rights and Asian values more generally, the establishment of an Asian Monetary Fund, or the formation of an East Asian Economic Group. However, by the late 1990s, with ASEAN once again taking the initiative, the ASEAN+3 concept was beginning to make headway. Ministerial meetings between ASEAN, China, Japan and South Korea were regularized, and informal summit meetings between the 13 countries became an accepted part of the East Asian diplomatic calendar. The Joint Statement on East Asia Cooperation issued by the ASEAN+3 Summit in Manila in November 1999 may have been short on practical commitments, but the symbolism was nevertheless potent. The ARF Chairman's statement of July 2000 welcoming the ASEAN+3 initiative[91] was itself an indication of a new diplomatic wind blowing through the region – a wind, it should be readily conceded, that was still very much of uncertain direction and strength. It remained to be seen how the ARF would in practice connect with this emerging East Asian dialogue, in particular the extent to which one forum would mesh in with or influence the other's agenda, ethos, or policy initiatives.

In Northeast Asia itself several developments had occurred – a more detailed examination follows in Chapter 8 – which pointed to a more intense level of diplomatic activity, especially in relation to the Korean conflict. The Agreed Framework which the United States and the Democratic People's Republic of Korea (DPRK) concluded in October 1994 and the subsequent creation of the KEDO in March 1995[92] had paved the way for more substantial, though periodically faltering, bilateral dialogues between North Korea on the one hand and South Korea, the United States and Japan on the other. The four-party talks (North and South Korea, the United States and China) which eventually got under way in December 1997 provided new evidence of the potential for multilateral dialogue, as did the proposal for a '2+2+2' framework (the four parties plus Russia and Japan). When it came, however, to the ARF's connection with and response to these developments, the same ambiguities applied as in the case of the East Asian dialogue. The ARF might offer words of encouragement to the relevant parties, and prod gently towards a negotiated solution of all outstanding differences, but it was not at all clear whether the ARF would assume a distinctive role in confidence-building in Northeast Asia, let alone contribute to conflict prevention or conflict resolution. The limitations of the ARF's ambitions and capabilities were equally apparent when it came to the intermittent tensions in the Russo–Japanese and Sino–Japanese relationships, and, if anything, more pronounced still when it came to the China–Taiwan dispute.

Though for partly different reasons, the ARF's relationship to South Pacific issues and to the South Pacific Forum was similarly problematic. ARF discussions and statements would increasingly refer to security developments in the South Pacific, whether in relation to Fiji, the Solomons, or Bougainville, as overlapping with the ARF's 'geographical footprint'. But the implications of such overlap remained unstated. The issues might intrude into the discussions of ARF ministerial and senior officials, but it was not clear what function the ARF might perform other than that of exhorting the parties to establish cease-fires, restore law and order, and respect democratic principles. Would the ARF itself have a role to play in promoting such outcomes? Would it liaise in a more direct or sustained fashion with South Pacific multilateral mechanisms? If so, with what aims in mind, and by what means? To the extent that a number of ARF members had critical interests to defend in the Pacific, whether it be the United States, France, Australia or New Zealand, ARF intrusion might be less than welcome should their interests be threatened by such intrusion. These uncertainties and ambiguities, while closely linked to the dynamics of particular conflicts and the sensitive balance of interests in particular sub-regions, did nevertheless reflect the larger features of the region's geopolitical and economic landscape. Here again we come face to face with the complexities of the region's evolving architecture – a question to which the final chapter will devote more sustained attention.

NOTES

1. See Nicole Gallant and Richard Stubbs, 'APEC's Dilemma: Institution-Building around the Pacific', *Pacific Affairs*, 70 (2), Summer 1997, 203–18.
2. See Mark Beeson and Kanishka Jayasuriya, 'The Political Rationalities of Regionalism: APEC and the EU in Comparative Perspective', *Pacific Review*, 11 (3), 1998, 311–36.
3. See John Ravenhill, 'APEC and the WTO: Which Way Forward to Trade Liberalization?', *Contemporary Southeast Asia*, 21 (2), August 1999, 220–370.
4. See, for example, Kenneth Flamm and Edward Lincoln, 'Time to Reinvent APEC', *Brookings Policy Brief Series*, 26, November 1997; also Robert G. Gilpin, 'APEC in a New International Order', in Donald C. Hellman and Kenneth B. Pyle (eds), *From APEC to Xanadu: Creating a Viable Community in the Post-Cold War Pacific*, Armonk, NY: M.E. Sharpe, 1997, pp. 14–36.
5. *APEC A Decade of Progress*, A report prepared for APEC Ministers Responsible for Trade, Darwin: Department of Foreign Affairs and Trade, 2000, p. vi.
6. Ibid., p. 13.
7. Jane Khanna, 'Asia-Pacific Economic Cooperation and Challenges for Political Leadership', *Washington Quarterly*, 19 (1), Winter 1996, 258.
8. See Andrew Elek (ed.), *Building an Asia-Pacific Community. Development Cooperation within APEC*, Brisbane: Foundation for Development Cooperation, 1997.
9. Statement by the Chairman, Senator the Hon. Gareth Evans, APEC Ministerial-level Meeting, Canberra, 6–7 November 1989, Documentation, Department of Foreign Affairs and Trade, Canberra, 1989.
10. Gareth Evans, Address to the Australian Business Asia Forum, Sydney, 3 November 1994, p. 7.
11. See *Australia and APEC: A Review of Asia Pacific Economic Cooperation*, Report of the Senate Foreign Affairs, Defence and Trade References Committee, July 2000, p. 15.
12. The ambivalence of ASEAN members was an important part of the sub-text of ASEAN's 21st Economic Ministers' Meeting held immediately after APEC's inaugural meeting. See Joint Press Statement, Brunei Darussalam, 30 November–1 December 1989, at http://www.aseansec.org/print.asp?file=/economic/eco-221.htm (sighted on 25 September 2002). Interestingly, some 12 years later much the same sub-text coloured Rudolfo Severino's address to the APEC Ministerial Meeting, Shanghai, 18 October 2001, *ASEAN Economic Bulletin*, 18 (8), December 2001, 334–6.

13. Jiang Zemin's speech at the Seattle APEC Summit, *Xinhua*, 20 November 1993, translated in *FBIS-CHI 93*, 'Text of Jiang Speech', 22 November 1993, 11–13.
14. William Bodde Jr, *View from the 19th Floor: Reflections of the First APEC Executive Director*, Singapore: Institute of Southeast Asian Studies, 1994, p. 67.
15. For a more detailed description of the APEC framework, see *Australia and APEC*, pp. 43–52.
16. Bodde, *View from the 19th Floor*, p. 45.
17. *Australian*, 8 April 1992, p. 1.
18. *Australian*, 4 May 1992, p. 1.
19. *Age* (Melbourne), 10 April 1993, p. 8.
20. *Australian*, 21 April 1993, p.8.
21. Cited in Hadi Soesastro, 'ASEAN and APEC: Do Concentric Circles Work?', *Pacific Review*, 8 (3), 1995, 483.
22. Beeson and Jayasuriya, 'The Political Rationalities of Regionalism', pp. 314–15.
23. Ibid., p. 324.
24. See Peter F. Cowhey, 'Pacific Trade Relations after the Cold War: GATT, NAFTA, ASEAN and APEC', in Peter Gourevitch, Takashi Inoguchi and Courtney Purrington (eds), *United States–Japan Relations and International Institutions after the Cold War*, La Jolla, CA: Graduate School of International Relations and Pacific Studies, University of California, 1995, pp.183–226.
25. Rapkin, 'The United States, Japan, and the Power to Block: The APEC and AMF Cases', *Pacific Review*, 14 (3), 2001, 383.
26. Khanna, 'Asia-Pacific Economic Cooperation', p. 270.
27. Joan E. Spero, 'US Business and Economic Cooperation in the Asia-Pacific Region', *US Department of State Dispatch* (hereafter *Dispatch*), 5 (44), 31 October 1994, 729.
28. See *A Blueprint for APEC*, Report of the PBF handed to President Suharto as APEC Chairman, 15 October 1994.
29. *Australia and APEC*, p. 25.
30. See, for example, *Facing Globalization the APEC Way*, Report to the APEC Economic Leaders, APEC Business Advisory Council, Brunei Darussalam, 2000.
31. *Australia and APEC*, p. 106.
32. See Ravenhill, 'APEC and the WTO', p. 232.
33. Koro Bessho, *Identities and Securities in East Asia*, Adelphi Paper 325, London: International Institute for Strategic Studies, 1999, p. 65.
34. See Address by Gareth Evans, Minister for Foreign Affairs and Trade, to the Centre for International Business Affairs (CIBA) Forum on, 'Strategic Approach to Trade and International Investment', Melbourne, 13 August 1992 at http://members.aol.com/merranev/CIBA.html (sighted on 29 October 2002).
35. For a succinct exposition of the political pitfalls that make governments wary of following the free trade prescriptions of economic theory, see Ravenhill, 'APEC and the WTO', pp. 223–5.
36. See joint statement, APEC 5th Ministerial Meeting, Seattle, 17–19 November 1993, pp. 1–2, at http:www.apecsec.org.sg/virtualib/minismtg/mtgmin93.html (sighted on 24 September 2002).
37. See Bodde, *View from the 19th Floor*, pp. 47–8; *Australia and APEC*, pp. 14–16.
38. *APEC Pacific Business Forum Report*, 15 October 1994, pp. i–ii.
39. Ministry of Foreign Affairs, Japan, *Japan's Views on APEC*, Official Information, Osaka, 15 November 1995.
40. See Osaka Action Agenda, APEC, *Selected Documents 1995*, pp. 5–6.
41. Michael Wesley, 'APEC's Mid-Life Crisis? The Rise and Fall of Early Voluntary Sectoral Liberalization', *Pacific Affairs*, 74 (2) Summer 2001, 189.
42. APEC Economic Committee, *The Impact of Trade Liberalization in APEC*, November 1997, p. 2.
43. APEC Economic Committee, 'Assessing APEC Trade Liberalization and Facilitation – 1999 Update', September 1999, p. 10.
44. APEC Economic Leaders' Declaration, 'Connecting the APEC Community', Vancouver, 25 November 1997.

45. Wesley, 'APEC's Mid-Life Crisis?', pp. 195–6.
46. APEC Second Senior Officials Meeting, Chair's Report to the Ministers Responsible for Trade, Kuching, Malaysia, 11–20 June 1998; Summary Conclusions of the Third Senior Officials Meeting for the Tenth Ministerial Meeting, 13–15 September, 1998, Kuantan, Malaysia.
47. See John S. Wilson, *Standards and APEC: An Action Agenda*, Washington, DC: Institute for International Economics, 1995, pp. 57–84.
48. See Myrna S. Austria, 'APEC's Commitments on Investment', in Richard E. Feinberg and Ye Zhao (eds), *Assessing APEC's Progress: Trade, Ecotech and Institutions*, Singapore: Institute of Southeast Asian Studies, 2001, p. 62.
49. Merit E. Janow, 'Competition Policy and Regulatory Policy', in Feinberg and Zhao (eds), *Assessing APEC's Progress*, p. 75.
50. Leonardo A. Lanzona, 'Mobility of Business People in APEC', in Feinberg and Zhao (eds), *Assesing APEC's Progress*, pp. 79–82.
51. See APEC Committee on Trade and Investment, *2001 Annual Report to Ministers*, Shanghai, October 2001, p. 1.
52. 'China Proposes Measures for Asia-Pacific Co-operation', *FBIS-CHI*, 13 May 1996, p.11.
53. See Thomas G. Moore and Dixia Yang, 'China, APEC and Economic Regionalism in the Asia-Pacific', *Journal of East Asian Affairs*, 13 (2), Fall/Winter 1999, 388–9.
54. *Beijing Review*, 8–14 February 1999, p. 4.
55. See Statement by Rodolfo C. Severino, Secretary-General of ASEAN, at the 11th APEC Ministerial Meeting, Auckland, 10 September 1999 (sighted 5 December 2001 at http/www.aseansec.org/secgen/sg_apc.htm).
56. See *Australia and APEC*, pp. 157–73; also John McKay, 'Development of Economic Infrastructure', in Feinberg and Zhao (eds), *Assessing APEC's Progress*, pp. 145–52.
57. APEC First Ministerial Meeting, Canberra, 6–7 November 1989.
58. See Declaration, APEC Ministerial Meeting on Sustainable Development, Manila, 11–12 July 1996.
59. See APEC–PECC Workshop to improve Investor Confidence and Capital Mobilization in APEC's Energy Sector, Oakland, CAL, 19–20 April 1999.
60. See Rouben Azizian, 'The APEC Summit: From Acceleration to Consolidation', *New Zealand International Review*, 24 (6), November–December 1999, 3.
61. The full text is available at the APEC Secretariat website at http://www.apecsec.org.sg/download/pubs/LeadersStmtFightTerroNGrowth.pdf (sighted on 31 October 2002).
62. Rapkin, 'The United States, Japan, and the Power to Block', p. 381.
63. President Clinton, 'US–Asia Economic Engagement in the 21st Century', *Dispatch*, 5 (9), November 1994, 12–13.
64. This analysis closely dovetails that offered by John Ravenhill, *APEC and the Construction of Pacific Rim Regionalism*, Cambridge: Cambridge University Press, 2001, pp. 93–6.
65. Walter Hatch and Kozo Yamamura, *Asia in Japan's Embrace: Building a Regional Production Alliance*, Cambridge: Cambridge University Press, 1996, p. 192.
66. Japan's approach to APEC is examined in greater detail in Ravenhill, *APEC and the Construction of Pacific Rim Regionalism*, pp. 99–103.
67. Ibid., p. 385.
68. 'Jiang Addresses APEC Meeting', *Beijing Review*, 7–13 December 1998, 6.
69. Cited in Moore and Yang, 'China, APEC and Economic Regionalism in the Asia-Pacific, p. 370.
70. Noor Adlan, 'APEC and Asia's Crisis', *Far Eastern Economic Review*, 28 May 1998, 35.
71. See Stuart Harris, 'Asian Multilateral Institutions and their Response to the Asian Economic Crisis', *Pacific Review*, 13 (3), 2000, 509.
72. It is not therefore a case of a coherent, effective APEC agenda emerging from the convergence of American and Asian views (a formulation advanced, for example, by Seiji Finch Naya and Pearl Imada Iboshi, 'A Post-Uruguay Round agenda for APEC: Promoting Convergence of North American and Asian Views', in Chia Siow Yue (ed), *APEC Challenges and Opportunities*, Singapore: Institute of Southeast Asian Studies, 1994, pp. 72–3. It could be argued that APEC encompassed, if not all, then at least three of the four schools of thought identified by Aggarwal: open regionalism, inward-looking regionalism, pure 'GATT-ism',

and advocacy of an Asian bloc (see Vinod K. Aggarwal, 'Building International Institutions in Asia-Pacific', *Asian Survey*, 33 (11), November 1993, 1029–42).

73. Ravenhill, *APEC and the Construction of Pacific Rim Regionalism*, p. 169.
74. The presumption that ASEAN's preference for an open multilateral trading system pointed to a complementarity of interests between APEC and ASEAN was often asserted but seldom demonstrated. See Mohamed Ariff, 'AFTA and NAFTA: Complementing or competing?', in Chia (ed.), *APEC Challenges and Opportunities*, pp. 168–9.
75. See Gareth Evans, Address to the Seminar on 'Building the Confidence and Trust in Asia Pacific,' Canberra, 24 November 1994, p. 3.
76. See Ralph A. Cossa, 'Multilateral Dialogue in Asia: Benefits and Limitations,' *Korea and World Affairs*, 19 (1) Spring, 1995, p. 5; Desmond Ball, 'CSCAP: Its Future Place in the Regional Security Architecture', paper presented to the Eighth Asia Pacific Roundtable, Kuala Lumpur, 6-8 June 1994, pp. 11–12.
77. ASEAN, 27th ASEAN Ministerial Meeting, ASEAN Regional Forum, and Post-Ministerial Conferences with Dialogue Partners, Bangkok, 22–28 July 1994, Jakarta: ASEAN Secretariat, 1994, p. 62.
78. See 'Chairman's Statement of the Second ASEAN Regional Forum (ARF), 1 August 1995, Bandar Seri Begawan', *PacNet Newsletter*, 29, 18 August 1995. See also Jusuf Wanandi, 'Dialogue on Security Gains Momentum', *PacNet Newsletter*, 31, 1 September 1995.
79. Co-Chairmen's Summary Report of the Meetings of the ARF Intersessional Support Group on Confidence Building Measures, Honolulu, 14–16 November 1998, and Bangkok, 3–5 March 1999.
80. This argument is developed at greater length in John Garofano, 'Flexibility or Irrelevance: Way Forward for the ARF', *Contemporary Southeast Asia*, 21 (1), April 1999, 88.
81. Richard Sadleir, 'Eighth ASEAN Regional Forum: Outcomes', *AUS–CSCAP Newsletter*, 12, November 2001, 25–6.
82. See, for example, 'Co-Chairmen's Summary Report of the ARF Experts' Group Meetings on Transnational Crime held in Seoul, 30–31 October 2000 and in Kuala Lumpur, 16–17 April 2001', at http:www.aseansec.org/print.asp?=/amm/arf8doc4.htm (sighted on 25 September 2002).
83. Amitav Acharya, *Constructing a Security Community in Southeast Asia: ASEAN and the Problem of Regional Order*, London: Routledge, 2001, pp. 172–3; Ralf Emmers, 'The Influence of the Balance of Power Factor within the ASEAN Regional Forum', *Contemporary Southeast Asia*, 23 (2), August 2001, 282.
84. Amitav Acharya, 'The ARF Could Well Unravel', in Derek da Cunha (ed.), *The Evolving Pacific Power Structure*, Singapore: Institute of Southeast Asian Studies, 1996, p. 64.
85. See William J. Clinton, *A National Security Strategy of Engagement and Enlargement 1995–1996*, Washington, DC: Government Printing Office, July 1994, p. 28.
86. US Defense Department, *The United States Security Strategy for the East Asia-Pacific Region*, Washington, DC: 1998, p. 6.
87. Acharya, *Constructing a Security Community in Southeast Asia,* pp. 180–81.
88. A striking example of overstatement is provided in Robyn Lim, 'The ASEAN Regional Forum: Building on Sand', *Contemporary Southeast Asia*, 20 (2), August 1998, 117–35.
89. See Co-Chairmen's Summary Report of ARF ISG meetings held in Seoul (1–3 November 2000) and Kuala Lumpur (18–20 April 2001); also Sadleir, 'Eighth ASEAN Regional Forum: Outcomes', p. 26.
90. See Yong Deng, 'The Asianization of East Asian Security and the United States' Role', *East Asian Studies*, 16 (3/4), Autumn/Winter 1998, 103–4.
91. Chairman's Statement, Seventh Meeting of the ASEAN Regional Forum, 27 July 2000 (sighted 4 December 2001 at http://www.aseansec.org/menu.asp?action=3content=2).
92. For details, see Joseph A. Camilleri, *States, Markets and Civil Society in Asia Pacific: The Political Economy of the Asia-Pacific Region*, Vol. I, Cheltenham, UK: Edward Elgar, 2000, pp. 253–5.

7. ASEAN: the challenges of adaptation

The mid- to late 1980s may have ushered in the 'new regionalism', but the changing circumstances which made it possible had yet to run their course by the late 1990s. The very term 'post-Cold War' was suggestive of the new uncertainties for, while pointing to the end of an era in international relations, it gave little indication of what would replace it. As argued elsewhere, at least four distinct security models now competed for the attention of scholars and policy-makers alike: unipolarity, concert of powers, balance of power, and universal security.[1] Written in 1992, the study concluded that taken in isolation none of these four tendencies adequately described the dynamics of the post-Cold War order, and that for some time to come all four tendencies would coexist in uneasy tension as competing interests, projects and institutional arrangements vied for supremacy. Ten years later that conclusion remained just as valid.

Despite significant developments (for example, the UN's enhanced peacekeeping role, increasing intervention in intra-state conflicts, establishment of the International Criminal Court), the emergence of an effective global security system based on the enhanced authority of the United Nations and related multilateral institutions remained a distant prospect. Similarly, relations among the great powers, as much in the security as in the economic arena, at the regional as at the global level, reflected a curious mixture of intermittent and partial agreements on the one hand and profound and at times highly visible disputes and animosities on the other. Of the four tendencies, the assertion of US hegemony seemed the most pronounced, yet the outward manifestations of power (for example, military power projection, flexing of economic muscle, capacity to manipulate or neutralize international institutions, reluctance of any other major centre of power to challenge directly US dominance) were themselves deceptive, for they obscured the diminishing capacity of the United States to produce intended consequences or prevent unintended ones. The intractability of the Middle East conflict, increased US vulnerability to terrorist attack, the rise of Islam as a major force in international political life, and rising Chinese influence in Asia were but the most visible signs of the limits to US power.

The 'new regionalism' in Asia Pacific generally, and ASEAN in particular, was inevitably buffeted by a complex web of endogenous and exogenous, centripetal and centrifugal pressures. The purpose of this chapter is to analyse how these contradictory tendencies impacted on ASEAN, how ASEAN attempted to navigate through these turbulent waters, and what the implications of ASEAN's trajectory during this period might be for our understanding of the emerging multilateralism in Asia Pacific.

POLITICS OF INCLUSION

Of the many challenges facing ASEAN during the 1990s none was perhaps more indicative of its priorities than the way it would approach the issue of enlargement. To put it simply, the great attraction of an expanded ASEAN that encompassed the whole of Southeast Asia yet somehow remained a cohesive entity able to speak with one voice, was the greater diplomatic influence the Association would enjoy, and the enhanced capacity it would have to cement its pivotal role in the development of both existing and new regional institutions.[2] In presenting the case for enlargement, the ASEAN Secretariat rejected the idea that a larger, more diverse ASEAN would weaken or undermine the Association's cohesion. Southeast Asia's diversity, it was argued, was a fact of life which ASEAN's composition could not alter. An inclusive ASEAN, on the other hand, improved the prospect that Southeast Asian countries would deal with their differences peacefully and constructively. ASEAN's founding fathers had in any case made it clear from the outset that the Association would be open to all states in the region willing to subscribe to ASEAN's purposes and principles. Since its inception, the argument went on, member states had developed a complex code of conduct based on mutual trust, shared responsibility and reciprocal accommodation of each other's interests. This accumulated wisdom would greatly assist the enlargement process. ASEAN states had in the past exercised great care to temper ambitious integration policies and ensure that these did not cut across national sensitivities. There was no reason to think that an enlarged ASEAN would depart from this well-established principle.[3] On the other hand, by virtue of enlargement the ASEAN economies would have access to a larger market, which would make them more competitive by providing them with access to cheaper raw materials, lower-cost labour, and new export platforms, particularly in textiles, clothing and electronic assembly products.[4]

Well before the resolution of the Cambodia conflict, the new Indochinese initiative announced by Thai Prime Minister Chatichai Choonhavan in August 1988 had, as previously indicated, effectively transformed Vietnam from a serious security threat to a potentially lucrative market for ASEAN exports. Once Vietnam began withdrawing its forces from Cambodia – a move not unconnected with the decline of the Cold War and China's rising influence in the region – both Malaysia and Indonesia signalled that Vietnam's inclusion would help overcome regional antagonisms.[5] Though this view was not shared by others, Lee Kuan Yew included, the process of rapprochement soon gathered pace, greatly facilitated by the Agreement on a Comprehensive Political Settlement of the Cambodian conflict, concluded in October 1991.

From Hanoi's perspective, the improving relationship with ASEAN was highly beneficial in that it lessened its diplomatic isolation and effectively regionalized two conflicts, namely Cambodia and the South China Sea dispute, which Hanoi might otherwise have had to shoulder single-handedly. In the face of mounting Chinese pressure in the Spratlys dispute, the ASEAN connection probably strengthened Vietnam's resolve to stand its ground. Once China granted the American company, Crestone, an exploration contract in May 1992 in an area adjacent to the blocks that Vietnam had similarly earmarked for exploration, a number of incidents ensued. When Crestone began drilling in its allocated area, Vietnamese vessels gave chase to a Chinese survey ship. With Vietnam's admission to ASEAN, the South China Sea effectively became a regional conflict.[6] The normalization of relations with ASEAN had one other important effect: it opened up a new source of foreign investment at a time when Southeast Asian economies were experiencing average annual growth rates of 7 per cent, thereby lessening Vietnam's dependence on development funds from Hong Kong, Japan and Taiwan. From 1988 to 1992 foreign investment in Vietnam rose from $366 million to $1,939 million, of which ASEAN accounted for one-sixth.[7] By 1993 the 'ASEANization of Vietnam' was well under way.[8]

Though the entry of Laos into ASEAN in July 1997 was a much less complicated decision, the same could not be said of Cambodia or Burma. Hun Sen's coup of July 1997 led to a postponement of Cambodia's admission into the Association. ASEAN insisted that Cambodia's internal dispute would have to be settled through free, fair and credible elections, and nominated three of its members, Indonesia, the Philippines and Thailand, to serve as a troika to persuade the Cambodian parties to accept such an approach. Despite Hun Sen's initially positive reaction to ASEAN's mediation efforts, the troika's mission was made difficult by Hun Sen's subsequent accusations that ASEAN was interfering in Cambodia's internal affairs. The clear implication was that ASEAN had abandoned the principle of non-interference widely viewed as the linchpin of the 'ASEAN way'.[9] ASEAN, on the other hand, justified its actions by arguing that its attempt at mediation had proceeded with the approval of the relevant parties and did not propose to take sides. ASEAN also pointed to its special role in the resolution of the Cambodian conflict – a role clearly acknowledged by the 1991 Paris Peace Agreements. Moreover, the breakdown of Cambodia's internal order threatened to create instability along its borders, and in particular to increase the refugee flow into Thailand. Finally, ASEAN took pains to strengthen its credentials as an honest broker, carefully avoiding suspension of aid or other punitive actions against Cambodia of the kind entertained by Western governments.

None of this is to suggest that ASEAN's response was entirely coherent, or that it did not provoke significant differences and tensions within its own ranks. Not surprisingly, the proposal to admit Cambodia in December 1998 proved highly controversial. Thai Foreign Minister Surin Pitsuwan argued that Hun Sen's coup had undermined Cambodian stability, and that Cambodia could join ASEAN only after stability had returned to the country.[10] Nevertheless, the coalition that emerged between Hun Sen's Cambodian People's Party and Prince Ranaridth's FUNCINPEC following the July 1998 National Assembly elections had given sufficient legitimacy to Cambodia's existing power structure to provide ASEAN with the justification it needed to lift the moratorium on Cambodia's admission.

The dilemmas surrounding Burma's projected membership were if anything more acute. Cambodia's special case could at least be set in the context of a protracted conflict, itself the legacy of a larger conflict that had engulfed the whole of Indochina. Burma, on the other hand, had for many years pursued a consciously isolationist policy, avoiding any entanglement in regional conflicts. The State Law and Order Restoration Council (SLORC) created in the wake of the military coup of September 1988 had seemingly given the green light to a process of democratization by authorizing the general elections of May 1990, only to have them annulled once the results gave Aung San Suu Kyi's National League for Democracy (NLD) a clear parliamentary majority. For ASEAN, however, the human rights issues raised by the brutal suppression of the Burmese democracy movement were secondary to the strategic objective of reducing Burma's dependence on China and drawing it more closely into ASEAN. For Singapore, Burma offered significant trade and investment opportunities, while for Thailand border stability and border trade were important considerations.[11] There was little prospect therefore of ASEAN adopting the condemnatory tone of Western governments and in particular of the European Union. ASEAN opted instead for a policy of 'constructive engagement', which, it argued, perhaps more in hope than in expectation, would encourage the SLORC to adopt a process of gradual liberalization.

While calling on the SLORC to open a dialogue with Aung San Suu Kyi and to improve its human rights performance, ASEAN stood its ground in the face of Western pressure. Accordingly, Myanmar was granted observer status in July 1996 and admitted a few days later to the ARF. ASEAN's decision assumed added significance in that it came at a time of considerable friction between ASEAN and its Western dialogue partners over human rights and democracy issues. Critics of 'constructive engagement' argued that, far from advancing liberal reform, the policy was more likely to give the SLORC added international protection and legitimacy. The European Union and the United States, for their part, continued to denounce the SLORC but took no punitive action against ASEAN. Indeed, US Secretary of State Madeleine Albright went so far as to suggest that it was largely up to ASEAN to find a solution to Burma's problems.[12]

ASEAN's stance on Myanmar had not been an entirely consensual one. Both Thailand and the Philippines had expressed considerable misgivings about the decision, as had the ASEAN–ISIS group of think-tanks and a good number of NGOs, especially in the Philippines. Here was evidence that human rights questions were gradually assuming a higher profile in public advocacy in a number of ASEAN societies, enough at any rate to intrude into foreign policy discourse, and as a consequence into ASEAN deliberations. We return to this issue in later chapters, but it is worth noting here that by the late 1990s a slow but steady shift in the psychology of ASEAN diplomacy could be discerned, suggesting that the rigid demarcation between internal politics and inter-state relations, which had served as one of ASEAN's foundational principles, was visibly fraying at the edges. After all, the notion of 'constructive engagement', which was advanced as an argument for Burma's inclusion, was itself couched in language that acknowledged the relevance of human rights and pointed to the need for change in Burma's political order.

The challenges posed by enlargement were not, however, confined to the issue of 'non-interference'.[13] Both Burma and Cambodia raised the possibility that, in economic terms at least, ASEAN would have to function as a two-tiered association. Building 'One Southeast Asia' was easier said than done given the vast disparities in levels of income and industrialization. Such schemes as the Mekong River Basin, involving huge infrastructural investment, could not be expected to bridge the existing gaps in the short to medium term. How ASEAN would handle the competing demands of widening and deepening – a problem not unfamiliar to other regional groupings, the European Union included – was likely to determine its future political and economic viability. Would ASEAN be able to offer its economically least-developed members, in particular Burma, Laos and Cambodia, adequate infrastructural support and trade and other concessions to fast-track their economic development without at the same time retarding the development of more advanced member economies? Simply put, would ASEAN be able to devise economic strategies that delivered to all members sufficient incentives and rewards to strengthen the spirit of co-operation and withstand the intra-mural tensions that would periodically surface in bilateral and multilateral relations?

ECONOMIC INTEGRATION UNDER PRESSURE

In many respects the ASEAN of the late 1980s and early 1990s seemed at the height of its prestige and influence. It had achieved high international standing as the most effective experiment in Asia-Pacific multilateralism; it had proved relatively successful in containing frictions within its own ranks, and had contributed to conflict resolution, notably in Cambodia. Most conspicuously, perhaps, ASEAN was able to make capital of the impressive export performance and high levels of growth recorded by its leading member economies. However, by the mid-1990s many of these achievements would come under serious challenge. The slowing pace of export growth which became clearly visible in 1996 foreshadowed the more severe downturn associated with the 1997 financial crisis. Quite apart from the substantial damage done to these economies, the crisis exposed the limitations of most Southeast Asian economies, the limitations of ASEAN's institutional infrastructure, the conflicting interests and responses which the crisis would provoke, and the absence of effective mechanisms through which remedies could be collectively implemented.[14]

The first tangible attempt at a collective response did not come until early November 1997 when 14 countries from the Asia-Pacific region gathered in Manila, and agreed on a new framework for financial stability and regional co-operation. However, the agreement reached, widely known as the 'Manila framework', was less than adventurous. It called for a strengthening of the IMF's crisis management capacities, the establishment of a regional financial arrangement to supplement the IMF's resources, and the creation of a regional financial surveillance mechanism. The surveillance process, which was to be facilitated by a Permanent Secretariat formed by the finance ministers, would be housed in and financed by the Asian Development Bank, before being transferred to the ASEAN Secretariat in Jakarta.[15]

The Second ASEAN Informal Summit held in December 1997 endorsed these decisions, stressed the need to institutionalize regional surveillance and so avoid risks that might precipitate a future crisis, and called upon the IMF 'to undertake in-depth analysis of the structure of global financial markets and short-term capital flows, including the ongoing study of the operations of hedge funds and their impact on financial market activities'.[16] This general statement of position was followed by the Second ASEAN Finance Ministers Meeting in February 1998, which, in addition to setting in train the creation of a 'mutual monitoring system' with a permanent secretariat, established a framework for Bilateral Payments Arrangements (BPA) to encourage the use of ASEAN currencies in regional trade. It also considered two other ideas: linking all ASEAN currencies, possibly by pegging them to an external currency or basket of currencies; and expanding the ASEAN Swap Arrangement (ASA) which currently stood at $200 million, perhaps by inviting non-ASEAN countries to participate in the arrangement.[17] By the end of 2000 the ASA was enlarged to include all ten ASEAN members and its size increased to $1 billion. There is no denying that the financial crisis stung ASEAN into action, which is not to suggest that the various proposals under consideration were given adequate intellectual preparation or institutional follow-through.

When it came to direct financial assistance, ASEAN left it to member states to approach the IMF and the ADB for quick loans. Generally, ASEAN found the latter a more congenial organization. It appreciated the ADB's continued support for surveillance-related activities, including training of finance and central bank officials, and its readiness to accelerate project development financing and provide additional technical assistance. For the rest, ASEAN used a number of regional and global forums, including APEC, ASEM (Asia-Europe Meeting) II, the ASEAN PMC, and the ASEAN+3 dialogue to press the need for international assistance. Exhortations were made to the IMF to moderate the conditions of its lending policies and to review the practices of international currency trading and finance. The G7, the European Union, and individual OECD economies were urged to facilitate access for Southeast Asian exports, and China was commended for refraining from devaluing the renminbi.[18]

Notwithstanding this burst of multilateral activism, might not Michael Wesley be right to argue that 'East Asian regional institutions [had] fallen short of previous achievements in the use of collective diplomatic weight during the financial crisis'?[19] That ASEAN's response to the crisis revealed 'a considerable failure to wield global influence' is no doubt a valid observation, but the implicit claim that ASEAN or any other Asian regional organization had previously exercised such influence would seem a considerable overstatement. It is arguable that the crisis represented ASEAN's first major test, at least in the economic arena, precisely because this was the first time it had to face a challenge posed by players with global reach, over whom it had little or no influence. Though three states, the United States, Japan and China, were to different degrees and in quite different ways significant players in this game, it is fair to say that, so far as the dynamic of the financial crisis is concerned, the decisions of international banks, transnational corporations, hedge funds and international financial institutions were even less amenable to influence. By virtue of their technological prowess, organizational strength or financial mobility, these organizations were relatively immune to the pressure which Southeast Asian states could individually or collectively apply. Given that many of its members were badly hit by the crisis and that several of them were entering a period of political turmoil, ASEAN did well simply to retain a degree of cohesion. ASEAN advocacy played a part in placing reform of the international financial architecture on the political agenda. The ASEAN initiative for the establishment of an 'Asian monetary fund' backed by Japanese money may have been thwarted, but subsequent proposals for a more modest $30 billion fund met with less resistance.

ASEAN's diplomatic forays could not, however, obscure the fact that economic integration remained painfully slow. ASEAN leaders had decided to proceed with the creation of a free trade area in part because they saw this as a vehicle for a stronger ASEAN voice in international trade negotiations and greater leverage *vis-à-vis* trading partners.[20] The great fear was that, in a period of emerging trading blocs and in the absence of timely action, ASEAN would be swept aside. APEC's formation may also have spurred ASEAN into action. There was more to it, however, than just fear. A new mood of self-confidence was in the air. Policy-makers came to believe that ASEAN's domestic industries could withstand international competition. The Indonesian leadership, in particular, became a strong advocate of trade liberalization. The ASEAN Free Trade Area (AFTA) agreement seemed a handy instrument which ASEAN governments could use to make their domestic industries more receptive to the case for free trade, and to that extent more willing to operate within a regime of lower tariffs. The principal objective was not so much expanded intra-ASEAN trade as the creation of a large enough market to offer the foreign investor attractive economies of scale. The specific vision was of a Southeast Asian common market in which tariffs on all intra-ASEAN trade in manufactures and processed agricultural products would within 15 years be reduced to 5 per cent or less. In September 1994 the AFTA Ministerial Council agreed to shorten the timetable for these reductions to ten years, and to include unprocessed agricultural products in the Common Effective Preferential Tariff (CEPT) scheme.

The September 1994 meeting also agreed to a three-track process of tariff reduction. The first track covered products earmarked for accelerated tariff reductions (the 5 per cent or less target to be reached by 1 January 200). The second track comprised those products for which tariffs were to be reduced to 20 per cent within five years and to 0–5 per cent over the following five years. The third track was reserved for products which individual governments would exclude from the scheme. Two types of exclusion were entertained: short-term exclusion for products regarded as sensitive to domestic industry (such exclusions to be removed in five equal annual instalments beginning in 1995); and longer-term exclusions for products where defence of national security, public morals, and natural or cultural heritage values was deemed a high priority. Once products came under the CEPT scheme, all non-tariff barriers applying to them were to be removed over a period of five years. A safety valve was nevertheless provided enabling governments to withdraw products from the CEPT scheme for such time as imports were likely to cause 'serious injury' to domestic industries.[21] Out of 1,995 tariff lines 1,358 were placed under the CEPT scheme in 1996, while 402 were temporarily excluded. Products on the temporary exclusion list were, however, to be phased into the CEPT scheme in seven instalments from 1997 to 2003 (see Table 7.1).

The ASEAN Plan of Action adopted at the December 1998 Hanoi Summit sought to give trade liberalization added impetus by requiring the six original signatories of the CEPT Agreement to advance the implementation of AFTA by one year from 2003 to 2002. They also agreed to achieve a minimum of 90 per cent of their total tariff lines with tariffs of 5 per cent or less by the year 2000.[22] By February 1999, 85.24 per cent of tariff lines had been included, with 12.75 per cent temporarily excluded. The General Exception List and

Table 7.1   AFTA: Common Effective Preferential Tariff (CEPT) list (2001)

Country	Inclusion List	Temporary Exclusion List	General Exception List	Sensitive List	Total
Brunei	6,284	0	202	6	6,492
Indonesia	7,190	21	68	4	7,283
Malaysia	9,654	218	53	83	10,008
Philippines	5,622	6	16	50	5,694
Singapore	5,821	0	38	0	5,859
Thailand	9,104	0	0	7	9,111
ASEAN-6 total	*43,675*	*245*	*377*	*150*	*44,447*
Percentage	*98.26*	*0.55*	*0.85*	*0.34*	*100*
Cambodia	3,115	3,523	134	50	6,822
Laos	1,673	1,716	74	88	3,551
Myanmar	2,984	2,419	48	21	5,472
Vietnam	4,233	757	196	51	5,237
New members total	12,005	8,415	452	210	21,082
Percentage	*56.94*	*39.92*	*2.14*	*1.0*	*100*
ASEAN total	*55,680*	*8,660*	*829*	*360*	*65,529*
Percentage	*84.74*	*13.40*	*1.28*	*0.55*	*100**

Note: * Rounded.

Source: ASEAN Secretariat.

Sensitive List accounted for just over 2 per cent.[23] In 1999 the weighted average tariff rate for intra-ASEAN trade was 4.59 per cent.[24] By 2001, the average CEPT tariff rate for the six countries was down to 3.21 per cent. It was expected that by 2002 42,377 tariff lines representing 96.2 per cent of the Inclusion List of the original six members would have tariffs of 0–5 per cent.

Encouraging though these steps were, any assessment of ASEAN's trade liberalization agenda would need to take account of several counter-tendencies. To begin with, it was far from clear whether ASEAN's business communities were fully committed to the AFTA project. Several industries were still biding their time to see how serious ASEAN governments were about meeting AFTA timelines. From the outset AFTA had failed to elicit from the private sector the enthusiasm that its principal architects had anticipated. Sceptical of the capacity of ASEAN governments to implement the ambitious vision set out in the Framework Agreement, the tendency was for inefficient producers to put their energies into securing exemptions for their products. The more efficient producers were more likely to seek export markets outside ASEAN than they were to explore enhanced opportunities for regional free trade.[25]

AFTA ministerial meetings had, it is true, endeavoured to maintain the momentum generated by previous decisions. However, the setting and periodic review of AFTA targets seemed as much a political as an economic exercise, in which the emphasis was on establishing a moral and psychological climate conducive to future progress. Much less energy went into developing the detailed formulation, monitoring and enforcement of commitments characteristic of European or North American free trade agreements. As Ravenhill has argued, this lack of detail meant that many key issues were left unresolved and that the difficult negotiations would take place only when the decision could no longer be delayed.[26] It also meant that the institutional arrangements needed to cushion the effects of trade liberalization on the poorer member economies had yet to be carefully considered, let alone adequately addressed. Apart from offering these economies a longer lead time to achieve certain targets, few concrete steps had yet been taken to handle the uneven distribution of costs and benefits likely to result – in the short and possibly longer term – from an accelerated programme of trade liberalization.

Three other considerations raised questions about future progress. First, the removal of tariff barriers in the services sector was proving especially tortuous. A working group, established in 1995 to accelerate the process, paved the way for an agreement reached at the 1995 ASEAN Summit, which committed member countries to negotiate an intra-regional liberalization programme in seven sectors (financial services, tourism, telecommunications, maritime transport, air transport, construction, and business services).[27] However, agreement on such a programme proved elusive until the end of 1998 when the ASEAN economic ministers signed the Protocol to Implement the Initial Package of Commitments. A new round of negotiations to cover all remaining sectors commenced in 1999. Secondly, progress in the area of tariff reductions had not been matched by a comparable lowering of non-tariff barriers – a consideration that was perhaps even more troublesome than the first. ASEAN states sought to protect their respective industries by relying on such barriers as domestic standards, local content, government procurement practices and the arbitrary or non-transparent application of customs procedures. Though the full impact of non-tariff barriers on intra-ASEAN trade could not be easily calculated, the absence of reliable information was itself an indicator of the degree to which AFTA members were reluctant to expose themselves to full public scrutiny. Thirdly, and partly for similar reasons, ASEAN governments had refrained from establishing the administrative or juridical monitoring and enforcement of standards, with little or no attention given to the modalities of dispute resolution. The periodic tension between Malaysia and Singapore over trade in petrochemical products was but one striking instance of this unresolved difficulty. For its part, the ASEAN Secretariat remained seriously underfunded. Despite moderate expansion, the ASEAN Secretariat of the late 1990s could still count only on a relatively small number of senior officers to handle the complex issues of intra- and extra-ASEAN trade.

Given all these impediments to trade liberalization, the patchy record of ASEAN's intra-regional trade is not altogether surprising. Indeed, ASEAN governments had realistically refrained from assigning a high priority to increased intra-ASEAN trade. Nevertheless, for many observers this remained an important benchmark of the success and long-term viability of ASEAN economic integration. Intra-regional exports as a share of ASEAN's total exports did grow from 18.7 per cent in 1990 to 23.0 per cent in 1995, but, following the general decline in ASEAN's export performance in 1996 and the onset of the financial crisis in 1997, the trend was reversed with intra-regional exports in 1998 accounting for only 20.6 per cent of ASEAN's total exports. By 2000, ASEAN's export performance was beginning to recapture some of the ground lost in the preceding three years. In 2000, ASEAN total exports stood at $423.6 billion (an increase of 19.9 per cent over 1999) and imports at $360 billion (an increase of 22.8 per cent over 1999), but intra-ASEAN exports and imports registered even higher growth, rising by 26.3 per cent and 27.0 per cent, respectively. Intra-regional exports as a share of total exports had reached a new high of 23.1 per cent.[28]

There is, of course, more to economic integration than trade liberalization. Interestingly, however, when one turns from issues of trade to those of industrial collaboration or investment promotion, one finds the same mixture of achievement and failure, the same tension between rhetorical enthusiasm and operational constraint. Following a proposal made by the ASEAN Automotive Federation, agreement was eventually reached to proceed with the ASEAN Industrial Complementation (AIC) scheme, which was designed to facilitate exchange of automotive parts, with a view to realizing regional economies of scale. Under pressure from the Japanese motor vehicle industry, the scheme was reorganized in 1988, and subsequently extended to other sectors. By the mid-1990s eight car manufacturers and three countries (Malaysia, the Philippines and Thailand) were participating in the scheme. Another initiative, the ASEAN Industrial Joint Venture (AIJV), was launched in 1983. Designed to facilitate projects involving two or more ASEAN countries, the scheme offered products, which complied with rules of origin requirements, preferential margins for four years – an arrangement renewable up to four years. Under yet another scheme, the ASEAN Industrial Cooperation Organisation (AICO), which was established in November 1996, participating companies could take immediate advantage of the 0–5 per cent CEPT tariff rates instead of waiting for 2003. Within three years, several companies, including Matsushita, Toyota, Desno, Honda, Sony and Goodyear, had lodged applications. Yet for all these initiatives, national rivalries, corporate misgivings and inadequate organizational infrastructure tended to make the going relatively slow.

It was in part because of the roadblocks to integration that the discourse of ASEAN leaders and officials would periodically seek to give the ASEAN project a new lease of life. That was precisely the function of ASEAN Vision 2020 adopted by the second ASEAN Informal Summit in December 1997. The document referred to the regional grouping as 'a partnership in dynamic development' and spoke of accelerated liberalization of trade in services, the achievement of an ASEAN Investment Area by 2010, the free flow of investments by 2020, the establishment of a Trans-ASEAN Gas Pipeline and Water Pipeline and an integrated and harmonized trans-ASEAN transportation network (see Table 7.2). Three years later, ASEAN Secretary-General Rodolfo Severino attempted once again to instil a sense of urgency into the implementation of the ASEAN vision:

> ASEAN has to drop its non-tariff barriers fast. Trade must be made not only freer but also easier and cheaper. Customs procedures have to be streamlined and cleaned up. Product standards within ASEAN have to be harmonized. Air and maritime transport has to be liberalized. Other services have to be opened up. Infrastructure linkages – highway systems, railway lines, regional power grids, gas-pipeline networks – have to be put in place . . . ASEAN is turning its attention to all these measures for further economic integration.[29]

Both the Vision 2020 document and Severino's address are particularly instructive for what they tell us about ASEAN's history. That so much should need to be accomplished in such a relatively short period is a telling comment as much on the obstacles which had stood in the way of progress in the past as on the potential for progress in the future.

The concept of an ASEAN Investment Area (AIA), which was adopted in December 1995, envisaged four main activities: coordination of investment co-operation and facilitation programmes; promotion of greater investment awareness; opening up of industries; and extending national treatment status to all ASEAN investors. A Framework Agreement signed in October 1998 sought to give renewed impetus to the concept by setting a number of more specific objectives, including granting of national treatment to all ASEAN investors by 2010, opening up of all industries to ASEAN investment by 2010, and promoting the freer flow of capital, skilled workers and technology among ASEAN members.[30] Achieving any, let alone all, of these outcomes was likely to prove no less difficult than other attempts at integration. To oversee the process, an AIA Council was created, comprising the ASEAN Secretary-General, ministers and heads of agencies responsible for investment, but in line with the ASEAN approach, it was left to member countries to develop their own AIA action plans. By the end of 2000 several steps had been taken to maintain momentum: preparation of plans for the 2000–04 period; submission of 'temporary exclusion lists' and 'sensitive lists' for the granting of national treatment and the opening up of industries; establishment of a working group to develop comparable FDI data collection and reporting system, and the dissemination of six investment publications to promote the ASEAN region as a single investment area.[31]

Table 7.2   ASEAN compared with other regional economic groups (1999)

Organization	Members	Population (m.)	Nominal GDP ($bn)	Nominal GDP per capita ($)	Trade (Import & Export) ($bn)
ASEAN	10 countries	508.33	547.0	1,072	522.9
European Union (EU)	15 countries: Belgium, Denmark, Germany, Greece, Spain, France, Ireland, Italy, Luxembourg, the Netherlands, Austria, Portugal, Finland, Sweden, UK	375.37	8,455.2	22,400	4,321.7
North American Free Trade Agreement (NAFTA)	3 countries: US, Canada, Mexico	400.99	10,435.6	26,025	1,321.5
Mercado Comun del Sur (MERCOSUR)	4 countries: Argentina, Brazil, Paraguay, Uruguay	209.2	841.5	4,022	125.0

Note: ASEAN population is taken from World Bank, *2001 World Development Indicators*, whereas its nominal GDP and nominal GDP per capita figures are provided by the ASEAN Secretariat.
EU population, nominal GDP and nominal GDP per capita figures are taken from OECD, *OECD in Figures*, 2000 and 2001 editions.
NAFTA and MERCOSUR population, nominal GDP and nominal GDP per capital figures are taken from IMF, *International Financial Statistics*.
Trade figures are taken from IMF, *Direction of Trade Statistics Yearbook 2000*.

Source: *ASEAN–Japan Centre.*

A number of initiatives in other areas are worth noting, not least the ASEAN Framework Agreement on Intellectual Property Cooperation (1995), the ASEAN Agreement on Customs (1997), the ASEAN Framework Agreement on Mutual Recognition Arrangements (1998), and the ASEAN Framework Agreement on Facilitation of Goods in Transit (1998). In July 1998 the ASEAN Foundation was established to promote greater functional co-operation. More specifically, the Foundation was mandated to enhance interaction among the ASEAN peoples and to widen their participation in ASEAN activities, especially through human resource development. Another of its functions was 'to soften the social impact of the ongoing financial and economic crisis . . . and to alleviate poverty'.[32] In December 1998 the Hanoi Summit set out an extensive action plan, which, among other things, sought to streamline and harmonize policy development and legislation in the area of intellectual property, and approved the establishment of the ASEAN information infrastructure, partly with the aim of developing networks of centres and universities devoted to scientific and technological research and institutionalizing a system of science and technology indicators.[33]

The task of economic integration as conceived by ASEAN leaders required the private sector to be not only the engine of national economic growth but also a driving force for regional institutionalization. Almost from its inception in 1972, the ASEAN Chambers of Commerce and Industry was seen as an important vehicle for inter-country private sector interaction. Other private organizations contributing to the process included: the ASEAN Institute, made up of some 250 ASEAN-based companies, subsequently renamed the ASEAN Business Forum; the ASEAN Bankers' Association and its offshoot the ASEAN Finance Corporation, a merchant bank which began operations in Singapore in 1981; the ASEAN Insurance Council; the Federation of ASEAN Shipowners' Association; the ASEAN Ports Authorities' Association; and the ASEAN Tours and Travel Association. These and a great many other forums, centres and institutes played a useful role in establishing personal and organizational connections, and in performing a number of technical and coordinating functions. However, they generally lacked the resources, influence or organizational ethos required to make investment decisions consistent with the logic of regional integration.

ASEAN leaders, especially in the first six member countries, were generally supportive of a leading role for the private sector in the development of their economies. But at a regional level neither governments nor corporations had yet acquired the sophisticated organizational infrastructure or the necessary linkages to ensure that strategies and decisions were always compatible and mutually reinforcing. The inclusion of the four new members – Burma and the three Indochinese states – greatly complicated the task, given their much lower levels of industrialization, and the very different institutional ethos that continued to prevail, most conspicuously with regard to the relationship between the private and public sectors. By the end of the 1990s ASEAN leaders, now more conscious of the need to reduce the infrastructural, technological and income gaps within the Association, would often return to the theme of affirmative action. But the initiatives undertaken, including the convening of seminars and establishment of monitoring units, were at best likely to sharpen the analysis of the problem, but do little to address the problem at its source. And while ASEAN political elites might try as best they could to revitalize the strategies and mechanisms of economic integration, the region as a whole had to contend with powerful globalizing currents shaped largely by economic, financial and technological decisions over which they had relatively little control.

CONFLICT MANAGEMENT

In Southeast Asia, as in most other parts of the world, the end of the Cold War gave rise to new uncertainties but also new opportunities. To the extent that Soviet–American rivalry was no longer a decisive factor in regional affairs, new possibilities existed for containing, if not resolving, conflicts that had originated in, or been driven by, the dynamic of ideological and strategic bipolarity. Such difficult issues as the Cambodian conflict and Vietnam's future role in the region were likely to benefit from the easing of global tensions, and to that extent offered ASEAN new opportunities to press ahead with more inclusive policies. On the other hand, troubling questions surrounded the future direction of US–China, US–Japan and China–Japan relations. At issue was the likely shape of the triangular relationship between these three major centres of power, and its implications for regional security, most obviously for the two unresolved and potentially explosive legacies of the Cold War, Taiwan and Korea. Far from being able to insulate itself from the US–China–Japan triangle, ASEAN was, by virtue of its extensive and growing links with all three sides of that triangle, bound to influence and, more importantly perhaps, to be deeply influenced by the complex and largely unpredictable way in which the triangle was likely to function.

As with the approach developed in Chapter 5, there is much to be gained from examining ASEAN's intra- and extra-mural approaches to conflict management, so long as the close interconnections between the two levels of analysis are kept firmly in mind. Nor should we lose sight of the fact that security and economics are themselves closely intertwined, and, useful as the differentiation between them may be for purposes of analytical convenience, the two cannot in practice be treated in isolation. As indicated in the earlier chapter, ASEAN's development had been premised on the acknowledged importance of 'regional resilience'. This is another way of saying that each member regarded the security or resilience of the other ('national resilience'), as important to its own security or resilience. Understood in this sense, non-interference in the internal affairs of member states did not mean mutual indifference, but sensitivity to the political circumstances of others, to the vulnerability of their situation. This characterization of ASEAN's overarching philosophy, valid as it may be, runs nevertheless the danger of oversimplification. When ASEAN political elites thought of national and regional resilience, or even of national and regional security, what they had in mind first and foremost was the resilience and security of their respective states, and only indirectly, the resilience and security of their societies. The possibility that the interests of state and society might under certain conditions diverge or even conflict was certainly not in the forefront of their thinking.

The neglected 'societal' dimension of resilience and security is one to which we shall return, but for the moment it is enough to note the priority accorded by ASEAN's political elites to regime survival. Intra-mural conflict avoidance is to a large extent premised on that priority. As Leifer observes, ASEAN developed little by way of conflict resolution strategies other than restrained inter-governmental dialogue. ASEAN's preoccupation was almost entirely with conflict avoidance for one important reason: to have become overly involved with the rights and wrongs of any particular conflict, to have fleshed out the content or modalities of a peace process, would have been to invite an escalation or widening of the conflict, hence ASEAN's perennially low-key role.[34]

In this context, Leifer is no doubt right to point to ASEAN's diminished role in the Cambodian conflict once the Cold War came to an end. Moscow was now ready to reassess its relationship with Vietnam, Sino–Soviet ties were on the way to normalization, and Vietnam was completing the withdrawal of its forces from Cambodia. Yet, the Leifer interpretation may be misleading if it suggests that ASEAN was relegated to the sidelines simply by virtue of the newly found ability of the great powers to reach agreement among themselves. Two qualifications are worth making here. First, ASEAN retained an important role both during and after the 1991 international conference in Paris; secondly, ASEAN's preference for a low-key role was dictated in part by its realization that both Vietnam and Cambodia would soon be members of the ASEAN family, and that its role in the peace process would therefore need to be pursued with that in mind, in other words with considerable tact and less than full visibility.

It is precisely the same considerations which prompted ASEAN countries to play a less than conspicuous part in the East Timor conflict during both the prelude to the UN-sponsored vote of self-determination and its violent aftermath. ASEAN members did not wish to be publicly associated with policies which could be interpreted as hostile to the Indonesian government or as liable to precipitate the fall of the Suharto regime. Even after the UN decision to authorize the establishment of a multinational peace operation, ASEAN continued to pursue a relatively low profile both in its public declarations and in its support for the UN military presence in East Timor. Individual ASEAN members made varying contributions to the International Force on East Timor (INTERFET) and to the United Nations Transitional Authority in East Timor (UNTAET), but these occurred only after the Habibie government had agreed to international intervention and after the matter had been dealt with by the UN Security Council. East Timor hardly featured in ASEAN deliberations until after all the critical decisions had been taken elsewhere.

Cambodia and East Timor were particularly dramatic instances of the limitations of ASEAN's capacity for intra-mural conflict management. Each pointed in different ways to the decisive role played by major external actors. These limitations, however, were just as evident in ASEAN's seeming incapacity or unwillingness to deal with a range of bilateral frictions, as between Malaysia and Singapore or between Malaysia and the Philippines. What might be the explanation for this apparent inability to play a more interventionist peacemaking role? Part of the answer had no doubt something to do with ASEAN's inadequate institutionalization. It lacked highly developed mechanisms which could be effectively applied to handle actual or imminent conflicts involving one or more of its members. Though explicitly established by the Treaty of Amity and Cooperation as a dispute settlement mechanism, the High Council had not been constituted in the first 25 years of the Treaty's operation, and no member state had ever sought to have a dispute referred to it. This outcome is not surprising given that the Council was seen as a mechanism of last resort, that it was not empowered to take the initiative, and that parties to a dispute were not compelled to utilize the Council.[35] These provisions themselves reflected ASEAN's cultural style which was to shun potentially contentious attempts at intra-mural dispute settlement, and to concentrate instead on conflict avoidance and highly discrete and informal conflict management.[36] It was partly the realization of these limitations that prompted the ASEAN Ministerial Meeting in July 2001 to adopt Rules of Procedure for the High Council.[37]

Similar considerations explain the Thai initiative which resulted in the decision of the ASEAN Ministerial Meeting in July 2000 to approve the principles, purposes and procedures for the creation of an *ad hoc* ministerial 'troika'. The overriding purpose of the Troika was 'to address in a timely manner urgent and important regional political and security issues and situations of common concern likely to disturb regional peace and harmony'. It would be composed of the foreign ministers of the present, past and future chairs of the ASEAN Standing Committee, and come into being if requested by the ASC Chairman or by any ASEAN foreign minister. Its establishment and mandate would be subject to consensus; it would not be a decision-making body but would report to the ASEAN foreign ministers. In carrying out its mandate it would refrain from meddling in the internal affairs of ASEAN member countries. This, then, was a less radical departure than might seem at first sight. It was an attempt to give ASEAN a more clearly acknowledged role in conflict management, but in ways which did not cut across the longstanding principle of non-interference. There was more to this approach than diplomatic style. This was the natural reaction of governments which, democratic trimmings aside, had by and large operated on the principle that civil society was not integral to the task of policy-making. If the decisions of government were not be subjected to critical scrutiny by the domestic population, then it hardly made sense for those same decisions to be critically scrutinized by neighbouring governments. Indeed, external scrutiny carried the risk of inviting and legitimizing domestic scrutiny. The continuing stress on sovereignty and non-interference had as much an internal as an external rationale. It had as much to do with authority structures and regime survival as it had with external independence.

When it came to extra-mural conflict, ASEAN discourse was more comprehensive and to that extent more credible, which is not to say that it was fully coherent or effective. The ASEAN Vision 2020 adopted in December 1997 spoke of a Southeast Asia free from nuclear weapons and all other weapons of mass destruction, of a region whose rich human and natural resources would contribute to shared prosperity, and of ASEAN as 'an effective force for peace, justice and moderation in the Asia-Pacific and in the world'.[38] Inevitably a substantial gap separated the vision from actuality. It was one thing for ASEAN members to reach agreement after years of negotiation on the SEANWFZ Treaty, and quite another to secure the endorsement of the permanent members of the UN Security Council. In July 1999, Beijing announced its readiness to accede to the SEANWFZ Protocol, but the other great powers were far more reluctant to accommodate ASEAN's exhortations. Indeed, the first direct consultations between ASEAN and the nuclear weapons states did not occur until May 2001. The difficulties in extra-mural conflict management were equally apparent in the South China Sea dispute. As indicated in the previous chapter, ASEAN had achieved a degree of success in internationalizing the conflict, at least to the extent of engaging China in discussion of the issues involved both through the ASEAN–China dialogue and in ARF meetings. Yet, China's periodic reassertion of its claims, whether in the violent clash with Vietnam in 1988, its occupation of Mischief Reef in 1995, or expanded construction activities in 1999, posed a major challenge for ASEAN, not in the crude sense that China constituted a serious military threat, but in the deeper sense that it exposed ASEAN's lack of cohesion.

Against a backdrop of renewed strains in Sino–Philippine relations and a series of incidents in the South China Sea in May–July 1999, the Philippines and Vietnam drafted a code of conduct for consideration by the ASEAN Ministerial Meeting in July 1999. Agreement, however, proved elusive and in the light of objections voiced by other members, notably Malaysia, the draft code was referred to a working group chaired by Thailand. In November 1999 senior ASEAN officials met to review the draft code, but agreement was reached only after a special meeting between Malaysia, Vietnam and the Philippines. The agreement, which committed ASEAN to supporting the Vietnamese position – that the code be expanded to encompass the Paracels – was promptly rejected by Beijing. While restating their willingness to work towards an agreed code of conduct, the Chinese offered to resume discussions with the Philippines but only if these were confined to the Spratlys.[39] In subsequent ASEAN–China consultations both sides committed themselves to adopting a set of guidelines for managing the conflict and developing good-neighbourly relations. Agreement was reached on 4 November 2002 on a code of conduct, which encompassed co-operative activities of the less contentious variety, including marine environmental protection, marine scientific research, and safety of navigation and communication. The guidelines were designed to limit the use or threat of force and prevent the occupation of uninhabited reefs and shoals.[40]

Competing claims in the South China Sea constituted the most conspicuous but by no means the only source of tension between ASEAN and China. The South China Sea conflict was perhaps little more than a barometer of the wider but fluctuating relationship in which ASEAN anxieties had more to do with China's long-term ambitions. Of particular relevance in this context were China's expanding military capabilities. On one occasion even Singapore's Prime Minister Goh Chok Tong, generally not known for strident anti-Chinese rhetoric, spoke with apprehension about China's rising power and arms build-up, arguing that the time had come 'to bring into the open this underlying sense of discomfort, even insecurity, about the political and military ambitions of China'.[41] Another complicating factor in the relationship was the multi-ethnic composition of several ASEAN countries, with Chinese minorities accounting either for a significant proportion of the total population as ·in Malaysia or for a disproportionately large fraction of financial and commercial activity as in Indonesia and Thailand. These concerns no doubt weighed heavily in the minds of ASEAN's political elites, yet the 'China threat' thesis was distinctly less prominent in Southeast Asian than Western analyses of China's rise as a major centre of power.

While it is true that distrust of China has deep historical roots for a number of ASEAN countries, not least Vietnam, Malaysia and Indonesia, there is little evidence to suggest that ASEAN leaders thought it at all likely that China would seek to subjugate through conquest. Even in previous centuries when Chinese power was at its height, China was not so much out to invade and occupy territory as to extend its influence and establish the legitimacy of its central place in the universe.[42] China's current ambitions in all probability reflected the same overriding objective. ASEAN's task was therefore one of adjusting to the political realities of China's rising influence, but in ways which would not deprive it of a strong voice in shaping a new regional security framework. The policy of dialogue with China was designed to promote this strategic objective. Though officially, the ASEAN–China dialogue started in 1996, regular consultations first commenced in 1992. A number of mechanisms were established, including the ASEAN–China Joint Cooperation Committee, Senior Officials Consultations, the Joint Committee on Economic and Trade Cooperation, the Joint Committee on Science and Technology, and the ASEAN–China Business Council. Complementing these were the ARF ministerial meetings and in due course the ASEAN+1 and ASEAN+3 summits which began in December 1997. As already mentioned, the ASEAN–China experts group on economic co-operation was formed in November 2000. Its first report submitted in 2001 spoke glowingly of the prospects for expanded ASEAN–China trade, and referred to the proposed free trade area between ASEAN and China as an economic region with 1.7 billion consumers, a GDP of about $2 trillion and total annual trade of $1.23 trillion.[43]

Institutionalized dialogue and the rhetoric of co-operation could not, however, conceal a number of structural constraints bearing upon the relationship. Though trade with China was growing rapidly (ASEAN exports to China rose from $3.8 billion in 1993 to $10.8 billion in 1997), Japan, the European Union and the United States were still by far ASEAN's most important trading partners. Economic ties between China and ASEAN were in any case characterized as much by competition as by complementarity. Both the Chinese and the ASEAN economies had made the export of labour-intensive manufacturing products a centrepiece of their industrialization policies. Both were competing for foreign capital and technology to promote a more sophisticated industrial capacity. Southeast Asia's FDI inflows rose from $16.0 billion in 1993 to $27.8 billion in 1997 before dipping to $21.4 billion in 1998, whereas China's FDI inflows rose from $27.5 billion in 1993 to $44.2 billion in 1997, and reached $45.5 billion in 1998.[44]

Geopolitical considerations perhaps posed an even greater challenge for ASEAN. The central question here was the management of two distinct but closely connected triangular relationships: with China and the United States on the one hand and with China and Japan on the other. The Sino–US relationship carried both dangers and opportunities. At one level, it may be argued that a number of Southeast Asian countries individually and ASEAN as a whole sought to balance China's expanding influence in the region by maintaining close ties with the United States. Singapore pursued the most proactive policy in this direction. Through the 1990 Memorandum of Understanding and subsequent implementation agreements, Singapore undertook to host the Logistics Command of the US Seventh Fleet as well as US fighter aircraft on a rotational basis. As of 2000, US aircraft carriers were allowed to dock at Changi naval base. For its part, the Estrada government in the Philippines secured in May 1999 Senate approval for the Visiting Forces Agreement with the United States. Quite apart from the specific preferences and priorities of the Philippine armed forces, which had over the years developed close personal and organizational ties with their US counterparts, the agreement was seen by the Philippine governing elite as a useful bargaining chip in the Spratlys dispute with China. Several ASEAN countries were now prepared to hold joint military exercises with the United States and give the US Seventh Fleet access to repair and other facilities.

While welcoming the US military presence in the region, ASEAN was at the same time concerned not to align itself too closely with policies which might be interpreted by Beijing as a renewed attempt by the United States to forge an anti-China coalition. China, for its part, had an interest in preventing the emergence of such a coalition, hence its readiness to offer ASEAN countries a number of inducements. One of these was the prospect of enhanced economic co-operation. Another was the possibility of an ongoing bilateral and multilateral dialogue focusing on regional security in general and the South China Sea conflict in particular.[45] For ASEAN this was an opportunity to pursue a 'balance of politics' approach as a complement to the more traditional 'balance of power' policy.[46] ASEAN had no reason to support Beijing should the latter opt to achieve the reunification of Taiwan by force. Equally, an escalation of the Taiwan dispute and the worsening of Sino–American relations which would inevitably accompany it was likely to place ASEAN in an unenviable dilemma. To put it differently, ASEAN had little to lose and much to gain from a policy of equidistance from China and the United States, specifically designed to maintain co-operative relations with both great powers, while avoiding postures likely to antagonize one or the other. Placed in that context, developing multilateral dialogue mechanisms served a double purpose. It helped to create forums that facilitated ASEAN's delicate balancing act, and at the same time gave ASEAN a stronger voice in regional deliberations than might otherwise be the case.

When it came to Japan, extracting maximum advantage from the economic relationship remained the keystone of ASEAN's approach. This was hardly surprising given the importance of the Japanese economy to the region and the increasing interdependence between the ASEAN and Japanese economies. In the immediate aftermath of the 1997 financial crisis, ASEAN looked to Japan for both short-term assistance and long-term recovery. For its part, Japan had a strong incentive to come to the rescue. As on previous occasions ASEAN countries were disappointed by Japan's refusal to assume economic leadership, notably by the timidity with which it pursued the proposal to establish an Asian monetary fund. They were nevertheless appreciative of its generous financial support estimated to be in excess of $42 billion. To mitigate the social impact of the crisis, ASEAN countries were given access to Japan's 'special funds' in the World Bank, the ADB and the UNDP, and offered a 'solidarity fund' as a contribution to the ASEAN Foundation. Through the joint Program for Comprehensive Human Resources Development, the Japanese also offered to train some 20,000 administrators, experts, technicians and others over a five-year period. ASEAN also welcomed the participation of the Japanese private sector in the development of sub-regional growth areas, including the Mekong Basin Development Cooperation project. While continuing to press for improved access to Japanese markets and a reduced trade deficit with Japan, ASEAN countries saw their exports to Japan rise by 38.1 per cent from $37 billion in 1999 to $52 billion in 2000, and their imports during the same period by 19.7 per cent from $51 billion to $62 billion.[47]

By concentrating on the economic dimensions of the relationship with Japan, ASEAN was able to evade the pitfalls surrounding a number of highly sensitive political and security issues central to the Japan–US alliance on the one hand and the Japan–China relationship on the other. ASEAN saw little to be gained from openly supporting the upgrading of the defence relationship between Japan and the United States, since such support would provoke outright Chinese hostility. Japan's future strategic role in Asia Pacific was in any case the subject of much debate within ASEAN. In so far as ASEAN was at all prepared to articulate a view, it was to indicate acceptance of an enhanced Japanese contribution to regional security, so long as it was confined to peacekeeping operations authorized or at least legitimated by the UN as in the cases of Cambodia and East Timor. Such an approach was deemed less likely to attract Chinese opposition and more consistent with a longstanding ASEAN preference for maintaining a regional equilibrium among the great powers, while at the same time discouraging any one of them from a provocative projection of military capabilities.

It remains to say a word about the range of transnational challenges to security because they too required careful intra-mural and not infrequently extra-mural conflict management. By and large the ASEAN approach, not unlike that taken by the ARF, was one of strong rhetorical commitment but limited practical engagement. Nowhere was this duality more strikingly evident than with respect to environmental degradation generally and the Indonesian fires in particular. In 1997 and early 1998 much of Southeast Asia was affected by large and prolonged fires covering some 750,000 hectares of forest, primarily in the provinces of Kalimantan and Sumatra. The smoke haze, which soon spread to various parts of the region, especially Malaysia, Singapore and Brunei, constituted a serious health hazard, a severe blow to the tourism industry, and a major challenge to the efficacy of ASEAN collaboration.[48]

Though the Co-operation Plan on Transboundary Pollution adopted by ASEAN ministers in June 1995 had set admirable principles, objectives and strategies,[49] a wide gap soon emerged between declaratory and operational policy. The 1997 haze crisis made that gap starkly transparent. No coherent multilateral response emerged, only a series of relatively uncoordinated bilateral arrangements. The Regional Haze Action Plan agreed to in December 1997 stressed the need for regional monitoring, preventive measures, and fire fighting, with each area under the leadership of one ASEAN country. ASEAN's Haze Technical Task Force was asked to identify both short-term requirements and long-term needs, particularly for research and technology transfer. The ADB was called upon to strengthen ASEAN's technical capacity to prevent and mitigate transboundary atmospheric pollution, and to consider the establishment of a regional forest-fire research and training centre in Indonesia.[50] All these measures, however, were very much in the future tense; they did not amount to a concerted response to the crisis at hand. Undoubtedly, one of the factors which contributed to ASEAN's tepid response was the Suharto factor. It was after all the malpractice of companies close to the Suharto family – mismanagement, overlogging and the clearing of land for palm oil and other crops – which accounted for both the scale of the problem and the delicacy of the situation.[51] Were ASEAN to have pursued an interventionist policy, it would have seriously embarrassed the Indonesian President at a time when the financial crisis and IMF strictures had already placed his regime under severe strain. In the event, ASEAN policy-makers chose to tread warily but both public and media responses in a number of ASEAN countries made it clear that the principle of non-interference might not be the most appropriate guide to action when responding to security challenges that were transnational in scope and impact.

The forest fires in a sense gave added visibility to a number of other environmental challenges, all of which to a greater or lesser extent tested ASEAN's problem-solving capacity. In clear reference to the fires, Malaysia's Prime Minister called for the adoption of policies that were 'sustainable, clean and environment-friendly to avoid costs associated with environmental degradation', and stressed the need to 'address the problem of pollution from both the national and regional perspectives'.[52] In line with this renewed sense of urgency, the Plan of Action issued at the Hanoi Summit in December 1998 called for the full implementation of the ASEAN Cooperation Plan on Transboundary Pollution and in particular the Regional Haze Action Plan by 2001. It also envisaged the establishment of a regional research and training centre for land and forest-fire management by 2004, the strengthening of the ASEAN Regional Centre for Biodiversity Conservation, and enhanced institutional and legal capacities to implement Agenda 21 and other international environmental agreements by 2001.[53] Yet, the lack of detailed and binding agreements as well as the limited financial capacity of several ASEAN members to comply with the proposed course of action raised doubts as to whether implementation of this Plan would be any more effective than previous attempts. ASEAN had yet to endow its institutional arrangements with the independence and resources needed for regional initiatives to be brought to fruition.

Though ASEAN's responses to other transnational security challenges were not identical, they tended to conform to the same general pattern. ASEAN ministerial meetings would regularly draw attention to the seriousness of organized transnational crime, and to the need to stem the rising incidence of drug trafficking, arms smuggling, money laundering, trafficking in persons, and piracy. Similarly, the rapid spread of the HIV/AIDS epidemic through much of Southeast Asia became the subject of mounting concern.[54] Yet, apart from periodic workshops, task forces and reports, frequent references to the value of increased co-operation, and a handful of declarations, there was little by way of coherent or persistent follow-through.[55] Much the same could be said of the regional human rights regime. The 26th ASEAN Ministerial Meeting in July 1993 considered the establishment of an appropriate regional mechanism on human rights, thereby paving the way for an informal non-governmental Working Group for an ASEAN Human Rights Mechanism. By the end of the 1990s the process was still confined to periodic consultations between the Working Group and ASEAN officials. The human rights controversy is considered more fully in Chapter 9 in the context of the 'Asian versus Western values' debate and the rapidly evolving relationship between state and civil society. Suffice it here to say that the issue was especially sensitive because it impinged directly on ASEAN's relations with its Western dialogue partners, and more importantly because it raised difficult questions about authority and legitimacy, which challenged the very foundations on which was built the ASEAN political edifice.

ASEAN's response to September 11 was again indicative of this strategic ambivalence. Meeting in November 2001, ASEAN leaders chose to condemn in the strongest possible terms the terrorist attacks on the United States, and to commit themselves to strong anti-terrorist measures. These included among others the signing and ratification of all relevant anti-terrorist conventions, greater information/intelligence exchange and other forms of co-operation among law enforcement agencies, increased regional capacity-building designed to enhance the effectiveness of member countries in investigating, detecting, monitoring and reporting on terrorist acts.[56] In his address to the Extraordinary Session of the Islamic Conference of Foreign Ministers on Terrorism in April 2002, the Malaysian Prime Minister went several steps further. He defined armed attacks against civilians as acts of terror, and on the basis of that definition labelled Palestinian suicide bombers as terrorists.[57] But ASEAN was a long way from devising a coherent regional response to the twin challenges posed by terrorism and the 'war on terror'. In Malaysia's case but also that of Indonesia and the Philippines, government reactions were dictated primarily by domestic considerations. Political or military elites were in each instance subjected to enormous pressure by the United States. For the Mahathir government this was an opportunity to embarrass the Islamic opposition, Parti Islam Se-Malaysia (PAS); for the Philippine military to strengthen their ties with the United States and perhaps gain the upper hand against militant Islamic groups; and for Indonesia's military and the Indonesian government to mend fences with the United States, although great care had to be taken not to antagonize powerful elements of Islamic opinion on which the Megawati presidency depended for its effectiveness and perhaps survival. In short, ASEAN policy-makers, while conscious of the need for regionally agreed rules of behaviour and co-operation to address an increasingly thorny and expanding security policy agenda, could not always agree on to how to formulate them, and, even where they could agree, not at all persuaded of the value of monitoring and enforcing them.

ORGANIZATIONAL IDENTITY

Enough has been said to indicate that the culture and decision-making framework developed by ASEAN over the first three decades of its existence were put to the test by the vastly different circumstances in the closing years of the twentieth century. As a broad generalization, the formula for success devised by ASEAN's policy-making elites had sought to combine an international market orientation with varying degrees and forms of political authoritarianism. The low level of interest-group and public participation in the workings of ASEAN in one sense facilitated policy development. The relatively small number of political leaders, diplomats and bureaucrats involved in the process made for greater intimacy and negligible levels of public accountability. However, the strength of these institutional arrangements was also their weakness. Policy-makers entered into understandings and agreements which had not been adequately discussed by relevant interest groups, let alone by society at large, and which could not therefore count on high levels of public acceptance. Economic policies did, it is true, reflect and to a degree helped to mobilize increasingly influential constituencies supportive of foreign investment and export-driven industrialization. But in so far as market-driven internationalism had both winners and losers, the institutional cohesiveness from which it sprang was largely deceptive. Neither the internationalism nor the cohesiveness could conceal, let alone overcome, the inequalities and grievances to which they gave rise. The resulting regionalism lacked effective social and political roots and so could not easily withstand internal tensions or externally induced crises (see Table 7.3).

Most obviously elite cohesiveness did not succeed in doing away with bilateral tensions, whether between Malaysia and the Philippines, the Philippines and Singapore, or Singapore and Malaysia.[58] More importantly, the powerful pressures generated by the financial crisis of 1997 exposed the fragility of domestic political institutions, most dramatically but by no means exclusively in Indonesia. The Philippine, Thai and Malaysian governments all had to contend with the political backlash unleashed by the social and economic effects of the crisis, which not surprisingly were experienced most starkly by the already disadvantaged sections of society. In Malaysia's case, the economic crisis coincided with, and may have accentuated, a two-pronged political crisis

Table 7.3   ASEAN summits (1976–2002)

Summit	Place	Date
First ASEAN Summit	Bali	23–24 February 1976
Second ASEAN Summit	Kuala Lumpur	4–5 August 1977
Third ASEAN Summit	Manila	14–15 December 1987
Fourth ASEAN Summit	Singapore	27–29 January 1992
Fifth ASEAN Summit	Bangkok	14–15 December 1995
First Informal Summit	Jakarta	30 November 1996
Second Informal Summit	Kuala Lumpur	14–16 December 1997
Sixth ASEAN Summit	Hanoi	15–16 December 1998
Third Informal Summit	Manila	27–28 November 1999
Fourth Informal Summit	Singapore	22–25 November 2000
Seventh ASEAN Summit	Bandar Seri Begawan	5–6 November 2001
Eighth ASEAN Summit	Phnom Penh	4–5 November 2002

which saw Deputy Prime Minister Anwar Ibrahim fall out with Mahathir, and the governing party (United Malays National Organization) sustain heavy electoral losses with corresponding gains made by PAS. Anwar's dismissal from office, followed by his arrest on charges of corruption and sexual misconduct, led to the creation of the Parti Keadilan Nasional and to a vocal political movement committed to his release and political liberalization.

For ASEAN these events had far-reaching implications as the countries most seriously weakened by the crisis were also the ones that had traditionally been most influential in shaping the Association's institutional and policy development. Within ASEAN, Indonesia was only first among equals, but by virtue of its size, resources and strategic location it was also the one most likely to provide effective leadership. By early 1998 the Suharto government was haemorrhaging badly under the combined impact of the economic downturn and the IMF's subsequent intervention on the one hand and the mass outbreak of inter-communal violence in the provinces, notably in East Timor, Irian Jaya, Aceh and Ambon on the other. The highly volatile situation was compounded by the seemingly unaccountable actions of the Indonesian military, and the anti-Chinese elements within the wider society which the government seemed unable or unwilling to control. The fall of Suharto in May 1998 followed by the explosion of violence in East Timor before and after the UN-administered referendum of August 1999 strengthened the international community's resolve to intervene, with Jakarta eventually yielding to international pressure and allowing a UN-sanctioned but Australian-led international force to restore order and stability. The East Timor crisis had effectively deprived Indonesia of its leadership role within ASEAN. More than that it exposed ASEAN's inability to perform any kind of conflict management role and its abdication of that role to the UN and the Australian-led 'coalition of the willing'.

It is precisely against this backdrop that ASEAN's future role became the subject of internal contestation. While still Deputy Prime Minister, Anwar Ibrahim launched the debate with the proposal that ASEAN adopt a policy of 'constructive intervention'. There was no suggestion here that ASEAN should begin interfering in the internal affairs of member states, but rather that each state should initiate a process of political liberalization centred around the strengthening of civil society.[59] ASEAN's role would be to provide a helping hand in improving electoral processes, contributing to legal and administrative reforms, developing human resources, and generally solidifying the rule of law. To some extent ASEAN had already embarked upon this path, and its assistance to Cambodia was premised in part on developing these institutional capacities. Though Anwar's public foray had not directly deviated from the principle of non-interference, it is nevertheless clear that other elements of the Malaysian government were less than enthusiastic about his proposals. In his speech to the 30th ASEAN Ministerial Meeting, Malaysian Foreign Minister Ahmad Badawi pointedly reaffirmed ASEAN's more conventional approach:

ASEAN has been able to survive and progress all these years because each member-state has been free to develop politically and economically according to its own national ethos. We do not have a common secretariat that prescribes what policies member governments should adopt in our nation building tasks. And perhaps one of the most important principles that have governed intra-ASEAN relations has been that of non interference in one another's internal affairs. This principle has stood the test of time . . .[60]

Notwithstanding its obvious appeal to governments reluctant to have their performance subjected to greater domestic or international scrutiny, such an unreconstructed view of the future was unlikely to hold universal sway at a time of profound political and economic change.

It was left to the Thai and Philippine governments to begin to make the case for new directions. At the 31st ASEAN Ministerial Meeting in July 1998, President Estrada referred to the lessons to be drawn from the present crisis and in particular to the need for greater integration. More specifically, he identified a less restrictive form of regional dialogue as critical to the advancement of regional 'convergence': 'Let us be open to one another and freely and candidly exchange views no matter how controversial the issue . . . And let us muster the courage to strengthen our existing institutions and build the new ones we need'.[61]

Thai Foreign Minister Surin Pitsuwan was even more forthright, arguing that ASEAN had to move 'into a higher gear of regionalism on a higher plane of regional cooperation'.[62] The Thai case for reform was set out at greater length in an informal paper submitted to senior officials prior to the ministerial meeting. While recognizing that ASEAN members had a responsibility to uphold the principle of non-interference, the paper argued that such a commitment could not be absolute. It had to be subjected to 'reality tests' and flexibly applied.[63] Frank discussion of sensitive issues should not be confused with interference in domestic affairs. The Thai Foreign Minister chose to be even more explicit at the 12th Asia-Pacific Roundtable, pointing to the need for intra-ASEAN relations to be made 'more dynamic, more engaged, and . . . more constructive than before'.[64] The Thai concept of 'flexible engagement' was presented as a necessary response to three key developments: increasing global interdependence, the emergence of new transnational security threats, and mounting pressures for democratization.[65]

Whatever the merits of the case, the three other core states remained sceptical. The Malaysian Foreign Minister returned to the theme he had repeatedly rehearsed at regional gatherings: the principle of non-interference had served ASEAN well for over 30 years and was firmly embedded in numerous ASEAN agreements, including the Kuala Lumpur Declaration and the Treaty of Amity and Cooperation. Many of ASEAN's achievements were attributed to the willingness of member states to respect that principle, which did not in any case preclude them from freely expressing their views or even reservations.

Frank discussion was possible so long as this was done quietly, 'befitting a community of friends bonded in cooperation'.[66] Echoing the same commitment to 'pluralistic solidarity', the Singapore representative stressed that ASEAN was never envisaged as a supranational organization, and that the 'ASEAN Way' had more to do with process than outcome, and that this depended on carefully nurturing personal relationships between leaders. For his part, Indonesian Foreign Minister Ali Alatas stressed the 'very thin' dividing line between talking about transborder problems and interfering in domestic affairs. To cross that line would be to return to the tensions and suspicions characteristic of the period prior to the birth of ASEAN.[67]

ASEAN members were sharply divided about the need for institutional reform. Judging from the tenor of the discussions at the 1998 ASEAN Ministerial Meeting, a clear majority – the three core states, plus Vietnam, Laos, Cambodia and Burma – were still strongly committed to the retention of the status quo. Even the Philippines and Thailand had yet to elaborate the concrete implications of their proposals. Indeed, the arguments presented by the two governments lacked both clarity and specificity, and to that extent made it easier for the proposals to be rejected. If the intention was to empower ASEAN to deal with any number of bilateral tensions, it could be legitimately claimed that multilateral dispute settlement mechanisms were not always an appropriate conflict management mechanism. If, on the other hand, the Thai concept of flexible engagement was designed to allow ASEAN to intervene in those instances where the actions of one particular member were deemed to have an adverse impact on the security and welfare of several, if not all, other members, then it could be said that ASEAN had already embarked on such a course and that its handling of both the Cambodia and Burma problems was predicated on this understanding. There was, of course, a third reading of the proposed reform path, namely that ASEAN should develop clear standards or benchmarks of state conduct, which would apply as much to domestic as to external policies. The reference to democracy and human rights, and even environmental degradation, seemed consistent with this reading. The setting of standards would in turn require that processes and institutions be developed to monitor the observance of such standards. It was by no means clear that either Thailand or the Philippines were themselves ready to adopt such a course of action.

It would be misleading, however, to characterize the emerging debate as an empty rhetorical exercise. Most ASEAN members had acknowledged the need to quicken the pace of integration, a view reflected in the adoption of ASEAN Vision 2020 in December 1997. In a further development, the Joint Declaration for a Socially Cohesive and Caring ASEAN signed in Bangkok in July 2000 argued that integration would have to go beyond the economic arena to encompass a wide range of social policies and programmes aimed at delivering the fruits of integration to the less advantaged or more vulnerable sections of society. For this purpose, it would be necessary to construct a more robust partnership between the state and civil society, in particular between governments, the private sector, NGOs and local communities. This conclusion was even more firmly expressed in the report of the Eminent Persons Group (EPG) on Vision 2020. Created specifically to address the mounting criticisms of ASEAN's irrelevance, the EPG reaffirmed the principle that the peoples of ASEAN had to take ownership of ASEAN Vision 2020. In a wide-ranging report the EPG recommended that ASEAN take the lead in building a regional financial architecture in East Asia. Other proposals included the establishment of an ASEAN Volunteer Corps, the adoption of English as a common working language within ASEAN, more effective networking between the training institutes of member countries, and an expanded ASEAN Secretariat. Such a programme, it was argued, would enable ASEAN to contribute to the enhancement of social, cultural and educational outcomes in member countries, and to maintain and strengthen its guiding role within the ARF. By 2001 ASEAN, conscious of the multifaceted pressures emanating from above and below, was attempting to reposition itself. It remained to be seen whether these tentative first steps at reshaping the tenor of ASEAN discourse would be translated into durable and efficacious policies. At issue was not only the Association's organizational ethos and the adequacy of its resources, but the adaptiveness of the social and political institutions of member states and their individual and collective responsiveness to the challenges posed by the external environment.

ASEAN AND REGIONAL ARCHITECTURE

Generally speaking, ASEAN's priority in its relations with other existing or emerging regional organizations was to retain as far as possible its status as the core or driving engine of Asia-Pacific multilateralism. Such an objective was bound to encounter difficulties on many fronts, not least because other players had interests which did not necessarily point in the same direction. The difficulties were likely to be most acute in the economic arena, which helps to explain ASEAN's ambivalence towards APEC. As previously noted, most ASEAN countries had joined APEC for fear of being left out of any trade and investment facilitation arrangements which might be to their benefit, but many continued to entertain serious concerns about the speed of liberalization. Their preference, by no means confined to ASEAN leaders, was for an informal consultative body rather than an integrated free trade area which might work to their disadvantage.[68] At least as worrying, for Malaysia and to a lesser extent other ASEAN states, was the prospect of APEC developing the kind of momentum which could in due course downgrade ASEAN's institutional standing in the region, as much politically as economically. A third concern had to do with the relationship between the public and private sectors of the economy. The ASEAN view was clearly stated at the Fourteenth ASEAN–US Dialogue in July 1998:

> [T]he role of government as the prime mover in encouraging development cooperation should not be relegated. It should in fact complement the role of the private sector, not only in strengthening the economic development cooperation, but also in broadening cooperation areas not ventured by the private sector.[69]

APEC's undiluted neoliberalism threatened to tilt the balance drastically in favour of the private sector, and thereby deprive the state of its role in the regulation of the market.

These concerns were not uniformly shared by all ASEAN members. Differences of view existed with respect not only to the pace of liberalization but also to the most appropriate forms of economic regionalism. Should the emerging multilateralism assume an Asia-Pacific profile in which the United States was likely to dominate? Or, should it be a purely Asian grouping in which leadership was more likely to be exercised by Japan, and in years to come shared between Japan and China, presumably in ways which still enabled ASEAN to exert meaningful influence? Malaysia's proposal for an East Asian economic grouping was very much based on this latter perspective. More than ten years after the proposal had first surfaced, these differences still lurked in the background, reflecting as they did different stages of economic development, different economic needs and different domestic circumstances. Divisions within ASEAN, which APEC's formation had exposed, were temporarily lost from view because of the financial and political crises of the late 1990s and APEC's loss of momentum. Sooner or later, however, they were likely to re-emerge and to test ASEAN's cohesiveness and direction.

As indicated in the previous chapter, the view that ASEAN should play a pivotal role in the management of regional security, though again strongly championed by Malaysia, was in this case strongly and almost universally supported by other member states. ASEAN leadership in the development and organization of the ARF was meant to be the practical expression of this principle. The problem with this approach was that it effectively made the principle hostage to the ARF's progress and future viability. Should the ARF come to be seen as an ineffective mechanism for security dialogue and *a fortiori* of marginal utility in conflict prevention and conflict resolution, it is likely that ASEAN's leadership role would come under sharp scrutiny. By 2000 a number of unofficial or semi-official proposals were already circulating, the net effect of which would be to dilute or altogether eliminate ASEAN's control over the ARF's agenda and organizational development. Such a demotion of its role might have negative spin-offs for ASEAN, as much for its regional standing as for internal cohesion.[70]

Having taken the initiative in establishing the ARF, ASEAN now had to demonstrate that it had the intellectual and organizational capacity to perform the managerial role to which it had laid claim. Several problems awaited resolution. First, ASEAN had to show how its leadership of the ARF could facilitate the twin processes of conflict prevention and conflict resolution when its own intra-mural record had been less than entirely successful. The 1998 Hanoi Summit had insisted that ASEAN retain its chairing role, and to this end directed the ASEAN Secretary-General to provide the necessary support and services, and called for new initiatives to advance the ARF process from its current emphasis on confidence-building to promoting preventive diplomacy. It was not, however, readily apparent how these in-principle commitments would be translated into practice. The question at issue here was: how could a multilateral structure encompassing the Asia-Pacific region as a whole but adopting ASEAN's methods achieve more by way of regional security than ASEAN had thus far been able to achieve in Southeast Asia? More pertinently, could ASEAN's conflict management strategies and organizational style be applied to the much more demanding security environment of Northeast Asia? Several years after Vietnam, Laos, Cambodia and Myanmar had been admitted into ASEAN, it was still unclear whether enlargement would assist or impede ASEAN's leadership role within the ARF.

A second, though not unrelated, question immediately suggested itself. If doubts remained as to APEC's viability or even desirability as an Asia-Pacific construction in which the United States might become the dominant player, was not the ARF vulnerable to the same criticism? Might there not be a case to be made for a purely Asian grouping in security as much as in economic co-operation? Finally, the relationship between the ARF and the ASEAN Post-Ministerial Conference remained unclear. What was it that the ARF could achieve that the annual meeting between ASEAN and its dialogue partners could not? Admittedly, the ARF had developed an infrastructure and know-how in security dialogue which, though embryonic, were almost entirely lacking in the ASEAN PMC. None the less the division of responsibilities between the two fora had yet to be clarified, and this lack of clarity might in due course adversely affect the functioning of either or both organizations.

Notwithstanding the challenges of the 1990s and the plethora of unanswered questions ASEAN had not fallen apart.[71] On balance the organization had achieved a thicker institutional infrastructure and remained central to multilateral discourse in the Asia-Pacific. ASEAN's centrality ultimately rested not only on its ambiguous relationship to APEC or even its importance to the ARF, but also on two other key facets of its external diplomacy, namely the dialogue with its various partners and the ASEAN+3 arrangement. The medium- and longer-term implications of ASEAN+3 are explored in the next chapter. One general observation can nevertheless be usefully made here. Both mechanisms provided ASEAN with opportunities to press its point of view on a range of issues with the most influential players in the Asia-Pacific region. Each of these interlocutors had its own reasons for maintaining and even strengthening the dialogue, not least the fear that failure to participate might work to the advantage of one or more competitors. The mere existence of the mechanisms, and ASEAN's continuing capacity to enlarge, diversify and refine them in the light of changing circumstances, significantly enhanced its freedom of manoeuvre in shaping the emerging regional architecture.

A note of caution might nevertheless be entered here. In a keynote address in August 2000, ASEAN Secretary-General Rodolfo Severino spoke of political and cultural convergence as ASEAN's inevitable response to the twin pressures of globalization and regionalization. He envisaged an ASEAN that would move in the direction of 'greater openness, greater freedom, and greater pluralism'. He went on to stress the need for cultures and mindsets to adjust if Southeast Asia were to be competitive in the global economy. The region had to cultivate 'the capacity and inclination to turn knowledge into practical applications', and personal relationships had to be tempered by the objective application of law and rules in the conduct of government and business.[72] He was making the case – widely supported by influential political and professional elites – for a paradigmatic shift. While it had much to commend it, the proposed path also carried with it a number of dangers, not least for the multilateral agenda. ASEAN had to respond to the challenge of global competition, but its entire rationale and long-term viability as a distinctive regional project might be endangered if its political, cultural and intellectual role were to be reduced to injecting into Southeast Asia – and Asia more generally – the external influences that were propelling economic globalization. For ASEAN faced another equally critical challenge: how to cultivate its rich and diverse cultural and intellectual heritage and channel it in ways that could meet societal aspirations for prosperity but also peaceful and co-operative intercourse regionally and beyond.

NOTES

1. Joseph A. Camilleri, 'Alliances and the Emerging Post-Cold War Security System', in Richard Leaver and James L. Richardson (eds), *Charting the Post-Cold War Order*, Boulder, CO: Westview Press, 1993, pp. 84–94.
2. See Michael Leifer, ' International Dynamics of One Southeast Asia: Political and Security', *Indonesian Quarterly*, 24 (4), 1996, 361.
3. See Temsak Chalermpalanupap, 'ASEAN-10: Meeting the Challenges', paper presented at the Asia-Pacific Roundtable, Kuala Lumpur, 1 June 1999, at htttp://www.asean.or.id/secgen/ articles/asean_10htm (sighted 29 November 1999) .
4. This more optimist assessment of the prospects of an enlarged ASEAN was a feature of official Malaysian pronouncements on the question. See, for example, the official website of the Malaysian Foreign Ministry <http:/www.kln.gov.my/englishFr-foreignaffairs.htm> (sighted 13 December 2001).
5. Statements to this effect by General Try Sutrisno, then Commander of Indonesia's armed forces, and Malaysian Prime Minister Mahathir are cited in Amitav Acharya, *Constructing a Security Community in Southeast Asia: ASEAN and the Problem of Regional Order*, London: Routledge, 2001, p. 105.
6. See Leszek Buszynsky, 'ASEAN's New Challenges', *Pacific Affairs*, 70 (4), Winter 1997–98, 559.

7. Hari Singh, 'Vietnam and ASEAN: The Politics of Accommodation', *Australian Journal of International Affairs*, 51 (2), July 1997, 212.

8. Ibid., p. 214.

9. See Jürgen Haacke, 'The Concept of Flexible Engagement and the Practice of Enhanced Interaction: Intramural Challenges to the "ASEAN Way"', *Pacific Review*, 12 (4), 1999, 589–91.

10. *Straits Times*, 6 December 1998, p. 21.

11. Buszynsky, 'ASEAN's New Challenges', p. 563.

12. *Straits Times*, 28 July 1997.

13. The implications of enlargement for both intra- and extra-mural conflict management are examined in Herman Joseph S. Kraft, 'ASEAN and Intra-ASEAN Relations: Weathering the Storm', *Pacific Review*, 13 (3), 2000, 453–72.

14. For an incisive analysis of the risks and opportunities presented by the Asian financial crisis, see Amitav Acharya, 'Realism and Institutionalism and the Asian Economies', *Contemporary Southeast Asia*, 21 (1), April 1999.

15. See Jürgen Rüland, 'ASEAN and the Asian Crisis: Theoretical Implications and Practical consequences for Southeast Asian Regionalism', *Pacific Review*, 13 (3), 2000, 429–30.

16. Joint Statement of the Heads of State/Government of the Member States of ASEAN on the Financial Situation, Kuala Lumpur, 15 December 1997.

17. See Suthad Setboornsarng, 'ASEAN Economic Co-operation: Adjusting to the Crisis', in Institute of Southeast Asian Studies, *Southeast Asian Affairs 1998*, Singapore: Institute of Southeast Asian Studies, 1998, pp. 18–36.

18. See Michael Wesley, 'The Asian Crisis and the Adequacy of Regional Institutions', *Contemporary Southeast Asia*, 21 (1), April 1999, 56–7.

19. Ibid., p. 65.

20. See John Ravenhill, 'Economic Cooperation in Southeast Asia: Changing Incentives', *Asian Survey*, XXXV (9), September 1995, 854.

21. Ibid., 857–9.

22. 'Statement on Bold Measures', Sixth ASEAN Summit, Hanoi, 16 December 1998.

23. See Table 4.4 in Nattapong Thongpakde, 'ASEAN Free Trade Area: Progress and Challenges', in Than Mya and Carolyn L. Gates (eds), *ASEAN Beyond the Regional Crisis: Challenges and Initiatives*, Singapore: Institute of Southeast Asian Studies, 2001, p. 64.

24. Ibid., p. 65.

25. East Asia Analytical Unit, Department of Foreign Affairs and Trade, *ASEAN Free Trade Area: Trading Bloc or Building Bloc?*, Canberra: Australian Government Publishing Service, 1994, p. 45.

26. Ravenhill, 'Economic Cooperation in Southeast Asia', p. 859.

27. Thongpadke, 'ASEAN Free Trade Area', p. 54.

28. See Table 3 (Intra-ASEAN Trade 1999–2000) attached to Joint Press Statement, 'The Fifteenth Meeting of the AFTA Council, 14 September 2001', at http://www.aseansec.org/menu.asp?action=4&content=1 (sighted 4 December 2001).

29. Rodolfo C. Severino, 'Diversity and Convergence in Southeast Asia', Beijing, 28 August 2000, at http://www.aseansec.org/secgen/sg.dc.htm (sighted 5 December 2001).

30. The full text of the agreement may be found at http://www.aseansec.org/economic/aem/30/frm_aia.htm (sighted 4 December 2001).

31. *ASEAN Annual Report 2000–2001*, Jakarta: ASEAN Secretariat, 2001, p. 5.

32. See Statement by Indonesian Foreign Minister, Ali Alatas, at the opening of the 31st ASEAN Ministerial Meeting, Manila, 24 July 1998, FE/3289 S1/13.

33. ASEAN Plan of Action adopted by the Hanoi Summit on 16 December 1998, in BBC Summary of World Broadcasts (SWB), 18 December 1998, FE/3413 S1/4-6.

34. Asian executives were generally of the view that ASEAN played a minimalist role in dealing with regional security issues: 'Asian Executives Poll', *Far Eastern Economic Review*, 26 August 1999, 31.

35. See Vitit Muntarbohrn, *The Challenge of Law: Legal Cooperation among ASEAN Countries*, Bangkok: Institute of Security and International Studies, 1986, p. 19.

36. Michael Leifer, 'The ASEAN Peace Process: A Category Mistake', *Pacific Review*, 12 (1), 1999, 28–29.

37. See Joint Communiqué of the 34th ASEAN Ministerial Meeting, Hanoi, 23–24 July 2001.
38. See ASEAN Vision 2020 adopted by Second ASEAN Informal Summit, Kuala Lumpur, 14–16 December 1997 at http://www.kln.gov.my/KLN/statement.nsf/ ...9d48c84fe3c8256571000344f2?OpenDocument (sighted 9 April 1999).
39. See Carlyle A. Thayer, 'New Faultlines in ASEAN?', *Asia-Pacific Defence Reporter*, February–March 2000, 27.
40. See 'Declaration on the Conduct of the Parties in the South China Sea', 4 Novenber 2002 at http://www.aseansec.org/1316.htm (sighted 20 May 2003); also Liselotte Odgaard, 'Deterrence and Co-operation in the South China Sea', *Contemporary Southeast Asia*, 23 (2), August 2001, 303–4.
41. Cited in Denny Roy, 'The China Threat Issue', *Asian Survey*, 36 (8), 1996, 759.
42. See Wang Gungwu, 'China's Place in the Region: Search for Allies and Friends', *Indonesian Quarterly*, 25 (4), 1997, 421.
43. 'Forging Closer ASEAN–China Economic Relations in the Twenty-First Century', A Report submitted by the ASEAN–China Expert Group on Economic Cooperation, October 2001.
44. See N. Freeman, 'ASEAN Investment Area: Progress and Challenges', in Mya and Gates (eds), *ASEAN Beyond the Regional Crisis*, p. 88.
45. See Joseph Y.S. Cheng, 'China's ASEAN Policy in the 1990s: Pushing for Regional Multipolarity', *Contemporary Southeast Asia*, 21 (2), August 1999, 176–203.
46. This formulation is proposed by Allen Whiting, 'ASEAN Pressures China', *Far Eastern Economic Review*, 24 April 1997, 28.
47. 'The Eighth Consultation between the ASEAN Economic Ministers and the Minister of Economy, Trade and Industry of Japan, 12 September 2001, Hanoi at http://www.aseansec.org/menu.asp?action=4&content=1 (sighted 4 December 2001).
48. Early estimates of damage suggested that health costs and lost tourism revenues might amount to $1.38 billion (see *Business Times*, 26 February 1988, 77).
49. See Simon S.C. Tay, 'ASEAN Co-operation and the Environment', in Mya and Gates (eds), *ASEAN Beyond the Regional Crisis*, pp. 184–5.
50. These and other measures are described by Rodolfo Severino, 'Sovereignty, Intervention and the ASEAN Way', address delivered to the ASEAN Scholars' Roundtable organized by the Konrad Adenauer Foundation and the Singapore Institute of International Affairs, Singapore, 3 July 2000, at http://www.aseansec.org/secgen/sg_siaw.htm (sighted 5 December 2001).
51. The Meteorological Service Singapore apparently provided clear evidence 'that the fires were not the work of individual farmers, but large land-holding companies' (see Anthony L. Smith, *Strategic Centrality: Indonesia's Changing Role in ASEAN*, Singapore: Institute of Southeast Asian Studies, 2000, pp. 42–3).
52. 'Mahathir Courts Brave New Asia', *Australian*, 17 October 1997, 9.
53. 'Hanoi Summit', SWB, 18 December 1998, FE/3413 S1/7.
54. See the ASEAN Summit Declaration on HIV/AIDS, 5 November 2001, Brunei at http://www.aseansec.org/menu_7thsummit.htm (sighted 5 December 2001).
55. A more energetic approach to transnational crime would eventually emerge, but with the emphasis largely on information-sharing and capacity-building. See the steps taken to implement the ASEAN Plan of Action to Combat Transnational Crime, Kuala Lumpur, 17 May 2002, at http:www..aseansec.org/view.asp?file=/newdata/ammtcwp.htm (sighted on 4 June 2002).
56. See 'ASEAN Declaration on Joint Action to Counter Terrorism', 5 November 2001 at http://www.aseansec.org/menu.asp?action=3&content=3 (sighted 4 December 2001); Joint Communiqué, Special ASEAN Ministerial Meeting on Terrorism, 20–21 May 2002, Kuala Lumpur, at http:www.aseansec.org/view.asp?file=new data/sammter.htm (sighted on 4 June 2002).
57. See Prime Minister Mohamad Mahathir's speech at the Extraordinary Session of the Islmaic Conference of Foreign Ministers on Terrorism, 1 April 2002, at http://domino.kln.gov.my/ kln/statmen.nsf/ (sighted on 24 September 2002).
58. See Alan Collins, *The Security Dilemmas of Southeast Asia*, Singapore: Macmillan in association with Institute of Southeast Asian Studies, 2000, pp. 93–103; Acharya,

Constructing a Security Community in Southeast Asia, pp. 129–31; John Funston, 'Challenges facing ASEAN', *Contemporary Southeast Asia*, 21 (2), August 1999, 206; N. Ganesan, 'ASEAN's Relations with Major External Powers', *Contemporary Southeast Asia*, 22 (2), August 2000, 267.

59. *Straits Times*, 15 July 1997.
60. See Opening Statement by the Minister of Foreign Affairs of Malaysia at the Opening of the 30th ASEAN Ministerial Meeting, 24 July 1997 at http://kln.gov.my/KLN/statemen.nsf/ ...8a3a4eb557c82564fb000d0ff0?OpenDocument (sighted 9 April 1999).
61. See 'ASEAN Meeting in Manila', *SWB*, 27 July 1998, FE/3289 S1/1–3.
62. Ibid., S1/14.
63. 'In the Bunker', *Far Eastern Economic Review*, 6 August 1998, 25.
64. Suri Pitsuwan, 'Currency Turmoil in Asia: The Strategic Impact', Remarks at the 12th Asia-Pacific Roundtable, Kuala Lumpur, 1 June 1998.
65. See Haacke, 'The Concept of Flexible Engagement and the Practice of Enhanced Interaction', pp. 581–612.
66. 'ASEAN Meeting in Manila', *SWB*, 27 July 1998, FE/3289 S1/5.
67. *Far Eastern Economic Review*, 6 August 1998, 25.
68. These fears are described in Leszek Buszynski, 'ASEAN's New Challenges', pp. 566–7.
69. See statement by the Malaysian Foreign Minister, Ahmad Badawi, at the PMC 9+1 session with the United States, 28 July 1998, Manila at http:www.aseansec.org/menu.asp?action=3&content=5 (sighted 11 December 2001).
70. These possibilities are discussed by a number of authors, though not always with appropriate analytical subtlety. See Shaun Narine, 'ASEAN into the Twenty-first Century: Problems and Prospects', *Pacific Review*, 12 (3), 1999, 362.
71. For a similar assessment, see John Funston, 'ASEAN: Out of its Depth?', *Contemporary Southeast Asia*, 20 (1), April, 1998, 34–6.
72. Rodolfo Severino, 'Diversity and Convergence in Southeast Asia', Keynote Address to the Ninth Annual Conference of the Harvard Project for Asian and International Relations, Beijing, 28 August 2000 at http://www.aseansec.org/secgen/sg_dc.htm (sighted 5 December 2001).

8. Multilateralism by other means

Judged by almost any measure, be it membership, structure, decision-making processes or policy outcomes, ASEAN, APEC and the ARF all offer striking testimony to the pervasive diversity and diffuseness of Asia-Pacific multilateralism. Yet these three organizations do not fully capture, singly or collectively, the heterogeneity of the region. Nor do they fully explain how heterogeneity and multilateralism can coexist and how one can act as a stimulus for the other. The cultural, economic or political diversity of the Asia-Pacific region is not, as we have seen, an impediment to regionalism but a catalyst for a different kind of regionalism to the one that has emerged in Europe or North America.

Institutional innovation has been far from absent in Asia Pacific, but it has tended to be loose, *ad hoc*, diffuse and often contradictory. These features, though not unique to this region, have assumed a prominence and distinctive profile not to be found elsewhere. In common with but perhaps more sharply than other regions, Asia Pacific has experienced the powerful competitive dynamic that is simultaneously driving globalization and regionalization. As a consequence, the competing interests, visions, images and projects that characterize the Asia-Pacific mosaic have prompted a unique blend of intra-regional and inter-regional conflict and co-operation. The ongoing and still unresolved contest between those espousing an Asia-Pacific formation and those wedded to notions of Pacific Asia is but the most graphic manifestation of this contradictory phenomenon.

What follows is not an exhaustive treatment of the regional organizations which now complement ASEAN, APEC and the ARF, but a thematic account of the arrangements and initiatives which most usefully illuminate the present stage of Asia-Pacific multilateralism, that is its diversity, fluidity and contradictoriness. Five types of multilateralism – with appropriate case studies for each type – have been selected for particular attention: 'East Asianism' (ASEAN+3), inter-regionalism (ASEM), economic sub-regionalism (growth areas), *ad hoc* multilateralism (South China Sea Workshops, the Korean Peninsula Energy Development Organization – KEDO), and track-two multilateralism (Council for Security Cooperation in the Asia Pacific – CSCAP). Neither these five types nor the particular initiatives and arrangements which exemplify them constitute discrete phenomena. The boundaries that separate Asia Pacific from Pacific Asia, the regional from the inter-regional or the sub-regional, economy from security, public from private, and track one from track two are neither rigidly drawn nor permanent. Yet each type has its own centre of gravity, is located primarily on one or the other side of these divides, and sheds its own distinctive light on the complex interactions that constitute Asia-Pacific regionalism and connect it to national, transnational and global processes and institutions.

EAST ASIANISM

That Asia generally, and East Asia (or Pacific Asia) in particular, has an identity, a dynamic and an organizational logic of its own is not an entirely new idea. It is nevertheless the case that the vigour with which the idea was articulated during the 1990s now gave it greater political salience. It was perhaps most strikingly expressed by Malaysian Prime Minister Mohamad Mahathir and Japanese politician Shintaro Ishihara in their jointly authored book *The Voice of Asia*.[1] Though polemical in tone, the work offered rich insights into the new 'Asia' consciousness which sought to celebrate the Asian model of capitalism and the renaissance of Asian civilizations. The Malaysian government had in fact proposed as far back as December 1990, partly in response to APEC's formation, the establishment of the East Asia Economic Group (EAEG). Though the Malaysian proposal was not fully developed, it envisaged a regional trade organization comprising the member states of ASEAN, South Korea, China and Japan. Its express purpose was to defend East Asian interests *vis-à-vis* the European Union and NAFTA, and more generally give participants greater leverage in international negotiations on trade and other economic and financial issues.

Fearing that the Malaysian initiative would undermine attempts to construct an Asia-Pacific entity, the United States and Australia firmly opposed it, thereby circumscribing Japan's freedom of manoeuvre, and prompting misgivings within ASEAN's own ranks. In the face of strong opposition, the EAEG proposal was substantially diluted and relabelled the East Asia Economic Caucus (EAEC). ASEAN endorsement was now forthcoming, but on the understanding that this consultative arrangement would be open, outward-looking and GATT-consistent, would not cut across the APEC agenda, and would build on ASEAN's strength and enhance its identity. Though preliminary responses from China and South Korea were moderately encouraging, several obstacles still stood in the way, notably continued US hostility, Japan's unwillingness to participate, and the difficulties surrounding Taiwan's possible membership. ASEAN plans to host a meeting of trade ministers in 1995, which would have included the ASEAN Six, Korea, Japan and China, had to be abandoned once Japan made it known that it would not attend. The first significant East Asian meeting would not occur until February 1996 in preparation for the first Asia–Europe Meeting (ASEM) held in March 1996.

These obstacles certainly retarded the progress of the 'East Asia' concept, but did not altogether derail it. It was as if the idea simply lay dormant until a number of factors would in due course converge to give it a new lease of life. Of the influences endogenous to the East Asian region, none was more important than the dynamic of economic regionalization. The principal dimensions of East Asia's economic growth and its regionalizing implications are considered in some detail in the companion volume[2] and in Chapter 3 of this volume. Suffice it here to say that the extraordinary growth of East Asia's trade from 1970 to 1995 (averaging an annual rate of 16 per cent) resulted not only in a higher East Asian share of world exports (rising from 11.3 per cent in 1970 to 26.7 per cent in 1995) but in much higher levels of intra-regional trade (from 31.7 per cent in 1970 to 51.2 per cent in 1995).[3] After a brief hiatus associated with the financial crisis of the late 1990s, intra-regional trade soon resumed its upward curve, the volume of trade between ASEAN, China, Japan and South Korea rising from $158.2 billion in 1999 to $201.7 billion in 2000.[4] Trends in intra-regional trade were matched by comparable trends in intra-regional investment. In 1995, 53.6 per cent of FDI flows in East Asia were of East Asian origin, with the overwhelming proportion of these flows originating from Japan and the 'tiger' economies and moving to China and the ASEAN countries.

A second factor, of particular political importance, was China's evolving role in East Asia. China's neighbours, Japan included, were themselves more disposed to integrating the rapidly expanding Chinese economy into its regional environment. For their part, Chinese policy-makers were also far more responsive to the construction of an East Asian entity. In September 1997, Premier Li Peng described the 'rise of Asia' as 'an irreversible developmental trend', and East Asia's diversity as facilitating rather than hindering 'mutual exchanges, mutual complementarity and joint progress'.[5] Speaking at the inaugural ASEAN+3 Summit in December 1997, President Jiang Zemin referred to East Asia's cultural traditions as positively contributing to the development of East Asian economic co-operation, citing in particular the role of such values as 'self-respect and self-strengthening, arduous effort, industriousness, frugality, modesty and eagerness to learn'.[6] He went on to advocate a further strengthening of East Asian co-operation, and advocated the establishment of 'a rational economic structure in the region' that would be 'non-exclusive and non-discriminatory' and strike 'a balance among different interests'. In a clear departure from the misgivings of an earlier period, Chinese policy was now firmly committed to East Asian multilateralism, including not only 'friendly dialogues and consultations to build up confidence' but also concrete steps to develop regional financial co-operation.[7]

The 1997 financial crisis may well have provided the single most powerful stimulus to East Asian regionalism. What gave the crisis its potency was the confluence of external and internal influences, which brought home to East

Asian governments the fragility of the East Asian 'economic miracle'. They now had a clearer sense of the structural weaknesses of their national economies, and of the vulnerability of those economies to outside pressures variously exerted by capital markets, hedge funds, Western governments and the IMF. Internal weakness and external vulnerability had combined to expose the inadequacy of regional responses. Most instructive in this respect was Japan's abortive attempt to sponsor the creation of an Asian Monetary Fund (AMF). Confronted with the hostile reaction of the United States and the IMF Japan simply withdrew the proposal. Ironically, the initiative was itself inspired, at least in part, by Japan's sense of frustration at not being able to exercise within the IMF and the World Bank a degree of influence commensurate with its financial contribution to the two organizations.[8]

The AMF proposal was not, however, entirely abandoned, but refashioned in more modest clothing under the label 'New Initiative to Overcome the Asian Currency Crisis'/'Resource Mobilization Plan for Asia', more popularly known as the 'New Miyazawa Initiative'. It was announced by the Japanese Finance Minister at a meeting in October 1998, attended by the finance ministers and central bankers of Indonesia, Malaysia, Thailand, the Philippines and South Korea. The new Japanese plan, to be supported by the Japanese Export–Import Bank, envisaged a contribution of $30 billion, half of which would be earmarked for mid-term and long-term development, and the other half for the short-term capital needs of economies engaged in the painful process of financial reform. To obviate the hostility encountered by the previous plan, the New Miyazawa Initiative was presented more as an aid package than a currency stabilization scheme, and as part of a larger multilateral G7-sponsored $90 billion contingency facility intended primarily for Asia. The initiative was nevertheless intended to serve Japanese interests, hence the requirement that loans extended under the Miyazawa Initiative be allocated to projects proposed by wholly-owned Japanese companies, or in the case of joint ventures, to projects where Japanese companies had a majority stake. The Miyazawa Initiative also provided Japan with an opportunity to provide loans in yen, which would in practice help to internationalize its currency.[9] This initiative, however, no less than its predecessor, suffered from inadequate coordination between the relevant arms of the Japanese bureaucracy and a singular incapacity to project Japanese actions on to the regional stage with any degree of clarity or higher sense of purpose.[10] Japan had yet to acquire anything like the structural power at the disposal of US diplomacy.

The widely shared grievances generated by the financial crisis strengthened among East Asia's policy-making elites a sense of collective identity.[11] Though they did not generally use the same vehement language as the Malaysian Prime Minister, they all to a greater or lesser degree felt that their economies had been unjustifiably exposed to the inadequacies of the international financial system, the volatility of short-term capital movements, the rigid strictures of the IMF, and the unresponsiveness of the US government. The failure of the United States to contribute at all substantially to rescue operations, its hardline commitment to the Washington consensus, dutifully reflected in IMF policies, and the new opportunities created for foreign investors to acquire ailing East Asian enterprises at basement prices helped to breed a lingering dissatisfaction with the US-dominated global multilateral system, and a renewed interest in exploring the possibilities of enhanced regional multilateralism.[12] The Malaysian Minister for Foreign Affairs explicitly referred to the Asian financial crisis as underscoring the common destiny of Southeast Asian and Northeast Asian countries, and the need for them 'to consult together on problems confronting the region, evolve common understanding and approaches'.[13] Lee Kuan Yew warned that East Asia had no option but 'to follow the global trend towards regionalisation . . . because only then could Asia exercise its bargaining power against other regions'.[14] Other regional organizations, either because they posed a potential threat to future East Asian economic growth, or simply because they made it necessary to engage in consultative arrangements (as in the case of ASEM), had thus served as a powerful catalyst for East Asian regionalism.

This, then, was the backdrop to the slow but steady institutionalization of the ASEAN+3 process, inaugurated by the summit of December 1997. The leaders of China, Japan and Korea met, as a group and individually, with their ASEAN counterparts on the occasion of the ASEAN Summit in Kuala Lumpur. A second ASEAN+3 Summit was held in Hanoi in1998, at which time agreement was reached to regularize the event. Although initial summit meetings were confined mostly to economic issues, it soon became apparent that these gatherings would also offer a useful vehicle for political and security dialogue. The gravity of the financial crisis largely explains the initial priority given to meetings of finance ministers. Following a decision taken at the 1998 Summit, the first meeting of ASEAN+3 deputy finance ministers and central bank governors was held in March 1999 in Hanoi, at which emphasis was placed on the need for emerging economies to be involved in various fora dealing with issues of international financial architecture. The finance ministers of the 13 countries met for the first time in Manila in April 1999.

Several other initiatives would soon contribute to the steady thickening of the layers of interaction. Ministerial meetings were arranged to cover a wider range of policy portfolios. By 2001 economic and trade ministers, labour ministers, ministers of agriculture and forestry, and foreign ministers had met at least once, and were planning to meet with increasing regularity. These ministerial meetings were supplemented by an ongoing process of review and implementation involving meetings of senior officials. To add further substance to their interaction, East Asian leaders agreed at their Second Summit in December 1998, on Kim Dae-Jung's suggestion, to convene an East Asian Vision Group of 'eminent intellectuals', and at their Fourth Summit in Singapore in November 2000 established an East Asia Study Group to assess its recommendation. The report of the East Asian Vision Group was first considered at the Fifth Summit in November 2001.[15] Two other related developments are worth noting here. A Japan–China–South Korea dialogue was inaugurated on the occasion of the Third ASEAN+3 Summit, an event which was also regularized and whose first concrete result was a decision to launch among think-tanks in the three countries trilateral joint research on economic co-operation. Of longer standing were the ASEAN+1 summits already referred to in the previous chapter. By the end of 2001 the ASEAN+China Summit had already seen the creation of an ASEAN–China Expert Group and endorsement of the proposal to develop a 'Framework on Economic Cooperation' and establish an ASEAN–China Free Trade Area within ten years. The ASEAN+Japan Summit tended to focus on the possibilities of extending Japanese financial and technical assistance to ASEAN, although increasing attention was also devoted to the long-term requirements of a 'closer economic partnership'.[16]

These institutional arrangements tended to reflect policy priorities. Reference has already been made to the understandable salience of financial co-operation. A meeting of finance ministers in May 2000 agreed on the need to establish a well-coordinated economic and financial monitoring system in East Asia. To this end it identified the ASEAN+3 framework as a useful vehicle for the exchange of consistent and timely data and information on capital flows, and established a contact network to facilitate regional surveillance. More importantly perhaps, it advocated the establishment of a regional financial arrangement to supplement existing international facilities. As a first step it sought to strengthen the 'Chiang Mai Initiative', which involved an expanded ASEAN Swap Arrangement supported by a network of bilateral swap and repurchase agreement facilities within the ASEAN+3 framework.[17] By November 2000, the ASEAN Swap Arrangement had been enlarged to $1 billion. By May 2002, bilateral swap agreements with a combined size of $17 billion had been reached between Japan on the one hand and Korea, Malaysia, Thailand, the Philippines and China on the other, and between China and Thailand.[18] In addition, negotiations were under way for several other bilateral arrangements, which would eventually bring the total to well in excess of $30 billion. Though these measures did not yet amount to the establishment of an AMF, they very much pointed in that direction. Equally indicative of future trends, at least in the longer term, were proposals, supported by the Philippines and others, for an Asian currency unit modelled on the euro. The increased scale and speed of cross-border capital flows had created a powerful incentive for East Asian governments, chastened by the experience of the 1997 financial crisis, to pursue more ambitious forms of monetary co-operation. They had not only the incentive but also the means to do this, given the large financial reserves which they had accumulated in the wake of sustained trade surpluses

– at the end of 1999 China's reserves stood at $154.7 billion (by the end of 2002 that figure would rise to $286.4 billion). Globalization had become one of the key factors propelling East Asian regionalism.[19]

Notwithstanding the urgency of financial developments, the joint statement issued at the end of the Manila ASEAN+3 Summit made it clear that co-operation would extend to a great many other areas. These included economic relations (in particular trade, investment, technology transfer, promotion of tourism, industrial and agricultural co-operation), human resource development, scientific and technical research and development, and development co-operation. Significantly, the statement went on to commit the participants to continuing dialogue and collaboration in the political–security field and on a range of transnational issues.[20] These different policy areas were not in any case unconnected. From ASEAN's perspective one of the most useful spin-offs of the emerging East Asian partnership was the contribution which China, Japan and Korea could make to accelerate ASEAN integration. In this regard, considerable importance was attached to human resource development, infrastructure and information technology. ASEAN countries were especially keen to take advantage of training programmes and technical expertise in the areas of economic, financial and corporate restructuring, monitoring of capital flows, and the development of a regional early warning system. A meeting of ASEAN+3 economic ministers in May 2001 endorsed six collaborative projects: strengthening the competitiveness of ASEAN small and medium-sized enterprises (SMEs); training on practical technology for environmental protection; developing common skill standards for information technology engineers; building competence in conformity assessment of industrial standards; software development in the Mekong Basin Project; and sharing of resources in remote sensing and satellite image archives to help address environmental problems. A subsequent meeting in September endorsed the 'Asia e-Learning Initiative' which envisaged sharing information on e-learning trends and technologies and promoting interoperability of e-learning systems.[21]

These early attempts to institutionalize the twin processes of consultation and collaboration constituted primarily a statement of intention on the part of the 13 governments. They had yet to demonstrate the capacity to develop common policies and appropriate decision-making mechanisms. The approach adopted thus far pointed to a certain commonality of interests, namely a largely muted desire to be able to act with greater independence *vis-à-vis* the United States and to speak with a louder voice in international fora. On the other hand, ASEAN+3 was at pains not to project itself as in any sense inimical to US interests. The complex psychology underlying the ASEAN+3 experiment was perhaps most clearly articulated by Kim Dae-Jung:

> I see a great deal of possibility in this ASEAN-plus-three group further expanding and further solidifying as a forum for East Asia as a whole . . . It will be able to

speak for the region *vis-à-vis* the North American Free Trade Area, Latin America and the European Union, and engage these organizations in cooperation as well as in competition.[22]

There was little sense in inviting US hostility to the project. After all, several East Asian governments were militarily aligned with the United States, and many East Asian economies remained highly dependent on continued access to the North American market. All of which helps to explain the tenor of much ASEAN+3 discourse, with its emphasis on open regionalism and rejection of any predetermined blueprint.

The ASEAN+3 experiment had to contend not only with the possibility of external retaliation, but also with the reality of its internal limitations, namely the absence of effective leadership, and the presence of latent or overt tensions. East Asianism, it could be argued, was more likely to prosper if one of its members were to exercise effective leadership. There were, however, only three candidates eligible for such a role: Japan, China and ASEAN. Neither Japan nor China could easily assume that role, because that would be to invite the hostility of the other and create profound misgivings on the part of ASEAN. If, on the other hand, ASEAN were to continue to exercise a leadership role, with Japan and China more or less balancing each other, the pace and scope of East Asian co-operation would be constrained by ASEAN's modest leverage. As one observer has aptly put it, 'ASEAN may be able to lead Japan and China to the water, but is unlikely to be able to force them to drink'.[23] That, however, was too pessimistic an assessment of the evolving dynamic of East Asian regionalism, for any one of three reasons. First, it was not the case that political leadership would necessarily have to rest on economic clout. Secondly, East Asia might successfully develop an institutional framework in which shared leadership could coexist with lingering tensions and suspicions. Thirdly, the European experience suggested that substantial conflicts of interest and perception need not prove an insurmountable obstacle to sustained institutional growth.

INTER-REGIONALISM

Here we focus on the emerging inter-regional linkages between East Asia and the European Union. The phenomenon is highly instructive in that it anticipated and greatly accelerated the development of ASEAN+3. To this extent it may be said that inter-regionalism sustained, and was in turn sustained by, East Asianism. There is, it need hardly be said, a rich legacy which links the two continents, including intermittent movements of cultures and peoples, the patterns of ancient trade, often referred to as the old Silk Road, and the more recent economic, political and cultural dimensions of European colonialism. The post-independence period inevitably saw a decline of European influence in much of East Asia, a trend reinforced by the American ascendancy and the rigours of strategic and ideological bipolarity, which is not to say that Britain, France and the Netherlands did not, wherever possible, continue to cultivate old connections. It is, however, only in the post-Cold War period that these two longstanding established centres of political and cultural influence have sought to construct a more evenly balanced relationship. The European Union had already institutionalized its links with ASEAN through its status as a dialogue partner and its membership of the ASEAN PMC. Indicative of things to come was the EU's successful bid to join the ARF in July 1994. In the same year ASEAN and EU representatives agreed at their meeting in Karlsruhe to establish an 'Eminent Persons Group', which would in due course propose ways of enhancing inter-regional collaboration.

Conscious of East Asia's economic and political renaissance, the European Commission submitted to the European Parliament in July 1994 a report *Towards a New Asia Strategy*, which was duly accepted the following year. The opening to Asia was seen as integral to the EU's endeavours to develop a common foreign and security policy. However, the report prompted a number of criticisms, notably its tendency to treat virtually the whole of Asia as an undifferentiated mass, seemingly overlooking the fact that rapid export-oriented industrialization accompanied by high rates of economic growth was an almost entirely East Asian phenomenon. A strategy paper prepared by the Commission entitled *Creating a New Dynamic in EU–ASEAN Relations* went some way towards rectifying the problem of geographical delineation.[24] However, the theme of conditionality which permeated important sections of the paper drew highly negative reactions, most obviously in Southeast Asia. The EU's policy towards ASEAN appeared to rest on two premises, one predicated on the political agenda of the Maastricht Treaty, which stressed such values as democracy, human rights and the rule of law, and the other on the Union's interests in matters of international trade, including its commitments to the WTO. Under the banner of 'fair trade', the European Union pressed such disparate issues as those of international copyright, protection of Europe's labour-intensive industries, and the 'social clause', whereby Europe required Southeast Asian countries to amend their social legislation and industrial practices so as to align them more closely with European standards.[25]

Whatever the ideological rationale for the European case, the primary objective was to redress Europe's bilateral trade imbalances with Asia. Europe's combined trade deficit with the 12 major Asia-Pacific economies would reach $55 billion in 1997. The ASEAN governments for their part were not prepared to accept European attempts to redress the trade balance by use of the social clause. For them this was little more than a subterfuge whereby human rights, workers' conditions and environmental concerns were intruded into the negotiating process purely to secure a trade advantage. In opposition to European conditionality and the stress on human rights and social clauses, ASEAN countries asserted the twin principles of sovereignty and sustainable development. Similar considerations led ASEAN to reject repeated European pressures on the question of East Timor. Though European governments, led by Portugal, would consistently point to gross human rights violations by Indonesia's armed forces, ASEAN policy remained steadfast, insisting that East Timor came under Indonesia's sovereign jurisdiction, and that any ASEAN initiative would therefore constitute improper interference in Indonesia's internal affairs.[26] For ASEAN governments regional solidarity was essential if the sovereignty principle was to be salvaged, and salvaging that principle was a high priority since it helped to insulate them from unwanted international scrutiny of domestic political arrangements.

Notwithstanding these obvious points of contention, Asia had by the mid-1990s achieved renewed prominence in the minds of European policy-makers. Trends in overall trade and investment flows between the two regions had fluctuated somewhat since the early 1980s, but the economic relationship remained a substantial one. During its presidency of the Council of Ministers (July–December 1994), the German government drew repeated attention to East Asia's impressive economic performance, describing China and Southeast Asia as increasingly important markets and partners. East Asia's share of world trade had risen from 19.1 per cent in 1986 to 28.6 per cent in 1996, and was projected to rise to 32.4 per cent in 2010. The EU's share of East Asia's total trade had registered a significant rise from 11.6 per cent in 1985 to 15.0 per cent in 1990 – a proportion which it more or less maintained over the next five years. The EU had also made substantial investments in Japan and Korea, although its share of total FDI flows into East Asia had declined from 17.9 per cent in 1985 to 8.7 per cent in 1993, before recovering to 12.8 per cent in 1996. While East Asian FDI flows into Europe also fell during the first half of the 1990s, partly as a result of the prolonged Japanese recession, by 1996 Japan's total FDI stock in Europe had reached $113 billion. By the same year, South Korea, East Asia's second largest investor in Europe, had an accumulated FDI stock of $2.1 billion.[27]

It is true that of the 15 member states of the European Union, only four had a major economic stake in Asia, namely Britain, France, Germany and the Netherlands. Yet, European governments and enterprises generally had now 'embarked on a frantic commercial race towards Asia'.[28] The competitive search for new markets was the most powerful catalyst for the emerging Asia–Europe dialogue, but several other factors, including the end of the Cold War, China's rise as a major centre of power, Britain's imminent departure from Hong Kong, Europe's conspicuous exclusion from APEC, and US ambivalence towards trade liberalization and global multilateralism made the idea especially attractive to Europeans.[29] The expanding membership of the EU, the establishment of the European Monetary Union, and the progressive integration of Europe's financial markets gave added momentum to Europe's foray into Asia. These same developments had sensitized Asia's political and business elites to the importance of an integrated Europe as an economic and political partner.

There was now an evident desire on both sides to explore the possibilities of mutual accommodation, in part by placing the relationship in its tripolar context. Treating the EU, East Asia and North America as three distinct economic blocs, though at best a crude and at worst a misleading approximation of the configuration of economic power, is nevertheless a useful heuristic device. Measured in terms of the volume of trade, the EU constituted by far the largest bloc, its two-way trade totalling some $3,862 billion in 1996, that is 45.3 per cent of the combined exports and imports of the three blocs, with East Asia and North America accounting for 31.0 per cent and 23.7 per cent, respectively. Similarly, FDI flows in and out of the EU amounted to $2,420 billion in 1996 (45.1 per cent of combined inward and outward FDI), compared with $1,677 billion and $1,268 billion for North America (31.3 per cent) and East Asia (23.6 per cent), respectively.[30] On the basis of these admittedly crude indices, it is arguable that Europe and to a lesser extent East Asia were able to exercise far less economic leverage than their share of tripolar trade and FDI flows would indicate. Placed in this tripolar context, the decision to strengthen the Asia–Europe connection may be interpreted as a modest attempt by the two sides to counterbalance America's global dominance, which it derived in part from its commanding role in the transatlantic and transpacific relationships. All this having been said, it is also the case that the 'triadic powers', as Dent has labelled them, were connected in ways that were not entirely conflictual, and that global interdependence had given rise to a complex set of corporate alliances and governmental linkages that cut across the three blocs.[31]

With this economic and diplomatic backdrop in mind, the Singapore Prime Minister proposed in 1994 a meeting of European and Asian leaders. He saw the development of this bridge as a way of closing the triangular relationship between Asia, Europe and North America. Following ASEAN's endorsement of the proposal, the 1994 and 1995 EU summits responded positively to the idea. Facilitators were appointed during 1995 to prepare position papers, and a Communication was issued by the European Commission underscoring the compatibility of European and East Asian interests. Arrangements soon got under way for what came to be known as ASEM I, the first Asia–Europe Summit held in Bangkok in March 1996.

ASEM I was attended by ten Asian states, the EU member states and the European Commission. To get the meeting off to a good start, the Europeans agreed to give human rights a lower profile, although these were not entirely neglected. The meeting was seen as generating the necessary impetus for a series of initiatives that would set the future agenda of Asian–European rapprochement. Commitments made at that meeting included the decision to hold ASEM II in London in 1998 and ASEM III in Seoul in 2000, and in the intervening time to convene meetings of economic ministers and foreign ministers. Commitments were also made to establish the Asia–Europe Business Forum (AEBF), create an Asia–Europe Foundation (ASEF), an Asia–Europe

University Programme and an Asia–Europe Technology Centre, and prepare an Investment Promotion Action Plan, and an Asia–Europe Co-operation Framework which would elaborate the long-term principles of co-operation.[32]

To give effect to these commitments and generally sustain the dialogue process, European and East Asian leaders, had no option but to establish an appropriate consultative framework. The necessary mechanisms for negotiation, decision-making and coordination of agendas, projects and activities were established but with no secretariat and relatively little administrative infrastructure. To this end, decisions were taken to complement the biennial summit meetings with periodic meetings of foreign, economic, finance and science and technology ministers, as well as Senior Officials Meetings (SOMs), including the Senior Officials Meeting on Trade and Investment (SOMTI) and a range of coordinating committees, working groups and task forces.[33] It remained to be seen whether this skeletal organizational infrastructure could sustain the ambitious collaborative programme which emerged out of the first three ASEM summits (see Figure 8.1).

As with ASEAN+3, the 1997 financial crisis inevitably impacted on ASEM's evolution. The most obvious and immediate effect was to reduce the flow of East Asian FDI into Europe. A number of large Korean firms, including Daewoo and Hyundai, announced suspension of current or planned operations, while smaller ones withdrew entirely.[34] Even more dramatic was the impact on European banks which had lent heavily to Asian banks and companies. According to one estimate, as of June 1997 these loans amounted to $365 billion, suggesting a much higher level of exposure for European banks than for their American or Japanese counterparts. By October 1998, Europe as a whole had contributed some 20 per cent of the IMF's total rescue packages.[35] For Europe restoring East Asia's financial stability was a key objective.

Europe was also intent on taking advantage of new opportunities. Following IMF intervention East Asia's worst-hit economies had to accelerate foreign investment deregulation, thereby making it possible for foreign investors to acquire domestic assets at bargain prices. Far from derailing the ASEM project, the financial crisis gave it an additional *raison d'être*. In response to the crisis, the London Summit launched a number of initiatives, of which the most important was the establishment at the World Bank of the ASEM Trust Fund (ATF). Its principal task was to provide technical assistance and advice on restructuring the financial sector and on finding ways to redress poverty. By January 1999, ¤40 million had been committed to the Fund and a number of projects were under way. In October 2000, the Seoul Summit decided to extend the ATF into a second phase, but left it to the finance ministers meeting the following January to determine its modalities.

ASEM's agenda was not, however, restricted to the financial arena. The Asia–Europe Foundation which was established in February 1997, and to which the ASEM partners had pledged $22 million, organized a high-profile lecture

Figure 8.1   ASEM structure

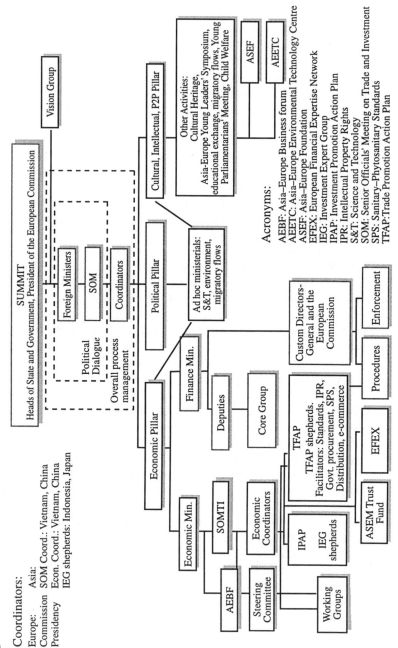

Coordinators:

Europe: Asia:
Commission   SOM Coord.: Vietnam, China
Presidency   Econ. Coord.: Vietnam, China
   IEG shepherds: Indonesia, Japan

SUMMIT
Heads of State and Government, President of the European Commission

Vision Group

Foreign Ministers

SOM

Coordinators

Political Dialogue

Overall process management

Political Pillar

Economic Pillar

Cultural, Intellectual, P2P Pillar

Ad hoc ministerials: S&T, environment, migratory flows

Other Activities:
Cultural Heritage,
Asia-Europe Young Leaders' Symposium,
educational exchange, migratory flows, Young
Parliamentarians' Meeting, Child Welfare

ASEF

AEETC

Finance Min.

Deputies

Core Group

Custom Directors-
General and the
European
Commission

Enforcement

Procedures

Economic Min.

SOMTI

Economic
Coordinators

IPAP

IEG
shepherds

TFAP
TFAP shepherds.
Facilitators: Standards, IPR,
Govt. procurement, SPS,
Distribution, e-commerce

ASEM Trust
Fund

EFEX

AEBF

Steering
Committee

Working
Groups

Acronyms:

AEBF: Asia–Europe Business forum
AEETC: Asia–Europe Environmental Technology Centre
ASEF: Asia–Europe Foundation
EFEX: European Financial Expertise Network
IEG: Investment Expert Group
IPAP: Investment Promotion Action Plan
IPR: Intellectual Property Rights
S&T: Science and Technology
SOM: Senior Officials' Meeting on Trade and Investment
SPS: Sanitary–Phytosanitary Standards
TFAP:Trade Promotion Action Plan

series, a summer school for undergraduates, the Young Parliamentarians' conference, and a number of seminars and conferences across a range of issues, including science, technology and economy as well as the more contentious questions of culture, human rights, and labour relations. Other initiatives saw the creation of the Asia–Europe Vision Group which had its first meeting in April 1998, an ASEMConnect electronic resource network for SMEs, and the Virtual Information Exchange (VIE) website designed to provide information on the investment regimes and opportunities of partners. The ASEM Summit in Seoul recommended greater co-operation between the educational institutions of the two regions, and to this end referred to the potential of the ASEM Education Hubs (AEH) and the Asia–Europe University (AEU). The meeting formally received the report of the Asia–Europe Vision Group, adopted the Asia–Europe Cooperation Framework 2000 and a wide range of new projects, including a conference on e-commerce and logistics, a roundtable on globalization, a seminar on information and telecommunications technology, a WTO trade facilitation conference, an anti-money laundering initiative, a symposium on combating transnational crime, an environment ministers' meeting, and an initiative on HIV/AIDS.[38]

Though less tangible, perhaps more significant in the longer term was ASEM's function in institutionalizing a rapidly evolving dialogue on almost the entire spectrum of global economic and security issues. The security agenda as set out under the Asia–Europe Cooperation Framework (AECF) encompassed: arms control, disarmament and non-proliferation of weapons of mass destruction; illicit trafficking in and accumulation of small arms and light weapons; global environmental issues; transnational crime, in particular money laundering, smuggling and exploitation of migrants; trafficking of women and children; international terrorism and piracy; and racism and xenophobia. The economic agenda envisaged dialogue on complementing and strengthening the open and rules-based multilateral trading system embodied in the WTO; establishing an enhanced business-to-business dialogue and co-operation between the two regions, with particular emphasis on the role of the AEBF; promoting co-operation in priority industrial sectors, including agro-technology, food processing, bio-technology, information and telecommunication, energy and environmental engineering. In the social, cultural and educational fields, AECF priorities included: enhancing student, academic and information exchanges, encouraging mutual recognition of degrees and licences between European and Asian educational institutions; and promoting a broad-based dialogue between all sectors of society, not least parliamentary representatives.[39]

It remains to highlight two features of the ASEM process: one bearing a striking resemblance to APEC, and the other suggesting a more distinctive approach. As with APEC, the ASEM process had from the outset sougth to cultivate the active involvement of the business communities of the two regions. Formed in 1996, the AEBF had met annually, and at its fifth meeting in Vienna in September 2000 finalized a series of detailed recommendations covering trade, investment, financial services, SMEs, information technology, physical infrastructure and life science. Detailed responses to these recommendations given by each of the ASEM partners were made public in August 2001. The responses varied considerably in the degree of enthusiasm with which the recommendations were received, and in the capacity of the various parties to act upon them. They did nevertheless point to a growing level of transparency within the ASEM consultative process. At its sixth meeting in Singapore in September 2001, the AEBF announced a number of new initiatives two of which are worth highlighting: 127 meetings had been arranged among SMEs with a view to developing business partnerships; and an AEBF website and e-conference platform had been established to provide a bridge between AEBF participants, ASEM governments and business communities. As in previous years and in line with the APEC experience, the theme running through most of the meeting's recommendations was the need for enhanced public–private sector partnerships with the focus on trade and investment liberalization and facilitation.

The other feature of the ASEM process was its keen interest in and support for global multilateral institutions. At first sight, support for the WTO was common to both APEC and ASEM. But the ASEM approach seemed more accommodating, at least rhetorically, of the interests and concerns of developing and least-developed countries. Meeting shortly before the Fourth WTO Ministerial Conference in Doha, the ASEM economic ministers agreed that the negotiating agenda should be sufficiently broad and balanced to reflect diverse interests, and offered clear support for a number of positions espoused by the developing world, in particular the need to address implementation-related issues, special and differential treatment, improved market access, and technical assistance for capacity building.[40] ASEM's emphasis was even more striking with regard to other multilateral organizations. The need to strengthen the role of the United Nations was repeatedly stressed, especially in the areas of peacekeeping, development, disarmament, arms control and human rights. ASEM foreign ministers agreed in May 2001 that their governments should consult regularly at an appropriate level before sessions of the UN General Assembly. In contrast to the APEC Statement of October 2002, the Fourth Asia–Europe Meeting in Copenhagen in September 2002 emphasized that 'the fight against terrorism must be based on the leading role of the United Nations and the principles of the UN Charter'.[41]

Within a relatively short period ASEM had acquired an institutional and policy momentum which could not have been readily anticipated on the eve of its inception. Yet the proliferation of meetings, statements and activities could not obscure a number of significant constraints bearing upon its trajectory. It is as if ASEM, not unlike APEC, had embarked upon a high level of activism almost for its own sake. The general sense of purpose which had brought it into being had yet to be translated into clearly specified objectives or benchmarks with which to measure ASEM's progress. The lack of specificity was attributable to any number of factors. It may be argued that in the first few years all that ASEM partners could reasonably hope to achieve was to familiarize themselves with each other's priorities and diplomatic style. Yet, familiarization could not of itself ensure commonality of views or policies. Quite apart from the obvious differences between the European Union and East Asia, the regional formations themselves were greatly preoccupied with their own internal affairs. Both the European Union and ASEAN were grappling with the competing demands of enlargement on the one hand and integration on the other. As for ASEAN+3 it was of even more recent origin than ASEM, and a long way from establishing policy coherence on many of the most pressing issues of regional and global security. The very composition of ASEM was itself problematic. New EU members would automatically become ASEM members, and several European countries were currently under consideration for possible EU membership. Should there be a corresponding increase in the Asian contingent? What of Australia and New Zealand which were already pressing their case? A rapidly expanding ASEM could not but further retard the formulation of common objectives and strategies.

While organizational difficulties were obvious enough, two other even more formidable impediments stood in the way of ASEM's progress. The first may be simply termed the US factor. As already intimated, the United States was so closely connected to both Europe and East Asia that US interests and power could not but influence, and often significantly circumscribe, any major European or East Asian initiative, ASEM included. These connections were mediated by states, markets and civil society, and evident as much in the cultural as in the economic and politico-strategic fields (see Figure 8.2). The Transatlantic Economic Partnership, the Transatlantic Business Dialogue and NATO were but the most visible institutional pillars of the Atlantic edifice, mirrored in the Pacific by APEC, PECC and the bilateral security arrangements linking the United States with Japan, South Korea, Taiwan, the Philippines, Thailand and Australia.

As Dent has argued, the Eurasian relationship was vastly inferior in economic and strategic muscle to its transatlantic and transpacific counterparts.[42] Dent goes on to list a number of factors which might entrench the structural weakness of the Eurasian bridge: continued US technological and entrepreneurial superiority; the possibility of a restructured and reinvigorated Japanese economy; the EU's 'introspective preoccupation with European integration'; limited commercial prospects in the EU for East Asian firms, 'the persistent underdeveloped socialization between Europe and East Asia'; and 'the lack of European security linkages'.[43] Though each of these factors is salient to the evolution of Europe–Asia relations, they need not all be seen as adversely impacting on the relationship. Indeed, it is arguable that anything which strengthens the European or East Asian poles (for example, greater European

Figure 8.2   Competitive interdependence: regional, inter-regional and global multilateralism

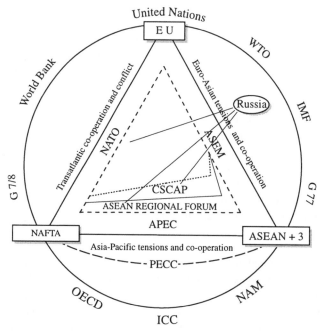

cohesion, Japanese economic recovery) may to that extent provide either or both poles with greater leverage *vis-à-vis* the United States, and to that extent enhance their capacity to develop the Eurasian side of the global geoeconomic and geopolitical triangle. Conversely, anything which solidifies the Eurasian connection may in turn help constrain US dominance of transatlantic and or transpacific institutional linkages. There was a long way to go before ASEM could acquire the critical mass needed to transform the existing tripolar balance.

The second impediment, and the one more likely to determine the ultimate fate of the ASEM experiment, was the conspicuous absence of civil society. Though projects and activities undertaken or planned after ASEM II sought to encourage people-to-people contacts, and ASEM III referred specifically to the importance of education and intellectual and cultural exchanges, these were very much icing on the cake, with governments as the only *patissiers*. It was not just that ASEM's formation and subsequent evolution were the product of a top-down approach, but that the two regional formations which were engaged in this bridge-building exercise, essentially the European Union and ASEAN+3, were themselves elitist constructions. Much has been said of the strikingly different status accorded to business on the one hand and the non-governmental or non-profit community sector on the other. ASEM official pronouncements made little mention of the role of civil society organizations working in such fields as the environment, development, education, indigenous rights, health, women's rights, legal reform, consumer protection, urban renewal, inter-cultural and inter-religious dialogue. As Paul Lim aptly observed, even the European Parliament and the national parliaments were 'marginal to the ASEM process'.[44] The standard explanation has emphasized the antipathy of East Asian governments to European notions of democracy and human rights, hence the EU's reluctance to press strongly for the promotion of these values. Though there is evidence to support it, the explanation is nevertheless deficient for it assumes that civil society is central to the European project. In reality, the European Union itself suffers from an acute democratic deficit, which is reflected in the limited powers of the European Parliament, and more importantly in the relative impotence of civil society organizations in the key deliberative organs of the EU, not to mention the less visible corridors of power in Brussels and other European capitals. The ASEM process was unlikely to become consultative and democratic so long as its parent organizations were themselves severely lacking in these qualities.

The difficulties alluded to in the preceding paragraphs were unlikely to prove fatal to the ASEM experiment. European and Asian governments were for a variety of economic and strategic reasons likely to keep the project alive. However, lack of popular support and enthusiasm could not but severely constrain ASEM's future development and the opportunities it might offer Europe and Asia to play a more active and creative role in the emerging norms, rules and regulatory frameworks of global governance. Here the initiative, at least in the early stages, might lie more with Europe than with Asia, given Japan's slow economic recovery and the preoccupation of most other East Asian governments with catch-up developmental strategies. By the same token, Europe's capacity for leadership was severely compromised by its seeming inability to formulate a viable alternative to the neo-liberal economic agenda of the 1980s and 1990s. This failure had troublesome ramifications for Eurasian dialogue, for it limited Europe's external capacity to promote reform of existing global institutional arrangements and its internal capacity to stem the tide of rising levels of racism and xenophobia.

ECONOMIC SUB-REGIONALISM

The phenomenon has been given a great many labels: sub-regional economic zones, growth triangles, growth polygons, natural economic territories, transnational export-processing zones. The phenomenon itself refers to economic integration processes which gained considerable impetus in the late 1980s in different parts of East Asia. Cutting across state boundaries, these processes link adjacent areas of separate countries, each contributing particular assets (for example, land, labour, capital, technology) in which they have a 'competitive advantage'. A number of key ingredients normally combine to produce a sub-regional economic zone: '*economic complementarity, geographical proximity, political commitment* and *infrastructure development*' (italics added).[45] These ingredients can, of course, combine differently in different zones. The degree of political commitment, for example, can vary considerably from one zone to another, and even from one government to another within the same zone. Political commitment often refers to government action aimed at removing barriers which are said to prevent the full realization of existing complementarities.[46]

One useful classification of these zones distinguishes between three categories:[47]

- *A metropolitan spillover into the hinterland* – here the territory of one or more countries constitute the core (that is, provide better infrastructure and economies of scale) while other countries constitute the periphery (that is, provide cheap land or labour).
- *Geographically proximate areas with common interests,* where the primary stimulus to economic exchange is not just physical proximity but ethnic or cultural affinity, which may have been previously impeded by domestic conflict or geopolitical alignments.
- *Joint development of natural resources and infrastructure,* where low-income countries intent on developing natural resource, manufacturing or service industries lack the necessary infrastructure, and must therefore engage in multinational projects which can attract the necessary capital and technology.

Though conceptually distinct, these categories inevitably overlap in practice, with private capital usually providing the driving engine but depending to a greater or lesser degree on government to facilitate the process.

The existing literature points to a long list of sub-regional economic zones. The most frequently cited are the growth triangles that have emerged under the ASEAN umbrella: the Brunei–Indonesia–Malaysia–Philippines East Asia Growth Area (BIMP-EAGA); the Indonesia-Malaysia–Singapore Growth Triangle (IMS-GT) also known as SIJORI; the Indonesia–Malaysia–Thailand Growth Triangle (IMT-GT), and the West–East Corridor (WEC) of the Mekong Basin which covers parts of Vietnam, Laos, Cambodia and Thailand, and is linked to the ASEAN Mekong Basin Development Cooperation Scheme. These triangles may be considered a form of unofficial regionalism designed to stimulate higher levels of investment, including FDI, given the relatively slow pace of ASEAN's economic integration. It is widely seen as an intermediate step in economic co-operation, that may bypass a number of the difficulties encountered by AFTA. Its main advantages are its relative informality, the smaller number of countries involved, and the complementarities to be gained by combining the different endowments of contiguous territories. Other zones include the Greater South China Economic Zone (encompassing Hong Kong, Macau, Taiwan and China's southern coastal provinces of Guangdong and Fujian), the Yellow Sea Rim (including China's northeastern provinces, the west coast of the Korean peninsula and the Japanese island of Kyushu), the Golden Quadrangle (connecting Thailand, Laos, Myanmar and western China) and the Tumen River Area Development Project (TRAD).

The aim here is not to investigate any one of these zones, but to examine the main factors facilitating or impeding the phenomenon in Northeast Asia, where political and strategic considerations have played a much larger role in determining the pace and character of economic sub-regionalism. In this context Northeast Asia may be said to include northeast China, eastern Russia, North Korea, South Korea, Mongolia and Japan. At face value all or most of the facilitating factors would seem to apply to Northeast Asia: geographical proximity, cultural affinities (at least between some territories), availability of infrastructure and complementarity of endowments. In addition, the Cold War had come to an end, market economies dominated the region, and economic development had become the standard catchword. Bilateral trade between neighbouring countries duly increased in the early 1990s: two-way trade between China and South Korea rose from $5.8 billion in 1991 to $8.2 billion in 1992, and $8.9 billion in 1993; Sino–Japanese trade reached $22.8 billion in 1991, $25 billion in 1992, and $39 billion in 1993; Sino–Russian trade also registered a sizeable increase, totalling $7.2 billion in 1993.[48] Close connections also emerged in FDI flows, with the Northeast Asian economies, and Japanese corporations in particular, accounting for the bulk of foreign investment in China. Contributing to and complementing higher levels of economic interaction were increased cultural and tourist flows and trans-urban co-operation, especially between Beijing, Seoul and Tokyo.[49]

Rising intra-regional trade and FDI flows in Northeast Asia pointed to deepening economic interdependence of the regional economies, but also to the diminishing importance of the United States as a market and source of investment for the Northeast Asian economies as well as to rising transpacific trade frictions. Between 1985 and 1997, the proportion of Northeast Asia's total exports accounted for by the United States had fallen from 36.1 per cent to 23.5 per cent. By contrast the proportion accounted for by intra-regional trade during the same period had increased from 22.9 per cent to 35.0 per cent.[50] The most dramatic shift had occurred in the case of Taiwan whose exports to the United States as a proportion of total exports fell from 57.9 per cent in 1985 to 27.6 per cent in 1997. On the other hand, during the same period the proportion accounted for by Northeast Asia had risen from 21.0 per cent to 38.8 per cent.[51] The rapidly increasing volume of intra-regional trade and investment flows coupled with 'mounting protectionism and emerging regionalism in Western Europe and North America' was widely expected to give added impetus to Northeast Asian economic integration.[52]

Sub-regional integrative processes were considered a particularly promising avenue given that they relied less on government initiative or inter-governmental agreement. The energy sector was identified as providing the greatest incentive for joint economic development, although large infrastructure construction projects in transport and telecommunications were also expected to get under way. Major ports in the region, including Dalian, Vladisvostok and Nakhodka might 'serve as the gateway to the heartland of Asia and Siberia'.[53] The Tumen River project, of which more later, was expected to encourage the expansion of transport links between China and Russia. East Siberia's oil, gas and hydroelectric resources were thought likely to contribute significantly to China's, Japan's and South Korea's energy requirements. China's oil consumption had grown rapidly since the beginning of the 1990s and was expected to exceed that of Japan by 2010. Domestic oil production was rising only modestly, and could not prevent increasing dependence on oil imports. While China was committed to the large-scale development of its own gas resources, it was estimated that by 2020 China might need to import as much gas as the European Union in 2020.[54] Gas demand was also expected to exceed supply in other Northeast Asian countries, including Japan, South Korea, Mongolia and North Korea.

Notwithstanding the size of the potential market, several difficulties had to be overcome, including climatic conditions, large-scale exploration to confirm the scale and accessibility of reserves, the maturation of the anticipated markets, establishment of large-scale transport infrastructure, and not least investment mobilization. Were Northeast Asia's natural gas requirements to be supplied from eastern Siberia, Yakutia and Sakhalin the investment required for oil and gas projects in these areas was estimated to be of the order of $40–70 billion. Natural gas in western Siberia might also be brought on stream via a 6,500-kilometre pipeline which could eventually be integrated with the gas projects in Eastern Siberia, Yakutia and Russia's Far Eastern region. If, on the other hand, Central Asia were to be the preferred source, an 8,000-kilometre pipeline might be constructed to run to Japan via China at an estimated cost of $23 billion.[55] Projects of this scale could not, however, be brought to fruition simply through the initiative of entrepreneurial capital, government intervention and inter-governmental co-operation would prove necessary at virtually every stage of the process.

Much was made of the complementarity of Northeast Asia's economies. Japan was well placed to provide capital, advanced technology, and industrial infrastructure, and its capital- and technology-intensive enterprises could take advantage of the natural resources, lower labour costs and sizeable markets offered by the other economies. Though on a smaller scale, South Korean, Taiwanese and Hong Kong capital and expertise could play a similar role. The 'flying geese' model, simplistically applied to describe the emerging East Asian division of labour linking economies at different stages of development,[56] was now thought to have relevance to economic complementarity in a Northeast Asian context, with the rapid industrialization of the 'tiger economies' and now China likely to contribute to a more horizontal division of labour.[57] But the supposed complementarity of needs and endowments, in so far as it treated national economies as the key units of analysis, tended to overlook the quite distinct interests and perceptions of industrial and financial enterprises on the one hand, and the interests and perceptions of states on the other.

The Cold War may have come to an end, but its legacy was still a potent factor in regional politics. The Korean conflict remained unresolved; the United States retained a pervasive military presence, not least in Korea and Japan; and Sino–US relations were at best precariously balanced between economic interdependence and political suspicion. Other deep-seated animosities whose origins could be traced back to a more distant past included the unresolved dispute over the Kurile Islands, the uneasy Sino–Japanese relationship, and periodic friction in Japan–South Korea relations. The political trust needed to translate economic complementarity into effective co-operation even at a sub-regional level had yet to be developed. Though powerful cultural and economic influences and personal connections had encouraged a complex network of commercial and financial ties between the PRC, Hong Kong and Taiwan, the strategic orientation of Japanese and Korean enterprises had more of a regional or even global than sub-regional focus. The entrepreneurial connections between China, Japan and South Korea on the one hand and Russia on the other were either tenuous or still at an embryonic stage.

Given these obstacles, the progress of Northeast regionalism was understandably slow. Even sub-regional projects, though they offered a more promising avenue for co-operative projects, tended to be limited in scope and to proceed with caution. The Yellow Sea Rim is a case in point. The sub-region covered mainly China's northeastern coastal provinces (Heilongjiang, Jilin and Liaoning), the west coast of the Korean peninsula and the island of Kyushu in Japan. While trade and other economic ties had expanded during the 1990s, by the end of the decade infrastructural development in roads, rail, shipping and air transport was still in its infancy. The Tumen River Area Development Project, given the specific character of the project, and the external institutional support it enjoyed, was widely considered to have better prospects of success. Yet, it too would find the going hard.[58]

The Tumen Project was spearheaded by the UNDP as a mechanism for regional dialogue and co-operation. Its main objectives were to promote sustainable economic growth in North Asia, and the Tumen region in particular; to strengthen economic, environmental and technical collaboration; and to make the region attractive for international investment, trade and business. The more specific aim was to mobilize resources for the construction of infrastructure needed for large-scale resource exploitation, trade and industrial development. The project was meant to encompass the territories adjacent to the Tumen

River and the littoral areas of the Japan Sea into which it empties, that is, Russia's Far East, Mongolia, northeast China (Jilin, Liaoning and Heilongjiang provinces), and North and South Korea. Two free trade zones were initially canvassed: a core Tumen River Economic Zone comprising Huchun in China, Najin in North Korea and Posyet in Russia, and a more extensive delta zone (Tumen Economic Development Zone) extending to China's Yanji, North Korea's Chongjin, and Vladivostok in Russia.

The first phase of the Tumen Project involved extensive planning and background studies, and was followed by a second phase which focused on investment promotion and development initiatives aimed at creating a growth triangle. The institutional framework for the project, established in December 1995 by the five member countries (China, North Korea, South Korea, Mongolia and the Russian Federation) consisted of two inter-governmental bodies (the Consultative Commission and the Coordination Committee) and the Tumen Secretariat. Meeting annually, the Commission had overall responsibility for the project and was composed of representatives at vice-ministerial level from the five member countries. The Coordination Committee, on the other hand, coordinated economic development, especially with regard to trade and investment facilitation, environment, and cross-border transport, and comprised representatives from the three riparian countries (China, North Korea and Russia). In addition, national teams made up of central and local government representatives were established by each of the five member countries, and Working Groups were formed to formulate economic co-operation policy in six sectors: trade and investment, transport, environment, energy, tourism, and telecommunications.[59]

The Tumen region had been selected because of its potential as a major entrepôt for international trade, its strong complementarities, vast natural and human resources, and accessibility to northeast Asian markets. Yet, despite a substantial organizational infrastructure, regular meetings, steadfast support by local governments in the Tumen region, and sizeable funding by the UNDP, the Asian Development Bank and the Canadian government (some $20 million in donor contributions over the first ten years), progress on the ground remained noticeably slow. Though a number of steps had been taken to create legal and institutional mechanisms as well as human capacity-building conducive to cross-border trade and transport, the anticipated investment flows and large infrastructure projects had yet to materialize. Political and security considerations remained major impediments. The general easing of tensions in the post-Cold War period and the early signs of a thaw in relations between North and South Korea did not translate into the resolution of the Korean conflict or of the Russo–Japanese territorial dispute. Economic and political considerations also played a part, in particular North Korea's relatively closed economy, Russia's internal difficulties, the Asian financial crisis, and the 'grandness of the scheme', which made it dependent on massive capital inflows that could not be easily mobilized. In such a climate, it proved exceedingly difficult to arrive at implementation arrangements which delivered benefits of comparable value to each of the relevant governments.

By the end of the 1990s the future of economic sub-regionalism in Northeast Asia was in the balance. Russia's economic performance was steadily improving, but the volume of its trade with the Americas had risen much more than with Asia, and trade with Japan remained in the doldrums. Moreover, with the exception of the Sakhalin projects, major Japanese investment proposals were not on the horizon. In any case, Russia's overall economic growth obscured major regional differences, with the Russian Far East lagging well behind. Plans for transportation corridors in Northeast Asia remained a subject of considerable research and discussion, but the private sector was unlikely to take the initiative without the active support of central government.[60] Effective coordination of government initiatives in turn depended on the sustained input of regional and global organizations. To put it simply, Northeast Asia had yet to construct the necessary synergy between the national, regional and global tiers of governance. Complex institutional arrangements were needed to address several closely interconnected problems, including uneven development within and between countries, the enormous disparities between national legal and administrative frameworks, and the periodic tensions generated by unresolved territorial disputes and the vulnerability of all states in the region to internally and externally induced political crises. Economic sub-regionalism offered a promising avenue for managing and channelling the expanding web of interdependence, but its effectiveness, as with other forms of regionalism, would ultimately depend on recasting the triangular relationship between state, market and civil society to make it more responsive to the imperatives of human security.

AD HOC MULTILATERALISM

As the label suggests, *ad hoc* multilateralism refers to institutional projects or processes that are objective, space and time specific.[61] They are designed to address a particular problem over a clearly delineated area, often within a given time frame. The institutional arrangements may be designed to encourage security, economic or functional co-operation, or some mixture of the three. Though multilateralism, including its *ad hoc* variant, is often viewed in much of the literature through a state-centric lens,[62] in practice it may involve track-one, track-two or even track-three processes or some combination of the three. Because of its specificity, *ad hoc* multilateralism is usually aimed at resolving or at least managing a particular conflict. It may involve no more than shuttle diplomacy, in which a third party – usually but not necessarily a government – attempts to mediate between two conflicting parties, be they states, ethnic communities or political movements. Alternatively, it may give rise to a complex institutional process which encompasses governments, inter-governmental agencies, and a range of non-state actors.

This necessarily selective survey focuses on *ad hoc* multilateralism as it impinges on the security domain, with particular emphasis on the military dimensions of security. It is, however, important to note that the approach has widespread applicability, and that during the 1980s and 1990s both governmental and non-governmental organizations in East Asia made increasing use of it as a problem-solving mechanism, not least in the area of environmental degradation. Rapidly deteriorating air quality in major cities, serious pollution and resource depletion in the Sea of Japan, the Yellow Sea and the East China Sea, the destruction of wetlands, expanding levels of deforestation and desertification, proliferation of nuclear and other highly toxic wastes – to name but a few of the more obvious environmental problems – prompted a series of bilateral and multilateral responses.[63] A number of regional initiatives had substantial governmental input, a comprehensive agenda and encompassed the entire region. Initiated by the Japanese Environment Ministry in 1991, the Environmental Congress for Asia and the Pacific had the participation of some ten countries, the UNEP and the World Bank. Others had a more limited brief, for example, the Program on Prevention and Management of Marine Pollution in East Asian Seas, established by the UNDP/Global Environmental Facility (GEF), with the involvement of several governments, including those of China and North Korea. Others had a sub-regional focus, confining themselves to Northeast Asia or Southeast Asia. Some were inter-governmental (for example, the Senior Officials Meeting on Environmental Cooperation in Northeast Asia, which first met in Seoul in February 1993; the Northwest Pacific Action Programme, which first met in Vladivostok in October 1991; the ASEAN Senior Officials Meeting on the Environment), while others were non-governmental (for example, the 1992 Seoul International Environmental Symposium). Not surprisingly, given the intractability of the problems in question, these multilateral initiatives tended to have a relatively long life or to lead to various forms of institutional innovation.

South China Sea Workshops

Two cases of *ad hoc* multilateralism have been selected for closer examination, one located in Southeast Asia and the other in Northeast Asia. Several references have already been made to the South China Sea workshops, primarily in connection with the Spratlys dispute. The focus here is on the role of key actors, their understanding of the dynamics of conflict and conflict management, and their capacity to influence the regional security agenda. The Korea Energy Development Organization, on the other hand, is highly instructive for the light it sheds on the competing interests that have kept the Korean peninsula in a quasi-permanent state of overt or latent conflict. The aim here is not so much to trace in detail the specific trajectory of these two projects or to evaluate their prospects for success or failure, but rather to illuminate the economic and geopolitical context which gave rise to them, and which they were meant to influence.

The momentum of the South China Sea workshops – often described as a track-two initiative – was in fact created and sustained largely by Indonesian diplomacy. Established in 1990, the workshops could not but mirror the ups and downs of the Suharto regime's political fortunes. Overwhelmingly East Asian in membership and inspiration, the initiative was nevertheless dependent on external funding. Intended primarily to prevent jurisdictional disputes from erupting into armed hostilities, it soon became apparent that the competing sovereignty claims to the Spratlys and the Paracels were but one variable in a rather complex equation. The workshops on 'Managing Potential Conflict in the South China Sea' could not but reflect the multifaceted character of the contemporary security agenda.

The workshops had one relatively clear objective: to promote the peaceful settlement of overlapping territorial and jurisdictional claims. However, the sheer weight of China's position with respect to the South China Sea generally and to the various territorial disputes in particular made it clear that the best that the workshops could hope to achieve would be to manage rather than resolve these conflicts. Beijing agreed to participate because it did not wish to be left out of the negotiating process. Multilateral dialogue offered one additional avenue through which it could articulate the official Chinese view. Its *ad hoc* character was especially welcome as its deliberations would not result in binding decisions. China could influence the discussions, yet retain full freedom of action. Beijing insisted from the outset that any mechanisms to be established should focus not on resolving conflicting sovereignty claims but on promoting co-operative projects. It proposed a number of scientific initiatives, including a joint expedition to investigate natural phenomena in the South China Sea, a joint study on meteorological conditions, and another study on promoting navigational safety in the South China Sea.[64] Chinese representatives argued that marine scientific research and environmental studies were useful not only in themselves but as confidence-building measures (CBMs). They were much less willing to entertain CBMs directly related to the easing of tensions associated with the Spratly and Paracel disputes. They argued against the participation of non-South China Sea states but entertained the possibility of seeking their collaboration in specific projects. They were adamant that the process could not extend official recognition to Taiwan, but welcomed the latter's participation as a way of enhancing the cross-Strait relationship.[65]

Faced with the constraints imposed by China's declared position, Indonesia as the initiating country was prepared to accept the Chinese approach at least as a first step. Scientific and technical collaboration, though it would not go to the heart of sovereignty claims, might nevertheless be mutually beneficial, and eventually spill over into the more sensitive areas of security dialogue. As a consequence, the workshop process fell between two stools. On the one hand, it had many of the features of an academic gathering, but the agenda and many of the participants were primarily focused on its political implications. On the other hand, while senior officials played a key role, they were meant to participate in a private capacity and their discussions were largely confined to technical issues. The exercise could be best described as *hybrid multilateralism*, located somewhere between track one and track two, between preventive diplomacy and technical or functional co-operation.

To facilitate progress in the development of substantive collaborative projects, technical working groups (TWGs) were established, in which experts other than diplomats and lawyers could fully contribute.[66] Five areas were identified as meriting particular attention: marine scientific research, marine environmental protection, safety of shipping navigation and communication, resource assessments, and legal matters. As discussion became increasingly technical, group of experts meetings (GEMs) were convened, with each GEM reporting to a TWG, and each TWG in turn reporting to the workshops which met annually, had general oversight of the process, and reached agreement on the programme of activities and meetings for the coming year.[67] Substantive discussion at all these meetings revolved around specially commissioned papers prepared by experts, with the agenda designed to generate a consensual approach to incremental collaboration. The TWG on navigational safety put forward a number of practical proposals. The GEM on training of mariners, to which it was connected, identified the wide variation in standards followed by regional training establishments as an important contributing factor to marine casualties. The 1997 GEM held in Kuching prepared a draft proposal for a hydrographic survey of the South China Sea. The TWG also considered contingency plans for pollution control and unlawful activities at sea.[68]

By 1999 ten consecutive workshops had been held, all of them in Indonesia. After a one-year interruption, largely a fallout of the Indonesian political crisis, the 11th Workshop was held in March 2001. Core funding had been provided by the Canadian International Development Agency, but with Brunei, Taiwan and Singapore funding their own participants, and other governments, notably, Indonesia, and international agencies, in particular UNEP, UNDP, the World Bank and the International Maritime Organization, contributing resources and expertise. ASEAN's principal dialogue partners, the United States, Japan, Australia and the European Union, had also expressed varying degrees of support for proposed activities. The decade-long experiment had mixed results: only four projects had been approved: one on biodiversity, another on climate and sea-level change, a third on data collection and scientific networking, and a fourth on monitoring the ecosystem of the South China Sea. All were still in various stages of implementation. Initial steps had also been taken to assess the mineral resource potential of the South China Sea. The legal implications of the Convention on the Law of the Sea and of other regional and global agreements had been examined but practical conclusions had yet to be reached. Different methodologies for joint development were under consideration as was the harmonization of marine environmental standards and regulations. The most concrete high-profile initiative was the *Anambas Expedition* which took place in March 2002. Its purpose was to explore the Islands of Anambas, situated within Indonesian waters, in the South China Sea, approximately 130 nautical miles northeast of the eastern entrance of the Singapore Strait.[69]

The Indonesian government had more than once made the case for elevating the workshop format from track two to track one, or at least adding to it a more formal dimension. A government-to-government dialogue might, for example, parallel rather than replace the existing informal process. The Chinese, however, steadfastly opposed such suggestions, arguing that official discussions would soon come to grief given the intractability and sensitivity of the issues involved. In any case, by the mid-1990s the first signs had emerged of a willingness on China's part to allow the Spratly and Paracel disputes to intrude into the official arena. As indicated in previous chapters, the issue had become a subject of discussion at ARF meetings, and in a more decisive way now formed part of the ASEAN–China dialogue. It is arguable that the South China Sea workshops, as the only multilateral forum regularly convened to deliberate on South China Sea issues, had helped to create a sufficient level of trust among the key protagonists to make this transition possible. Beijing, for its part, saw the diversification of multilateral mechanisms as a positive development in so far as it could be used to prevent any one mechanism from applying excessive pressure. When one particular mechanism appeared likely to move in directions that China did not favour, the possibility now existed for another mechanism to take the running, thereby deflecting the attention and energies of the offending mechanism. These two seemingly contradictory developments were in fact part of the intricate and still rapidly evolving institutional scaffolding of which the workshops were an integral part. The scaffolding was not robust enough to meet the highest standards of preventive diplomacy. It was, on the other hand, sufficiently textured to give expression to conflicting interests and perceptions, and at the same time give added impetus to regional dialogue and co-operation. In this sense, the workshop process had become a reliable barometer of the shifting geopolitical, economic and environmental pressures now bearing upon the region.

KEDO

Notwithstanding the vastly different circumstances obtaining in Northeast Asia, KEDO performed a similar function. At one level, it accurately reflected the deep-seated conflicts of interest between the North Korean and South Korean regimes as well as the alignments and policies underpinning US attempts to maintain hegemonic stability. At another level, it pointed to the increasingly powerful constraints as much on Washington's as on Pyongyang's freedom of action. The background to KEDO's establishment has already been canvassed in the earlier volume.[70] A brief summation of key events may nevertheless be helpful. In late September 1991 President Bush announced the unilateral withdrawal of all naval and land-based tactical nuclear weapons deployed abroad, effectively ending the deployment of some 100 US nuclear weapons in South Korea. A week later Mikhail Gorbachev reciprocated the US announcement. In early November, South Korean President Roh Tae Woo pledged that South Korea would not produce, possess, store, deploy or use nuclear weapons, or acquire nuclear reprocessing or uranium enrichment plants. On 31 December 1991, both Koreas formally made the same commitment by signing the Joint Declaration on Denuclearization of the Korean Peninsula. In January 1992, six years after becoming a party to the Nuclear Non-Proliferation Treaty (NPT), the DPRK signed a comprehensive safeguards agreement with the International Atomic Energy Agency (IAEA). This sequence of events seemed to advance a key US strategic priority: to forestall the development of a North Korean nuclear weapons capability.

The IAEA agreement was considered especially significant because it allowed for international inspection of North Korea's nuclear facilities. Unfortunately for the United States, this proved to be the beginning rather than the end of the story. The North Korean leadership concluded that there was much to gain from adopting a tough stance *vis-à-vis* IAEA inspections. Accordingly, it refused to submit two sites, believed to store nuclear wastes, to IAEA special inspections. North Korea's motivation was kept deliberately opaque. The most obvious reason for Pyongyang's refusal to co-operate with the IAEA was that it had something to hide – that it was in fact using ostensibly peaceful nuclear activities as a cover for a nuclear weapons programme. It is nevertheless feasible that North Korean thinking was more subtle. Pyongyang may have calculated that the prospect of a North Korean nuclear bomb might make Washington more amenable to negotiation. The United States might be willing to offer a number of concessions if North Korea in return took steps to honour its commitments to the IAEA. Following talks between the two governments, North Korea suspended its decision to withdraw from the NPT and agreed to the full and impartial application of IAEA safeguards. For its part, the United States gave assurances against the threat and use of force, including nuclear weapons, and pledged not to interfere in North Korea's internal affairs.

Though an inspection team arrived in North Korea in March 1994, a stalemate soon ensued with Pyongyang's refusal to allow IAEA inspectors access to a plutonium reprocessing plant at Yongbyon. Former US President Jimmy Carter helped to negotiate a breakthrough in June 1994 with North Korea agreeing to 'freeze' its nuclear weapons programme in return for high-level talks with the

United States. Following lengthy negotiations the two governments concluded the 'Agreed Framework' in Geneva in October 1994. North Korea gave three undertakings: (a) to freeze operation of its 5-megawatt reactor and plutonium reprocessing plant at Yongbyon, and construction of two other reactors, and eventually dismantle all three nuclear facilities; (b) to allow the IAEA access to all nuclear facilities to enable it to determine the extent to which materials may have been diverted for weapons use in the past; and (c) to remove 8,000 spent nuclear reactor fuel elements to a third country. In exchange, Pyongyang was to receive two light-water reactors (LWRs) with a total generating capacity of 2,000 MW(e) by 2003, and shipments of heavy fuel oil elements during construction of the LWRs at a rate of 500,000 metric tons annually.[71] KEDO was formally established by the United States, Japan and South Korea in March 1995 with the express purpose of giving effect to this agreement.

While KEDO was entrusted with the implementation of the Agreed Framework, the broader aim, explicitly referred to in its mission statement, was to strengthen the international non-proliferation regime and improve the prospects for peace and stability on the Korean peninsula. For the United States, KEDO's financial, technical and environmental tasks were meant to serve a security objective. For the DPRK, the ostensible purpose was to satisfy the country's energy requirements. Yet, behind these declared objectives lay a less tangible but perhaps more profound dynamic, namely a contest for geopolitical ascendancy in the Korean peninsula and beyond.

KEDO's three founding members were soon joined by the European Union (through the European Atomic Energy Community), New Zealand, Australia, Canada, Indonesia, Chile, Argentina, Poland, the Czech Republic and Uzbekistan. However, KEDO's Executive Board, which set the organization's general direction, was made up exclusively of US, Japanese and South Korean representatives. KEDO's Executive Director (an American) and its two Deputy Directors (nominated by Japan and South Korea) were responsible for day-to-day operations. US, Japanese and South Korean experts made up the bulk of KEDO staff, and the KEDO Secretariat was located in New York. KEDO and the DPRK concluded an agreement in December 1995, whereby KEDO would provide the DPRK with the two LWRs on a turnkey basis. The reactor model to be selected by KEDO would be of advanced US-origin design and technology, and the project would conform to standards equivalent to those of the United States and the IAEA, with an anticipated delivery date of 2003. North Korea, for its part, undertook to freeze its existing graphite-moderated reactors and related facilities and refrain from building new ones. However, site surveys were not completed until October 1999 and preliminary works until February 2000. The Turnkey contract, which became effective in February 2000, envisaged completion of the first LWR by January 2008.

Successful completion of the project would depend on resolution of a number of difficulties. Skilled labour and a sophisticated infrastructure were indispensable if such a large, multi-billion, technologically complex project were to come to fruition. Highly sensitive issues had to be addressed, including nuclear safety and protection against liability in the event of a major nuclear accident.[72] Through regular meetings with the DPRK's regulatory authority, the State Nuclear Safety Regulatory Commission, KEDO sought to strengthen North Korea's national regulatory framework and secure adherence to international conventions. The financial arrangements would prove equally difficult. The entire project was conservatively estimated to cost some $4.6 billion, of which South Korea was to provide $3.2 billion, Japan $1 billion, the United States $115 million and the European Union $80 million.[73] Between March 1995 and December 2001 only $1.38 billion had been committed, of which South Korea and Japan accounted for $604.5 million and $292.6 million, respectively.[74] The annual delivery of 500,000 metric tons of heavy fuel oil to North Korea also proved problematic, with KEDO pointing to unpredictable and fluctuating oil prices, the total annual cost rising from $83 million in 1998 to $180 million in 2000.

Without understating the magnitude of these technical and financial difficulties, it can be fairly said that the overriding obstacle was political. The Framework Agreement could not obscure the periodic strains in the US–North Korean relationship, which were inevitably reflected in delays to the construction schedule. While the agreement centred primarily on the possible linkage between nuclear power and nuclear weapons, US attention soon turned to the development and transfer of missile systems, components and technology. In a series of bilateral meetings in 1996–97, Washington pressed Pyongyang to refrain from deploying its medium-range Nodong missile and to end sales of Scud missiles and their components. In April 1998, it imposed additional sanctions on North Korea for transferring missile technology and components to Pakistan. In August 1998, North Korea launched a three-stage Taepo dong rocket with a range of 1500–2000 kilometres, in response to which Japan suspended its signature of the cost-sharing agreement for the LWR project. The spotlight turned again to nuclear issues in December 1998, when the United States requested North Korea to place a suspected underground nuclear facility at Kumchang-ni under international scrutiny. A US inspection team visited the nuclear site in May 1999, but found no evidence of nuclear activity or violation of the Agreed Framework. It was not, however, until William Perry, whom President Clinton had appointed as North Korea policy coordinator, presented his report to Congress in September 1999 that high-level discussions got under way with a view to the long-term normalization of diplomatic relations. The turnkey contract between KEDO and the DPRK was duly signed in December 1999.

The improved climate in US–DPRK relations was reflected in the joint US–DPRK statement on international terrorism of 6 October 2000. In the US–DPRK joint communiqué of 12 October 2000, the two sides agreed on the desirability of greater transparency in carrying out their respective obligations under the Agreed Framework. Yet, tensions remained. In the latter part of 2000, the United States was reportedly considering renegotiation of the Agreed Framework. Citing as reasons longer lead times for nuclear power construction, difficulty in obtaining nuclear liability insurance, and the backwardness of North Korea's economy, US officials openly canvassed alternative energy technologies. Interpreting it as a politically motivated attempt to delay construction, North Korea threatened to withdraw from the project and resume its own nuclear power programme. The advent of the Bush administration in January 2001 deepened the strains in the relationship. A number of senior US officials and Republican senators were now vociferously calling for changes to the agreement, though Secretary of State Colin Powell seemed committed to honouring existing obligations. Following a review of North Korea policy, President Bush declared in June 2001 his willingness to resume 'serious discussions' on a 'broad agenda', including 'improved implementation of the Agreed Framework'. For his part, Kim Jong-Il had made it known that he intended to maintain the existing North Korean moratorium on ballistic missile flight tests through at least 2003. Parallelling this more conciliatory mood, the second half of 2001 saw an active round of KEDO–DPRK negotiations, the issuance of a construction permit and the start of excavation work. By December 2001, 1,100 personnel were working at the Kumho site.[75]

Contradictory signals nevertheless continued to emanate from Washington. In his State of the Union address on 29 January 2002, President Bush accused North Korea of 'arming with missiles and weapons of mass destruction, while starving its citizens', and described it, along with Iraq and Iran, as constituting 'an axis of evil, arming to threaten the peace of the world'. Yet, barely a week later, at a Senate Foreign Relations Committee hearing, US Secretary of State Colin Powell confirmed that North Korea was continuing to observe the missile flight-test moratorium and adhere to its obligations under the Agreed Framework. Press reports were nevertheless beginning to circulate that, following its nuclear posture review, the United States might in certain circumstances entertain a preemptive nuclear strike, and that North Korea might constitute a possible target. On 1 April 2002, President Bush announced that he would not certify North Korea's compliance with the Agreed Framework, but qualified the decision by waiving applicable US law that would have prevented the United States from continuing its financial support for KEDO. To explain the apparent contradiction, US officials argued that the President's refusal to certify compliance did not mean that the DPRK had violated the Agreed Framework but that it needed to co-operate more fully with IAEA verification activities.[76] Pyongyang insisted that it was not required to provide the IAEA with unfettered access to its nuclear-related sites until a 'significant portion' of the first light-water reactor had been completed. Washington, on the other hand, maintained that the IAEA needed three to four years to complete its accounting of North Korea's past nuclear activities. Inspections would therefore need to begin immediately if IAEA accounting were to coincide with the completion of 'a significant portion' of the first reactor, expected in 2005.[77] Was this a case of genuinely diverging interpretations of the Agreed Framework? Was the United States stretching the meaning of the agreement to its limits in order either to maximize pressure on North Korea or to reconcile sharply opposing views within the Bush administration? Was North Korea intent on pursuing its nuclear weapons programme? Each of these interpretations offered useful insights but only one slice of a complex reality.

The KEDO initiative received a major setback in October 2002, when the US State Department announced that the North Korean authorities had admitted to developing nuclear weapons. The admission was reportedly made in discussions with US Assistant Secretary of State James Kelly after he had presented the North Koreans with new evidence that they had acquired enriched uranium and were therefore in breach of the 1994 agreement. A day later US Secretary of Defense Donald Rumsfeld claimed that North Korea had built a small number of nuclear weapons. The reactions of both protagonists to these dramatic revelations were themselves highly instructive. While refusing to confirm publicly the validity of the US account, North Korea argued that it was entitled to possess nuclear weapons and 'other more powerful weapons to defend itself'. In its next move Pyongyang made it known that it was ready to address US concerns if Washington would guarantee its sovereignty and right to economic development. The state news agency KCNA quoted a foreign ministry official as saying: 'It is a reasonable and realistic solution to the nuclear issue to conclude a non-aggression treaty between the DPRK [North Korea] and the US if the grave situation of the Korean peninsula is to be bridged over'.[78] While dismissing the North Korean proposal, the Bush administration, in striking contrast to its position on Iraq, seemed willing to pursue diplomatic channels, which is not to say that it was ready to shed the ambiguity of its diplomacy.

On 14 November 2002 KEDO announced that it was suspending heavy-fuel oil deliveries to North Korea in response to Pyongyang's uranium-enrichment plans. Two weeks later the IAEA adopted a resolution calling upon North Korea to 'clarify' its 'reported uranium-enrichment programme'. North Korea rejected the resolution, describing it as biased in favour of the United States. On 9 December 2002, Spanish and US forces intercepted and searched a ship carrying North Korean Scud missiles and related cargo for delivery to Yemen. The shipment was nevertheless allowed to proceed as the United States lacked the necessary legal authority to seize the cargo. On 12 December, North Korea informed the IAEA that it would restart its one functional nuclear reactor and reopen the other nuclear facilities frozen under the Agreed Framework. It subsequently ordered international inspectors out of the country, and cut all seals and disrupted surveillance equipment on the reactor, its spent fuel pond, the fuel reprocessing plant, and the fuel fabrication plant. On 10 January 2003, it announced its withdrawal from the NPT, effective 11 January, arguing that it was not required to give three-months notice in advance of withdrawing since notice of withdrawal had already been given on 12 March 1993 – the decision to withdraw some ten years earlier had been merely 'suspended'.

What are we to make of this destabilizing sequence of events? The advent of the Bush administration had clearly deepened the strains in the relationship. The open repudiation of Kim Dae-Jung's 'sunshine policy' and the 'axis of evil' speech had set alarm bells ringing in Pyongyang. Deeply unsettled by US notions of pre-emptive strikes and regime change, the North Korean leadership now saw itself a possible target of US global unilateralism. Its primary interests had not changed. These were regime survival, assistance for its battered economy, and international recognition. The United States was considered central to all three objectives, hence its insistence on bilateral negotiations between the two countries and a non-aggression treaty with the United States.

The DPRK's more assertive nuclear strategy was designed to promote the same three objectives in the altered circumstances of the Bush presidency. It formed part of a stick and carrot strategy – a stick designed to serve as a deterrent against a possible US military strike, and a carrot offering the United States the prospect of an agreement which could effectively freeze North Korea's nuclear weapons programme. Once Pyongyang became convinced of the hostility of US intentions – possibly some time in the latter half of 2001, it decided to reactivate its nuclear ambitions in order to give its dual strategy added teeth. As before, it wanted to create the impression of enough nuclear capability to draw the United States into negotiations, but not so much as to preclude the future possibility of a verifiable nuclear freeze.

The Bush administration now faced a crucial dilemma. One option was to seek a credible and durable agreement with North Korea – this would necessarily require some form of negotiation. The other option was for Washington to impose its will by a coercive strategy involving a mix of political, economic and military sanctions. The second option was more dangerous than the first. It could not guarantee the denuclearization of the North, and might provoke a military conflagration that would engulf the two Koreas and possibly the rest of Northeast Asia. Generally speaking, key countries in the region, while alarmed by Pyongyang's words and actions, had a strong preference for the first option.

Despite provoking Washington's displeasure, both Kim Dae-Jung and his successor, Roh Moo-hyun, saw no alternative to the policy of economic assistance and patient negotiation. In response to the crisis, the new Roh government enunciated three principles: zero tolerance for North Korea's nuclear weapons development, a peaceful resolution of the crisis through dialogue, and South Korea's active participation in the process. The three principles had been carefully crafted to advance a more specific goal, namely that of preventing 'North Korea and the United States from crossing each other's red lines'.[79] Even Koizumi's Japan, which had been severely jolted by North Korea's nuclear brinkmanship, its resumption of missile testing across the Sea of Japan and admission that it had kidnapped Japanese citizens for intelligence training, remained persuaded that Pyongyang was interested in a comprehensive settlement that embraced nuclear weapons development, wider security issues and economic and political co-operation. Significantly, a meeting of the Trilateral Coordination and Oversight Group (TCOG) – a consultative body consisting of the United States, Japan and South Korea – produced a statement on 7 January 2003 indicating that the United States was now 'willing to talk to North Korea about how it will meet its obligations to the international community', and reiterating the previously stated US position that Washington had 'no intention of invading North Korea'.

Not surprisingly, the announcement that China would host talks between the United States and North Korea was met with widespread relief. The outcome of the trilateral forum held in Beijing on 23–25 April was predictably ambiguous. North Korea advanced 'a bold new proposal' for the settlement of the nuclear issue but at the same time confirmed that it had nuclear weapons,[80] and that it had started reprocessing plutonium from more than 8,000 spent fuel rods at Yongbyon.[81] For its part, the United States insisted that it was prepared to engage only in multilateral talks, that these should also include South Korea and Japan, and that the purpose of such talks should be to commit North Korea to a verifiable nuclear freeze, not to reward 'bad behaviour'.

How, then, is KEDO's function to be understood? KEDO was first and foremost a mechanism born of the profound conflict of interests between the American and North Korean states. The Agreed Framework, on which it was predicated, was an attempt by each side to advance certain interests – for the DPRK to obtain economic benefits and diplomatic recognition from its arch enemy, and for the United States to prevent North Korean acquisition of weapons systems which might blunt its own military preponderance in the region. To this extent the Agreed Framework, hence KEDO, could be seen as an instrument designed to reconcile these competing interests. There were, however, other DPRK and US interests which, though not integral to the agreement, could not but influence how each side viewed its provisions. US administrations were loath to act in ways which might consolidate the North Korean regime's grip on power. The DPRK was reluctant to accede to an intrusive inspection system either because it was not convinced of the desirability of abandoning the nuclear option, or at least not convinced of the wisdom of forgoing the leverage which it could exercise only so long as it could credibly threaten to pursue that option either immediately or at some unspecified time in the future. In other words, the Agreed Framework and KEDO were hostage not only to the clash of interests between two states but also to the contradictory interests pursued by each state, which were inevitably reflected in periodic policy shifts.[82]

The ambiguities surrounding US and North Korean policies were in any case compounded by the role of other actors, in particular Japan and South Korea, the other two key members of KEDO. Japan, for its part, had a strong interest in preventing North Korea from developing a missile capability which might pose a direct threat to it. It financial support for KEDO was the price it was prepared to pay to achieve such an outcome. Continuing tensions, however, between Japan and the DPRK might endanger such support within the Japanese Diet. By the same token Japanese diplomacy was fearful of the breakdown of KEDO arrangements, which a worsening of the US–DPRK relationship might provoke.

As for South Korea, Kim Dae-Jung's 'sunshine policy's was in part dependent on preventing the irreversible breakdown of the Agreed Framework or at least of the step-by-step process of reciprocal accommodation,[83] which was viewed as fundamental to the long-term resolution of the crisis. Its large financial commitment to KEDO was a direct expression of that policy, and an integral part of Seoul's continuing attempts to consolidate the embryonic dialogue between the two Koreas. More than that, the LWR project provided Seoul with the most tangible instrument it could use to prevent US–DPRK tensions from escalating to the point of endangering its own policy of engagement with North Korea.[84] Japanese and South Korean priorities might not proved decisive in shaping KEDO's future, but they could not but impact on the US policy-making process. In this sense, the KEDO process served as a barometer of the conflictual relationship between the United States and North Korea and of the fragile relationship between the two Koreas and between Japan and North Korea, but also of the fluid and at times contradictory relationship between the United States and its principal allies in East Asia.

TRACK-TWO MULTILATERALISM

In previous chapters reference has been made more than once to the role of track-two organizations, primarily in the economic arena. In this connection, much emphasis has been placed on the Pacific Economic Co-operation Council for its role in bringing together the academic, business and policy-making elites of the Asia-Pacific region. Over the course of the 1980s and into the 1990s, PECC is credited with helping to forge, if not a consensus, at least a substantial body of opinion in support of the notion of open regionalism, which in turn paved the way for APEC's formation. The validity of this assessment may be open to debate. Much less debatable is the more general proposition that track-two multilateralism has played a significant part in the evolution of Asia-Pacific regionalism. Indeed, it is arguable that this mechanism, better described as the 'unofficial' channel for political, economic, and security dialogue, has been particularly well suited to the psychology of Asia-Pacific diplomacy. It has provided governments in the region with a highly flexible instrument for circumventing some of the pitfalls impeding regional dialogue in the post-Cold War period.

Track-two mechanisms, precisely because they operate on the basis of informality, inclusiveness and non-attribution, enable government officials to participate in their 'unofficial' capacity, and to engage in frank and open discussion of issues that governments would normally consider too sensitive or controversial.[85] To the extent that these mechanisms also include academics and experts of various kinds, including representatives of non-state institutions, they encourage the articulation of a wider range of views and perceptions, and permit conclusions to be drawn which need not commit any of the relevant governments. On the other hand, they enable information, ideas and proposals to percolate through official channels and eventually capture the attention of policy-making elites at the national and regional level. Our analysis will concentrate on the CSCAP experience because of the salience of track-two multilateralism in the security domain, and because of CSCAP's acknowledged contribution to security dialogue.

The decline of Cold War rivalries in the late 1980s prompted a great many seminars, conferences, research projects and other activities, all attempting in one way or another to think through the implications for regional security. ASEAN-ISIS, the Pacific Forum in Honolulu, the Japan Institute of International Affairs (JIIA) and the Seoul Forum for International Affairs would play a leading role in shaping the emerging track-two dialogue.[86] In November 1992 a meeting of representatives from strategic studies institutes in ten countries (Australia, Canada, Indonesia, Japan, Malaysia, the Philippines, Singapore, South Korea, Thailand and the United States) agreed to establish the Council for Security Cooperation in the Asia Pacific. National CSCAP committees (formally designated as 'member committees') were quickly formed in each of these ten countries, and were followed over the next eight years by member committees in Russia, North Korea, Mongolia, Vietnam, Europe, India, Cambodia and Papua New Guinea.[87]

CSCAP's primary function was to facilitate political and security dialogue involving 'scholars, officials and others in their private capacities'. To this end CSCAP proposed to organize working groups on a range of security issues, make policy recommendations to inter-governmental organizations, convene regional meetings, co-operate with other institutions actively engaged around issues of regional security, and produce and disseminate publications relevant to its objectives. Apart from its member committees, CSCAP's structure comprised a Steering Committee, two co-chairs (one drawn from within and the other from outside ASEAN), and a number of working groups. The Steering Committee was assisted by a secretariat provided by ISIS Malaysia, and by a number of sub-committees dealing with such issues as finance, oversight of working groups, and future planning. Provision in the CSCAP Charter was also made for regular general meetings (open to all members of CSCAP member committees), the first three being held in 1997, 1999 and 2001.

Though the member committees differed considerably in size and cross-section of membership, range of interests, style of work and frequency of meetings, they were all expected, within the limits of their resources, to participate in the deliberations and activities of the working groups. These were seen from the outset as constituting the core of CSCAP's intellectual and political contribution to security dialogue. Working groups were established in June 1994 to cover four key areas: Confidence and Security Building Measures (CSBMs), Concepts of Cooperative and Comprehensive Security, Maritime Cooperation; and the North Pacific, followed by a fifth, Transnational Crime, in December 1997. By 2000 the five working groups had held a combined total of some 40 meetings and produced 12 edited collections of papers.[88]

Given the weight attached by CSCAP to its working groups, a brief word about each of them may help to convey something of the scope and limitations of this experiment in track-two multilateralism. More importantly from our perspective, it may illuminate the geopolitical and geocultural context within which CSCAP had to operate. The working group on CSBMs concentrated on two main areas: enhanced transparency of government activities that had a direct or indirect bearing on regional security, for example defence white papers and conventional arms registers; and preventive diplomacy, which included the formulation of basic principles as well as elaboration of practical initiatives, in particular an enhanced role for the ARF Chair. Under the general rubric of transparency, the working group also addressed issues of nuclear proliferation by turning its attention to the 'back end' of the nuclear fuel cycle, hence to the sensitive question of spent fuel management, including weapons grade plutonium. To this end it established in collaboration with the Sandia National Laboratory in New Mexico a web site providing details of nuclear power facilities in Asia.[89]

The Working Group on Maritime Cooperation was equally energetic, producing two CSCAP memoranda and five volumes of edited papers covering almost the entire range of maritime security issues.[90] CSCAP Memorandum No. 4, *Guidelines for Regional Maritime Cooperation*, published in December 1997, attempted to encapsulate a regional consensus on maritime co-operation principles, especially in relation to safety of navigation and marine environment practice. The working group's agenda inevitably touched on some of the most sensitive aspects of East Asian regional security, including freedom of navigation in contested jurisdictions, illegal fishing, illegal population movements, piracy, drug trafficking, and not least territorial disputes. To give coherence to this highly diverse agenda and at the same time make it more palatable to the diverse interests represented within the CSCAP family, the working group made order the centrepiece of its brief. Order seemed the *sine qua non* for managing, if not resolving, all of the problems under discussion, be it ocean pollution, freedom of navigation, fishing, piracy or maritime boundaries. Not surprisingly, the Law of the Sea soon emerged as a fruitful area of exploration, with a view to ascertaining both areas of common ground in interpretations of the existing legal order, and prospects for further development of maritime law. The first result of this effort was CSCAP Memorandum No. 5, *Cooperation for Law and Order at Sea*, published in February 2001, soon followed by further meetings to prepare another memorandum on the Law of the Sea.[91]

The other three working groups, though they canvassed many issues, found it, each for different reasons, more difficult to develop the necessary focus and momentum needed to produce proposals of immediate policy relevance. The Working Group on Comprehensive and Cooperative Security offered, through CSCAP Memorandum No. 3 (published in December 1995), a useful starting point for the emerging discourse on what was widely acknowledged to be an important but elusive set of concepts. Its subsequent meetings and publications, however, ranged over so many elements of the comprehensive security agenda from so many perspectives as to preclude any possibility of arriving at common conclusions, let alone agreed recommendations. The Working Group on the North Pacific had the advantage of dealing with a relatively well-delineated sub-region. Among the many issues explored, two were the subject of sustained attention, namely the dangers of nuclear proliferation in Northeast Asia, and the prospects for institutional innovation, both of them of profound interest but sharply contested and surrounded by lingering suspicion and mistrust. As for the working group on Transnational Crime, it was, despite initial reservations, widely perceived to have turned the spotlight on a set of troublesome trends which could no longer be ignored. Probably more so than in the case of the other four, an important function of this fifth working group was to develop a clearer understanding of the nature and scope of the problem, and to survey the arrangements which national law enforcement agencies and international organizations had thus far developed in response to it. The issues considered included drug trafficking, the illicit transfer of arms and nuclear materials, illegal immigration, money laundering, counterfeiting, and other forms of corporate fraud. In later meetings, the focus narrowed around issues pertaining to electronic crime, and use of illegal travel documents. In the aftermath of September 11, the working group inevitably turned its attention to terrorism, concentrating on its criminal manifestations, links to criminal organizations, the various issues relating to terrorist financing, and on terrorist activities in the Asia-Pacific region. A CSCAP memorandum on terrorism was proposed, with initial preparatory work under way in the first half of 2002.

The CSCAP experience was a contradictory one. It undoubtedly enabled the policy-making process at both national and regional level to draw on a larger and more varied body of expertise and informed opinion than might otherwise be the case. To illustrate, the defence white paper model proposed by the Working Group on CSBMs was adopted by the ARF's CBM Intersessional Support Group, and at least in part by China, Vietnam and Mongolia. As indicated in Chapter 6, the approach to preventive diplomacy, including principles and practical measures, elaborated by the same working group were eventually adopted with modifications by the ARF ministerial meeting in July 2001. Similarly, the Working Group on Maritime Cooperation was able to engage in useful exchanges with different elements of the ARF process, including the ARF Track-Two Conference on Preventive Diplomacy and the ARF ISG on CBMs.[92] CSCAP may also be credited with influencing the ARF's decision to add transnational crime and maritime security to its agenda in 1999. The following year, the Thai Foreign Minister, Surin Pitsuwan, in his capacity as ARF Chairman, made known to CSCAP the ARF's wish to enhance the role of the ARF Chair in promoting interaction between track-one and track-two diplomacy in general, and between the ARF and CSCAP in particular. As a first step, it was proposed that the CSCAP Co-Chairs should transmit to the ARF Chair the conclusions and recommendations resulting from CSCAP deliberations. The opportunity was enthusiastically taken up by the CSCAP Steering Committee, and a number of possible mechanisms were subsequently discussed, including periodic exchange of information between the two organizations, attendance by CSCAP officers at certain ARF meetings and by ARF senior officials at CSCAP meetings, and a formalized arrangement whereby CSCAP working groups could make a regular input into ARF deliberations.[93]

Since its inception, CSCAP had sought to cultivate a close relationship with the ARF. Indeed, it would not be an overstatement to suggest that for many key players within CSCAP the principal yardstick of the organization's effectiveness was the degree to which its contribution was valued by the ARF membership. Put briefly, CSCAP's primary institutional goal was to gain the ARF's confidence as a prelude to establishing itself as the privileged second-track organization to which the first track, namely the ARF, would turn regularly for research and policy advice. CSCAP's overriding rationale was to act as a catalyst for an enhanced regional security dialogue, with the ARF serving as the principal agent and arena for such dialogue. These assumptions about CSCAP's role carried a number of far-reaching implications.

Having defined its function largely in terms of support for the first track, CSCAP had to ensure that its own membership, structure, organizational ethos, and policy recommendations were acceptable to the ARF, or at least palatable enough not to endanger the possibility of a productive association with it. In addressing the dilemma between independence and policy relevance, CSCAP had chosen to retain its formal autonomy while at the same time carefully circumscribing its practice. Currently serving foreign ministry, defence and other government officials constituted a relatively small fraction of the membership of most national committees. On the other hand, the rest of the membership usually comprised retired policy-makers and diplomats as well as academics and experts who had either served in an advisory capacity for their respective governments or whose policy outlook did not radically depart from the official worldview. To the extent that national CSCAP committees depended for their continued operation on varying degrees of government funding, and actively sought the involvement of government in their activities, there were limits to which their analysis and recommendations could be critical of government policy.

The close correlation in security outlook between CSCAP member committees and national governments meant that the geopolitical dynamic which underpinned the ARF process tended to reproduce itself within CSCAP. On contentious questions, be it developments in East Timor, Cambodia or Burma, or human rights more generally, discussion within CSCAP might be a little freer, fuller, better informed, and encompass a wider range of views. There was little likelihood, however, that the CSCAP process could generate a meeting of minds significantly in advance of what might be expected to emerge from ARF consultations. Indeed, the reluctance to antagonize any major party to a conflict or controversy meant that CSCAP would in practice avoid formal discussion of the issue, and refrain from developing a problem-solving response. Emulating ASEAN's and the ARF's predilection for low-key diplomacy, CSCAP was unwilling to examine in any depth, either at steering committee or working group level, any of the unresolved conflicts of the region, be it the Kurile Islands, Korea, Taiwan, or the Spratlys. Ironically, the ARF was, if anything, more likely than CSCAP to give attention to these troublesome disputes. Like ASEAN and the ARF, CSCAP had internalized the maxim that, when addressing either internal or external conflicts, regional organizations could not be seen to call into question the principle of sovereignty or its concomitant, non-interference in the internal affairs of another country. CSCAP's reluctance to move forward with notions of comprehensive, let alone human, security, except at the highest level of generality, stemmed largely from this assumption. Conflict resolution at one end and human rights or even environment at the other were troublesome precisely because they raised the possibility that a third party might be seen as sitting in judgement over the conduct of one or other state.

There is a third dimension to the CSCAP–ARF relationship which is worth noting. By tying its fortunes so closely to those of the ARF, CSCAP had in effect deprived itself of strategic options. CSCAP's efficacy as a track-two organization had been made almost entirely dependent on the ARF's future progress. To be more specific, CSCAP could be said to have acquired a vested, though in one sense perfectly legitimate, interest in seeing to it that the ARF successfully handled two complex and interconnected transitions: one from confidence-building to conflict prevention and conflict resolution, and the other from narrowly defined to wider notions of security. As a consequence, CSCAP's own future now revolved around two closely related but as yet unanswered questions. First, did CSCAP have the intellectual capacity, unity of purpose and political clout needed to steer the ARF in the desired direction? Secondly, what if, despite CSCAP's best efforts, the ARF project did not live up to expectations? These questions are revealing not only for the light they shed on CSCAP's trajectory but for what they tell us about the region's emerging architecture.

As regards the first question, it was certainly not a foregone conclusion that CSCAP was organizationally equipped to guide the future direction of regional security dialogue. Though it had conducted several useful studies and elaborated a number of well-thought-out practical proposals, it had by and large shied away from advancing ideas about regional architecture or offering any assessment of the ARF's performance. To put it simply, it had avoided, except in marginal ways, the key conceptual and institutional questions surrounding regional security in the Asia-Pacific context. This was no mere accident or oversight. It reflected in part the reluctance of several membership committees to entertain options deemed unlikely to have the support of their respective governments. Other committees that did not operate under the same constraints were nevertheless averse to elaborating proposals that might cause embarrassment to fellow CSCAP committees. Unintentionally perhaps, CSCAP had thus far stopped short of developing the intellectual and organizational independence it needed to map out a path for regional security co-operation that was distinctive, let alone at odds with prevailing trends.

As for the second question, it was not immediately apparent how soon or how effectively the ARF's discernible loss of momentum would be reversed. That so much attention should have been directed to the issue of terrorism at the July 2002 ARF meeting was in itself an indication that the organization functioned as an essentially reactive forum. The annual meeting was first and foremost an opportunity for member states to respond either to the latest pressures emanating from major centres of power, in this case the United States, or to their short-term domestic priorities. These two considerations largely account for the ARF's seemingly enthusiastic but in practice carefully modulated support for the 'war on terror'. There was little evidence to suggest that the organization had constructed, or would soon construct, a medium- to long-term plan which would in time equip it to identify potential conflicts and take the necessary preventive or remedial action. The question facing CSCAP was whether it had the disposition or the means to develop objectives, strategies and activities that could be usefully pursued even if the ARF should over the next decade fail to move beyond its present marginal role.

UNANSWERED QUESTIONS

The various attempts at multilateralism examined in this chapter point to the multifaceted character of Asia-Pacific regionalism. More importantly, they indicate the profound dilemmas that confront the regionalist project not only in Asia Pacific but in almost every other region. Apart from the continuing tension, intellectual as much as political, between national and regional governance, and the compromises needed to negotiate these tensions across the range of policy issues, regional co-operation has to contend with several large and perplexing questions. Keeping in mind the specific circumstances of the Asia-pacific region, these may be simply but not inaccurately stated as follows: if it is accepted that security and economy are increasingly interconnected, how is that nexus to be adequately reflected in regional institutions? If it is in the nature of globalization that regions are themselves increasingly interconnected, how can regional distinctiveness and cohesion be reconciled with inter-regional coordination? In the case of Asia-Pacific is the United States to be considered an integral member of the region, or merely an external power with extensive interests in the region? Is the overriding task the construction of an Asian (perhaps East Asian) or a Pacific Community? Regardless of the answer to that question, how can regional institutions most effectively handle the hegemonic power and aspirations of the United States, and the possible collision of interests between actual and potential hegemons and between global and regional hegemony? When it comes to issues of military security how are notions of common and co-operative security to be reconciled with the collective defence arrangements that are pre-eminently the legacy of the Cold War? There is one last question, which has implicitly or explicitly surfaced in much of the previous analysis and which will loom large in all future regionalist discourse: is civil society vital to the success of the regionalist project? If so, are there effective ways of integrating the voices of civil society into emerging regional processes and institutions? None of these questions is amenable to a simple or definitive answer. The next two chapters will at least begin to explore them.

NOTES

1. Mahathir Mohamad and Shintaro Ishihara, *The Voice of Asia: Two Leaders Discuss the Coming Century*, New York: Kodansha International, 1995.
2. Joseph A. Camilleri, *States, Markets and Civil Society in Asia Pacific: The Political Economy of the Asia-Pacific Region*, Vol. I, Cheltenham, UK: Edward Elgar, pp. 64–112.
3. See Yong-Kul Won, 'East Asian Economic Integration: A Korean Perspective', *Journal of East Asian Affairs*, 15 (1), Summer/Spring 2001, 79; also IMF, *Direction of Trade Statistics Yearbook*, 1996.
4. See the Fourth ASEAN Economic Ministers and the Ministers of People's Republic of China, Japan and Republic of Korea Consultation, 12 September 2001, Hanoi, Joint Press Statement, at http://www.aseansec.org/menu.asp?=4&content=1 (sighted on 4 December 2001).
5. Premier Li Peng's Speech at the '21st Century Forum', *China Report*, 33 (1), 1997, 118, 122.
6. 'Join Hands in Cooperation and Build a Future Together', *Beijing Review*, 5–11 January 1998, 8.
7. Ibid., p. 9.

8.   See Koichi Hamada, 'From the AMF to the Miyazawa Initiative: Observations on Japan's Currency Diplomacy', *Journal of East Asian Affairs*, 13 (1), Spring/Summer 1999, 42.
9.   Ngai-Ling Sum, 'A Material-Discursive Approach to the "Asian Crisis": The Breaking and Remaking of the Production and Financial Orders', in Peter W. Preston and Julie Gilson (eds), *The European Union and East Asia: Interregional Linkages in a Changing Global System*, Cheltenham, UK: Edward Elgar, 2001, pp. 148–9.
10. Hamada, 'From the AMF to the Miyazawa Initiative', pp. 46–7.
11. See Paul Kelly, 'United States of East Asia', *The Weekend Australian*, 29–30 April 2000, 22.
12. See C. Fred Bergsten, *The New Asian Challenge*, Washington, DC: Institute for International Economics, 2000, Working Paper 00/4, p. 3; also by the same author, 'Towards a Tripartite World', *The Economist*, 15 July 2000, 20.
13. Statement by Malaysian Minister for Foreign Affairs Syed Hamid Albar at the Intan, Kuala Lumpur, 12 August 1999.
14. Lee Kuan Yew, 'A More Self-Assured East Asia in the Making', *Straits Times*, 17 August 2000.
15. *ASEAN Annual Report 2000–2001*, pp. 106–8.
16. See Press Statement by the Chairman of the Seventh ASEAN Summit and the Three ASEAN+1 Summits, 6 November 2001, Bandar Seri Begawan at http://www.aseansec.org/menu_7thsummit.htm (sighted on 5 December 2001).
17. See Joint Ministerial Statement of the ASEAN+3 Finance Ministers' Meeting, 6 May 2000, Chiang Mai, at http://www.aseansec.org/menu.asp?action+4&content+7 (sighted on 4 December 2001).
18. See Joint Ministerial Statement of the ASEAN+3 Finance Ministers' Meeting, 10 May 2002, Shanghai, at http://www.aseansec.orgprint.asp?file=/newdata/afmmshanghai.htm (sighted on 4 June 2002).
19. This argument is well made by Douglas Webber, 'Two Funerals and a Wedding? The Ups and Downs of Regionalism in East Asia and Asia-Pacific after the Asian Crisis', *Pacific Review*, 14 (3), 360–61.
20. See Joint Statement on East Asia Cooperation, 28 November 1999 at http://www.aseansec.org/menu.asp?action=2&content=1 (sighted on 4 December 2001).
21. See Joint Press Statement of the Fourth ASEAN Economic Ministers' and the Ministers of PRC, Japan and South Korea Consultation, Hanoi, 12 September 2001 at http://www.aseansec.org/menu.asp?action=4&content=1 (sighted on 4 December 2001).
22. Cited in Michael Richardson, 'Wary of rivals, East Asia Weighs Closer Integration: Security and Free Trade Pacts under Discussion', *International Herald Tribune*, 26 November 1999.
23. Webber, 'Two Funerals and a Wedding?', p. 363.
24. See Jacques Pelkmans, 'A Bond in Search of More Substance: Reflections on the EU's ASEAN Policy', in Chia Siow Yue and Joseph L.H. Tan (eds), *ASEAN and EU: Forging New Linkages and Strategic Alliances*, Singapore: Institute of Southeast Asian Studies, 1997, pp. 36–45.
25. For a fuller discussion of the different strands in European thinking as reflected in the deliberations of the European Parliament, see Eero Palmujoki, 'EU–ASEAN Relations: Reconciling Two Different Agendas', *Contemporary Southeast Asia*, 19 (3), December 1997, 274–5.
26. Leaders' statements at the Fifth ASEAN Summit in Bangkok in December 1995 all echoed the same position.
27. These figures are cited in Sahng-Gyoun Lee, 'EMU and Asia–Europe Economic Relations: Implications and Perspectives', *Journal of East Asian Affairs*, 13 (1), Spring/Summer 1999, 66.
28. See François Godement, *The New Asian Renaissance*, London and New York: Routledge, 1997, p. 278.
29. See Yeo Lee Hwee, 'ASEM: Looking Back, Looking Forward', *Contemporary Southeast Asia*, 22 (1), April 2000, 116.
30. These figures are drawn from Christopher M. Dent, 'ASEM and the "Cinderella Complex" of EU–East Asia Economic Relations', *Pacific Affairs*, 74 (1), Spring 2001, Table 1 and Figure 1, p. 27.
31. Ibid., p. 29.

32. See Chairman's Statement on the Asia–Europe Meeting, Bangkok, 2 March 1996 at http://www.asem.inter.net.th/ASEM/chairman/index.html (sighted on 25 September 2002).
33. See Hwee, 'ASEM: Looking Back, Looking Forward', p. 128.
34. See Brian Bridges, 'Europe and the Asian Financial Crisis: Coping with Contagion', *Asian Survey*, XXXIX (3), May/June 1999, 461–2.
35. Ibid., p. 466.
36. Ibid., p. 461.
37. See Chairman's Statement, Third Asia–Europe Finance Ministers' Meeting, 13–14 January 2001, Kobe, at http://www.europa.eu.int/comm/external_relations/asem/min_other_meeting/fin_min3.htm (sighted on 4 December 2001).
38. For a full list of these projects and initiatives, see Chairman's Statement of the Third Asia–Europe Meeting, Seoul, 20–21 October 2000, at http://www.europa.eu.int/comm/external_relations/asem/asem_summits/asem3_stat.htm (sighted on 4 December 2001).
39. Asia–Europe Cooperation Framework (AECF) 2000 at http://www/europa.eu.int/comm/external_relations/asem/asem_process/aecf_2000.htm (sighted on 4 December 2001).
40. See Chairman's Statement, Third Economic Ministers' Meeting, Hanoi, 10–11 September 2001, at http://www.europa.eu.int/comm/external_relations/asem/min_other_meeting/eco_min3.htm (sighted on 4 December 2001).
41. See Chairman's Statement, ASEM 4, Copenhagen, 23–24 September 2002; 'ASEM Copenhagen Declaration on Cooperation against International Terrorism'; and 'ASEM Copenhagen Cooperation Programme on Fighting International Terrorism' at http://www.um.dk/asem/erklaeringUK.asp (sighted on 29 October 2002).
42. Dent, 'ASEM and "the Cinderella Complex"', pp. 30–31.
43. Ibid., pp. 32–3.
44. Paul Lim, 'The Unfolding Asia–Europe Meeting (ASEM) Process', in Preston and Gilson (eds), *The European Union and East Asia*, p. 101.
45. East Asia analytical Unit, Department of Foreign Affairs and Trade, *Growth Triangles of Southeast Asia*, Canberra: Department of Foreign Affairs and Trade,1995, p. 1. See also Min Tang and Myo Thant, 'Growth Triangles: Conceptual and Operational Considerations', in Myo Thant, Min Tang and Hiroshi Kakazu (eds), *Growth Triangles in Asia: A New Approach to Regional Economic Cooperation*, Oxford: Oxford University Press for the Asian Development Bank, 1994, pp. 1–13.
46. Amos A. Jordan and Jane Khanna, 'Economic Interdependence and Challenges to the Nation-State: The Emergence of Natural Economic Territories in the Asia–Pacific', *Journal of International Affairs*, 48 (2), Winter 1995, 433.
47. See Chia Siow Yue and Tsao Yuan Lee, 'Subregional Economic Zones: A New Motive Force in Asia-Pacific Development', in C. Fred Bergsten and Marcus Noland (eds), *Pacific Dynamism and the International Economic System*, Washington, DC: Institute for International Economics, 1993, pp. 225–69.
48. See 'Official Prospects for Northeast Asia "Economic Bloc"' (published in *China Daily*, 25 May 1994), *FBIS-CHI-94-101*, 25 May 1994, 2; Shi Min, 'The Basis, Features and Prospects of Northeast Asian Economic Cooperation', in Jang-Hee Yoo and Chang-Jae Lee (eds), *Northeast Asian Economic Cooperation: Progress in Conceptualization and in Practice*, Seoul: Korea Institute for International Economic Policy, 1994, pp.17–18.
49. For an examination of the Beijing–Seoul–Tokyo (BESETO) Co-operative Scheme and its potential contribution to the North East Asian region, see Hieyeon Keum, 'Globalization and Inter-City Cooperation in Northeast Asia', *East Asia: An International Quarterly*, 17 (12), Summer 2000, 97–114; also Yeong-Joo Han, 'The Necessity and Role of a Cooperative System among the Northeast Asian Mega-Cities', in *The Future of Northeast Asian Mega-Cities*, Seoul: Seoul Development Institute, 1994.
50. Kevin G. Cai, 'Is a Free Trade Zone Emerging in Northeast Asia in the Wake of the Asian Financial Crisis?', *Pacific Affairs*, 74 (1), Spring 2001, 8, Table 1.
51. Ibid., Table 2.
52. Ibid., p. 33.
53. 'Official Prospects for Northeast Asia "Economic Bloc"', p. 3.
54. See Vladimir I. Ivanov and Eleanor Oguma, 'Energy Security and Sustainable Development in Northeast Asia: Prospects for Cooperative Policies', Report to International Workshop, Niigata, 26–28 June 2001, pp. 23–4.

55. Ibid., p. 25.
56. For a critique of the 'flying geese' model, see Camilleri, *States, Markets and Civil Society in Asia Pacific*, pp. 100–106.
57. Cai, 'Is a Free Trade Zone Emerging in Northeast Asia?', pp. 20–23.
58. Lee Hong-pyo, 'Yellow Sea Regional Economic Cooperation', *Korea Focus*, 6 (3), 1998, 67–78.
59. For a useful overview of these arrangements, refer to 'The Institutional Framework of the Tumen Programme' at http://tumenprogramme.org/tumen/programme/instframework (sighted on 11 June 2002).
60. See 'Outline of the Results of the 2002 Northeast Asia Economic Conference in Niigata' at http://www.erina.or.jp/FRorum/Forum2002/eresult.htm (sighted on 11 June 2002).
61. See David Capie and Paul Evans, *The Asia-Pacific Security Lexicon*, Singapore: Institute of Southeast Asian Studies, 2002, pp. 10–11.
62. See Robert Scalapino, 'Historical Perceptions and Current Realities Regarding Northeast Asian Regional Cooperation', NPCSD Working Paper No. 20, York University, Toronto, 1992; Susan L. Shirk, 'Asia-Pacific Security: Balance of Power or Concert of Powers?', paper prepared for the Japan Institute of International Affairs–Asia Society Conference on 'Prospects for Multilateral Cooperation in Northeast Asia: An International Dialogue', Tokyo, 18–20 May 1995.
63. See Taek-Whan Han, 'Current Development in Northeast Asian Environmental Cooperation', in Yoo and Lee (eds), *Northeast Asian Economic Cooperation*, p. 263.
64. See Statement by Wang Yinfan at the Second Workshop in July 1991, reproduced in M. Singgih Hadipranowo et al. (eds), *The Second Workshop on Managing Potential Conflicts in the South China Sea*, Jakarta: Research and Development Agency, Indonesia, p. 31.
65. For a useful exposition of Chinese attitudes and objectives, see Lee Lai To, *China and the South China Sea Dialogues*, Westport, CT: Praeger, 1999, pp. 60–74.
66. Ian Townsend-Gault, 'Preventive Diplomacy and Pro-Activity in the South China Sea', *Contemporary Southeast Asia*, 20 (2), August 1998, 184.
67. Ibid, p. 185.
68. Ian Townsend-Gault, 'Managing Potential Conflicts Arising from the Safety of Shipping, Navigation and Communication in the South China Sea', in Stephen Bateman and Stephen Bates (eds), *Shipping and Regional Security*, Canberra Papers on Strategy and Defence No. 29, Canberra: Strategic and Defence Studies Centre, Australian National University, 1998, pp. 27–9.
69. 'Exercise Anambas Launched', *Ascribe Higher Education News Service*, 22, March 2002.
70. Camilleri, *States, Markets and Civil Society in Asia Pacific*, pp. 252–4.
71. See 'Chronology of US–North Korean Nuclear and Missile Diplomacy', *Arms Control Association Fact Sheets*, April 2002 at http://www.armscontrol.org/factsheets/dprkchron.asp (sighted on 18 June 2002).
72. See comments by Marc Vogelaar, director of KEDO's Public and External Promotion and Support Division, in *Arms Control Today*, May 2002, at http://www.armscontrol.org/act/2002_05/pressmay02.asp (sighted on 18 June 2002).
73. *Tokyo Kyodo News Service in English*, 3 June 1999.
74. *KEDO Annual Report,* 2001, p.14.
75. Ibid., pp. 5-6.
76. See Statement by Ambassador Charles Pritchard to the KEDO General Conference, 23 May 2002.
77. Alex Wagner, 'Bush Challenges North Korean Adherence to Nuclear Freeze', *Arms Control Today*, April 2002, at http://www.armscontrol.org/act/2002_04/nkapril02.asp (sighted on 18 June 2002).
78. See 'North Korea Puts Nuclear Weapons on the Table', *The Guardian*, 26 October 2002.
79. See Haksoon Paik, 'Steering between Red Lines: A South Korean View', *Arms Control Today*, May 2003 (sighted at http://www.armscontrol.org/ on 23 May 2003).
80. 'DPRK Foreign Ministry Spokesman on US Attitude toward DPRK–US Talks', *Korean Central News Agency*, 25 April 2003.
81. Glenn Kessler, 'North Korea Says It Has Nuclear Arms', *The Washington Post*, 25 April 2003, A1.

82. See the analysis advanced by Robert Gallucci, former Assistant Secretary of State under both the Bush and Clinton administrations, in 'Progress and Challenges in Denuclearizing North Korea', *Arms Control Today*, May 2002 at http://www.armscontrol.org/act/2002_05/pressmay02.asp (sighted on 18 June 2002).

83. Phillip C. Saunders, 'Confronting Ambiguity: How to Handle North Korea's Nuclear Program', *Arms Control Today*, March 2003 (sighted at http://www.armscontrol.org/ on 23 May 2003).

84. See Statement by Ambassador Sun-sup Chang, ROK Representative and Chair of the KEDO Executive Board, 23 May 2202.

85. Capie and Evans, *The Asia-Pacific Security Lexicon*, pp. 213–14.

86. See Desmond Ball, 'A New Era in Confidence Building: The Second-Track Process in the Asia/Pacific Region', *Security Dialogue*, 25 (2), June 1994, 157–76.

87. Desmond Ball, *The Council for Security Cooperation in the Asia Pacific (CSCAP): Its Record and Its Prospects*, Canberra: Strategic and Defence Studies Centre, ANU, 2000, pp. 10–11.

87. Ibid., p. 15.

89. See Sheldon Simon, 'Evaluating Track II Approaches to Security Diplomacy in the Asia-Pacific: The CSCAP Experience', *Pacific Review*, 15 (2), 2002, 177–9.

90. Sam Bateman and Stephen Bates (eds), *Calming the Waters: Initiatives for Asia Pacific Maritime Cooperation*, Canberra Papers on Strategy and Defence No. 114, Canberra: Strategic and Defence Studies Centre, ANU, 1996; Sam Bateman and Stephen Bates (eds), *The Seas Unite: Initiatives for Asia Pacific Maritime Cooperation*, Canberra Papers on Strategy and Defence No. 118, Canberra: Strategic and Defence Studies Centre, ANU, 1996; Sam Bateman and Stephen Bates (eds), *Regional Maritime Management and Security*, Canberra Papers on Strategy and Defence No. 124, Canberra: Strategic and Defence Studies Centre, ANU, 1998; Sam Bateman and Stephen Bates (eds), *Shipping and Regional Security*, Canberra Papers on Strategy and Defence No. 129, Canberra: Strategic and Defence Studies Centre, ANU, 1998; Sam Bateman (ed), *Maritime Cooperation in the Asia-Pacific Region: Current Situation and Prospects*, Canberra Papers on Strategy and Defence No. 132, Canberra: Strategic and Defence Studies Centre, ANU, 1999.

91. Sam Bateman, 'CSCAP Maritime Cooperation Working Group', *AUS-CSCAP Newsletter*, No. 12, November 2001, 33–4.

92. Ball, *The Council for Security Cooperation in the Asia Pacific*, pp. 50–51.

93. Ibid., p. 53.

9. Clash or dialogue of civilizations? State and civil society

Notions of culture and civil society have intruded more than once in earlier chapters, but their role in contemporary regionalism has yet to be subjected to careful scrutiny. These two closely interlinked yet distinct notions are critical to an understanding of the rapidly evolving and contradictory phenomenon that is Asia-Pacific multilateralism.

Four key questions (or sets of questions) best encapsulate the relationship between culture and society on the one hand and regionalism on the other. The first has to do with the perceptions of key players: how do states and non-state actors perceive the role of cultural and civilizational influences in the task of regional institution-building? To what extent have these influences been used as instruments of policy, and with what outcomes? A second question readily arises from the first: to the extent that values, traditions and symbols – by no means reducible to the pronouncements or policies of governing elites – have influenced regionalism in Asia Pacific, have they generally made for coherence and cohesion, or for confusion and contestation? In determining the impact of these influences it is not enough to focus simply on the region, whose delineation is in any case open to intense debate. We have to pose a third question: how have the various strands of cultural and political discourse played out nationally, inter-regionally and even globally, and how have these in turn affected regional developments? All of which leads to a fourth question: are cultural and civilizational influences in Asia Pacific conducive to the participation of civil society in regional construction? If so, what are the mechanisms through which the voices of civil society can be articulated and integrated into the policy-making process?

To these highly complex and contentious questions there are no simple or single answers. Each of these questions is, however, thrown into sharp relief when set against the backdrop of the 'Asian versus Western values' debate. Having reached a crescendo in the mid-1990s, the debate continued to occupy a prominent place in intellectual and political discourse in much of Asia and therefore merits detailed examination.[1] The case for a distinctive Asian ethic is considered at length in *States, Markets and Civil Society*. Its constituent themes may be briefly summarized as follows: (a) the claim that cultural difference matters and that human rights, though universal in nature, must be interpreted and applied regionally in the light of Asia's specific cultural and religious

267

traditions; (b) the centrality of family values, as a result of which familial and kinship ties are said to play a politically decisive role in East Asia in both Confucian and non-Confucian societies; (c) the stress on respect for authority generally and political authority in particular; (d) the priority accorded to social and economic development, hence the primacy of social and economic over civil and political rights; (e) the need to subordinate the interests of individuals to the interests of the community as a whole, and especially to the need for social cohesion and political stability; (f) reaffirmation of the principle of state sovereignty as a buffer against interference in the internal affairs of states, and indirectly as a way of preserving cultural difference; (g) rejection of Western dominance, that is, the attempt to deny the West the right to impose its cultural, political or economic preferences by presenting them as an expression of universal values.[2] Especially relevant to our analysis here is the underlying assumption common to most, if not all, of these claims that East Asia possesses a culturally and politically distinctive ethos, notwithstanding the many different nationalities, ethnicities and religions which it encompasses. In developing modern political systems East Asian societies had to give due recognition to this ethos which, it is argued, set them apart from the liberal democratic West. By virtue of their excessive stress on individualism, and the lack of social discipline which they inspire, Western values were poorly suited to East Asian traditions and aspirations. It is this claim more than any other which made 'Asian values' a major bone of contention in the domestic and international politics of the region and between Asia and the West.

The 'Asian versus Western values' debate was, it should be said, more of a political than an intellectual exercise.[3] At issue, at least so far as the main protagonists were concerned, was not so much cultural or historical analysis as a contest for power. For a number of Asia's political elites the notion of an 'Asian Way' was attractive in that it offered a powerful rationale for their management of economy and politics. Asian values, they contended, had provided their societies with the necessary foundations on which could be erected the twin pillars of high economic growth and political stability. For Western governments, on the other hand, liberal democratic values coupled with free markets constituted the ideological bedrock which had sustained and justified Western dominance since the end of the Second World War. For the United States, human rights advocacy was an important instrument of diplomacy, which, if anything, gained added momentum with the end of the Cold War.

By the early 1990s 'values' and 'rights' had become codewords for distinguishing between acceptable and unacceptable forms of governance. At stake was the legitimacy of political rule in many parts of East Asia.[4] The uncensored exchange between Presidents Bill Clinton and Jiang Zemin broadcast live to a mass television audience in China on 27 June 1998 was profoundly symbolic of this larger political debate. The exchange was significant not because an American president was lecturing his Chinese host on human rights, or because the latter refused to concede an inch, but because it demonstrated that, while operating in radically different political systems, both leaders were under enormous pressure from different quarters to confront the issue at the highest level and in full public view. Coming soon after Kim Dae-Jung's victory in Korea and Suharto's fall in Indonesia in the wake of widespread student protests, the US–China dialogue was testimony to the fact that human rights had now become central to Asian political discourse both within and between countries.

Yet a good deal of confusion surrounded the human rights controversy. Like the Asian values debate with which it was inextricably linked, it involved both a contest for power and a contest of ideas and principles. If we are to explore the ramifications of human rights discourse and practice for Asia-Pacific regionalism, we must first revisit the longstanding debate surrounding the competing claims of universalism and cultural relativism. Given a plurality of cultural traditions, the doctrine of cultural relativism asserts that moral claims depend for their validity on the cultural context from which they derive.[5] Such claims or values may be imposed on others by *force majeure*, but imposition should not be confused with universal acceptance or validity. In cautioning against the pretentious claims to moral superiority of any culture, the relativist argument preaches the virtue of tolerance and the need for coexistence between diverse cultural or ethical preferences which may not be mutually consistent. The question is: how is cultural relativism – read here the notion of Asian values – to be understood? Is it a doctrine which is itself moral in that it seeks to maximize human dignity and well-being by exposing the moral obnoxiousness of cultural imperialism? Or, is its support for cultural autonomy to be equated with a retreat from moral argument, and indifference to the worst excesses in human conduct? This question, though it may at first sight appear unduly abstract, has, as we shall see, highly concrete and far-reaching ramifications for regionalism in Asia Pacific.

How then might we most profitably place the four key questions outlined above in the context of the 'Asian values' and human rights controversies? Our approach is a relatively simple one. It is to ascertain how different actors intervened in this multidimensional discourse, in pursuit of what ends, and with what consequences for the regionalist project. We begin with a brief examination of the way different East Asian political and economic elites used different cultural narratives to organize and delineate national political space, that is to say, the space within which they exercised – or hoped to exercise – authority. We shall then consider whether the various formulations of 'pan-Asianism' were an expression of East Asia's economic and political renaissance, and, if so, whether or not they formed part of a larger geopolitical design. Could, for example, pan-Asianism or East Asianism be understood as an attempt to construct a regional formation at odds with prevailing Western conceptions of a Pacific Community? These first two parts of the analysis will set the stage for a more extensive treatment of cultural and religious diversity in the Asia-Pacific context. We propose to explore whether such diversity makes for incompatibility and possible collision, or whether it allows for complementarity and dialogue. Here the focus is on the delineation and organization of global as much as regional space. Finally, we shall consider how civil society, as distinct from the state, has intervened in this discourse, and how such intervention has manifested itself both nationally and regionally, and with what consequences for institutional innovation in Asia Pacific.

ORGANIZATION OF NATIONAL SPACE: THE CULTURAL DIMENSION

We have already alluded to the attempt by a number of East Asian governments to use the notion of a distinctively Asian set of values as justification for centralized political control. Given that these arguments are reviewed extensively in *States, Markets and Civil Society*, they need not detain us for long. Our primary focus here is the debate which these arguments have provoked, and its implications for the organization of political space.

The argument for an authoritarian system of government normally rests on the premise that the individual in East Asian societies is viewed not as an isolated being but 'as a member of a nuclear and extended family, clan, neighborhood, community, nation and state', and that as a consequence 'East Asians believe that whatever they do or say, they must keep in mind the interests of others'.[6] In other words, the interests of the individual must somehow be balanced with the interests of family and society. It is this collective ethos which is said to typify Asian consciousness and to stand in sharp contrast to the atomized individual of the liberal West, hence the emphasis on duties and responsibilities as opposed to individual rights. A SLORC publication offers a politicized version of this argument:

> We are not Caucasians, we are Asians, and we wish to preserve our own national identity. So the democracy we want is the kind that is most suitable for us and not an imitation of the West. As a sovereign nation no one should try to force us into a mould that is completely out of character with our people. The same holds true for human and civil rights . . . Freedom for us does not mean licence, and rights bring along in its wake responsibilities and duties.[7]

The views outlined here are not dissimilar to those expressed by any number of other Asian leaders. Among the leading exponents of a distinctively Asian model of development were former Prime Minister Lee Kuan Yew and other members of the 'Singaporean school', including Ambassador Tommy Koh and Kishore Mahbubani (permanent head of the Ministry of Foreign Affairs).[8] The latter referred to American human rights advocacy as 'a suicide pill' which, no matter how sugar-coated, 'no government in the region [would] swallow'. Citing the cases of China and Vietnam, Mahbubani stressed their common determination to resist US efforts to 'pry open the government they [had] in place'. For them the choice was not 'between dark repression and enlightenment', but between the existing regime and either 'the chaos of the past' or 'a future anarchy'.[9]

Not content to defend existing political practice, some Asian leaders went so far as to highlight the West's moral and political degeneration. Mahathir pointed to the stultifying effect of 'materialism, sensual gratification and selfishness . . . the breakdown of established institutions and diminished respect for marriage, family values, elders and important customs, conventions, and traditions'.[10] He contrasted the weak performance of Western economies with 'those not-so-liberal democracies with governments that play a major role in the economy'. In his view, successful development required 'political stability, long-range vision, and consistency'.[11] In taking the offensive, Mahathir and others were in fact engaged in a defensive operation aimed at solidifying an official culture capable of facilitating rapid industrialization. The appeal to tradition served an economic as much as a political agenda. As David Martin Jones has aptly put it, the strategy 'reinvented Confucian culture and modified Islamic practice teaches habits that facilitate collective mobilization toward development targets and provide technocratic planners with an invaluable resource'.[12] His perceptive analysis merits closer attention. The main thrust of his argument is that state education and mass media campaigns aimed at inculcating discipline and respect for authority were made more palatable to the extent that they also promised a better economic future. This was a message likely to strike a chord with the expanding middle classes precisely because they were the 'material beneficiaries of the East Asian economic miracle'[13] and the ones who, by virtue of education, employment and patronage, were most readily susceptible to the dissemination of 'official' norms and values. A number of East Asia's authoritarian regimes, notably South Korea under Park Chung Hee and Chun Doo Hwan and Indonesia under Suharto, did depend for their survival on military power and more generally on the repressive apparatus of the state. But Jones is surely right to emphasize the equally, if not more important, role of the middle classes. For it is they who would increasingly provide the bureaucratic, managerial and entrepreneurial networks and skills on which depended the continued viability of the conformist political culture. For Jones, the archetypal manifestation of this phenomenon was the Singaporean regime which had, under the guiding hand of the People's Action Party, 'syncretically blended an apparent commitment to a liberal market economic policy with a reinvented concern for Asian values of hierarchy and deference'. This, he concludes, was a blend 'peculiarly suited to the anxiously apolitical new middle classes of Pacific Asia'.[14]

The Jones thesis is instructive in two respects. On the one hand, it rightly questions the facile connection that is often assumed to exist between growing material affluence and political liberalization. On the other hand, it leaves relatively unexplored the collectivist ethic of Pacific Asian political cultures and the capacity of the state to manage crises and balance conflicting interests and perceptions.[15] To begin with, East Asia is not a religious or cultural monolith. How, then, can the same set of 'Asian values' speak to such a diverse array of religious and ethical traditions? One way of handling the question might be to argue that this unifying ideological system was potent precisely because it served the needs of capitalism – and indirectly at least the material aspirations of the emerging middle classes – at a critical stage of its development in East Asia. No doubt, there is a great deal to be said for such an interpretation. Yet it captures only one slice of a complex social reality. To begin with, different East Asian societies were at different stages of economic development. But quite apart from the enormous variations in industrial capacity, technological sophistication, income and educational levels, Singapore, South Korea, China, Malaysia and Indonesia diverged markedly in terms of their historical experience and contemporary political outlook.

It is not surprising, then, that the political culture of different societies should have assumed a different political complexion, and that political leadership in each society should have experienced a particular ebb and flow in keeping with its own political traditions and history. To say that East Asian societies have a deep attachment to community tells us little of the way community is understood and experienced, or of attitudes to the state. Indeed, in most East Asian societies, China, Indonesia and South Korea included, we see evidence of a lively and at times intense debate on alternative models of government and attitudes to the West. East Asia may have been home to Lee Kuan Yew, Suharto and Mahathir, but it was also home to Corazón Aquino, Abdurrahman Wahid and Kim Dae-Jung. Burma may have lived through the repression of successive regimes for several decades, but it also gave birth to Aung San Suu Kyi's popular democracy movement.

Kim Dae-Jung's reading of Chinese and Korean history no doubt reflects his own political predilections, but the fact remains that, for him, both societies offer fertile soil for the democratic tradition. He refers in this context to a number of 'democratic' practices:

> In China and Korea powerful boards of censors acted as a check against imperial misrule and abuses by government officials. Freedom of speech was highly valued, based on the understanding that the nation's fate depended on it. Confucian scholars were taught that remonstration against an erring monarch was a paramount duty. Many civil servants and promising political elites gave their lives to protect the right to free speech.[16]

The idea of freedom or *merdeka* became 'the key word of an aroused people' during the Indonesian revolution of 1945–49.[17] For most the idea had a collective meaning, namely freedom from colonial rule and the independence of a nation. Yet, especially for young people, it also meant the exhilaration of political activism, escape from the constraints of family and other forms of authority, and a sense of personal liberation.[18] In Burma's case, the democracy movement is perhaps best understood as the synthesis of different cultural traditions. Writing in 1988, Aung San Suu Kyi depicted dictatorship as standing in contradiction to Buddhism, for it thwarted the potential of each man to 'realize the truth through his own will and endeavour and to help others to realize it'.[19] Conversely, she saw no contradiction between indigenous values and 'concepts which recognize the inherent dignity and equal and inalienable rights of human beings . . . and which recommend a universal spirit of brotherhood'.[20] These expressions of freedom do not signify that Asia's cultural and political traditions were indistinguishable from those of the West. Nor do they suggest that the 'democratic' strand of Asian political discourse was somehow more authentic or representative than its authoritarian counterpart. Rather what they indicate is a complex mosaic of discourses and practices reflecting the needs of different political elites. In appealing to different traditions or to different interpretations of the same tradition, Asian elites were attempting to delineate and organize political space in ways which resonated with different constituencies or addressed different socio-economic and political conditions.[21]

PAN-ASIANISM: ORGANIZATION OF REGIONAL SPACE

The analysis thus far has sought to correct the notion of a monolithic Asian cultural tradition in which a clearly defined set of norms or values commands universal acceptance. This is not to deny, however, the blossoming of Asian consciousness and identity over the last several decades. During the 1980s and 1990s, Asia's political leaders would occupy a far more conspicuous place on the world stage. At different times and in different contexts Japan, China and ASEAN would give voice to a renewed sense of pride and achievement, reflected in frequent allusions to the 'Asian Way' and even to an emerging pan-Asian vision.[22] Haas describes the new Asian diplomacy as a 'process of unlearning Anglo-European practices' coupled with 'a "rediscovery", selective, of course, of more traditional Asian methods for conflict resolution'.[23] The argument here is not that Asian elites had somehow managed to rediscover an authentic Asian past, but that politicians, intellectuals and business leaders were now sufficiently self-confident to challenge the dominant European discourse, and in the process to experiment with various attempts at self-definition. Some formulations were noticeably strident, others relatively moderate. Some entailed an idealized reading of pre-colonial Asia, while others attempted a more subtle blend of the best features of Asia's and Europe's cultural legacies. They all in varying degrees addressed the relationship between the old and the new, between the public and private spheres, and between state and religion.

To establish the cultural foundations for a system of Asian values, it was not enough to return to the past. The rediscovery of national cultures and traditions would not of itself engender a regional identity or a sense of shared heritage, since each tradition and culture retained its own symbolic, aesthetic and ethical character. A distinctive Asian heritage had to be grounded in an ethical or metaphysical tradition whose geographical extension was not confined to one or two societies. That was precisely the attraction of Confucianism.[24] Though it had its roots in China, its influence over the centuries had spread, albeit unevenly, to a number of other countries, including Japan, Korea, Vietnam and other parts of Southeast Asia. Indeed, it is arguable that the spread of Confucianism was itself a measure of the expansion of China's regional influence. Its extensive reach aside, Confucianism owed its prominence in Asian values discourse to one other factor: its ethical world-view seemed particularly well suited to the normative framework which a number of Asia's elites were intent on constructing as part of their nation- and state-building strategies.

The next section will offer a more detailed examination of the Confucian ethic. Suffice it here to say that, however broad its appeal, Confucianism could not adequately encompass or represent East Asia's religious and cultural diversity. It could not, of itself, provide a wide enough platform on which to construct an East Asian, let alone Asian, cultural project. Modern Asian polities endeavouring to forge a regional consciousness had therefore to appeal to something more pervasive and in a sense more tangible than ancient cultural or civilizational legacies. The rejection of Western dominance fulfilled precisely this function. Rejection varied in form and intensity with time, place and political context, but the colonial experience and the resentment it provoked was widespread, if not universal.

In the most recent period, the attack centred on the attempts of Western governments to impose their particular conceptions of governance and human rights. As Tun Daim Zainuddin, a senior adviser to the Malaysian government, put it,

> No one, no country, no people and no civilization has a right to claim that it has a monopoly of wisdom as to what constitutes human rights. What qualifies the Western Liberal democrats to become judge and executioner of . . . nations and citizens of other countries?[25]

Perhaps the most serious charge was that of hypocrisy. Balihari Kausikan reminded his Western readers that it was, after all, the West 'that launched two world wars, supported racism and colonialism and perpetrated the Holocaust and the Great Purge'.[26] In the United States, it was argued, slavery was accepted for several decades after the US Constitution came into force, and legalized segregation had only recently been terminated. Racial and other forms of discrimination remained unresolved problems in a great many Western societies. Double standards were said to be equally evident in foreign policy with human rights often subordinated to economic and political interests. The United States and other Western powers had often engaged in overt and covert forms of military intervention to overthrow democratically elected governments, or alternatively supported dictatorships and other authoritarian regimes with appalling human rights records.

Asia's perception of Western dominance had another important dimension to it. Whereas the West was preoccupied, however selectively, with the rights of individuals, it seemed less sympathetically disposed to the rights of small states, or more generally to the rights of communities and cultures situated at the periphery of the world system. As a leading Malaysian intellectual observed:

> As globalisation intensifies in scope and speed, the global actors and interests that are dictating our future are going to impact more and more upon the lives – and rights – of human beings in this region. It is not inconceivable, given their determination to perpetuate their dominant power, that these largely western global actors would cripple any attempt by Asia Pacific nations to assert their rights at the regional level or international level.[27]

The 1997 financial crisis showed this sentiment to be remarkably prescient. Even the dynamic economies of East Asia, supposedly underpinned by 'strong states', seemed singularly incapable of withstanding the pressures exerted by the world's financial markets. Though Mahathir's emotive response to his country's financial crisis and his diatribes against the IMF and international currency markets were often dismissed in the West as political theatre, in Malaysia and other parts of Southeast Asia they were widely welcomed as an accurate and legitimate response to Western and, more specifically, US hegemony. Mahathir was able to contrast the West's insistence on applying human rights and good governance to the internal affairs of Asian countries with its refusal to apply the same principles to the management of the world economy. As for the conditionality rules imposed by multilateral aid and lending organizations as well as by governments, they were seen as just another instrument used in the name of human rights to enhance the West's economic and diplomatic leverage over poor and newly industrializing economies. The advocacy of an Asian ethic may therefore be interpreted, at least in part, as an attempt by East Asia's elites to stake new ground. While prepared to engage with a rapidly globalizing world, they were less favourably disposed to forms of globalization which made it in practice indistinguishable from Americanization or Westernization.

In the Asian mind the contemporary predicament was inextricably linked with the memory of the colonial past. Mahbubani describes the response of Asia's intellectuals as 'an effort to define their own personal, social and national identities that enhances their sense of self-esteem in a world in which their immediate ancestors had subconsciously accepted the fact that they were lesser beings in the Western universe',[28] Islamic revivalism in Indonesia is perhaps best understood as an attempt to find in the pre-colonial past the religious and intellectual resources needed to resist the pervasive influence of the colonialist legacy. It would be highly misleading, however, to suggest that the anti-colonial project is simply a nostalgic return to the past. On the contrary, the recovery of tradition was part of a conscious strategy 'to discover alternatives to the Western narratives and Western conceptual architecture'.[29] For Anwar Ibrahim, religion was 'the singular most important force resisting the tendency towards uniformity ... the moral armour ... that will ensure that the world remains multicultural, rather than being dominated by a single colossus'.[30] The attempted synthesis of religion and culture on the one hand and politics on the other was oriented as much to the future as to the past.

This was by no means a new undertaking. Earlier versions of the same project had featured prominently in nineteenth and early twentieth century Asian history. Intellectuals in China, Japan, India and Southeast Asia had sought to devise responses to the challenge of modernity by drawing inspiration from the richness of their respective traditions but also from the many points of connection between them. Asian societies and cultures were connected as much by the numerous interactions of the pre-colonial era as by the humiliating and shared history of the colonial period. Though often amorphous and subject to widely varying interpretations, the idea of 'Asia' acquired considerable currency in intellectual, artistic and religious circles. Japanese art historian Okakura Tenshin (1862–1913), the Bengali religious leader Vivekenanda (1863–1902), Chinese philosopher Liang Qichao (1873–1929) and Indian poet Rabindranath Tagore (1861–1941) were among the notable contributors.

Tagore's message to Asia's intellectuals was a particularly poignant one. He pointed to the failings of modernism and to Europe's future self-destruction, and contrasted this with the prospect of a renewed Asian civilization that could approach the West in 'a spirit of true sympathy'. Presenting himself to audiences in China and Japan as the 'representative of Asia', he envisaged 'an associated Asia' which, despite the barriers of language and communication, would constitute 'a powerful combination'. From Siam to Japan he discerned 'kindred stocks', and from Japan to India 'much of religion and art and philosophy which [was] a common possession'.[31] Tagore had in mind an Asian entity with a uniquely spiritual character, seeking 'strength in union, with an unwavering faith in righteousness, and never in the egoistic spirit of separateness and self-assertion'.[32] During the inter-war years Tagore's message had a mixed reception, particularly in China which was in the throes of civil war and in Japan, engulfed as it was by a tide of nationalistic fervour. Yet the pan-Asian vision had not been entirely extinguished. As we saw in Chapter 3, the Bandung spirit was an attempt to bring it back to life, though in this instance it was inevitably coloured and perhaps distorted by the dynamic of the Cold War. With the demise of Cold War rivalries and the increased confidence that came with East Asia's strong economic performance, the idea of an Asian renaissance soon acquired renewed impetus.

In *The Voice of Asia*, Malaysian Prime Minister Mahathir and Japanese politician Shintaro Ishihara celebrated in somewhat provocative language the advent of 'the Asian era'. Ishihara offered the following contrast of the fortunes of 'East' and 'West': 'Everything considered, Asia's problems are the minor aches and pains of a powerful Olympian ready to compete for the gold medal, while the West's troubles are those of the out-of-shape has-been, staggering to the sidelines'.[33] Even as close a friend of the United States as Singapore had the permanent head of its Foreign Affairs Ministry express himself in the following uncompromising language:

> America cannot turn off the economic explosions it helped begin in East Asia. Indeed, like a chain reaction, the dynamism will continue in Asia until most Asian countries approach the standard of living of industrialized countries. And economic growth has ignited cultural confidence in East Asian minds. The Asian renaissance is here to stay, with or without American involvement.[34]

In sum, the notion of an Asian renaissance had a wider support base than was often acknowledged by governments or media in the West. 'Asian values' soon became codewords for the renewed interest in the 'Asia' idea or, as some preferred to label it, the 'Asianization of Asia'. The sentiment found widespread expression not only in Malaysia or China, but in Korea, Japan, Thailand and even the Philippines.[35]

Pan-Asianism suffered nevertheless from a number of weaknesses. To begin with, the vigour of East Asia's economic performance and the psychological self-confidence which it instilled were severely punctured by the 1997 financial crisis. The political and economic difficulties associated with the crisis and Japan's prolonged recession restricted the capacity of East Asian governments, many of which were now reliant on IMF rescue packages, to persist with the ideological campaign they had previously waged in defence of 'Asian values'. Secondly, East Asian industrialization, precisely because of its export orientation, was in part dependent on Western markets. Commercial, technological and financial interaction with Western economies had provided much of the impetus for East Asian regionalization. Thirdly, the concept of a distinctive Asian ethic or civilization had to take account of the long-term homogenizing effects of globalization. Fukuyama may have overstated the argument, but East Asia's economies had already been compelled to undergo a painful process of deregulation and liberalization, and with it might come disruption of longstanding familial traditions and a shift towards more individualistic lifestyles associated with industrial and post-industrial Western societies.[36] The dominance of English as the diplomatic and commercial *lingua franca* in much of Asia was itself an indicator, if not of cultural homogenization, then at least of continuing Western dominance. Finally, by placing constraints on the development of civil society, the East Asian state had curtailed its own capacity to draw upon the immense cultural capital accumulated over the preceding centuries of civilizational development. A stifled or subdued society could not so easily cultivate its artistic, intellectual, ethical and spiritual resources and insights. Nor could it productively connect with other societies to facilitate the discovery and growth of a distinctively Asian ethic.

The handling of these weaknesses varied greatly within and between societies. Whereas the Thai, Indonesian and South Korean governments endeavoured to manage the financial crisis by largely complying with IMF prescriptions, the Malaysian government adopted an uncompromising stance. In diagnosing the crisis, Mahathir placed responsibility for it squarely on the shoulders of currency speculators. He spoke of a Western conspiracy aimed at undoing East Asia's successful industrialization and at reasserting Western economic dominance. When it came to remedies, he proposed a two-pronged strategy: government intervention, including imposition of capital controls, on the one hand and greater regional co-operation on the other. At the level of both diagnosis and practical response, Mahathir chose to elaborate a distinctively Asian response and to emphasize the divergence between Asian and Western interests. Though other Asian political elites were generally less outspoken, they nevertheless contributed to the multitude of ASEAN meetings, working groups, declarations and initiatives, and to the expanding network of consultative arrangements associated with ASEAN+3. The results of such diplomatic activity were often modest, particularly when it came to managing intractable financial, economic, environmental or security problems. Yet, the meetings themselves and the less formal arenas of exchange, whether in business, cinema, television, education or religion, were contributing to an incremental and multifaceted regionalism. Given the various constraints bearing upon China, Japan and ASEAN, not least the periodic tensions between them, regional leadership remained relatively low-key. On the other hand, as previous chapters have indicated, all three were at different times and in different settings able to influence in significant ways the shape of regional discourse.

What, then, do these cultural crosscurrents tell us about the organization and delineation of regional space? Is Huntington's 'clash of civilizations' at all helpful in making sense of Asia's gradually evolving political landscape?[37] There is no intention here to undertake yet another exposition of the Huntington thesis or to rehearse the many critical responses that have ensued.[38] Suffice it to say that the nub of the thesis is best expressed in Huntington's own formulation:

[T]he fundamental source of conflict in this new world will not be primarily ideological or primarily economic. The great divisions among humankind and the dominating source of conflict will be cultural . . . [The] principal conflicts of global politics will occur between nations and groups of different civilizations. The clash of civilizations will dominate global politics.[39]

The deficiencies of this formulation should be obvious enough. Two, however, merit closer attention.

It is difficult, to put it mildly, to distinguish either in theory or in practice between the ideological and the economic on the one hand and the cultural on the other. The competing interests, perceptions and policies that are central to any major international conflict are normally shaped by a complex blend of political, cultural and economic influences. To take one example, any serious reading of the Middle East conflict must give due regard to the triangular relationship between the three Abrahamic faiths – Christianity, Judaism and Islam – but also to the economics of oil and the geopolitics of the region. The second difficulty with the Huntington formulation is that it obscures the nature of the conflicting parties. Ultimately, it is states not cultures that wage international war. It is states that develop, deploy, threaten and actually use military capabilities. A conflict, then, is civilizational only in the sense that the states in question are driven by civilizational loyalties and aspirations, which brings us to the second observation. In practice, the boundaries of states and cultures, let alone civilizations, do not neatly coincide. The translation from culture to state is an intensely political exercise. As often as not, culture and in particular potent symbols and images of the enemy are shaped or manipulated by dominant elites to serve a range of political, economic or military interests.

Placed in this more nuanced conceptual setting, the putative conflict between Asian and Western values is as much a political as a cultural construct. The often acrimonious exchanges between East Asian and Western governments on a range of human rights issues were not civilizational, if by that is meant that their respective policies were driven first and foremost by diverging ethical conceptions. US denunciations of Malaysia's system of justice, for example Vice-President Al Gore's inflammatory language at the 1998 APEC Summit, at which he took issue with the host state's treatment of Anwar Ibrahim, and similarly, Mahathir's denunciation of Western currency speculators were first and foremost attempts by one side or the other to mobilize support for its vision of a new regional order. Washington's strong preference was for the construction of a Pacific Community in which it could as the dominant partner guide the processes of regionalization. At the very least it was striving for a set of interlocking economic and security organizations, including revamped Cold War alliances, which would enable it to obstruct or substantially dilute initiatives deemed inimical to its interests. By contrast, a number of East Asian political elites were more attracted to an exclusively Asian regional framework that would be a substitute for, or function in parallel with, transpacific arrangements. The aim here was to enhance their freedom of action within their own polities, and at the same time increase the leverage which they could exercise within Pacific, inter-regional or even global institutions. Pan-Asian as much as pan-Pacific narratives were designed to serve primarily political and geopolitical ends. To describe these competing designs as 'a clash of civilizations' would be to obscure rather than illuminate. Cultural and civilizational differences were no doubt important, but they did not of themselves constitute some kind of immutable fault-line. Indeed, as we shall be at pains to show, cultural and civilizational influences were amenable to both divisive and co-operative strategies.

CULTURAL AND RELIGIOUS DIVERSITY: IMPLICATIONS FOR HUMAN RIGHTS DIALOGUE

Reference has already been made to the human rights dimension of the 'Asian values' debate. However, if this debate is viewed primarily through the lens of official pronouncements we are likely to shed relatively little light on the civilizational or cultural context of human rights discourse and on the implications for regional dialogue. The analysis proposed here rests on two assumptions: first, that since the late 1980s human rights have moved much closer to the centre stage of regional diplomacy; and secondly, that this trend is unlikely to be reversed in the foreseeable future. Events in China, Burma, Cambodia, Indonesia/East Timor, to name only the most dramatic examples, and the international response to these events amply demonstrated that human rights could no longer be divorced from the wider regional dialogue, whether conceived in a transpacific or purely Asian context.

We begin this analysis by briefly revisiting the Western conception of human rights. Daniel Skubik describes the Western, and more specifically Anglo-American, tradition in terms of the following key attributes: (1) individuality (each human being is considered to be a separate, distinct whole; (2) moral agency (each person, is a free, autonomous agency; (3) moral equality (each individual is deemed inherently equal); (4) rationality (each individual has access to reason); (5) individual integrity (each person has an inherent dignity concomitant with his or her individuality). It is primarily these attributes which explain the Western preoccupation with negative rights understood as freedom from undue interference or repression by political authority.[40] Negative rights, which stress personal autonomy, are often contrasted with positive rights (freedom to) which emphasize the needs of others and support principles of justice. Though the Western conception has its origins in the Judeo-Christian notion that all men are equal in the sight of God, its modern expression is inextricably linked to the growth of capitalism and to the rise of the merchant and manufacturing classes that gradually displaced the power of monarchs and feudal lords. Over time it became an integral part of the culture of modernity with its emphasis on rationality, efficiency, predictability, scientific advance and productivity. The net effect has been to rupture the traditional attachments to local community and to create instead mobile and atomized populations whose claim to humanity rests more and more on the assertion of individual rights *vis-à-vis* an impersonal, distant and bureaucratized governmental apparatus.

Partly as a consequence of its global economic, political and military dominance the West has come to believe in the universality of its culture and to measure progress in the light of its own achievements. Western epistemology, with its bias for analytical thinking, has tended to segment and interpret society in zero-sum or adversarial terms where one of the primary functions of conflict is to identify winners and losers. Galtung has characterized 'Western social cosmology' as a complex process of fragmentation and marginalization which separates one individual from another, material from non-material needs, and the private from the public sphere. Though civil and political freedoms are considered the norm in the public sphere, they can coexist, both normatively and practically, with the widespread incidence of poverty and inequality in the private sphere.[41]

To draw attention to these shortcomings is not to ignore the very substantial contribution of the Western human rights tradition, but rather to indicate that it does not hold a monopoly on human rights discourse. Vincent rightly reminds us that there are 'three worlds of democracy': one modelled on civil and political rights (John Locke); the second on social and economic rights (Karl Marx); and the third on collective rights (Jean Jacques Rousseau). While all three tendencies have found philosophical and political expression in the West, it is fair to say that the Lockean view has been predominant. The same three tendencies are also to be found in Asia, but here the mix has assumed a different and more subtle complexion. The contemporary international human rights regime has, of course, been guided largely by the West, which helps to explain the dominance of the liberal democratic tradition. Many of the international human rights instruments were shaped at a time when the vast majority of Asian and African societies had scarcely asserted their right to self-determination. Even in the aftermath of political independence, most Third World countries, though formally participating in human rights forums and institutions, could exercise only limited leverage over a process that was still driven largely by Western perceptions and priorities. The 'Asian versus Western values' debate of the late 1980s and 1990s may therefore be interpreted as a reaction to this phenomenon. Though their motives varied widely, East Asian elites, encouraged by their economic success, found it useful to challenge the assumption of a universal human rights consensus. Whether they judged the prevailing Western discourse as prejudicial to their political and economic interests, or whether they hoped to use cultural and civilizational arguments to advance alternative conceptions of regional integration, the net effect was to call into question the hegemonic control of human rights discourse.

The ensuing acrimony, for example between the United States and China or between the European Union and ASEAN, seemed at first sight to give added weight to the notion of an impending clash of civilizations. On closer inspection, the notion of an unbridgeable civilizational divide between cultures that privilege rights and those that privilege duties is simply unsustainable. To substantiate this claim we shall briefly survey the social cosmology contained in four of Asia's most influential religious and ethical systems: Hinduism, Buddhism, Confucianism and Islam. The normative structure of any culture is, of course, a complex phenomenon which cannot be reduced to a religious or ethical tradition, however dominant it may be. On the other hand, for most of the societies under consideration the religious and ethical world-view is so closely interconnected with other social and cultural variables as to offer useful insights into the dynamics of social and political discourse. The point of the exercise, it should be stressed, is not to establish some fictitious identity between Asian and Western cultural traditions, but rather to explore the implications of differences, commonalities and complementarities for regional geopolitics, regional identity and regional organization.

Hinduism

The Hindu faith, one of the oldest world religions, still holds a remarkable sway over the cultural and political life of modern India. The Hindu tradition and the caste system which it sustains and legitimizes are, it would seem, fundamentally at odds with notions of freedom and equality. Duties and privileges are assigned on the basis of status or position as specified by caste, age and sex. On the other hand, the Hindu tradition has tolerated and even encouraged periodic challenges to the prevailing hierarchical order. The caste system itself represents an intricate set of reciprocal relationships, with each group in theory at least respecting 'the rights and dignity of the others'.[42] The notion of right, it is true, remains wedded to the concept of duty or *dharma*, one of the four values, the others being wealth (*ārtha*), happiness (*kāma*) and liberation (*mokṣa*). For many in the Hindu tradition, however, *dharma* is not only an end in itself, but the necessary means for the achievement of the other three values. Dharma represents an ideal of society, including 'the righting of injustices, the restoring of balance which men in their ignorance or out of selfish passions had disturbed'.[43]

It is instructive to note that modern Hinduism has sought to breathe new life into the five social freedoms and five individual virtues derived from an older Hindu tradition. The five freedoms refer to freedom from violence, freedom from want, freedom from exploitation, freedom from violation or dishonour, and freedom from early death or disease. The five individual virtues comprise absence of intolerance, compassion or fellow feeling, knowledge, freedom of thought and conscience, and freedom of fear and frustration or despair.[44] These are not, it is true, the standard liberal formulation of individual freedoms, but a delicately balanced framework of norms in which rights exist in relation to obligations.[45] Set in the context of ancient India, it required the king to uphold the law but also to be subject to the law. By virtue of his duties, as enshrined in sacred and customary laws, the king administered a system of justice based 'on equality before the law and equal protection of law'.[46]

Complementing these ancient strands in Hindu thought has been the influence of British law and education, the combined effect of which was reflected in the agenda of various social change movements, notably the Indian independence movement. Especially revealing in this respect is the contribution of Mohandas Karamchand Gandhi. Though a Hindu by birth, Gandhi could not but be influenced by the many other religious traditions with which he came into contact from early childhood. Especially influential was his Jainist friend and guide, Rajchandra Mehta, for whom religion was a 'discipline of spiritual self-perfection (*sādhanā*) through which we are able to know ourselves'.[47] Gandhi concluded that Hinduism was consistent with such a view of religion, but from his understanding of the Hindu metaphysic he derived a social morality based on certain key principles, in particular the unity of man, life and creation, non-injury or non-violence (*ahimsā*) and the indivisibility of humanity and of human salvation.[48] For Gandhi, man was an integral part of the cosmos, which consisted of 'different orders of being ranging from the material to the human, each autonomous and standing in a complex pattern of relationship with the rest within a larger framework'.[49] The cosmic order was a co-operative product which depended on each of these orders, not least the human order, playing its part. So, while remaining faithful to the Hindu notion of *dharma* and drawing on 'an ethic of community, responsibility and loyalty', he was able to establish the principle that each human being is entitled to equal consideration and concern, and 'has an equal right to the necessaries of life'.[50] Obedience of the law was, for Gandhi, 'necessarily willed and reasoned'.[51] He subordinated political obligation to a moral standard, to 'loyalty to God and His Constitution'.[52] The state's authority could be accepted only to the extent that its laws were just and its actions non-repressive. Where laws were unjust and the state's conduct repressive, the citizen could appeal to his conception of truth (*satya*) to challenge the authority of the state so long as the means chosen were consistent with *ahimsa*. From these principles Gandhi derived a long list of rights, including the right to vote, the right to participate in the affairs of government, the right to resist bad government, and the right to liberate one's country from foreign rule.[53]

The Gandhian legacy represents an uneasy blending of the cosmic harmony of *dharma* and the doctrine of individual rights. Elements of that synthesis are evident in the Indian constitution, although some have interpreted its elaborate statement of fundamental rights (for example, liberty of thought, expression, belief, faith and worship; equality of status and of opportunity; right against exploitation) as tilting the balance too far in favour of rights and neglecting ethical notions of self-discipline, co-operation and responsibility.[54]

Buddhism

Buddhism, which emerged as an alternative faith to Hinduism in the fifth century BC, took one strand in Hindu thought, namely the renunciation of self, to its ultimate conclusion. In opposition to the class or caste system, Gautama Buddha established the community of practitioners as a society of equals. The new religion undermined the status of the high-born priestly caste and the metaphysical system on which it was based. Accordingly, Buddha's teaching stressed impermanence rather than permanent being, radical ignorance rather than knowledge, and suffering rather than bliss.[55] The Buddhist vision of reality is of 'innumerable, incalculable universes in infinite expanse, all filled with sentient beings, hellions, hungry ghosts, beasts, humans, titans, and the many gods'.[56] Though Buddhas do not create these universes, they enter into all of them, and in so doing create an environment conducive to the liberation and enlightenment of sentient beings.

For our purposes several salient features of Buddhist teaching are worth highlighting. The process of evolution (*karma*) which produces human beings represents a series of successful adaptations, in which each individual is the product of countless generations of personal achievement. Upon this evolutionary foundation is built the edifice of 'responsible individualism', namely the notion that every individual must take responsibility for his or her actions, since the consequences of those actions will form an integral part of his or her future experience. The knowledge that evolution can be negative as well as positive provides the incentive in the continuing quest for enlightenment, that is the cultivation of intelligence or wisdom to the transcendent degree. The accumulation of positive *karma* is made possible by the 'eightfold noble path' which in ascending order consists of right views, right thought, right speech, right action, right livelihood, right effort, right mindfulness and right contemplation.[57] There are two important points to note here: first, we are all endowed with the potential for enlightenment and liberation; secondly, the radical transformation (or renunciation) of self 'does not mean the loss of personality, individuality, or moral responsibility', but the realization of an egoless but truly human personhood.[58]

There is, then, in Buddhist thought a delicate balance between the achievement of individual enlightenment and the interdependence and interconnectedness of all existence. On the one hand, human beings are viewed not anthropocentrically, but as an integral part of all existence, sentient and non-sentient. That is why they are seen as transient or impermanent, and why any notion of absolute self-identity or enduring self-hood is an illusion. On the other hand, the life of the individual is a unique experience, a unique combination of past and present relationships and experiences. Just as a person is a historical product, being born, living and dying in the world, so the historical world is affected by the creative powers of the individual. As Taitsu Unno puts it, 'here we find the absolute affirmation of the individual, irreplaceable and unique, but at the same time subservient to all things for the good of the many'.[59] It is precisely this understanding which has helped to make the associated notions of non-injury (*avihimsa*) and compassion central to Buddhist teaching on the treatment of sentient beings.[60]

Writing in the third century BC, the Indian emperor Ashoka, a convert to Buddhism, stressed that all sects deserved reverence:

> For he who does reverence to his own sect while disparaging the sects of others wholly from attachment to his own, with intent to enhance the splendour of his own sect, in reality by such conduct inflicts the severest injury on his own sect.[61]

For Ashoka the object of government was non-injury, restraint, impartiality and mild behaviour applied to all creatures. We may not find in Buddhist cultures the Western liberal notion of individual rights,[62] but we do find a highly developed sense of the dignity of human life and of the responsibility that each person has as a free and rational moral agent to construct his or her life. The fulfilment of each individual is the purpose of the whole, provided that fulfilment is understood not as material acquisition but as enlightenment and liberation. In this context, culture and language are especially valued in so far as they contribute to the communication and sharing of understanding over time and space.

The monastic, spiritually centred institutions which assumed responsibility for government in Tibet from the fifteenth to the seventeenth centuries are perhaps the most significant attempt to date to give practical application to Buddhist teaching. A policy of non-violence (no army, few police), unfettered access to learning, wide social mobility and universal commitment to the enlightenment of each individual became the hallmarks of this Buddhist experiment.[63] The main thrust of Buddhist political principles can also be gleaned from frequent advice offered to rulers. These principles have been described in terms of (1) individualistic transcendentalism, (2) non-violent pacifism, (3) religious pluralism with an educational emphasis, (4) compassionate welfare paternalism, and (5) reliance on a powerful central authority to affirm the rights of individuals.[64] It is the failure of the Burmese government to abide by these principles which prompted Aung San Suu Kyi to conclude in her essay *In Quest of Democracy* that a fundamental contradiction existed between Buddhism and the Burmese dictatorship. Conversely, she saw no contradiction between 'indigenous values' and 'concepts which recognize the inherent dignity and equal and inalienable rights of human beings, which accept that all men are endowed with reason and conscience and which recommend a universal spirit of brotherhood'.[65]

One concluding observation is especially pertinent to our analysis. Whereas Western liberalism treats each individual as a disparate, static, almost closed entity, the Buddhist conception considers human experience as a totally open, holistic phenomenon which transcends the division between the mental and the physical and aspires to an emptiness which is not sheer nothingness but openness to everything. As such it offers a healthy antidote to the crude rationalism and psychological reductionism which have so profoundly influenced the modern liberal conception of human rights.

Confucianism

The Confucian ethical code, as expressed in the *Four Books*: *The Analects*, the *Great Learning*, *The Doctrine of the Mean*, and *The Book of Mencius*, has largely shaped the Chinese understanding of social relationships. Its two most important contributions were to affirm the perfectibility and educability of the individual and to extend to the commoner a code which was principally derived from the rules and rituals governing the conduct of nobility in feudal China.[66] As with the Hindu and Buddhist traditions, though without reference to their supernatural or metaphysical cosmology, the Confucian notion of human dignity is embedded not so much in the abstract, purely rational, calculating, autonomous individual favoured by Western liberalism as in the person considered in relationship to other persons. It is the set of complex inter-personal relationships, that is the social context, which confers on personhood its meaning and content, hence the importance of manners, customs and traditions in defining obligations and inextricably linking personal histories.

The Confucian ethic is not, as we shall see, antithetical to notions of justice, but the primary function of law is the maintenance of social harmony. There is considerable scope for individual lives to be aesthetically enriched, but such enrichment stems from a profound sense of shared humanity which connects the individual with others, that is with contemporaries across space, but also across time, with elders and ancestors on the one hand, and children and descendants on the other.[67] Such spatio-temporal continuities reflect and nurture the 'humaneness' or 'humanity' of Confucian ethics and help to explain the subordinate role of law itself.

Human relationships and expectations, whether in the context of family or community, are normally governed not by law but by reciprocity based on civility, respect, affection and tradition. Recourse to the law, in the sense of penal codification and administration of punishment, is only a last resort, a less than optimal method of resolving conflict, since it represents 'official interference in the normal processes of community life and . . . the violence or coercion of externally imposed rule'.[68] The organization of human relations generally and the satisfaction of human needs in particular revolve around *rites* rather than laws. Indeed rites or *li*, understood as 'the formal definition and concrete embodiment of principle',[69] are the closest Confucian approximation to the Western conception of rights. It is *li* or the system of rites which orders five basic status relationships: ruler–subject, father–son, husband–wife, elder brother–younger brother, and friend–friend. By ordering and providing standards of rightness for these relationships, *li* orders society as a whole. The function of ritual is to socialize each member of society into his or her role, to coordinate the different roles in society, in short to preserve and transmit culture.

In ritualized behaviour lies the key to the Confucian vision of social harmony, not simply because it fosters social cohesion, but in the more important sense that social relationships allow individual persons to express their uniqueness and develop their creativity. The ritual-ordered community envisaged by Confucius has been aptly described as 'programmatic – a future goal that is constantly pursued . . . an open-ended aesthetic achievement, contingent upon particular ingredients and inspiration like a work of art'.[70] The emphasis on ritual as an alternative to law is designed to provide more flexible, less adversarial mechanisms for the resolution of conflict. It also opens up the possibility of a social system that is both more diverse and more inclusive.

To complete this brief sketch, it remains to say a word about the function and importance of duties and obligations. Much has been written about the Confucian insistence on the need for harmony in social relationships, notably the kind of harmony which rests on hierarchy, status, deference and uniformity, which is, in other words, preoccupied with duties as opposed to rights.[71] Yet there is in Confucian thought and practice a strong commitment to legitimacy. To put it differently, there are clear expectations as to how authority is to be exercised, for duties apply at least as much to those of high rank as they do to those of lower rank. In the Neo-Confucian context, the principles of reciprocity and humaneness required officials to 'govern the people with humaneness', 'clean up the penal system', 'be fair in administering tax collections', and 'establish charitable granaries'.[72] The Mandate of Heaven made it incumbent on any ruler or regime to respect the universal life-giving principles constitutive of human nature, notably the inherent dignity of man. For Kim Dae-Jung the ultimate goal of government in Confucian political philosophy is to bring peace under heaven (*pingtianxia*). Such key government functions as 'public safety, national security, and water and forest management' are subsumed under the wider concept of 'peace under heaven', which includes 'peaceful living and existence for all things under heaven'.[73]

The Neo-Confucian scholar, Lu Liu-Liang, described the moral imperative of rulership in the following terms: 'The Son of Heaven occupies Heaven's position [*t'ien wei*] in order to bring together the common human family within the Four Seas, not just to serve the self-interest of one family'.[74] Here we have, at least by implication, something akin to the Lockean view of natural rights, which government must respect if it is to have legitimacy, except that in this case the term 'rite' is used to denote fundamental institutions and principles, whereas 'right' is reserved for conduct appropriate to particular times, places and circumstances. Where these rites are violated, where rulers ignore or thwart the ordinances of heaven, the legitimacy of rulership is thereby undermined. The duties of rulers to take care of the interests of their people imply a corresponding right on the part of the people to overthrow tyranny, a notion which finds clear and repeated expression in several Confucian classics, not least in the works of Mencius. Rulers who live up to their duties cannot be assailed, but those who do not forfeit their claim to power and may even be executed for their misdemeanours.[75] Here de Bary rightly reminds us that for

Mencius the ruler–minister relation may be more telling than the ruler–subject relation. For the minister the critical consideration is adherence to what is right – 'undying loyalty attaches to principle not rights'.[76] To refer to this doctrine as the 'right of revolution' is an unwarranted modern reinterpretation, but 'remonstration against an erring monarch' is considered a paramount duty of the responsible official. To this extent at least we may legitimately speak of an incipient doctrine of rights and responsibilities.

So far as the relationship of Confucianism to Chinese political life is concerned, the most notable institutional development was the introduction by the Han Dynasty of the examination system which was to underpin a vast administrative empire and provide a major vehicle for social mobility.[77] By expanding the opportunities for political participation, and dispensing more widely the distribution of rewards, the examination system may be said to have created an incipient welfare system, which helps to explain the longevity of Confucian institutions and the absence of the kind of intellectual and political ferment that was to engulf Europe from the Renaissance and Reformation through to the Enlightenment. A number of writers have also attributed to the Confucian legacy the observable tendency of modern China, as of other East Asian societies, to fashion a highly organized social order intent on delivering job security, social welfare and public safety.[78] The preoccupation with social and economic rights and relative neglect of civil and political rights are said to be part of the same legacy. Reference is also made in this context to several features of the contemporary Chinese constitution, in particular the inseparability of rights and duties and the practice of deriving rights from one's ongoing membership of society. By withdrawing from community participation or failing to perform certain duties, individuals can disqualify themselves from the exercise of certain rights. The same principle, namely the emphasis on wholeness rather than individuality, on the rights of all parties as distinct from one person's rights against another's, is said to characterize more generally the East Asian consensual tradition, hence the dislike of industrial strikes, trade union militancy and adversarial politics.

There is an element of truth in all these claims, but it should not be assumed that the Confucian influence alone accounts for all or any of these aspects of contemporary political life. In China's case, several influences are at work. For example, the legalist school of thought, while still embracing social harmony as a key objective, substantially deviates from the Confucian analysis, emphasizing laws (*fa*) rather than rites (*li*), and the consistent and predictable application of codified rewards and punishments without regard to status. The more recent and profound influence has been that of Marxism, with its stress on community over individuality and on centralized planning as a legal form of state control.[79] Equally important has been the preoccupation with social and economic rights (for example, work, education), often defined in terms of duties, but also with collective rights (for example, right of self-determination, right to development) usually presented as part of a larger international campaign against colonialism, racism, imperialism and hegemonism.[80]

What emerges from this discussion is that the contemporary Chinese state has merely appropriated those cultural influences and ethical prescriptions which most closely approximate its own organizational interests, ideology and political vocabulary. The Chinese communist state does not embody, any more than any other state, the diversity of religious and ethical traditions which make up its cultural inheritance. To give one example, the Jiang Zemin leadership was keen to exploit the nationalist theme in so far as it could strengthen and legitimize the state and indirectly at least the Communist Party, but much less keen to explore the relationship between nation and citizenry. Yet, that connection had been integral to the awakening of national sentiment in early twentieth century China, to which neo-Confucianism made an important intellectual contribution. Writing at the time, Liang Qichao, a leading neo-Confucian scholar, argued for a new 'public morality' that would enable people to fulfil their responsibilities towards others and towards themselves. In his essay on *Renewing the People*, he referred explicitly to the citizenry as 'an assemblage of individual persons' whose strength was constitutive of the strength of the state. Describing the state as 'a tree' and the consciousness of rights as 'its roots', he warned that 'if the roots are destroyed, the tree will wither and die no matter how strong its trunk or vigorous its leaves'.[81] The moral of this story is clear enough. There exists within any civilization, especially one as large and as rich as China's, a wealth of normative tendencies, some of which at least pose a challenge to the prevailing political orthodoxy. So it is with Confucianism. There are important elements of its social cosmology, not least its view of moral human nature, its conception of rites and reciprocity, its emphasis on the need for humane and legitimate governance, which are only marginally reflected in contemporary Chinese political practice, but have considerable relevance for the future development of human rights discourse and the application of conflict resolution norms and procedures both nationally and internationally.

Islam

Though Islam is often associated with the societies of North Africa and the Middle East its demographic centre of gravity lies in South and Southeast Asia, with its adherents accounting for the majority of the population in Pakistan, Bangladesh, Malaysia, Brunei and Indonesia, and for significant minorities in India and the Philippines. Notwithstanding the image of political extremism which Islamic fundamentalism conjures up in the Western mind, and much of the ill-informed stereotyping prevalent in the Western media, the closely related concepts of rights and duties are an integral part of the Islamic faith. Islamic scriptures, beliefs and traditions may not entirely accord with the Western secular philosophy of human rights, but a spate of pronouncements and declarations by religious and political leaders suggest that the connections are both numerous and illuminating.

Of particular interest is the Memorandum prepared in 1970 by the Saudi Ministry of Foreign Affairs in response to a United Nations request. The Saudi government, not noted for its democratic credentials, had been asked to clarify its position on the 1948 Universal Declaration and the International Covenant on Social, Economic and Cultural Rights.[82] The Memorandum cited the following rights as safeguarded in Islamic law: the dignity of the human person, prohibition of racial discrimination, unity and dignity of the family, freedom of conscience, protection of the goods of others, inviolability of the home, concern for the poor, and the right to knowledge and health. Reservations were expressed in relation to three issues raised by UN statements: the right of a Muslim woman to marry a non-Muslim man; the right of Muslims to change their religion; and the right to strike and form unions. The document became the subject of extensive discussions between Saudi and European jurists as well as with officials of the Catholic Church.

Another indication of Islamic attitudes to human rights came with the 1980 Colloquium of Kuwait jointly sponsored by the International Commission of Jurists, the Union of Arab Advocates and the University of Kuwait. In his inaugural address, the Emir of Kuwait reaffirmed the Islamic commitment to human rights: 'To preserve the dignity of man, it is necessary that society guarantees him food, drink, lodging, clothing, education and employment as well as his right to express his opinion, participate in the political life of his country and to be assured of his own security and his kin'.[83] The Colloquium reached the following conclusions: (1) *the Qur'ān* and the *Sunna* present a total way of life which assures both men and women their freedom and their rights; (2) minorities in Islamic countries have the right to practise their faith, to engage in work of their choice, and to avail themselves of public resources; (3) Islam gives learning and science an honoured place in the community, and recognizes freedom of opinion and expression; (4) Islamic law is based on the principle of social equality; (5) in the area of penal law Islamic principles have regard to individual security (for example, prohibition of torture and false arrest) and the well-being of society. The Colloquium conceded that Islamic practice did not always match Islamic law, and insisted on the need for a periodic review of the *Shari'ah* (that is, codification of Islamic law) to deal with the unforeseen circumstances of modern life.[84]

A more conservative statement, prepared by the foreign ministers of the Organisation of the Islamic Conference for consideration by the 1981 summit meeting, affirmed the principle of human equality, without distinction of race, colour, language, religion, sex, political affiliation or social situation.[85] Numerous other Islamic scholars, jurists and religious leaders have since returned to the same theme, arguing for the compatibility of human rights and

Islamic faith, and setting out the basic principles in Islam which define and legitimate these rights.[86] These individual affirmations are to varying degrees mirrored in the constitutions of Islamic states and in their endorsement of the Universal Declaration.

It is nevertheless the *Qur'ān* which remains the most authoritative source of Islamic support for the concept of rights. The right to life and property ('Your blood and your property are sacrosanct until you meet your Lord'), the right to freedom and expression, the right to freedom of religion and conscience ('There is no compulsion in religion'), the right to equality ('No Arab has superiority over a non-Arab as no non-Arab has superiority over an Arab'), equality before the law, and protection of social and economic rights, find sustenance in the *Qur'ān* and the *Sunna* of the Prophet.[87] So does the overarching principle of legitimate governance:

> The nation that lived before you were destroyed by God because they punished the common man for their offences and let their dignitaries go unpunished for their crimes ... It is not considered obedience to God to obey a person who acts against the Good people.[88]

Yet, in seeking to liberate human beings from servitude and grant them equal status, Islam, it is true does not share the liberal passion for individual rights.

For Islam, human rights are not merely or even primarily the rights of individuals, but the rights of the community. In Islamic democracy freedom is affirmed as the necessary foundation for the establishment of a stable community, in which people co-operate for the sake of the common good. Conversely, the function of the stable community and of the resultant political system is to utilize resources so as to satisfy human needs and promote human creativity. The four types of freedom identified by Islam (personal freedom, freedom of expression, freedom of religious beliefs, and freedom of private ownership) form part of an 'egalitarian, community-oriented approach to freedom', which distances itself from individualistic liberalism in order to stress participation in cultural creation.[89]

There is one other important difference. Whereas the modern Western conception of democracy is often associated with the notion of popular sovereignty, in Islamic theory, as indeed in medieval Christendom, rulers are but God's representatives on earth; their rule ultimately rests on divine authority. The Islamic state becomes a vehicle for God's will, which among other things requires it to prevent all forms of exploitation and injustice and to nurture instead qualities of purity, beauty, goodness, virtue, success and prosperity.[90] While it affirms the principle of human dignity and recognizes the concepts of participation, consultation and justice, Islamic law interprets these as much in terms of duties as of rights. The emphasis on obligation, which derives from the twin ideas of obedience to God and attachment to the collective good, translates into a range of specific duties, for example, the duty of a ruler to his people, the duty of the rich to the poor, or the duty of the individual to the community, notably the community of believers.

These duties and obligations draw their inspiration from the principles of the *Shari'ah*, that is the laws derived from the *Qur'ān*, the *Sunna* (the way of life based on Muhammad's example), the *Hadith* (sayings and actions attributed to the Prophet), *Ijma* (the consensus of opinion shared by religious scholars), and the *Itjihad* (the counsel of judges on a particular case). The state enjoys legitimacy to the extent that its laws and policies are in accord with the principles of the *Shari'ah*. There are two aspects of the Islamic conception of legitimacy, namely consultation and accountability, which are worth noting because they are central to governance and, by implication, to the complex relationship between human rights and conflict resolution. On matters other than those regulated by the *Qur'ān* or the *Hadith* consultation (*Shura*) is considered a prerequisite for the functioning of government. The leader is required to consult with the people on all community affairs, and to do so in honesty and good faith. The duty to consult (and the right to be consulted) is closely connected to the notion of accountability, that is, in exchange for accepting leadership the leader must exercise power within the limits laid down by the *Shari'ah*. Once leaders fail to perform their functions or duties (for example, internal and external security, proper management of public property, administration of social justice) on behalf of the community, their authority lapses and so does the community's duty to obey.[91] Here we come remarkably close to the Lockean conception of the social contract.

The place accorded the notion of rights within the Islamic tradition is impressive to say the least, yet, judged from the vantage point of liberal individualism, it seems deficient. The rights of women, the right to strike and to form unions, and freedom of religion for both Muslims and religious minorities are often cited in this respect. We confine our attention to two categories: women and religious minorities. So far as women are concerned, veiling, seclusion and non-contact with marriageable males are just a few of the restrictions which, it is argued, seriously violate the rights of women in Islamic societies. Three reservations are relevant here. First, such restrictions are not confined to the Islamic world; they have been prevalent in a number of Middle Eastern and Mediterranean civilizations from ancient to rather recent times. Secondly, the *Qur'ān* may be credited with the introduction of several reforms (for example, the obligation on husbands to provide a dowry, thereby creating a contract between a woman and her husband; the prohibition of female infanticide; recognition of property rights for women before and after marriage).[92] Thirdly, many societies where Islam predominates have moved decisively to extend the economic, social and political rights and opportunities available to women. The treatment of women under the Taliban in Afghanistan or even in Saudi Arabia differs markedly from prevailing mores and practices in Lebanon, Egypt, Indonesia or Malaysia.

As for the question of religious minorities in Muslim countries, the traditional understanding is that if they submit to Muslim sovereignty they can reach an agreement for a charter of rights and duties with the Islamic state, known as a compact of *dhimmh.* Under this compact, they may be expected to pay a special poll-tax, but are in exchange guaranteed the right to security of life and property, freedom of worship, and a degree of internal autonomy to conduct their personal affairs in accordance with their religious beliefs.[93] Religious tolerance, it should be noted, was a distinguishing feature of the reign of Moghul emperor Akbar (1556–1605). One of his enactments proclaimed: 'No man should be interfered with on account of religion, and anyone [is] to be allowed to go over to a religion he pleased'.[94] Akbar was no democrat, but he was careful to organize his court in ways that respected different religions and combined their respective artistic talents and intellectual insights. It is nevertheless true that where modern nation-states have sought to translate *Shari'ah* principles into constitutional and legislative arrangements, the net effect has often been to place serious limitations on the exercise of religious freedom. As a generalization, guarantees for freedom of conscience appear to have fared better in those countries where Islam, though it may be the majority religion, is not accorded official status.

In concluding this cursory analysis of the relationship of Islam to human rights, it is worth highlighting the severe and rising tensions which exist between tradition and modernity within the Islamic faith. The reassertion of traditional symbols, norms and institutions is in large measure a response to long years of Western political and cultural domination and to widespread disillusionment with Western lifestyles and the Western model of development.[95] It would appear that jumping on to the 'traditional' bandwagon may be a convenient strategy used by clerical and political elites to advance their power and influence in society. In this sense, Islamic resistance to liberal democratic concepts of human rights may be symbolic of larger political or cultural undercurrents.

The fact remains that within most Islamic countries there are reformist tendencies – some religious, others secular – committed to the institutionalization of human rights. These tendencies are well exemplified in the pronouncements and actions of prominent Southeast Asian leaders, including Mahathir and Anwar Ibrahim in Malaysia, and Abdurrahman Wahid in Indonesia. Equally instructive are the attempts of Islamic movements to nurture reform by developing 'a comprehensive and coherent Islamic methodology'. Central to this project is the advocacy of a return to the earliest sources of the Islamic faith, the *Qur'ān* and the *Hadith* – a parallel tendency is observable in the contemporary efforts to renew the Christian tradition – with a view to stressing their egalitarian and reformist ethos. A second but closely related strategy seeks to question the validity of certain literal prescriptions of the *Qur'ān*, which, it is argued, may have made sense in the context of 'the reformist possibilities of its own times',[96] but are clearly out of step with the vastly altered circumstances of modern life. For many in the Islamic world, reform of the *Shari'ah* is an entirely feasible project, which can draw its inspiration and validation from the fundamental sources of Islam itself. Placed in this context, Islam's capacity to participate in the emerging human rights discourse may be much greater than is often assumed in the West.[97]

The preceding analysis has hardly done justice to the complexity of the human rights problématique as it currently confronts the peoples and states of the Asia-Pacific region. To begin with, the four traditions we have surveyed by no means exhaust the cultural or religious diversity either of the region as a whole or of its constituent societies. Secondly, civilizational discourse is not static. The multiplicity of influences, both indigenous and external, which are helping to shape the political culture of these countries, are furiously interacting with each other and are, in the process, contributing to the slow but steady transformation of norms and expectations. Thirdly, implications of the normative and cultural dimensions of social and political organization for the evolution of contemporary regionalism in Asia Pacific require closer examination. In this sense, the evidence presented here has merely set the stage for the analysis that is to follow in the next chapter.

Enough has been said, however, to suggest that, for all their differences, Hinduism, Buddhism, Confucianism and Islam share with Western liberalism and the Judeo-Christian tradition from which springs a sense of the dignity of human life, a commitment to human fulfilment, and a concern for standards of 'rightness' in human conduct.[98] Another normative strand common to all traditions is the notion of humane and legitimate governance, although the criteria used to measure legitimacy may vary considerably from one tradition to another. There is, one may reasonably conclude, sufficient common ground between these religious and ethical world-views to make possible an ongoing regional conversation about human ethics in general, and about rights and responsibilities in particular.[99]

This is not to deny or obscure the many unique characteristics that distinguish each of the civilizational currents and cultural formations. However, it does not necessarily follow from this that differences are inimical to normative discourse either among East Asian societies or between them and Western societies. The emerging regional dialogue may benefit as much from complementarity as from commonality. Indeed, it is arguable that each of the four traditions we have reviewed can richly contribute to the universality and comprehensiveness of the evolving human rights regime. Though each tradition has its own distinctive ethos and symbolism, five dimensions may be said to characterize their collective contribution. First, they provide a richer and more varied conception of political space, by establishing a closer connection between human rights and the range of human needs, notably those of the disadvantaged (hence the emphasis on social and economic rights). Secondly, they offer a more holistic understanding of the human condition by establishing a closer connection between rights and obligations and between the individual and the community (hence the dual emphasis on rights and responsibilities). Thirdly, they help to situate human rights within a larger social context applying them not so much to individuals as disaggregated atoms but as members of larger collectivities (hence the emphasis on the rights of peoples – not only the right to self-determination but the right to a healthy environment, the right to food, and the right to security, and the right to a share of the common heritage of humanity).

The other two dimensions flow from the preceding three but have an importance of their own. The first involves a rejection of Western hegemony, that is, a rejection of the view that the West enjoys a monopoly on the definition of human needs and human rights. Western liberal formulations (and the idea of progress on which they rest) are not seen as applying universally across time and space. Human rights standards may be universal in scope at any one time, but how these standards are understood and applied is likely to change over time. This brings us to the last aspect of the non-Western contribution to human rights discourse, namely the emphasis on consensual decision-making. If participation is one of the criteria of legitimate governance of nation's affairs, then presumably the same criterion applies when the arena shifts from national to international governance, be it regional or global. In other words, an international human rights regime is more likely to command universal respect to the extent that it proceeds by way of negotiation, involves all parties concerned, and incorporates the insights of their respective traditions.

None of this is to suggest that human rights discourse and practice and the wider normative framework governing state conduct are likely to evolve without pain or confusion. States have a tendency to appropriate normative and ethical ideas and symbols to achieve desired outcomes. Official rhetoric is used to find favour with influential constituencies, be they domestic or international. The preceding analysis offers no more than a map for the possible trajectory of civilizational dialogue. Such a possibility may or may not materialize depending on two equally important and interdependent variables: the extent to which the state allows the voices of civil society sufficient political space to express themselves, and conversely the extent to which those discursive practices of civil society that draw on the deepest civilizational insights can influence the behaviour of the state.

CIVIL SOCIETY: REGIONAL IMPLICATIONS

As noted in the earlier volume, civil society is more than 'the amalgam of social movements and non-governmental organizations of progressive or liberal disposition'.[100] It encompasses a wide range of values, interests and forms of association – from nuclear and extended families, to clans and villages and local neighbourhoods, craft guilds, unions and professional associations, groups for leisure and charity, and religious, cultural and sporting organizations. What is distinctive about these agencies is that they can influence and be influenced by the state, but that they occupy a public space which functions side by side with, yet independently of, the state. Contrary to some interpretations and prognostications, there is no reason to suppose that civil society cannot flourish in any part of East Asia.

At first sight it may seem as if Confucian principles do not sit comfortably with notions of civil society. However, as Edward Shils persuasively argues, the Confucian conception of social civility is not altogether dissimilar from the ethic of civil society in that it rests on the responsible but critical participation of the educated class in the affairs of government. The intellectual demonstrates civility by serving the ruler, but also by refusing to serve when the ruler's ways are inconsistent with the Way. This may be understood as a Confucian approximation of the Western idea of a sphere of public opinion. Shils goes on to suggest that even the family constitutes part of Confucian civil society in that it contributes to the maintenance of public order and social harmony. Civil society includes the actions of those who 'bring peace to the old', 'have trust in friends', 'cherish the young', or have 'eagerness to learn'.[101] True enough, authority plays an important part in the Confucian universe, but the balance of responsibilities associated with different social roles makes for a diffused, ultimately reciprocal authority.[102] There is not a single line of authority, but a plurality of authorities, each taking on a profile that is specific to a given social role and the *li* that accompany it.[103] Fruitful connections can also be established between civil society and the concepts of *dharma* in Hinduism, *avihimsa* in Buddhism, and *shura* in Islam.

Philosophical discourse aside, the recent East Asian experience points in the same direction. As we observed in *States, Markets and Civil Society*, civil society across Pacific Asia had gradually 'acquired a richer and more variegated organizational texture, especially in the context of family, religion and work, and partly as a consequence, its political space has intruded with increasing frequency and intensity into the political space traditionally occupied by the state'.[104] Civil society activism mirrors and reinforces the democratization of the state. The role of the middle class in relation to this dual trend is, as we have noted, somewhat ambivalent. Increasing prosperity and social security may be conducive as much to the politics of contentment as to the politics of dissent. On the other hand, the rapidly expanding network of educational, professional, cultural and recreational associations, even when they do not give rise to oppositional politics, tend to widen the public sphere and to multiply the social pressures bearing upon the state. In any case the phenomenon of a rising middle class cannot be considered in isolation from a number of other factors, notably the end of ideological bipolarity, the vulnerability of the state to external shocks, the rise of ethnic and religious separatism, elite dissension, and the corrosive effect of corruption. Though these factors would combine differently in different societies, the cumulative effect has been to diminish the efficacy of authoritarian controls, whether in Taiwan, South Korea, China, Vietnam, Indonesia or Malaysia.

In Taiwan's case, rapid economic growth led to the rise of professional and social organizations, and to the establishment of numerous think-tanks variously connected with political figures, wealthy businessmen and academics. A wide range of issues, including environment, consumer protection, women's affairs, indigenous rights, nuclear safety, housing, education and health, gave rise to an extraordinary proliferation of groups of varying size and permanence, to which increased media freedom and diversification greatly contributed.[105] Significantly, the development of civil society also gathered pace in China's vastly different political circumstances. Not surprisingly, the early 1990s saw a spate of Western and Chinese writings inquiring into the likely evolution of Chinese civil society.[106] The Chinese leadership's steadfast pursuit of the modernization strategy coupled with the traumatic events of June 1989 helped to place the spotlight on the future relationship between civil society and the ruling Communist Party. Each country was, of course, characterized by a distinctive set of sociological and political developments. These are extensively canvassed in the literature, and in the survey offered in *States, Markets and Civil Society*.[107] Suffice it here to restate one general but important conclusion. The voices emanating from civil society became more assertive and self-confident; authoritarianism was increasingly under challenge; the centralization of power and authority was eroding gradually if unevenly, and varying notions of political and cultural pluralism assumed a new prominence in public discourse.

Two related questions immediately arise. Did the democratization of political space and the flowering of civil society have any discernible influence on Asia-Pacific regionalism? How did they connect, if at all, with the currents of East Asia's religious and ethical traditions? So far as the first question is concerned, we should expect greater civil society activism to be reflected sooner or later in policy formulation and implementation, although the connection may not always be direct or uniform. The 'Asian values' argument, though it was articulated by Malaysian and Singaporean political elites during the 1990s, was in part a response to changing economic and political conditions in their respective societies. Paradoxically, this was also the period when human rights acquired a more substantial institutional profile in a number of Southeast Asian states.

Of particular importance was the establishment of national human rights institutions. Following the demise of the Marcos regime, itself the expression of a large popular movement, the Philippines adopted a new constitution in 1987. A comprehensive bill of rights was enshrined in Article III of the Constitution, which the Philippines Commission on Human Rights was required to protect through a mixture of mediation, conciliation and arbitration mechanisms. The Indonesian National Human Rights Commission was established by presidential decree in 1993 and subsequently strengthened by legislation. In Thailand, the consultative process associated with the drafting of the 1997 constitution opened the way for the establishment of the National Human Rights Commission, whose brief was to monitor and promote compliance with the country's international treaty obligations.[108] Owing to bureaucratic and political squabbling it did not begin functioning until July 2001. Malaysia's Human Rights Commission was established in 1999, largely in response to the changing political climate associated with the trial of Deputy Prime Minister Anwar Ibrahim. Similarly, the attempts of the Thai and Philippine governments to inject human rights principles more conspicuously into the regional dialogue in the aftermath of the 1997 financial crisis were themselves a measure of the shifting cultural climate of these countries, as was the ratification of several human rights treaties by ASEAN states during the 1990s.[109]

These and other institutional developments, while significant in their own national context, also influenced and were influenced by the tenor of inter-governmental consultation and co-operation, not least at the regional level. Civil society ferment gave considerable impetus to this process. The focus here, however, is not so much on the direct impact of civil society on national policy-making as on the regionalization of civil society discourse. Indicative of this trend were the efforts of ASEAN-ISIS to raise the regional profile of human rights issues. Given the close association of its member national institutes, ASEAN-ISIS developed a cautious but persistent approach to human rights advocacy. It proposed that ASEAN human rights diplomacy should be guided by the following principles: (1) interdependence; (2) comprehensiveness; (3) situational uniqueness; (4) co-operation, not conflict; (5) uniform criteria for conditionalization; (6) use of sanctions as a last resort; (7) non-discrimination; (8) justice and equitable distribution; and (9) combining the international and domestic dimensions.[110]

Unlike the second track, the Asian track-three phenomenon comprised mainly communities and organizations 'largely marginalized from the centre of power', and intent on challenging mainstream government positions and priorities.[111] Notable examples were Focus on the Global South, Asia-Pacific Research Network, Asia Monitor Resource Centre, Pacific Asia Resource Centre, Committee for Asian Women, Center for Asia-Pacific Women in Politics, the Asian Human Rights Commission, the Alternative ASEAN Network on Burma, the Asian Forum for Human Rights and Development, the Forum on Alternative Security, and the Asia-Pacific Coalition for East Timor.[112] To these must be added a great number of trade union and professional associations (for example, International Labor Organization for Asia and the Pacific, Union Network Asia Pacific, Education International – Asia and the Pacific Regional Office).[113] Track-three organizations varied widely in size, resources, level of technical expertise, and organizational infrastructure, but they generally subscribed to notions of comprehensive and human security, concentrating primarily on issues of peace, disarmament and conflict resolution, gender equality, human rights, environment, political reform and socio-economic development. They pursued a wide range of strategies, encompassing education, advocacy and protest.

In some cases, the emphasis was on influencing policy through direct participation in regional consultations and negotiations. To illustrate, NGO networking and collaboration played an important part in the adoption in October 1994 of the Manila Declaration on the Agenda for Action on Social Development in the ESCAP region. The 'Regional Social Development Agenda', as it came to be known, was adopted in preparation for the 1995 World Summit on Social Development at an Asia-Pacific ministerial conference at which were represented 35 governments and 45 NGOs. The non-governmental sector was formally recognized as performing key functions in alleviating poverty and social marginality, empowering women, safeguarding children, dealing with problems posed by ageing populations, integrating disabled persons into mainstream society, and repairing damage inflicted by modernization policies and market forces in such areas as drug abuse, HIV/AIDS, migration and environmental pollution.[114] Another significant NGO contribution was made in March–April 1993 by the Asian Forum of NGOs which met in parallel with the official UN regional consultation. The NGO declaration issued at the end of the meeting affirmed the universality and indivisibility of both streams of human rights – civil and political on the one hand, and social, economic and cultural on the other.[115] The NGO position, though it met with little positive response from East Asian governments, was reaffirmed, at least in its fundamentals, by the Vienna World Conference on Human Rights.

By the early 1990s a more critical perspective on the role of civil society was rapidly gaining ground. At the initiative of the Korean Citizens' Coalition for Economic Justice, the Asia-Pacific Civil Society Forum was established in 1995.[116] Its aim was to harness societal energies around the call for new regional structures and processes which could challenge existing development models favoured by dominant states and globalizing markets. Notions of accountability, democracy and sovereignty were proposed as central to national economic management. Even more influential was Focus on the Global South, an organization attached to Chulalongkorn University in Bangkok, which, by virtue of its regional expertise, high-profile advocacy, and the growing impact of its conferences and publications, soon acquired a leading role in shaping critical intellectual currents in the region. The trend emerged slowly at first, gaining impetus from APEC's formation in 1989 but did not reach its peak until after the Asian financial crisis in 1997. Indicative of the same trend was the declaration sponsored by the Asia Pacific Sustainable Development Initiative on the occasion of the November 1996 APEC Summit. Echoing the language of the UNDP's 1996 Human Development Report, the Declaration described

APEC's economic liberalization agenda as compromising the sovereignty of member economies, and as sacrificing 'social, cultural, environmental and human rights to purely economic concerns'. It called on APEC to 'undertake a transparent and participatory process to develop measurable indicators to assess – and mitigate – environmental, equity, gender, generational and cultural impacts of all APEC trade liberalization initiatives, including the Individual Action Plans'.[117]

A few months later, a regional conference convened by Focus on the Global South called for a people-centred approach to security that gave priority to 'protection of life, livelihoods, communities, cultures and the environment'. To this end it established an alternative security network with the specific aim of 'democratizing' security policy and discourse in the Asia-Pacific region.[118] The following year a nine-day Asia-Pacific People's Assembly attended by more than 600 delegates urged regional governments to ratify international human rights treaties, and singled out the Malaysian, Indonesian, Chinese, Mexican, Australian and US governments as pursuing policies contrary to their human rights obligations. The South Asia and Southeast Asia Peace Activists' Conference held in Dhaka in February 2000 again stressed the need for a co-operative security system and called on the ASEAN Regional Forum to facilitate effective civil society participation in its deliberations. In October 2000, the ASEM 2000 People's Forum, parallelling the official ASEM III Summit in Seoul, voiced strong opposition to neo-liberal economic globalization and in particular to ASEM proposals for trade and investment liberalization.[119]

East Asian governments were generally not prepared to move in the direction favoured by the discontented voices of civil society. Especially on human rights issues, many governing elites were unsympathetic to proposals that might strengthen the regional human rights regime, or endow civil society organizations with greater legitimacy or greater capacity to monitor the observance of human rights. ASEAN did, it is true, pay increasing lip service to the role of civil society in regional construction, and sought to integrate elements of civil society into its activities. But this was more by way of allocating civil society functions and tasks, especially in the social, cultural and educational arenas, whose scope and content had been predetermined by governments. Even when ASEAN-ISIS proposed in mid-1999 the establishment of an ASEAN People's Assembly, a kind of track-three forum comprising mainly NGOs working on socio-economic development but located within ASEAN,[120] the proposal was delayed for several months to accommodate opposition from the Vietnamese and Lao governments. In many respects the regionalization of civil society mirrored the difficulties experienced by civil society at the national level.

Yet, the general trend remained one of qualitative and quantitative growth. In his analysis of the revitalization of Asia, Anwar Ibrahim placed much stress on the resurgence of civil society, which he portrayed as the continuation of the cultural and intellectual reform movements of the nineteenth century. He envisaged a new Asia buffeted by democratic and reactionary currents, but increasingly integrated by a dual process of institutionalization:

> Governments will endeavour to coordinate activities on a regional scale and the people will also have a life of their own. Ideas, views and voices will compete like products in the market-place. Governments will collaborate for mutual interest, as will workers, artists and nature lovers, just a few of the pan-regional groups that will certainly emerge.[121]

These were prescient words. Written several years before his trial and imprisonment, they anticipated the subsequent flowering of civil society not only in his own country, but in Indonesia, the Philippines, Thailand, South Korea and Taiwan. The growth of civic culture was far from uniform. It encompassed a multiplicity of movements, associations and networks, and the full panoply of objectives, strategies and organizational forms. Some, especially those connected with religious revivalism, tended to have a polarizing effect within and even between societies. Others expressed and reinforced a burgeoning regional consciousness, which, far from jettisoning cultural or religious attachments, sought to connect them with contemporary social and political challenges. The phenomenon was necessarily inchoate, absorbing and expressing a variety of messages and impulses. It was not susceptible to precise territorial or spatial definition. It undoubtedly had a significant transpacific dimension, yet its potency and centre of gravity were strikingly East Asian or pan-Asian. Even the many voices that now spoke the language of human rights did so from an Asian perspective, from an existential appreciation of the post-colonial moment and a recognition that learning from and dialogue with the West need not mean acceptance of cultural or political hegemony.

NOTES

1. Joseph A. Camilleri, *States, Markets and Civil Society in Asia Pacific: The Political Economy of the Asia-Pacific Region*, Vol. I, Cheltenham, UK: Edward Elgar, 2000, pp. 389–91.
2. Fareed Zakaria, 'Culture is Destiny: A Conversation with Lee Kuan Yew', *Foreign Affairs*, 73 (2), March–April 1994, 109–26; Kishore Mahbubani, 'The Pacific Impulse', *Survival*, 37 (1), Spring 1995, 105–20; Balihari Kausikan, 'Asia's Different Standard', *Foreign Policy*, 92 (3), Fall 1993, 24–41.
3. See Alan Dupont, 'Is There an Asian Way?', *Survival*, 38 (2), Summer 1996, 24.
4. This chapter draws heavily on earlier research, and particularly on two papers: Joseph A. Camilleri, 'Human Rights, Cultural Diversity, and Conflict Resolution: The Asia Pacific Context', *Pacifica Review: Peace, Security and Global Change*, 6 (2), 1994, 17–41; and Joseph A. Camilleri, 'Regional Human Rights Dialogue in Asia Pacific: Prospects and Proposals', *Pacifica Review: Peace, Security and Global Change*, 10 (3), 1998, 167–85.
5. See R. John Vincent, *Human Rights and International Relations*, Cambridge: Cambridge University Press, 1986, chapter 3; also Ruth Benedict, *Patterns of Culture*, London: Routledge, 1935; George E. Marcus and Michael Fischer, *Anthropology as Cultural Critique*, Chicago: University of Chicago Press, 1986, pp. 45–64.

6. See Tommy Koh, 'The 10 Values Undergird East Asian Strength and Success', *The International Herald Tribune*, 11–12 December 1993, 6.
7. Kyi Kyi Hla, *Myanmar Perspectives*, 12, 1996, 53–4.
8. For an early version of Mahbubani's argument see 'The Dangers of Decadence: What the West Can Teach the East', *Foreign Affairs*, 72 (4), 1993, 10–14.
9. Kishore Mahbubani, 'An Asia-Pacific Consensus', *Foreign Affairs*, 76 (5), 1997, 155.
10. 'Will East Beat West? Exclusive: A Challenge from Two Asian Statesmen', *World Press Review*, 42 (12), December 1995, 10.
11. Ibid., p. 11.
12. David Martin Jones, 'Democratization, Civil Society, and Illiberal Middle Class Culture in Pacific Asia', *Comparative Politics*, 30 (2), January 1998, 152.
13. Ibid.
14. Ibid., p. 162.
15. Camilleri, *States, Markets and Civil Society in Asia Pacific*, pp. 414–15.
16. Kim Dae Jung, 'Is Culture Destiny? The Myth of Asia's Anti-Democratic Values', *Foreign Affairs*, 73 (6), November/December 1994, 192.
17. Anthony Reid, 'Merdeka: The Concept of Freedom in Indonesia', in David Kelly and Anthony Reid (eds), *Asian Freedoms: The Idea of Freedom in East and Southeast Asia*, Cambridge: Cambridge University Press, 1998, p. 155.
18. Ibid., p. 156.
19. Aung San Suu Kyi, *Freedom from Fear and Other Writings*, Harmondsworth, Middlesex: Penguin, 1991, p. 175.
20. Ibid., p. 176.
21. For a comparative study of the political uses made of cultural symbols by Mahathir and Lee Kuan Yew, see Alfred L. Oehlers, 'Asian Values: Mahathir and Lee Kuan Yew', in Abdul Rahman Embong and Jürgen Rudolph (eds), *Southeast Asia into the Twenty First Century: Crisis and Beyond*, Bangi: Penerbit Universiti Kebangsaan Malaysia, 2000, pp. 207–22.
22. See Yoichi Funabashi, 'The Asianization of Asia', *Foreign Affairs*, 72 (5), Winter 1992, 75–85.
23. Michael Haas, 'Asian Culture and International Relations', in Yongsuk Chay (ed), *Culture and International Relations*, New York: Praeger, 1990, p. 177.
24. See Masakazu Yamazaki, 'Asia, a Civilization in the Making', *Foreign Affairs*, 75 (4), July/August 1996, 106–17.
25. *New Straits Times*, 28 July 1997, p. 14.
26. Kausikan, 'Asia's Different Standard', p. 34.
27. Chandra Muzaffar, 'Taking Another Look at Human Rights', *New Straits Times*, 19 August 1995, p. 11.
28. Kishore Mahbubani, 'Can Asians Think?', *National Interest*, 52, Summer 1998, 35.
29. Anthony Milner, '"Asia" Consciousness and Asian Values', Faculty of Asian Studies, Australian National University, at http://www.anu.edu/asianstudies/cons_vals.html (sighted 26 September 2002).
30. Anwar Ibrahim, 'Globalisation and the Cultural Re-Empowerment of Asia', in Joseph A. Camilleri and Chandra Muzaffar (eds), *Globalisation: The Perspectives and Experiences of the Religious Traditions of Asia Pacific*, Kuala Lumpur: JUST, 1998, p. 3.
31. Tagore's interview with *Manchester Guardian* (20 July 1916), reproduced in *Modern Review*, 20 (3), September 1916, 344–45.
32. Rabindranath Tagore, *Talks in China: Lectures Delivered in April and May 1924*, Calcutta: Visva-Bharati Bookshop, 1925, pp. 21–2.
33. Mahathir Mohamad and Shintaro Ishihara, *The Voice of Asia: Two Leaders Discuss the Coming Century*, New York, NY: Kadansha International, 1995.
34. Mahbubani, 'An Asia Pacific Consensus', pp. 154–5.
35. Evidence for Asia's cultural resurgence is to be found both in the writings of Asian intellectuals and in the analysis of Western scholars. See Yotaro Kobayashi, 'Re-Asianize Japan', *New Perspectives Quarterly*, 9 (1), 1992, 2–23; Noordin Sopiee, 'The Development of an East Asian Consciousness', in G. Sheridan (ed), *Living with Dragons*, St Leonards: Allen & Unwin, 1995, pp. 180–93; Anwar Ibrahim, *The Asian Renaissance*, Singapore:

Times Books International, 1996; Anthony Milner and Deborah Johnson, 'The Idea of Asia', in John Ingleson (ed), *Regionalism and Subregionalism in APEC*, Melbourne: Monash Asian Institute, 1997, pp. 1–19.

36. Francis Fukuyama, 'Asian Values and the Asian Crisis', *Commentary*, 105 (2), February 1998, 23–8.

37. Samuel P. Huntington, *The Clash of Civilizations and the Remaking of the World*, New York: Simon & Schuster, 1997.

38. See, for example, Faroud Ajami, 'The Summoning', *Foreign Affairs*, 72 (4), 1993, 2–9; Pal Ahluwalia and Peter Mayer, 'Clash of Civilizations or Balderdash of Scholars?', *Asian Studies Review*, 18 (1), 1994, 186–93.

39. Samuel P. Huntington, 'The Clash of Civilizations', *Foreign Affairs*, 72 (3), 1993, 22.

40. Daniel W. Skubik, 'Two Perspectives on Human Rights and the Rule of Law: Chinese East and Anglo-American West', *World Review*, 3 (2), June 1992, 31.

41. Johan Galtung, 'International Development in Human Perspective', in John W. Burton (ed), *Conflict: Human Needs Theory*, London: Macmillan, 1990, p. 313.

42. For a useful overview of this analytical approach, see Kenneth W. Thompson (ed), *The Moral Imperatives of Human Rights: A World Survey*, Washington, DC: University Press of America for the Council on Religion and International Affairs, 1980; Adamantia Pollis and Peter Schwab (eds), *Human Rights: Cultural and Ideological Perspectives*, New York: Praeger, 1980.

43. Margaret Chatterjee, *Gandhi's Religious Thought*, London: Macmillan, 1983, p. 19.

44. Unpublished essay by Mark Juergensmeyer, cited in Robert Traer, *Faith in Human Rights: Support in Religious Traditions for a Global Struggle*, Washington, DC: Georgetown University Press, 1991, p. 129.

45. See Peter Bailey, *Human Rights: Australia in an International Context*, Sydney: Butterworths, 1990, p. 43.

46. Yougindra Koushalani, ' Human Rights in Asia and Africa', *Human Rights Law Journal*, 4 (4) 1983, 407–8.

47. Cited in Sibnarayan Ray, *Gandhi India and the World*, Melbourne: Hawthorne Press, 1970, p. 35.

48. See Bikhu Parekh, *Gandhi's Political Philosophy*, Delhi: Ajanta, 1989, p. 104.

49. Ibid., p. 86.

50. Louis Fischer (ed), *The Essential Gandhi: His Life, Work and Ideas*, New York: Vintage Books, 1983, p. 284.

51. Ram Rattan, *Gandhi's Concept of Political Obligation*, Calcutta: Minerva Associates, 1972, p. 73.

52. *The Collected Works of Mahatma Gandhi*, Delhi: Publications Division, Ministry of Information and Broadcasting, Government of India, 1963, IX, p. 507.

53. Rattan, *Gandhi's Concept of Political Obligation*, pp. 91–2, 95.

54. See P.V. Kane, *History of Dharma'sastras*, 2nd edn, Poona: Bhandarkar Oriental Research Institute, 1968, p. 1669; also John B. Carman, 'Duties and Rights in Hindu Society', in Leroy S. Rouner (ed), *Human Rights and the World's Religions*, Notre Dame: University of Notre Dame Press, 1988, pp. 126–7.

55. See Taitsu Unno, 'Personal Rights and Contemporary Buddhism', in Rouner (ed), *Human Rights and the World's Religions*, p.131.

56. Ibid., pp. 133-4.

57. See Arthur Danto, *Mysticism and Morality: Oriental Thought and Moral Philosophy*, Harmondsworth, Middlesex: Penguin Books, 1987, p. 74.

58. Unno, 'Personal Rights and Contemporary Buddhism', p. 140.

59. Ibid., p. 161.

60. See Ian Mabbet, 'Buddhism and Freedom', in Kelly and Reid (eds), *Asian Freedoms*, p. 21.

61. Cited in Amartya Sen, 'Human Rights and Asian Values: What Lee Kuan Yew and Le Peng Don't Understand about Asia', *The New Republic*, 217 (2–3), July 1997, 37.

62. Some have even argued that Buddhism lends itself to a bill of rights, including the right to select the government, the right to fair and equal treatment under the law, and freedom from discrimination on the basis of race, creed, economic class, or gender. See John M.

Peek, 'Buddhism, Human Rights and the Japanese State', *Human Rights Quarterly*, 17 (3), 1995, 527–40.

63. Unno, 'Personal Rights and Contemporary Buddhism', p. 156.
64. For an analysis of these two contrasting views, see Kenneth K. Inada, 'A Buddhist Response to the Nature of Human Rights', in Claude E. Welch and Virginia A. Leary (eds), *Asian Perspectives of Human Rights*, Boulder, CO: Westview Press, 1990, pp. 94–8.
65. Cited in Josef Silverstein, 'The Idea of Freedom in Burma and the Political Thought of Daw Aung San Suu Kyi', in Kelly and Reid (eds), *Asian Freedoms*, p. 199.
66. Hung-Chao Tai, 'Human Rights in Taiwan: Convergence of Two Political Cultures', in James C. Hsiung (ed), *Human Rights in Asia: A Cultural Perspective*, New York: Paragon House, 1985, p. 90.
67. Henry Rosemont, Jr, 'Why Take Rights Seriously? A Confucian Critique', in Rouner (ed), *Human Rights and the World's Religions*, p. 178.
68. W. Theodore de Bary, 'Neo-Confucianism and Human Rights', in Rouner (ed), *Human Rights and the World's Religions*, p. 178.
69. Ibid., p. 196.
70. Robert T. Ames, 'Rites as Rights: The Confucian Alternative', in Rouner (ed), *Human Rights and the World's Religions*, p. 201.
71. Vincent, *Human Rights and International Relations,* p. 41.
72. de Bary, 'Neo-Confucianism and Human Rights', p.191.
73. Kim Dae-Jung, 'Is Culture Destiny', p. 194.
74. Cited in de Bary, 'Neo-Confucianism and Human Rights', p. 195.
75. James Legge (trans.),*The Chinese Classics, Vol. II, The Works of Mencius*, Hong Kong: Hong Kong University Press, 1970, Book 1, part II, chapter 8, p. 167.
76. William Theodore de Bary, *Asian Values and Human Rights*, Cambridge, MA: Harvard University Press, 1998, p. 19.
77. For an analysis of the implications of social mobility, see James C. Hsiung, 'Human Rights in an East Asian Perspective', in Hsiung (ed), *Human Rights in Asia*, pp.7–8.
78. Ibid., pp. 2–22.
79. See Skubik, 'Two Perspectives on Human Rights', pp. 38–9; Richard W. Wilson, 'Rights in the People's Republic of China', in Hsiung (ed), *Human Rights in Asia*, pp. 109–28.
80. 'On the Question of Human Rights in the International Realm', *Beijing Review*, 25 (30), 26 July 1982, pp. 13–17, 22.
81. Cited in de Bary, *Asian Values and Human Rights*, p. 114.
82. In this section I have drawn on L.P. Fitzgerald, *The Justice God Wants: Islam and Human Rights*, Melbourne: Collins Dove, 1993, pp. 19–21.
83. *Human Rights in Islam*, Geneva: International Commission of Jurists, 1982, p. 25.
84. Ibid., pp. 22–5; also Traer, *Faith in Human Rights*, pp. 111–12.
85. Fitzgerald, *The Justice God Wants*, pp. 26–27.
86. Traer, *Faith in Human Rights*, pp. 113–14.
87. See Allabbukhsh K. Brohi, 'Human Rights and Duties in Islam: A Philosophic Approach', in Salim Azzam (ed), *Islam and Contemporary Society*, London: Longman, 1982, pp. 231–52.
88. Cited in Abdul Aziz Said and Jamil Nasser, 'The Use and Abuse of Democracy in Islam', in J.L. Nelson and V.M. Green (eds), *International Human Rights: Contemporary Issues*, Standfordville, NY: Human Rights Publishing Group, 1980, p. 64.
89. Said and Nasser, 'The Use and Abuse of Democracy in Islam', pp. 75–6.
90. See Abdul A'la Mawdudi, *Human Rights in Islam*, London: Islamic Foundation, 1980, pp. 9–11.
91. Said and Nasser, 'The Use and Abuse of Democracy in Islam', pp. 68–71.
92. See Adullahi A. An-Na'im, 'Religious Minorities under Islamic Law and the Dilemma of Cultural Relativism', *Human Rights Quarterly,* 9 (1) February 1987, 10–14.
93. For a fuller list of these reforms, see Kathleen Taperell, 'Islam and Human Rights', *Australian Foreign Affairs Record*, 56 (12), December 1985, 1183.
94. Cited in Sen, 'Human Rights and Asian Values', p. 8.
95. See Elizabeth Mayer, 'The Dilemmas of Islamic Identity', in Rouner (ed), *Human Rights and the World's Religions*, pp. 99–100.
96. See Nikki R. Keddie, 'The Rights of Women in Contemporary Islam', in Rouner (ed), *Human Rights and the World's Religions*, pp. 76–93.

97. An-Na'im, 'Religious Minorities under Islamic Law', pp. 14–18.
98. See Chandra Muzaffar, 'From Human Rights to Human Dignity', in Peter Van Ness (ed), *Debating Human Rights: Critical Essays on the United States and Asia*, London: Routledge, 1999, pp. 25–31.
99. See Edward Friedman, 'Asia as a Fount of Universal Human Rights', in Van Ness (ed), *Debating Human Rights*, pp. 32–55.
100. Camilleri, *States, Markets and Civil Society in Asia Pacific*, p. 357.
101. Edward Shils, 'Reflections on Civil Society and Civility in the Chinese Intellectual Tradition', in Tu Wei-ming (ed), *Confucian Traditions in East Asian Modernity,* Cambridge, MA: Harvard University Press, 1996, pp. 49–51.
102. Russell Arben Fox, 'Confucian and Communitarian Responses to Liberal Democracy', *Review of Politics*, Special Issue on Non-Western Political Thought, 59 (3), Summer 1997, 576.
103. Ibid., p. 577.
104. Camilleri, *States, Markets and Civil Society in Asia Pacific*, p. 403.
105. Thomas B. Gold, 'Civil Society in Taiwan: The Confucian Dimension', in Tu Wei-ming, *Confucian Traditions in East Asian Modernity*, pp. 254–5.
106. See Richard Madsen, 'The Public Sphere, Civil Society, and Moral Community', *Modern China*, 19 (2), April 1993, 183–98; Thomas Gold,'The Resurgence of Civil Society in China', *Journal of Democracy*, 1 (1), Winter 1990, 18–31; Lucian Pye, 'The State and the Individual: An Overview', *China Quarterly*, 127, September 1991, 443–66; Shu Yun-Ma, 'The Chinese Discourse on Civil Society', *China Quarterly*, 137, March 1994, 180–93.
107. Camilleri, *States, Markets and Civil Society*, pp. 354–426.
108. Maznah Mohamad, 'Towards a Human Rights Regime in Southeast Asia: Charting the Course of State Commitment', *Contemporary Southeast Asia*, 24 (2), August 2002, 230–51.
109. See Philip Eldridge, *The Politics of Human Rights in Southeast Asia*, London: Routledge, 2002.
110. The approach adopted by ASEAN-ISIS and details of the yearly ASEAN Colloquium on human rights are outlined at http://www.aseanisis.org/human_rights.htm (sighted on 18 September 2002).
111. Navnita Chadha Behera, Paul Evans and Gowher Rizvi, *Beyond Boundaries: A Report on the State of Non-Official Dialogues on Peace, Security and Cooperation in South Asia*, Toronto: University of Toronto–York University Joint Centre for Asia Pacific Studies, 1997, p. 19.
112. See *Directory of International NGO Community in the Asia Pacific Region by Theme* at http://www.caprn.bc.ca/directory/ngo.htm (sighted on 18 September 2002); also David Capie and Paul Evans, *The Asia-Pacific Security Lexicon*, Singapore: Institute of Southeast Asian Studies, 2002, p. 217.
113. See *International Trade Union Federations and Labour Organizations in Asia Pacific* at http://www.caprn.bc.ca/directory/intl_lu.htm (sighted on 18 September 2002).
114. UN Economic and Social Commission for Asia and the Pacific, *Enhancing the Role of NGOs in the Implementation of the Agenda for Action on Social Development in the ESCAP Region*, New York: United Nations, 1995, pp. 11–44.
115. Bangkok NGO declaration, reproduced in *Law and Society Trust Fortnightly Review*, 1 May 1993, 5–21.
116. See *Proceedings of First Asia-Pacific Civil Society Forum*, 11–14 August 1995.
117. Declaration of the International Conference on Confronting the Challenge of City, Liberalization: Sustainable Development Cooperation and APEC, Quezon, 20–21 November 1996, presented to the APEC Leaders Meeting, Subic Bay, Philippines, 25 November 1996.
118. *The Nation*, 3 April 1997, 7.
119. See *Focus on Security*, 3 (7), 20 November 2000.
120. ASEAN-ISIS, 'ASEAN-ISIS at the Turn of the Century: A Mission Statement', adopted at the ASEAN-ISIS Heads Meeting held in conjunction with the Asia Pacific Roundtable, Kuala Lumpur, 29 May 1999.
121. Anwar Ibrahim, *The Asian Renaissance*, p. 134.

10. Comprehensive security: an emerging architecture for Asia Pacific

The interacting and often contradictory processes of integration and fragmentation associated with globalization have radically altered the economic and political landscape of the Asia-Pacific region. The rapid pace of technological change, most dramatically evidenced in information and communication systems, and the transnationalization of production, trade and finance have produced a striking shift in the international division of labour. East Asia's rapid industrialization is but the most dramatic manifestation of this trend.

The dismantling of old industries and establishment of new ones, with all that this implies for employment, education and training, infrastructure, taxation, social welfare and financial flows, had created severe social, political and environmental pressures. By the end of the 1990s a growing gap was readily discernible – by no means confined to Asia Pacific – between societal expectations and institutional performance.

The complex set of interconnected insecurities greatly exceeded the problem-solving capacities of states and other institutions. The decline of ideological and strategic bipolarity may have eased international tensions and facilitated the resolution, or at any rate the management, of regional conflicts, but it also created new uncertainties, which compounded the unpredictability of international economic, financial and cultural currents. What, if anything, would replace the ideologies, alliances and military capabilities that had sustained the bipolar international order over more than four decades? What policies might be expected to cope with the challenges posed by the integrative and disintegrative tendencies of a rapidly globalizing world? The problem, as much conceptual as organizational, was likely to dominate the first two decades of the twenty-first century.

THE NEW SECURITY AGENDA

The globalization of insecurity assumed different guises and gave rise to different responses in different settings. However, states and societies everywhere confronted much the same task: to identify and then connect the disparate threads that constituted the web of global insecurity. In Asia as elsewhere efforts were made to broaden and reinvigorate the security policy debate. In Europe the idea of fashioning a wider security agenda first emerged in response to Cold War divisions. Co-operative behaviour was gradually institutionalized through CSBMs and eventually more ambitious arms control and disarmament agreements, expanded economic contacts between East and West, and a more robust human rights regime. These three constitutive elements of the Helsinki process played an important part in the demise of the Cold War, and the subsequent development of the Organization for Security and Cooperation in Europe (OSCE).

Europe was not alone in developing a broader conception of security. A parallel though distinctive discourse was discernible in Asia, where scholars and practitioners turned their attention with increasing enthusiasm to the notion of 'comprehensive security'. In the case of Japan the term dates back to 1976, when it first featured in the Liberal Democratic Party's election platform.[1] A more substantial study commissioned by the Ohira government argued that the function of security policy was to protect core values, which required, in addition to defence against military attacks, territorial integrity, economic viability and political stability. The report stressed the importance of internal as well as external threats to security, and the need to utilize, often in combination, military, diplomatic, economic, political and cultural resources to suit different circumstances.[2] Two noteworthy features of this early Japanese elaboration of the concept were the perceived security–economy nexus and the emphasis on minimizing reliance on military force.

Discussion of comprehensive security was not confined to Japan. As noted in Chapter 4, the concept of '*Ketahanan Nasional*' or national resilience underpinned Indonesia's security policy during the Suharto years. The 'Guidelines of State Policy' promulgated in 1973 referred to

> a dynamic condition of will-power, determination, and firmness with the ability to develop national strength to face and overcome all manner of threats internal and external, direct or indirect, that may endanger the Indonesian national identity and the total way of life of the nation and its people.[3]

Malaysia endowed the concept with an important external or regional focus. In 1984, Deputy Prime Minister Musa Hitam described Malaysia's doctrine of comprehensive security in terms of 'three pillars':

> The first is the need to ensure a secure Southeast Asia. The second is to ensure a strong and effective ASEAN community. The third, and most basic, is the necessity to ensure that Malaysia is *sound, secure and strong within* (italics added).[4]

Economic growth, he went on to argue, was a necessary component of comprehensive security, for it made possible a viable programme of social justice, contributed to inter-ethnic harmony, hence social cohesion and national unity, and allowed for the modernization of Malaysia's armed forces. Central to the way ASEAN as a whole – not just Indonesia or Malaysia – understood comprehensive security and the related notion of national resilience was the emphasis placed on threats to internal security and, with it, a preoccupation with the wide-ranging tasks of nation-building.[5] It is, however, the case that by 1984 the accent was as much on 'regional' as on 'national' resilience. For Noordin Sopiee, regional resilience required 'the building of mutual trust, confidence, and goodwill between the ASEAN states', for which purpose it was necessary to prevent external intervention in the region and foster 'the development of institutions, conventions, procedures, and practices for the peaceful resolution of conflict'.[6]

The next significant advance in the Asian context did not come until the establishment of the CSCAP Working Group on Comprehensive and Cooperative Security. In 1996 CSCAP published a memorandum setting out 'an overarching organizing concept for the management of security in the region'.[7] Comprehensive security was defined as 'sustainable security' in all fields (personal, political, economic, social, cultural, military, environmental) in both the domestic and external spheres, essentially through co-operative means.[8] Under economic issues were listed a number of macroeconomic indicators of national strength – competitive capability, food and energy sufficiency – but also economic factors impinging directly on everyday life – poverty, unemployment, and dislocations caused by structural reform. A long list of other threats to security followed, including drug abuse, epidemics, corruption, insurgency, ethnic and religious extremism, threats to life and personal liberties, and a range of environmental challenges. The intention here was to underline the 'multifaceted' and 'multidimensional' character of comprehensive security. Finally, the memorandum drew attention to several underlying principles: the interdependence of various dimensions of security, the perception of security as a co-operative enterprise, acknowledgement of the possible benefits of self-reliance in defence, the value of inclusive processes and institutions, a preference for non-military solutions to conflict, and support for the accepted norms of international conduct.

The CSCAP memorandum was an important landmark in the security discourse of the Asia-Pacific region for it brought together many of the strands of European academic writing in the 1980s and 1990s, in ways which resonated with and built upon the Asia-Pacific experience. On the one hand, a serious attempt was made to apply notions of political, societal and environmental security, which were now seen as complementing and qualifying the more established notions of military and economic security. Though it did not explicitly use the language and philosophy of human security, the CSCAP notion of comprehensive security did focus attention, at least indirectly, on the preservation of human values and the well-being of nations and communities. On the other hand, emphasis was placed on the economic and social foundations of domestic and international security and on the difficulties which ethnic, religious and cultural frictions posed for plural societies.[9] In other words, the CSCAP document sought to allay the anxieties of East Asian governments, most of which were preoccupied with the impact of far-reaching economic and social transformation on the fragile fabric of their political institutions.[10]

The revamped notion of comprehensive security, with its stress on income, food, energy and environmental security, might at first sight be expected to discomfort governments that had traditionally given relatively low priority to such concerns. On the other hand, it offered a methodology that could enhance the prospects of political stability and regime survival. Several other elements in the CSCAP notion of comprehensive security were also likely to strike a responsive chord: the recognition that security policy must reflect the diversity and emerging multipolar power structure of the Asia-Pacific region;[11] the consequent need for a co-operative approach based on consultation and consensus;[12] a shift in strategic outlook focusing on uncertainties rather than threats; and the wish to promote a second-track diplomacy that made more effective use of the knowledge and expertise of the security studies community.[13] Not surprisingly, many of these propositions had already found – or would soon find – their way into the declaratory policies of East Asian governments and regional organizations, which is not to deny the substantial gap that often separated declaratory from operational policy.

Notwithstanding the intellectual and political sophistication of the CSCAP document, the notion of comprehensive security needed further refinement. For comprehensiveness to acquire greater policy relevance, especially in the multilateral context, a number of connections had to be clearly established. Most obviously, high and rising military expenditures threatened a society's economic, ecological and political resources to the point of endangering its core security values.[14] Several other connections, some less palatable than others, readily suggested themselves: between economic and military security (for example, disruptive implications of using water and other scarce resources to gain strategic advantage,[15] higher rates of economic growth resulting in higher and destabilizing levels of military spending); between energy and environmental security (adverse consequences of heavy reliance on fossil fuels);[16] between energy policy and nuclear proliferation (reprocessing of spent nuclear fuel);[17] and between large and unplanned cross-border population movements and regional instability.[18]

The question arises: what precisely is the link between a given issue, be it environment, economy, access to food, migration or human rights, and national, regional or global security? The short answer is insecurity, or to be more precise 'personal insecurity'.[19] Here we have in mind the fears and anxieties that are a byproduct of war, poverty, hunger, disease and discrimination. Closely related to all these forms of insecurity are the tensions and rivalries that set one community against another. Social and economic insecurity sets the stage for political polarization, whether based on race, ethnicity, nationality or religion.

It is worth noting that of the 61 major armed conflicts between 1989 and 1998, 58 were intra-state conflicts. The phenomenon, sometimes inappropriately referred to as 'failed' or 'collapsed' states, points precisely to the increasing incidence and intensity of human insecurity and the inability of fragile local and national institutions to cope with the ensuing pressures. Frequent and expanding forms of multilateral intervention in intra-state conflicts are the unfortunate but sometimes necessary consequence of this trend.

Nor is insecurity in its various dimensions the preserve of the South. Industrial restructuring and financial deregulation have resulted in severe social and economic dislocation in many parts of the North. It is hardly surprising that in times of social and economic anxiety and in the face of rising numbers of migrants, guest workers, refugees and asylum seekers, racism and xenophobia should have become increasingly prevalent in Britain, France, Germany and Australia. If to this should be added the fears of environmental degradation, terrorist attack, and the losing battle against rising levels of drug abuse, the heightened and seemingly pervasive experience of individual and collective anxiety becomes readily understandable.

The emphasis on insecurity is deliberate, for it reminds us that security is primarily not a physical but a psychosocial experience. After all, fear of physical attack is itself a psychosocial phenomenon. Analytically, what is critical to security is the maintenance of a 'legitimated social order', which has enough pattern and regularity, and sufficiently resonates with the deeper needs and aspirations of its members to inspire confidence in the future.

It follows from this brief exposition (about which more later) that grappling with personal and social insecurity is crucial to the notion of comprehensive security. This proposition has an important corollary, which, consciously or otherwise, is often overlooked. If a given event, practice or relationship (for example, illicit trade in drugs, money laundering, people smuggling, refugee flows, illegal labour migration, piracy) arises out of or generates personal insecurities, both its origins and consequences may overspill national boundaries and require simultaneous action at the local, national, bilateral, regional or global level. To illustrate, the mass exodus of 'boat people' in the aftermath of the Vietnam War provoked ill-judged and ultimately counter-productive national responses in several host countries, which eventually gave way to a more rational collective approach, in particular the Comprehensive Action Plan for Indochinese Refugees.[20] To put it simply, comprehensive security calls for a holistic approach to the prevention and resolution of conflict, which takes fully into account human insecurities and the close interconnections between the policies of different states, between citizens and foreigners, and between governmental and non-governmental agencies.

This approach has particular significance for Asia Pacific given that in the post-colonial era a range of indigenous minorities, overseas communities, ethnic separatist movements, migrants, guest workers and refugees have continued to challenge either the legitimacy of existing institutions or the meaning and content of national identity. Despite marked differences between countries, the phenomenon is evident as much in Australia, New Zealand and Canada, as it is in China, Indonesia, Malaysia or the Philippines. Underlying or compounding these insecurities are a number of factors, in particular instability in civil–military relations, leadership succession problems, regional inequalities in wealth and income distribution, and systematic violations of human rights.[21]

While governments generally acknowledged the link between personal, national and regional insecurity, they tended to avoid careful diagnosis of the linkages, or prescription of effective treatment. Much stress was placed on the principle of non-interference in the internal affairs of another country. Such a principle was no doubt integral to any emerging normative framework that sought to preserve national autonomy and to safeguard against unwarranted external intervention. Yet this is only one of the principles that must underpin a multi-layered approach to comprehensive security. The principle must in any case be distinguished from the relatively dated, absolutist and often obfuscatory notion of sovereignty developed largely in sixteenth century Europe to describe and respond to political conditions far removed from those prevailing in Asia Pacific in the early years of the twenty-first century.[22]

If it is true that global and for that matter regional social space can no longer be understood as 'inter-sovereign state, social space', then a state-centric approach to comprehensive security is bound to be seriously defective.[23] The conceptual shift from state security to human security does not express a mere ethical preference. It is a considered response to the phenomenon of globalization, which generates higher levels of insecurity and simultaneously reduces the capacity of the state to offer effective remedies. In so far as the globalizing market produces economic inclusion for some and economic exclusion for others, the resulting disparities in welfare, both within and between societies, are likely to generate tensions that can in turn erupt into violence. The rape and murder of ethnic Chinese in Indonesia in the midst of the financial and political crisis of 1997 was one striking manifestation of this tendency. So was the large and growing number of refugees and internally displaced persons arising from environmental, economic, or military insecurity. In many parts of the world – Asia Pacific was no exception – the security of the state, in particular the security of its military apparatus, found it difficult to deliver security for those under its jurisdiction. Expressed a little differently, the state, operating under conditions of globalization, was often poorly equipped and at times little inclined to satisfy the security needs of its population. Conversely, the very same conditions were beginning to endow individuals and societal organizations with added incentives as well as enhanced resources and expertise to perform a number of security functions.

LINKING MULTILATERALISM AND COMPREHENSIVE SECURITY

Enough has been said to indicate that all states, because they have to operate in an environment of economic, technological and political interdependence, are under increasing pressure to pool their efforts and create co-operative frameworks and mechanisms designed to enhance policy coordination across a wide range of issues. This is not to say that multilateralism is a uniform or monolithic trend. It assumes different forms and serves different purposes in different places at different times. As noted in Chapter 1, multilateralism can operate globally, but also regionally and sub-regionally, along the first, second or third track, or a combination of the three, either formally or informally, in relation to one or several areas of policy.

For all its versatility, multilateralism is no panacea. The problem of security, or to be more precise insecurity, precisely because it is multidimensional, cannot be resolved by a single institutional strategy. It requires recourse to a wide range of processes and mechanisms, including those that operate nationally and subnationally, as well as bilaterally between states. It is nevertheless the case that multilateral approaches, especially at the regional level, can perform a number of useful functions.[24]

First is the normative function, which refers to the capacity of regional institutions and processes, be they governmental or non-governmental, formal or informal, to give meaning and legitimacy to more encompassing notions of security. Regions, it should be noted, are not artificial constructions derived purely from geographical proximity but products of history shaped by diverse forms of cultural, economic and political interaction. At a time of rapid geopolitical and geoeconomic change, marked by the increasing diffusion of power, they provide useful avenues for redefining not only security but also the functions and modalities of co-operative behaviour. They enhance the prospects for peacemaking and peacebuilding by establishing the institutional context within which interests can be effectively articulated and reconciled and comforting identities can emerge and mature. As Michael Barnett puts it, regional institutions are 'a locus for socialization, a place where norms and values are transferred from one actor to another and new identities and beliefs are formed'.[25] They provide the space and the catalyst for forging more co-operative approaches to security.

The second function refers to implementation. Regional multilateralism can help give effect to the concept of comprehensive security, either by providing an overarching umbrella for discussion and negotiation across the entire policy and conflict spectrum, or by dovetailing institutional initiatives, often of the informal variety, with the specific requirements of particular issues, conflicts or sub-regions. In other words, multilateralism can be conflict-specific, function-specific or time-specific. As we have already observed, the comprehensiveness and versatility of the multilateral process has been a distinguishing feature of the ASEAN dialogue.[26] To the extent that the primary focus of comprehensiveness in security is the multifaceted management of the complex relationship between insecurity and conflict, multilateral institutions have to concern themselves with all facets of conflict management, including early warning and prevention, containment and minimization of violence, and termination of conflict, whether through coercion, conciliation, mediation, arbitration, or other forms of negotiation.[27]

This brings us to the third function of regional multilateralism, which is that of strengthening, connecting and harmonizing the numerous efforts in comprehensive security being undertaken at the national, bilateral or global level. It is not enough for multilateral institutions to frame principles and conventions. These have to be effectively internalized by the governmental apparatus of member states. Multilateral dialogue can do much to encourage the separate ministries and bureaucracies of national and provincial governments (for example, foreign affairs, defence, intelligence, police, immigration, health, environment) to coordinate their activities, assessments and recommendations, when these are pertinent to comprehensive security. Multilateralism thus becomes a vehicle for a more integrated approach to national policy-making. At the other end of the spectrum there is much to be said for improved collaboration between regional and global institutions in ways which mutually reinforce their legitimacy, mitigate in each case the constraints imposed by meagre resources and in appropriate circumstances pave the way for concerted action, whether in conflict prevention, peacekeeping or peacebuilding.[28] Asia-Pacific security dialogue has yet to connect in systematic fashion with the UN system or, more generally, with the emerging global security agenda.

One other critical linkage in the emerging regional security architecture has yet to receive the attention it deserves, notably that between the state and civil society. For multilateralism to reach its full potential it must run along all three tracks. It must, in other words, involve not only states, but also markets and civil society. These three tracks cannot, however, function in isolation. They must, even while retaining their autonomy, intersect and overlap to produce the synergies that are needed to maintain a 'legitimated social order', as much regionally as nationally.

THE MULTILATERAL LANDSCAPE

Before considering the future prospects and agenda of Asia-Pacific multilateralism, it is necessary to reflect, however briefly, on the ground covered in previous chapters. The multilateral edifice that gradually emerged in the post-Cold War period was notable for the sheer complexity of the structure, the absence of any apparent grand design, the *ad hoc* method and timing which characterized the process of construction, and the multiplicity of actors which periodically influenced the process. Many organizations established during the Cold War years had survived, although, it is true, most of them, with the exception of ASEAN, the Pacific Islands Forum, ESCAP, and the Asian Development Bank, continued to serve narrowly defined functions and had remarkably little institutional infrastructure at their disposal. However, by the late 1990s the cluster of organizations covering different parts of Asia Pacific presented, at least outwardly, an impressive façade.

It may be useful at this point to return to the typology elaborated in Chapter 1, but with some fine-tuning to take account of contemporary developments. In line with Yamamoto's terminology, it is helpful when considering regional institutions to distinguish between 'macro-regionalism', which refers to geographically coherent, region-wide institutions, and 'mega-regionalism', which denotes looser but larger institutional constructions spanning two or more continents.[29] The most significant macro-regional organization to emerge after the Cold War was ASEAN+3, whereas three mega-regional organizations developed during the same period, namely APEC, the ARF and ASEM. None of these regional formations had a substantial bureaucratic structure. Though each of them spawned many meetings and initiatives, they remained first and foremost consultative arrangements likely to yield broad declaratory agreements and indicative benchmarks rather than binding targets or obligations. In the Asia-Pacific context, the mega-regional/macro-regional distinction was important in one other respect. It pointed to a fundamental and as yet unresolved ambiguity in the very nature of the regional project. While East Asia constituted in some sense the fulcrum of all four organizations, ASEM was an inter-regional organization connecting East Asia and the EU, APEC centred primarily around East Asia and the NAFTA partners, and the ARF was a loose security forum driven by ASEAN but including all the major East Asian players apart from Taiwan, the United States and its English-speaking Pacific allies, Russia and the European Union. APEC and the ARF in particular were Asia-Pacific constructions in which the United States and its allies exercised substantial, though not always decisive influence. Regionalism in Asia Pacific was, it seemed, an amorphous or at least highly variable construct given to diverse geographical and institutional manifestations, each representing distinct configurations of power and interest.

Nor, as we have seen, was institutional innovation limited to these four geographically diffuse but high-profile initiatives. ASEAN, a sub-regional but inclusive, geographically compact but functionally polymorphous organization, remained, despite its ups and downs and the unevenness of its performance, the principal engine of Asian regionalism. ASEAN views and priorities still offered the most convenient litmus test for evaluating the prospects of any new regional proposal. Several other pieces had been injected into the regional jig-saw puzzle: some conflict-specific as with the Cambodian peace process and the KEDO arrangements, others functioning less formally as with the South

China Sea workshops, and others even further removed from high diplomacy, driven largely by market forces but with varying degrees of government input as with a number of growth triangles. Several other projects, both old and new, some operating along the second track (for example, PECC, CSCAP), others exploring third-track possibilities (for example, Asian Forum on Human Rights and Development) attested to the fact that Asia-Pacific regionalism had come of age, at least in the limited sense that it now encompassed states, markets and civil society, functioned at a multiplicity of levels from *ad hoc* sub-regionalism all the way to official mega-regionalism, and ranged across the entire policy spectrum – from military security, to trade, environment, health and education.

The picture that emerges from the preceding discussion is not of a fully-fledged Asia-Pacific multilateral framework able to deliver anything resembling comprehensive security. By the same token there were unmistakable signs of progress made possible by a unique historical conjuncture. Diverse factors of uneven duration and force had cumulatively propelled Asia-Pacific regionalism. A few are worth restating here. The most obvious and most important was the growth of a pan-Pacific trading and investment region, which included East Asia, North America and Oceania, but whose geographical boundaries were susceptible to change in the face of shifting patterns of economic activity and competitive advantage. Asia Pacific was best understood as a 'zone of economic interdependence' rather than a trading bloc or even free trade area, whose dynamism rested in part on access to a large US market, Japanese penetration of Asian supplier networks, and the steady growth of 'Greater China'.[30] Geopolitics too was a factor. Beginning hesitantly in the late 1980s but with increasing vigour during the Clinton years, the United States embraced the concept of multilateral security dialogue as one of the four pillars of the 'new Pacific Community'. A comparable shift in Japanese attitudes also played a part. Tokyo's interest in raising its international profile in ways that would not stir regional anxieties but might make its economic dominance more palatable made it more amenable to notions of regional co-operation. As we observed in previous chapters, the leadership role of ASEAN was especially helpful, as was the unique contribution of a number of small and middle powers, in particular Indonesia, Malaysia, Australia and Canada. The particular diplomatic style favoured by a number of Asian governments, and most closely associated with ASEAN's practice, also proved helpful in defusing the contentiousness of new proposals. The ASEAN emphasis on longer time horizons and policy perspectives, and the preference for informal structures and processes, consensual approaches to decision-making, multidimensional or comprehensive notions of security, and the principle of non-interference in the internal affairs of other countries helped to make multilateralism both more enticing and less threatening than might otherwise have been the case. Less direct but no less significant was the role of influential elements of the business and academic communities and as time went on of the expanding number of civil society networks, all with a crucial stake in regionalization.[31]

These and other factors certainly eased the path of multilateralism, but they did not make it irreversible. Neither economic dynamism nor complex interdependence offered a sufficient guarantee of success. Indeed, their combined effect was a contradictory one, on the one hand providing the glue holding the emerging Pacific Community together, and on the other generating competitive pressures driving societies and economies apart. Side by side with the many positive developments were a number of equally potent economic, geopolitical and cultural forces, which, if not properly addressed, could endanger continued progress towards a multilateral framework of comprehensive security.

Indicative of the magnitude of the task ahead were the negative possibilities inherent in rapid industrialization and large and unpredictable financial flows. The list is now relatively well known and includes rising military expenditures and acquisition of potentially destabilizing offensive weapons systems and platforms,[32] proliferation of nuclear capabilities, environmental degradation, disparities of wealth and income within and between states, and the consequent suspicions and fears harboured by the less prosperous and successful *vis-à-vis* those exercising economic dominance (for example, Japan, overseas Chinese, Singapore).[33] Though many regional or sub-regional conflicts had been contained in the post-Cold War period, few had been definitively settled. Latent bilateral tensions, many of them predating the Cold War (for example, Sino–Japanese rivalry, Japan–Korea tensions, India–Pakistan conflict, competing territorial claims in relation to the Spratlys, the Kuriles or Northern Territories, and the Senkaku or Diaoyutai Islands), periodically threatened to break out into military hostilities. Equally troublesome were unresolved separatist claims (for example, Tibet, Kashmir, Aceh, Papua) and issues of divided sovereignty (China–Taiwan, Korean Peninsula). The East Timor crisis sparked by the referendum of 30 August 1999 cast in stark relief the inadequacy of existing regional security arrangements. None of the regional mechanisms, ASEAN included, could be activated to perform a conflict prevention or peacekeeping function. Belatedly Australia took the diplomatic initiative and assumed leadership of the INTERFET force created under UN auspices to restore order in East Timor. Other than the opportunities for bilateral and multilateral consultations offered by the APEC Leaders' Meeting in Wellington, which fortuitously coincided with the peak of the crisis, no regional initiative was forthcoming in support of the principle of East Timorese self-determination.[34] It was left largely to NGO advocacy, aided by the international media, to mobilize the necessary political will for a concerted international response.

In the immediate aftermath of the Cold War the overarching geopolitical context seemed to offer a window of opportunity for co-operative institution-building, but contradictory forces were at work. With the demise of the Soviet

Union, it was not clear whether bipolarity would give way to unipolarity or multipolarity. Uncertainty and instability were likely to accompany either trend. The 1980s and early 1990s pointed to the relative decline of US dominance and the corresponding rise of China and Japan as major centres of power. As from the mid-1990s the US economy had recovered something of its former levels of growth, capacity for technical innovation, and productivity. By the end of the 1990s, the American state was once again ready to flex its military muscle and pursue its unilateralist impulses – a trend which became especially pronounced during the early years of the Bush presidency. This was a period of transition during which unipolarity and multipolarity coexisted uneasily, with varying degrees of mistrust and misunderstanding punctuating the triangular relationship between the United States, China and Japan. Set against the highly fluid geopolitics of the period, those travelling along the multilateralist path had embarked upon a steep learning curve, made all the more difficult by the relative lack of familiarity with, or confidence in, such processes, and by the cultural, political and economic heterogeneity of the region.[35]

Compounding these hazards was the absence of effective great power leadership. The United States, Japan and China, each for different reasons lacked the will or the capacity to design, let alone construct, the institutional edifice appropriate to the new political and economic conditions of the post-Cold War period. In the case of the United States, the relative decline of its economic leverage coupled with its diminishing moral authority had eroded the leadership position it once occupied. While US policy in the 1990s was more amenable to multilateral concepts and proposals, there was still a strong tendency to subordinate their function to the bilateral and multilateral alliances and coalitions of an earlier period. This predisposition became all the more pronounced with the advent of the Bush administration in January 2001, and the decision of the President to place security policy in the hands of a relatively small group of confidants and advisers, notably Vice-President Dick Cheney, Secretary of Defense Don Rumsfeld, Deputy Secretary of Defense, Paul Wolfowitz, and National Security Advisor, Condoleeza Rice, for whom unilateralism was generally the preferred strategy. The events of September 11 seemed at first to reinforce this strategic priority and privileged once again the forward projection of military power and the reinvigoration of military alliances and coalitions.

Japan, the only Asian candidate for regional leadership, was still struggling to gain political legitimacy.[36] Though it had since the late 1980s adopted a higher profile in regional security discussions[37] and was instrumental in the formation of both APEC and the ARF, it was still far from articulating a coherent institutional blueprint for the future.[38] China, for its part, though it had indicated support for a variety of bilateral and multilateral security dialogue mechanisms,[39] was largely preoccupied with the task of economic reform and national unification. Jiang Zemin, Li Peng, Zhu Rongji and other members of the Chinese inner policy circle were reluctant to commit substantial intellectual and political capital to institutional arrangements, particularly if these were to distract China from its domestic priorities. It is hardly surprising, then, that the burden of leadership should have fallen on small and middle powers and a variety of non-state actors, who, for one reason or another, were less encumbered by the past and more disposed to creative thinking about regional architecture and the conventions and institutions needed to bring it to fruition. On the other hand, these less powerful actors, regardless of the potency of their ideas and imaginations, lacked the economic muscle, diplomatic infrastructure and organizational resources necessary for such an undertaking.[40]

A NEW THRESHOLD

Enough has been said to indicate that the creation of a regional architecture in Asia Pacific consistent with the principles of comprehensive security was unlikely to be the handiwork of an existing or aspiring hegemon. In all probability it would not arise under conditions of 'hegemonic stability', but in slow and tortuous fashion as part of a still unfolding historical process, in which, notwithstanding US unilateralist pretensions, power would remain diffuse and decisions would depend for their legitimacy on consensus rather than diktat. Here we return to the question that has repeatedly surfaced in our analysis: what would be the geographical expression of this architecture? Did the evolutionary process identified in previous chapters point to Pacific Asia or to Asia Pacific? At the time of writing it was neither possible nor necessary to choose between the two trajectories. Both had a reasonably long history and had developed sufficient momentum to translate the idea into concrete institutional form. Both ideas gave expression to powerful sentiments and powerful interests, and both could serve useful functions. Neither was likely, at least in the foreseeable future, to achieve pre-eminence over the other. The issue was not whether to promote a Pacific or an East Asian community, but rather how to make use of both arenas to maximize co-operative interaction within and between them and minimize friction and wasteful duplication of effort.

It follows from this evolutionary perspective that much could be gained from simultaneously pursuing a number of institutional niches. While the path to be followed could not be expected to be painless or unilineal, it did not follow that the entire journey need be at the mercy of *ad hoc* improvisation. A measure of politically prudent yet conceptually inventive planning, at least on the part of certain actors, was both feasible and necessary. This is presumably the function of what is referred to in the literature as 'architecture',[41] but may be more appropriately described as 'design'. The notion, as relevant to politics as it is to music and architecture, refers to the way the overall arrangement of the parts contributes to the finished product. Design and construction can exhibit formality or informality, inclusiveness or exclusiveness, uniformity or diversity. However, for a regional structure to be both durable and comfortable, its design and construction have to be inclusive of diverse needs, levels of economic development, and cultural and political traditions. They need to reflect a pluralist, cosmopolitan, multi-layered architecture, incorporating a great many styles, formal and informal, and a range of organizational arrangements – bilateral and multilateral, sub-regional, regional and inter-regional, governmental and non-governmental – each performing its own function, and none overwhelming the others.

Declaration of Principles

Essential to any regional project, however polymorphous its rationale and structure, is the enunciation of the principles that are to underpin the comprehensive security framework. This is precisely the function served in an earlier period and primarily for Southeast Asia by the ZOPFAN Declaration and the Treaty of Amity and Cooperation. What was now needed was a revised declaration or statement, which spoke to Asia Pacific as a whole and set out a more encompassing, yet more clearly defined set of principles.[42] The point of such a declaration would not be to set in concrete the foundations of a new structure, but rather to spell out the principles that should at this stage of the region's economic, cultural and political evolution inform the processes of institutionalization and strengthen conditions of mutual trust and mutual benefit. Conceivably, such an objective could be met by expanding or amending an existing declaration, as contained, for example, in the Treaty of Amity and Cooperation, or alternatively by drafting an entirely new document.

Whichever route was followed, the declaration would seek to define the norms of state conduct by giving moral, and in certain respects legal, force to three distinct but closely interrelated notions: common security, economic interdependence, and multicultural and multiracial harmony. Within such a framework each state would accept the multi-ethnic and multi-religious character of the Asia-Pacific community and of most of its constituent units.[43] Equally, it would accept that its security is inseparable from that of its neighbours,[44] and that mutual security needs to be advanced by co-operative behaviour across the spectrum of policy areas relevant to comprehensive security.

As part of the common security objective a general endorsement could be given to the principle of non-provocative defence. As argued elsewhere, a non-provocative defence policy would give priority to the peaceful settlement of disputes; exhaust all peaceful avenues, including international mediation, conciliation and arbitration, before entertaining the use of force, and then only in response to a direct threat to the security of the nation; abstain from the forward projection of military power except for purposes of keeping the peace as legitimately mandated by global and regional institutions; resort to the use of force in strict compliance with the provisions of the laws of armed conflict and international law generally; and formally renounce any notion of 'pre-emptive strike'.[45] The ethos of non-provocative defence would reinforce efforts to reduce the volume of arms transfers in and out of the region. It would strengthen attempts to formulate a set of generally acceptable guidelines governing the supply of arms, particularly to governments whose conduct is deemed inimical to the peace and stability of the region.

This overarching statement of norms would be given form and content by a subsidiary set of principles. Signatories to the declaration would first commit themselves to the twin tasks of confidence-building and transparency, understood as the willingness to implement 'both formal and informal measures, whether unilateral, bilateral, or multilateral that address, prevent, and resolve uncertainties among states'.[46] This more comprehensive approach to confidence-building would encourage states to develop declaratory and operational practices designed to clarify their military intentions and capabilities, reduce uncertainties about potentially threatening military activities and alliances, and constrain opportunities for surprise attack or the coercive use of military force. Its rationale being the fundamental transformation of threat perception, the confidence-building process would embrace the gamut of conventional and unconventional security concerns, including environment and refugee flows, which had special relevance for Asia Pacific.

The declaration would also commit the signatories to predictable and legitimate behaviour in the context of *regional resilience*, particularly with respect to bilateral or regional conflicts (for example, Northern Territories, South China Sea). This approach could be extended even to a highly sensitive conflict designated by one or other party as an internal matter (for example, China–Taiwan, Indonesia–Papua). In this context, it would be helpful to refer in such a declaration to the benefits of consultative and other collaborative arrangements linking regional and global organizations, for example the ARF and the UN Security Council.[47]

Unpalatable as the prospect might seem to some governments, the declaration could not fulfil its purpose unless it made respect for fundamental social, economic, cultural, civil and political rights a keystone of state conduct. The declaration would foreshadow regional co-operative action aimed at minimizing and, where possible, eliminating gross violations of these rights.[48] This principle is crucial not only to the linkage between domestic and external security, but also to any wider commitment to political and economic forms of democratic governance. There is no implication here that democratic forms would have to emulate Western models of governance. The analysis developed in the previous chapter makes it clear that, despite the authoritarian tendencies evident in the recent history of several Asian states, there is much in the religious and ethical traditions of Asia Pacific that is sympathetic to notions of legitimacy, accountability and participation. Over the previous decades, the region had witnessed a series of vigorous social and political campaigns around issues of popular democracy, human rights and self-determination. The opportunities for achieving common ground and developing standards by which to evaluate processes and institutions were considerably greater than was often supposed.[49] We shall presently return to the human rights implications of comprehensive security, for they provide an invaluable, perhaps indispensable, bridge between economy and security on the one hand and between the state and civil society on the other.

The foregoing list of principles is not an exhaustive one, but it does indicate the main contours of the normative framework that could underpin multilateral approaches to comprehensive security in Asia Pacific. The actual content of any declaration would inevitably be the subject of much debate and disagreement, not least around such notions as sovereignty and non-interference in the internal affairs of other countries. By seeking to reconcile diverging interests, perceptions and world-views the negotiating process was likely to prove as important as the outcome itself. It needed to engage the widest possible public in each country and draw on the region's diverse religious and cultural traditions. Any eventual agreement could not therefore be viewed as the last word on the subject. It would be another stage or threshold in an ongoing conversation. On the other hand, once reached, a consensus on principles would provide governments with a useful guide for the development of national human rights institutions, and the region as a whole with a convenient benchmark by which to assess institutional performance. Reflective of the needs and experiences of the different states and peoples comprising the region, the declaration could be a self-contained document. Alternatively, all or part of the declaration could be inserted into an existing agreement, or featured in more specific documents (for example, Preamble to the Southeast Asian Nuclear Weapons Free Zone), or even informal statements (for example, proposed code of conduct in the South China Sea). It is worth noting in passing that the enunciation of principles, even when it is not enshrined in a legally binding document, can serve as an effective confidence-building mechanism in its own right. In using declaratory policy to serve this purpose, ASEAN had already set a precedent which future multilateral diplomacy could develop and refine.

Institutional Reform

What, then, were the institutional arrangements, formal or informal, which, building on existing foundations, were most likely to advance in Asia Pacific the comprehensive security agenda outlined in the preceding pages? Here, it is useful to begin by considering Asia Pacific as a mega-region, which is not to suggest that the mega-region had political or organizational priority over the macro-region, in this case, East Asia.

How might Asia Pacific be geographically defined? Our preferred definition is one that encompasses the ASEAN countries, China, Mongolia, the two Koreas, Japan, Russia, the United States, Canada, Australasia, and the whole of Oceania. The rationale for so delineating the region was relatively straightforward. East Asia constituted the political and economic fulcrum for the entire project. The other countries were selected because they had an extensive pattern of interaction with East Asian countries. The inclusion of the United States was unavoidable given its economic, geopolitical and cultural omnipresence. It was, and would in the foreseeable future continue to be, a primary player in the resolution of outstanding conflicts (for example, China–Taiwan, the two Koreas) and in the region's trade and investment flows. Australia, New Zealand and Canada were included because of their close connections with both East Asia and the United States, the Pacific island states because they gave concrete expression to the notion of a 'Pacific' Community. To have meaning such a community could not confine itself to the rimlands of Asia and the Americas. It had to encompass the entire Pacific basin and its peoples, numerically small and geopolitically lightweight though they were. Their very vulnerability and currently high levels of dependence on the United States, Japan, Australia and New Zealand, if anything strengthened the case for their inclusion.[50] To mitigate the problems posed by a large and unwieldy forum, Pacific Island states could be represented through the intermediary of the Pacific Islands Forum. Latin American participation would be optional and limited to countries able to make a strong case on the basis of extensive economic or other links with the Asian rimlands.

Mega-regional processes, mechanisms and conventions constitute just one of the tiers in any comprehensive security framework. It is, however, a crucial tier because it connects national, subnational and transnational as well as regional and sub-regional tiers of governance. For these linkages to be fully developed in the Asia-Pacific context, the mega-regional tier had to be given coherence and direction. Put simply, Asia-Pacific regionalism needed a highly visible roof or umbrella. This could take the form of an altogether new organization expressly created for the purpose. Alternatively, it could emerge as an extension or refinement of an existing institution. Whichever option was chosen, the aim would be to establish at the highest level a widely representative entity embracing all the countries of the region and placing on its agenda all the issues which have a bearing on comprehensive security.

Could any existing organization provide the basis for the proposed forum? By virtue of membership, both APEC and the ARF came close, but neither exactly fitted the bill. APEC in its first ten years was preoccupied with questions of trade and investment and only indirectly with the larger security agenda. To force it to take on much more in the security realm would be to risk overload and loss of coherence.[51] The ARF, on the other hand, precisely because it was primarily a meeting of foreign ministers and their officials, tended to lack the authority and all-embracing character of APEC. A possible way forward was to revamp the APEC Leaders' Meeting and give it a wider brief. Renamed the Asia-Pacific Leaders' Meeting, it would consider the entire gamut of economic and security issues, giving due attention to interconnections as much as to comprehensiveness. It would continue to meet annually, reviewing and where appropriate hastening progress in trade and economic relations more generally, while at the same time exerting much greater influence on future regional diplomacy. It would provide an authoritative umbrella for comprehensive security dialogue and give continuing impetus to the work of both APEC and the ARF.

Supporting this roof would be a number of pillars or region-wide interlinking structures, some of which would be located on the first track (inter-governmental organizations), others on the second track (epistemic communities in close proximity to governments) and others still on the third track (civil society organizations). So far as the first track is concerned, APEC and the ARF would constitute the principal mega-regional pillars, though by no means the only ones. Issues of membership, agenda, and greater inter-organizational coordination (not least between APEC and the ARF) would require careful consideration. Over a ten-year period, APEC would progressively reconsider its mandate and its narrowly defined focus on trade and investment liberalization and begin to devote systematic and proactive attention to a number of unconventional security issues that impinged directly or indirectly on economic policy (for example, environment, development, energy security, labour migration, labour laws, narcotics trade). Complementing this shift in policy focus would be a concerted opening to civil society, through the establishment of an APEC Civil Society Advisory Council, an APEC Trade Union Advisory Council, participation of non-governmental organizations in APEC working groups, and public policy forums held in all APEC member countries, where such contentious issues as the trade/development/environment nexus could be widely canvassed.[52] APEC would also need to consider a modest expansion of its membership to allow for more adequate representation of the less-developed economies of the South Pacific and Southeast Asia.

As for the ARF, unconventional security issues (for example, environment, piracy, transnational crime and human rights) would increasingly intrude into all three stages of its anticipated development (confidence-building, conflict prevention and conflict resolution). The ARF's function on these various fronts would not necessarily be to implement detailed action programmes. Rather it would monitor progress being made, often within other existing mechanisms, and ensure effective coordination across the spectrum of security issues and policies, and between relevant national agencies and regional organizations. In the field of conventional security, a pressing objective would be greater transparency in relation to threat assessment, defence doctrine and military procurement. Other agenda items would presumably include additional CSBMs, regional action to stem the proliferation of weapons of mass destruction, mechanisms for conflict resolution, and in the longer term the possibility of a conflict prevention centre.[53] But perhaps the most taxing challenge facing the ARF would be to manage a security dialogue that constructively accommodated shifts in the regional distribution of power and effectively dealt with 'problem' states (for example, Myanmar, North Korea) in ways likely to strengthen the regional normative consensus.

Constructing more regular and efficient communication flows between APEC and the ARF would enhance the effectiveness of both organizations. Greater coordination, particularly at the level of senior officials, should help to ease problems posed by overlapping functions, most likely to arise in relation to security. Two areas seemed especially promising, namely drug trafficking and other forms of transnational economic crime, and protection of the marine environment.[54] There was, however a third area where coordination might be possible, namely in relation to the future presence and role of the United States. To the extent that US security commitments continued to be seen by a number of governments as an important factor in Asia's economic and political stability, and that enhanced access to Asian markets was one of the key elements likely to shape US policy in Asia, both APEC and the ARF had a direct interest in managing the multiple tensions likely to accompany the transition from hegemony to complex interdependence. Though the three bilateral relationships involving the United States, China and Japan were likely to be decisive, skilfully coordinated multilateral diplomacy could play a useful supporting, and at times agenda-setting, role.

For reasons that have already been canvassed, region-wide institutions operating in the second track were also expected to assume an increasingly important role. Reference has already been made to the important functions which PECC and later CSCAP performed by combining the insights of scholars and practitioners. With the institutional growth and experience gained in its first ten years, CSCAP seemed well placed to expand its activities and contribute to the more effective coordination of the second-track process. A useful first step might be for PECC and CSCAP to be linked by more effective consultative mechanisms, including joint seminars, workshops and regional briefings, especially around unconventional security issues of interest to both organizations.

So far as CSCAP's own development was concerned, two possibilities readily suggested themselves. The first was a bolder and more direct CSCAP contribution to the ARF process, which would among other things require CSCAP to accelerate work already under way (for example, maritime security, transnational crime), and to initiate new activities in anticipation of the ARF's future development (particularly in the area of preventive diplomacy and conflict resolution). To justify its existence CSCAP had to go beyond the relative safety of its existing working groups, and begin to address some of the region's more intractable intra-state and inter-state conflicts. Most conflicts were in any case likely to be a dichotomous blend of the domestic and the international. Candidates for immediate attention included the China–Taiwan dispute, the Korean conflict, and the tensions created by separatist tendencies, whether in China, Indonesia or the Philippines.

CSCAP had to demonstrate that it had the political credibility, intellectual resources, and organizational skills to develop conflict prevention and conflict resolution programmes based on international experience and local know-how. As a first step CSCAP might produce detailed studies offering sustained analysis, policy recommendations and transitional strategies. Then would come the equally taxing task of mobilizing the interest, and where possible the support, of relevant policy communities. In the more sensitive areas of security dialogue a serious programme of research, consultation and advocacy was likely to take the best part of five years before coming to fruition.

This leads us to a second but not unrelated possibility. The CSCAP process has thus far relied primarily on specialists – be they scholars or practitioners – drawn largely from the relatively narrow field of security studies. However, by definition comprehensive security requires a wider range of specializations. CSCAP's effectiveness could therefore be enhanced by the judicious involvement of other epistemic communities – environmental and medical scientists, lawyers and judges, parliamentarians and civil servants, sociologists and psychologists, to name a few. How these knowledge communities could be effectively harnessed, and how they would relate to existing second-track mechanisms were questions that had yet to receive serious attention. However, as the security agenda expanded and the multilateral process gathered pace, it was likely that the need for other second-track functions, not least a systematic monitoring function, would become increasingly apparent.

Notwithstanding the importance of mega-regional institutions, be they first track or second track, oriented primarily to economic or to political security issues, the fact remains that in a region as large and diverse as Asia Pacific, the success of multilateral co-operation would in good measure be governed by macro-regional and sub-regional organizations and processes. These were the supporting pillars, energizing and giving practical effect to the concerns and priorities of the regional structure. Some were geographically and others functionally based, but important gaps remained. There was also scope for further development and refinement of existing arrangements. For reasons of space we confine ourselves to a few key observations.

At the macro-regional level, ASEAN+3 had already emerged as the most significant political expression of 'pan-Asian' consciousness and of East Asian economic interdependence. Whether ASEAN+3 as a whole would make rapid strides towards the establishment of a free trade zone was an open question, but it could be confidently predicted that the expansion of trade and investment flows would exert a powerful integrative pressure. The commercial, financial and family networks underpinning the 'Greater China area' were likely to maintain the momentum of the preceding decade, at least for the foreseeable future. Similarly, Japanese capital would continue its penetration of East Asian markets, although greater competition might be expected from Taiwanese, South Korean and even Chinese capital as these economies continued to mature. Greater political integration was also likely, at least in the form of more elaborate and sustained consultative arrangements. However, for these to acquire more than cosmetic value they would need to address three key issues: the actual and potential conflicts relating to the Spratly Islands and more generally the South China Sea, the related issues of energy and environment, and future developments in regional architecture. Addressing these questions did not mean arriving at comprehensive and lasting agreements. Rather it meant establishing a framework conducive to in-depth consultation, and to the management of conflicting views and interests. In the medium to longer term, the test of ASEAN+3's contribution to comprehensive security would be measured by its capacity to fashion a *modus vivendi* between its three major centres of power and influence (China, Japan and ASEAN) and to generate a sufficiently distinctive and coherent set of ideas that could guide its own internal development as well as its external relationships, in particular its input into APEC, ASEM, the ARF, and even global institutions. To put it more dramatically, ASEAN+3 had to develop a set of structures and policies which, though taking account of the close connections between several of its members and the United States, could nevertheless offer, in keeping with East Asia's cultural and political traditions, an alternative or at least independent perspective to that emanating from Brussels or Washington.

At the sub-regional level, ASEAN and the Pacific Islands Forum were the two leading institutions. ASEAN, particularly now that its membership had expanded to cover the whole of Southeast Asia, had a key role to play in maintaining intra-mural stability and co-operative behaviour. Beyond that, by virtue of its longer history, more established institutional culture, and strategic location between the North Pacific, South Pacific and South Asia, ASEAN was likely for the foreseeable future to retain a catalytic function, partly as the pace-setter in the development of a regional normative consensus, partly as the main engine of institutional innovation within the ARF, and partly as a model of multilateral dialogue, which other parts of the Asia-Pacific region might adapt to suit their particular circumstances. Such an outcome, however, was far from assured. To perform these three functions ASEAN could not rest on its laurels. It needed to internalize three closely related principles to which it had thus far paid occasional lip service but had in practice swept under the carpet: standards of humane and legitimate governance; active national and regional participation of civil society in ASEAN activities and decision-making processes; and a readiness to develop crisis-prevention norms and strategies capable of addressing a range of intra- and inter-state conflicts in Southeast Asia.

The first principle involved a much clearer agreement on human rights norms, as they would apply to individual Southeast Asian polities, and to the role of ASEAN's principal deliberative and administrative organs in setting and implementing these norms. The conditions of success on this front are more fully considered later. The second principle required that ASEAN's top-down efforts to involve civil society in region-building increasingly make way for a bottom-up approach whereby non-governmental agencies active around issues of environment, development, human rights and political reform, but also a number of religious, ethnic, cultural and professional associations as well as independent trade unions, would be regularly consulted and their advice and recommendations routinely integrated into ASEAN's policy-making processes. To give effect to the third principle, ASEAN would need to acquire sophisticated analytical and research capabilities designed to buttress its crisis prevention strategy. An independent crisis prevention centre would be a useful way of pooling information and proposals, and of translating these into concrete recommendations for the consideration of summit and foreign ministers' meetings. These initiatives, useful though they were, had to be subjected to periodic monitoring, the primary purpose of which would be to assess the overall efficacy of ASEAN's intra- and extra-mural diplomacy. ASEAN initiatives in this sphere were likely to have widespread ramifications for other parts of East Asia. ASEAN's lead might also be helpful in clarifying the options available to Northeast Asian countries in developing comparable communication arrangements.

In sharp contrast to ASEAN, the Pacific Islands Forum remained on issues of economic and political security at the margins of region-wide dialogue. On the other hand, the Forum had played an important intra-mural role, giving its members, notably the smaller island states, a greater voice in environmental and nuclear issues, and a greater capacity to coordinate positions in the United Nations and other multinational forums. Although Australia, New Zealand and to a lesser extent Papua New Guinea had a significant presence in APEC, ASEAN PMC and the ARF, the smaller states had no such representation, and little prospect of it in the foreseeable future. These multilateral organizations might nevertheless be amenable to granting the Forum either full or associate membership, thereby improving the lines of communication and ensuring that the priorities of Pacific micro-states, especially their understandable preoccupation with issues of development, climate change and marine environment, were more effectively integrated into a comprehensive security agenda for the Asia-Pacific region.

The pressing need for a North Pacific multilateral security forum has been the subject of much discussion. The Agreed Framework between the United States and North Korea, the subsequent establishment of KEDO, the inter-Korean rapprochement in the wake of Kim Dae-Jung's Sunshine policy, and Prime Minister Koizumi's overtures to North Korea indicated a temporary easing of tensions. Promising though they were, these developments were offset by contradictory trends and highly destabilizing concentrations of military capability. In any case, they did not address the outstanding conflicts of the region, attend to the multiple interconnections between them, or adequately mobilize the interests and energies of all relevant protagonists. An enduring diplomatic forum, to which Japan, Russia, the United States, China, the two Koreas, and possibly Canada and Mongolia could give their undivided attention, remained a high priority. A great many desirable initiatives had been proposed at different times: information-sharing, military consultations and exchanges, a Northeast Asian nuclear weapons-free zone, informal discussions at ministerial or senior officials' level, and working groups on specific issues. It was not so much a case of choosing between this or that proposal, but of proceeding simultaneously on several fronts, pursuing both first- and second-track diplomacy, and within the first track both generic and specific initiatives, with a view to achieving the necessary level of synergy.

While permanent institutional arrangements could serve useful functions at all levels, a case could also be made for *ad hoc* mechanisms. The Cambodian peace process had set an important precedent. The combined efforts of the Indonesian, Australian and other governments helped to launch and then sustain a multilateral conflict-resolution mechanism which proved sufficiently robust to warrant comparable third-party efforts with respect to other conflicts. A great many lessons were learnt from that experience, particularly in connection with what may be termed the micro-politics and micro-economics of large-scale peacekeeping operations,[55] and the indecent haste with which the international community sought to terminate the UN's involvement in both peacekeeping and peacebuilding. In subsequent years the South China Sea workshops and KEDO, although operating at a lower level of intensity and with less visible success, continued to point to the usefulness of a conflict-specific approach. Two observations seem apposite in the light of recent experience. *Ad hoc* multilateral arrangements tailored to the requirements of particular conflicts had a place in the tool-kit of comprehensive security, but success would normally be governed by two factors: the adequacy of the intellectual, organizational and financial resources which one or more actors were prepared to commit to the initiative; and the availability of institutional back-up for monitoring progress and ensuring a continuing third-party presence until the peacekeeping or peacebuilding process acquired the necessary robustness.

A recurring theme of this chapter has been the need for more extensive coordination and communication flows between different facets and tiers of the emerging regional security framework. This requirement might at first sight suggest an intricate and costly bureaucratic apparatus, but such an outcome was neither necessary nor desirable. As a first step an informal working group could be established at either first- or second-track level – perhaps a CSCAP working group or a group convened by the ARF Senior Officials Meeting. It could be mandated to perform the following tasks: (a) prepare a detailed inventory of currently functioning regional dialogue mechanisms impinging on all issues relevant to comprehensive security; (b) identify those policy areas where the security dimension was not adequately addressed or where it prompted unnecessary or wasteful duplication; (c) recommend measures to ensure reliable and regular monitoring of the rapidly developing regional security dialogue.

A separate working group could be asked to prepare an annual report to the ARF Senior Officials Meeting, setting out what actions had been taken either collectively or by individual member states, at either first- or second-track level, in line with previous ARF agreements, recommendations and proposals. In the interests of comprehensiveness this function could be extended to cover other dialogue mechanisms, which the ARF may have sponsored or with which it was closely connected. By making information flows more efficient and more flexible, the proposed arrangements would not only enhance regional resilience and cohesion, but offer national governments a greater incentive as well as a greater capacity to integrate notions of comprehensive security into their own decision-making structures and processes.

It remains to say a word about the extra-regional dimensions of security co-operation. The relationship with other regions, notably the European Union, North America (in this later case, possibly through APEC) and with the United Nations was critically important. Here we limit ourselves to a few brief observations covering ASEM and the UN system. In ASEM's case, three key functions are worth highlighting. First was the intrinsic benefit to be derived from closer commercial, financial, technological and cultural links and exchanges between the two regional formations, which might have as one of their positive spin-offs a more mature inter-civilizational and human rights dialogue. Equally significant was ASEM's potential to facilitate an East Asian–European collaborative relationship that might curb the excesses of US unilateralism, and over time persuade US policy-makers of the virtues of an international concert of powers as a first step towards the progressive democratization of global governance.[56] In this regard, one of ASEM's main challenges was to create the psychological and political conditions whereby both Asian and European policy-makers would find it comfortable and advantageous to place on their agenda the future structural and policy reorganization of key global institutions, including the UN Security Council, other parts of the UN system, the IMF, the World Bank and the WTO.

By virtue of its Charter, the United Nations was committed to a comprehensive approach to security, a view that was steadily reinforced during the 1990s through the interventions of the UN Secretariat as well as the deliberations of the Security Council. In *An Agenda for Peace* Boutros Boutros-Ghali called for closer links between the UN and regional organizations, partly with a view to strengthening the legitimacy of the international organization, and directly or indirectly enlarging the pool of resources at its disposal. However, this could not be a one-way street. Regional organizations had themselves much to gain from closer interaction,[57] as the Cambodian peace process,[58] the Comprehensive Action Plan on Indo-Chinese Refugees, the East Timor crisis, and the unfinished business of bringing to trial the perpetrators of monstrous crimes in Pol Pot's Cambodia clearly indicate. Viewed from an Asia-Pacific perspective, such links could be put to productive use in relation to arms control (for example, nuclear non-proliferation, UN arms register), conflict prevention (for example, Law of the Sea) and peacebuilding (for example, application of international criminal law with respect to Cambodia and East Timor).

Other possible areas for fruitful co-operation included uncontrolled or illegal migration, narcotics smuggling, border disputes, human rights, resource management and protection of the environment. The attention intermittently given by the ARF to peacekeeping was suggestive of other possibilities, including the establishment of a regional peacekeeping centre, which might oversee the preparation and development of systematic training programmes, and provide the necessary early warnings about latent local and regional conflicts. Co-operation between the UN on the one hand and the ARF, ASEAN and the Pacific Islands Forum on the other could prove particularly useful in addressing a number of intra-state conflicts, for example in Indonesia (Aceh, Papua), the Philippines (Mindanao), and in what is sometimes referred to as the 'Melanesian arc of instability', including Papua New Guinea/Bougainville, the Solomons, and potentially Fiji. In different ways and to varying degrees ASEAN, the ARF, and even APEC and CSCAP could liaise more effectively with the relevant regional arms of the UN system (for example, UN Regional Centre for Peace and Disarmament in Kathmandu, and ESCAP, as well as with the UN Secretariat, numerous UN agencies and programmes, and the Secretary-General's special representatives). These and other forms of collaboration (for example, UN observer status at various regional forums) could enhance the analytical skills of both regional and global organizations, make for a more effective division of labour between them, and pave the way for joint initiatives in confidence-building and conflict prevention.

HUMAN RIGHTS: A KEY TO REGIONAL DIALOGUE

There is, of course, more to comprehensive security than better policy coordination. Several important areas of policy had thus far received less attention in the Asia-Pacific region than they deserved. Arms transfers, transnational crime, environment, migration flows and treatment of refugees readily came to mind. In each case the principal stumbling blocks were not so much organizational deficiencies as political sensibilities. As a concluding note to this chapter we propose to examine one such policy area, arguably the most contentious, namely human rights. Three main considerations underlie this choice. First, human rights policies can shed light on the role of the state and the grounds on which its stakes its legitimacy. Secondly, they underscore the actual and potential contribution of civil society to the comprehensive security agenda. Thirdly, they illuminate the prospects for regional dialogue across the cultural and religious divide.

As our analysis of the 'Asian versus Western values' debate has already indicated, official and semi-official pronouncements in the 1990s tended to oscillate between high-sounding generalizations about universalism or cultural relativism and acrimonious exchanges that risked damaging important bilateral relationships. Whether in relation to Burma, Tibet, East Timor, Papua, Aceh, the use of the Internal Security Act in Malaysia, or the plight of Aborigines and asylum seekers in Australia, it is doubtful whether the complex questions of human rights abuse could be adequately resolved at the bilateral level. At the same time, these questions could not be left entirely in the hands of those most directly involved, namely those claiming sovereign jurisdiction or those subjected to gross victimization.

Asia Pacific, not despite but because of the plurality of religious and ethical traditions which it encompasses, was well placed to put to constructive use both differences and complementarities. A human rights dialogue grounded in the cultural traditions of the Asia-Pacific region might, in fact, enhance the comprehensiveness of the international human rights regime, in part by clarifying the linkages between human rights and human needs, between rights and obligations, and between the individual and the community.[59] The task of developing a normative and operational human rights framework attuned to local circumstances could only proceed dialogically.[60] The human rights component of comprehensive security highlighted an aspect of regionalism, which, though by no means unique, had been largely neglected. Comprehensive security, to the extent that it directs attention to the security of society as a whole, and not just that of the state and its armed forces, necessarily involves a great many of society's constituencies. If the European experience had any lessons for Asia Pacific, it was that without substantial societal involvement and support, the regional project risked being derailed. Much could be done to strengthen the second and third tracks, and to incorporate into the multilateral project the energies and resources of the legal, medical, educational, scientific and other professions, not to mention religious, cultural and social organizations concerned with such issues as economic development, health, environment, media, urban planning, or industrial relations.

One other important connection between human rights and comprehensive security is worth stressing. Fundamental human rights may be described as 'minimum satisfiers', that is, as that cluster of human claims and entitlements which are recognized as legitimate (in that they meet basic human needs) and just (in that they do not privilege some at the expense of others). The setting, monitoring and enforcement of human rights standards performed, by virtue of the relationship between rights and needs, a function that is universal in scope and character. Yet rights also have an important cultural dimension. Their establishment and subsequent development is an ongoing evolutionary process which rests on cultural interaction and cultural synthesis. Human rights may therefore be described as socially learned or culturally derived satisfiers. At any given time, human rights norms will have universal applicability, but many cultural strands or influences may have contributed to the formulation of these norms, and cultural and socio-economic differences are bound to affect how these norms are applied in different places and at different times.

Another way of characterizing the human rights project is to see it as a bridge between governance and the satisfaction of basic needs. It provides an instrument for evaluating the institutions and processes of government from a human needs perspective. It focuses attention on policies, decisions and outcomes. It establishes a public arena where civil society and the individuals and groups that constitute it can participate in the processes of governance, thereby fulfilling a number of needs both directly (for example, identity, recognition) and indirectly (for example, material sustenance). Set in this context, human rights protection becomes one of the important indicators of the legitimacy of the state. Once this premise is accepted, legitimacy can no longer be grounded exclusively in the principle of state sovereignty, and repressive regimes cannot invoke that principle either to justify the violation of human rights standards or to shield such violation from international scrutiny.

If the analysis developed in Chapter 9 is at all valid, then the Asia-Pacific region was well placed to contribute to, but also to benefit from a universal, needs-based, but evolving conception of human rights. There was much that Asian traditions, in particular, could contribute to such a dialogue: a richer and more varied conception of political community, which could strengthen the intellectual and practical connection between human rights and human needs; a more effective balance between rights and obligations; a clearer appreciation of the relationship between social and economic rights on the one hand, and civil and political rights on the other; a strong sense that no culture or civilization had a monopoly on the formulation of human rights; and a readiness to explore a consensual approach to the negotiation of an international human rights regime.

Asian perspectives might over time come to moderate the legalistic and individualistic ethos which still dominated much of human rights discourse. A third generation of human rights might emerge, which would affirm the related rights to security, survival and sustainability, that is the right of groups and individuals – even those of unborn generations – to be reasonably secure about their prospects of physical well-being, now increasingly under threat by weapons of mass destruction and environmental degradation.[61] Several Asian initiatives were indicative of the changing intellectual climate. In its 1994 report, the Commission for a New Asia identified the 'challenge of human rights and responsibilities' and the 'challenge of democracy and the rule of law' as two of the six central challenges that Asia would face in the coming years. Though not exclusively Asian in inspiration but with significant Asian input, the InterAction Council, whose membership comprised more than 20 former presidents and prime ministers, including Helmut Schmidt, Malcolm Fraser, Valéry Giscard d'Estaing, Jimmy Carter, Pierre Trudeau, but also Kenneth Kaunda, Lee Kuan Yew, Kiichi Miyazawa and Anand Panayerachun, drafted a Universal Declaration of Human Responsibilities. The Council's Chairman, Malcolm Fraser, offered the following rationale for the initiative:

> The Universal Declaration of Human Rights properly addresses itself to the protection of individuals against the abusive power of governments, our proposed declaration of human responsibilities places obligations on governments, on institutions and corporations as well as on people themselves. The totality provides a balance which ... is presently lacking.[62]

The proposed declaration, though little more than a statement of principles, offered a normative benchmark by which to evaluate the efficacy and legitimacy of existing institutions, be they national or international, economic or political. The Asian Human Rights Commission (AHRC), founded in 1986 by a prominent group of jurists and human rights activists in Asia, initiated an exhaustive consultative process over a two-year period (1994–96), involving thousands of individuals and organizations across Asia, and culminating in May 1996 in the adoption and widespread distribution of a consensual document *The Asian Human Rights Charter.*[63]

A great many actors, in addition to governments, were now intent on occupying the terrain of debate, negotiation and implementation. Diverse communities and organizations, some operating locally, others nationally, regionally or internationally, were involved. The function of government would be as much to reflect as to steer the debate, to coordinate as to set the agenda. Perhaps the most important contribution of governments would be to establish and solidify the regional channels of communication and negotiation, and eventually the mandate of regional institutions entrusted with monitoring and promoting human rights standards.

Attempts to regionalize the human rights agenda in Asia Pacific could not simply emulate the European, American or African experience. The mechanisms to be established had to respect local needs and circumstances. A more durable and comprehensive human rights regime at the regional level would need to mirror but also enhance the implementation of human rights standards at the national level. It would comprise a carefully modulated blend of measures involving domestic reform, diplomacy, cultural exchange, and technical and economic assistance.

Human rights education would be critical to the success of any long-term strategy. A key objective would be higher levels of community awareness of national and international human rights laws and standards currently in force or soon to be adopted.[64] In the absence of an informed public, governments would lack the confidence to take the necessary initiatives, and even if they did their actions would lack the necessary credibility in the eyes of neighbours or the region as a whole. Well-coordinated and adequately resourced community awareness campaigns would need to involve all levels of government (local, provincial and national), educational institutions, the media, business groups, trade unions, professional associations, religious and other non-governmental organizations. They could be initiated either by existing or newly established national human rights commissions. The principal aims of such campaigns would be to disseminate in accessible form the texts of human rights instruments, to promote a higher media profile on human rights issues, and to introduce the study of human rights in schools and universities. The higher education system would itself need to be resourced to conduct appropriate human rights research and training. In all of this the focus would not be simply on human rights in general or in the abstract; explicit attention would be given to the national and regional context. Precisely because human rights are an intensely cultural issue, government policies could not make headway unless they were grounded in cultural literacy, that is, greater familiarity with the languages, histories, religions and philosophies of the region. One initiative that could over time significantly enhance the efficacy of a regional human rights regime would be the establishment within each country of at least one centre for inter-civilizational dialogue.[65] Such centres – in all likelihood attached to universities – would co-operate in fostering research, education and public discussion on the major cultures, religions and civilizations of the region. They would host or encourage meetings, seminars, conferences and exchanges involving intellectuals, artists, and religious and community leaders drawn from diverse Asian and Pacific traditions.[66]

Two other initiatives worthy of consideration had both a unilateral and a multilateral dimension. The first was especially relevant to Western governments, which, having traditionally portrayed themselves as champions of human rights, might be amenable to introducing mechanisms designed to subject their own human rights performance to international scrutiny. This could take the form of government-commissioned reports on such contentious issues as indigenous rights, race relations, women's rights, and the treatment of migrants, guest workers and refugees (relevant in varying degrees to the United States, Canada, Japan, Australia and New Zealand). Such reports, to be tabled and discussed in the legislatures of the host state, would be prepared by panels whose membership might comprise eminent judges, scholars, retired diplomats and political or religious leaders known for their independence and representative of the region's cultural diversity. Apart from its obvious benefits in facilitating the resolution of complex problems, such a process could help gain wider acceptance for the related principles of transparency and international monitoring, and at the same time provide a useful antidote to 'West-centric' human rights discourse and practice.

The second initiative envisaged the development of robust national action plans. The 1993 World Conference on Human Rights endorsed an Australian proposal calling on UN member states to prepare such plans as a way of improving their observance of human rights standards. The proposal could be given added force by requiring national action plans: (a) to have a stronger regional focus (that is, governments in the region would be strongly encouraged to prepare such plans); (b) to state clearly what each government considered the main deficiencies in the country's current human rights record, and how the proposed plans were likely to remedy these deficiencies; (c) to establish specific goals, strategies and a timetable for anticipated improvements; (d) to be presented to a regional forum, in addition to any UN or other international forums, where these plans could be discussed and periodically reviewed.[67]

Unilateral initiatives, important as they were, were unlikely to be sustained for long unless they rested on solid multilateral foundations. There now existed internationally an elaborate international human rights infrastructure, whose legitimacy derived principally from the UN system, and which, despite serious limitations, performed three key functions: the setting, monitoring and enforcement of standards. The more effective performance of these functions depended in part on regional institutions whose membership, ethos and mode of operation were attuned to the region's political, economic and, above all, cultural particularities. With this in mind, several modest yet significant steps appeared politically feasible in the emerging Asia-Pacific environment.

Given the well-known diplomatic sensitivities of the region, and a lingering suspicion of formal institutions, it seemed preferable, at least initially, to proceed with a track-two human rights forum, which would not immediately commit governments to a particular position or course of action. Building on the work and experience of the Asia-Pacific Workshops on Human Rights, such a forum would bring together academics, community leaders, NGO representatives, experts drawn from UN and related human rights organizations, representatives of business associations, and government officials and experts participating in a non-official capacity. Operating within a relatively informal framework participants would be able not only to exchange views, but to promote human rights education strategies, review the role of other regional and national institutions in the implementation of human rights, and submit ideas and proposals for the consideration of governments.

To complement and underpin the work of such a forum, a Regional Centre for Human Rights Dialogue and Co-operation might be established to perform specific research and training functions. With substantial funding from one or more of the developed economies (for example, Australia, Canada, Japan), such a centre, located in Hong Kong, Manila or Bangkok, would operate under a charter guaranteeing its independence. Governed by a board culturally and geographically representative of the region, it would promote debate, research and analysis across the full range of individual and collective rights, bringing to bear a strong inter-cultural focus. It would provide interested governments with a range of professional services, including facilitation of national educational strategies, regular publication of reports to be submitted to governments, and various forms of research and technical assistance, notably in the preparation of national action plans.

There was also a case for consolidating and formalizing the work of regional workshops convened to strengthen co-operation between national human rights institutions. An Asia-Pacific organization created for this purpose could compare, and draw lessons from, different national experiences, especially with respect to the ratification and implementation of international human rights instruments.[68] It could also help to identify the main areas of need for economic assistance and technical support in the development of national human rights institutions, and provide a focal point of coordination between UN human rights organizations and national human rights institutions. Though many of these tasks would be largely technical in character, they would have a natural spillover effect in other areas of inter-governmental co-operation.

The development of an institutional infrastructure of the kind foreshadowed here would enhance the public visibility of human rights dialogue, shelter it from unnecessary acrimony, and provide significant points of reference and contact for the rapidly growing number of scholars, lawyers, civil servants and journalists with a professional interest in human rights. It would nevertheless be useful to invigorate and legitimize regional human rights discourse by the adoption of a Regional Charter of Human Rights and Responsibilities. Drawing on track-two and track-three initiatives referred to above, such a Charter could be drafted as a stand-alone document, or form part of a larger document setting out principles of regional co-operation (for example, the proposed Regional Declaration of Principles). It would serve a number of important functions: (a) bring a regional focus to international human rights agreements and negotiations by directing particular attention to the needs and circumstances of societies and polities in Asia Pacific; (b) strengthen the commitment of governments to human rights standards, but without its provisions having legally binding force; (c) periodically set priorities for the regional implementation of human rights (for example, treatment of refugees, elimination of torture, rights of indigenous peoples).

The preceding steps would, individually and collectively, contribute over time to a psychological climate more conducive to political initiative. Probably sooner rather than later, governments would find it helpful to exchange views and coordinate initiatives through periodic meetings, which could operate in one of several ways. They could bring together either foreign ministers or ministers with responsibility for national human rights institutions. Alternatively, human rights issues could be included on the agenda of the ASEAN Regional Forum, and other regional organizations (for example, ASEM) whose functions were likely to impinge on human rights issues (for example, labour rights). Ministerial meetings convened specifically to discuss human rights issues might in the first instance be held irregularly and informally, but such meetings could eventually be convened annually and develop a more systematic agenda. In time conditions may have been created for the adoption of a legally binding Regional Convention on Human Rights and Responsibilities. An Asia-Pacific convention could not be a replica of the European model, with its concentration on civil and political rights, its elaborate institutional infrastructure, and its provisions for legally enforceable decisions by the European Court of Human Rights. Instead, it might be authorized to investigate human rights abuses, or at the very least to conciliate, report and recommend. That in itself would represent dramatic progress.

The proposals outlined above were not necessarily indicative of what governments, even those with strong declaratory policies in support of human rights, would actually do. Few governments in East Asia, or for that matter in Asia Pacific, were as yet intellectually or politically disposed to developing the proposed regional processes, mechanisms and forums, or to committing the necessary resources. Most governments would tend to follow rather than lead. In this sense, the ideas canvassed here did not purport to predict the future. They were suggestive of possibilities rather than probabilities. They did nevertheless point to what was at least an embryonic trend. Side by side with the multiple manifestations of religious fundamentalism and political dogmatism associated with the competing ideologies of terrorism and anti-terrorism was a greater sensitivity among educated elites to cultural and civilizational diversity. Among governments one could discern a growing though still grudging recognition that their performance was now subject to both domestic and international evaluation. The multiple roles, actors and process that would necessarily form part of a regional human rights dialogue were slowly and tentatively taking shape.

A MORE EFFECTIVE FRAMEWORK FOR REGIONAL DIALOGUE

The agenda for multilateral co-operation presented in this chapter does not offer an exhaustive survey of the possible or the desirable. It does, however, bring into stark relief the immense difficulties but also promising opportunities surrounding the institutionalization of regional dialogue. To live up to its promise, Asia-Pacific regionalism would have to pass three daunting tests. First, regional processes and mechanisms would need to involve fully, and in a sense strengthen, the state and its agencies. Regional policies and priorities would be unattainable unless states were prepared to make available the necessary organizational and financial resources. In this sense, states could be expected to retain a substantial veto power with respect to both the content and pace of regionalism. On the other hand, to perform their most critical functions, notably security and economic well-being, states would have to coordinate their actions with those of other states. The second half of the twentieth century had witnessed a distinct trend towards a multi-tiered system of governance, in which regional and global institutions complemented the regulatory role of national governments (with varying degrees of devolution to local and provincial government). The trend was likely to gather pace during the first half of the twenty-first century.

Regionalism in its various guises was in good measure a response to globalization, or to be more precise to the diminishing capacity of the state to manage the national economy in the era of rapidly globalizing markets. In the neo-liberal perspective regional organizations offered an additional vehicle through which the competitive logic of the market could further penetrate the organization of economic activity. There was, however, an alternative perspective, which viewed the development of regional and global institutions as the necessary antidote to the unplanned and unforeseen consequences of globalization. The task of these institutions was to breathe new life into the regulatory ethic, and subordinate the market to politically determined priorities. A multi-tiered system of governance, in which regional institutions would play an increasingly prominent role, might be better equipped to discipline the market in ways conducive to the achievement of widely debated and carefully negotiated environmental, social and economic objectives.

This brings us to the third test. Open regionalism in the Asia-Pacific context would be meaningless unless it meant openness to the voices and needs of civil society. The success with which the comprehensiveness of the security agenda could be addressed, in Asia Pacific as elsewhere, would in no small measure depend on the capacity of regional institutions to harness the diverse insights, resources and expertise of civil society organizations – not just regionally, but nationally and globally. The stress on 'social comprehensiveness' would no doubt greatly complicate the task. On the other hand, to overlook or underestimate the complexities and interconnections might be to simplify the task but in practice render it unachievable. In pursuing this vision institutional innovation in Asia Pacific would have to strike a balance between mindless inclusiveness and rigid compartmentalization, between unattainable architectural elegance and faulty design.

NOTES

1.   See J.W.M. Chapman, R. Drifte and I.T.M. Gow, *Japan's Quest for Comprehensive Security: Defence–Diplomacy–Dependence*, London: Frances Pinter, 1983; also Yoshinobu

Yamamoto, 'A Framework for a Comprehensive Co-operative Security System for the Asia-Pacific', in Jim Rolfe (ed.), *Unresolved Futures: Comprehensive Security in the Asia-Pacific*, Wellington: Centre for Strategic Studies, 1995, pp. 18–19.

2. See R.W. Barnett, *Beyond War: Japan's Concept of Comprehensive National Security*, Washington, D.C: Pergamon Brassey's, 1986, pp. 1–6.
3. Cited in Muthiah Alagappa, 'Comprehensive Security: Interpretations in ASEAN Countries', Research Paper and Policy Studies No. 26, Berkeley, CA: Institute of East Asian Studies, University of California, pp. 57–8.
4. Speech given in Singapore on 2 March 1984, *Foreign Affairs Malaysia*, March 1984, 17 (1), 94.
5. See Alan Dupont, 'Concepts of Security', in Rolfe (ed.), *Unresolved Futures*, p. 7.
6. Noordin Sopiee, 'Malaysia's Doctrine of Comprehensive Security', *Journal of Asiatic Studies*, XXVII (2), 1984, 259–65.
7. *The Concepts of Comprehensive Security and Co-operative Security*, CSCAP Memorandum No. 3, 1995.
8. Ibid., p. 2.
9. See Mohamed Jawhar Hassan, 'The Concept of Comprehensive Security', paper presented at the second meeting of the CSCAP Working Group on Concepts of Comprehensive Security and Co-operative Security, Kuala Lumpur, 27–29 August 1995, pp. 5, 9.
10. Peter Katzenstein, 'Regionalism in Comparative Perspective', *Cooperation and Conflict*, 31 (2), June 1996, 144–5.
11. CSCAP Memorandum No. 3, p. 2.
12. Mohamed Jawhar Hassan, 'The Concepts of Comprehensive Security', p. 9.
13. Pauline Kerr, 'The Security Dialogue in the Asia-Pacific, *Pacific Review*, 7 (4), 1994, 400.
14. See Joseph A. Camilleri, 'Security: Old Dilemmas and New Challenges in the Post-Cold War Environment', *GeoJournal*, 34 (2), 1994, 2.
15. Vincent Gable, 'What is International Economic Security?', *International Affairs*, 71 (2), 1995, 305–24.
16. See Thomas F. Homer-Dixon, 'On the Threshold: Environmental Changes as Causes of Acute Conflict', *International Security*, 16 (2), Fall 1991, 77–116.
17. Lawrence Scheinman, *The International Atomic Energy Agency and World Nuclear Order*, Washington, DC: Resources for the Future, 1987, pp. 187–98.
18. Jonas Widgren, 'International Migration and Regional Stability', *International Affairs*, 66 (4), 1990, 749–66; Myron Weiner, 'Security, Stability and International Migration', *International Security*, 17 (3), Winter 1992/93, 91–126.
19. The analysis is developed at greater length in Joseph A. Camilleri, 'Globalization of Insecurity: The Democratic Imperative', *International Journal on World Peace*, XVIII (4), December 2001, 3–18.
20. See Pierre Michel-Fontaine, 'The Comprehensive Plan of Action (CPA) on Indo-Chinese Refugees: Prospects for Post-CPA, and Implications for a Regional Approach to Refugee Problems', *Pacifica Review: Peace, Security and Global Change*, 7 (2), October–November 1995, 39–60.
21. For a detailed survey of the scope and impact of these problems in a Southeast Asian context, see Amitav Acharya, *A New Regional Order in Southeast Asia: ASEAN in the Post-Cold War Era*, Adelphi Papers 279, August 1993, 17–27.
22. Even Chinese scholars were beginning to concede by the mid-1990s that the principle of sovereignty did not constitute an insuperable barrier to regional or international intervention. See Wenrong Qian, 'The United Nations and State Sovereignty in the Post-Cold War Era', *Pacifica Review: Peace Security and Global Change*, 7 (2), October-November 1995, 135–46.
23. The implications of globalization for security in Asia Pacific are clearly drawn out in Christopher W. Hughes, 'Conceptualising the Globalisation-Security Nexus in the Asia-Pacific', unpublished paper.
24. See Gareth Evans, *Cooperating for Peace*, Sydney: Allen & Unwin, 1993, p. 29.
25. Michael Barnett, 'Partners in Peace? The UN, Regional Organizations, and Regional Stability', *Review of International Studies*, 21 (4), 1995, 424.

26. This view was clearly reflected in the Thai Prime Minister's Keynote address to the 27th ASEAN Ministerial Meeting in Bangkok, 22 July 1994, *ASEAN Documents Series*, 1994, p. 2.

27. For an instructive representation of the contribution of regional institutions to security, using the Cambodian conflict as an example, see Muthiah Alagappa, 'Regionalism and the Quest for Security: ASEAN and the Cambodian Conflict', *Australian Journal of International Affairs*, Vol. 46 (2), Winter 1993, 439–68.

28. Joseph A. Camilleri, 'Major Structural Reform' in E. Aksu and J. Camilleri (eds), *Democratizing Global Governance*, Basingstoke, UK: Palgrave Macmillan, 2002, pp. 265–8.

29. See Ryuhei Hatsuse, 'Regionalisms in East Asia and the Asia-Pacific', in Yoshinobu Yamamoto, *Globalism, Regionalism and Nationalism: Asia in Search of its Role in the Twenty-first Century*, Oxford: Blackwell, 1999, pp. 108–9.

30. Katzenstein, 'Regionalism in Comparative Perspective', p. 129; for a more nuanced interpretation, see Alexander B. Murphy, 'Economic Regionalization and Pacific Asia', *Geographical Review*, 85 (2), April 1995, 134–9.

31. See Desmond Ball, 'Strategic Culture in the Asia-Pacific Region', *Security Studies*, 3 (1), Autumn 1994, 44–74; also Mohamed Jawhar Hassan, 'The Concept of Comprehensive Security', pp. 12–13.

32. J.N. Mak and B.A. Hamzah, 'The External Maritime Dimension of ASEAN Security', *Journal of Strategic Studies*, 18 (3), September 1995, 133–6.

33. See Mohamed Jawhar Hassan, 'Economic Pragmatism and Its Implications for Security and Confidence-Building among States in the Asia-Pacific Region', in *Disarmament: Topical Papers*, No. 13, New York: UN Department of Political Affairs, 1993, p. 74.

34. Wade Huntley and Peter Hayes, 'East Timor and Asian Security', *Bulletin of Concerned Asian Scholars* (Special Issue), 31 (1–2), at http://www.nautilus.org/napsnet/sr/East_Timor/index.html (sighted on 18 September 2002).

35. See Edward A. Olsen and David Winterford, 'Multilateral Arms Control Regimes in Asia: Prospects and Options', *Asian Perspective*, 18 (1), Spring–Summer 1994, 21.

36. Joseph A. Camilleri, 'Asia-Pacific in the Post-Hegemonic World', in Andrew Mack and John Ravenhill (eds), *Pacific Cooperation: Building Economic and Security Regimes in the Asia-Pacific Region*, Boulder, CO: Westview Press, 1995, p. 194.

37. See Liu Jiangyong, *Building a Multilateral Security Dialogue in the Pacific*, Pacific Economic Paper No. 235, Canberra: Australia–Japan Research Centre, ANU, September 1994, pp. 6–8.

38. The inability of successive governments to endow Japanese foreign policy with a coherent multilateral foundation is emphasized by Taniguchi Makoto, 'Without an Independent and Multilateral Foreign Policy, There is No Future for Japan: Some Proposals for Japan's Foreign Policy', see *Japan in the World* at http://www.iwanami.co.jp/world/text/ForeignPolicy01.html (sighted on 11 October 2002).

39. See Qian Qichen's opening speech to the symposium on 'Post-Cold War Security Situations in Asia/Pacific and Its Prospects', Beijing, 11 May 1994, cited in Paul Evans, 'The Prospects for Multilateral Security Co-operation in the Asia-Pacific Regions,' *Journal of Strategic Studies*, 18 (3), September 1995, 210; also Banning Garrett and Bonnie Glaser, 'Multilateral Security in the Asia-Pacific Region and its impact on Chinese Interests: A View from Beijing', *Contemporary Southeast Asia*, 16 (1), June 1994, 31–2.

40. Richard Higgott offers an instructive analysis of the non-structural basis of power in 'Competing Theoretical Approaches to International Cooperation: Implications for the Asia Pacific', in R. Higgott, R. Leaver and J. Ravenhill (eds), *Pacific Economic Relations in the 1990s: Cooperation or Conflict*, Sydney: Allen & Unwin, 1993, pp. 290–311; see also R. Higgott, A.F. Cooper and J. Bonner, 'Asia-Pacific Economic Cooperation: An Evolving Case Study in Leadership and Co-operation Building', *International Journal*, 45 (4), Autumn 1990, 823–66.

41. The concept of architecture is one that Gareth Evans gradually applied in the development of Australia's regional diplomacy (see his address to the 1994 Pacific Rim Forum, Beijing, 27 October 1994, p. 2).

42. Such a proposal has been widely canvassed, especially in track-two forums. See Paul M. Evans, 'Towards a Pacific Concord', paper presented at the 10th Roundtable, Kuala Lumpur, 5–8 June 1996; Mohamed Jawhar Hassan, 'Towards a Pacific Concord – Carrying the Debate Forward', in D. Dickens (ed.), *No Better Alternative: Towards Comprehensive and Cooperative Security in the Asia-Pacific*, Wellington: CSCAP/CSS, New Zealand, 1997, pp. 145–60.

43. Yukio Satoh, *Policy Co-ordination for the Asia-Pacific Security and Stability*, ANU, Strategic and Defence Studies Centre, Working Paper No. 305, 1996.

44. For a version of these norms set in a Northeast Asian context see William T. Tow, 'Northeast Asia and International Security: Transforming Competition to Collaboration', *Australian Journal of International Affairs*, 46 (1), May 1992, 13–14.

45. Joseph A. Camilleri, 'New Approaches to Regional Security: The Asia-Pacific Context', in Gary Smith and St John Kettle (eds), *Threats Without Enemies*, Leichhardt, NSW: Pluto Press, 1992, p. 172.

46. See Report of US, CSCAP, Taskforce on CSBMs, revised draft of 11 October 1994, p. 3; also James A. Boutilier (ed.), *Final Report of Cooperative Research Workshop*, prepared for the Non-Proliferation, Arms Control and Disarmament Division, Department of External Affairs and International Trade, Canada, April 1993, pp. 58–60.

47. See Sarasin Viraphol and Werner Pfennig (eds), ASEAN-UN Cooperation in Preventive Diplomacy, Bangkok: Ministry of Foreign Affairs, 1995, pp. 79–93.

48. The phrase 'comprehensive human rights and freedoms' is a particularly appropriate one because it highlights the need to encompass both individual and collective rights, both civil and political as well as social and economic rights, and to draw upon both Asian and Western traditions in the development of a viable human rights regime. For a useful illustration of this approach see *Towards a New Asia*, A Report for the Commission for a New Asia, Kuala Lumpur, 1994, pp. 21–30. The notion of 'comprehensive human rights and freedoms' is also helpful in that it draws attention to the conceptual and practical connections between human rights and comprehensive security.

49. For an insightful analysis of current trends and future possibilities, see Anwar Ibrahim, *The Asian Renaissance*, Singapore: Times Books International, 1996, pp. 47–60.

50. The case for greater connection between the South Pacific and Asia Pacific is well made by Robert Ayson, 'New Zealand and Asia-Pacific Security: New Rationales for Engagement', *Contemporary Southeast Asia*, 22 (2), August 2000, 389–406.

51. *The Agenda for Cooperative Security in the North Pacific*, Vancouver, 21–24 March 1993, Conference Report July 1993, p. 19.

52. See Jack Barkenbus, 'APEC and the Environment: Civil Society in an Age of Globalization', East–West Center, Asia-Pacific Issues Paper, No. 51, March 2001.

53. For a fuller discussion of the ARF's prospective agenda see Trevor Findlay, 'South-East Asia and the New Asia-Pacific Security Dialogue', in *SIPRI Yearbook 1994*, Stockholm: SIPRI, 1994, pp. 143–5.

54. See Yukio Satoh, *Policy Co-ordination for the Asia-Pacific Security and Stability*, revised version of the paper presented to the Conference on Europe in the Asia-Pacific, Bali, 28–31 May 1996, pp. 8–9.

55. For a range of interpretations of the UNTAC (UN Transitional Authority in Cambodia) experience, see articles by Uch Kiman, Lt General J.M. Sanderson, Ken Berry, Yeshua Moser-Puangsuwan and Kien Serey Phal, in *Pacifica Review: Peace Security and Global Change*, Special Issue: The United Nations after the Cold War, 7 (2), October–November 1995, pp. 61–133; also Michael W. Doyle, *UN PeaceKeeping in Cambodia: UNTAC's Civil Mandate*, Boulder, CO: Lynne Rienner, 1995.

56. See Camilleri, 'The Politics of Reform', in Aksu and Camilleri (eds), *Democratizing Global Governance*, pp. 272–83.

57. See Benjamin Rivlin, 'Regional Arrangements and the UN System for Collective Security and Conflict Resolution: A New Road Ahead', *International Relations*, 11 (2), August 1992, 69–107.

58. The scope and limitations of such collaboration are examined by Wener Pfennig, 'Cambodia: On Lessons of the Past and Prospects for Future ASEAN–UN Cooperation', and Chem Widya, 'Cambodia: Future ASEAN–UN Cooperation', in *ASEAN–UN Co-operation in Preventive Diplomacy*, pp. 175–92.

59.   See Joseph A. Camilleri, 'Human Rights, Cultural Diversity and Conflict Resolution: The Asia-Pacific Context', *Pacifica Review: Peace Security and Global Change*, 6 (2), 1994, 17–41.

60.   For an insightful attempt at such a synthesis, see *Towards a New Asia*, pp. 21–30.

61.   See Faroud Ajami, 'Human Rights and World Order Politics', in R. Falk, S. Kim and S. Mendlovitz (eds), *Towards a Just World Order*, Boulder, CO: Westview Press, 1982, pp. 371–99.

62.   Address given to the UNESCO Conference, Melbourne, 30 March 1998.

63.   The Charter enshrined the principle of the 'universality and indivisibility of rights', made 'sustainable development and protection of the environment' a central plank of its conceptual framework, focused on the rights 'to life', 'to peace', 'to democracy', 'to cultural identity and the freedom of conscience', and 'to development and social justice'. It drew particular attention to the rights of 'vulnerable groups': women, children, differently abled persons, workers, students, prisoners and political detainees. See Asian Human Rights Charter at http://www.ahrchk.net/charter/mainfile.php/eng–charter/77/ (sighted on 14 October 2002).

64.   This was one of the strongest themes running through the recommendations of the Australian parliamentary inquiry into regional dialogue on human rights, *Improving But ... Australia's Regional Dialogue on Human Rights*, Joint Standing Committee on Foreign Affairs, Defence and Trade, Commonwealth of Australia, June 1998, pp. 117–41.

65.   The only such centre in the region established at the University of Malaya produced, under Chandra Muzaffar's intellectual leadership a number of significant publications, including Osman Bakar and Cheng Gek Nai (eds), *Islam and Confucianism; A Civilizational Dialogue*, Kuala Lumpur: University of Malaya Press, 1997; Osman Bakar, *Islam and Civilizational Dialogue: The Quest for a Truly Universal Civilization*, Kuala Lumpur: University of Malaya Press, 1997.

66.   The Fourth Asia–Europe Summit held in Copenhagen on 22–24 September 2002 gave explicit endorsement to the theme of civilizational dialogue, and as a follow-up to the summit, the governments of China, Denmark, France, Indonesia, Malaysia and Singapore undertook as a joint initiative to convene a conference on promoting understanding among cultures and civilizations in ASEM.

67.   See Australian Government, *International Human Rights Policy and Activities 1994–1995*, prepared by the Department of Foreign Affairs and Trade, Canberra, September 1996, p.19.

68.   Of the 12 key human rights instruments: (1) International Covenant on Economic, Social and Cultural Rights (CESCR), (2) International Covenant on Civil and Political Rights (CCPR), (3) Optional Protocol to the International Covenant on Civil and Political Rights (CCPR-OP1), (4) Second Optional Protocol to the International Covenant on Civil and Political Rights, (5) International Convention on the Elimination of All Forms of Racial Discrimination (CERD), (6) Convention on the Elimination of All Forms of Discrimination against Women (CEDAW), (7) Optional Protocol to the Convention on the Elimination of All Forms of Discrimination against Women (CEDAW-OP), (8) Convention against Torture and Other Cruel, Inhuman or Degrading Treatment or Punishment (CAT), (9) Convention on the Rights of the Child (CRC), (10) Optional Protocol to the Convention on the Rights of the Child (CRC-OP-AC), (11) Optional Protocol to the Convention on the Rights of the Child (CRC-OP-SC), (12) International Convention on the Protection of the Rights of All Migrant Workers and Members of Their Families (MWC), as of 21 August 2002, the number ratified + signed for each of the ASEAN+3 countries was as follows: Brunei 1; Cambodia 7 + 2; China 5 + 3; Indonesia 4 + 3; Japan 6 + 2; Laos 3 + 2; Malaysia 2; Myanmar 2; Philippines 8 + 3; Republic of Korea 7 + 2; Singapore 1 + 1; Thailand 5; Vietnam 7. All 13 countries had either ratified or acceded to the 1949 Geneva Conventions, but only six had become parties to the additional 1977 protocols. As of July 2002, when the Rome Statute of the International Criminal Court came into force, four countries (Cambodia, the Philippines, South Korea and Thailand) had signed it, and only one country (Cambodia) had ratified it.

Select bibliography

This bibliography refers mainly to some of the more useful secondary source material available in books, monographs and articles. For primary sources consult the notes for each chapter.

A'la Mawdudi, Abdul, *Human Rights in Islam*, London: Islamic Foundation, 1980.

Abulgani, Roslan, *The Bandung Connection: The Asia–Africa Conference in Bandung in 1955*, translated by Molly Bondan, Jakarta and Singapore: Gunung Agung, 1981.

Acharya, Amitav, 'Regional Military–Security Cooperation in the Third World: A Conceptual Analysis of the Relevance and Limitations of ASEAN (Association of Southeast Asian Nations)', *Journal of Peace Research*, 29 (1), 1992, 7–21.

Acharya, Amitav, 'An Arms Race in Southeast Asia?', in Derek da Cunha (ed), *The Evolving Pacific Power Structure*, Singapore: Institute of Southeast Asian Studies, 1996, pp. 83–8.

Acharya, Amitav, 'The ARF Could Well Unravel', in Derek da Cunha (ed), *The Evolving Pacific Power Structure*, Singapore: Institute of Southeast Asian Studies, 1996, pp. 63–9.

Acharya, Amitav, *Constructing a Security Community in Southeast Asia: ASEAN and the Problem of Regional Order*, London: Routledge, 2001.

Acharya, Amitav and Richard Stubbs (eds), *New Challenges for ASEAN: Emerging Policy Issues*, Vancouver: University of British Columbia Press, 1995.

Adlan, Noor, 'APEC and Asia's Crisis', *Far Eastern Economic Review*, 28 May 1998, 35.

Adler, Emanel and Michael N. Barnett, 'Governing Anarchy: A Research Agenda for the Study of Security Communities', *Ethics and International Affairs*, 10, 1996, 63–98.

Aggarwal, Vinod K., 'Building International Institutions in Asia Pacific', *Asian Survey*, 33 (11), November 1993, 1029–42.

Aggarwal, Vinod K. and Charles E. Morrison (eds), *Asia-Pacific Crossroads: Regime Creation and the Future of APEC*, New York: St. Martin's Press, 1998.

Ahluwalia, Pal and Peter Mayer, 'Clash of Civilizations or Balderdash of Scholars?', *Asian Studies Review*, 18 (1), 1994, 186–93.

Ajami, Faroud 'The Summoning', *Foreign Affairs*, 72 (4), 1993, 2–9.

Akaha, Tsuneo and Frank Langdon (eds), *Japan in the Posthegemonic World*, Boulder, CO: Lynne Rienner, 1993.

Akao, N., 'Strategy for APEC: A Japanese View', *Japan Review of International Affairs*, Special Issue on APEC and Regional Perspectives, 9 (3), Summer 1995, 169–77.

Akamatsu, Kaname, 'A Historical Pattern of Economic Growth in Developing Countries', *The Developing Economies*, 1, March–April 1962, 3–25.

Alagappa, Muthiah, 'US–ASEAN Security Relations: Challenges and Prospects', *Contemporary Southeast Asia*, 11 (1), June 1989, 1–37.

Alagappa, Muthiah, 'Regional Arrangements and International Security in Southeast Asia: Going Beyond ZOPFAN', *Contemporary Southeast Asia*, 12 (4), March 1991, 269–305.

Alagappa, Muthiah, 'Regionalism and the Quest for Security: ASEAN and the Cambodian Conflict', *Australian Journal of International Affairs*, 46 (2), Winter 1993, 439–68.

Albert, Michel, *Capitalism against Capitalism* (trans. Paul Haviland), London: Whurr, 1993.

Albright, M., 'Building a framework for American leadership in the 21st century', *US Department of State Dispatch*, 8 (2), February 1997, 1–9.

Angle, Stephen, C. *Human Rights and Chinese Thought: A Cross-Cultural Inquiry*, Cambridge: Cambridge University Press, 2002.

Antolik, M., *ASEAN and the Diplomacy of Accommodation*, London: M.E. Sharpe, 1990.

Anwar, Dewi, Fortuna, 'Twenty Five Years of ASEAN Political Cooperation', in Hadi Soesastro (ed), *ASEAN in a Changed Regional and International Political Economy*, Jakarta: CSIS, 1995, pp. 108–28.

Anwar, Ibrahim, *The Asian Renaissance*, Singapore: Times Books International, 1996.

Anwar, Ibrahim, 'Globalisation and the Cultural Re-Empowerment of Asia', in Joseph A. Camilleri and Chandra Muzaffar (eds), *Globalisation: The Perspectives and Experiences of the Religious Traditions of Asia Pacific*, Kuala Lumpur: JUST, 1998, pp. 1–4.

APCS Forum Secretariat, *Proceedings of Asia Pacific Civil Society Forum*, Seoul, 11–14 August 1995.

Aranal-Sereno, M. and Santiago, J. (eds), *The ASEAN: Thirty Years and Beyond*, Quezon City: Institute of International Legal Studies, University of the Philippines Law Center, Philippines, 1997.

Arase, David, 'Pacific Economic Cooperation: Problems and Prospects', *Pacific Review*, 1 (2), 1988, 128–44.

Asada, M., 'Confidence Building Measures in East Asia: A Japanese Perspective', *Asian Survey*, 28 (5), May 1988, 489–508.

ASEAN Secretariat, *ASEAN Economic Co-operation: Transition and Transformation*, Singapore: Institute of Southeast Asian Studies, 1997.

Asia Pacific Foundation, 'Asian Regionalism, Asia-Pacific Bilateralism and Canada', *Canada –Asia Commentary*, 17, December 2000, 1–5.

Asia Pacific Foundation, 'APEC After Shanghai', *Canada–Asia Commentary*, 21, November 2001, 1–5.

Askandar, Kamarulzaman, 'ASEAN and Conflict Management: The Formative Years of 1967–1976', *Pacifica Review: Peace, Security and Global Change*, 6 (2), 1994, 57–69.

Azizian, Rouben, 'The APEC Summit: From Acceleration to Consolidation', *New Zealand International Review*, 24 (6), November–December 1999, 2–5.

Bailey, Peter, *Human Rights: Australia in an International Context*, Sydney: Butterworths, 1990.

Bakar, Osman and Cheng Gek Nai (eds), *Islam and Confucianism: A Civilizational Dialogue*, Kuala Lumpur: University of Malaya Press, 1997.

Baker, J., 'International Conference on Cambodia held in Paris', *Department of State Bulletin*, (89) 2151, October 1989, 25–7.

Baker, James A. III 'America in Asia: Emerging Architecture for a Pacific Community', *Foreign Affairs*, 70 (1), Winter 1991–92, 1–18.

Balassa, Bela, 'The Lessons of East Asian Development: An Overview', *Economic Development and Cultural Change*, 36 (3), Supplement, 1988, S273–90.

Ball, Desmond, 'Arms and Influence', *International Security*, 18, Winter 1993/ 1994, 88.

Ball, Desmond, 'A New Era in Confidence Building: The Second-track Process in the Asia/Pacific Region', *Security Dialogue*, 25 (2), June 1994, 157–76.

Ball, Desmond, 'CSCAP: Its Future Place in the Regional Security Architecture', Canberra: Australian National University, Strategic and Defence Studies Centre, June 1994.

Ball, Desmond, 'Strategic Culture in the Asia-Pacific Region', *Security Studies*, 3 (1), Autumn 1994, 44–74.

Ball, Desmond, *The Council for Security Cooperation in the Asia Pacific (CSCAP): Its Record and Its Prospects*, Canberra: Strategic and Defence Studies Centre, Australian National University, 2000.

Ball, W. Macmahon, *Japan: Enemy or Ally?*, New York: John Day, 1949.

Barkenbus, Jack, *APEC and the Environment: Civil Society in an Age of Globalization*, East–West Center Paper, No. 51, March 2001.

Bateman, Sam (ed), *Maritime Cooperation in the Asia-Pacific Region: Current Situation and Prospects*, Canberra Papers on Strategy and Defence No. 132, Canberra: Strategic and Defence Studies Centre, Australian National University, 1999.

Bateman, Sam, 'CSCAP Maritime Cooperation Working Group', *AUS–CSCAP Newsletter*, No. 12, November 2001, 33–4.

Bateman, Sam and Stephen Bates (eds), *The Seas Unite: Initiatives for Asia Pacific Maritime Cooperation*, Canberra Papers on Strategy and Defence No. 118, Canberra: Strategic and Defence Studies Centre, Australian National University, 1996.

Bateman, Sam and Stephen Bates, (eds), *Calming the Waters: Initiatives for Asia Pacific Maritime Cooperation*, Canberra Papers on Strategy and Defence No. 114, Canberra: Strategic and Defence Studies Centre, Australian National University, 1996.

Bateman, Sam and Stephen Bates (eds), *Regional Maritime Management and Security*, Canberra Papers on Strategy and Defence No. 124, Canberra: Strategic and Defence Studies Centre, Australian National University, 1998.

Bateman, Sam and Stephen Bates (eds), *Shipping and Regional Security*, Canberra Papers on Strategy and Defence No. 129, Canberra: Strategic and Defence Studies Centre, Australian National University, 1998.

Bauer, Joanne, R. and Daniel A. Bell, *The East Asian Challenge for Human Rights*, Cambridge: Cambridge University Press, 1999.

Beeson, Mark, 'Reshaping Regional Institutions: APEC and the IMF in East Asia', *Pacific Review*, 12 (1), 1999, 1–24.

Beeson, Mark and Kanishka Jayasuriya, 'The Political Rationalities of Regionalism: APEC and the EU in Comparative Perspective', *Pacific Review*, 11 (3), 1998, 311–36.

Behera, Navnita Chadha, Paul Evans and Gowher Rizvi, *Beyond Boundaries: A Report on the State of Non-Official Dialogues on Peace, Security and Cooperation in South Asia*, Toronto: University of Toronto–York University Joint Centre for Asia Pacific Studies, 1997.

Bell, R., T. McDonald and A. Tidwell (eds), *Negotiating the Pacific Century: The 'New' Asia, the United States and Australia*, Sydney: Allen & Unwin, 1996.

Benedict, Ruth, *Patterns of Culture*, London: Routledge, 1935.

Berger, Mark T., 'A New East–West Synthesis? APEC and Competing Narratives of Regional Integration in the Post-Cold War Asia-Pacific', *Alternatives*, 23 (1), 1998, 1–28.

Bergsten, C. Fred (ed), *Whither APEC? The Process to Date and Agenda for the Future*, Washington, DC: Institute for International Economics, 1997.

Bergsten, C. Fred, 'Towards a Tripartite World', *The Economist*, 15 July 2000, 20–22.

Bergsten, C. Fred, *The New Asian Challenge*, Washington, DC: Institute for International Economics, 2000, Working Paper 00/4.

Bergsten, C. Fred and Marcus Noland (eds), *Pacific Dynamism and the International Economic System*, Washington, DC: Institute for International Economics, 1993.

Bessho, Koro, *Identities and Securities in East Asia*, Adelphi Paper 325, London: International Institute for Strategic Studies, 1999.

Blank, S., 'The New Russia in the New Asia', *International Journal*, XLIX (4), Autumn 1994, 874–907.

Bodde Jr, William, *View from the 19th Floor: Reflections of the First APEC Executive Director*, Singapore: Institute of Southeast Asian Studies, 1994.

Bora, B. and C. Findlay (eds), *Regional Integration and the Asia-Pacific*, Melbourne: Oxford University Press, 1996.

Borthwick, Mark, *The Pacific Century: The Emergence of Modern Pacific Asia*, Boulder, CO: Westview Press, 1992.

Bowles, P., 'ASEAN, AFTA and the "New Regionalism"', *Pacific Affairs*, 70 (2), Summer 1997, 219–34.

Boyd, Gavin, 'Pacific Community Building', in Gavin Boyd (ed), *Regionalism and Global Security*, New York: Pergamon, 1984.

Boyd, G. (ed), *Regionalism and Global Security*, New York: Pergamon, 1984.

Bracken, P., 'Maritime Peacekeeping in Northeast Asia', *Journal of East Asian Affairs*, 12 (2), Summer/Fall 1998, 577–98.

Bridges, Brian, *Europe and the Challenge of the Asia Pacific: Change, Continutiy and Crisis*, MA: Edward Elgar, 1999.

Bridges, Brian, 'Europe and the Asian Financial Crisis: Coping with Contagion', *Asian Survey*, XXXIX (3), May/June 1999, 461–2.

Brohi, Allabbukhsh K., 'Human Rights and Duties in Islam: A Philosophic Approach', in Salim Azzam (ed), *Islam and Contemporary Society*, London: Longman, 1982, pp. 231–52.

Bronowski, Alison (ed), *Understanding ASEAN*, New York: St. Martin's Press in association with the Australian Institute of International Affairs, 1982.

Bundy, B., S. Burns and K. Weichel (eds), *The Future of the Pacific Rim: Scenarios for Regional Cooperation*, Westport, CT: Praeger, 1994.

Buszynsky, Leszek, 'Declining Superpowers: The Impact on ASEAN', *Pacific Review*, 3 (3), 1990, 257–61.

Buszynsky, Leszek, 'ASEAN Security Dilemmas', *Survival*, 34 (4), Winter 1992–93, pp. 90–107.

Buszynsky, Leszek 'ASEAN's New Challenges', *Pacific Affairs*, 70 (4), Winter 1997–98, 555–77.

Byung-joon, Ahn, 'Regionalism in the Asia-Pacific: Asian or Pacific Community?', *Korea Focus*, 4 (4), July–August 1996, 5–23.

Caballero-Anthony, Mely, 'Mechanisms of Dispute Settlement: The ASEAN Experience', *Contemporary Southeast Asia*, 20 (1), April 1998, 38–65.

Cai, Kevin G., 'Is a Free Trade Zone Emerging in Northeast Asia in the Wake of the Asian Financial Crisis?', *Pacific Affairs*, 74 (1), Spring 2001, 6–46.

Camilleri, Joseph A., 'The Cold War', in Max Teichmann (ed), *Power and Policies: Alignment and Realignments in the Indo-Pacific Region*, Melbourne: Cassell Australia, 1970, pp. 16–24.

Camilleri, Joseph A., *The Australia–New Zealand–US Alliance: Regional Security in the Nuclear Age*, Seattle, WA: University of Washington Press, 1987.

Camilleri, Joseph A., 'Alliances in the Emerging Post-Cold War Security System', in Richard Leaver and James L. Richardson (eds), *Charting the Post-Cold War Order*, Boulder, CO: Westview Press, 1993, pp. 81–94.

Camilleri, Joseph A., 'Human Rights, Cultural Diversity, and Conflict Resolution: The Asia–Pacific Context', *Pacifica Review: Peace, Security and Global Change*, 6 (2), 1994, 17–41.

Camilleri, Joseph A., 'Asia-Pacific in the Post-Hegemonic World', in Andrew Mack and John Ravenhill (eds), *Pacific Cooperation: Building Economic and Security Regimes in the Asia-Pacific Region*, Boulder, CO: Westview Press, 1995, pp. 180–208.

Camilleri, Joseph A., 'Regional Human Rights Dialogue in Asia Pacific: Prospects and Proposals', *Pacifica Review: Peace, Security and Global Change*, 10 (3), October 1998, 167–85.

Camilleri, Joseph A., *States, Markets and Civil Society in Asia Pacific: The Political Economy of the Asia-Pacific Region,* Vol. 1, Cheltenham, UK: Edward Elgar, 2000.

Camilleri, Joseph A., 'Globalization of Insecurity: The Democratic Imperative', *International Journal of World Peace*, XVIII (4), December 2001, 3–36.

Camilleri Joseph A. and J. Falk, *The End of Sovereignty? The Politics of a Shrinking and Fragmenting World*, Aldershot, UK: Edward Elgar, 1992.

Camilleri, J. and Chandra Muzaffar (eds), *Globalisation: The Perspectives and Experiences of the Religious Traditions of Asia Pacific*, Kuala Lumpur: JUST, 1998.

Camroux, David, 'The Asia-Pacific Policy Community in Malaysia', *Pacific Review*, 7 (4), 421–33.

Cantori, Louis J. and Steven L. Spiegel (eds), *The International Politics of Regions: A Comparative Approach*, Englewood Cliffs, NJ: Prentice-Hall, 1970.

Capie, David and Paul Evans, *The Asia-Pacific Security Lexicon*, Singapore: Institute of Southeast Asian Studies, 2002.

Castells, M., 'Four Asian Tigers with a Dragon Head: A Comparative Analysis of the State, Economy and Society in the Asian Pacific Rim', in R. Appelbaum and J. Henderson (eds), *States and Development in the Asian Pacific Rim*, Newbury Park, CA: Sage, 1992, pp. 27–32.

Cerny, Philip G., 'Globalization and the Changing Logic of Collective Action', *International Organization*, 49 (4), Autumn 1995, 595–625.

Chan, G., '"Three Chinas" and International Organizations after 1997', *Journal of Contemporary China*, 6 (16), November 1998, 435–48.

Chang, King-yuh, 'Building the Pacific Community: An Incrementalist Approach', *Korea and World Affairs*, 7, Summer 1983, 218–26.

Chatterjee, Margaret, *Gandhi's Religious Thought*, London: Macmillan, 1983.

Chatterjee, Srikanta, 'ASEAN Economic Co-operation in the 1980s and 1990s', in Alison Bronowski (ed), *ASEAN into the 1990s*, London: Macmillan, 1990, pp. 58–82.

Chee, Stephen (ed), *Leadership and Security in Southeast Asia*, Singapore: Institute of Southeast Asian Studies, 1991.

Cheeseman, Graeme, 'Asian-Pacific Security Discourse in the Wake of the Asian Economic Crisis', *Pacific Review*, 12 (3), 1999, 333–56.

Chen, Edward and C.H. Kwan (eds), *Asia's Borderless Economy: The Emergence of Sub-Regional Zones*, Sydney: Allen & Unwin, 1997.

Cheng, Joseph Y.S., 'China's ASEAN Policy in the 1990s: Pushing for Regional Multipolarity', *Contemporary Southeast Asia*, 21 (2), August 1999, 175–203.

Cheng, Joseph Y.S., 'Sino–ASEAN Relations in the Twenty-First Century', *Contemporary Southeast Asia*, 23 (3), December 2001, 420–51.

Chia Siow Yue (ed), *APEC Challenges and Opportunities*, Singapore: Institute of Southeast Asian Studies, 1994.

Chiu, H., 'Exploration and Exploitation of Ocean Reserves in the Western Pacific: The Legal and Political Implications for Regional Cooperation and Joint Prosperity', *Korean Journal of International Studies*, 15 (1), Winter 1983–84, 17–37.

Choy, Chong Li, *Open Self-Reliant Regionalism: Power for ASEAN's Development*, Singapore: Institute of Southeast Asian Studies, 1981.

Christensen, T., 'China, the U.S.–Japan Alliance, and the Security Dilemma in East Asia', *International Security*, 23 (4), Spring 1999, 49–80.

Christopher, W., 'Developing APEC as a Platform for Prosperity', *US Department of State Dispatch*, 4 (48), 29 November, 1993, 823–4.

Christopher, W., 'Transforming the APEC Vision into Reality', *US Department of State Dispatch,* Supplement, 5 (9), November 1994, 3–5.

Clad, J., 'Regionalism in Asia: A Bridge Too Far?', *Southeast Asian Affairs 1997*, Institute of Southeast Asian Studies, Singapore, 1997, pp. 3–14.

Clark, Cal and Steve Chan (eds), *The Evolving Pacific Basin in the Global Political Economy: Domestic and International Linkages*, Boulder, CO: Lynne Rienner, 1992.

Clinton, W., 'Building a New Pacific Community', *US Department of State Dispatch*, 4 (28), 12 July 1993, 485–8.

Clinton, W., 'Fundamentals of Security for a New Pacific Community', *US Department of State Dispatch*, 4 (29), 19 July 1993, 509–12.

Collins, Alan, 'Mitigating the Security Dilemma the ASEAN Way', *Pacifica Review: Peace, Security and Global Change*, 11 (2), June 1999, 95–114.

Collins, Alan, *The Security Dilemmas of Southeast Asia*, Singapore: Macmillan in association with Institute of Southeast Asian Studies, 2000.

Cossa, Ralph, A., 'Multilateral Dialogue in Asia: Benefits and Limitations', *Korea and World Affairs*, 19 (1), Spring 1995, 106–20.

Cossa, Ralph, A. (ed), *Asia Pacific Confidence and Security Building Measures*, Washington, DC: Center for Strategic and International Studies, 1995.

Cossa, Ralph, A., 'Track II and Northeast Asia', National Bureau of Asian Research Conference on National Strategies in the Asia Pacific: The Effects of Interacting Trade, Industrial and Defence Policies, Monterey, CA, 28–29 March 1996.

Cossa, Ralph and Akiko Fukushima, 'Security Multilateralism in Asia: Views from the United States and Japan', An IGCC Study Commissioned for the Northeast Asia Cooperation Dialogue VIII, Moscow, 11–12 November 1998.

Cossa, R. and J. Khanna, 'East Asia: Economic Interdependence and Regional Security', *International Affairs*, 73 (2), 1997, 219–34.

Cotton, James, 'The North Korea/United States Nuclear Accord: Background and Consequences', *Korea Observer*, 26 (3), Autumn 1995, 321–44.

Cotton, James, 'ASEAN and the Southeast Asian "Haze": The Prevailing Modes of Regional Engagement', Canberra: Australian National University, Department of International Relations, Working Paper No. 1999/3, 1999.

Cox, Michael, 'From the Truman Doctrine to the Second Seapower Détente: The Rise and Fall of the Cold War', *Journal of Peace Research*, 27 (1), 1990, 25–42.

Cox, R.W., 'Social Forces, States and World Orders: Beyond International Relations Theory', *Millennium Journal of International Studies*, 10 (2), Summer 1981, 126–55.

Cox, R.W., *Production, Power and World Order: Social Forces in the Making of History*, New York: Columbia University Press, 1987.

Cox, Robert W., 'Multilateralism and World Order', *Review of International Studies*, 18, 1992, 161–80.

Crawford, B., 'The New Security Dilemma under International Economic Interdependence', *Millennium*, 23 (1), 1994, 25–55.

Crawford, Sir John, *'The Pacific Basin Cooperative Concept'*, Australia–Japan Economic Relations Research Project, Research Paper No. 70, August 1980.

Crawford, Sir John and Saburo Okita (eds), *Raw Materials and Pacific Economic Integration*, Canberra: Australian National University Press, 1978.

Crone, D., 'The Politics of Emerging Pacific Cooperation', *Pacific Affairs*, 65 (1), Spring 1992, 68–83.

Crone, D., 'Does Hegemony Matter? The Reorganisation of the Pacific Political Economy', *World Politics*, 45 (4), July 1993, 501–25.

Cronin, P., 'Does Multilateralism Have a Future in Asia?', in R. Cossa (ed), *The New Pacific Security Environment: Challenges and Opportunities: The 1992 Symposium*, Washington, DC: National Defense University, 1993.

de Bary, William Theodore, *Asian Values and Human Rights*, Cambridge, MA: Harvard University Press, 1998.

Denoon, D.B.H. and E. Colbert, 'Challenges for the Association of Southeast Asian Nations (ASEAN)', *Pacific Affairs*, 71 (4), Winter 1998, 505–23.

Dent, Christopher M., 'The ASEM: Managing the New Framework of the EU's Economic Relations with East Asia', *Pacific Affairs*, 70 (4), Winter 1997/1998, 495–516.

Dent, Christopher M., 'ASEM and the "Cinderella Complex" of EU–East Asia Economic Relations', *Pacific Affairs*, 74 (1), Spring 2001, 25–52.

Dernberger, R., 'Economic Cooperation in the Asia-Pacific Region and the Role of the P.R.C.', *Journal of Northeast Asian Studies*, 7, Spring 1988, 3–21.

Deutsch, Karl W., et al., *Political Community and the North Atlantic Area*, Princeton, NJ: Princeton University Press, 1957.

Dibb, P., *The Emerging Strategic Architecture in the Asia-Pacific Region*, Centre for Strategic Studies, Canberra: Australian National University Press, 1996.

Dickens, D. (ed), *No Better Alternative: Towards Comprehensive and Cooperative Security in the Asia-Pacific*, Wellington: CSCAP/CSS, New Zealand, 1997.

Dirlik, Arif, *What is in a Rim? Critical Perspectives on the Pacific Region Idea*, 2nd edn, Boulder, CO: Westview Press, 1998.

Djisman, S. Simandjuntak, 'Regionalism and Its Implications for the Asia Pacific', *Economic Review*, American Economic Association, Papers and Proceedings, 82 (2), May 1992, 79–83.

Djiwandono, J. Soedjati, 'ASEAN Regionalism and the Role of USA', *Indonesian Quarterly*, 12 (1), January 1984, 62–72.

Djiwandono, J. Soedjati, 'Indonesia and the Asia-Pacific Region in the 1990s: Prospects for Regional Co-operation', *Indonesian Quarterly*, 15 (2), April 1987, 243–51.

Djiwandono, J. Soedjati, 'ZOPFAN: Is It Still Relevant?', *Indonesian Quarterly*, XIX (2), Second Quarter 1991, 115–30.

Djiwandono, J. Soedjati, 'Defence Cooperation Between Member-States of ASEAN', *Indonesian Quarterly*, 24 (4), 1996, 339–51.

Dokken, Karin, 'Environment, Security and Regionalism in the Asia-Pacific: Is Environmental Security a Useful Concept?', *Pacific Review*, 14 (4), 2001, 509–30.

Donowaki, Mitsuro, 'The Pacific Basin Community', in Hadi Soesastro and Han Sung-joo (eds), *Pacific Economic Co-operation: The Next Phase*, Jakarta: Centre for Strategic and International Studies, 1983.

Dorian, J., D. Fridley and K. Tresser, 'Multilateral Resource Cooperation Among Northeast Asian Countries: Energy and Mineral Joint Venture Prospects', *Journal of Northeast Asian Studies*, 12 (1), Spring 1993, 3–34.

Douglas, S. and S. Douglas, 'Economic Implications of the U.S.–ASEAN Discourse on Human Rights', *Pacific Affairs*, 69 (1), Spring 1996, 71–87.

Downer, Robert L. and Bruce J. Dickson (eds), *The Emerging Pacific Community: A Regional Perspective*, Boulder, CO: Westview Press, 1984.

Drysdale, Peter, 'The Proposal for an Organization for Pacific Trade and Development Revisited', *Asian Survey*, XXIII (12), December 1983, 1293–303.

Drysdale, Peter, 'The Pacific Trade and Development Conference: A Brief History', Australia–Japan Research Centre, Paper No. 112, Canberra: Australian National University, Research School of Pacific Studies, June 1984.

Drysdale, Peter, *International Economic Pluralism: Economic Policy in East Asia and the Pacific*, Sydney: Allen & Unwin in association with the Australia–Japan Research Centre, Australian National University, 1988.

Drysdale, P. and H. Patrick, *An Asian-Pacific Regional Economic Organization: An Exploratory Concept Paper*, Washington, DC: Washington Library of Congress, Congressional Research Service, 1979.

Dua, André and Daniel C. Esty, *Sustaining the Asia Pacific Miracle: Environmental and Economic Integration*, Washington, DC: Institute for International Economics, 1997.

Duffy, Charles A. and Werner J. Field, 'Whither Regional Integration Theory?', in Werner J. Field and Gavin Boyd (eds), *Comparative Regional Systems*, New York: Pergamon Press, 1980, pp. 497–522.

Dupont, Alan, 'Is there an Asian Way', *Survival*, 38 (2), Summer 1996, pp. 13–34.

Dupont, Alan, *East Asia Imperilled: Transnational Challenges to Security*, Cambridge: Cambridge University Press, 2001.

Dutt, N., 'The United States and the Asian Development Bank', *Journal of Contemporary Asia*, 27 (1), 1997, 71–84.

East Asia Analytical Unit, *Growth Triangles of South East Asia*, Canberra: Department of Foreign Affairs and Trade, 1995.

Eldridge, Philip, *The Politics of Human Rights in Southeast Asia*, London: Routledge, 2002.

Elek, Andrew, *From Osaka to Subic: APEC's Challenges for 1996*, Pacific Economic Paper No. 255, Australia–Japan Research Centre, Canberra, April 1996.

Elek, Andrew (ed), *Building an Asia-Pacific Community. Development Cooperation within APEC*, Brisbane: Foundation for Development Cooperation, 1997.

Elliott, Lorraine, 'Environmental Challenges', in Daljit Singh and Anthony Smith (eds), *Southeast Asian Affairs 2001*, Singapore: Institute of Southeast Asian Studies, 2001, pp. 68–81.

Embong, Abdul Rahman and Jürgen Rudolph (eds), *Southeast Asia into the Twenty First Century: Crisis and Beyond*, Bangi: Penerbit Universiti Kebangsaan Malaysia, 2000.

Emmers, Ralf, 'The Influence of the Balance of Power Factor within the ASEAN Regional Forum', *Contemporary Southeast Asia*, 23 (2), August 2001, 275–91.

Emmerson, D., 'ASEAN as an International Regime', *Journal of International Affairs*, 41 (1), Fall 1987, 1–16.

Etzioni, Amitai, *Political Unification*, New York: Holt, Rinehart & Winston, 1965.

Evans, Paul, 'The Prospects for Multilateral Security Co-operation in the Asia/Pacific Region', *Journal of Strategic Studies*, 18 (3), September 1995, 202–17.

Fairbank, John K. (ed), *The Chinese World Order: Traditional China's Foreign Relations*, Cambridge, MA: Harvard University Press, 1968.

Feinberg R. and Y. Zhao (eds), *Assessing APEC's Progresss: Trade, Ecotech and Institutions,* Singapore: Institute of Southeast Asian Studies, 2001.

Fesharaki, Fereidun, 'Energy and the Asian Security Nexus', *Journal of International Affairs*, 53 (1), Fall 1999, 85–99.

Fifield, Russell H., *National and Regional Interest in ASEAN*, Singapore: Institute of Southeast Asian Studies, Occasional Paper No. 57, 1979.

Fischer, Louis (ed), *The Essential Gandhi: His Life, Work and Ideas*, New York: Vintage Books, 1983.

Fitzgerald, L.P., *The Justice God Wants: Islam and Human Rights*, Melbourne: Collins Dove, 1993.

Flamm, Kenneth and Edward Lincoln, 'Time to Reinvent APEC', *Brookings Policy Brief Series*, 26, November 1997.

Fox, Russell Arben, 'Confucianal and Communitarian Responses to Liberal Democracy', *The Review of Politics*, Special Issue on Non-Western Political Thought, 59 (3), Summer 1997, 561–92.

Frankel, J., *APEC and Regional Trading Arrangements in the Pacific*, Working Paper No. 94-1, Washington, DC: Institute for International Economics, 1994.

Frankel, J. and M. Kahler (eds), *Regionalism and Rivalry: Japan and the US in Pacific Asia*, Chicago: University of Chicago Press, 1993.

Frost, F., 'The Peace Process in Cambodia: Issues and Prospects', Australia–Asia Papers No. 69, CSAAR, Griffith University, 1993.

Fukui, H. and S. Fukai, 'The Role of the United States in Post-Cold War East Asian Security Affairs', *Journal of Asian and African Studies*, 33 (1), 1998, 114–33.

Fukushima, Akiko, 'Japan's Emerging View of Security Multilateralism in Asia', in IGCC Study commissioned for the Northeast Asia Cooperation Dialogue VIII, Moscow, 11–12 November 1998.

Fukuyama, Francis, 'Asian Values and the Asian Crisis', *Commentary*, 105 (2), February 1998, 23–8.

Funabashi, Yoichi, 'The Asianization of Asia', *Foreign Affairs*, 72 (5), Winter 1992, 75–85.

Funabashi, Yoichi, *Asia Pacific Fusion: Japan's Role in APEC*, Washington, DC: Institute for International Economics, 1995.

Funston, John, 'ASEAN: Out of its Depth?', *Contemporary Southeast Asia*, 20 (1), April 1998, 22–37.

Funston, John, 'Challenges facing ASEAN', *Contemporary Southeast Asia*, 21 (2), August 1999, 205–19.

Gallant, Nicole and Richard Stubbs, 'APEC's Dilemmas: Institution-Building around the Pacific Rim', *Pacific Affairs*, 70 (2), Summer 1997, 203–18.

Galtung, Johan, 'International Development in Human Perspective', in John W. Burton (ed), *Conflict: Human Needs Theory*, London: Macmillan, 1990, pp. 247–64.

Gamble, Andrew and Anthony Payne, 'Conclusion: The New Regionalism', in Andrew Gamble and Anthony Payne (eds), *Regionalism and World Order*, London: Macmillan, 1996.

Gandhi, *The Collected Works of Mahatma Gandhi*, Delhi: Publications Division, Ministry of Information and Broadcasting, Government of India, 1963, IX.

Ganesan, N., 'ASEAN's Relations with Major External Powers', *Contemporary South East Asia*, 22 (2), August 2000, 258–78.

Gangopadhyay, Parthay, 'Patterns of Trade, Investment and Migration in the Asia-Pacific Region', in G. Thompson (ed), *Economic Dynamism in the Asia-Pacific: The Growth of Integration and Competitiveness*, London: Routledge in association with the Open University, 1998, pp. 20–54.

Gangwu, Wang, *China and the Chinese Overseas*, Singapore: Times Academic Press, 1991.

Garofano, John, 'Flexibility or Irrelevance: Way Forward for the ARF', *Contemporary Southeast Asia*, 21 (1), April 1999, 74–94.

Garrett, Banning and Bonnie Glaser, 'Multilateral Security in the Asia-Pacific Region and its Impact on Chinese Interests: A View from Beijing', *Contemporary Southeast Asia*, 16 (1), June 1994, 14–34.

Gelman, H., 'Gorbachev's Policies in East Asia after Two Years', *Journal of Northeast Asian Studies*, Spring 1988, 46–54.

Gibb, Richard, 'Regionalism in the World Economy', in Richard Gibb and Wieslaw Michalak, *Continental Trading Blocs: The Growth of Regionalism in the World Economy*, Chichester: John Wiley & Sons, 1994, pp. 1–36.

Gill, B., 'North-East Asia and Multilateral Security Institutions', *SIPRI Yearbook 1994*, Stockholm: Stockholm International Peace Research Institute, 1994.

Gilpin, Robert G., 'APEC in a New International Order', in Donald C. Hellman and Kenneth B. Pyle (eds), *From APEC to Xanadu: Creating a Viable Community in the Post-Cold War Pacific*, Armonk, NY: M.E. Sharpe, 1997, pp. 14–36.

Godement, François, *The New Asian Renaissance*, London and New York: Routledge, 1997.

Gold, Thomas, B., 'The Resurgence of Civil Society in China', *Journal of Democracy*, 1 (1), Winter 1990, 18–31.

Graham, N., 'China and the Future of Security Cooperation and Conflict in Asia', *Journal of Asian and African Studies,* 33 (1), 1998, 94–113.

Grant, Richard L., 'Security Cooperation in the Asia-Pacific Region: An Introduction', in Desmond Ball et al., *Security Cooperation in the Asia-Pacific Region,* Honolulu: Pacific Forum/CSIS, 1993, pp. 1–7.

Haacke, Jürgen, 'China's Participation in Multilateral Pacific Cooperation Forums', *AUSSENPOLITIK,* 48 (2), 1997, 166–76.

Haacke, Jürgen, 'The Concept of Flexible Engagement and the Practice of Enhanced Interaction: Intramural Challenges to the "ASEAN Way"', *Pacific Review,* 12 (4), 1999, 589–91.

Haas, Ernest, 'The Challenge of Regionalism', *International Organization,* 12 (4), Autumn 1958, 440–58.

Haas, Ernest, *The Obsolescence of Regional Integration Theory,* Berkeley, CA: Institute of International Studies, University of California, Research Series No. 25, 1975.Haas, Ernest, *The Obsolescence of Regional Integration Theory,* Berkeley, CA: Institute of International Studies, University of California, Research Series No. 25, 1975.

Haas, Michael, 'International Subsystems: Stability and Polarity', *American Political Science Review,* 64 (1), 1970, 98–123.

Haas, Michael, *The Asian Way to Peace: A Study of Regional Cooperation,* New York: Praeger, 1989.

Haas, Michael, *The Pacific Way: Regional Cooperation in the South Pacific,* New York: Praeger, 1989.

Haas, Michael, 'Asian Culture and International Relations', in Yongsuk Chay (ed), *Culture and International Relations,* New York: Praeger, 1990.

Haas, P.M., 'Obtaining International Environmental Protection through Epistemic Consensus', *Millennium Journal of International Studies,* 19, 1990, 347–63.

Halliday, Fred, *The Making of the Second Cold War,* London: Verso, 1983.

Hamada, Koichi, 'From the AMF to the Miyazawa Initiative: Observations on Japan's Currency Diplomacy', *Journal of East Asian Affairs,* 13 (1), Spring/Summer 1999, 33–50.

Hamel-Green, Michael, 'Alternative Security Approaches in the South Pacific, *Pacifica Review: Peace, Security and Global Change,* 9 (2), November/December 1997, 19–38.

Hamilton, G. (ed), *Business Networks and Economic Development in East and Southeast Asia,* Hong Kong: Centre of Asian Studies, University of Hong Kong, 1991.

Hamzah, B.A., 'ASEAN and the Remilitarization of Japan: Challenges or Opportunities?', *Indonesian Quarterly,* XIX (2), Second Quarter 1991, 141–68.

Harding, Harry, *A Fragile Relationship: The United States and China since 1972,* Washington, DC: Brookings Institution, 1992.

Harding, Harry, *China at the Crossroads: Conservatism, Reform or Decay*, Adelphi Paper, 275, March 1993.

Harding, H., 'Prospects for Cooperative Security Arrangements in the Asia-Pacific Region', *Journal of Northeast Asian Studies*, Fall 1994, 31–41.

Hariato, Farid, *Oriental Capitalism*, Toronto: Centre for International Studies, University of Toronto, 1993.

Harland, B., *Collision Course: America and East Asia in the Past and the Future*, Singapore: Institute of Southeast Asian Studies, 1996.

Harris, Stuart, 'Varieties of Economic Cooperation', *Pacific Review*, 4 (4), 1991, 301–11.

Harris, Stuart, *Concepts and Objectives of Pacific Economic Cooperation*, Pacific Economic Paper No. 213, Australia–Japan Research Centre, Australian National University, Research School of Pacific Studies, November 1992.

Harris, Stuart, 'Policy Networks and Economic Cooperation: Policy Coordination in the Asia-Pacific Region', *Pacific Review*, 7 (4), 1994, 380–95.

Harris, Stuart, 'The Economic Aspects of Security in the Asia/Pacific Region', *The Journal of Strategic Studies*, 18 (3), September 1995, 32–51.

Harris, Stuart, 'Asian Multilateral Institutions and their Response to the Asian Economic Crisis', *Pacific Review*, 13 (3), 2000, 495–516.

Harris, Stuart, 'China and the Pursuit of State Interests in a Globalising World', *Pacifica Review: Peace, Security and Global Change*, 13 (1), 2001, 15–30.

Harrison, Selig S., *Japan's Nuclear Future: The Plutonium Debate and East Asian Security*, Washington, DC: Carnegie Endowment for International Peace, 1996.

Hart-Landsberg, M. and P. Burkett, 'Contradictions of Capitalist Industralization in East Asia: A Critique of "Flying Geese" Theories of Development', *Economic Geography*, 74 (2), April 1998, 87–110.

Hatch, Walter and Kozo Yamamura, *Asia in Japan's Embrace: Building a Regional Production Alliance*, Cambridge: Cambridge University Press, 1996.

Hay, Keith A.J., 'ASEAN and the Shifting Tides of Economic Power at the End of the 1980s', *International Journal*, XLIV, Summer 1989, 641–59.

Hellmann, D., A. Watanabe, T. Kikuchi and K. Pyle, 'America, Japan, and APEC: The Challenge of Leadership in the Asia-Pacific', *National Bureau of Asian Research (NBR) Analysis*, 6 (3), APEC Study Center, University of Washington, November 1995.

Hemming, A., 'ASEAN Security Cooperation after the Cold War: Problems and Prospects', *Indonesian Quarterly*, 20 (3), Third Quarter 1992, 286–97.

Henderson, D., 'International Economic Integration: Progress, Prospects and Implications', *International Affairs*, 68 (4), 1992, 633–53.

Herr, R., 'The United Nations, Regionalism and the South Pacific', *Pacific Review*, 7 (3), Routledge, 1994, 261–9.

Higgott, Richard, 'Economic Cooperation: Theoretical Opportunities and Practical Constraints', *Pacific Review*, 6 (2), 1993, 103–17.

Higgott, Richard, 'Ideas, Identity and Policy Coordination in the Asia-Pacific', *Pacific Review*, 7 (4), 1994, 367–79.

Higgott, R., 'The International Political Economy of Regionalism: The Asia–Pacific and Europe Compared', in William D. Coleman and Geoffrey R.D. Underhill (eds), *Regionalism and Global Economic Integration: Europe, Asia and the Americas*, London: Routledge, 1998.

Higgott, R. and R. Stubbs, 'Competing Conceptions of Economic Regionalism: APEC versus EAEC in the Asia Pacific', *Review of International Political Economy*, 2 (3), Summer 1995, 516–35.

Higgott, Richard, A.F. Cooper and J. Bonner, 'Asia-Pacific Economic Cooperation: An Evolving Case Study in Leadership and Cooperation Building', *International Journal*, 45 (4), Autumn 1990, 823–66.

Higgott, R., R. Leaver and J. Ravenhill (eds), *Pacific Economic Relations in the 1990s: Cooperation or Conflict*, Sydney: Allen & Unwin, 1993.

Hofheinz, Roy and Kent E. Calder, *The East Asia Edge*, New York: Harper & Row, 1982.

Holdridge, J., 'U.S. Dialogue with ASEAN and ANZUS', *Department of State Bulletin*, 82 (2067), October 1982, 29–32.

Hongying Wang, 'Multilateralism in Chinese Foreign Policy: The Limits of Socialization', *Asian Survey*, XL (3), May/June 2000, 475–91.

Hsiung, James C. (ed), *Human Rights in Asia: A Cultural Perspective*, New York: Paragon House, 1985.

Hu, Chun-tien, 'Challenges to Economic Cooperation in the Asia-Pacific Region', *Issues and Studies*, 35 (1), January/February 1999, 131–46.

Huisken, Ron, 'Civilizing the Anarchical Society: Multilateral Security Processes in the Asia-Pacific', *Contemporary Southeast Asia*, 24 (2), August 2002, 187–202.

Hung-Chao Tai, 'The Oriental Alternative: A Hypothesis on East Asian Culture and Economy', *Issues and Studies*, 25, 1989, 10–36.

Huntington, Samuel P., 'The Clash of Civilizations', *Foreign Affairs*, 72 (3), Summer 1993, 22–49.

Huntington, Samuel P., *The Clash of Civilizations and the Remaking of the World*, New York: Simon & Schuster, 1997.

Hurrell, Andrew, 'Regionalism in Theoretical Perspective', in Louise Fawcett and Andrew Hurrell (eds), *Regionalism in World Politics: Regional Organization and International Order*, Oxford: Oxford University Press, 1995, pp. 37–73.

Huxley, Tim, 'ASEAN Security Co-operation – Past, Present and Future', in Alison Bronowski (ed), *ASEAN into the 1990s*, London: Macmillan, 1990, 112–37.

Hwee, Yeo Lee, 'ASEM: Looking Back, Looking Forward', *Contemporary Southeast Asia*, 22 (1), April 2000, 113–44.

Inada, Kenneth K., 'A Buddhist Response to the Nature of Human Rights', in Claude E. Welch and Virginia A. Leary (eds), *Asian Perspectives of Human Rights*, Boulder, CO: Westview Press, 1990, pp. 94–8.

Inoguchi, Takashi and Courtney Purrington (eds), *United States–Japan Relations and International Institutions after the Cold War*, La Jolla, CA: Graduate School of International Relations and Pacific Studies, University of California, 1995.

Institute of Southeast Asian Studies, Singapore and the International Institute for Strategic Studies, London, papers presented at an international conference *Regional Security Developments and Stability in Southeast Asia*, 1980.

Ivanov, Vladimir I. and Eleanor Oguma, 'Energy Security and Sustainable Development in Northeast Asia: Prospects for Cooperative Policies', Report to International Workshop, Niigata, 26–28 June 2001.

Jaggi, G., *ASEAN and AFTA: Chronology and Statistic*, Working Paper No. 95-4, Washington, DC: Institute for International Economics, 1995.

Jang-Hee Yoo and Chang-Jae Lee (eds), *Northeast Asian Economic Cooperation: Progress in Conceptualization and in Practice*, Seoul: Korea Institute for International Economic Policy, 1994.

Jawhar, Mohamed, 'Managing Security in Southeast Asia: Existing Mechanisms and Processes to Address Regional Conflicts', *Australian Journal of International Affairs*, 47 (2), October 1993, 210–20.

Jayasuriya, K., 'Singapore: The Politics of Regional Definition', *Pacific Review*, 7 (4), 1994, 411–20.

Ji Guoxing, 'The Multilateralisation of Pacific Asia: A Chinese Perspective', *Asian Defence Journal*, 7, 1994, 20–24.

Job, B., 'Matters of Multilateralism: Implications for Regional Conflict Management', in D. Lake and P. Morgan (eds), *Regional Orders: Building Security in a New World*, Philadelphia, PA: Pennsylvania State University Press, 1997, pp. 165–94.

Johnson, Chalmers, 'Rethinking Asia', *The National Interest*, Summer 1993, 20–28.

Jones, David Martin, 'Democratization, Civil Society, and Illiberal Middle Class Culture in Pacific Asia', *Comparative Politics*, 30 (2), January 1998, 147–69.

Jordan, Amos A. and Jane Khanna, 'Economic Interdependence and Challenges to the Nation-State: The Emergence of Natural Economic Territories in the Asia-Pacific', *Journal of International Affairs*, 48 (2), Winter 1995, 433–62.

Jorgensen-Dahl, Arnfinn, 'ASEAN 1967–1976: Development or Stagnation?', *Pacific Community*, 7 (4), July 1976, 519–35.

Kacowicz, Arie M., 'Regionalization, Globalization and Nationalism: Convergent, Divergent, or Overlapping?', *Alternatives,* 24 (4), October–December 1999, 527–56.

Kahin, George McTurnam and John Wilewis, *The United States in Vietnam,* Ithaca, NY: Delta, 1967.

Kane, P.V., *History of Dharma'sastras,* 2nd edn, Poona: Bhandarkar Oriental Research Institute, 1968.

Kao, John, 'The Worldwide Web of Chinese Business', *Harvard Business Review,* 71, March–April 1993, 24–34.

Kappagoda, N., *The Multilateral Development Banks, Vol. 2: The Asian Development Bank,* Boulder, CO: Lynne Rienner, 1995.

Katzenstein, P., 'Regionalism in Comparative Perspective', *Cooperation and Conflict,* 31 (2), June 1996, 123–59.

Katzenstein, Peter J. and Takashi Shiraishi (eds), *Network Power: Japan and Asia,* Ithaca, NY: Cornell University Press, 1997.

Kausikan, Balihari, 'Asia's Different Standard', *Foreign Policy,* 92 (3), Fall 1993, 24–41.

Kelly, David and Anthony Reid (eds), *Asian Freedoms: The Idea of Freedom in East and Southeast Asia,* Cambridge: Cambridge University Press, 1998.

Kerr, Pauline, 'The Security Dialogue in the Asia-Pacific', *Pacific Review,* 7 (4), 1994, 397–408.

Keum, Hieyeon, 'Globalization and Inter-City Cooperation in Northeast Asia', *East Asia: An International Quarterly,* 17 (12), Summer 2000, 97–114.

Khanna, Jane, 'Asia-Pacific Economic Cooperation and Challenges for Political Leadership', *Washington Quarterly,* 19 (1), Winter 1996, 257–75.

Khoo How San, 'ASEAN as a "Neighbourhood Watch Group"', *Contemporary Southeast Asia,* 22 (2), August 2000, 279–301.

Kihl, Young Whan, 'Intra-Regional Conflict and the ASEAN Peace Process', *International Journal,* XLIV, Summer 1989, 598–615.

Kim Dae Jung, 'Is Culture Destiny? The Myth of Asia's Anti-Democratic Values', *Foreign Affairs,* 73 (6), November/December 1994, 189–94.

Kim, Kook-Chin, 'A Plea for the Asia-Pacific Regional Cooperation', *Korea and World Affairs,* 7, 1983, 208–17.

Kim, S., *China and the World: New Directions in Chinese Foreign Relations,* Boulder, CO: Westview Press, 1989.

Kim, Samuel, 'Mainland China and a New World Order', *Issues and Studies,* 27 (11), November 1991, 1–43.

Kim, Sung-Han, 'Comprehensive Security Effects of the East Asian Economic Crisis', *Journal of East Asian Affairs,* 13 (2), Fall/Winter 1999, 412–34.

Kimura, M., *Multi-Layered Regional Cooperation in Southeast Asia After the Cold War,* Tokyo: Institute of Developing Economies, 1995.

Klintworth, G., 'China's Evolving Relationship with APEC', *International Journal,* L (3), 1995, 488–515.

Kobayashi, Yotaro, 'Re-Asianize Japan', *New Perspectives Quarterly*, 9 (1), 1992, 2–23.

Kohona, P., 'The Evolving Concept of a Pacific Basin Community', *Asian Survey*, 26 (4), April 1986, 399–419.

Kojima, K. (ed), *Pacific Trade and Development*, Center Paper No. 9, Japan Economic Research Center, East–West Center, Honolulu, 1968.

Kojima, K. (ed), *Pacific Trade and Development II*, Center Paper No. 11, Japan Economic Research Center, East–West Center, Honolulu, 1969.

Kojima, Kiyoshi, 'The "Flying Geese" Model of Asian Economic Development: Origin, Theoretical Extensions, and Regional Policy Implications', *Journal of Asian Economics*, 11, 2000, 375–401.

Korhonen, P., *Japan and the Pacific Free Trade Area*, London: Routledge, 1994.

Kotkin, Joel, *Tribes: How Race, Religion and Identity Determine Success in the New Global Economy*, New York: Random House, 1993.

Koushalani, Yougindra, 'Human Rights in Asia and Africa', *Human Rights Law Journal*, 4 (4), 1983, 403–42.

Kraft, Herman Joseph S., 'ASEAN and Intra-ASEAN Relations: Weathering the Storm', *Pacific Review*, 13 (3), 2000, 453–72.

Krauss, Ellis S., 'Japan, the US, and the Emergence of Multilateralism in Asia', *Pacific Review*, 13 (3), 2000, 473–94.

Krauss, Willy and Wilfrid Lütkenhorst, *The Economic Development of the Pacific Basin: Growth Dynamics, Trade Relations and Emerging Cooperation*, New York: St. Martin's Press, 1986.

Ku-Hyan Jung and Jang-Hee Yoo (eds), *Asia-Pacific Economic Cooperation: Current Issues and Agenda for the Future*, Korea Institute for International Economic Policy, 1996.

Kurus, Bilson, 'Understanding ASEAN', *Asian Survey*, 33 (8), August 1993, 819–31.

Lanxin, Xiang, 'The China Debate and the Civilisation Debate', *Issues and Studies*, No. 10, October 1998, 79–92.

Lau Teik Soon, 'ASEAN and the Bali Summit', *Pacific Community*, 7 (4), July 1976, 536–8.

Lau Teik Soon, 'ASEAN Diplomacy: National Interest and Regionalism', *Journal of Asian and African Studies*, XXV (1–2), 1990, 114–27.

Lee Hong-pyo, 'Yellow Sea Regional Economic Cooperation', *Korea Focus*, 6 (3), 1998, 67–78.

Lee Lai To, 'ASEAN and the South China Sea Conflicts', *Pacific Review*, 8 (3), 1995, 531–43.

Lee Lai To, *China and the South China Sea Dialogues*, Westport, CT: Praeger, 1999.

Lee Lai To, 'China's Relations with ASEAN: Partners in the 21st Century?', *Pacifica Review: Peace, Security and Global Change*, 13 (1), February 2001, 61–72.

Lee Sahng-Gyoun, 'Multilateral Security in Europe and Northeast ASIA: In Search of New Alternatives', *The Journal of Far East Asian Affairs*, Spring/Summer 1998, 12 (1), 1–22.

Lee Sahng-Gyoun, 'EMU and Asia–Europe Economic Relations: Implications and Perspectives', *Journal of East Asian Affairs*, 13 (1), Spring/Summer 1999, 51–72.

Lee, Sang-Gon, 'Transboundary Pollution in the Yellow Sea', in H. Edward English and David Runnals (eds), *Environment and Development in the Pacific: Problems and Policy Options*, New York: Addison Wesley Longman in association with the Pacific Trade and Development Conference, 1998.

Legge, James (trans.), *The Chinese Classics, Vol. II, The Works of Mencius, Book 1*, Hong Kong: Hong Kong University Press, 1970.

Leifer, Michael, *Conflict and Regional Order in Southeast Asia*, Adelphi Paper, 162, London: International Institute for Strategic Studies, 1980.

Leifer, Michael, *ASEAN and the Security of Southeast Asia*, London: Routledge, 1989.

Leifer, Michael, 'ASEAN as a Model of a Security Community?', in Hadi Soesastro (ed), *ASEAN in a Changed Regional and International Political Economy*, Jakarta: Centre for Strategic and International Studies, 1995, pp. 129–42.

Leifer, Michael, 'The Extension of ASEAN's Model of Regional Security', in R. Cobbold (ed), *The World Reshaped, Vol. 2: Fifty Years after the War in Asia*, London: Macmillan, 1996, pp. 136–53.

Leifer, Michael, 'International Dynamics of One Southeast Asia: Political and Security', *Indonesian Quarterly*, 24 (4), 1996, 357–64.

Leifer, Michael, *The ASEAN Regional Forum*, Adelphi Paper 302, London: International Institute for Strategic Studies, 1996.

Leifer, Michael, 'The ASEAN Peace Process: A Category Mistake', *Pacific Review*, 12 (1), 1999, 25–38.

Leviste Jr, Jose P. (ed), *The Pacific Lake: Philippine Perspectives on a Pacific Community*, Manila: Philippine Council for Foreign Relations, Inc. and SGV Foundation, Inc., 1986.

Lim, Robyn, 'The ASEAN Regional Forum: Building on Sand', *Contemporary Southeast Asia*, 20 (2), August 1998, 117–35.

Lincoln, Edward J., *Japan's Rapidly Emerging Strategy toward Asia*, Paris: OECD, 1992.

Liu Jiangyong, *Building a Multilateral Security Dialogue in the Pacific*, Pacific Economic Paper No. 253, Canberra: Australia–Japan Research Centre, ANU, September 1994.

Lizée, Pierre P., 'Civil Society and Regional Security: Tensions and Potentials in Post-Crisis Southeast Asia', *Contemporary Southeast Asia*, 22 (3), December 2000, 550–69.

Lloyd, P. and L. Williams (eds), *International Trade and Migration in the APEC Region*, Melbourne: Oxford University Press, 1996.

Looney, Robert E. and P.C. Frederiksen, 'The Economic Determinants of Military Expenditure in Selected East Asian Countries', *Contemporary Southeast Asia*, 11 (4), March 1990, 265–77.

Lord, W., 'Building a Pacific Community', *US Department of State Dispatch*, 6 (3), 16 January 1995, 34–40.

Lubis, T., 'Human Rights Standard Setting in Asia: Problems and Prospects', *Indonesian Quarterly*, 21 (1), First Quarter 1993, 25–37.

Luck, E., 'Layers of Security: Regional Arrangements, the United Nations, and the Japanese–American Security Treaty', *Asian Survey*, 35 (3), March 1995, 237–52.

Luhulima, C.P.F, 'ASEAN, the South pacific Forum and the Changing Strategic Environment', *The Indonesian Quarterly*, 20 (2), second quarter 1992, 207–218.

MacIntyre, A., 'Ideas and Experts: Indonesian Approaches to Economic and Security Cooperation in the Asia-Pacific Region', *Pacific Review*, 8 (1), 1995, 159–72.

Mack, Andrew, 'Reassurance versus Deterrence Strategies for the Asia-Pacific Region,' Working Paper 103, Peace Research Centre, Australian National University, Canberra, 1991.

Mack, Andrew and John Ravenhill (eds), *Pacific Cooperation: Building Economic and Security Regimes in the Asia-Pacific Region*, Boulder, CO: Westview Press, 1995.

Mackie, J.A.C, 'Overseas Chinese Entrepreneurship', *Asia-Pacific Economic Literature*, 6, May 1992, 41–64.

Maddock, R., 'Environmental Security in East Asia', *Contemporary Southeast Asia*, 17 (1), June 1995, 20–37.

Madsen, Richard, 'The Public Sphere, Civil Society, and Moral Community', *Modern China*, 19 (2), April 1993, 183–98.

Mahathir, Mohamad, 'Regionalism, Globalism and Spheres of Influence: ASEAN and the Challenge of Change into the 21st Century', ISEAS Singapore Lecture, Singapore, 1988.

Mahathir Mohamad and Shintaro Ishihara (trans. F. Baldwin), *The Voice of Asia: Two Leaders Discuss the Coming Century*, New York: Kodansha International, 1995.

Mahbubani, Kishore, 'The Dangers of Decadence: What the West Can Teach the East', *Foreign Affairs*, 72 (4), 1993, 10–14.

Mahbubani, Kishore, 'The Pacific Impulse', *Survival*, 37 (1), Spring 1995, 105–20.

Mahbubani, Kishore, 'The Pacific Way', *Foreign Affairs*, 74 (1), January/February 1995, 10–14.

Mahbubani, Kishore, 'An Asia-Pacific Consensus', *Foreign Affairs*, 76 (5), 1997, 149–58.

Mahbubani, Kishore, *Can Asians Think?*, *The 1988 National Interest*, 52, Summer 1998, 27–35.

Maidment, Richard and Colin Mackerras (eds), *Culture and Society in the Asia-Pacific*, London: Routledge, 1998.

Mak, J. and B.A. Hamzah, 'The External Maritime Dimension of ASEAN Security', in D. Ball (ed), *The Transformation of Security in the Asia/Pacific Region*, London: Frank Cass, 1996, pp. 123–46.

Manning, Robert A., 'The Asian Energy Predicament', *Survival*, 42 (3), 2000, 73–88.

Manning Robert A. and Paula Stern, 'The Myth of the Pacific Community', *Foreign Affairs*, 73 (6), November–December 1994, 79–93.

Marcus, George E. and Michael Fischer, *Anthropology as Cultural Critique*, Chicago: University of Chicago Press, 1986.

Martinez, Patricia M., 'The Islamic State or the State of Islam in Malaysia', *Contemporary Southeast Asia*, 23 (3), December 2001, 474–503.

Masakazu Yamazaki, 'Asia, a Civilization in the Making', *Foreign Affairs*, 75 (4), July/August 1996, 106–18.

Matsunaga, N., 'APEC and PECC', *Japan Review of International Affairs*, Special Issue on APEC and Regional Perspectives, 9 (3), Summer 1995, 195–8.

Matsunaga, N. and J. Singh (eds), *Enhancing Peace and Cooperation in Asia*, New Delhi: Institute for Defence Studies and Analyses, 1996.

Matsuzaka, Hideo, 'Future of Japan–ASEAN Relations', *Asia Pacific Community*, 20, Summer 1983, 11–22.

Maznah Mohamad, 'Towards a Human Rights Regime in Southeast Asia: Charting the Course of State Commitment', *Contemporary Southeast Asia*, 24 (2), August 2002, 230–51.

McCore, William, *The Dawn of the Pacific Century: Implication of the Three Worlds of Development*, New Brunswick, NJ: Transaction Publishers, 1993.

Meldrum, B. and J. Cotton, 'The U.S.–DPRK Agreed Framework, KEDO, and "Four-Party Talks" – The Vicissitudes of Engagement', *Issues and Studies*, 34 (11/12), November/December 1998, 121–43.

Millar, T.B. (ed), *Britain's Withdrawal from Asia: Its Implications for Australia*, Canberra: Strategic and Defence Studies Centre, Australian National University, 1967.

Miller, Benjamin, 'International Systems and Regional Security: From Competition to Co-operation, Dominance or Disengagement?', *Journal of Strategic Studies*, 18 (2), June 1995, 52–100.

Milner, Anthony and Deborah Johnson, 'The Idea of Asia', in John Ingleson (ed), *Regionalism and Subregionalism in APEC*, Melbourne: Monash Asian Institute, 1997, pp. 1–19.

Min, Shi, 'The Basis, Features and Prospects of Northeast Asian Economic Cooperation', in Jang-Hee Yoo and Chang-Jae Lee (eds), *Northeast Asian Economic Cooperation: Progress in Conceptualization and in Practice*, Seoul: Korea Institute for International Economic Policy, 1994, pp. 15–29.

Mio, Thant, Min Tang and Hiroshi Kakazu (eds), *Growth Triangles in Asia: A New Approach to Regional Economic Cooperation*, Oxford: Asian Development Bank/Oxford University Press, 1994.

Mitford, Paul, 'Japan's Leadership Role in East Asian Security Multilateralism: The Nakayama Proposal and the Logic of Reassurance', *Pacific Review*, 13 (3), 2000, 367–98.

Mitrany, David, *A Working Peace System*, Chicago: Quadrangle Books, 1961.

Mochizuki, Mike M., 'Japan as an Asia-Pacific Power', in Robert S. Ross (ed), *East Asia in Transition: Toward a New Regional Order*, Armonk, NY: M.E. Sharpe, 1995, pp. 124–59.

Moller, B., 'A Common Security and NOD Regime for the Asia-Pacific?', *Pacifica Review: Peace, Security and Global Change*, 9 (1), 1997, 23–43.

Moon, Chung-in, 'Economic Interdependence and the Implications for Security in Northeast Asia', *Asian Perspective*, 19 (2), Fall–Winter 1995, 29–52.

Moore, Thomas G. and Dixia Yang, 'China, APEC and Economic Regionalism in the Asia-Pacific', *Journal of East Asian Affairs*, 13 (2), Fall/Winter 1999, 361–411.

Mori, K., 'China's Pivotal Role in the Asia-Pacific Community', *Japan Review of International Affairs*, 9 (3), Summer 1995, 228–34.

Morimoto, S., 'A Security Framework for the Asia/Pacific Region', in Des Ball (ed), *The Transformation of Security in the Asia/Pacific Region*, London: Frank Cass, 1996, pp. 218–31.

Moulder, Frances V., *Japan, China, and the Modern World Economy: Toward a Reinterpretation of East Asian Development ca. 1600 to ca. 1918*, Cambridge: Cambridge University Press, 1977.

Muddathir, 'Abd al-Rahim, *Islam and Non-Muslim Minorities*, Penang: JUST World Trust, 1997.

Muntarbohrn, Vitit, *The Challenge of Law: Legal Cooperation among ASEAN Countries*, Bangkok: Institute of Security and International Studies, 1986.

Murphy, Alexander B., 'Economic Regionalization and Pacific Asia', *Geographical Review*, 85 (2), April 1995, 127–40.

Muzaffar, Chandra, 'Taking Another Look at Human Rights', *New Straits Times*, 19 August 1995, p. 11.

Muzaffar, Chandra, *Rights, Religion and Freedom*, London: Routledge, 2002.

Mya, Than and Carolyn L. Gates (eds), *ASEAN Beyond the Regional Crisis: Challenges and Initiatives*, Singapore: Institute of Southeast Asian Studies, 2001.

Naess, Tom, 'Environmental Co-operation around the South China Sea: The Experience of the South China Sea Workshops and the United Nations

Environment Programme's Strategic Action Programme', *Pacific Review*, 14 (4), 2001, 553–73.

Nagatomi, Y., 'Economic Regionalism and the EAEC', *Japan Review of International Affairs*, Special Issue on APEC and Regional Perspectives, 9 (3), Summer 1995, 206–11.

Narine, Shaun, 'ASEAN and the ARF: The Limits of the "ASEAN WAY"', *Asian Survey*, XXXVII (10), October 1997, 961–78.

Narine, Shaun, 'ASEAN and the Management of Regional Security', *Pacific Affairs*, 71 (2), Summer 1998, 195–214.

Narine, Shaun, 'ASEAN into the Twenty-first Century: Problems and Prospects', *Pacific Review*, 12 (3), 1999, 357–80.

Ngai-Ling Sum, 'Greater China and the Global–Regional–Local Dynamics in the Post-Cold War Era', in Ian G. Cook, Marcus A. Doel and Rex Li (eds), *Fragmented Asia: Regional Integration and National Disintegration in Pacific Asia*, Aldershot, UK: Avebury, 1996, pp. 53–74.

Nicholas, R.M, 'ASEAN and the Pacific Community Debate: Much Ado about Something', *Asian Survey*, 21 (12), 1981, 1197–210.

Noble, Gregory W. and John Ravenhill (eds), *The Asian Financial Crisis and the Architecture of Global Finance*, Cambridge: Cambridge University Press, 2000.

Nobuo, Okawara and Peter J. Katzenstein, 'Japan and Asian-Pacific Security: Regionalization, Entrenched Bilateralism and Incipient Multilateralism', *Pacific Review*, 14 (2), 2001, 165–94.

Nukazawa, K., 'APEC: A Body in Search of a Spirit', *Japan Review of International Affairs*, Special Issue on APEC and Regional Perspectives, 9 (3), Summer 1995, 212–16.

Nye, Joseph S. (ed), *International Regionalism*, Boston, MA: Little Brown, 1968.

Oakman, Daniel, 'The Politics of Foreign Aid: Counter Subversion and the Colombo Plan 1950–1970', *Pacifica Review: Peace, Security and Global Change*, 13 (3), October 2001, 255–72.

Odgaard, Liselotte, 'Deterrence and Co-operation in the South China Sea', *Contemporary Southeast Asia*, 23 (2), August 2001, 292–306.

Olsen, Edward, A., 'The role of Taiwan in ASIAN Multilateral Security: Towards the 21st Century,' *The Journal of East Asian Affairs*, Spring/ Summer, 1998, 25–53.

Pacific Campaign for Disarmament and Security, 'ASEAN Regional Forum in Jakarta: A Nongovernmental Perspective', Pacific Campaign for Disarmament and Security, Resource Office, March 1997.

Palat, Ravi Arvind (ed), *Pacific-Asia and the Future of the World-System*, London: Greenwood, 1993.

Palmer, Norman D., *The New Regionalism in Asia and the Pacific*, Lexington, MA: Lexington Books, 1991.

Palmujoki, Eero, 'EU–ASEAN Relations: Reconciling Two Different Agendas', *Contemporary Southeast Asia*, 19 (3), December 1997, 269–85.

Palmujoki, Eero, *Regionalism and Globalism in Southeast Asia*, Basingstoke: Palgrave Macmillan, 2001.

Parekh, Bikhu, *Gandhi's Political Philosophy*, Delhi: Ajanta, 1989.

Park, H., 'Multilateral Security Cooperation', *Pacific Review*, 6 (3), 1993, 251–66.

Payoyo, Peter Bautista, 'Ocean Governance in the ASEAN Region and the United Nations Convention on the Law of the Sea', *Pacifica Review: Peace, Security and Global Change*, 9 (2), November/December 1997, 57–72.

Peattie, Mark R., 'The Japanese Colonial Empire', in Peter Duus (ed), *The Cambridge History of Japan, Vol. 6: The Twentieth Century*, Cambridge: Cambridge University Press, 1988, pp. 217–65.

Peek, John M., 'Buddhism, Human Rights and the Japanese State', *Human Rights Quarterly*, 17 (3), 1995, 527–40.

Petri, Peter A., 'The East Asian Trading Bloc: An Analytical History', in Ross Garnaut and Peter Drysdale (eds), with John Kunkel, *Asia Pacific Regionalism: Readings in International Economic Relations*, Pymble, NSW: HarperEducational in association with the Australia–Japan Research Centre, Australian National University, 1994, pp. 107–24.

Poindexter, J., 'Regional Security, Collective Security, and American Security', *Department of State Bulletin*, 86 (2113), August 1986, 64–7.

Polanyi, Karl, *The Great Transformation: The Political and Economic Origins of Our Time*, Boston, MA: Beacon, 1957.

Pollis, Adamantia and Peter Schwab (eds), *Human Rights: Cultural and Ideological Perspectives*, New York: Praeger, 1980.

Polomka, P., 'Asia Pacific Security: Towards a "Pacific House"', *Australian Journal of International Affairs*, 44 (3), December 1990, 269–80.

Preston, Peter W. and Julie Gilson (eds), *The European Union and East Asia: International Linkages in a Changing Global System*, Cheltenham, UK: Edward Elgar, 2001.

Pryor, Pamela, T.I., 'The Pacific Islands and ASEAN: Prospects for Inter-Regional Co-operation, *The Indonesian Quarterly*, 16 (1), January 1988, 48–71.

Pye, Lucian, 'The State and the Individual: An Overview', *China Quarterly*, 127, September 1991, 443–66.

Radtke, K. and R. Feddema (eds), *Comprehensive Security in Asia: Views from Asia and the West on a Changing Security Environment*, Boston, MA: E.J. Brill, 2000.

Ramacharan, Robin, 'ASEAN and Non-Interference: A Principle Maintained', *Contemporary Southeast Asia*, 22 (1), April 2000, 60–88.

Rapkin, D., 'The United States, Japan, and the Power to Block: The APEC and AMF Cases', *Pacific Review*, 14 (3), 2001, 373–410.

Rattan, Ram, *Gandhi's Concept of Political Obligation*, Calcutta: Minerva Associates, 1972.

Ravenhill, John, 'Economic Cooperation in Southeast Asia: Changing Incentives', *Asian Survey*, XXXV (9), September 1995, 850–66.

Ravenhill, John, 'APEC and the WTO: Which Way Forward to Trade Liberalization?', *Contemporary Southeast Asia*, 21 (2), August 1999, 220–37.

Ravenhill, John, *APEC and the Construction of Pacific Rim Regionalism*, Cambridge: Cambridge University Press, 2001.

Ray, Sibnarayan, *Gandhi India and the World*, Melbourne: Hawthorne Press, 1970.

Rigg, Jonathon D., *Southeast Asia: A Region in Transition*, London: Unwin Hyman, 1991.

Rolls, Mark G., 'ASEAN: Where From or Where To?', *Contemporary Southeast Asia*, 13 (3), December 1991, 315–32.

Room, A., 'Naming the Pacific', *Pacific Review*, 1 (2), 1988, 181–5.

Rosecrance, Richard, 'Regionalism and the Post-Cold War Era', *International Journal*, XLVI, Summer 1991, 373–93.

Ross, Robert S. (ed), *East Asia in Transition: Towards a New Regional Order*, Armonk, NY and London: M.E. Sharpe, 1995.

Rouner, Leroy S. (ed), *Human Rights and the World's Religions*, Notre Dame, IN: University of Notre Dame Press, 1988.

Roy, Denny, 'The China Threat Issue', *Asian Survey*, 36 (8), 1996, 758–71.

Rozman, G., 'Comparisons of the Modern Confucian Values in China and Japan', in G. Rozman (ed), *The East Asian Region: Confucian Heritage and its Modern Adaptation*, Princeton, NJ: Princeton University Press, 1991, pp.157–203.

Rozman, G., 'A Regional Approach to Northeast Asia', *Orbis*, 39 (1), Winter 1995, 65–80.

Rozman, G., 'Flawed Regionalism: Reconceptualizing Northeast Asia in the 1990s', *Pacific Review*, 11 (1), 1998, 1–27.

Rüland, Jürgen, 'ASEAN and the Asian Crisis: Theoretical Implications and Practical Consequences for Southeast Asian Regionalism', *Pacific Review*, 13 (3), 2000, 421–52.

Russett, Bruce M., *International Regions and the International System: A Study in Political Ecology*, Chicago: Rand McNally, 1967.

Russett, Bruce, 'Delineating International Regions', in J. David Singer (ed), *Quantitative International Politics: Insights and Evidence*, New York: The Free Press, 1968, pp. 317–52.

Russian Delegation, 'Declaration on Principles of Security and Stability in the Asia-Pacific Region', paper presented at ASEAN–ISIS 10th Asia-Pacific Roundtable, Kuala Lumpur, 5–8 June 1996.

Sadleir, Richard, 'Eighth ASEAN Regional Forum: Outcomes', *AUS–CSCAP Newsletter*, 12, November 2001.

368 *Regionalism in the new Asia-Pacific order*

Said, Abdul Aziz and Jamil Nasser, 'The Use and Abuse of Democracy in Islam', in J.L. Nelson and V.M. Green (eds), *International Human Rights: Contemporary Issues*, NY: Human Rights Publishing Group, 1980, pp. 61–84.
Saito, S., 'East Asian Regionalism: A Plan for Phased Economic Cooperation', *Japan Review of International Affairs*, 9 (3), Summer 1995, 252–8.
Sakamoto, Y., 'An Alternative to Global Marketization: East Asian Regional Cooperation and the "Civic State"; paper presented at the Hallym University Symposium, Seoul, 29 May 1998.
Saravanamuttu, Johan, 'Militarization in ASEAN and the Option for Denuclearization in South-East Asia', *Interdisciplinary Peace Research*, 2 (1), 1990, 40–64.
Saravanamuttu, Johan, 'The Southeast Asian Development Phenomenon Revisited: From Flying Geese to Lame Ducks?', *Pacifica Review: Peace, Security and Global Change*, 10 (1), February 1998, 111–26.
Scalapino, R. and M. Kosaka (eds), *Peace, Politics and Economics in Asia: The Challenge to Cooperate*, Washington, DC: Pergamon-Brassey's, 1988.
Scalapino, R., S. Sato, J. Wanandi and S. Han (eds), *Asian Security Issues: Regional and Global*, Berkley: University of California, 1988.
Schofield, Julian, 'War and Punishment: The Implications of Arms Purchases in Maritime Southeast Asia', *Journal of Strategic Studies*, 21 (2), June 1998, 75–106.
Schubert, James N., 'Toward a "Working Peace System" in Asia: Organizational Growth and State Participation in Asian Regionalism', *International Organization*, 32 (1), Winter 1978, 425–40.
Searle, Peter, 'Ethno-Religious Conflicts: Rise or Decline? Recent Developments in Southeast Asia', *Contemporary Southeast Asia*, 24 (1), April 2002, 1–11.
Segal, Gerald, *Rethinking the Pacific*, Oxford: Clarendon Press, 1990.
Segal, Gerald, '"Asianism" and Asian Security', *The National Interest*, Winter 1995–96, 58–65.
Seki, Mitsubiro, *Beyond the Full-Set Industrial Structure: Japanese Industry in the New Age of East Asia*, Tokyo: LTCB International Library Foundation, 1994.
Sen, Amartya, 'Human Rights and Asian Values: What Lee Kuan Yew and Le Peng Don't Understand about Asia', *The New Republic*, 217 (2–3), July 1997, 33–40.
Shi Yongming, 'ASEAN: A Strong Voice in the Post-Cold War World', *Beijing Review*, 3–9, February 1997.
Shirk, S., 'Chinese Views on Asia-Pacific Regional Security Cooperation', *Analysis* (National Bureau of Asian Research), 5 (5), 1994, 5–13.
Shu Yun-Ma, 'The Chinese Discourse on Civil Society', *China Quarterly*, 137, March 1994, 180–93.

Simandjuntak, Djisman S., 'Instability of Global Environment and ASEAN Economic Co-operation', *The Indonesian Quarterly*, 17 (1), first quarter, 1989, 55–68.

Simandjuntak, Djisman S., 'Reinventing ASEAN Between Globalism, Regionalism and Nationalism', *The Indonesian Quarterly*, 22 (2), second quarter, 1991, 179–90.

Simon, Sheldon W., *The ASEAN States and Regional Security*, Stanford, CA: Hoover Institution Press, 1982.

Simon, Sheldon, *The Future of Asian-Pacific Collaboration*, Lexington, MA: D.C. Heath, 1988.

Simon, Sheldon, W., 'ASEAN Security in the 1990s', *Asian Survey*, 29 (6), 1989, 580–600.

Simon, Sheldon W., 'The Regionalization of Defense in Southeast Asia', *Analysis*, 3 (1), National Bureau of Asian Research, 1992.

Simon, Sheldon, 'Evaluating Track II Approaches to Security Diplomacy in the Asia-Pacific: the CSCAP Experience', *Pacific Review*, 15 (2), 2002, 167–200.

Singh, Biveer, *ZOPFAN and the New Security Order in the Asia-Pacific Region*, Malaysia: Pelanduk Publications, 1992.

Singh, Hari, 'Vietnam and ASEAN: The Politics of Accommodation', *Australian Journal of International Affairs*, 51 (2), July 1997, 215–29.

Skubik, Daniel W., 'Two Perspectives on Human Rights and the Rule of Law: Chinese East and Anglo-American West', *World Review*, 3 (2), June 1992, 28–45.

Smith, Anthony L., *Strategic Centrality: Indonesia's Changing Role in ASEAN*, Singapore: Institute of Southeast Asian Studies, 2000.

Smith, Esmond D., 'China's Aspirations in the Spratly Islands', *Contemporary Southeast Asia*, 16 (3), 1994, 274–94.

Sneider, Richard, 'The Evolving Pacific Community – Reality or Rhetoric?', in R. Hewett (ed), *Political Change and the Economic Future of East Asia*, Honolulu: Pacific Forum, University of Hawaii Press, 1981, pp. 33–43.

Sneider, Richard and M. Borthwick, 'Institutions for Pacific Regional Cooperation,' *Asian Survey*, 23 (12), December 1983, 1245–54.

Snitwongse, K., 'ASEAN's Security Cooperation: Searching for a Regional Order', *Pacific Review*, 8 (3), 1995, 518–30.

So, A.Y. and W.K. Chiu, 'Modern East Asia in World-Systems Analysis', *Sociological Inquiry*, 66 (4), 1996, 471–85.

Soesastro, Hadi, 'Pacific Economic Co-operation: The History of an Idea', in Ross Garnaut and Peter Drysdale (eds), *Asia-Pacific Regionalism: Readings in International Economic Relations*, Pymble, NSW: HarperEducational in Association with the Australian–Japan Research Centre, Australian National University, 1994, pp. 77–88.

Soesastro, Hadi 'ASEAN and APEC: Do Concentric Circles Work?', *Pacific Review*, 8 (3), 1995, 475–93.

Soesastro, H. and A. Bergin (eds), *The Role of Security and Economic Cooperation Structures in the Asia Pacific Region: Indonesian and Australian Views*, Jakarta: Centre for Strategic and International Studies, 1996.

Soesastro, H. and J. Wanandi, 'Towards an Asia Europe Partnership – A Perspective from Asia', *Indonesian Quarterly*, 24 (1), 1996, 38–58.

Soeya, Y., 'The Evolution of Japanese Thinking and Policies on Cooperative Security in the 1980s and 1990s', *Australian Journal of International Affairs*, 48 (1), May 1994, 87–95.

Soeya, Y., 'Japan's Multilateral Diplomacy in the Asia-Pacific and its Implications for the Korean Peninsula', *Asian Perspective*, 19 (2), Fall–Winter 1995, 223–41.

Solingen, Etel, 'ASEAN, Quo Vadis? Domestic Coalitions and Regional Co-operation', *Contemporary Southeast Asia*, 21 (1), 1999, 30–53.

Song, Young Sun, 'Prospects for a New Asia-Pacific Multilateral Security Arrangement', *Korean Journal of Defense Analysis*, 5 (1), Summer 1993, 185–206.

Sopiee, Noordin, 'ASEAN and Regional Security', in Mohamed Ayoob, *Regional Security in the Third World: Case Studies from Southeast Asia and the Middle East*, London: Croom Helm, 1986, pp. 221–34.

Sopiee, Noordin, 'The Development of an East Asian Consciousness', in G. Sheridan (ed), *Living with Dragons*, St Leonards: Allen & Unwin, 1995, pp. 180–93.

Spero, Joan E., 'US Business and Economic Cooperation in the Asia-Pacific Region', *US Department of State Dispatch*, 5 (44), 31 October 1994, 728–30.

Stargardt, A.W., 'The Road to Bandung: The Emergence of the Asian System of Powers', *Monographs in Asian Diplomatic History*, Cambridge: Cambridge Project on Asian Diplomatic History, 1992.

Stubbs, Richard, 'Asia-Pacific Regionalization and the Global Economy: A Third Form of Capitalism?', *Asian Survey*, 35 (9), September 1995, 785–97.

Sudarsono, Juwono, 'The Role of Governmental and Private Interests and Organizations in ASEAN Co-operation', *The Indonesian Quarterly*, 16 (1), January 1988, 15–26.

Sudo, See Sueo, *The Fukuda Doctrine and ASEAN: New Dimensions in Japanese Foreign Policy*, Singapore: Institute of Southeast Asian Studies, 1992.

Sueo, S. and N. Makato (eds), *Road to ASEAN-10: Japanese Perspective on Economic Integration*, New York: Japan Center for International Exchange, 2001.

Suhartono, R.B., 'ASEAN Approach to Industrial Co-operation', *Indonesian Quarterly*, XIV (4), October 1986, 505–21.

Suisheng Zhao, *Power Competition in East Asia from the Old Chinese World Order to Post-Cold War Regional Multipolarity*, London: Macmillan, 1998.

Sukma, R., 'ASEAN and the ASEAN Regional Forum: Should "The Driver" Be Replaced?', *Indonesian Quarterly*, 27 (3), Third Quarter 1999, 236–55.

Sum, Ngai-Ling, 'A Material-Discursive Approach to the "Asian Crisis": The Breaking and Remaking of the Production and Financial Orders', in Peter W. Preston and Julie Gilson (eds), *The European Union and East Asia: Interregional Linkages in a Changing Global System*, Cheltenham, UK: Edward Elgar, 2001, pp. 125–53.

Sung-Han, Kim, 'The Role of the ARF and the Korean Peninsula', *Journal of East Asian Affairs*, 12 (2), Summer/Fall 1998, 506–28.

Suthad Setboonsarng, 'ASEAN Economic Co-operation: Adjusting to the Crisis', in Institute of Southeast Asian Studies, *Southeast Asian Affairs 1998*, Singapore, Institute of Southeast Asian Studies, 1998, pp. 18–36.

Suu Kyi, Aung San, *Freedom from Fear and Other Writings*, Harmondsworth, Middlesex: Penguin, 1991.

Tagore, Rabindranath, 'Interview with *Manchester Guardian* (20 July 1916)', reproduced in *Modern Review*, 20 (3), September 1916, 344–45.

Tagore, Rabindranath, *Talks in China: Lectures Delivered in April and May 1924*, Calcutta: Visva-Bharati Bookshop, 1925.

Tang, J. (ed), *Human Rights and International Relations in the Asia-Pacific Region*, New York: Pinter, 1995.

Tang, Min and Myo Thant, *Growth Triangles: Conceptual Issues and Operational Problems*, Economic Staff Paper, No. 54, Asian Development Bank, February 1994.

Tang, Min and Hiroshi Kakazu (eds), *Growth Triangles in Asia: A New Approach to Regional Economic Cooperation*, Oxford: Oxford University Press for the Asian Development Bank, 1994.

Tay, S. and O. Talib, 'The ASEAN Regional Forum: Preparing for Preventative Diplomacy', *Contemporary Southeast Asia*, 19 (3), December 1997, 252–68.

Taylor, Paul, 'A Conceptual Typology of International Organization', in A.J.R. Groom and Paul Taylor (eds), *Frameworks for International Co-operation*, London: Pinter, 1990.

Tehranian, Majid (ed), *Asian Peace: Security and Governance in the Asia-Pacific Region,* London: I.B. Tauris, 1999, pp. 12–26.

Tehranian, Majid and David W. Chappell (eds), *Dialogue of Civilizations: A New Peace Agenda for a New Millennium*, London: I.B. Tauris, 2002.

Teló, Mario (ed), *European Union and New Regionalism: Regional Actors and Global Governance in a Post-Hegemonic Era*, Aldershot, UK: Ashgate, 2001.

Terada, Takashi, 'The Origins of Japan's APEC Policy: Foreign Minister Takeo Miki's Asia-Pacific Policy and Current Implications', *Pacific Review*, 11 (3), 1998, 337–63.

Terada, Takashi, *The Japanese Origins of PAFTAD: The Beginning of an Asian Pacific Economic Community*, Pacific Economic Papers, No. 292, Canberra: Australia–Japan Research Centre, June 1999.

Terada, Takashi, *The Genesis of APEC: Australian–Japan Political Initiatives*, Pacific Economic Papers, No. 298, Canberra: Australia–Japan Research Centre, December 1999.

Terada, Takashi, 'Directional Leadership in Institution-Building: Japan's Approaches to ASEAN in the Establishment of PECC and APEC', *Pacific Review*, 14 (2), 2001, 195–20.

Thant, M., M. Tang and H. Kakazu (eds), *Growth Triangles in Asia: A New Approach to Regional Economics Cooperation*, Hong Kong: Oxford University Press, 1994.

Thayer, Carlyle A., 'New Faultlines in ASEAN?', *Asia-Pacific Defence Reporter*, February–March, 2000, 26–27.

Thompson, Kenneth W. (ed), *The Moral Imperatives of Human Rights: A World Survey*, Washington, DC: University Press of America for the Council on Religion and International Affairs, 1980.

Thompson, William R. 'The Regional Subsystem: A Conceptual Explication and a Prepositional Inventory', *International Studies Quarterly*, 17 (1), March 1973, 89–117.

Titarenko, M., 'The Soviet Concept of Security and Cooperation in the Asia-Pacific Region', *Journal of Northeast Asian Studies*, Spring 1988, 55–69.

Tomoda, S., 'Japan's Search for a Political Role in Asia: The Cambodian Peace Settlement', *Japan Review of International Affairs*, 6 (1), Spring, 1992, 43–60.

Tow, William, 'Regional Order in Asia Pacific', in Ramesh Thakur and Carlyle A. Thayer (eds), *Reshaping Regional Relations: Asia-Pacific and the Former Soviet Union*, Boulder, CO: Westview Press, 1993, pp. 261–84.

Tow, William T., Ramesh Thakur and In-Taek Hyun (eds), *Asia's Emerging Regional Order: Reconciling Traditional and Human Security*, Tokyo: United Nations University Press, 2000.

Townsend-Gault, Ian, 'Preventive Diplomacy and Pro-Activity in the South China Sea', *Contemporary Southeast Asia*, 20 (2), August 1998, 171–91.

Traer, Robert, *Faith in Human Rights: Support in Religious Traditions for a Global Struggle*, Washington, DC: Georgetown University Press, 1991.

Tso, Allen Y., 'Foreign Direct Investment and China's Economic Development', *Issues and Studies*, 34 (2), February 1998, 1–34.

Tu Wei-ming (ed), *Confucian Traditions in East Asian Modernity,* Cambridge, MA: Harvard University Press, 1996.

Tucker, William E., 'ASEAN's Economic and Strategic Significance', *Asia Pacific Community*, 16, Spring 1982, 39–45.

United Nations, Economic and Social Commission for Asia and the Pacific, *Challenges and Opportunities of Restructuring the Developing ESCAP Economies in the 1990's, with Special Reference to Regional Economic Cooperation*, Development Papers No. 12, Bangkok: United Nations, 1992.

United Nations, Economic and Social Commission for Asia and the Pacific, Social Development Division, *Enhancing the Role of NGOs in the Implementation of the Agenda for Action on Social Development in the ESCAP Region*, New York: United Nations, 1995.

United Nations, Economic and Social Commission for Asia and the Pacific, *What ESCAP Offers Asia and the Pacific*, New York: United Nations, 1996.

Valencia, M., 'Economic Cooperation in Northeast Asia: The Tumen River Scheme', *Pacific Review*, 4 (3), 1991, 263–71.

Valencia, Mark J., 'Preparing for the Best: Involving North Korea in the New Pacific Community', *Journal of Northeast Asian Studies*, XIII (1), Spring 1994, 64–76.

Valencia, M., *China and the South China Sea Disputes*, Adelphi Paper 298, London: International Institute of Strategic Studies, 1995.

Valencia, M., 'Asia, the Law of the Sea and International Relations', *International Affairs*, 73 (2), 1997, 263–82.

Valencia, Mark, 'Energy and Insecurity in Asia', *Survival*, 39 (3), 1997, 85–106.

Van Ness, Peter (ed), *Debating Human Rights: Critical Essays from the United States and Asia*, London: Routledge, 1999.

Väyrynen, Raimo, 'Regional Conflict Formations: An Intractable Problem of International Relations', *Journal of Peace Research*, 21 (4), 1984, 337–59.

Vincent, R. John, *Human Rights and International Relations*, Cambridge: Cambridge University Press, 1986.

Wade, R., *Governing the Market: Economic Theory and the Role of Government in East Asian Industrialization*, Princeton, NJ: Princeton University Press, 1990.

Walsh, J., 'A Pillar of the Community: The Role of APEC in US Policy', *Journal of East Asian Affairs*, 7 (2), 1995, 545–62.

Wanandi, J., 'Security Cooperation in the Asia Pacific', *Indonesian Quarterly*, 22 (3), 1994, 198–204.

Wanandi, J., 'The Regional Role of "Track Two" Diplomacy: ASEAN, ARF, and CSCAP', *Japan Review of International Affairs*, Special Issue on APEC and Regional Perspectives, 9 (3), Summer 1995, 155–68.

Wanandi, Jusuf, 'Developing the Regional Security Architecture: The Road Ahead', Paper presented at the 10th Asia-Pacific Roundtable, Kuala Lumpur, 5–8 June 1996.

Wang Gungwu, 'A Machiavelli for Our Times', *The National Interest*, Winter 1996/97, 69–73.

Wang Gungwu, 'China's Place in the Region: Search for Allies and Friends', *Indonesian Quarterly*, 25 (4), 1997, 419–30.

Watanabe, A., 'What is Asia-Pacific Regionalism?', *Japan Review of International Affairs*, Special Issue on APEC and Regional Perspectives, 9 (3), Summer 1995, 189–94.

Weatherbee, Donald, E., 'The Foreign Policy Dimensions of Subregional Economic Zones', *Contemporary Southeast Asia*, 16 (4), March 1995, 421–32.

Webber, Douglas, 'Two Funerals and a Wedding? The Ups and Downs of Regionalism in East Asia and Asia-Pacific after the Asian Crisis', *Pacific Review*, 14 (3), 339–72.

Weixing Hu, 'China and Asian Regionalism: Challenge and Policy Choice', *Journal of Contemporary China*, 5 (11), 1996, 43–56.

Wendt, Alex, 'Anarchy is What States Make of It: The Social Construction of Power Politics', *International Organization*, 46, Spring 1992, 391–425.

Wenrong Qian, 'The United Nations and State Sovereignty in the Post-Cold War Era, *Pacifica Review*, 7 (2), October–November 1995, 135–46.

Wesley, Michael, 'The Asian Crisis and the Adequacy of Regional Institutions', *Contemporary Southeast Asia*, 21 (1), April 1999, 54–73.

Wesley, Michael, 'APEC's Mid-Life Crisis?' The Rise and Fall of Early Voluntary Sectoral Liberalization', *Pacific Affairs*, 74 (2), Summer 2001, 185–204.

Wiessala, Georg, 'An Emerging Relationship: The European Union's New Asia Strategy', *World Affairs*, 3 (1), January–March 1999, 96–112.

Wilson, John S., *Standards and APEC: An Action Agenda*, Washington, DC: Institute for International Economics, 1995.

Wiseman, G., 'Common Security in the Asia-Pacific Region', *Pacific Review*, 5 (1), 1992, 42–59.

Won, Yong-Kul, 'East Asian Economic Integration: A Korean Perspective', *East Asian Economic Integration*, 15 (1), Summer/Spring 2001, 72–95.

Wong, Diana, 'Regionalism in the Asia-Pacific – A Response to Kanishka Jayasuriya', *Pacific Review*, 8 (4), 1995, 683–8.

Woods, L., 'Non-governmental Organisations and Pacific Cooperation: Back to the Future?', *Pacific Review*, 4 (4), 1991, 312–21.

Woods, Lawrence T., 'A House Divided: The Pacific Basin Economic Council and Regional Diplomacy', *Australian Journal of International Affairs*, 45 (2), November 1991, 264–79.

Woods, L., 'Learning From NGO Proponents of Asia-Pacific Regionalism: Success and its Lessons', *Asian Survey*, 35 (9), September 1995, 812–27.

World Press Review, 'Will East Beat West? Exclusive: A Challenge from Two Asian Statesmen', *World Press Review*, 42 (12), December 1995, 6–11.

Wright-Neville, David, 'The Politics of Pan Asianism: Culture, Capitalism and Diplomacy in East Asia', *Pacifica Review*, 7 (1), 1995, 1–26.

Wu, Leifer, 'International Exchange and Cooperation on Human Rights', *Beijing Review*, 19–25 October 1998, 10–13.

Xinbo, Wu, 'Changing Roles: China and the United States in East Asian Security', *Journal of Northeast Asian Studies*, 25 (1), Winter 1996, 35–56.

Xiong, Guangkai, 'The New Security Concept Initiated by China', *International Strategic Studies*, 65 (3), July 2002, 1–5.

Yahuda, Michael, 'The "Pacific Community": Not Yet', *Pacific Review*, 1 (2), 1988, 119–27.

Yamakage, S., 'Plotting APEC's Future: A Case for Holding the ASEAN Course', *Japan Review of International Affairs*, Special Issue on APEC and Regional Perspectives, 9 (3), Summer 1995, 199–205.

Yamakage, S., 'An Asia-Pacific Community as a Regional Order: Possibilities and Limitations of APEC', *Asia-Pacific Review*, 1, 1995, 117–26.

Yamamoto, Tadashi, *Emerging Civil Society in the Asia Pacific Community*, Singapore: International Institute of Strategic Studies, 1995.

Yamamoto, Yoshinobu, 'A Framework for a Comprehensive Co-operative Security System for the Asia-Pacific', in Jim Rolfe (ed), *Unresolved Futures: Comprehensive Security in the Asia-Pacific*, Wellington: Centre for Strategic Studies, 1995.

Yamamoto, Yoshinobu, *Globalism, Regionalism and Nationalism: Asia in Search of its Role in the Twenty-first Century*, Oxford: Blackwell, MA, 1999.

Yamazawa, I., 'Implementing the APEC Bogor Declaration', *Japan Review of International Affairs*, Special Issue on APEC and Regional Perspectives, 9 (3), Summer 1995, 178–88.

Yanga, Chitoshi, *Japan since Perry*, Handen, CT: Archion Books, 1966.

Yee, Herbert S., 'China and the Pacific Community Concept', *World Today*, February 1983, 70–71.

Yeo, Lee Hwee, 'ASEM: Looking Back, Looking Forward', *Contemporary Southeast Asia*, 22 (1), April 2000, 113–4.

Yergin, Daniel, Dennis Eklof and Jefferson Edwards, 'Fueling Asia's Recovery', *Foreign Affairs*, 77 (2), March–April 1998, 34–50.

Yong Deng, 'The Asianization of East Asian Security and the United States' Role', *East Asian Studies*, 16 (3/4), Autumn/Winter 1998, 87–110.

Young, Oran R., 'Political Leadership and Regime Formation: On the Development of Institutions in International Society', *International Organization*, 45 (3), Summer 1991, 281–308.

Young, Soogil, 'East Asia as a Regional Force for Globalization', in K. Anderson and R. Blackhurst (eds), *Regional Integration and the Global Trading System*, New York: Harvester/Wheatsheaf, 1993, pp. 126–44.

Young Sun Song, 'Prospects for a New Asia-Pacific Multilateral Security Arrangement', *Korean Journal of Defense Analysis*, 5 (1), Summer 1993, 185–206.

Yue, Chia Siou and Joseph L.H. Tan (eds), *ASEAN and EU: Forging New Linkages and Strategic Alliances*, Singapore: Institute of Southeast Asian Studies, 1997.

Zakaria, A.H., 'The Pacific Basin and ASEAN: Problems and Prospects', *Contemporary Southeast Asia*, 2 (4), March 1981, 332–41.

Zakaria, Fareed, 'Culture is Destiny: A Conversation with Lee Kuan Yew', *Foreign Affairs*, 73 (2), March–April 1994, 109–26.

Zarsky, L., 'The Prospects for Environmental Cooperation in Northeast Asia', *Asian Perspective*, 19 (2), Fall–Winter 1995, 103–30.

Zarsky, L. and J. Drake-Brockman, 'Trade, Environment and APEC: Imperatives and Benefits of Regional Cooperation', Asia Foundation Report No. 18, December 1994, May 1997.

Zhao, Suisheng, 'Soft Versus Structured Regionalism: Organizational Forms of Co-operation in Asia-Pacific', *Journal of East Asian Affairs*, 12 (1), Winter/Spring 1998, 96–134.

Zhenyuan, Guo, 'Changes in the Security Situation of the Asia-Pacific Region and Establishment of a Regional Security Mechanism', *Foreign Affairs Journal* (Beijing), 29, September 1993, 38–47.

Zhu, Y., 'The Tumen River Delta Project and Northeast Asian Regional Economic Cooperation', *Issues and Studies*, 32 (3), March 1996, 96–120.

Index